For Galen Hershberger
With congratulations on
the completion of the
M. S. degree
and all good wishes
Herman B Wells
July 7, 1979

INDIANA UNIVERSITY

Midwestern Pioneer

Vol. III / Years of Fulfillment

INDIANENSIS UNIVERSITATIS SIGILLUM
LUX
ET VERITAS
MDCCCXX

INDIANA UNIVERSITY

Midwestern Pioneer

Vol. III / Years of Fulfillment

THOMAS D. CLARK

INDIANA UNIVERSITY PRESS

Bloomington & London

Published in Canada by Fitzhenry & Whiteside Limited, Don Mills, Ontario

Manufactured in the United States of America

Library of Congress catalog card number: 76–48523
ISBN: 0–253–32996–5
vol. I ISBN: 0–253–14170–2
vol. II ISBN: 0–253–32995–7
vol. IV ISBN: 0–253–37501–0
complete set ISBN: 0–253–32997–3

For

Elizabeth Marye Stone

CONTENTS

List of Illustrations

following pages 138 and 298

PREFACE

WITHIN THE scope of three decades, 1938–68, Indiana University underwent phenomenal expansion of both institutional organization and educational objectives. No division of the university escaped the eternal impact of time and redirection. Prior to these seminal decades there already existed in Bloomington the discernible forms of a university of valid quality. Over a century there had developed a strong tradition for good teaching and an abiding respect for scholarship. A small army of excellent scholars had at one time or another served Indiana in the early years of their professional development and had left behind the enthusiasm of youth. Lingering on the staff was a respectable corps of scholars who by 1937 had grown worn and aged in the service. Under more conducive circumstances many of them would have distinguished themselves in their chosen professional fields. A good example was William Lowe Bryan who earlier had shown promise of becoming an important American psychologist; instead he spent his academic life caught in the toils of more prosaic university administration.

It is not the purpose of this concluding volume to engage in making comparisons of Indiana University faculties and administrators out of context of time, or against a background of social and political conditions in Indiana and the nation. These, of course, had a profound bearing upon the university at every stage of its growth. At no time did the institution forget that it not only was a public institution, but that legally it was at the apex of the Indiana educational system. Because of this fact it had always to be sensitive of the strong competitive forces that at times threatened to deprive it of this important location in the public educational structure.

In the concluding chapter of volume II the fact is discussed that in 1937 the Indiana General Assembly belatedly enacted a law establishing an acceptable pension system for Indiana University. This law quickly produced major changes in both faculty and administrative personnel. The overage president, several deans, and most heads of departments had passed the biblical limits of threescore and ten. Few major universities, perhaps none, have been confronted with the necessity of changing so many staff members in key positions as Indiana in 1938. To replace William Lowe Bryan, the Board of Trustees elevated young Herman B Wells, dean of the School of Business, to be acting president. By this act the trustees unwittingly introduced a revolutionary age in university management. No one, including Herman B Wells himself, foresaw the turn of historical events that would so quickly result in the reordering of the university.

Like David Starr Jordan in another century, Wells came to the presidency in one of those seminal moments when fundamental reorganization could take place without upsetting public or campus emotions. The acting president laid no claims to broad or intensive scholarship, but he did have an appreciation for the indispensable and superior human and intellectual qualities that could mean the difference between progress and the drift into the mire of mediocrity on a university campus. Wells was not alone in this conviction. By his side were such competent colleagues as Herman Briscoe, Fernandus Payne, W. W. Wright, Fowler V. Harper, Alfred Charles Kinsey, Henry L. Smith, Paul Weatherwax, and others.

On the heels of the mass retirements there began an arduous hunt for highly competent professor-scholars who would raise Indiana's star in the academic firmament. Lacking financial support and facilities to support the new breed of scholars in many fields, prospective professors were given promises far exceeding anything the university had been able to supply in the past to draw them to Bloomington. Within themselves these promises in their fulfillment became goals. In the early years of the Wells administration a wide chasm was opened between Indiana University's past as a modest liberal arts institution with two professional appendages and one which sought aggressively to compete with its Old Northwest neighbors in many areas of higher education. The gathering of a new faculty at Indiana University after 1937 remolded, if it did not shatter, every shred of institutional tradition and history.

Indiana University entered its years of major mid-twentieth

century expansion with a solid backlog of graduates who in New Deal and World War II years were in decision-making positions in the state and nation. Among these were Paul V. McNutt, Ralph Gates, Sherman Minton, John Hastings, a good congressional delegation, a small army of legislators and state officials, and a large number of judges of the courts. Besides this powerful political support there were dependable friends in the Indiana Medical and Bar associations. It lacked, however, direct associational appeal to Indiana farmers, but compensated for this in part in the rapid expansion of its School of Business and its essential public services. Without this substantial support, plus that of a publicly influential Board of Trustees few major changes could have been so readily accomplished.

In Bloomington in the waning years of the Great Depression there was an air of excitement and expectation that challenged many residual scholars to realize their genuine potentials. Professors who had served under two presidential administrations sensed in 1938 not only changes in the general tenor of the university, but a relaxation of ancient social and intellectual mores which permitted much broader social and academic freedoms. In numerous interviews with this group of professors and administrators this conception was repeated almost by rote, and it was this important but somewhat intangible fact that embodied the new era for Indiana University.

Fortunately in 1942 there were already on the faculty staff members with special training and capabilities who soon proved so vital to the national war efforts. Among these was President Wells himself who saw broad service in administrative and diplomatic areas. In the decade, 1942–52, Indiana University grew from a respectable provincial institution serving what was called an isolationist state into one with broad international perspectives. Helping this change along was the subsequent influx of veterans with their insistent demands for housing, laboratory and library facilities, adequate teaching, and a general reassessment of both the university curriculum and objectives. The postwar years saw a sudden rise in student numbers place an almost intolerable strain on academic qualitative standards, and in these years Indiana University faced the sternest test in its history as an institution of valid academic growth and intellectual maturity. This was a period of the rise of severe complexities, of sharp historical contradictions, and of constantly seeking a clear path to the future. The successful breaking of the stifling parity formula, which held Indiana public universities and colleges in an appropriational vise, broke the shackles of academic serfdom and opened a new vista of growth.

In subsequent years Indiana University garnered some of the bitter harvest of the closing 1960s and early 1970s. There was revealed to it not only the currents of national unrest during the crisis of an aimless and needless war, but also the complex causes of internal campus dissatisfactions. The latter were often the fruits of too rapid expansion in numbers, a questioning of basic intellectual objectives, cardinal educational policies of both modern Indiana and American society, and the age-old art of classroom teaching itself came under heavy and muddled fire. At the same time the lines of classical instructional procedures and the rendering of broad specialized public services in nonacademic areas drew closer together. Within this context the history of modern Indiana University is that of a vibrant academic community functioning under constant pressure of reexamining and redirecting its aims to achieve the broad original mandate to head the state's system of public education. To continue to merit this position required sharp and often daring departures from the traditions of "more stable times."

There was never a period in the first century and a half of Indiana University's history when the State of Indiana gave it financial support commensurate with demands made upon the institution. Likewise there was never a time when the university received more than half of its total operational support from the Indiana treasury. Behind the history of fiscal operation was the process of generating extra funds, first from the disposal of public lands, then from foundation support derived from special funds. The latter was a reflection of the administrative genius in operating Indiana University. From Andrew Wylie to Elvis J. Stahr extralegislative public support and resources have meant the difference between academic successes or dismal public failure. Financing the university has been an ancient and continuing theme of its operational history.

During the long years of its existence Indiana University has generated a towering volume of records of a diverse nature. These documents portray the operation of various parts of the institution.

Collectively they comprise the total official picture of the rise of a public university in a rural agrarian state and society. Fortunately the disastrous fires of earlier years did not destroy the essential records. Too, the various university administrations have been conscious from the beginning of the importance of the historical document. Though there was earlier lack of an organized archival facility, the precious materials have survived. In the period covered by this volume both Herman B Wells and Elvis J. Stahr knew the importance of university records, and their files are full and complete. I have had full and free access to all materials pertaining to the university and its staff, including those special files marked "confidential." It is a disappointment to me that it has been physically impossible to have documented all three volumes with the inclusion of footnotes referring to the hundreds of factual sources. It was a hard decision to forego such documentation, but no one, including the author, realized at the outset that the text would run to such extensive length. Every effort within the context of style has been made to indicate internally the sources from which statements and conclusions have been drawn. I personally have spent an arduous decade searching the records; I also had the assistance of researchers who read basic documents and papers. Represented in the bibliography of this volume is a phenomenal body of basic source materials which we used. Specifically we read Board of Trustees records, minute books of faculty bodies, of organizations, and ad hoc committees. We also read through hundreds of thousands of pieces of personal and official correspondence, examined minute books, reports, plans, analyses, and memoranda of all sorts. As in the case of every piece of research as extensive as this one the historian turns away frustrated by the fact he has had to be so highly selective of materials and subjects treated. I hope the list of personal interviews with individuals so intimately associated with Indiana University's past reflects long hours of asking questions and the thousands of miles traveled in an effort to establish a human dimension of the university. These are now available in both transcribed and sound tape forms in the Lilly Library collection of oral history.

I sorely missed a major documentary resource because there is no significant collection of professorial papers. Our colleagues and their heirs have been reluctant to preserve such personal papers. Some professors, suffering equinoctial strokes of housekeeping cleaned their files annually and systematically erased themselves from the university's historical record. Those who came to end of careers, and sensed those first soul-disturbing moments of feeling professionally useless, have too often dumped mellowing accumulations of dog-eared records into waste baskets as blithely as they did piles of semester-end blue books. The Indiana University archival collection is weak in this area, and perforce the story of many a professorial career has faded in memory for lack of personal documentary accumulations.

I have prepared an extensive separate body of major documents covering the full century and a half of university operation. These are to be published separately. Besides this extensive documentation my voluminous notes are now in the University Archives, and are readily available for scholarly examination. Obviously a university historian has to be certain that he goes through the files of both the student and local regional newspapers. These sources may or may not always be precisely as reliable as the official documents, but they reflect eloquently at the grass-roots level the tenor of campus and regional life and activities. The *Indiana Daily Student* proved to be a dependable gauge of the student mind in succeeding eras; it revealed campus irritations, the whimsicalities of adolescent university life, the day-to-day course of affairs in general, and often conducted the "great" debates on matters of student dissatisfactions. The columns of the paper shouted with unrestrained joy over university victories, and sobbed in despair over failures to solve instantly scores of problems and shortcomings. In all, the paper was one of the best available calendars of university affairs. We searched the files of the *Daily Student*, and it is often cited as a source of information. At the same time we searched with equal diligence the files of the Bloomington and nearby metropolitan dailies of Indianapolis and Louisville. Beyond this we sifted through volumes of newspaper clippings preserved in institutional scrap books. These give rather broad national coverage. We also examined extensive files of periodical publications.

Always I have had to be selective of the subjects which I have covered. Many times I turned away from topics I hoped I could cover more thoroughly because of the awesome demands of space. I wish I could have cast the history of Indiana University against a much fuller comparative background of its academic "blood sisters" in the so-called "Big Ten" consortium of public universities. No doubt this is a meaningful measure which reflects with much accuracy the accomplishments and shortcomings of all members of this group. Almost from the outset the history of Indiana University has been measured on the comparative scale of its Old Northwest neighbors. To do this intelligently the historian of an individual institution would have to cast his work on a more innovative scale than has yet seemed practical.

I am conscious that in this final volume I have had to deal disproportionately with current history. I have had to write about people who are yet hale and hearty, and who retain vivid memories, and who have locked in these memories their "own Indiana universities." Often I found it difficult to get from active participants in the decision-making acts of the immediate past just what precisely did happen. This was especially true when I sought to draw from them those human nuances which are so vital a part of academic history and decisions. Nevertheless, I have served too long in professorial ranks not to understand that every professor has his own particular slant on the unspoken "whys" and "whats" that took place behind the curtains of university operations and publicity.

Having served on scores of committees, and as a member of a state university board of trustees, I think I understand that university directors of publicity do not fill their days in the preparation of adverse public statements. Inside its organization every university has at least four loosely formed categories of human beings who make up its staff. There are dedicated professors and administrators who serve diligently and unselfishly. There are those absorbed scholars who give little thought or care to what happens on the campus so long as they and their work are left alone. Always there are the "front runners" who in their own opinions feel they bear the burdens of the whole institutional responsibility, and with them are the self-appointed guardians who draw the university uncritically to their bosoms, dress up in the school colors on festive occasions, join in the ceremonial shoutings and tribal moanings, and go home undecided whether they are the spirit of youth reincarnated or institutional cases of arrested arthritic adolescence. Some of the latter do little to raise the stones of the intellectual pyramid above the ground swirl of dusty mediocrity. Finally, there are the congenitally sorehead malcontents who look forward daily to the intellectual collapse and moral disintegration of the whole thing—university, state, and world.

So far as I am aware, I have no personal interest to serve in the publication of this history beyond that of being as factually correct and objective as is humanly possible. As a member of the Indiana University faculty I engaged in no internecine feuds; I carried on no personal vendetta with anyone along the Jordan. I set out blithely to write a "professor's history of Indiana University," and on many occasions found myself overwhelmed by strong administrative personalities such as David Starr Jordan, William Lowe Bryan, Herman B Wells, and Elvis J. Stahr. Add to these a small army of capable deans, a highly respectable number of topflight teachers, and an appreciable assembly of productive research scholars, and the historian finds his modest talents taxed to balance his approaches.

If a reader should chance to ask that question which turns an author's very soul on the spit of psychological torture, "Why I didn't deal with more incidents, appreciate more personal contributions, treat more departmental and school histories, and comprehend more understandingly the underlying twentieth century forces which shaped the history of Indiana University?" I can only reply in guilt-ridden humility that the full panoply of the university's history will be made visible when campus historians write the stories of schools, departments, and branches. There cannot be presented a full personal story of the university until some autobiographies and biographies are written.

For my part I wanted, as a historian interested in the development of American society and culture, to write the history of an important people's university. I have long desired to understand how the idea of a democratic university as projected by Thomas Jefferson and some of his contemporaries has developed since 1818. Too, I have wanted to have an opportunity to trace in some detail the social and institutional developments that were made along the great American frontier in the first half of the nineteenth century. Indiana is an ideal place to view this phenomena, and Indiana University has been a solid example of a people's university that has grown without disruption from its beginnings as little more than a one-room school on the edge of a backwoods clearing in Monroe Township into a complex and sophisticated university with intellectual tentacles reaching deep into the soil and soul of its homeland, and even around the globe. Its social and intellectual commitments are as broad as the scope of mankind and his aspirations. I found the University on a raw social and physical frontier and I have closed its first century and a half on the edge of a broader and more complex frontier clearing. The central challenge of the people's university is yet as stern in its modern contemporary setting as it was in the young nationalistic age when Thomas Jefferson debated his university plan with Virginia legislators. There still remains the timeless issue of purposes as set forth by James D. Maxwell and Andrew Wylie.

The author of so extensive a work is placed under heavy obligation to many people. He has depended upon them for all kinds of assistance from the searching of sources to the actual writing and preparation of the manuscript. Throughout Mrs. Mary B. Craig and Miss Dolores M. Lahrman have constantly provided me assistance and guidance in the use of the Indiana University Archives. Early in this project George Challou and Thomas Buckley ferreted out materials of the earlier administrations and that of President Wells in particular. The assistance of Eric Gilbertson, Leo LaSota, John Woerner, Don Gossom, Howard Jones, James H. Jones, Charles Zimmerman, Don Zimmer, Kathryn Shoupe, Loren Fraser, Robert Burrows, and Naomi Ramirez was indispensable. I wish especially to acknowledge the indefatigable assistance of Barbara Buckley Saunders and Eileen Walters. They were indeed faithful in performing all of the nagging chores so necessary in keeping track of research assignments, filing notes, typing, doing research themselves, and dealing with scores of other problems.

Chancellor Herman B Wells was generous indeed in spending long hours taping interviews, and in conversations about his administration. Elvis J. Stahr was equally as generous in giving interviews, organizing this project administratively, and in rendering other assistance. Chancellor Wells has read this manuscript; he suggested correcting some factual errors and further exploration of topics, and recalled facts which bore upon the making of decisions. In no case did he suggest "editorial" changes in the treatment of his administration.

Miss Jane Rodman of the Indiana University Press has been magnificent in her editing. It would be an unforgivable oversight on my part if I did not express appreciation to the directors of the

Press, Bernard Perry, and his successor, John Gallman, for their generosity in undertaking so expensive and demanding a publication. I no doubt could have struggled through this task without the faithful support of Dorothy Collins, but it now seems unreasonable to make such a supposition. She was generous beyond all reasonable call in her many efforts to work out perplexing problems. My wife, Elizabeth Turner Clark, found in the Indiana University community much joy, and she became engrossed in the research and writing of this history. She gave me that support so necessary to an author.

All the people mentioned above and scores of others sought faithfully to bring about an objective portrayal of a century and a half of Indiana University history. I alone, however, trod the thorny path of responsibility for the writing of this book, its shortcomings, its conclusions, and its perspectives.

THOMAS D. CLARK

INDIANA UNIVERSITY

Midwestern Pioneer

Vol. III / Years of Fulfillment

[I]

"Put Not New Wine in Old Bottles"

AT INDIANA UNIVERSITY an old era ended in 1937 and the old leader retired to his ivory tower. The new leader was a young, untried, and to many, unknown dean of the Business School. Acting President Herman B Wells came into office at one of the most dramatic moments in Indiana and American educational history. From 1937 to 1946 the United States and the world would make the heaviest calls on capable human resources ever in the history of civilization. These demands would shatter the old objectives and ideals of the Bryan period and destroy the complacency of academia in Bloomington. Herman B Wells proved alert to the signals of the time and determined not to allow his institution to dawdle away its precious days at the foot of the Big Ten educational ladder.

A month before he retired President William Lowe Bryan revealed a curious uncertainty about his faculty colleagues. He sent a far-ranging questionnaire to faculty and honor graduates in which he sought an evaluation of the faculty he was leaving behind. There were 217 staff and professorial names on the Bryan list which was sent to 1,756 individuals, 211 of whom were faculty members at Indiana University. Of this number 439 questionnaires were completed and returned. When the results were tabulated there was an interesting contrast between the ratings of former students and the professors. Professors rated 12 of their colleagues at the top, while former students rated 19, and expressed 100 per cent confidence in their choices. No professor was at the top of both lists, but F. Lee Benns in history came closest with 96 and 97 per cent, and 115 others were rated a comfortable 80 per cent. There was a wide diversity between the ratings of strong faculty personalities; R. C. Buley, for instance, was rated 68 per cent by his colleagues and 100 per cent by his former students. The professors rated 25 of their colleagues below 60 per cent, and the students rated 22 this low, with the eight lowest names appearing in the same order on both lists. One professor with fourteen years' tenure was dismissed as a result of the poll, but he gained a temporary reinstatement from President Wells and the trustees.

Bryan's survey was not explained, and perhaps it revealed little more than expressed opinions. There is no documentation that Wells was influenced by it; he had too many other problems to deal with to take time studying opinion polls. One of these was getting his colleagues to say specifically what they wished to do, and what financial aid they needed to accomplish their purposes. He had scarcely been in office a year before he revealed one of his most pronounced administrative traits. He requested each faculty member to suggest concrete needs for a well-defined teaching or research project. He said the university's appeal for funds from the legislature would be greatly strengthened if the administration could say exactly how much money it needed, and how the money would be spent. He wished to avoid general statements and a mere request for money in a lump sum. "For example," he said, "don't ask for $100, but ask for $100 for early American astronomical works."

Two days after he admonished his colleagues on the importance of specificity he revealed another approach to administrative-faculty relations. He wrote Professor H. H. Carter, head of the Department of English, "I want to tell you how interesting your talk of yesterday was to me. You put first things first in an admirable way. Your statement that the chief function of the university is to develop the minds and character of our students, that we should strive for quality, not for quantity, that we should place emphasis upon fundamentals and not upon frills or gadgets, that we should refrain from engaging in needless competition for the mere sake of competition is one which I wish again to dedicate such powers as I have to you in carrying out this program."

President Wells believed the teaching function of Indiana University was the central mission of the institution. His letters and public statements ring with a deep sincerity on the subject. He wrote Charles R. Clarke, "The teaching function is the most important of all the functions here, and the principal reason for our being. I come from a family of teachers. My father was so expert in his classroom technique that his students from all over the world now write him. . . . Every member of the staff here is rated on three scores: first, upon his teaching; second, upon his research and scholarly activity; and, third, upon his public service. We feel that these are the three-fold functions which we all have to discharge in a state university. None of our men, with a few rare exceptions, is so loaded with work that it is impossible for him to perform excellently in each of three fields. I pledge you that I shall make a feature of my administration, whether it be short or long, the promotion of good, sympathetic, inspirational teaching."

It was the commitment of an eager young man in search of success. In a reminiscence he said, "A university cannot render distinguished service to its constituency without a distinguished faculty; therefore the selection of faculty personnel is of first importance." He was determined to build a solid faculty as the very foundation stone of the university. The new president was scrupulously careful never to express criticism of his predecessor's administration, but his every action pointed him in an opposite direction to that pursued in the past. He rationalized that the changes which he effected in the university were made within the context of radically changing times and social conditions rather than as corrections of the historic past.

Historically, men and university had been caught without an adequate retirement system, and most of the older professors had remained in service too long. There was no doubt on this point in anybody's mind, even that of the elderly professors. In Wells' first five years 24 elderly faculty members retired under the Teachers Insurance and Annuity plan, 122 were no longer connected with the university, 84 more were on temporary leave, and 23 went on sabbatical leave to do research. The university was now operating with only a slender core of the old Bryan professors still on its faculty roll.

In August 1937 Herman B Wells addressed to the deans and the Board of Trustees an extensive communication entitled "A Memorandum Concerning a Fact Finding Program for Indiana University." This document proposed the organization of a special committee to make a thorough internal study of the university and all its academic programs. The acting president suggested that the committee attempt to have its report ready by the time the trustees selected and installed a permanent president. The committee, however, took two years to report, and the trustees would only take one year to select Wells as permanent president.

This was a period in the history of American higher education in which many universities and several foundations concerned themselves with the adequacy of general academic programs. The trustees and deans approved Wells' suggestion, and in November 1937 the acting president appointed a committee of three professors—Herman T. Briscoe of Chemistry, Fowler V. Harper of Law, and Wendell W. Wright of Education—to make the study. Their mandate was a broad one, and in time the committee called upon faculty members for assistance and information. Almost at the outset the committee adopted the precept that "The principal business of the University is to advance knowledge and to train the minds of its students."

On January 11, 1940, the searching two-volume report was presented to the faculty for consideration. After full and sometimes bitter debate it was adopted. Perhaps no other report in the history of Indiana University had such far-reaching influence. From 1940 to 1962 it served as a detailed blueprint by which the Wells administration operated, and it was the basis on which most of the fundamental changes in the operation of the institution were made during this quarter of a century. (This subject is treated in considerable detail in *Indiana University/Midwestern Pioneer: In Mid-Passage*, II, 364–383.)

The early years of the Wells administration constituted one of the most important periods in Indiana University history. Not even David Starr Jordan had restructured both the faculty and the aims of the university so thoroughly. New standards had been set for the institution and the blueprint for achieving them was in hand. There continued to be a central emphasis on teaching, and there lingered on some of the traditional folksy provincial spirit which tended to make the campus a snug human island in Hoosier society. The addition of new research-oriented professors, the ending of the great national depression, and the increasing tensions of impending worldwide conflict thrust Indiana University not only outward from the campus, but well beyond the confines of Indiana itself.

Both Herman B Wells and his advisors understood that the new age in which they functioned demanded sensitive approaches and acceptance of change. Dean Fernandus Payne was direct in expressing his opinions in this area. The dean of the Graduate School thought he knew what he wanted Indiana University to become, and with native stubbornness he demonstrated a determination to insure its development in the face of all criticism. The young acting president had been in office only a week when Dean Payne sent him recommendations concerning several departments that he felt needed decisive and immediate attention. Professor U. S. Hanna of the Mathematics Department, said Payne, should be retired immediately. In his opinion a younger man should be appointed temporarily to the post. Kenneth P. Williams should be asked to replace Schuyler Colfax Davidson as temporary head of the department. Payne urged that the acting president should move quickly to strengthen this key department.

Physics, Dean Payne said, should be reorganized and redirected. He felt American science was in new stages of growth, especially in the field of atomic and nuclear physics. There was nobody at Indiana who was capable, said the dean, of organizing a modern department of physics. A new department head should be sought on the outside and brought to Bloomington within the year, and a new physics faculty should be organized around him. Botany was in serious need of reorganization and restaffing. Under an aged head, said its critics, it had been allowed to drift into a state of mediocrity. The department had declined in efficiency and had lost its prestige during the past two decades.

The situation in music was similar to that in physics and botany. Payne said Winfred Merrill was the only member of the staff who should be asked to serve longer. Merrill's decided talents, Wells was told, were less those of a modern academic executive and more those of a sensitive artist. In the Department of French, Professors George David Morris and Jotilda Conklin were praised as good teachers and should be carried on the faculty roll for another year. The latter were the fortunate ones, few passed the dean's penetrating scrutiny with such favorable praise.

Within two weeks after Dean Payne's sharply appraising letter reached the acting president, the Bloomington *Daily Telephone*, July 22, 1937, announced the retirement of Professors D. M. Mottier, A. L. Foley, and U. S. Hanna. With this announcement important blocks of the old Bryan faculty were toppled.

Almost at the very moment Herman B Wells knew that he was to serve as acting president, James B. Conant of Harvard sent him a confidential list of outstanding professors in the fields of physics, chemistry, geology, and botany. He suggested these men would comprise an excellent and highly informed advisory committee to help Wells fill the key vacancies at Indiana. How much Conant's advice to Wells and Payne amounted to at the outset of the new administration is not clearly revealed in the record of the university. A note appeared in the minutes of the Board of Trustees in late 1937 saying that Conant was employed as advisor to the acting president and the deans to help them locate and hire scientists in the various fields.

At the opening of the new academic year in September 1937 Wells had written Walter A. Jessup of the Carnegie Foundation that he and Dean Payne had been in Indianapolis interviewing scientists. He was positive there were good men available in both physics and botany who had already established fine reputations and who would accept offers from Indiana University. He said, "We have checked their records with very great care to prevent any possibility of departments unloading upon us men whom they wish to get rid of themselves."

During the year Indiana administrators traveled far in search of good men. Between interviews with prospective candidates for the Indiana vacancies they consulted educational leaders like E. H. Lindley, Lotus Coffman, Walter Jessup, and others. The appearance of Herman B Wells or Dean Fernandus Payne on another university campus was an omen of trouble for that institution. They were in search of the most promising scholars they could hire. They sought in these men personal attributes and administrative qualities that would enable them to assume most of the burden of building good modern departments.

Back in Bloomington the university firmament assumed a somewhat rosy glow. Wells again wrote Walter Jessup that favorable budgetary developments would give Indiana University adequate funds with which to rehabilitate its physics, mathematics, and botany departments. For once in the history of the university there was no really stifling financial situation blocking the way. This was indeed a burst of premature enthusiasm.

Wells and Payne were aware that they were making decisions almost daily that would influence the university far into the future. They were tearing up traditional departmental organizations that had grown old and set in the ways of aged heads who had spent the lean years in guiding their programs into ever-narrowing scopes of earlier personal interests. Many of the men had not kept up with the new researches and publications in their fields, and some of them even refused to allow their younger colleagues to venture into fresh scientific experiments. The result was that in 1937 Indiana University's scientific departments especially were inadequately led and equipped either to allow the liberalization of departmental programs or to project the university out into the world of modern American scholarship.

Professor Paul Weatherwax in a letter of January 28, 1938, to Wells said that in the past twenty years the Department of Botany had declined in morale, lost its objectives, and lowered the quality of its instruction and was now uncooperative with other science departments in the institution. "I am inclined," he said, "to think that it was due to the absence of any definite system of appointment and the lack of a clear picture of what is needed." He was certain that fresh leadership was needed.

The botany situation was remedied in May 1938 when the highly promising Ralph Cleland of Goucher College was made professor and head of the department. In the employment of Cleland, Wells conducted an active wooing campaign, and before the botany professor consented to leave Goucher he asked and received the promise of an additional greenhouse, an acre of land on the university reservoir watershed, and an appreciable increase in salary plus non-salary benefits. The employment of Professor Cleland involved two or three cardinal historical facts in Indiana University. Wells was determined to get his man, the science department lacked modern equipment, and the acting president demonstrated the assurance he could secure funds to make changes if he could be specific about concrete university needs in terms of definite personalities.

While Wells was celebrating the employment of Ralph Cleland he had internal faculty problems to ponder. Jack Geiger of the music faculty wrote to ask him for a promotion and received the answer, "If I were dictator of this institution rather than only its somewhat ponderous chief errand boy, I would like to make it a full professorship." More persistent, however, was Stephen Sargent Visher of geography. Visher flooded the president's office with off-prints, self-commendations, and observations on faculty members listed in the various prestige biographical volumes and the low state of geography in the university.

Six months after Ralph Cleland arrived in Bloomington the jubilation over his employment was justified. The Rockefeller Foundation awarded him a $20,000 research grant. Not only was this an expression of faith in the man, but by meeting the terms of his employment the university indicated that it was restructuring all its science programs. Judge Ora Wildermuth wrote Wells in January 1939, "This [Rockefeller] gift indicates to me that you got a good man for this job, on which I want to congratulate you, and which further vindicates my position that what we need badly on the campus is really some learned men."

The self-congratulations over the promise of Professor Cleland had hardly died away before Wells faced a protective challenge in the staff. New York University approached the famous folklorist Stith Thompson with an invitation that he join its faculty. Wells began an investigation in reverse in which he inquired of leading men in Thompson's field in the East of the professor's worth and was told he stood above most men in his field in general reputation. Earlier both Bryan and Wells had refused Thompson the rank of research professor; instead he was given the title of professor of English and folklore with a $750 increase in salary.

Wells' determination not to lose good men created some friction at home. In the Thompson case it was with H. H. Carter, Dean Selatie Stout, and Dean Fernandus Payne. Wells, however, stood his ground because he considered a major personnel issue to be at stake. If he let Thompson go, then he would signal to the faculty that the university did not expect to hold its own older scholars. He wrote Thompson, "I want to make it clear that I personally was responsible for the terms we agreed to in connection with your staying."

There was an air of change on the campus, and faculty members were anxious to give Wells advice. The fiery and authoritarian Alfred Kinsey had observed in a confidential document that he was unhappy about the methods of recruiting new faculty. "My attention," he wrote Wells, "had been drawn to Dr. Van Osten's decision to turn down the offer made to him by our university. This is the first time I had known that an offer was made Dr. Van Osten, and, as far as I am aware, no one else on our staffs, except Dr. Payne, had known anything about it. I am reminded that the last addition to our Zoology Department staff was also made without the previous knowledge of the staff as a whole. I wish to protest that this method of making faculty appointments is ruinous to the morale of the faculties involved, and inefficient because it fails to utilize all modern wisdom that is available. . . . It seems premature to make replacements and additions until the university's survey committee has made its report. I have reason to believe that the faculty as a whole has become greatly concerned with this aspect of the matter in the past few weeks."

Kinsey thought the administration should wait until the self-study committee had made its report and then go after new faculty members. He believed that the committee would make recommendations for faculty reorganization which would change all present ideas of needs. His document caused Wells to hold a personal conference with Kinsey on March 25, 1938, but it seems not to have slowed down the search for new professors.

Wells was tugged at from all sides by faculty members concerning the employment of new professors. In April Fowler V. Harper of the self-study committee wrote, "I have been concerned lest the university was not sufficiently demonstrating its devotion to the ideals of science and learning in the matter of affording academic sanctuary to German and Austrian refugees. . . . I think that the institution could profit doubly by adding two or three additional exiled scholars to the staff. It should do so for the good of its soul and for the objective value in making such additions." Wells agreed to keep an eye out for possible refugee scholars who could meet his standards.

While Harper strongly favored hiring refugees, some of his colleagues believed the university should refrain from employing outsiders. To them "pure" Hoosiers should be trained for the new jobs. Writing from retirement in Florida, Logan Esarey told Wells, "In one of the few talks I attempted at a faculty meeting, I argued for an Indiana university to hire Hoosiers and develop along Hoosier lines. I am still of that opinion. Yale is a great university, but we don't want Yale in Bloomington, neither do we want Columbia any closer than New York City." With tongue in cheek, more or less, he spoke in favor of hiring Indiana graduates because "It is barely possible that Indiana men and women, trained in our own institutions, may possibly understand Indiana better than some wandering Jew from Vienna, or even Jerusalem!"

Rolla Roy Ramsey joined the faculty chorus, claiming that Dean Payne had ruined everything. "I think Dean Payne is prejudiced," he wrote the president, "and has been prejudiced all his life against the Physics Department, and has been jealous of any success that has been made here!" If a new head of physics were found, Ramsey was ready to predict dire trouble for him. "I tremble," he wrote, "when I think of the possibility of the head of the Physics Department being cast in the sea of strife and jealousies existing on the campus, with a cyclotron tied around his neck." Thus the campus chorus rose in its crescendo. Professors wanted change, but within the context of their own narrow perspectives and specialities.

Wells and Payne listened to everybody who had a word to add on the subject of faculty employment, but they stuck to their stated purpose to hire top-quality scholars. Payne was at the point in 1939–40 of discussing appointment details with several candidates. Repeatedly he gave Wells reports on prospective candidates, appraising their worth in various ways. An example was his appraisal of Professor Allan C. G. Mitchell, head of the physics department at New York University. Indiana administrative interest had focused on Mitchell to be head of the department at Indiana. The New York professor proposed to Payne and Wells a budget that contained several large items, the most important of which was a cyclotron. On top of equipment and building expenditures, Mitchell and Payne had discussed a tentative salary of $6,000. Never before had the university been called to make such a heavy appropriation to a single academic department. Dean Payne felt the equipment cost could be spread over several years because it would take at least two years to build the cyclotron.

Wells personally waged an avid campaign to get Mitchell to come to Indiana University. He promised the new physics building, two additional professors, a $20,000 addition to a $37,000 departmental budget, and other increases. When the Mitchell appointment was finally announced, the wife of an older professor expressed the feeling in an angry letter that her husband had been passed over unfairly by the administration. The young president proved equal to the unpleasant chore of placating disgruntled professors and their wives. He wrote the physics professor's wife that he would have appointed her husband, but that he was too old to shoulder the laborious duties of reorganizing and modernizing a progressive physics department. The burden, the president said, of supervising the construction of the new building and purchasing equipment would be injurious to her husband's health.

The addition of Allan C. G. Mitchell to the science faculty ushered in another age of experimentation. Just as Professor Ramsey had helped to establish wireless communication in the field of radio science, Mitchell and his colleagues were to embark upon wide experimentation in nuclear physics. A memorandum in the administration file boasts that the new cyclotron at Indiana would be, when completed, the second largest in the United States. Already, as early as May 1939, steel supports for the 170,000-pound magnet were in place.

Earlier Wells impressed the trustees in April 1938, when he made his first comprehensive report on his search for a new faculty. After the board meeting Albert Rabb wrote, "We were all much impressed by the diligence and thoroughness with which Dean Payne and yourself had canvassed the respective fields; and this fact strengthened our belief that you should go ahead and use your own best judgment on the appointments within the limits mentioned. I knew you were going at the matter in such an admirable way, and of course I knew how important such appointments will be." Wells and Payne on this occasion had all but overwhelmed the trustees with information concerning the new faculty appointments.

An attraction offered prospective faculty members was the opportunity to do research in their special fields. In the process of changing administrations, the close introspection of the self-study, and the highly competitive market for talented and productive professors had changed the course of development in Indiana University. Almost as important as the institution of the new retirement system was the introduction of the research-oriented sabbatical leave. These were provided for the first time in 1939–40. A professor who could convince a committee that he wished to do research and had a project well in hand could expect to secure a semester's relief from teaching with pay every seventh year. This plan helped set the university on a modern scholarly course which made it competitive for research professors with its neighbors.

The ardent search for serious staff members went on during the summer of 1938. Robert L. Sanders was chosen to be dean of the Music School to succeed Winfred Merrill. In turn Wells recommended the appointment of S. T. Burns to the music faculty as professor of public school music. So anxious was he to employ Burns that he wrote him letters, sent him telegrams, called him on the telephone, and visited him personally. On August 12, 1938, Burns accepted the headship of public school music, saying he did so because of the president's sincere desire to have him join the Indiana faculty.

Sanders also recommended the appointment of William E. Ross as assistant professor of voice because he had "a bit of the perennial undergraduate's feeling of which he is master. . . ." He was, said Sanders, able to penetrate the minds of midwestern male undergraduates. Also, he was a first-class promoter, "he would make a Kiwanis, Rotary, or school group sit up and take notice."

Wells and Payne appeared to be determined to refute the conclusions drawn by August de Belmont Hollingshed, assistant professor of sociology, in "Climbing the Academic Ladder," *American Sociological Review*, June 1940. This author had concluded that staff members at Indiana were promoted from a lower rank to the next above, never skipping a rank, and as a result an instructor had a slim chance of becoming professor; and alumni seemed to have much better choices of appointments to the faculty, to salary raises, and to promotions." Salary raises, however, seemed to have little or no relation to promotions, publications counted for little, and the greatest internal emphasis was placed on teaching.

These conclusions were drawn before the inflow of Wells' new appointees occurred. Each new man promised to add a real luster to the staff. Ralph Cleland, A. C. G. Mitchell, Tracy Morton Sonneborn, and Jerome Hall were among the first. Sonneborn brought to the zoology faculty the research and teaching strength which both administration and faculty had discussed so frequently, but which still awaited realization in the new faculty. He had received his doctorate at the Johns Hopkins University in 1928, and for more than a decade he devoted his energies to research. He came to Indiana University because he was given assurances that he would be able to continue his research with adequate support from the administration.

Jerome Hall was hired as professor of law in September 1938, at a higher salary than the head of his department received, and even higher than those of some deans in the university. He had degrees from Chicago, Columbia, and Harvard, and was professor of law at Louisiana State University. In Indiana Hall lived up to the predictions of Dean Bernard Gavit that he was an outstanding man in the fields of criminal law and jurisprudence.

A key appointment that troubled Wells was the selection of a dean for the Dental School. The president appealed to Walter Jessup for advice and guidance, and perhaps consolation. The difficulty was to appoint an academic man who could raise the standards of the school, and at the same time maintain reasonably good relations with the contentious State Board of Dental Examiners. The new dean would have to become licensed in the state and this presented some anxieties. Pressure in Indiana was strong to have an outright "proprietary" dean appointed from the ranks of practicing dentists. Jessup told Wells he faced a tough struggle, as had other university presidents across the country, but he felt sure that with tact, skill, and diplomacy Indiana would be able to establish a true university school of dentistry. He admonished the president to keep his eye open as he moved along, and not to allow himself to be caught in the predicament of President John Bowman of the Johns Hopkins University who had employed a dean with a fine academic record but who could not pass the examination of the Board of Dentistry and be licensed to practice in Maryland.

Wells' year as acting president was unbelievably busy. He reported to the Board of Trustees in September 1938 that some new faculty appointments came as the culmination of an intensive search for new and acceptable professors. He and Payne had traveled 33,414 miles to consult with 50 advisors, and to interview 190 prospective new staff members. He told the trustees that most of this great expenditure of energy had been made in the selection of departmental heads. The secondary appointments, nevertheless, were just as important. "No person," he said, "has been appointed to any position during the past few months who has not won the right to that appointment by the competitive process of selection." No doubt Wells was pleased with the commendation of the *Indianapolis Times* that his effort toward restructuring the Indiana faculty "was the greatest since David Starr Jordan in 1889."

The faculty at the opening of the new school year, 1938–39, was still not up to full complement. Yet to be added were heads of the departments of economics, zoology, mathematics, German, chemistry, business, and dentistry. Dean Fernandus Payne of the Graduate School was the key administrator in the selection of the new faculty. It is clearly revealed in the correspondence file of the administration that Wells relied upon his dean for advice and information. This he did at times to the consternation of some of his colleagues. There was a constant flow of advice from faculty members who wanted a hand in all decisions.

By August 1939 Wells had filled two key administrative posts in the university. Arthur Martin Weimer, a former professor and head of the economics and social services and real estate departments in the Georgia School of Technology was made dean of the School of Business. Dr. William Hopkins Crawford, son-in-law of Guy Stanton Ford, president of the University of Minnesota, was appointed dean of the School of Dentistry. Crawford was a graduate of the University of Minnesota and was recommended to Wells by Walter Jessup. Wells again exhibited unusual presidential zeal in the employment of Crawford.

Each new major addition to the staff stirred faculty emotions to some degree. There was special concern about the person who might be appointed dean of the College of Arts and Sciences. A faculty member who enjoyed the respect of the university community wrote Wells on September 26, 1941, that he felt it worthwhile for him to express some ideas about his colleagues whom he believed to be unsuited for the deanship. He listed their personal attributes and weaknesses which ranged from being a dull fellow lacking personal force to being a fine scholar though temperamentally unsuited for the job. His laconic descriptions were "erratic," "impossible," "too sensitive," "not bad," "strongheaded," "dictator," "not strong enough," "too volatile," "opinionated," "out of harmony with your administration," and "has a wife who is too bossy." All of these, of course, were personal judgments which touched only slightly on the intellectual and scholarly qualifications of the men listed.

The campus chatter and speculation kept pace with Wells and Payne's travels, and with faculty changes. No one, not even President Wells, could be certain how much influence all this had upon attracting new staff members to the campus, perhaps none. There is ample evidence that most of the time Wells knew what he wanted in a professor to fill a specific position and he was determined to hire the right person. Dean Payne, never a man of uncertainty, was stubborn and determined enough to see that candidates measured up to the administration's criteria.

By 1942 Judge Ora Wildermuth said that he was bewildered by all the changes proposed to the trustees, and asked President Wells to prepare a statement describing the faculty turnover during the past five years. In this period an average of 28 faculty members a year were either retired or dropped for stated reasons. In all, 146 professors out of a Bloomington faculty of approximately 225 members were changed. Of this latter number Wells said 94 had joined the faculty since 1937. Possibly no other old-line American university had undergone such a complete revision of its faculty roll in so brief a time. Wells informed the trustees and his faculty colleagues in August 1942 that, "A university cannot render distinguished service to its constituency without a distinguished faculty; therefore, the selection of faculty personnel is of first importance. During these five years, more time and effort have been spent by the administrative officers of the University in examination and selection of faculty than in the performance of any other duty." He was sure that inauguration of the sabbatical leave program in 1939–40 would lighten considerably the problem of improving the quality of faculty personnel, and it was a material inducement in the employment of new staff. Wartime conditions had disrupted the university's normal operation, and in 1942 the institution had no actual evidence of the effect the granting of sabbatical leaves would have in the future.

In his five-year report under the new administration Dean Fernandus Payne said the graduate faculty in 1942 differed radically from that of 1937. Sixteen new heads of departments had been appointed to vacancies that had been created by deaths, retirements, or resignations. The changes listed by Dean Payne virtually liquidated the mainstay of the Bryan faculty. In another way a revolution had occurred. The university increased its funds for research from $10,000 in 1937 to $26,000 in 1942. Cleland, Sonneborn, and William Ricks had received substantial grants from national foundations and the United States Government. In addition, six professors had been awarded grants from outside sources. Despite threats of war, and the actual outbreak of the European conflict, Indiana University kept up its momentum of change.

Commenting upon the revolution in faculty reorganization in his more or less tongue-in-cheek letter to President Wells, Logan Esarey said, "I have discussed the following points with Ferd Payne quite often. Of course, Ferd is Dean of the Graduate School, but the Graduate School is only a drop in the bucket compared with the Liberal Arts School. He is very much enthused with the idea of employing men skilled in research. I presume he is not opposed to hiring teachers but when your heart is set on one thing, there is danger of neglecting others. If I were to mention one thing that Indiana University needs, and has needed for many years; it would be fifty first-class liberal arts teachers. What is worse, such men are not on the market. It is hard to pick one before he is developed and impossible to buy him after he is developed." Esarey admitted to Wells he did not know where "I am going in this letter." Wells, however, could have responded that he did know where he wanted to go in the organization of a new faculty.

The fervor with which Wells and Payne sought to reconstitute the faculty spread far beyond the professorial community. It was a dense student indeed who was not aware by 1940 that great emphasis was being placed on professors, teaching, and research. If he listened to anything President Wells said, or read the interviews which the campus reporters held with deans and professors, the student knew that somehow he had an important stake in the building of the new faculty and in the effort to bolster the quality of professors already on the campus. The changes being brought about by the Wells administration filtered downward to everybody on the campus. In January 1940 the *Daily Student* and the campus Chamber of Commerce proposed that students be given an opportunity to rate professors in such an objective way as to bring about an improvement of teaching. The big questions were how precisely this could be done, and how could the results of ratings be communicated to individual faculty members, and what bearings the ratings would have on the professors' future standing in the university.

Dean Kate H. Mueller, who had had some experience with student faculty rating at the University of Minnesota, expressed the opinion that those individuals with the highest ratings suffered in the eyes of their colleagues. She advised that great care be exercised in the formulation and administration of such rating devices as might be used. She told the students that ten years hence they would view their associations with professors in an altogether different light. Other members of the faculty expressed varying opinions about student ratings. Dean Bernard C. Gavit of the Law School felt that the results of the ratings should be kept private, except to show individuals the results of their own appraisals. Dean R. L. Sanders of the Music School shared this opinion.

Generally students favored the idea. Only two of forty-two professors interviewed by the *Daily Student* reporter expressed any objection to a faculty rating plan. Responses to queries from 49 universities were on the whole favorable. Most of the respondent universities, however, expressed caution and offered suggestions about the administration of the rating forms and the evaluation of the results.

On the Indiana campus there was considerable discussion of the ratings as plans were slowly being made for a future administration of the tests. Many professors expressed the feeling that only students with "A" and "B" standing should be allowed to make the ratings. Professor William H. Jellema of the Department of Philosophy pleaded the cause of the "D" student, saying it was he who had been short-changed by his professor, and he was best able to assess teaching failures. Herman T. Briscoe of chemistry and Merrill E. Roff of psychology said advancements of professors in Indiana University were made upon research accomplishments as well as upon classroom lectures. There was little enthusiasm certainly in this quarter for the rating device.

The *Daily Student* kept up the campaign and by the opening of the fall semester it seemed a test could be made of the idea by rating the faculty of the School of Business. Before the forms were placed in the hands of students in October of that year it was decided first to rate Professor John F. Mee of the Personnel and Placement Bureau of the School of Business. After Professor Mee was rated, the tests would then be sent to DePauw for a comparative evaluation. The *Daily Student* said of its faculty rating scale, "It is intended to improve teaching practices by bringing before the faculty a concise summary of students' views regarding teaching methods." Once the ratings were evaluated there seems to be little dependable documentation as to their use in determining the professors' eligibility for tenure and promotion—or to aid them in the improvement of teaching itself.

Of much more fundamental importance was the report of the committee on promotions made in February 1940. Dean Selatie Stout sent this report to the faculty at that time and it caused some dissatisfaction in the staff, largely because it proposed to change fundamentally the line of professorial progression. The rank of professor, said the report, was the highest honor the university could bestow on a staff member. "They should," said the committee, "not only have published a scholarly work that has been acknowledged by scholars in their general field of interest in which their leadership is widely acknowledged, and have formed objectives and plans of research that promise additional significant contributions in succeeding years." This may well have been an official administrative attitude.

Internally the faculty was in a constant state of change. Never before in the history of the university had the current conditions in the nation and the conditions on the campus created so much fluidity in the American university community. The retirement plan continued to prune away older staff members and to make faculty additions mandatory. For instance, in the spring of 1940, five old wheelhorse professors reached the age of seventy; these were Burton Dorr Myers, Henry Thews Stephenson, Frank M. Andrews, Mark P. Helm, and John P. Foley. While these vacancies were being created, President Wells announced June 8, 1940, the promotion of Herman T. Briscoe to be dean of the Faculties. This was a new position created, said Wells, because "the work of the President's office had become too great" and he needed someone to be in charge of academic affairs in his absences from the campus, which at that time were frequent. Briscoe came to the new position well-prepared for the duties assigned to it. He had served with distinction as chairman of the self-study committee, and had won the respect and confidence of the faculty in his handling of sensitive and controversial matters. He also had a good reputation as a teacher. Perhaps Briscoe had gained as much respect for the manner in which he kept his two colleagues on the self-study committee in line with the essential charge of that body's commitment.

Some of the older faculty members were disturbed by all the changes going on about them. So much was being said about hiring new professors and installing new heads of departments and about excellence in teaching and research that some of the older staff began to wonder about their own security. Some found it hard to believe the new administration meant to grant as much personal academic freedom as it appeared to do on the surface. It was clear that Wells and his advisors were determined men and what they determined to do was not always clear to the old-timers. Nevertheless the president must have been a bit taken aback when on October 5, 1939, he received a letter from an old faculty faithful and his personal friend Oliver P. Field, telling him he wished to change the data appearing on his personnel record. He wanted to indicate he had become an "independent Republican." Wells responded, "Personally I have no interest in any man's political or religious affiliation. In fact, I have been tempted recently to break with custom and eliminate questions concerning politics and religion from the questionnaire."

The new president was never allowed to forget that he stood squarely over the historic chasm between the staid past and the throbbing modern future. No matter how many excellent professors he hired, there were moments when he had to make some degree of peace with the past. Such was a problem Dean Kate Mueller brought to him. She had been swamped with complaints from mothers principally about Professor Alfred C. Kinsey's unusual course on marriage. The Dean of Women said the mothers charged Kinsey with showing his class slides illustrating sexual intercourse, and with giving advice on the use of contraceptives. Generally Kinsey was accused of creating a greater air of social freedom among students. He was said to have told one frustrated female student, "You should go out and find a healthy male and have relations with him." It was also said that Kinsey told his students that an engaged woman should not refuse to have intercourse with her fiancé, and as a final charge the professor was accused of using the marriage course to further his own research purposes.

Other grim realities crept out of the past. Despite Wells' enthusiastic report to Jessup, the vigorous recruiting activities at times were sustained on little more than a prayer that legislators confronted with concrete propositions could not refuse reasonable requests for budgetary increases. At the time William Lowe Bryan retired from the presidency, faculty salaries ranged from $1,748 for instructors to a top of $5,520 for deans, or 8 to 12 per cent less than was budgeted for these positions in 1930–31, and before the cuts of the depression period. The average for professors was approximately $4,100.

From the outset Wells was thoroughly aware of the salary situation. He, however, did not propose to improve professorial incomes by consenting to the establishment of a general salary scale. An attempt was made by another university to hire Professor John Richard Scott, pediatrician in the Medical School, and Wells proposed to meet the offer. He wrote William A. Kunkel, a trustee, in July 1937 that he did not expect the substantial merit increase in the salary he offered Dr. Scott to carry the implication that all professors would have their ranks and salaries adjusted accordingly. Nevertheless the matter of salary adjustments in the closing years of the Depression placed heavy pressures upon both the university administration and the state.

Aside from the Waterman professorship and the Patten Foundation and Mahlon Powell lecture endowments, Indiana University had no significant private sources or endowment. On May 23, 1938, Herman B Wells wrote President Frank P. Graham of the University of North Carolina about the school's Kenan endowment for professorships. Wells was under the impression that Kenan funds were used to supplement salaries derived from public sources, and no doubt thought that such an arrangement could be made at Indiana University. Graham informed him, however, that all the Kenan income was used to pay the entire salaries of the Kenan professors. He said, "It enabled us to bring a strong faculty through the depression in spite of the fact that scores of calls were coming from all over the country." Wells' concern was not primarily with staving off invitations to his staff but with organizing a strong new staff.

The question of professorial salaries and promotions was vital in a period of rising prices and expanding faculties across the land. Involved immediately on the Indiana campus was the matter of faculty morale. It did little good to bring onto the campus superior professors who would daily associate with disgruntled colleagues. Wells spoke to the local chapter of the American Association of University Professors in May 1942 and requested that body to suggest a mode for improving teaching. The special committee gathered an extensive amount of information from several universities and in a remarkably short time had a report in hand. The professors asked for administrative recognition of good teaching as central to imparting a liberal education. If distinguished service professorships were established, good teaching, it said, should be a prime prerequisite. Departmental procedures should be democratized, a published time should be set each year for departmental members to discuss salaries, and the administration should publish a basic formula for promotions. Also, it should make a list of those individuals who in the past five years had not been given raises in salaries, and should explain why this condition was allowed to persist. The committee felt that a chart should be maintained for each individual faculty member to show what progress the professor made over a reasonable period of time.

The special committee report came at a time when the university found itself more deeply involved financially than ever before. Almost immediately after the bombing of Pearl Harbor on December 7, 1941, the institution adopted a program of acceleration which provided for the shortening of the time required for graduation. The university calendar was divided into three full terms. President Wells announced on May 1, that faculty members would receive extra pay in the form of a "bonus," for the "third semester." This announcement drew an immediate cautionary comment from Dean Bernard Gavit who told Wells that the word "bonus" should be eliminated from further university publicity because the institution could not properly grant such payments to members of the faculty. Gavit thought that the administration "may avoid unwarranted criticism and political activity if the use of this word is avoided and additional payment made and described as compensation for additional services."

The Administrative Council devised a somewhat complex scale of pay which set the "midterm" rate generally at 15 per cent, however, the actual scale of pay was set by at least three beginning dates. The war and the emergency basis on which the university operated after 1941 almost destroyed the traditional procedures of the institution. These internal wartime changes, however, did not entirely deter the great manhunt which continued for new faculty members.

By 1941 the faculty situation in one area at least had come into clearer focus. A study revealed that a number of retirements would occur in the immediate future in several departments. History, education, and English alone would lose seventeen professors within a decade. The Administrative Council noted that "Before these persons are replaced, however, careful consideration should be given to teaching load and opportunity for productive research *in these fields as compared with other departments* of the University." Two significant changes occurred at the end of the first semester of that year when Professor Charles J. Sembower retired, and Henry H. Carter relinquished the headship of the Department of English to Russell Noyes. In history, W. O. Lynch and Logan Esarey ended long careers. Thus several major professorships were left open, and the administration would continue to search for promising young men who would add considerable strength to the growing staff.

Wells evidently believed in 1942 that the task of faculty recruitment would be far simpler in the non-science fields. In response to an inquiry from President Gregg M. Sinclair of the University of Hawaii he said Indiana had not established a uniform rating system for making faculty promotions. "Here at Indiana," he told Sinclair, "we have only a general uniformity within the various ranks. We try constantly to avoid and eliminate injustices on this score. However, two considerations seemingly make impossible a fixed scale. The first is the supply and demand of competent individuals in the various subjects and ranks. The second is the competition with non-academic careers in certain areas." In physics, chemistry, and law, he said the competition was keener and the going rate of salaries higher. Not so in history and the foreign languages. "In the latter areas," he said, "there is not a great deal of competition from the non-academic world."

The president knew well the competition for competent men in several fields. He had carried on a relentless search for science professors, and then non-academic employers had taken them away. In November 1940 Karl T. Compton, president of the Massachusetts Institute of Technology, requested the loan of Professor Allan C. G. Mitchell to work on a project of vital public need. Mitchell told Wells that he would work with E. O. Lawrence and that he was not at liberty to reveal the nature of the project. Kenneth P. Williams of mathematics was on hand to participate actively in his third war and was given leave to do research for the United States Government. The aged E. Roscoe Cummings was granted a similar leave. C. L. Christenson was given leave to work with a war agency, and Fowler V. Harper went to the vital Manpower Commission. Three more physicists, Lawrence M. Langer, Emil J. Konopinski, and Franz N. D. Kurrie, were asked to do vital war research in 1942. In January of that year Mitchell had moved from Cambridge to Chicago where his work became even more secretive.

The following August Mitchell wrote Herman T. Briscoe concerning the promotion of Emil J. Konopinski. It was his belief that Wells and Briscoe had agreed to the promotion of the bright young theoretician, and he told them Konopinski had turned down invitations to do vital public research in physics and mathematics in order to serve the university. It is evident that Mitchell knew far more than he told the two administrators because in January Konopinski wrote Ward G. Biddle about his retirement annuities, giving the significant Metallurgical Laboratory, University of Chicago, as his address; this was the code name for the Manhattan Project.

At a time when Indiana's scientists in physics, botany, bacteriology, and mathematics were leaving the campus almost in droves to do war research, President Frank Sparks of Wabash College, in a spirit of desperation, appealed to President Wells for assistance in finding a physics professor. Wells told his neighbor that, "Finding a top-flight physicist is like finding a white blackbird. Our own situation has been desperate for some months because we were unfortunate enough to be staffed with nuclear physicists and the Government seems to think all of them are essential to winning the war in research laboratories on either the East or West coast. I am not quite sure whether the Government thinks they are essential or whether the men themselves are seeing that the Government thinks they are essential. . . ." Wells told Sparks that Indiana University was operating its Department of Physics with a staff made up of one woman, an overage male professor, and graduate assistants. Wells no doubt wrote this frank letter in the midst of his own desperation. His courtship of nuclear physicists and the heavy expenditure for building and equipment seemed in mid-1942 to be for naught. Obviously he had little inkling of what was happening in the world of nuclear physics, nor did he comprehend what all this boded for the future of the sciences in Indiana University.

Two ghosts haunted Indiana University in this period. First was the ancient one which had dwelt in the science departments for more than a century. Indiana as a "separate" liberal arts university lacked the scope of application of scientific findings that Purdue and other land grant universities had. There were no schools of engineering and agriculture, or other applied areas to challenge the Indiana scientists. Their work had to be confined almost altogether in the areas of theoretical and pure research. This handicapped the university in the hiring of men, and in securing funds to equip adequate laboratories and to maintain the necessary interrelationships of the various strands of theoretical and applied interests. A second handicap was the fact that in 1942 an entirely new area of physics was in a state of almost instant incubation.

The physics equipment at the time the brilliant Allan C. G. Mitchell and his young colleagues appeared on the Bloomington campus was next to the best in the country. The decision of the United States Government to develop the atomic bomb and to explore far and wide the field of nuclear physics made the modest $30,000 cyclotron and other equipment at Indiana obsolete almost overnight.

If Wells' physicists moved to the scenes of intensive wartime research, there was the cheering note that his favorite botanist, Ralph Cleland, remained in Bloomington while his colleague, Raymond E. Zirkle, answered the call to go to Oak Ridge, Tennessee. In June 1940, when Dean Selatie Stout informed the president that Cleland had just been elected editor-in-chief of the *American Journal of Botany*, he replied, "I have your letter of June 24 about Cleland. Of all the men I have added to the staff during my past two years, I do not know any I prize more." This pride was to be further justified when the head of the Department of Botany was elected a fellow in the National Academy of Science. Only Carl Eigenmann of the Indiana faculty had been accorded this honor. Cleland responded to Wells' letter of congratulation, saying he was not so calloused as to fail to express a deep loyalty to a university which had stood so ready to extend assistance to its scholars. He was certain Indiana University had a great future.

A locally cherished by-product of the ardent administrative search for new faculty members was the fact that the number of "starred names" appearing in *American Men of Science* had increased. Much had been made of the fact by the self-study committee that so few professors had been accorded this distinction before 1938. The new edition of *Who's Who in America* also carried the biographical sketches of 52 professors, not a phenomenal increase, but the upward trend was encouraging. There were indicators that the "new" faculty was intellectually active. A. J. Locke and A. B. Hollingshed, sociologists, were awarded research grants by the Social Science Research Council. The university itself established eight faculty research fellowships which Dean Payne announced would be available in the fall semester of 1942. There were other rewards and honors which came to professors which indicated that, even in wartime, Indiana University was establishing its new role as a scholarly research institution.

Despite the favorable indications of constructive change which had become visible during the past five years, a few homegrown thistles still blossomed in the garden. In May 1943 *Science* carried a story that a National Research Council Fellow had been given an appointment to Indiana University in the field of mathematics. The appointment had actually been made in honor of Professor Emil Artin. The appointee's name was Rosenbloom, and the award carried military deferment. The head of the Department of Mathematics, however, refused to accept the appointment on the grounds that there was not enough work on the campus to justify military deferment. Professor Ralph Cleland wrote President Wells a critical note about this incident, saying that the mathematics load was so heavy that the head of the department was teaching two sections without pay during a semester's leave. Frank K. Edmondson also wrote the president that Artin did not wish "to aggravate the already intolerable situation in the Mathematics Department." Both correspondents felt that the real reason for rejection of the National Research Council Fellowship was the name of the fellow. "Presumably," said Cleland, "because his name is Rosenbloom, he would not be with us." Wells wrote Cleland and Edmondson that he was ill when their letters arrived, and that neither he nor Briscoe was certain how to proceed. Nevertheless, the issue had to be dealt with. It is to be doubted that Kenneth P. Williams, a man whom his colleagues considered eminently fair, had an anti-Semitic bias in this case. Williams had a long and ardent military career, and most likely believed as a matter of principle that the Social Science Research Council Fellow should not be given military deferment. In 1943 Indiana University could ill afford a charge of racial bias. Rosenbloom did not come to Bloomington, but the record is unclear as to the solution of the problem.

By mid-1943 Indiana was deeply involved in war work on its campus, and a considerable number of its staff members were on leave to serve in government offices and laboratories in Washington and elsewhere. At the beginning of the war Wells had shown some anxiety if not resentment that his staff was being drawn away, but by July of the latter year he too was before the Board of Trustees reviewing the request of the War Manpower Commission for the services of Vice President Herman T. Briscoe. Paul V. McNutt, chairman of the commission, had asked the trustees to reverse an earlier refusal to give Briscoe leave and allow him to go to Washington. At the same time Wells informed the board that the State Department had requested that he accept at once the position of Deputy Director of Foreign Economic Co-ordination. This request came with strong backing from President Franklin D. Roosevelt. Wells was certain that he could return to Bloomington frequently and that he and Robert Ittner, Ford P. Hall, and Frank E. Horack could, in occasional conference with Briscoe, keep the university functioning properly. The trustees voted, after much discussion, to allow the two top administrators to extend their government services as long as it was in the best public interest to do so.

The search for new faculty members and the great momentum to advance Indiana University in its major fields of activity were of necessity virtually ended. One of the most important appointments Wells had to make in the midst of wartime was that of a dean of the College of Arts and Sciences. Dean Selatie E. Stout reached the mandatory retirement age, and Dean Fernandus Payne of Graduate Studies was made acting dean. The trustees voted to offer him the job, and if he refused it, then the president was instructed to offer it to Albert F. Kohlmeier, head of the Department of History, for the year 1943–44.

On September 11, 1943, the Board of Trustees adopted a major statement of academic freedom and faculty tenure. In the area of academic privilege the professor was guaranteed absolute freedom so long as he discussed subjects within the scope of his competence. He was not permitted to introduce irrelevant and controversial matter from outside his field of proficiency, and when he wrote and spoke outside of the institutional classrooms on any subject he subjected himself to the same conditions of responsibility as any other citizen. This conformed to and went beyond the American Association of University Professors' policies. Tenure was to be considered at the end of seven years' probationary service. A staff member might also claim three years of service in another university plus three years at Indiana. An instructor could not be dismissed without cause, and adverse charges were to be stated in writing. He could then employ an advisor or counsel to defend him before all committees and bodies which had the power of decision in his case, before the issue was finally placed before the Board of Trustees. This statement of policy had grown out of a report by the University Committee on Promotions.

On May 18, 1943, Briscoe wrote Wells about the thinking of the committee, and Wells responded with an interesting statement of his point of view. He told the committee he was unable to concur with it because he did not conceive that promotions should be made on the basis of years of acceptable teaching and service. He thought that "Acceptable, competent teaching is a prerequisite for beginning employment and something more than tenure must be added in order to merit promotion. This 'something more' in my judgment might be either exceptional teaching, a satisfactory output in research both as to quantity and quality, or very important public service on behalf of the institution." He also thought that in certain of the vocational fields special policy had to be instituted.

In a way the adoption of the promotion and tenure code was a capstone to the first phase of the Wells administration. The war disrupted further reorganization of the university along the strong lines established after 1937. Wells and his more progressive colleagues, however, had laid a foundation for a modern public university, having employed a good core of promising and competent research professors. By 1945 the stays of the old Indiana University had given way. Changes of deans, heads of departments, and older professors had swept out nearly all of the men who linked the institution emotionally and philosophically with the past, and the institution was brought fully into the main stream with America and the world.

Between 1937 and 1946 a significant revision or amplification of the curriculum had occurred, and listings of classroom offerings revealed an acceptance of the new age while clinging to some of the old. Like every other public American university in the land, Indiana had accepted heavy national instructional and research responsibilities during the war, and had willingly allowed itself to be drawn into national and international public affairs. Rebuilding large areas of the war-torn world would give American universities a new sense of their ever-broadening public charges.

In Bloomington, Wells and his administrative colleagues grew tremendously in perspective, experience, concept, and understanding of the greater role of higher public education in the daily affairs of the American people. They were able to redirect Indiana University after 1945 into intellectual channels that would have threatened it with closure in 1936. The fact that a course in Russian history could be offered for the first time in 1943 without stirring public wrath was indicative of this era of greater curricular freedom.

[I I]

Reassessment and Revision

PROBABLY NO ASPECT of American cultural and intellectual life in the 1930s revealed greater uncertainties or confusions than did university curricula. One stumbles through course offerings in college catalogs in almost complete bafflement, if not stupefaction. Alice herself would have been even more nonplussed in this great intellectual wonderland. The course listings and departmental organizations in the Indiana University catalog reflected to some degree an awareness that a public university owed its contemporary age a vast responsiveness, but even more they reflected great loyalty to the classics domination of the past, to personal selfishness, and to outmoded concerns of another age. There were extensive islands of vested professional interest that all but defied change and invasion.

The conditions and the times at the beginning of the Wells administration led to the seeking of new educational directions. The self-study report, of course, had an impact upon the educational approaches of Wells and his colleagues. Too, Herman B Wells had a highly sensitive notion of what the public should receive from the university. Nothing in his educational background and experience had wedded him to the classical liberal arts. Because of this he could be persuaded to venture out into areas that would have been frowned upon in the past.

A good example of this age of departures was the addition of a state police training course. This new program had an enrollment of 100 prospective policemen and Professor James J. Robinson of the Law School was the director. At the same time President Wells informed the trustees that Indiana labor unions had inquired about the possibility of an educational program oriented toward their specific interests. Teacher-librarians had asked the university to offer a course in the availability and organization of library materials. Others were asking for wide diversifications of the university offerings, some of which went far afield into areas of pure vocationalism.

No doubt one of the most dramatic requests was that made in a petition signed by the officers of various campus organizations asking that a course in marriage be offered in one of the appropriate departments. In June 1938 an announcement was made that zoology professor Alfred C. Kinsey and several of his colleagues would give such a course to seniors and graduate students. Kinsey would assume organizational responsibility, but most of the lectures would be given by professors of law, economics, ethics, medicine, sociology, and biology. No one that summer could have predicted that Indiana University in agreeing to sustain a set of lectures on domestic family affairs had set its feet upon the high road toward investigating human sexual behavior. With this decision Herman B Wells and the Board of Trustees revealed a determination to keep the university an island of intellectual freedom in a sea of bigotry and social conservatism. Within a year Kinsey's marriage course had a registration of 245 students, and was an established part of the institution's curriculum.

Seventy-six Kiwanis clubs in Indiana in the fall of 1940 volunteered in co-operation with Indiana University to offer courses in citizenship training throughout the state. Thomas A. Cookson, chairman of the joint committee, said this extension course would be used to instruct first voters, foreign-born residents, and the public in general in the rights and obligations of citizenship. While professors and Kiwanians tackled the mountainous task of creating informed and responsible citizens, Cecilia Hennel Hendricks of the English Department, organized a short course in writing under the coy explanation that it was "designed to foster the writing instinct acclaimed as inherent in Hoosiers." This dispensation of knowledge was expanded in time to include courses in music and community living, and in curriculum-making itself.

In a far more fundamental way both faculty and administration in 1939 concerned themselves with undergraduate students, especially freshmen and sophomores. Herman Briscoe almost single-handedly devised an advisory system which supplanted an older plan and prepared the way for instituting the Junior Division. The new program consisted of counseling, tests, and faculty-student conferences. It was an attempt to prevent the university from becoming wholly impersonal. President Wells wrote Ross Bartley of the University News Bureau, asking for a well-timed release of publicity so the new plan would receive the maximum public notice. "In my opinion this program strikes at the only serious criticism to which Indiana University has been subjected for some time."

Wells and Bartley, however, were premature in their desire to change the traditional courses of study on the campus. There was opposition, some of it bitter, toward the lower division plan. The idea was by no means a revolutionary one, and it seemed to promise a solution to one of Indiana University's greatest problems. Too many students came to the university as freshmen ill prepared to begin mature work. They still needed counseling and guidance which they had not received in their high schools, and which the traditional colleges of the university were not equipped to give them. Since 1938 it had seemed imperative to the Wells administration and to a great many faculty members that a change in undergraduate instruction was mandatory. The most innovative change in the general instructional program of the university in the 1940s would be the organization of a junior division.

In its searching analysis of the quality and response of students, the self-study committee made somewhat general recommendations that the first two years' work in the university be organized and directed under a separate administration and curriculum from those of the established colleges. The committee expressed the belief that the problems and needs of students were more intense during the freshman and sophomore years. Behind this, however, was the hint that committee members had made a more than casual inquiry into the Yale, Nebraska, and Chicago plans. Certainly Fowler V. Harper, an admirer of Robert Maynard Hutchins, knew something of the Chicago College experiment with what was called a "two-year elective course." The Chicago plan was instituted in 1933 and was designed principally for students who did not seek degrees, but who said they wanted the greatest possible choice of courses. Only English composition and military training were required.

This issue was long debated by the faculty after the report of the self-study committee was presented to them on January 11, 1940. Almost every degree of opinion that could be expressed about this new approach to undergraduate teaching was publicized. Some faculty members were violently opposed to the proposal, largely because they saw in it changes in faculty organization, and because they believed the experiment had not proved successful in other institutions. No doubt one of the strongest segments of opposition stemmed from a dislike of the Hutchins revolution at the University of Chicago.

One of the most fascinating developments in Indiana University faculty history would be the acceptance of the lower division by unanimity. The faculty had engaged in a considerable amount of debate, and three major facts stood out in the debates prior to 1942. Many deans and professors claimed to see in the proposal a direct threat to the curricular structures of their colleges and departments. There was, many said, a paucity of information on the subject; and there was pronounced opposition to the two-year plan because it was said it would "water down" the content of courses, and would delay by two years a student getting down to serious college study.

Oliver P. Field of the Department of Government addressed a long letter to Herman B Wells on January 17, 1942, two days after the faculty approved the Junior Division, saying that in 1939 "The air in the University was one of confusion and tenseness." He informed Wells that part of this was caused by the pressure Fowler V. Harper had put on Herman T. Briscoe to favor the Chicago College plan. He said that he and Carl Franzen had done some behind the scenes manipulating, and had succeeded in getting Briscoe to visit Yale. Once in New Haven the dean was won over immediately by the Yale plan's success. In Bloomington, however, faculty members were chary of anything coming from an eastern university. Harper, said Fields, preferred to study the Nebraska adaptation of the Yale program, and he and his colleagues expressed themselves as feeling more certain when they viewed the lower division program as it was applied in a state university. Fortunately Nels August Bengston, who had been transplanted from Yale to Nebraska to organize the program, visited Bloomington in 1939 in search of a head for the Nebraska department of geography. He agreed to meet with a select faculty committee and convinced its members that a lower division would help solve most of Indiana's instructional problems in the first two years. One can hardly dispute Oliver Field about his facts, but it is clear in the record that all this background maneuvering served only to keep the idea alive, and it did not bring about the actual adoption of the program.

Had it not been for the emergencies in instruction created by World War II, there are ample reasons for believing that the plan never would have been adopted. On January 15, 1942, after a fortnight of intensive consideration of the subject by a joint committee of faculty, students, and administrators, the Junior Division was unanimously approved, and the next day the Board of Trustees gave its consent. The first students were enrolled in the division in May 1942.

For Indiana the idea of two years' general training had stemmed from the nagging realization that large numbers of students came to the university poorly prepared and improperly motivated to embark upon college studies. This, in fact, had been a haunting perception since the doors of the institution had opened in 1825. Constantly it was a subject of faculty debates, and since the 1880s was reflected in the university's attempt to remedy the condition by certification of high school training.

Indiana actually established its lower division plan on the foundations of what it called the elective program that had been in existence since 1932. Robert L. Yeager administered the elective studies until 1940, when Arthur B. Leible became director. Leible in 1942 made a comprehensive report on the 268 students whom he had interviewed. The larger group felt they could not remain at the university for four years because of a lack of money and time. The smaller group expressed itself as frankly not being interested in getting a full college education, but sought to take easy courses while they enjoyed college life. The elective program was merged into the Junior Division in May 1942.

At its inception in January 1942 Wendell W. Wright was made dean of the Junior Division. In an elaborate outline he listed six objectives of the new branch which included intensive testing, counseling, better curriculum making, improvement of the teaching of freshman courses, and a re-study of the ancient student problems of adjustment and self-discipline. There would be, promised Wright, both professional and student counselors. Every entering student was to be interviewed and advised as to the courses he should take. Those who were prepared to take regular courses and knew what they wanted to major in would be allowed to pursue work to this end.

The new dean was thorough in defining and describing the objectives of the Junior Division. One approach he made was to send parents a statement of the ambitions of Indiana University for its students, and he asked them to respond by stating expectations which they held for their child. Herman B Wells was idealistic indeed in saying what he thought the new division should accomplish. "The purpose of the new guidance program," he wrote, "is to prepare the young men and women who come to Indiana University as thoroughly as possible for the place in the world that they can best occupy. Adequate instruction by competent instructors is not the University's sole obligation to its students. It must go further. It must help students analyze these problems. It must assist students in learning how to study, how to select and arrange their courses, how to fit their university work to their eventual profession or occupation, how to save time, how to make the adjustments which come with the transition from home and high school to the University, and how in the case of those earning their way to fit university work and outside work together."

By 1946 all freshman students, except veterans, entering the university had to register in the Junior Division. Those in the upper 50 per cent of classes in commissioned high schools were admitted without condition to the Junior Division. Those in the lower 50 per cent were required to come to the campus for conference and special guidance. Only those out-of-state students who ranked in the upper third of their high school classes were to be admitted to Indiana University.

President Wells in 1948 reported that the Junior Division had come to be a decisive factor in helping students to adjust to academic demands. University responsibilities, however, in counseling had now become continuous from matriculation to graduation. New norms had been set in the field of predictable listing in at least a half-dozen interest areas and in institutional planning. Almost 3,000 students were registered in the division each semester.

Under the leadership of Pressly S. Sikes, who was appointed

dean of the Junior Division in February 1946 when Wendell W. Wright became dean of the School of Education, the program continued to expand. It had 85 faculty counselors in 1952, and these advisors visited 309 high schools to begin preparation of incoming students for the transition to college classes. Every year professional and student counselors met with freshmen at McCormick's Creek State Park near Bloomington, where they had opportunities to ask and answer questions in a relaxed atmosphere. These advisors gave instructions to new students, and otherwise helped them orient themselves to university work.

During the academic year, 1957–1958, the university committed itself further to first-year students by instituting a program entitled "location of talented students" or LOTS. This project sought to work with the high schools in locating their gifted students, and then making available to them some estimate of their possibilities in the university. In this year the Junior Division staff undertook a careful analysis of the experiences of the 2,137 students who had entered the university in September 1957. The major objectives of this search were to determine how many had dropped out, and why they did so. An earlier grade analysis produced mixed opinions about the effectiveness of counseling when 27 per cent showed a grade improvement of one or two letters between two semesters, 17 per cent dropped by one or two letters, with 56 per cent demonstrating no change. No one could say positively by 1963, when there was a reassessment of the program, whether or not the Junior Division had come even close to the realization of the ideals expressed for it in 1942. An enormous amount of intellectual energy had gone into its administration, and it kept the university community alert to the weaknesses of high school training in Indiana on the one hand, and to the fact that gifted students could become lost in the overwhelming numbers of a public multi-university throng. Certainly the Junior Division proved a useful means of administering the mushrooming post-World War II student body, giving the university the best approach to the individual student. It helped keep alive to some extent a spirit of institutional and personal concern for the student as he passed through overburdened classrooms. Its intellectual accomplishments were to be measured in other ways, and within the changing context of American higher education itself. Perhaps the large number of dropouts proved the necessity of the experiment. Certainly the fact that the majority of students attained a rather low level of grade record reflected the fact that there was some validity after all in the modification of the traditional liberal arts processes of instruction.

It would be difficult to call what Indiana University did in the field of curriculum revision, 1938–46, actual reform; it was more nearly the expansion of courses with new names listed after them in the catalog. In September 1939 the *Daily Student* listed almost a score of new courses, but none was pedagogically revolutionary or original in nature. For instance, John Stempel, head of the Department of Journalism, announced a five-year curriculum for budding journalists, but the fifth year consisted of graduate work leading to the master's degree. Music offered more specialized vocal and instrumental courses, and the best history could do was suggest a senior course in historiography, and its first course in Russian history to be taught by F. Lee Benns. So it was in other departments in the College of Arts and Sciences.

The art of teaching did not escape a considerable amount of scrutiny, especially in light of the critical appraisal of the faculty made by the self-study committee. There were all sorts of suggestions as to how this central function of the university might be carried on, and nearly all of the traditional methods were criticized. The critics, however, offered no demonstrably better mode of classroom instruction. One plan which some professors, and especially those in the School of Business, believed promising was a reading or "cram" period just prior to examination week. President Wells, as dean of that school, had instituted the plan, but in 1939 Dean Selatie Stout of the College of Arts and Sciences thought it better to lengthen the examination period and not institute the "cram" week.

More major and graduate courses were added, especially in those departments which heretofore only offered elementary and service courses. Bacteriology offered a major for the first time in 1941, despite the existence of a strong department of zoology, and the first year of medical training in Bloomington. On this score President Wells opened correspondence with President Elliott of Purdue suggesting establishment of a joint committee of three professors from each institution to revise curricula of the schools drastically so as to curtail wasteful duplication of courses and instruction. He suggested occasional meetings of departmental staffs, and cooperative research projects in such fields as zoology at Indiana and the Experiment Station at Purdue. He thought such a project could be undertaken in research on the endocrinal glands and hormones.

By the opening of the first semester in 1942, Indiana University began to feel a genuine pinch for classroom teachers. As more professors were drawn into war services or into the armed branches of the government, there arose a more urgent demand for graduate teaching assistants. Never before had graduate students been regarded so highly as potential university teachers. There were too few of them available; heretofore the professorial staff had been ample, there were no extra funds, and university tradition itself had mitigated against the use of apprentice instructors. In February 1942 R. L. Shriner of the Department of Chemistry wrote President Wells that several major departments would be short of classroom instructors unless they could hire graduate students and remit fees. In this way, he thought, Indiana could attract good teaching assistants at a time when it suffered the greatest difficulty finding instructors.

For the next year Robert Ittner, assistant to the President, conducted a fairly complete investigation of comparative graduate assistants' pay and fees among several universities. In a highly competitive situation with its neighboring schools, Indiana was found to be at a great disadvantage. In 1942–43 the university had 168 assistants, and a year later the number had dropped to 126, with some of the key departments like chemistry and physics losing disastrously. "The reason," Ittner told Wells, "lies in the fact that assistants desirable to us are also desirable to other schools. Professor Shriner and Dean Payne have stated this reason repeatedly." In his opinion the employment of graduate assistants was not merely a means of securing cheap teaching assistance, but it helped to give an additional dimension to teacher training itself.

Ittner recommended that Indiana University pay its graduate assistants $67.50 a month and remit fees. He was not certain how this would serve the university in its competition for assistants, perhaps it was $150 low on the term. His suggestion was not carried out because the administrative council would not waive the in-state fees, and set the graduate stipends at $350 and $400 per semester. A. L. Kohlmeier, acting dean of Faculties, also disagreed with Ittner. He believed Indiana in 1943 could not attract graduate assistants of desirable quality at any price for the simple reason they were not available in wartime.

While university departments struggled with revising, if not revolutionizing, their traditional curricula, a certain atmosphere of reform that was more audible than real prevailed. Again that elder statesman, Logan Esarey, gave Wells free and unsolicited advice. Reformers he said were "wilful cattle" searching the weak places in the academic fence. They proposed "ring-around-the-rosie" courses to supplant "logic and Homer." To hear them tell it, he said, attendance in Indiana University classes was a penalty the student had to pay. The reformers tried constantly to "cut their patterns more and more narrow," to say nothing of the general university offerings.

Logan Esarey, in retirement, however, wandered in the historic Elysian Fields. The realities of the times shaped demands and changes that he could not comprehend. Indiana University had new areas of learning to explore in keeping with its revised objectives. Always fairly attentive if not actually strong in the fields of foreign languages, the university was called upon in August 1942 to demonstrate an even higher competence in the area. When it seemed that World War II would again involve the United States in Turkish affairs, and elsewhere in the Middle East and the Orient, the American Council of Learned Societies encouraged several American universities to engage in intensive instruction in the more limited language fields. Indiana was chosen to give courses in Turkish, and instruction was placed under the direction of Charles F. Voegelin, associate professor of Anthropology. Fortunately there were available on the campus Ishmail Eqilimez, Nejat Key, and Velit Daag, graduate students, who served as instructors in their mother tongue.

Seven students were enrolled in Turkish and for seven hours a day for six days a week they were drilled in the language. Charles Voegelin reported in November that they were already capable of not only traveling in Turkey, but they could get along without an interpreter. So successful was the first intensive language course that this program of instruction was expanded. The American Council of Learned Societies offered to pay the tuition of students enrolling in both Turkish and Russian. By this time Voegelin had been made head of both the Department of Anthropology and the Division of Eastern European Areas and Languages. This division laid a foundation for major expansion, not only for the teaching of a variety of specialized languages, but also the study of social, economic, and political areas where they were spoken.

Speaking before the Bloomington Rotary Club in July 1943, Professor Voegelin said Indiana University was one of the ten American schools giving intensive language training as a part of the defense effort. The university, he said, gave instruction in nine Balkan languages, and he believed this training would aid materially in shortening the war. In 1945 the United States Army permitted the university to reveal publicly that emphasis in the language field had been placed on Russian, and that this was one of two such programs in the country. Approximately 200 men were trained in the language at the university, and a third of this number served overseas. The institution, at the peak of the wartime language program, had sixteen highly specialized instructors, and these were directed by Voegelin and Thomas Sebeok.

At the time the languages of eastern Europe and the Orient were being taught so intensively, eight new courses were added to the regular university curriculum. These were in North and South American art, archaeology, and the American Indian languages. There were also courses in cryptanalysis and Latin American economy and the war. Hubert Herring wrote Herman B Wells, January 30, 1945, that he had just talked with a man named Borella, head of an educational division in the Office of the Coordinator of Inter-American Affairs, and had suggested that he build in a state university an education program dealing with Latin America. "I can see a wonderful program," he told Wells, "heading out of Bloomington with some work on the campus, with extension work in lectures and forums, with study groups who want to lend a hand. I believe you could get some money for it, if that outfit manages to make its point with Congress." Wells replied that he was not only interested in Herring's suggestion because of a desire "to spread good will to our Latin American brothers but also because it would be good to have you on the campus." Already, Indiana University in the midst of a world war, was launched upon a program of international interest which in time would lead it to expand its curriculum.

Despite its deep concern with wartime measures in the early

1940s, the university actually carried on a program of internal expansion and self-examination which bore little if any relationship to the international crisis. In December 1942 an announcement was made that a social work curriculum leading to the bachelor of science degree would be instituted the following January. Edwin H. Sutherland was director of the program, and by 1945 the social work department had been enlarged. A graduate study plan was developed by the Indianapolis Community Fund and Department of Social Service. An annual sum of $6,000 was appropriated for five years to train resident students of Marion County on condition that the graduates would accept any offer made by the Community Fund. Herman B Wells said, "In planning the future of the Social Work School the University is very eager to co-operate in any way with the welfare agencies of Indianapolis, and we realize that no school can have a strong program without their help."

The new social work program bore some relationship to Dean Kate H. Mueller's concern with women graduates of the university. She and M. Catherine Evans made a survey of female graduates who attended the university between 1933 and 1944 in order to determine what had happened to them. In this decade 2,675 women of known address had graduated, and of these 1,487 completed and returned the questionnaire. The majority had married and were housewives. Those who were employed indicated that they were dissatisfied with their work. This was especially true of those who had majored in English and the sciences. The liberal arts graduates earned the lowest pay, and fewer of these found jobs directly related to their academic fields of interests. This fact was further reflected because liberal arts graduates had declined from 57 to 48 per cent in the decade. The graduates of the School of Business felt they had fared no better, but they complained their cultural and domestic training was neglected. The fields of sales and business services were so ill paid there was a question as to the validity of the vocational emphasis of the school. Dean Mueller's study revealed that typing and stenographic skills were still the essential pathway for women into a business career.

The Mueller report concluded that, "The so-called cultural subjects in the curriculum are not subject to any such healthy modification from current demands. Any organization as ponderous as an educational system is by its very nature insensitive in its lag behind the educational needs of the individual student. An open-minded analysis of the role of woman as a citizen, home manager, cultural leader for the family would certainly call for a redistribution of her time over groups other than six groups now required in the Bachelor of Arts degree." Dean Mueller and her colleague Catherine Evans were in fact criticizing the basic philosophy behind both the Junior Division and the program of majors of the College.

Wells himself indicated faith in the Dean of Women's survey. He asked faculty members to rank twelve outstanding colleges and universities in the respondent's academic field of research. This questionnaire was mailed on February 17, 1944, and when a month later the faculty had not responded, he reminded them he needed the information to enable the administration to assess the weaknesses and strengths of Indiana University's teaching and research interests.

On the same date the faculty questionnaire was mailed, a second one was sent to teaching assistants and tutors asking for their assessment of the university's academic resources so that the information could be applied to projects proposed to governmental agencies. The president told the assistants, "In preparing proposals to the government commissions for teaching and research projects, it is of the utmost importance that we know our strengths and weaknesses, and that we have an accurate compilation of the special research interests of our faculty." Shrewdly the president sought information in the first questionnaire for making comparative analysis to be used in planning the post-war curriculum and making faculty additions. The purpose of the second one was a desire to enable the institution to prepare itself to seek government war and postwar contracts.

There seems never to have been a moment when the university administration did not concern itself with expansion and improvement. Robert Ittner wrote chairmen of twelve departments on October 9, 1943, that Wells had requested him to secure an estimate of what expenditures would be involved in the creation of first-rate departments in their areas. This estimate was to ignore present conditions, lack of space and research staff, and all other traditional conditioning factors. "The University," he said, "hopes to have adequate space for its needs; we hope also to have a faculty large enough to take care of any important aspect of your department's work." Ittner said the administration believed it would be able to provide the necessary equipment as rapidly as it would come on the market after the war. This boldness in planning and stating specific sums of money needed to the General Assembly of Indiana was the genius of the Wells administration. This specificity of planning would explain much of Indiana University's growth after 1945.

Henry R. Hope of the Department of Fine Arts revived in 1944 one of William Lowe Bryan's early dreams. He proposed that Indiana University organize a school of architecture, and made extensive inquiries on the subject. Finally he wrote Wells that everybody "has poured cold water on the plan." He named especially the well-known Dean Rexford Newcombe of Illinois, and Professor Turpin Bannister of Rennselaer Polytechnic Institute. A month after Hope's discouraging note, Ward G. Biddle wrote the President that such a school should be established, indicating there was outside pressure for such an addition to the university's curriculum. "I talked to Malcolm and Eggers and Higgins about it," he said. In the same letter Biddle told Wells the School of Business should organize a course for training airline executives. "That suggestion," Biddle said, "came to us from a T.W.A. man who feels there are great possibilities in that field."

At the end of the war everybody seems to have been full of ideas of what Indiana University might do to broaden its instructional program. With the end of the war in sight in 1944, and following the withdrawal of military units from the campus, the future began to loom brighter. In the new world of nuclear physics, for instance, there was demand not only for the most sophisticated instruction, but also for a simplified instructional course. A non-mathematical lecture course entitled *Descriptive Survey of Physics* was added to the curriculum for students interested only in a general knowledge of the subject. At the same time other new courses were added to the curriculum which reflected war experiences in and out of the university.

One course, however, had no war-related background, and even defied Dean Mueller's findings for explanation. Margaret Wilson, head resident counselor, divided women students into seven groups and gave instruction in social conduct by having them plan teas, receptions, and various other social functions.

The new world co-ed in Indiana University was still regarded as a prime candidate for social leadership and the preserver of refined culture.

While Dean Mueller and Margaret Wilson concerned themselves with the training and refining of women, Robert Ittner of the president's office raised the perennial issue of the elective system with Wells. It is clear that Ittner had never sat long hours with academic empire builders debating what subjects, and how many of them, a student should take in four years. He proposed to allow students to take intensive courses in single fields. The "four groups" in his opinion dominated most of American liberal arts education. He felt group IV should allow the student to choose all his work in one subject. "*The student*," said Ittner, "*would not only have a good grasp of three particular subjects; he would also have a good grasp of the approach and the method of work of these three general disciplines*. There would still be room left for interdisciplinary teaching if professors did their work well." Ittner suggested an administrative battle on a well-trampled field. Many a liberal arts committee across the nation had raised the question of the pedagogical usefulness of the elective system, entangled as it was in the mire of vested departmental interests. Beyond this Ittner proposed tackling the time-honored Jordan tradition in Indiana University.

Everybody sought new academic directions in 1945. The Indiana School of Business viewed the task of selling $140 billion of goods annually in the postwar world as stretching the entrepreneurial imagination. If 60,000,000 American workers were to be kept employed, salesmen had to perform a miraculous job of selling. This was an area in which the returning veteran could be employed with real profit. Indianapolis sales executives, in cooperation with the School of Business, planned an intensive sales training seminar to be known as the Bowes-Indiana Specialized Training Program. It was planned by Robert M. Bowes of Bowes Seal Fast Corporation of Indianapolis. Professor Brooks Smeeton was in charge of the program, and instruction was offered by staff members of the School of Business. The period of training was four months, and as *Printer's Ink* said, "It is one answer to the question of what to do with the office boy who marched off to war and returned a major." The first classes began in September 1945, and all but four of the first registrants were veterans.

The returning veteran offered a major academic challenge to every area of study in the university. Some were college students whose academic careers had been disrupted. Others were high school graduates who now took advantage of the benefits of the G. I. Bill of Rights, and who had not originally planned to enter college. All of them, whatever their backgrounds and original intentions, had maturing experiences in army camps and on battlefields. There was a staggering problem of adjustment for both veteran and university. In August 1945 a refresher course was added to the curriculum. Instruction was offered in three areas, English grammar, mathematics, and reading and study methods. Much of this instruction was offered on an individual basis to students who wished to improve their chances in college. Dean Wendell W. Wright of the Junior Division supervised the program; much of which consisted of intensive counseling. Veterans who were graduates of the School of Business were offered an opportunity to return to the university for six weeks of reorientation, reading, conferring with professors, and otherwise preparing themselves to make applications for jobs through the Guidance and Placement Bureau. For those who wished to start their own businesses, there was a special seminar on "problems of small businesses."

The university administration concerned itself with instruction on a broad front. Two world wars, an increasing interest in general gymnastics, Y.M.C.A. and Y.W.C.A., and the great emphasis on intercollegiate sports had all contributed to a concentration on physical culture in the university. Since the days of David Starr Jordan's presidency, Indiana University had conducted some kind of courses in physical education, often in the most informal manner. In the patriotic outbursts of the World War I era physical fitness almost became a test of national loyalty. A sound and fit body was a patriotic offering to the cause of democracy itself. Even more stress was placed on this aspect of human readiness during the periods of military occupation of the campus during World War II. Following the end of the war, the *Indianapolis Star* announced, November 5, 1945, that the University Board of Trustees had approved the consolidation of instruction in health, physical education, and recreation into a single school which would begin functioning as soon as a dean could be employed. The scope of the new division was to be broad, and would include athletics, intramural sports, physical education, and professional training in health and safety in recreation. It was decided, however, not to include nursing in this grouping.

Back of the organization of the new school were several historical strands, one of which added a genuine touch of romance. On November 12, 1940, the Board of Trustees added a touch of romance and drama to the physical education program by agreeing to a merger of the National Normal College of the American Gymnastic Union with the university. This institution was the oldest continuously operating physical training school in the United States. Its roots extended back into the middle of the nineteenth century when a heavy German migration poured into the Ohio Valley. Fathers of the American Turnvereins were Charles Beck, Charles Follen, and Francis Lieber. These in turn were followers of the great German physical culturist, Friedrich Jahn. Turner societies were formed in many of the larger American cities, and attempts were made to start a central training school that would prepare instructors for the local societies. It was not until 1860, however, in the national convention at Rochester, New York, that an agreement was reached to establish a teacher seminary somewhere in a large city to be supported by membership dues of a penny a week. Six years later in the national convention in St. Louis plans were completed to open classes in a seminary in New York City. The school was then moved to Chicago in 1871, and back to New York the next year. The moving spirit behind the physical culture seminary, 1872–98, was George Brosius, graduate of the Milwaukee Turnverein. He was dedicated to the notion that better living made a better world. After years of conflicts among the Turnverein Seminary, the National German-American Teachers Seminary, and the German-English Academy, the three institutions were merged into the Normal College of the North American Gymnastic Union, and the trustees located the institution in Indianapolis on August 31, 1907. In the latter place it operated independently until its merger with Indiana University in 1941.

Early in 1941 the struggling Normal College had reached an agreement with Indiana University for its students to come to Bloomington for the fourth year of their work, and to receive the Bachelor of Physical Education from the School of Education. Dean H. L. Smith sent Professor W. W. Patty to Camp Brosius on Elkhart Lake in Wisconsin to appraise the Normal School's instructional work, and to make co-operative plans for the future. On November 18, 1941, President Wells met with the trustees of the Normal College in the board room of the Indianapolis Atheneum and worked out a merger agreement between the two institutions. The title of the school would be changed to the American Gymnastic Union of Indiana University. In turn, the university was to receive title to the old Fleck Hotel at Camp Brosius, the kitchen, classrooms, gymnasium, and tent bases, plus fifteen acres of land. The very fine library collection of physical culture literature was to become a part of the university collection. There was no property in Indianapolis, but the school published a reputable physical journal, and was the homesite of the national physical culture fraternity. Besides this Indiana University was left at liberty to continue offering classes in the Atheneum gymnaisum or any other place it chose, and all former graduates of the Normal College were to be added to the Indiana alumni roll. President Wells appointed W. W. Patty as director of the new division, and it became the ninth college of the university.

As a direct result of the merger of the Normal College Indiana University for the first time in its history entered a gymnastic team in Big Ten competition in the fall of 1941. Most of the contestants came from the gymnastic classes in Indianapolis.

By the end of the war in 1945 Indiana University, in its numerous national defense programs, had become heavily committed to the idea of physical fitness as a great national asset. Herman T. Briscoe wrote Provost Coleman R. Griffith of the University of Illinois on January 19, 1945, that the director of athletics was also head of the department of physical education for men. Physical education for women was offered as a separate unit, but both were in the School of Education. However, the administration, said Briscoe, was considering bringing all physical education into a single division under the supervision of an academic dean.

Nine months later Briscoe advised Wells that it now seemed wise to create a new school of physical education, health, and recreation. He gave as reasons the coordination of the use of existing facilities. The work given in Indianapolis and at Camp Brosius should also be coordinated with the Bloomington curriculum. Briscoe told the president the time had come to develop a professional approach to training in the five major fields suggested in the new school program. Each division would be presided over by a head professor; even competitive collegiate athletics should be placed under the administration of the school, though Big Ten Conference rules forbade separation of athletic control from the general faculty.

Enrollment in the university increased rapidly, postwar planning made a new demand for efficiency in instruction, and the Wells administration demanded a rounded program that would measure up to those in the better universities. Such a program, however, had to be developed by use of existing physical educational facilities at hand. At its September 1945 meeting the Board of Trustees created the new physical education school. In informing the faculty of the board's action, President Wells said the move was in keeping with earlier recommendations of the self-study committee. He promised that as soon as a dean could be hired the School of Health, Physical Education, and Recreation would be organized.

The following March a university rule was adopted that all students registered in the Junior Division would be required to take two years of physical training. Edna Munro was said to have made plans for the instruction of 1,678 women students with nine staff members. The central administration then waited to see how many students would elect courses in the new school before employing a full complement of instructors. Briscoe wrote Wells on April 16, 1946, that W. W. Patty had agreed to accept the deanship of the school, and this appointment was confirmed in June. Two years later there were thirty-seven staff members in the school. Soon thereafter a four-year major was being offered in dance to meet the demand for high school teachers of the art. Jane Fox announced that the requirements for this course would be anatomy, music appreciation, stage craft, make-up, costuming, dance competition, art, and psychology. This required preparation no doubt was enough to make a dance major at least a tantalizing conversationalist, as well as a gracefully coordinated human being.

Lack of space and physical facilities handicapped the work of the School of Health, Physical Education, and Recreation until October 1960, when the thirty-year-old fieldhouse and the stadium were made available for instruction. It was the first time, said

Patty's successor, Arthur S. Daniels, that intramural sports had been given adequate facilities to serve the student body. "This lack of physical equipment," he wrote, "has caused a lag in Indiana's indoor intramural sports plan that some other Big Ten schools have managed to overcome by setting up separate facilities for intra-murals."

During the months when the university was reformulating its physical education and health programs at the end of the war, the School of Music broadened its curriculum to offer courses leading to the bachelor of science in music. Students seeking this degree were not only to concentrate on music, but also to take work in business, radio communication, journalism, and speech. Professor Newell Long said commercial music firms had asked that such training be offered at the collegiate level. He thought Indiana University was the first university in the country to respond to such a request.

At the end of World War II there was constant pressure by specialized interest groups for the university to offer instruction in many professional and vocational fields. The university's postwar records give eloquent testimony to this fact. One of the most insistent of the professional demands was made by the Indiana optometrists. They were led by Dr. John P. Davey of Indianapolis, who made the strong case that his profession was as deserving of public support as were the medical doctors.

President Herman B Wells instructed Dean of the Faculties Herman T. Briscoe in November 1945 to discuss the subject of establishing a school of optometry with Dr. W. D. Gatch, dean of the School of Medicine. Wells wanted to determine whether there would be conflict between the Department of Ophthalmology, and a school of optometry. Briscoe asked Gatch to explore the subject fully with Dr. Robert Masters, in doing so he obviously wished to avoid one of Dr. Gatch's predictably blunt answers. Dr. Masters opposed the idea, largely because he believed the optometrists would not be properly trained surgically to treat the human eye. Gatch was pointed in observation, "I strongly agree with all Dr. Masters has said," and he joined Masters in opposing the new school. He wrote Briscoe that he had discussed the idea with the executive committee of the Indiana Medical Association. "They are all opposed to it," he said, "on the grounds that anyone who treats the diseases of the eye may jeopardize the eyesight, health, or even the life of his patient. I can give many more reasons for my opposition of the establishment of this school. . . ." Wells told Masters, following the meeting of the trustees on December 10, 1945, that the board had accepted his suggestion to defer action on the school. He said that the optometrists had approached the university to create the school, and the administration had prescribed three conditions: the curriculum would be of collegiate quality, there would be no conflict with ophthalmology in the School of Medicine, and the legislature would finance the added program. Thus far Wells and Briscoe expressed themselves as being satisfied about the collegiate rank, but they were uneasy about the other questions.

Dean Briscoe continued to search for answers to the fundamental questions that blocked development of a school of optometry. He wrote Dr. Charles Sheard of the Mayo Clinic that personally he looked upon the proposal with great favor, because "there is a real job here to be done by an educational institution within the state." Leaders in optometry had indicated they would support a sound curriculum. "Our hesitation in approving the proposal is caused by several factors, including our present restriction on space, the difficulty of finding qualified personnel, and the attitude of certain medical groups," said Briscoe. He was sure the university wanted to get the new curriculum off to a successful start, and did not wish to see it handicapped by unsympathetic opponents. On the other side there was considerable pressure from the optometrists for the university to give publicity to the proposed new school in the professional journals at least, and Briscoe agreed that the university had to give the subject some publicity if it expected to attract students, even though the new division had not been established.

In the absence of President Wells, Herman T. Briscoe informed the public on December 31, 1947, that the Board of Trustees had approved the request of the Indiana Board of Optometry to establish the school, provided the optometrists could carry out their financial promises to support the school. The board had also authorized publicity of the new curriculum of preprofessional work to be started in the fall of 1948. The Medical Advisory Council, however, held a meeting under the guidance of Dr. John Ditmars Van Nuys in which the trustees' action was sharply criticized. The university's Administrative Committee agreed to hold up further publicity until representatives of the Medical Advisory Board had an opportunity to appear before the Board of Trustees at a future meeting. When they did appear on February 7, 1948, they opposed the organization of the optometry program. This opposition had an impact, which was indicated in Briscoe's letter to A. K. Bell of Kokomo on March 4. He told Bell, "We do not plan now or in the near future to develop any curriculum in optometry science."

The optometrists, however, were determined. In 1951 they persuaded the Indiana legislature to establish an optometry program in Indiana University, and to give the new department necessary financial aid. Dr. John Davey, leader of the drive to establish the school, had refused to surrender to the medical doctors in the long fight. He had spearheaded the drive to secure legislative support in the face of powerful opposition. It was Davey whom Wells congratulated when Governor Henry Schricker signed the optometry bill into law.

Herman B Wells said in his report that year that "a curriculum in optometry will be established. It will consist of two years of preprofessional and three years of professional work." The course would lead to the granting of a master's degree in optometry. In 1951–52 the first year of preprofessional work would be given, to be followed two years later with professional courses. That year the first students were enrolled, and the university employed Dean Henry Hofstetter of the Los Angeles School of Optometry to direct the school. Wells wrote in his State of the University message that "Because of the great need for optometrists and because of the rich background and outstanding reputation of Professor Hofstetter, we are confident that this program will flourish and soon begin to make its contribution to the physical well-being of our state."

The new division was first located in the basement of the new Health Center building, but quarters in this location were severely limited. When Hofstetter asked for 2,500 feet of floor space, the division was more permanently located in the student lounge area of the Medical Building (now Myers Hall).

In September 1953 nineteen Hoosier students entered professional training in optometry, and the new school was properly launched. The medical doctors, already in a state of shock, must have been excited even more when Dean Hofstetter announced that instead of using human cadavers, the optometrists would use monkeys. Hofstetter advised the oppointment of practicing Bloomington optometrists as clinical associates to serve university students. Three years later President Wells reported that the Division of Optometry had at last completed its organization of a professional training program, and by June 1956 the first master's degrees in optometry would be conferred on sixteen candidates.

The long struggle to overcome opposition to the establishment of the Division of Optometry was reminiscent of that which accompanied the organization of the School of Medicine. There was more than a hint of the narrow professional attitudes of the medical professors in opposing the new addition to the university curriculum. The record in this case is almost as revealing in what it suggests but does not say openly, as for what was accomplished.

Expansion of the university in the Wells era resembled somewhat the need for change that had earlier challenged David Starr Jordan and William Lowe Bryan, except that Wells and his staff led the university much further away from the classical liberal arts tradition. The creation of the Junior Division, organization of departments of social work and library science, the Division of Optometry, and the School of Health, Physical Education, and Recreation filled in some of the areas that were inadequately served by the more traditional university curriculum. Only in this period of extraordinary curriculum expansion did Indiana University finally escape many of the restrictive bonds placed upon it in the post-Civil War years when it failed to gain land-grant college status.

Along with the creation of new divisions the expansion of the university's general instructional program in content course areas was a major concern during the first two decades of the Wells administration. Older schools and departments within the university expanded their curricula semester by semester without creating undue attention. Every new course and every new program, however, exerted additional pressure on both faculty and administration to provide instruction and physical facilities. A rapidly rising student enrollment increased demands for new professors and classrooms. Beyond this, the new generation of postwar students brought to the campus a higher degree of sophistication and background training than had ever been true in the univerity's history. It was with justifiable pride that Herman B Wells reported to the trustees in June 1960 that

> The course of World War II and circumstances of the post-war era have propelled America into a new position of world leadership. The rapid rise of our country to this position in the short span of two decades has occurred to an important extent as the result of forces which we ourselves neither generated nor even significantly directed. Not having sought this position over decades or generations as other leading nations have done in earlier periods of history, we perhaps also have not been as well prepared for it as we now wish to be. Our rapid rise to world power prominence has affected *all* of our institutions—political, economic, and cultural; but probably none of our institutions has undergone changes more profound and far-reaching in recent years than our major universities.
>
> Like other universities of our type, Indiana University has changed in response to America's new role in the world; we have accepted enthusiastically and, I believe, effectively a large share of new responsibilities.
>
> These new responsibilities we now see reflected in our teaching, research, and in the direct services which we render in the public interest at home and around the world.

[III]

Unraveling the Great American Academic Myth

Life Magazine in all its wondrous ways of approaching a story was not altogether wrong in 1942 about the texture of American student life at the end of the 1930s. The magazine, however, gave evidence of editorial irresponsibility and sloppiness in trying to present a segment of society that it neither understood nor took pains to examine with any degree of comprehension and objectivity. In Bloomington there hovered over the campus of Indiana University a disturbing inner feeling of boredom and lethargy. The "Good Ole Days" of the 1920s now seemed far away. The Great Depression had taken its toll of human spirit and blitheness that not even the ebullience of Rooseveltian recovery could restore. The self-study committeemen had grave doubts that local students were more seriously inclined toward their studies, or that the depression had motivated them to make more serious demands of the university itself.

"Gustave," in a letter to the *Daily Student*, February 17, 1940, lamented social change or, as he called it, lack of campus spirit. He pleaded for a return to the days when writers filled the paper and handbills with vituperative letters and charges. He recalled earlier times when students had written moving letters reminiscing about the "good old days." The writer thought a few headbreaking "boresses," cap burnings, fist and skull fights between lawyers and medics, pro-squirrel versus anti-squirrel arguments, and a free-for-all assault on prom kings would revive Indiana University. "I'm telling you," he wrote, "the present student body is as wishy-washy as a cracker in a rain storm. The fighting spirit has died a horrible death. No one wants to argue. The only evidence of a revival noticed recently was when approximately 1,000 students booed a Purdue basketball player. And I bet if he had booed back the whole 1,000 would have run. I have a gripe but can't find anybody to listen to me. The present student body is as hard to insult as a drunk co-ed." In "Gustave's" opinion the students, since the advent of Dale Carnegie, had come to believe milk toast was the breakfast of champions. He expressed the feeling that students were too well satisfied with the administration. If the administration should turn really dictatorial and lay down a few unreasonable laws, they might shuck off their apathy in a hurry. It was felt, however, that students were babied into a state of stupefaction, and no editorial against apathy would accomplish anything.

Stephen M. Corey, a rugged old Disciples of Christ theologian from the University of Chicago, rocked the complacency of the student lake in March 1941, when he told an Indiana University audience that American students spent too much time with matters that did not mean anything. He said, "About the only way you can tell some have been to college is by the way they dress, the way they shake hands or the way they dance. Conversation doesn't indicate any intellectual developments that have come from a college education." This was an irritating blow to which the *Daily Student* replied, "Of course, students can't reply to his charges openly, but they do say to themselves that it is nice to know how to dress, dance and shake hands, and incidentally—recognize an old fogy when they hear one."

Maybe Dr. Corey did border on fogyism, but the vacuity of the *Daily Student* itself in this period indicates he had company. During the 1930s there was, of course, a greater liberalization of American social life in general. Repeal of the Volstead Act and revocation of the Eighteenth Amendment by popular vote perhaps did not lead to an actual increase in drinking, it simply brought out into the open an established pattern which had been in the shaping since 1918. In Bloomington, students, like those in every other American university, did not exactly die of thirst before repeal. There seems to have been ample evidence by 1933 that drinking of illegal liquor took place at the dances and at all other student gatherings. Smoking became more prevalent and the retreats of university authority in these areas were made stubbornly from one deeply excavated redoubt to another until the last stronghold of licensing local saloons within or near prohibitive distances of university and church buildings was reached.

Immediately after Halloween in 1937 that stalwart arbiter of student morals and social behavior, Dean of Women Agnes Wells, opened assault on Nick Hrisomalos' English Hut. This student oasis was located at 423½ East Sixth Street, and within the shadow of the new Administration Building. Dean Wells said it was too close to both the university and a church. She signed a petition to the Indiana State Alcoholic Beverage Commission asking that body to rescind the Greek saloonkeeper's license, which had been granted under the 1935 Indiana statute, because the English Hut was less than 200 feet from a church.

Hardly had the petition protesting the presence of Nick's English Hut gone the round of signers before a second front was opened against the liquor interest. At a football game on November 22, 1937, the Seagram's Distilling Company of Louisville, whose president was Fred Willkie ('12), committed two indiscretions. It had an airplane tow a Seagram's streamer above the football field during a game. Young President H. B Wells was asked to protest to the distilling company, even though a claim was made that the upper air was free territory. At the stadium gates Seagram's dared the forces further by distributing bright red megaphones with its advertising imprinted on them. In December the Louisville distiller apologized to the university for this overzealous sales pitch.

In connection with the Hrisomalos incident the State Alcoholic Beverage Commission answered the Bloomington dry petitions in part by proposing that students be issued identification cards showing that they were twenty-one or older. Dean Wells, ignoring the ingeniousness of undergraduates, expressed satisfaction with the proposal because it would prevent underage students from breaking the law, and place a heavy legal responsibility on the seller. Maybe Dean Wells had fallen under the spell of local drys who brought the Indianapolis anti-saloon play, "Prisoner at the Bar," to Bloomington late in 1938. This performance was introduced by President Emeritus William Lowe Bryan.

The Dean of Women had the grim satisfaction of closing Nick's English Hut. On November 22, 1937, the *Indiana Daily Student* said, "Nick's English Hut, long a favorite stamping ground of Indiana University consumers of alcoholic beverages, tonight will close its doors for eternity. Nick Hrisomalos, proprietor of the Hut, was tapped on the shoulder by the I. U. powers that be and the next thing he knew the state board was informing him that his alcoholic drinks selling permit would not be renewed. The Hut it seems, is too near the campus for its own good, to say nothing of the good of teen-aged students to whom anything stronger than root beer is a handicap to their education."

Dean Wells may have rendered Nick Hrisomalos a mortal blow, but the times were to palsy her hand of authority. In Detroit Henry Ford was busy seeing to it that students ranged well beyond the campus and deanly grasp. Boys and girls, even in adolescence, knew where within easy reach of Bloomington the best moonshine and homebrew could be obtained, and from "English Huts" far removed from the domain of Dean Wells.

In other areas of student dissipation old attitudes persisted. Girls had begun to smoke in the open, and boys sported cigarettes as a matter of course. Three years after President Bryan had retired the issue of the weed, however, still showed vitality. In 1940 the argument had shifted from one of morals to a threat to university property. Smoking on the campus, said the student newspaper, had become a dangerous fad. Fires had been started the year before by careless smokers, and already in the new semester the Chemistry Building had been damaged by fire. "It is needless to point out to any mental flyweight, that priceless unreplaceable materials is in the Library, and would not only be a serious loss to the University but to the state as well," said the *Daily Student*. Only student will to stop smoking would accomplish its end, and only social pressures would strengthen the will, thought the editor.

Currents of change ran strong in these years on the Indiana University campus. While Dean Wells jousted furiously with a well-nigh defenseless son of Eros, and President Wells scolded Seagram's distillers and his old friend Fred Willkie, students directed their interests into many other channels. Frank R. Elliott announced proudly that Indiana students would appear on the Pontiac Variety Show of the National Broadcasting Company. This was a trivial and superficial gesture that revealed an interest on the part of the university in gaining national attention. Within three years university supporters had reason, however, to doubt the wisdom of such commercial publicity.

That fall students broke the tedium of campus life by dipping into the past in a search for nostalgia. The honorary sophomore organization, Skull and Crescent, decided that it would revive the tradition of the "rhinie pod" by making freshmen wear class caps. An upperclassman walk would be established and it was to remain undefiled by the tread of freshmen. This sacrosanct walkway was to include areas from Maxwell to Kirkwood halls. Sophomores were asked to wear "sophomore blue" pants, and the other classes were requested to adopt distinctive clothing. This revival, however, died a-borning because the first order of class trousers had not appeared on the campus before wartime shortages of dyestuffs occurred. Freshmen also continued to use the high and mighty walkways.

Skull and Crescent sailed further out from shore by proposing an end to the "Old Oaken Bucket" tradition, and that there should be no female workers in the "Men's Grill" in the Memorial Union. Even the *Daily Student* chimed in and said, "We'd like to see this one sanctuary preserved for men." Men, however, did not disavow all interest in the female population. They were taken in by an advertisement of a sex movie entitled "Forbidden" shown in November 1937. The theatre was crowded by boys who came to savor an hour of pure salaciousness, and were bored to sleepiness when the movie instructed parents how to inform their children about sex. There were childbirth scenes, interspersed with venereal horrors, and fatherly admonitions about masturbation. A few brazen ones uttered whistling-in-the-dark wisecracks to prove they were blasé, but generally the audience was subdued into impenetrable silence. The "women's" showing of the same picture was poorly attended, perhaps female innocents had no sensuous curiosity. This movie was a prelude to a campus-wide campaign to persuade students to take Wasserman tests in a fight against syphilis.

The co-ed student in Indiana University in 1937 was still very much under surrogate care of the dean of women. She could not leave the campus for an overnight visit except on written permission of her parents. If she went for a ride in a student-driven car, she had to sign an application for permission in the dean of women's office, giving the name of the driver. The girls, however, were clever at giving rules a twist, and of fraternizing with the boys. They gave dances, paid taxi bills, bought drinks, and paid other expenses. Three ingenious lasses, just before Christmas vacation in 1937, talked Bloomington policemen into arresting their dates and literally dragging them to a waiting car.

In a far less authoritarian way President Herman B Wells ended a long and troubled chapter in university history in February 1940, when he announced that all freshmen women would have to live in dormitories. For the first time the university had available sufficient campus housing to enforce such a rule. The president explained the rule was intended to help girls adjust to college life, improve their scholarship, and encourage good social relationships. At the same time a university committee was appointed to consider women's education. This resulted in the preparation and publication of the booklet, *Indiana University Plans Careers for Women* (1941). An advisor was appointed to instruct women students in choices of vocations, and their educational planning.

While the women battled for social freedoms and prepared themselves for vocations they took time to deal with some of the finer phases of life at Indiana University. During the year 1939–40 the girls sought equal rights with men to lead cheering at athletic events. They appeared at all football games that season and made some real headway in asserting themselves. Then suddenly they were ruled off the field by the Athletic Committee which was made up of such professorial and staff stalwarts as Herman T. Briscoe, Bernard C. Gavit, Zora Clevenger, W. R. Breneman, Lee R. Norvelle, and Ward G. Biddle. The Union Board was informed the girls would no longer be allowed along the sidelines at games.

Students became more and more a central concern of the university's administration. The handwriting on the wall of academe was clear, times were changing, and between the end of the depression and the outbreak of World War II in Europe many of the old student-university associations underwent a fundamental change in the area of human relationships on the campus.

The self-study survey had taken a hard critical look at students, their capabilities, and their responses to learning. Generally the report indicated a fairly low esteem for undergraduate accomplishments. In the era just ending the state university had never catered so thoroughly to the whole gamut of society as in the 1930s. F. Scott Fitzgerald may have portrayed a college generation in *This Side of Paradise*, and Epes Todd, *Not to Eat, Not for Love* (1933), a succeeding and somewhat more introspective one, but neither pictured precisely campus life at Indiana University. Perhaps a more accurate description of the fundamental changes which came to the American campus was contained in Lynd Montrose's *Winds on the Campus*. In the area of campus economics, students in Bloomington were far more restricted than were those of affluent eastern schools. Professor James E. Moffat of the Department of Economics and Professor Mary Crawford determined by a survey in 1939 that the average Indiana student spent $619.57 a year, and the high and low ranges were from $180.50 to $2,017.75. Food and room rent absorbed 47.4 per cent of the total amount.

For the first time Indiana University authorities, in the closing years of the depression decade, undertook to control the automobile menace by requiring the purchase of a special student tag, and by prohibiting student parking on the campus between 8:00 A.M. and 5:00 P.M. Even this early it was discovered that it was all but impossible to regulate use of automobiles because the arm of campus authority was too short to reach the fugitive machine.

Use of automobiles in the decade of the 1930s gave new dimensions to student activities in Indiana University. Only the intensity of the depression tempered this invasion which necessitated tight restrictions. It would be impossible to sound the moral depths of change or to describe the revolutionary features of this new age of student mobility. Students became highly attuned to social life elsewhere, and the campus ceased to be the major focal center of many of their social affairs. To concerned observers of these years the campus gave the impression of being a place of student apathy. Chris Savage, a campus editor, said Indiana students were under heavy criticism because of their apparent lack of interest in cultural things. They seemed never to have visited the mezzanine art gallery in the Bookstore or the Steele studio in the Library. He hoped the acquisition of the

Thomas Hart Benton murals for the new Auditorium and the Business Building would kindle an interest in art on the campus. Savage apologized for the class-coke routine of the student body. He believed the pursuit of higher learning was for many people a will-o'-the-wisp. Apparently they pursued Owen Meredith's philosophy:

We may live without poetry, music and art
But where is the man who can live without dining?

It was an established fact that Indiana University students could not live without dining in 1939, but they were exposed to serious hazard in catering to the custom. Out of 80 local Bloomington restaurants only 11 received an "A" rating from the district sanitarian. Men spent less money for their sustenance than women, even in the microbic-ladened holes in the walls, and they preferred to spend much of their time in purely male company. On May 3, 1939, the men's lounge in the Memorial Union was opened, and was described as a "safe relaxation refuge for men only—safe from the encroachment of co-eds, dances, meetings, record hours, lectures or any other programs which have forced the men of this university to give up the old men's lounge." There was even objection to the presence of a female cashier, and, horror of horrors, a suggestion was made that beer be served in the lounge as in the student union at the University of Wisconsin.

If one turned back into American university history as Ernest Earnest did in the *Academic Procession* (1953), or as *Life Magazine* attempted to do in 1942, he would conclude that student life at the close of the depression was largely superficial. The last of the "red hot mamas," red shoes, high-pinched bras, rolled stockings, and empty heads were slinking off the scene with a shake of the hips, and a seductive beckon of the head. The Indiana *Arbutus* features were misleading in this direction. A closer inspection of group pictures or individual senior photographs reveals quite another thing. Girls actually appeared sedate, and their facial expressions were those of sober young Hoosiers crossing the bar from adolescence to maturity. There appeared not to be a "red hot mama" among them. The "big men on the campus" strode about inflated with self-importance, and the "chesty" athlete sometimes gave far more evidence of being at an all-campus hop than on the receiving end of a forward pass. There were "necking parties," it only took two people and a Ford car to organize one, and no doubt some campus widows engaged in "chain dating" to inflate their flagging egos. This was the coloration which, like the muddy streaks of confluent streams where one ran clear and the other murky, gave off more appearance than substance.

The number of Indiana students who could truly be called "Joe Colleges" and "Betty Co-eds" was small. There were many reasons to support this view. There was marked apathy on the part of most students so far as a formal expression of interest in campus queens and razzle-dazzle was concerned. Cheerleaders, class officers, and other college popularity contests were left to the superficial and over-ambitious.

In March 1939 the *Daily Student* was highly critical of the stereotyping of Indiana students with the derogatory names of "Joe College" and "Betty Co-ed." It blamed, however, the collegians themselves for producing variety shows and other entertainments which used such giddy characters. In the paper's opinion the old college rah-rah spirit was dead, and the campus should reflect the images of the moment.

Elections for popular student offices often revealed a remarkably small minority vote. For instance, in April 1938, only 499 men cast votes in the selection of a prom queen, and the winner apparently received only 189 votes. Earlier Ruth Smith was elected president of Associated Women Students, and only 600 ballots were cast out of a possible 2,000 votes. Seventy-six beauties competed in the *Arbutus* beauty contest. The *Daily Student* commented that elections that year were the hottest ever for student body president, with the old distinctions between "organized" and "independent" disappearing. "It," said the paper, "was the fairest ever," and this no doubt partially accounted for the ridiculously small vote.

Some students in January 1939 were charged with flagrant dishonesty in the area of academic performance. It was discovered that the English Department's final examination in freshman literature had been stolen and either sold or given to students. This was discovered because of the remarkable similarity of answers given on papers. Some of the cheaters admitted they had seen copies of the questions, and that these had been distributed in fraternity houses.

An internal survey was made that year after the English Department incident, and it was revealed that 67 per cent of the student body had no qualms about cheating. Sunday town-hall meetings were devoted to the discussion of academic honesty with Professor M. L. Anshen of the School of Business speaking for the faculty. Students charged lack of good faculty-student relations, the inability of professors either to make fair examinations or to draft them without maliciousness; students were charged with cramming; and, finally, it was concluded that examinations served no constructive purpose. The Associated Women Students and the Board of Standards assumed otherwise. A campaign was planned to reach 1,789 women undergraduates registered in the university for the second semester of 1940. These bodies proposed in public discussions to clarify faculty examination rules, and to eliminate cheating from the campus. Another point of view held, "Taxes and poor relatives will always be with us, says an adage. It ought not to be necessary to add cheaters to the omnipresent category."

Cheating no doubt reflected a part of the conflict in the modern American university student that showed more than a mere desire to receive a respectable course mark. Either psychologists had come to have a much more profound understanding of human nature, or post-depression times had developed sharper conflicts within the psyche of students. A survey of 160 Indiana students in March 1939 revealed that there were innumerable emotional conflicts which handicapped them. Most important of which were the problems of substituting college life for the environment of the home. The complexity of social organizations on the campus not only confused students, but irritated many of them to the point of inner rebellion. Impersonal professors created further conflicts, and so did interfraternity and group rivalries. There is evidence that students of this era were beset by serious emotional problems. A campus editorial on February 15, 1939, indicated that a considerable number of students had withdrawn from the university because of a lack of adequate assistance in the area of mental hygiene.

Cheating was still a serious campus issue in 1941, and Judge Frank M. Martin ('03) of Lawrence County said gambling was another. He indicated Indiana students were quite active about the poker tables in the stonebelt town of Bedford, and that fraternity houses on the campus sheltered games. Both President Wells and Dean of Men Clarence E. Edmondson denied this was true, and they were supported by the Monroe County prosecutor who said that no complaints of local gambling had been brought to his attention.

Despite charges of apathy on the part of students, and the nostalgia of the public and press for a carefree campus atmosphere in which students acted as irresponsibly as animals, there was an awareness of public and world problems in a core of serious people. The *Indiana Daily Student* editor felt the local co-eds should refuse to wear silk stockings until Japan withdrew from Manchuria. At the same time the paper expressed the opinion that pacifism (it called it a "leftist tendency") was dying out. During Christmas holidays of 1938 there were national meetings of several student organizations in which the nonpacifists voted in the majority. This was especially true of the National Student Federation of Americans for Adequate Defense. The *Daily Student* said "the pacifists and pink sections" were outvoted decisively as planks calling for national defenses were presented.

An incident occurred before the Sigma Alpha Epsilon fraternity house in October 1938 which reflected student opinion. As a Halloween joke the S. A. E.'s unfurled a large black and white swastika on their front lawn. During dinner they proclaimed a nazi creed, and then goose-stepped outdoors. Almost immediately they were set upon by a mob of students with buckets, water hose, missiles, and other bruising instruments. The fraternity men were glad to surrender their swastika, especially in the face of a police sortie. The student paper said, "The S. A. E.'s have decided that I.U. is no place for nazism, Halloween or no Halloween." How much of this was a staged college antic may be open to question; the resulting bruises, however, were real.

That fall David B. Richardson, in an expression of student opinion, said criticism of Hitler and his pride in Aryan stock should be tempered. Americans were equally as offensive in their racial prejudices toward Negroes and Jews. Negro athletes, he said, were barred from Big Ten basketball, baseball, and tennis. It was almost impossible for a Negro to graduate from West Point. There were "Jim Crow" railway cars. Jews, he said, were leaders in developing the movie industry and in business, and some Chinese were famous for great inventions and art, and all of them were not allowed to live in the average American suburban town. "Let those who shoot off their mouths about the great racial cruelties of Hitler look to their own land of liberty," said Richardson, "where equality is a word not a practice."

A public forum held in Alumni Hall in October 1939 discussed the United States and the European War. The gathering took the position that Americans abhorred Hitlerism, and all it stood for. The *Daily Student* editor expressed the belief that "War and all its complements creates paradoxes." One of these, he thought, was America's desire to remain neutral, but at the same time wanting to see Hitlerism destroyed. It was pointed out in the meeting that British and French citizens were already subjected to regimentation. Professor Ernest Marshall Linton expressed opposition to such an idea, and the audience gave him a loud cheer.

A student polled 100 of his fellows on the subject of whether or not they would supply aid to the allies: 92 said, "Let them help themselves, and if they fail, Germany would be so badly weakened that it could not attack the western hemisphere." Ten students placed war blame on the German people, 68 favored revision of neutrality policies, and 68 favored a strict cash-and-carry policy. In case of a treaty with Germany 20 students favored vindictiveness toward the Germans, and 60 favored humane revision of the Treaty of Versailles.

On Armistice Day 1938 Indiana University had held a ceremony with brass band music and a military review, a year later, however, the mood had changed. The Armistice Day celebration consisted of a proclamation of peace and orchestral music. "Thus preachment of the doctrine of peace and exhibition of the type of culture that thrives in peace time will take the place of military madness," said the *Daily Student* editor. "It seems to us entirely fitting and proper."

In that year Edward W. Pugh, Jr., of Stanford University extended Indiana an invitation to send a delegation to the Japanese-American Student Conference in Tokyo in July 1940. President Wells appointed Dean Fernandus Payne to have charge of arranging for the university's representation. There had been, however, anti-Japanese opposition on the campus because of the Manchurian situation, and in a poll taken in 1939, 375 students stated a decidedly pro-Chinese sentiment. Only 27 thought Japan was justified in its invasion of China; 197 wanted to place an embargo against export of munitions of war, and 184 hoped the United States would refuse to sign a new trade treaty with Japan until that nation withdrew from China; 161 girls said they would cease wearing silk stockings, socks, and ties, and 49 per cent of the men would give up silken garments compared with 40 per cent of the women.

A student non-aggression committee was formed as a branch of a New York organization with Professors A. B. Hollingshed, C. L. Lundin, and Mrs. A. R. Lindesmith as officers. Just before this the Sigma Delta Chi professional journalism fraternity had perpetrated a propaganda hoax and had narrowly escaped a brush with the Dies Committee. The organization had sponsored a speech by a Dr. Karl X. Boehmer, a phony radical Nazi, so it was said, to test student concern and alertness. Apparently the hoax did not stir a ripple, and students went about their affairs to the horror of the jokesters. Essentially the fraternity members concluded the campus was a place of apathy. It might have appeared otherwise, however, had the hoax taken place a day or two later. Major Hampden Wilson, a Dies Committee investigator, appeared in Bloomington. He was on a tour of fifty colleges to discover the existence of cells of the American Student Union, which he branded an instrument of communism. President Wells told Major Wilson that there was no branch of the union at Indiana University. He said that Hoosier students were for the most part conservative, and refused to subscribe to "isms."

President Wells no doubt was unaware that an organizer for the American Student Union had come to the campus in October 1937. An unnamed co-ed was in charge of the drive to establish a chapter, but she must have been a victim of the prevailing student apathy. There were chapters at Chicago, Minnesota, Purdue, Butler, Northwestern, and John Herron Art School. This organization supported a peace movement and equality among students regardless of race, creed, sex, politics, and nationality. It favored making the Reserve Officers Training Corps optional rather than compulsory, and campaigned for more democracy in student-faculty relationships. There is no evidence that a chapter was ever organized at Indiana.

Even though the student body appeared apathetic, perhaps it was mostly uninformed about current world conditions. The

Committee on Peace Education acted as sponsor for peace week in April 1940. A peace convocation was held, pamphlets were distributed, a peace poster contest was conducted, and on the evening of April 19 Richard Corwin's peace play, *They Fly Through the Air with the Greatest of Ease*, was performed. In addition, a religious workshop was held to promote peace.

All of this was serious business that interested professors and thoughtful students. Joe College and Betty Co-ed may have been in the majority at this time, but it is doubtful. They were the noisiest of students, and on every festive occasion made certain they were on public display, but in the everyday grind most students appeared to be fundamentally of serious minds. Students complained about some conditions in the university, often not knowing precisely what their dissatisfactions were about. One impetuous lass at least was certain. She stamped her foot and declared herself "free, white, and twenty-one," and she wanted the institution to give attention to peace matters close to home and revoke the 10:00 P.M. curfew restrictions on girls. While the lass with romance in her soul and dance in her feet wanted more time to savor the evenings, other students gave attention to the presidential campaign of 1940. This contest held for them an intimate meaning because a member of the university family was in the race. A poll of the campus showed Wendell Willkie leading with 63 per cent, Franklin D. Roosevelt had 30 per cent support, and Donald Duck and Mickey Mouse one-half of 1 per cent each.

President Herman B Wells could be numbered among those people in the closing of the 1930s who was sentimental about the past, but deeply concerned about the future. For three years he had conducted a crusade to add well prepared and promising professors to the staff. He also favored raising social and intellectual standards of the school. In September 1940 he undertook to unite a sense of continuity with the past with a promise for the future when he administered the Athenian Oath to 2,500 students from the steps of the Student Building. This oath had been devised by William Lowe Bryan, and had been administered for some time as a gesture to Indiana University's earlier commitment to the classical tradition. In this ceremony Susan Stull acted the part of the "Spirit of Indiana" in which she pleaded for loyalty to the past from underclassmen. These modern Athenians were embarking upon what Wells viewed as the career of the "new university."

Everybody agreed acts such as the administering of the Athenian Oath were sincere and stimulating, but the need was for genuine intellectual stirrings on the part of everybody. "Recently," said the campus editor, "the *Daily Student* sought to absolve students of the charge that they show a lethargic interest in the cultural and intellectual life of the University, by showing that there are few opportunities for students to participate in the cultural and intellectual aspects that are supposed to be an essential part of any modern university. Such opportunities, as was pointed out before, simply do not exist on this campus." The subject was a touchy one with faculty and administration, but notwithstanding, the university was challenged to offer more imaginative intellectual stimulation. Students, it was said, were enrolled in the university to learn how to make a living, and were not learning how to live. That was largely the institution's fault. It was too expensive to bring in notable speakers from the outside, but there were plenty of bright professors who could stimulate students in non-class lectures. Specifically, it was said that Albert L. Kohlmeier could give students an appreciation of American colonial beginnings and the formation of the United States Constitution. Fowler V. Harper had much to offer in the interpretation of the law in social and political growth, and in explaining the workings of governmental agencies. The University was challenged to prove students wrong by offering some non-credit lectures. No appreciable use was made of the Library except to read required assignments, and there were many other areas where students failed to respond to their essential purposes. "But a great deal more of the criticism," said the student author, "is ill-founded. How can students take an interest in the 'intellectual side' of the University if opportunities and means are lacking?" Until the university stirred intellectual interests, the students would ignore the carping of "professional critics," and relax by drinking "cokes" in the commons.

The constant lamentation about apathy on the campus had some aftereffects that the authors could never have anticipated. The general impression outside the university was that the Indiana campus in earlier years had been a glorified country club, a reputation the institution had been trying hard to outlive since 1935. Then the caricature of the college man and woman in the

1930s seemed to be brought into clear focus by all the complaints of social and intellectual failure on the campus. If, in fact, campus intellectual life in America moved along at a disturbingly complacent pace, as so many critics said it did, then that tempo was rudely interrupted in November 1942, when *Life Magazine* sent its reporter-photographer Walter Sanders to the Indiana campus to "take a farewell look at doomed folkways." The magazine's editors pretended to believe in two faulty premises: First, that the traditional American college spirit and campus folkways were dying, even though just the month before the publication had shown students and universities engaged in war services. Second, the editors expressed the belief that an entirely new set of campus mores and customs would appear in universities. In a mock sentimental note, *Life* said, "Boys who are already in the army will read these pages and feel a little sad because it [the old razzle-dazzle] will never come again."

Before his visit to the Indiana campus the *Life* reporter had secured a copy of John Visher's '42 booklet *Our Indiana* which listed "do's and don'ts" for freshmen to follow. The reporter chose the "don'ts" and presented them in fourteen pictures in a five-page spread as recognized practices. It was said that the students who posed for the pictures were amateur actors and were led to believe that they were illustrating dramatically John Visher's "don'ts." The various pictures showed students tromping the memorial plaque in the Memorial Union, jitterbugging, a campus "big man" politician, "snaffling," lounge lizards asleep, "pin hanging," and flirting in the Library. One especially intriguing picture was of a co-ed sitting on the corner of a professor's desk exposing as much thigh as the *Life* reporter thought his editors would tolerate. The picture was labeled "apple polishing." The photographs were so obviously posed and overacted that only an innocent could have credited them as fact.

Appearance of the November 23 issue of *Life* with the Indiana pictures sent a tremor through a good part of the American undergraduate world. On the Indiana campus the picture story was viewed as a well-nigh disastrous slap in the face, if not a downright betrayal by Henry R. Luce's empire. The *Daily Student* editor wrote, "While we do not make the claim that the students of this university are as war-minded and as war conscious as they might be, we do feel that such a one-sided presentation of the picture is definitely unfair to this institution." The paper frankly admitted that some things pictured were true, but it denied that a student sense of custom and tradition, and even of propriety, had been pushed into the background.

By November 1942 Indiana University was deeply involved in "the broadest war program of any institution in the Nation." From *Life Magazine's* article and pictures, however, a reader got the impression that its students had never heard of the great international conflict. The student editor felt the institution had within recent years, lived down the damaging country club reputation, but with the appearance of the misleading article parents would be reluctant to patronize the university.

At the University of California in Los Angeles, a student editor of the *Daily Bruin* condemned the *Life* article. "Just because a crafty reporter-photographer got a few publicity struck youngsters in a midwestern university to pose for him to illustrate what he wanted to portray of college life was no reason why all American undergraduate society should be indicted," said the *Bruin*. Further, "The immature adolescents who inanely scamper across the pages of *Life* are no more representative of the average American undergraduate than the article itself is of *Life's* usually sound judgment."

On December 2 the Harvard *Crimson* editor crushed both Henry R. Luce and *Life Magazine*. It thought somebody should make up Luce's mind for him. One week his magazine illustrated war efforts in American colleges, and the next it supplied fodder to Nazi propagandists. "If *Life's* editors," said the *Crimson*, "are to be listened to, students in our colleges are having a riot of a time making pick-ups in libraries, wearing zoot suits and playing havoc with the sanity of their professors." If *Life* was correct then the Harvard paper felt certain the axis powers had nothing to fear because the American undergraduate was devoid of brains and the ability to care. However, it appeared *Life's* editors were the Americans who lived in a vacuum. They gave little evidence in the Indiana article of knowing about the highly specialized services which institutions of higher education were rendering the war effort. "The real picture," thought the *Crimson*, "would have been less picturesque. It would have been dull, and purposeful and earnest. What's more important, it would have been the picture that students have helped to make, the one they're proud of—whether it's photogenic or not."

The real belly blow to the Luce empire, however, came not

from student editors and campus petitioners, but from its old nemesis Colonel Robert McCormick's lordly *Chicago Tribune*. In defending Indiana University the paper struck out at the Associated and United presses as the "pantywaist" or "insect" press. A part of this general insect breed, said the *Tribune*, was the Time-Life-Fortune axis of Henry R. Luce; "One of the men for whom the draft age was reduced from 45 to 38," said the editor. In the case of the "student-end-of-an-age debacle" at Indiana University, the Chicago editor said, "The other day more than a thousand students, faculty members, and alumni of Indiana University sent an open letter to *Life Magazine* denouncing as 'completely falsified' a pictorial feature of student life which the magazine printed on Nov. 23.

"Some slick little photographer for the magazine produced a booklet setting forth what student opinion considered improper behavior, and asked that students with experience in dramatics assist him in making a photo feature of the booklet. But when Life offered the pictures to its readers, it was not in this light of the 'do's and do not's' of students behavior, but as a 'candid' view of daily life on the campus. . . . The smart aleck editors then drew from this choice bit of fakery the moral that students of all American colleges, and of Indiana especially, are 'still living cozily in a world of fantasy; with no awareness there is a war.' Life was careful to omit that a great proportion of the students whom it libeled were taking courses directly preparatory to war services." The magazine was further ridiculed by the Chicago paper for its seeming intent to present American students in the most superficial light.

From around the country letter writers denounced Henry R. Luce and his organization. As the *Chicago Tribune* said, Indiana students, faculty, and alumni addressed an open letter to Henry R. Luce in which they said his editorial policy must be, "Never let the facts stand in the way of a good story." This stinging rebuttal concluded, "We Hoosiers, proud of our reputation of our loyalty in War or Peace, resent any such article as *Life's* (which intentionally or otherwise) ridicules our university and undermines public confidence in our university and its unstinted efforts to hasten the Winning of the War.

"To say the least, *Life* owes Indiana University, its students, faculty members, alumni, and friends, a prompt (see Webster) apology." The *Alumni Magazine* then reviewed fully the impressive war activities of the university, every paragraph of which demolished *Life's* shabby thesis about American student life and attitudes. After a tremendous pounding across the nation, and from Indiana in particular, *Life Magazine* in its issue of February 1, 1843, apologized to the university under the heading, "—With These [a new series of pictures] Life Makes Its Apologies for an Injustice Done to Indiana University." Internal evidence, however, seems to indicate that the editorial staff lost little time searching Webster's Dictionary for a definition of the word. The substance of apology was about as "oily" as the original story. The editors said, "*Life* found the booklet [*Our Indiana*] topical and humorous enough to send photographer Walter Sanders to the campus to illustrate its 'do's and don't's' and its guide to local customs." Then they explained, "When the story was published, however, a regrettable editorial misunderstanding resulted in an unfair interpretation of the pictures. The Indiana scenes were presented not as carefully posed 'Do's and Don'ts' from the booklet but as a general pattern of undergraduate behavior which was about to be swept away by a lowering of the draft age. Not only the willing boys and girls (most of them amateur actors) who helped photographer Sanders to get the dramatized pictures but also the student body felt outraged at such journalistic treatment." The magazine then commended the students for their etiquette booklet, and ran sixteen new pictures over negative captions presenting a much more serious and sedate Indiana University.

On the campus the *Daily Student* accepted the apology in about the same terms as *Life's* evasive explanation of its editorial blundering. "What Life Magazine does not state," said the paper, "is that the apology was made only after Henry R. Luce, editor of Life, and others connected with that publication, had been swamped with letters, newspaper articles, telephone calls and even telegrams from university alumni and friends who protested the distortion, unfairness and inaccuracy of the Nov. 23 pictures." In a more fundamental vein *Life* failed to admit that its editors were living in November 1942, and not "cosily in a world of fantasy far removed from the human realities of the world around them."

The *Chicago Tribune* had no notion of letting the Life-Time-Fortune axis rest in peace. It said of the apology, "Life Magazine,

Henry Robinson Luce's gift to the barber shops, has got around about two months late to apologizing to Indiana University, its faculty, students, and alumni." A factor behind Luce's apology was encouragement from Westbrook Pegler that he do so. Even *Life* did not want to tangle with Pegler, and Pegler, in turn, was encouraged to enter the fight by an Indiana alumna who was infuriated by the story. When Pegler asked President Wells what the administration expected to do about the libel, Wells told him nothing because he wanted the story to die without further injury to the institution. Pegler then told him he was going to pursue the matter.

A bit of turmoil over the *Life* story occurred off the campus. One of the students posed in an undignified posture was the daughter of a prominent Presbyterian clergyman, and this had repercussions in that church's circles, especially in Indianapolis. People pretended, at least, to see in the girl's actions a less than desirable home atmosphere; on the other hand there was sharp resentment that the young lady had been abused by "Henry Robinson Luce's smart aleck" photographer. If *Life* truly meant to mark the end of a collegiate era with a roaring thunderclap, it could scarcely have done a better job of what one critic called "yellow Hearstian journalism."

So loud was the criticism of student lack of interest in campus and public affairs that it came within range of presidential notice. In March 1941, President Herman B Wells appointed a special committee to oversee cultural matters on the campus. This group made plans to use local resources to broaden the horizon of concern and information. Albert L. Kohlmeier, Hugh E. Willis, and Fowler V. Harper were asked to lecture on American institutions and law. Provisions were made for a future panel to carry on other discussions in the same general areas. Oliver P. Field of the Political Science Department had charge of the campus lectures, and the first series happily proved competitive with both student apathy and spring sports.

Another assault was made upon the rock of campus unawareness when A. B. Hollingshed of the Department of Sociology conducted a one-man propaganda analysis to determine how alert students were as to the quality of world leadership. He asked them to adjudge world leaders within the context of five categories. They rated Winston Churchill first, Franklin D. Roosevelt second, and there followed in order Charles A. Lindbergh, Chiang Kai-Shek, Wendell L. Willkie, Martin Dies, William Knudson, Sidney Hillman, Paul Renaud, Premier Konoye, Adolf Hitler, Josef Stalin, and Benito Mussolini. Hitler had improved his position three points over Professor Hollingshed's first survey, but Benito clung firmly to the lowest rung.

In another area student interest was being awakened. A constitution establishing self-government was ready for detailed consideration early in May. This document was to begin an era of parliamentary nit-picking. Arguments were soon underway on issues of "town" representation, the legislative process, veto powers, and the powerful administrative council. Student self-government was indeed a long step from the days of Andrew Wylie, Cyrus Nutt, David Starr Jordan, and even William Lowe Bryan when student affairs remained under the strict administrative thumb. This move signified both a more liberal presidency of the institution, and changing conditions generally all through the American academic world. Perhaps the emotionalism of wartime and the democratic issues of the moment had much to do with the beginnings of student self-government. Historically, a greater barrier to student political freedoms was the granite-like wall between the Greek letter fraternities and the nonfraternity students. The Greeks nominated hand-picked candidates and organized tightly controlled campaigns in their behalf. "Honors" had a far-different meaning to the fraternities than to the "barbs." In a move to break the traditional slating of office seekers, the student newspaper put forward in 1942 the name of Leona Menze for prom queen, and later withdrew her nomination with the statement, "For we have made our point." In fuller explanation the editor said, "We have watched the growing feeling in student politics. There seems no rhyme or reason other than one votes blindly because he's organized or he isn't. Certainly we have reached a stage in life where liking and respecting a candidate as a person and as a leader should be the prime consideration—but for Indiana University students, we suspect this is too much to ask." Leona Menze (maybe a hoax) appears to have frightened both sides and to have exposed the shallowness of student responses to campus elections.

Indiana University probably deserved in some measure its reputation of being a good country club institution in the 1930s. During the years 1925–45, it must have been among the most highly organized campuses in the country. There were the student Chamber of Commerce, the Y. M. C. A. and Y. W. C. A., the Flying Club, Saddle Club, the Union Board, Board of Aeons, Board of Standards, Pershing Rifles, the Flame Club, the Top Hat Club, Townettes, and the Cosmopolitan Club. Besides these, every academic subject and professional college was represented by at least one club. There were more than twenty campus organizations open only to women, and the men's organizations were numberless.

In 1940 an attempt was made to bring about a sweeping reordering of campus societies, clubs, and organizations. Dean C. E. Edmondson and Dean Kate Mueller advocated placing a sharp limitation on the number of activities in which a student could participate. They proposed establishment of a point system ranging from 1 to 100 by which they could determine the stage at which the maximum might be established. President Wells approved this move, and in November he wrote the boards of Aeons and Standards, "I congratulate you upon the constructive beginnings which you have made in the solution of a difficult problem of limitation of extracurricular activities. I recognize that no beginning plan will prove correct in all details, but the direction of the program which you have outlined seems to me to be sound and I am happy to give my approval to it." In March 1941 Dean Mueller announced a system of checks which she would use to determine the eligibility of girls to participate in organized activities.

While deans of men and women, and various student groups were engaged in 1940 and 1941 in curbing organizational activities, a new custom was established that involved a few more student activities in extracurricular interests. The Sigma Delta Chi Fraternity planned to give a Brown Derby to the best-liked professor on the campus, but was unable to obtain such an item in Bloomington. Julian Ferguson wrote asking Alfred E. Smith to contribute one. The "Happy Warrior" responded to this request in the very best style of alert politician: "I have your letter of recent date," he told Sullivan. "I am sending forward by parcel post a brown derby duly autographed. It is one I have worn myself for a short time." Al did not specify what he meant by "a short time." Perhaps he meant he had passed it over his thinning locks. This award was to be made annually at the Gridiron banquet.

As the university became more deeply immersed in war services and responsibilities, efforts were made to give students serious challenges. A student war council was appointed to act as a clearing body for campus problems and to respond to complaints and petitions. It was expected to make recommendations to the deans of men and women, and to help adjust all other matters of daily campus concern. This student committee even had the potential power to concern itself with campus social affairs, and deans Kate H. Mueller and Robert E. Bates acted as faculty advisors.

At the opening of the spring semester in 1942, the student affairs committee faced the dilemma of maintaining the social calendar in the face of radically reduced student numbers and sharply revised wartime schedules. Some rules were waived because of the presence on the campus of military personnel. Social events were allowed on week nights because the Federal Government had decreased the "play time" of the various services personnel in Bloomington. Indiana girls, however, saw their social privileges shrink from 12:30 P.M. to 10:30 P.M. on work-a-day nights, principally on Friday nights.

An additional student committee of eighteen members was appointed to deal with such matters as promoting war and service-related campaigns of all sorts. They supplied volunteer clerical help, promoted interest in special defense courses set up by the university, participated in bond and savings fund drives, and did many errands. No doubt the desire to popularize the newly instituted compulsory physical fitness and mental education program was an important fact back of the appointment of the student committee. No aspect of the war program was to create more tension than the physical fitness one. Students complained about the stringency of its physical requirements, low credit allowance, and what they deemed unreasonable instructional demands of the Physical Education Department.

At Purdue, said Indiana students, men were required to take only three hours of physical education a week as compared with five and six hours at Indiana. Indiana, it was said, placed more emphasis on calisthenics and less on obstacle races. The *Daily Student* felt there ought to be some things men liked to do instead of all that jumping over horses, standing on one's head, diving onto mats, and cutting somersaults. Instead of proving exciting, physical education had become a grinding dull chore. Five days a week was enough of the grind. "Surely every week day," said the editor, "is enough to build better physical specimens in Indiana."

An appeal was made to the University War Council to let up on the spartan fitness program. Students assured the administration of their zeal for reduction in the amount of gymnastic drill in every way they knew. This dissatisfaction spilled over into the area of credit for all academic work. There was strong objection to the reduction of three-hour courses to two and a half hours' credit. In student opinion no time was really saved by the three-semester year, or the elongated summer session if the administration insisted on reducing credits allowed. "We propose that the summer semester be made a 'third semester,' as advertised, so more three hour courses will run for 3 hours." Student proponents of this idea felt, in July 1942, that the time had come for decision because "the bone of contention has been chewed dry and bare." But the faculty still seemed reluctant to act. By 1942, for large numbers of students, the university had become a place of wartime drudgery. Even many of the cherished summertime social events scheduled for 1942 were dropped by the wayside, including plans for the traditional senior prom which were still incomplete.

The campus took on the façade of an institution pushing at every point to cram knowledge of the world into students. A map case was established in the Memorial Union Building to keep them informed about the geographical locus of the daily news, and to outline the theatres of war. Four co-eds, Lorraine Holsinger, Rachel Stoner, Rosemary Hendricks, and Margaret Hotola, discussed women in wartime on the university's radio program, "Editorial of the Air." A campaign to elect a "Bond Queen" rivaled the election of a prom queen in popularity, and votes were purchased at a penny apiece. Indiana University's quota was $10,000, but Norma Deckard garnered $8,979.10, and Betty Porter $5,129.10, and the prediction was they would earn $35,000 between them before the polls were closed.

By this time the war had become an emotional issue on the campus. Students complained that old dating rules were outmoded by conditions on the campus. Social life during much of the war was erratic because of the military schedules for men and women. Because of this both military and regular students felt strongly that university social rules should be relaxed to permit them to enjoy moments of free time whenever they occurred. This meant the development of a new concept of social relationships throughout the week instead of over weekends. It was argued that U. S. O., dugouts, church centers, and other places of service entertainment allowed dancing on Sunday afternoons. A proposal was made by the Student Affairs Committee that men be allowed to visit sorority houses, dormitory foyers, assembly rooms, and other social centers for daily dancing from 6:30 to 7:30 P.M., but that the traditional hours on Friday and Saturday evenings still be observed. This indeed was a daring step into the future.

Perhaps Indiana University never did alleviate all its wartime social snags, nor did it relax many of the pressures exerted on the old social routine by the presence of so many diversified military and special services groups on the campus. Unhappily the male student population was for the most part in uniform, and it could not be fitted handily into the orthodox instructional and campus programs. Complaints were many and constant. The Student War Council and other special committees could only struggle to adjust problems; they never really solved them.

Four years of distraction of campus routine by the war had highly discernible effects upon student life. By September 1944 it seemed reasonably apparent that the war was entering its final phases. The time had come to plan a revival of student government, and to return to the ways of campus life undistracted by military activities. It was felt that all classes and groups should exercise voices in campus government. Past student bodies, it was said, had done more griping than governing. In the future students had to prove themselves more responsive to their campus political interests. The newly established governmental organization demanded action or the overall Student Council would become an autocratic body exerting greater influence than the old organization-bound slates of the past.

The story of the organization of student self-government at Indiana University is indeed a complex one, and the issue involved almost all the central facts of student-university relationships. From September 1937 to February 15, 1944, a campaign was under way to inaugurate a system of student self-government. The university administration seemed convinced that one of the best safeguards it could develop against the maladjustments and internal conflicts sure to result from a rising enrollment was to place serious responsibility in the hands of students. It was dramatically clear in 1937 that the ancient system of choosing class officers, and officers for central student organizations was woefully out of date in all the American university system, and in Indiana University in particular. There was even a hint of corruption in connection with the annual elections. Student indifference seemed a sure sign of these facts. Only twelve Indiana students had filed for forty-two class offices by the deadline in 1937. Part of this failure was due to the adoption of a merit point system administered by "Committee X" which attempted to eliminate political ballyhoo and partisan pulling and hauling in campaigns. There was also the issue of balancing men and women nominees on tickets.

Further complicating student political affairs was the fact that three top campus organizations exerted a wide influence. The Board of Aeons, an exclusive body composed of twelve top leadership men chosen by the president of the university and founded in 1921, had almost a veto influence. Second was the self-perpetuating Union Board. This powerful student group was charged with preferring organized over unorganized candidates for replacement on the board. It was contended that the Union Board split the campus into almost two irreconcilable political camps. Finally, there was the Associated Women Students which exercised a powerful voice in establishing guidelines in general matters of student decorum. Besides these, of course, were numerous other organizations which exerted some influence on campus affairs.

The general confusion of student issues in 1938 attracted the serious attention of the faculty self-study committee, and it was decided by this critical body that the university should take positive steps to determine the possibility of establishing a representative form of student government. Correctly, it was contended that students in Indiana University were being governed without representation, and in the turmoil of the late 1930s, when democratic government at all levels of society was being emphasized, this condition had to be corrected. The faculty and administration were of the opinion students should have a voice in solving not only their peculiar campus problems, but many academic ones as well.

As the spring semester of 1938 drew to a close the idea of organizing a central student self-governing body caught on, and three propositions were submitted for a campus-wide choice. Students were asked to decide whether they wanted to be governed by a council dominated by the administration, by a student-controlled board, or on an equality level with university officials.

More than a year elapsed before another active step was taken in the direction of instituting self-government. The Associated Women Students instituted the Board of Standards composed of three seniors, two juniors, and one sophomore. This body was required to meet weekly with the Dean of Women to adjudicate matters involving women students. At the same time the Board of Standards became active, Jacob Wittman published the results of his survey of student self-government. In fifty-three universities it was said that such a form of government functioned satisfactorily. Wittman stung local pride by concluding that, compared with a dozen of the institutions he considered progressive in the management of student affairs, Indiana University appeared to be very poor. At that moment a new student constitution seemed to be on the verge of adoption at the University of Missouri, and it was the result of a successful student survey. For Indiana, however, the most impressive example of student government was at the University of Wisconsin, which had maintained such a plan for the past thirty-five years.

Agitation for the self-governing issue in Bloomington resulted in the holding of town hall meetings, some of them presided over by the Reverend Frank Beck, the campus religious leader. J. E. Patrick, manager of the Indiana Memorial Union, said, "In a university community of some 5,000 students it should be reasonable to expect those students to want to devise some system of government in which all would have an opportunity to participate." Dean Selatie E. Stout of the College of Arts and Sciences welcomed the idea, and so did Dean of Women Kate Mueller and Professor Herman T. Briscoe, who had charge of the Freshman Vocational Guidance Program and was chairman of the self-study committee. In the town meeting fault was found with the Board of Aeons because it was not a representative body, to which Edward Hutton ('40) replied on December 2, 1939, "If as a result of the Town Hall meeting Sunday, it can be shown that the student body really wants a new, more dramatic form of student government, then the Board of Aeons is more than willing to reorganize itself to comply with student demand."

The *Indiana Daily Student* was forehanded. It drafted a plan of representative government in which nine proportional representative districts would elect twenty-seven delegates to a constituent assembly, but nine co-eds must be assured election because, "The co-eds would be more familiar with campus problems, better leaders and a steadying influence." The paper then outlined the details of the proposed government admitting, "Perhaps it is far from perfect, but it applies actual Federal Government methods to the campus and thus it is, in effect, a college laboratory in political science." It was said every student would become a better citizen under such a system.

The town hall meeting on December 4, 1939, was attended by slightly more than a hundred students out of an enrollment of approximately 5,000. Indicative of the central problem was the unresolved question of "How can student opinion be aroused so student government may be had?" There were replies to this question, but none really answered it. The discussion brought up many campus irritations, but generally it was desultory.

Between December 1939 and February 1944 constant discussion and debate took place over the self-governing issue. Not even vital concern with war issues crowded it out of the record. Convocations, town hall meetings, classroom assignments, campus newspaper coverage, survey committee reports, and internal reviews became monotonous parts of campus life. The *Daily Student* continued to blast campus indifference. On February 3, 1940, the editor said, "Town Hall's program Sunday night (scheduled for tomorrow [Feb. 4]) is designed to try if it can to pry students from their retreat of indifference by encouraging them to constructive thinking." There was reason for this comment; a petition asking President Wells to appoint still another committee to investigate self-government had lain for some time on a Memorial Union desk and had accumulated only 200 signers. The petition had finally to be withdrawn and passed around by hand. It was necessary to find 3,000 signers or the plea would be unconvincing to the university administration.

On and on went the campaign to institute student government, and the endless discussions and editorializing, suggestions of plans, and the critical destruction of them. Despite all the noisy dialogue and commotion there were still students who asked naïvely, "What this student government is all about?" In desperation the *Daily Student* on November 1, 1941, published its proposed constitution of an "Indiana University Student Congress." Two more years, however, were to elapse before any positive steps were taken.

In the midst of the war the matter of student self-government was brought to a head on December 10, 1943, when an elected provisional student council of twelve began work on a self-governing constitution. This action came at the end of two weeks of intensive campaigning which was climaxed by a convocation in which a thousand students voted to proceed with framing a constitution. President Wells had promised self-rule "when the students prove they really want it." On January 1, 1944, he was also quoted as saying, "I have long favored student self-government and I shall be glad to do anything in my power to aid in the movement."

The provisional council of twelve worked rapidly, and by January 28, 1944, their constitution was ready to be voted upon by the student body. The constitution was adopted 831 to 65, hardly an enthusiastic response from so large a student body. There followed a post-adoption whispering campaign against self-government in which opponents pretended to believe it was the handiwork of "an ambitious and enterprising group of politicians," and that it was after all "revolutionary" in purpose. It was said also that the new plan was the "devilish devisement" of the *Daily Student* staff. On February 15, 1944, the faculty, after making a few minor amendments, unanimously approved the document, and it received the same approval from the Board of Trustees.

In his *Annual Report* for 1943–44, President Wells commented, "One of the surprising, and yet most hopeful and encouraging, events of this chaotic period was the foundation on the Bloomington campus of a plan of student self-government. Despite the reduced civilian student body, sufficient leadership existed to enable the students to write a constitution and to petition the faculty and Board of Trustees for its adoption."

There was more than a nostalgic note in the plea for instigation of student self-government. In some way it was hoped returning veterans and the in-rush of a newer generation of postwar students would reclaim the past, and approach the future with as little change as possible. Dean of Men Robert E. Bates in the spring of 1945 undertook to define what he believed would be the realities of the years immediately ahead. His observation, appearing in the president's *Annual Report*, 1944–45, recognized the fact that wartime and the presence of military personnel on the campus had made heavy inroads into university custom and tradition. He wrote: "If the activities program is to retain a peripheral status common in universities in times past, the work of this office should be limited largely to general supervision and regulations. If, on the other hand, this phase of student life is to be considered an integral part of the University educational program, it then becomes the responsibility of this office to see that it is conducted in such a way as to contribute most effectively to the education of the student. It is the opinion of the Dean of Men that the latter point of view should be adopted."

Dean Bates was indeed perceptive of change, and his office did become largely involved in the "education of the students." Student life was to remain an integral part of the university's program in the postwar years, but in an entirely different manner. Looking back over the past four years, President Wells, almost wistfully, reported to the Board of Trustees in his annual summary: "Student conduct was exemplary. . . . the inherent wholesomeness and integrity of our students, supported and counseled by the guiding wisdom of our Deans of Men and Women, met the new social situations in admirable and praiseworthy manner. As a consequence, the wartime letdown in behavior apparent to even a casual visitor in any large city was not discernible here." There was change, which became highly noticeable in every phase of student life and activities, both President Wells and Dean Bates wrote, before the veterans came back to the campus bringing with them their independent viewpoints and vast experiences as men and women of war.

World War II, like the first great world conflict, had a tremendous impact, first upon the structure of American society itself, and then upon the new generation of university students. Professor Leonard Lundin, who had been most active, first in efforts to maintain peace, and then in helping to explain the issues of the war before he too joined the army, found it a remarkable fact that veteran-students had matured so much in points of view and intellectual responses. Callow youth who had drifted along in the placid old stream of college life in 1940 came home in 1945 ready to question and dispute professors. They had "been there" and had first-hand views of many things that formerly had been only vague abstractions to them. Most of all they were anxious to get on with their disrupted education. The narrow old provincialisms of comfortable rural Indiana were destroyed forever. For the returning students Indiana University took on new meanings after 1945; for the most part in the field of the practicalities of earning a living.

If much of the old razzle-dazzle of the campus folkways in the 1930s survived in 1945, it was difficult to discern. Students were either more mature in their thinking and approaches or more positive and mature in their demands. They were mobile and liberated to the extent that the old campus restrictions were all but swept aside. It would be difficult indeed to sustain the point of view that they were more concerned with internal governing affairs in the areas of fundamental application, but they were anxious to get their work done and to begin making up for lost years of their lives.

It is true that the great debate over student self-government went on ad infinitum, voting patterns, however, revealed fewer organizational influences and a marked unconcern with the old issues that had seemed so important in earlier years. Pleas for a voice in the running of the university itself and the making of rules and curricula created a cacophony of sound without revolutionizing procedures in these areas. Innovations were made, but there was no wholesale revolution. The Indiana University students with active service experience in the immediate postwar years scarcely had a speaking acquaintance with the mores and folkways of the immediate past campus generation; theirs was a new academic generation that brought the currents of life in the state and on the campus into closer harmony with the realities of the times.

[IV]

Professorial Pageantry in a Changing World

WHATEVER PROFESSORIAL STANDARDS Herman B Wells and Fernandus Payne may have set for Indiana University in 1937–40 in their search for new staff members, they had to revise them sharply in 1945. In less than a decade American higher education underwent a revolution not of its making. Not only had World War II disrupted usual campus procedures, but it had made enormously heavy demands for all kinds of scientific support, and for use of the whole gamut of trained and experienced personnel. In those years the course of both world and national history was redirected. Advances in the various scientific and diplomatic fields were breathtaking. The moral and intellectual ravages of the war in Western Europe placed demands on university professors almost to the extent of robbing American institutions of their ablest instructors and research men. After 1940 governmental demands for university specialists were so heavy that if there had been no other effects of the war this alone would have crippled schools and departments in Indiana University.

Paul V. McNutt, administrator of the Federal Manpower Commission, December 8, 1942, requested the loan of Dean Herman T. Briscoe. He wrote Wells, "I am wondering if it is asking too much to request the loan of Briscoe for a few weeks while we are formulating in concrete terms policies governing the utilization of the universities?" Wells consented to release his Dean of Faculties within the week. He explained to the Faculty Council that Briscoe's office would represent all the colleges and universities which were to become involved with federal training programs, and it would also begin to formulate plans for postwar education. Briscoe was to be away from the campus intermittently for the next four years, and in 1944 he was appointed Director of the War Manpower Training Bureau to succeed President Edward Charles Elliott of Purdue. This appointment placed both the dean and the university in the forefront of postwar educational planning and in knowledge of what was happening nationally.

During the earliest months of the war Herman B Wells was engaged in various brief war assignments, but in August 1943 he was invited by Secretary of State Cordell Hull to come into the State Department as an advisor on the affairs of the occupied countries. The Board of Trustees was not entirely enthusiastic about granting leaves to the two top university administrative officials. A major bone of contention, as expressed by Judge Ora Wildermuth, president of the board, and Governor Henry Schricker, was payment of the president's and dean's salaries. If the leaves were for some period of time, the trustees believed the University would be subjected to unnecessary public criticism. "But under no circumstances," wrote Wildermuth, "should the funds of the State of Indiana be used to provide employees for the Federal Government." More than Hoosier frugality, a sense of separation of state and federal responsibilities and concern for the management of the university disturbed the president of the Board of Trustees. There had been much discussion in the trustees' meetings he told Wells, "and to which I have fully subscribed, that there was so much government boondoggling going on that [I] doubt whether any good would come out of either of these positions."

Wells was released, but on condition that he would spend at least two days a week in Bloomington. This placed upon him an arduous burden of travel, and a seven-day work week. The *Indianapolis News*, October 18, 1943, said, "One of the busiest men in the state is President Herman B Wells, of Indiana University, what with trying to keep the University on an even keel and at the same time attending his government duties in Washington.

He spends Mondays through Friday in Washington as a member of the vitally important planning committee of the Office of Economic Co-operation. The committee has the task of setting up the organization to straighten out the economic affairs of occupied countries. Friday nights, he hops a plane and comes back to Indiana to spend a busy Saturday and Sunday on I. U. affairs. . . ."

What was true of Wells and Briscoe was also true of many members of the faculty and staff. Scientists, School of Business specialists, medical and nursing personnel, political scientists, and even musicians and artists were asked to perform special war services. It was true that a generous number of university professors and staff went from Bloomington to war services in 1916–18, but not in such proportionate numbers, and to such diversified positions as in the later crisis. With regularity the trustees in their meetings granted leaves of absence with the repetitive notation "For the duration and six months after cessation of hostilities." The list of absentee professors, or of professors still on the campus but engaged in war services, was almost as extensive as the regular faculty roll itself. It would be impossible to make more than a general appraisal of the impact that their collective war services had on the course of the war. Conversely, it would be difficult to measure the impact that the war leaves had on the professors' future views and attitudes.

There is no doubt that Herman B Wells' experience as deputy director of the Office of Foreign Economic Co-operation in the Department of State, 1943–44, as advisor on liberated areas to the Department of State, then as delegate to the San Francisco Conference of the American Council on Education in 1945, and as a member, with ministerial rank, of the Allied Mission for observing the Greek elections in 1946 gave him a breadth of vision that he could never have achieved under the traditional conditions of state university administration. Later he was to serve as advisor on cultural affairs to General Lucius Clay in the United States Military Command in West Germany, 1947–48. This experience brought him into direct association with the mainstream of affairs in wartorn Europe. Even more important, circumstances there gave him an opportunity to make useful comparisons of higher educational approaches in the western world.

Dean Briscoe's services likewise took him well beyond the confining walls of a campus administrative office. His fellow dean,

Bernard C. Gavit of the School of Law, served as general counsel to the War Manpower Commission. At the same time Arthur M. Weimer, dean of the School of Business, was commissioned a specialist officer in the Quartermaster Corps, and served in this position throughout the war. Other members of the School of Business staff were in service in varied economic and administrative concerns of the Federal Government.

Thus it was that in 1945 the president, deans, and many of the professors returned to the campus much as did returning military veterans. They had vastly broadened their experiences and outlooks; some of them had helped to project the American university system into postwar European educational reconstruction. For the returning professors the prosaic daily routine of classes, picking up delayed research projects, and struggling with curricula revisions proved a complex transition. Rapidly expanding enrollment, the in-rush of veterans, and the constant confusion of new campus expansion and construction, and the appearance of new, and for the most part, younger professors brought immediate changes, not only in university procedures, but in the way of life in the Bloomington community. For the first time in Indiana University history there appeared a sharply discernible division between the "Old Guard" and the "Young Turks." The endearing intimacies that had prevailed historically in university relationships became, after 1945, less clearly defined. So noticeable was this change that President Wells in a subsequent presidential report asked departments to perpetuate in some fashion the comprehensive accomplishments of their predecessors. He felt departmental histories should be written to keep the record continuous and green. Visual reminders should be displayed. He said the university histories were outdated, and some means should be found for the present faculty to identify itself with the alumni of the university. He acknowledged that "This is more difficult as we grow in size, although not impossible. Difficult because of the increased intellectual competitiveness which we have fostered as a necessary prerequisite to increased scholarly productivity."

Part of the unsettling change on the campus was caused, of course, by the coming and going of transitory faculty members. The years immediately after the cessation of military hostilities saw a vast increase in faculty mobility in American universities and colleges. Never before could so many professors change positions so easily and without destroying intellectual roots. Although staff members could move with relative ease from one institution to another, younger professors often found new employment policies that allowed them to stay for stated periods to prove their worth, and then either be promoted and given tenure or be separated from the faculty. Dozens of Indiana staff members returned to postwar federal service with various foreign commissions, or they went on leave to accept Fulbright appointments or to do research on grants from the various foundations. Indiana, like every other major American university in this era, used as one gauge of vitality the number of professors it had airborne every week of the year. This was the age of the professional university specialist and consultant, and many a professor lengthened his curriculum vita with a listing of the opportunities he was given to be away from the campus and the classroom on public missions.

Frank E. Horack of the School of Law presented a revealing background analysis of the instructional situation in the university in February 1945, five months before the war ended. There were 93 professors, 45 associate professors, 89 assistant professors, and 416 teachers and teaching assistants. More than 500 classroom teachers were below professorial rank, and 60 per cent of the instructional chores were performed by this less experienced personnel. This situation was not unique to Indiana University; all across the United States university and college staffs had been depleted during the war. This condition was to create many of the deficiencies in American higher education during the next three decades. This was the basic challenge that now confronted the university in building a modern faculty.

An age-old American tradition was shattered for both professors and literally thousands of students. As sections of basic courses were expanded to accommodate several hundred students in a single classroom, faculty-student relationships became more formal and impersonal. Graduate assistants, most of whom were wholly without instructional experience, were assigned to smaller segments of lecture sections to conduct what were called "quiz sections." No doubt a small army of students would have failed courses if they had been asked to identify their professors by name and to give a resumé of their background and position in the university, or to say where their offices were located.

Reflective of some of the conditions in Indiana University,

Robert Ittner wrote John W. Ashton, dean of Arts and Sciences, June 26, 1947, that the past fall the administration was under such great pressure to provide enough instructors that little or no attention had been given graduate teaching assistants. Some of these had been assigned full instructor loads without receiving comparable rank or pay. Ittner did not raise the question of teaching adequacy, but he did question whether the university was pursuing the wisest policy in its pay scale. "It is true," he said, "that our standard stipend of $900 to $1,000 (depending on a year's previous service or graduate work) is roughly one-third of a beginning instructor's salary. However, we feel that a graduate assistant is not as valuable as an instructor, and that he deserves less compensation for his *services*." Ittner said the assistant's compensation was based on bringing a graduate student's stipend up to a bare subsistence level, and because of this the pay could not be doubled or tripled no matter how heavy the work load.

At the opening of the spring semester in February 1946, long queues of students formed before registration tables in the Fieldhouse, and departmental staffs worked diligently to supply instructors for multiplying sections. Just before this crush of registration occurred, Tony Somers of the American Federation of Labor presented Fowler V. Harper of the School of Law a charter of the American Federation of Teachers. This organization was successor to the University Teachers' Union. A similar movement was underway at Wisconsin, Ohio State, Minnesota, Cornell, and Yale. The Indiana chapter said its purposes were to promote progressive and domestic policies as they applied to professors, students, and administrators. Specifically the officers mentioned faculty salaries and promotions, and terms of employment. They said the new organization would work with problems not considered by the American Association of University Professors. No specific number of members was given in the news stories, but G. W. Gaiser of the Department of English said the organization had the largest initial enrollment in the history of the American Federation of Teachers.

The Federation did not have to wait long before it had a test case of "domestic democracy." In the spring of 1946 the Department of English failed to reappoint Marshall W. Stearns who had been a member of that staff since 1942. Russell Noyes, chairman of the department, wrote Stearns, "The vote of disapproval is directed not against your scholarship, nor in the main your teaching, but against your failure to prove yourself a loyal and dependable member of the department." Stearns replied that reaction against him was caused by his somewhat overzealous activities in the Teachers' Union and the local chapter of the National Association for the Advancement of Colored People. Fowler V. Harper represented him, and there followed a volley of angry letters between the law professor and Dean John W. Ashton. A faculty committee was appointed to hear charges and to receive evidence, the result of which was a compromise proposed by Stearns himself. He suggested that he be reappointed for a year, and he would take a leave of absence without pay. The faculty committee reported it found no breach of academic freedom, but said the standing committee of the Department of English "had been dissatisfied with the showing of Mr. Stearns as a teacher." President Wells accepted Stearns' resignation, August 8, and he immediately accepted appointment to an instructorship at Cornell University.

No one at Indiana University in the spring of 1946, when the English Department considered Marshall W. Stearns' teaching performance, could have said with certainty what constituted good teaching for great masses of students. Earlier in the Wells administration students had introduced a scheme for rating professional teaching performances. This question was reintroduced by Dean Herman T. Briscoe in a letter to the college deans, April 10, 1946. He said students had discussed this matter with him, and he felt each academic dean would want to present the idea to his college faculty. Briscoe was positive that faculty rating was not a condition which the central administration wished to impose on teaching staff.

The Student Council, working with Professor Carl Franzen of the School of Education and an experienced planner of tests, set out to devise an experimental program. Franzen said, "There, no doubt, will be divided opinion on the validity of the ratings as to whether the expenditure of time and money required to carry out the program would be justified, but we hope to receive helpful information on the points from those whom the plan would affect." A four-page multiple-choice questionnaire was contemplated to seek information from students about instructors' personal characteristics and the quality of their lectures and discussions, and to encourage a general student appraisal of the basic worth of courses. Sample questions submitted did not reach above a subjective student judgment level, nor did they seem actually to get at the root of good teaching. There was indeed a wide gap between the Indiana student questions of 1946 and the time-honored Socratic and Mark Hopkins approaches to teaching. While students and professional testers spent hours debating how best to test the faculty, a more forthright proposal was published by the editor of the *Daily Student*, November 8, 1947. "The majority of I. U. instructors," he wrote, "work on the assumption that all students have the mentality of retarded ground squirrels and students sometimes feel that most instructors are something plucked out of a jar of formaldehyde." He believed neither proposition was correct. To dispel such gloomy attitudes he proposed informal get-togethers in which everybody proved to everybody else that the milk of humanity flowed freely in Hoosier veins.

The debate on faculty ratings went on intermittently until March 1950, when the question was turned over to a special committee to study the matter further and to devise a workable set of tests. Nobody seems to have recalled, publicly at least, that this proposition was debated extensively less than a decade before. The test that was finally prepared differed little from the basic format proposed by Carl Franzen. It was refined from year to year in the future, but without reflecting any real capability of mature testing of teaching as an art. The questions in large measure were either of a surface personal nature or called upon students to make subjective value judgments. In later years the Board of Academic Review published a booklet, which could be bought for $1.50, that revealed the collective feelings of students toward individual professors and courses in the College of Arts and Sciences during the first semester of 1966–67. This, however, turned out to be more of a guide to courses and professors for far-ranging students than to qualified teaching.

There was a combination of excitement and restlessness on the Indiana University campus after 1945. The university community experienced more fundamental internal changes in the first postwar years than had occurred in more than a century and a quarter of institutional history. As a veritable procession of new professors were appointed to the faculty, and as the average number of years of service dropped phenomenally, there were growing sensitivities over issues which in earlier years had not been excessively irritating or had been smoothed over because of deep-seated institutional loyalties. Freedoms, academic and political, had become more significant issues in a changing world, and with the growing complexities of professor-university relationships. Individual staff members found themselves more and more removed from direct participation or communication with the central administration.

In the era when American social and political issues had become of such vital importance in national life, professors everywhere were deeply concerned with the course and solution of current problems. Most of them had either served in the military forces or they had engaged in various government services and political planning during the war. After the termination of fighting, hundreds of them were again employed either as specialized administrators or consultants by state and federal governments. Indiana University's professors were no exception. From President Herman B Wells to instructional specialists, faculty members occupied key and even sensitive positions in governmental affairs. Inevitably the forces let loose by the ending of the war and attempts to re-order much of world civilization involved issues and freedoms that manifested themselves on the American university campus.

On a more provincial level there arose in Indiana the issue of professorial participation in local and state politics. Traditionally two attitudes had prevailed on this question. Professionally the professor stood above the mundane machinations of Hoosier practical politics. It was falsely assumed for more than a century that it was too dangerous for state university professors to become involved in politics because their partisanship would cloud the objectivity of their teaching; too, appropriations to the university might be endangered. Gradually this historical attitude was revised. Reflective of this fact were the nominations of Ernest M. Linton of political science, George Schlafler of physical education, and Marshon DePoister of sociology for local and state offices by the Monroe County Prohibition Party. All three withdrew their names, but not because of timidity at taking an active part in politics. In April 1956 Dean of the Junior Division Pressly Sikes was sworn in as a member of the Bloomington City Council.

The issue of academic freedom became somewhat more sensitive only once after 1945. The Marshall W. Stearns case was settled quietly and perhaps amicably. In an off-campus incident ninety-one Indiana professors protested to President Lincoln B. Hale of Evansville College the firing of George Parker. The Indiana petitioners said the only act in question that Parker had committed was to sit on the platform when Vice President Henry A. Wallace spoke in the Evansville Coliseum in April 1948. This was hardly an act of professorial indecorum.

During the 1940s and 1950s the Indiana faculty showed remarkable independence toward the American Legion and the various national loyalty investigating committees that came to the campus. The body collectively, however, was never called upon actually to act beyond the various protestations of the American Association of University Professors, and this organization's most impressive expression of displeasure was against the Catholic protesters in the Kinsey case. The association has had a long history at Indiana, and the chapter from the outset has been active in questions of academic freedom, with some of the local professors such as Ralph Fuchs and James A. Woodburn serving as national officers. Wells had been a member in full standing until 1938, and then he became an associate member.

An interesting case of faculty-university relationship arose in the Department of Journalism in December 1959, when the contract of fifty-two-year-old Associate Professor Jerome Ellison was not renewed. Ellison, a Wisconsin graduate, was a cartoonist, former editor of the *Reader's Digest*, managing editor of *Collier's Magazine*, *Liberty Magazine*, and director of the Bureau of Overseas publications of the Office of War Information. He was author of an extensive number of published articles, and was employed in the Department of Journalism in 1955 to teach periodical writing and publication. Four years later he published an article in the *Saturday Evening Post* entitled, "Are we Making a Playground out of College?" The article was both critical and controversial, and the author said it had stirred unfavorable reaction on the Indiana campus.

John E. Stempel, head of the Department of Journalism, said the decision not to renew Ellison's appointment was made by professors with tenure in the department on the grounds that Ellison's teaching, counseling, and sharing of departmental duties "did not meet the requirements we wanted in a person retained on a permanent basis." Stempel told the *Daily Student*, December

16, 1959, "We've been talking this over for two years and we felt it was time to act." Ellison charged that he was removed from his position for saying in the *Post* article that there was too much frivolity on the university's campus. President Wells commented that "I'm absolutely confident the article did not have anything to do with his [Ellison's] not being reappointed. This office simply takes the recommendation of the department in such matters. It's the policy of the University not to give reasons when a man is not recommended for reappointment."

Ellison indicated that his writing was in itself an expression of freedom. He said, "If I can help free the pens of young people for the thrill and challenge of writing all they can see of the truth, then I will have taught what I came here to teach, and losing this job will have been a small enough price to pay." Almost as a veiled threat he told the campus reporter there were many more stories to be written for the *Post*, one of which was ready to be submitted to the publishers on the subject of educational practices in state universities.

Concern for academic freedom at Indiana University was rather severely tested in this era, 1945–55. Some pressures, however, came from outside the institution, and in most instances were either senseless, or were attempts of narrow political and special interests to have their way. Charles M. Hewitt, assistant professor of business, was called before a state House of Representatives committee investigating "good faith" in dealer-manufacturer relationships. Representative Court Rollins claimed Hewitt had attempted to pass off theory for fact, basing his statements on the contents of the professor's doctoral dissertation. This even though Hewitt had cited generously from court decisions and Federal Trade Commission reports. He had concluded that dealers were at the mercy of large corporations that cancelled contracts on short notice and without giving valid reasons. Rollins went far beyond the scope of the hearing and impugned Hewitt's capacity to teach in the university, since he had never operated his own business. At that time he was serving as advisor to both the national and state automobile dealers associations.

Rollins told the *Daily Student* reporter that he had questioned Hewitt's fitness to teach. The campus editor, in turn, declared Rollins' attack in poor taste, saying, "It is unfortunate that a state legislator must resort to personal digs to challenge the testimony of a college professor before a legislative committee." Students rushed to Professor Hewitt's defense in an open letter. They not only declared Rollins wrong in every detail, but that he was an underprivileged person because he had not been fortunate enough to take a course under Hewitt. Rollins never made clear what precisely in Hewitt's testimony had provoked his attack; a possible implication was that the legislator may have represented corporate interests.

A similar case of external pressure and criticism arose in October 1960, when Robert J. Pitchell, an associate professor of government, criticized the laxity of tax assessments in Lake County. Speaking before the Indiana Municipal League in Indianapolis, he claimed costly automobiles were assessed at $92.00 apiece when the statewide average was $500. Michael Jankovich, an assistant assessor, branded the statement absurd and ridiculous and demanded an apology. He said the Lake County assessments were $506. Pitchell had cited not only the local assessment records signed by Sam Beushmig, assessor, and Jankovich's superior, but also the state records. The Lake County records, however, had later been revised, but this fact had not been reported to the Indiana Tax Commission in time to be placed in the published report. Pitchell refused to make an apology, and Professor J. B. Kessler heaped more coals on the heads of the northern assessors by saying, he, not Pitchell, had made the statement and he intended to stand by it. Jankovich backed down in light of the original record, and in 1963 Pitchell became president of Roosevelt University in Chicago.

Faculty freedoms were not always expressed in terms of academic or public pressures. An issue of an altogether different nature arose in 1945. The automobile had not completely disrupted campus tranquility before William Lowe Bryan left the presidency. When Herman B Wells became acting president, however, the names of Packard, Ford, and Chevrolet had become almost revered ones in America. Wells, given the image by the national press at least, was a joyful proponent of the automobile. Narrow campus drives and limited vacant spaces for parking lots created major administrative problems, and these became even more acute as the accelerated building program got underway. No one knew how to deal with this important campus dilemma. The best university officials could do was to adopt urban practices of levying fines on parking offenders. This, however, was aggravated by the fact that students had to pay their fines because their names appeared on delinquent lists, and even a Phi Beta Kappa candidate could be denied his degree because of outstanding parking charges. The university exercised no such control over faculty members. In May 1954 the *Daily Student* started a campaign against delinquent professors. Reporters noted that only two per cent of professor-violators paid fines that year. The next fall only 25 out of 559 fines collected had come from professors. Associate Dean of Faculties Ralph Collins denied his office was a collection agency, and he was willing to see that onerous task of enforcement go to any group who had enough zeal to administer parking rules. The Faculty Council accepted the challenge and voted to publish monthly the names of professors and staff members who were in arrears. A month later the rate of payment had gone up some, but still the parking problem was aggravated by professorial resistance where walking to work was involved.

These were, of course, relatively minor aspects of faculty-administration relationships. A far more fundamental fact was the continuing crusade begun in 1937 to find and employ the best professors available in a highly competitive job market. These efforts were constantly jeopardized by failures of the Indiana General Assembly to supply adequate support to a rapidly expanding university. Professors employed during the earlier years of the new administrative regime were now producing exciting teaching and research. Tracy M. Sonneborn, Ralph E. Cleland, Allan C. G. Mitchell, Emil J. Konopinski, Lawrence Langer, and others had become major scholars in their fields. Old-timers such as Alfred C. Kinsey, Stith Thompson, Edward Buehrig, Paul Weatherwax, Arthur Weimer, William R. Breneman, R. C. Buley, O. O. Winther, and Russell Noyes had met competition at home and abroad with creditable work indeed. After major scientific and administrative accomplishments during the war, A. C. G. Mitchell in 1948 worked on to extend knowledge of nuclear matter. For his war work he was presented the Naval Ordnance Award and other important government citations. He participated during the immediate postwar years in research in the use of radioactive isotopes supplied by the Oak Ridge Laboratory. This was part of a nationwide research project that utilized the talents of the most sophisticated physicists.

At the same time Emil J. Konopinski, Lawrence Langer, and Kenneth Ford worked in somewhat the same general area of nuclear physics. Dr. Edward Teller said in a *Science Magazine* article, February 1955, that it was Konopinski's inspired guess in 1942 about the effectiveness of tritium in a hydrogen bomb which made its development possible. Teller said Konopinski and Cloyd Martin, Jr., proved that a thermonuclear reaction such as the explosion of the hydrogen bomb could not ignite the atmosphere, the oceans, or deserts. Konopinski, said Teller, had made certain that no known question in nuclear physics went unexplored.

Dr. Renato Dulbreco, a bacteriologist working under the supervision of the famous scientist, S. E. Luria, received widespread publicity in November 1949 for his discovery that an ultraviolet short wave would kill a specific virus, and that a hardly visible light ray would bring it back to life. This discovery was made in connection with the special research Luria and Hermann J. Muller were doing for the American Cancer Society.

For the academic year 1948–49, 286 faculty members out of 735 reported that they had published articles and books. Four years later this number had increased to 450 out of 820 professors reporting. There was an evergreen debate among faculty members as to the relationship between research and teaching. If the faculty reports on publication are to be accepted as any sort of dependable measures, it was obvious that a majority of professors doubted that sustained research and publication were necessary adjuncts to either their intellectual development or teaching competence.

The *Daily Student* conducted a highly limited survey of the subject in November 1955, in which four professors interviewed expressed the thought that original knowledge was derived from research. They believed that the instructor owed it to himself, his students, colleagues, and the university to help to expand the fields of general knowledge. Not to do research, said Georg Neumann, an anthropologist, was to exploit what other men had discovered. "Research and teaching are so interwoven," he said, "that I can't say I'm reading this book for research and this for teaching. Research in no way takes away from teaching and both benefit from each other." Richard Moody of the Department of Speech felt that research sharpened his sense of values, and so the argument went. Henry Remak thought some professors and institutions had gone to extremes in promoting research, and should give more attention to teaching. He told a reporter, "A man outstanding in fields other than teaching is still valuable to the University and can be used in advanced courses." Remak said a professor's publications were something substantial to judge him by, and "the most productive professor is the best teacher." He was sustained in this point of view by William R. Breneman who had established a solid campus-wide reputation as an outstanding teacher, and had achieved deep respect as a scholarly biologist.

There was little doubt in anybody's mind but that research was important to professorial advancement. This became especially evident as many departments organized advisory or executive committees. These helped to make policies of hiring, dismissal, promotions, and tenure. In December 1955 Associate Dean of Faculties Ralph Collins outlined promotional and tenure policies of the university by saying, "Tenure is not connected in any way with promotion—the teacher does not have to be at a certain stage in the division [ranks] to be considered for this protection." He also said that rapid promotion in less than five years of service was extremely rare at Indiana.

In his *Annual Report* for 1959–60, President Wells wrote, "To turn out college teachers with no grasp of research that will enable them to build on the foundations of older knowledge and ideas to give them a new independence in their fields is no less a watering down of higher education than to have fewer (but better trained) teachers working with larger groups of students. In the long run higher education will suffer less from the latter than from being saddled with some generations of teachers who have never experienced the excitement and challenge of creative research."

The president noted in this same report that only 10 per cent of the faculty had been on the campus for twenty years, and 40 per cent had come in the last four years. A decade before he had reported the faculty had been increased in the years 1946 to 1948 by 45 per cent. This mobility and expansion were due to many factors, some of which originated with individual professors, while others were generated by the university. "Our increase in size and the development of research and graduate studies," said Wells, "have required many additional men and women. Our increasing standards of performance have resulted in the release of many men who in an earlier period might have been retained." In 1949 alone 62 faculty members were released, while 52 promotions were made, nine of whom were raised to the full rank of professor.

Whether or not the hoary debate over the relationships of teaching and research was ever resolved, even in part, Indiana University professors made impressive showings in their accomplishments. Professor Harry Engle and Stephen Greene of the Department of Fine Arts won awards in February 1946 in the Kearney Memorial Regional Exhibit of the Milwaukee Institute. One of the most impressive publications in the history of the faculty to date was Kenneth P. Williams, *Lincoln Finds a General* (1949–52, 5 volumes). The chairman of the Department of Mathematics showed more interest in the military and history than in his chosen field. The Grant study was massive, detailed, and exciting. The Macmillan editors recommended it for the Pulitzer Prize, and Bernard DeVoto, the critical outside reader for the publishers, suggested the work be published without imposition of volume limitation. This hefty work grew out of Williams' longtime interest in the military, and a desire to do a better job of analyzing the role of Grant in the Civil War than he believed historians had done. Using the 300 volumes of the ponderous *War of the Rebellion Records*, the mathematician produced what must be considered, source-wise, a narrowly technical historical analysis, but nevertheless a fascinating and precise one. Oliver P. Fields of the Department of Political Science wrote Herman B Wells, August 2, 1946, "That nothing that is likely to happen in mathematics [because of Williams] will be likely to compare with this work if he can complete it." Fields was wise in adding the conditional, Williams did not live to complete the seven projected volumes. Reviewers of the five published volumes largely justified Oliver P. Fields' faith in the author.

President Wells was able in 1945 to persuade the Rockefeller Foundation to support the university's major research program in genetics. A $95,000 grant enabled the university to employ Hermann J. Muller of Amherst College. Dean Fernandus Payne had been especially anxious to employ Muller. The two men had attended Columbia University at approximately the same time, and both studied under the direction of the famous geneticists Thomas Hunt Morgan and E. B. Wilson. In retrospect, Dean Payne, long after his retirement, considered employment of Hermann J. Muller to be one of the most courageous acts of the Wells administration.

The graduate dean informed the trustees, in the president's *Annual Report* for 1945–47, "We now have three of the leading geneticists of the country on our faculty. The other two are Tracy M. Sonneborn of the Department of Zoology and Ralph E. Cleland of the Department of Botany." The fifty-five-year-old Muller soon became one of Indiana's most distinguished scholars. Born in New York City, he received three degrees from Columbia University. From 1915 to 1918 he was an instructor at Rice Institute in Houston, Texas. He returned to Columbia as an instructor, but two years later he was back at the University of Texas as a professor. In the latter years of his Texas professorship he also served as the senior geneticist of Vavilov's Institute of Genetics in Moscow. Muller in these years was of communist leanings, if not actually a party member. This political excursion, however, had been a sobering experience, and later he was a clear spokesman against the excesses of Communism, even to appearing before the special congressional committees on Americanism.

After his Moscow period Muller served as lecturer and instructor in the University of Edinburgh, and then as visiting professor in Amherst College. In his field he was a pioneer in the use of X ray to produce gene mutations and thus bring about hereditary changes. When he arrived in Bloomington in July 1945, he brought with him a carefully guarded suitcase that contained his laboratory stock of precious fruit flies, or *Drosophila*. By this time he had attracted wide attention in the field of genetics, and in 1946 he delivered the Pilgrim Trust Lecture in London; this was an annual science recognition lecture given alternately in the United States and England. At the same time Muller was elected to membership in the Swedish Royal Academy of Sciences, and the *Monthly Science News*, publication of the British Council, carried as its lead article an account of his work, declaring him a leader in the field of genetic research.

Muller had been in Bloomington only a year when he was awarded the Nobel Prize in Medicine and Physiology. At the moment the award was announced in Stockholm that he had been selected for the prize, announcement was also made by the American Cancer Society that it had granted $45,000 to support his research. In talking with reporters Muller said he had started experiments with X rays twenty years before at the University of Texas. In two decades he had been able to produce mutations in fruit flies ranging from changes in size, body conformations, the growing of hair, and even the sprouting of extra heads. He denied his experiments would lead to the production of a race of supermen, but he hoped they would develop knowledge of hereditary changes. He warned that changes in hereditary genes were most harmful when artificially stimulated, and that the effects of the Hiroshima bomb would not be known for many generations.

Professor Muller had hardly been handed the diploma of the Nobel Prize before he found himself involved in a hot and sensitive debate over the effects of radiation both from explosion of the atom and hydrogen bombs, and the use of atomic energy for industrial purposes. He viewed potential dangers as insidious because they could not be determined with a limited number of generations. The same danger existed in the generous use of the X ray by inexperienced medical personnel.

In Bloomington, when the news of Muller's Nobel Prize was announced, Indiana University decked Science Hall with American flags. The institution "burst" with pride because of the high recognition of its professor of genetics. Administrative officials were quick to express joy at the honor, and they communicated this to the public through numerous newspaper interviews. The Library of Congress informed President Wells that it was honoring the Nobel Laureate with a month-long exhibit of Muller's writings and his portrait. In late January 1947, after the Nobel awarding ceremony on January 10, 1947, the diploma, gold medal, and other souvenirs were displayed in the lobby of the Memorial Union. *Life Magazine* published pictures and a story of Dr. Muller's work. Never before had the scholarly work of an Indiana University professor received such widespread and favorable publicity unless it was the Kinsey report on the sexuality of the American male.

For the scientist in the laboratory with his favorite *Drosophila*, life underwent fundamental changes after Stockholm. He now had an attentive worldwide audience, and his work in the field of X ray and radiation had profound and timely meaning for the existence and stability of the human race. Already involved in cancer research, he and Dr. S. E. Luria were given substantial additional financial support to explore the field of radiation in relation to cancer and its causes. Luria was responsible for investigating virus growth on the genetics of virus hosts specificity. Muller was to continue to study mutations arising from different radiated conditions of the fruit fly.

Dr. Muller was now drawn into a major scientific debate in the general area of the effects of X ray and nuclear radiation. He said that men exposed to heavy radiation should not attempt fatherhood. He thought the Japanese who survived Hiroshima and Nagasaki would wish they had been killed if they could see their pitiful descendants a thousand years hence. "Since most mutations are recessive," said Muller, "and most populations are already ladened with numerous mutations inherited from the distant past, the demonstration of production of new mutations and the measurement of their frequency ordinarily requires very special genetic techniques." These were matters of profound social concern. Perhaps 10 per cent of the future population should be asked to avoid parenthood. Radiologists were warned to refrain from use of radiation to stimulate production or to produce sterility that might be temporary. He felt the medical profession was permanently damaging the American life stream through improper use of X rays. There was in his opinion no dosage low enough to be without danger.

It was in the political-national defense areas that Muller saw ever greater threats. He feared political development would not keep up with scientific advances. This was especially true in the field of expanded application of nuclear energy and resulting widespread radiation. If nations did not blow each other up with nuclear bombs, they would kill off the human race by loading its plasma with too many mutated genes. Muller lectured on this subject all across America and abroad, and it was inevitable in this sensitive era of post-Hiroshima he should create anxieties and controversy.

In October 1948 Muller resigned from the Academy of Sciences of the United States of the Soviet Republics; he had been a member of the Russian Academy since 1933. In his letter of resignation he charged the Soviets with dropping from membership their truly significant geneticists, while stooping to take into the academy the charlatan T. D. Lysenko. Under Lysenko's baleful influence the Russian Academy had denounced the principles of genetics. The Soviets accepted Muller's resignation without regret, and he was cartooned in a party magazine as a crocodile seated at a desk with a $10,000 check in his hand.

Inevitably the wrath of a genetics professor would be stirred by the vacillating policies of the Atomic Energy Commission. Either because of idiotic bureaucratic blundering or by willful design Muller was denied at least one opportunity to criticize federal policies. He was invited in 1955 to participate in the United Nation's Geneva Conference on the peaceful use of the atom. Muller was given no instructions beyond the mere invitation and title of the conference. He proceeded to prepare his paper, and almost immediately after it was mailed he received firm instructions from the Atomic Energy Commission that no mention must be made of military use of nuclear energy. He had mentioned Hiroshima briefly in the paper. As a result of this inclusion Muller's name was stricken from the roll of participants. He told the Washington *Post* and the *Times-Herald* that the Atomic Energy Commission was making a conscious effort to play down public anxieties over the large doses of radiation with which humanity was threatened. He was then requested not to attend the international conference by Bryan Urquhart, executive assistant to the Secretary General of the Geneva meeting. Urquhart implied that Muller's reasoning was false. Dr. George L. Weil of the Atomic Energy Commission, and technical director of the conference, said Muller was not continued as a member of the American delegation nor was his paper, "How Radiation Changes the Genetic Constitution," accepted despite the fact it had been approved originally. The commission, through Lewis L. Strauss, also made the lame excuse that the paper referred to Hiroshima while the purpose of the conference was narrowly restricted to the peaceful use of the atom. Under the rules of the United Nations, it was said, such material could not be presented. In a reduced version of the paper the offensive material had been removed, but by that time the argument had gone too far for amicable readjustment. Muller said his objections were not to personalities but to failures of the conference to discuss fully and honestly the dangers of radiation in human genetics.

This controversy generated considerable heat and publicity. It even got into the political area. William G. Bray, congressman from the Bloomington district, wrote Lewis L. Strauss for details of the barring of Muller from the Geneva Conference. Bray told Strauss that the American people should be told the facts about radiation. On October 3, 1955, the chairman of the Atomic Energy Commission said the dispute had arisen because of a "regrettable snafu." He contradicted this by saying Dr. Muller's personal appearance in Geneva, in the opinion of the commission's officials, "would have stirred up unwanted discussion." Strauss said Muller's paper would be published in the record of the conference, thus refuting the basic contention of the Atomic Energy Commission that the power of decision was not in its hands.

Muller continued to be an energetic advocate of extreme caution in the area of radioactive exposure. In 1956 he was elected president of the American Humanist Association, and later that year he was authorized by the State Department to speak at the International Radiation Conference in Copenhagen. Until a week before the meeting of the conference there was again the question of whether or not the Atomic Energy Commission would block his speech. This, however, was resolved by the State Department taking a hand in assuring Muller's appearance in Denmark. In the report of the National Academy of Science for 1956, Muller made a strong statement regarding the possible damages of radiation. Despite this fact President Dwight D. Eisenhower, in commenting upon the report, said the findings of the academy indicated that fall-out tests produced only a fractional amount of the radiation that individuals received from natural sources and medical X rays. What the Indiana scientist said specifically was, "Unless this control [of the test of the hydrogen bomb] is achieved in the short time open to us before thermo-nuclear weapons have become available to more countries still, and before continental guided missiles have become a reality, we will find ourselves in a situation even more ungovernable and menacing than that of today." Muller thought that the only advantage of nuclear weapons was the possibility they would delay war long enough to allow people to find out how to get along with one another; nuclear energy he realized was with us to stay.

Muller was to enjoy many scientific triumphs. His predictions had the essential elements of truth in them. Other nations did develop nuclear bombs, and others in the 1970s were striving to do so while men talked of the suicidal dangers of such weapons. In July 1958 Muller delivered the keynote speech at the Conference on War and Health in Brussels, and was awarded the Darwin-Wallace Commemorative Medal by the United Nations International Exposition. A year later he read the leading paper at the University of Chicago celebration of the Darwin Centennial. This paper stirred a bit of absurd controversy on the part of some Indiana clergymen, mainly because an *Indianapolis Star* reporter had published an erroneous quotation. The two main points of the address dealt with direct insemination of women with semen from superior males, and development, gradually, of methods by which superior couples could produce as many children as possible, and the children in turn would be placed with an adoption agency for proper placement. As usual, the critics reacted without first reading the paper which was available to them in *Perspectives in Biology*, published by the University of Chicago Press.

Columbia University had already awarded Muller an honorary doctorate, and in April 1961 he was given the Alexander Hamilton Award in recognition of his scientific findings and his crusade against radiation. In what almost amounted to a philosophical valedictory, Muller in November 1961 counseled the United States to remain calm in the face of Russia's having detonated a nuclear bomb. "We must," he wrote, "on the one hand demonstrate our sincere desire to join in the taking by both sides of control steps toward bi-lateral disarmament." He was named "Humanist of the Year" by the American Association of Humanists in April 1963, and soon after Muller retired from Indiana University to join the staff of the Institute of Advanced Learning in the Medical Sciences at the City of Hope, Duarte, California. He went west principally to enjoy the softer climate.

Even though Muller's accomplishments were indeed impressive, they did not overshadow those of his colleagues who were equally as capable and devoted scholars. Ralph E. Cleland was highly productive, a fact which was recognized by his election to the presidency of the Botanical Society of America in 1947. Otis P. Starkey became president of the American Society of Professional Geographers, and Dean Bernard C. Gavit held the same office in the Association of American Law Schools. No less important than Hermann J. Muller's work in genetics was that of Tracy M. Sonneborn. He discovered sexes in ciliated protozoa, and later the role of genes, cytoplasm, and environmental control of heredity. By these discoveries he took man a broad step closer to understanding the processes of life. In 1946 he was co-winner of the American Association for the Advancement of Science prize for an outstanding research paper, and a decade later he won the Kimber Genetics Award of the National Academy of Science. Sonneborn's work was to receive additional recognition by his election to the presidency of the American Genetics Society in 1949, and the American Society of Zoologists in 1956. International recognition came to the distinguished geneticist in the form of honorary memberships in genetic and zoological societies. The *Indianapolis News* told Hoosiers, "The high distinction that has come to these educators is a tribute to the school they represent as well as the recognition of their professional standing. It will be regarded as additional evidence of the University's success in strengthening its faculty by the addition of men whose leadership in their field is unquestioned."

In 1951 R. Carlyle Buley won the Pulitzer Prize in history for his solid two-volume study of the Old Northwest after 1815. (This honor is described in volume II.) Buley was a highly interesting member of the faculty. He was indeed a provocative teacher, a meticulous research scholar, and a fine literary stylist. He, however, embraced an ultra-conservative tradition in American history and politics, and changes in the faculty and university programs disturbed him. In the Department of History he felt the new leadership was taking the subject far afield from Hoosier moorings. To him both curriculum content and teaching emphasis had been prostituted to the new spirit of internationalism. Speaking at the Governor's Educational Conference in Indianapolis, May 15, 1958, Buley was quoted by the Associated Press as saying the "don't give a damn" attitude of Americans would be more responsible for the defeat of the nation than Russian missiles. He deplored current educational standards, and said modern public school teachers were more entranced with methodology than solid content. He branded textbooks as being full of bias and propaganda. The Associated Press quoted him further as being extremely critical of "UNESCO education, hot rods, the radio, and television. We are reaping the benefits not only of so-called 'progressive education,'" he declared, "but also following the UNESCO line—that is, not teaching the history of our country until the histories of all other countries have been taught for fear [if] the history of our country was taught first these pupils might be prejudiced in favor of that country." From the above it is obvious that Professor Buley spoke in some heat, if not anger.

Buley found himself engaged at once in an unexpected and vigorous campus debate with Walter H. C. Laves, chairman of the Department of Government, and with William Riley Parker of English, and Henry R. Hope, chairman of the Department of Fine Arts. Laves had just published a book in collaboration with Charles H. Thompson on UNESCO. Besides this, he had been chairman of the United States National Commission for UNESCO, a deputy director of UNESCO, and a member of the Governing Board of the UNESCO Commission for the Social Sciences. Parker had served as vice chairman of the United States Commission for UNESCO, and Henry R. Hope had been active in the general field of international education. Laves and Parker denied that Buley had correctly interpreted the policies of the international organization. Hope did agree that American high school students were foggy on the subject of the nation's history, as was so eloquently documented at the outset of the war by the *New York Times*, and subsequently in Indiana by Buley's colleagues Maurice Baxter, Robert H. Ferrell, and John Wiltz. These scholars had used a Lilly Endowment grant to make an intensive study of the teaching of American history in the state's schools. Hope, however, did not believe this fact to be chargeable to UNESCO; quite to the contrary, he felt UNESCO encouraged first the understanding of the history of one's own country. Buley had spoken largely on the basis of a diagnostic test which he had given 90 Indiana freshmen and the results indicated to him intellectual mayhem. The intra-campus debate stirred by this speech, and the generous newspaper publicity of it did little to resolve either the problems of international education or the teaching of American history. Nevertheless, it revealed more clearly the fact that the Indiana faculty had become quite cosmopolitan in its thinking and attitudes.

Indiana University had made a major effort to employ displaced scholars from the Nazi regime and from elsewhere in Middle Europe. Many of these made genuine contributions to both teaching and research. Eberhard Hopf, who was one of them, later chose to stay in Bloomington rather than return to the University of Heidelberg as professor of mathematics. The appearance on the campus of continental scholars gave the university a new intellectual dimension and perspective. The Department of History, for instance, was to reflect this fact when Robert F. Byrnes became chairman in 1958. The addition of S. Y. Teng in Chinese history and language, the creation of the Russian and East European Institute, and the offering of courses by specialists in the history of most of the areas of the world was a sharp departure from the past. Charles Leonard Lundin, veteran of the history staff, was an authority in the complex field of nationalism.

What was true of history was also true of most other departments. Walter H. C. Laves of government achieved an extensive record indeed in the field of United States foreign relations. From the outset he participated in the work of the United Nations and UNESCO. Aside from this, he served in 1948 on the Commission of Education and International Affairs of the American Council on Education, a commission once directed by Herman B Wells. Laves' colleague, Edward Buehrig, likewise was an active scholar in international education, especially in the field of teaching. William Riley Parker of English and a distinguished Milton scholar, Frank Edmondson of astronomy, Henry R. Hope of fine arts, Louis Shere of economics, and John F. Mee of business took the name and reputation of Indiana abroad. Frank K. Edmondson headed the United Nations delegation to the General Assembly of the International Astronomical Union in 1964, and that same year the Republic of Chile decorated him with the Bernardo O'Higgins Order of Merit for his contributions to the development of astronomy in that country.

In the field of specialist services to the United States government, Robert C. Turner, professor of business administration, served the Truman Administration in 1948 as a member of the Council of Economic Advisors. In this position he helped to draft many of the President's speeches on economic subjects. Later, in 1961, Turner was appointed assistant director of the Bureau of the Budget by President John F. Kennedy. Charles S. Hyneman of political science served in numerous federal positions ranging from administrative analyst for the United States Bureau of the Budget to director of Foreign Broadcast Intelligence Service of the Federal Communications Commission. More important, however, were his penetrating studies of the processes of government. W. George Pinnell, associate dean of the School of Business, served on the Kennedy Committee of Area Development, and

Louis Shere was appointed by President Harry Truman in July 1950 as a tax specialist on the panel of American experts to help rehabilitate economic conditions of the Philippines. Three years later President Dwight D. Eisenhower appointed Shere to the Council of Economic Advisors.

No doubt one of the most important public service posts served by an Indiana University professor was Roy V. Peel's position as Director of the United States Bureau of the Census in 1950. At home, numerous professors served the State of Indiana in many advisory posts. Frank E. Horack, professor of law, was appointed by Governor Henry Schricker in 1951 to the Indiana Commission on Uniform State Laws. In 1966 Professor Leon Wallace of the School of Law headed Governor Roger D. Branigin's commission to determine the Ohio River boundary with Kentucky. This commission produced an interesting document which traced a fascinating history of the boundary from earliest English explorations, but it was more intriguing in its description of the vagaries of a wayward river. The road between Bloomington and Indianapolis was crowded with professors on missions of governmental and social services. Scores of Indiana specialists rendered endless public services in almost every capacity imaginable. Industry and government made free use of professional and expert talents in the postward years of economic expansion. For instance, sociologists such as Clifford Kirkpatrick were called upon to help analyze social trends for the purposes of making industrial projections in the fields of consumer and housing industries.

It was, however, in the fields of academic affairs that professors made their most creditable and lasting contributions. After 1945 Indiana staff members were awarded Guggenheim, Social Science Research Council, American Philosophical Society, Rockefeller Foundation, Lilly Endowment, and American Council of Learned Societies grants. A relatively large number received Fulbright appointments, both for teaching and research purposes. Representative of many of the scholarly grants was the one for $9,000 given to P. J. Vatikiotis by the Social Science Research Council for a year's study in the Middle East. Paul Weatherwax received in 1944 one of the first Guggenheim awards made to an Indiana University professor to study the corn plant in South America.

Among the most significant specialized studies made by

Indiana professors were those of Charles F. and Erminie Wheeler Voegelin in linguistics and anthropology in conjunction with the American Philosophical Society, and later the Department of Interior. Charles F. Voegelin served as research associate of the Library of the American Philosophical Society in 1946, and as editor of the *International Journal of Linguistics.* He was so-author of the *Franz Boaz Collection of American Linguistics.* Erminie Wheeler Voegelin was vice president of the American Folklore Society in 1947, and president in 1948. She shared a Guggenheim award with her husband in 1947 to study the North American Indians and Eskimos.

In doing research for the Department of Interior in the history of the treaties made with the various Indian tribes of the Old Northwest leading up to and including the Treaty of Greenville, 1795, the Voegelins made a major collection of basic historical materials relating to Indian history in the Ohio Valley and around the Great Lakes. The final report by Erminie Wheeler Voegelin was a searching study of Indian relations and treaty transactions. It was the basic document used by the Department of Interior in defense of the United States Government in the suit brought by the associated tribes to reclaim the lands ceded in the Greenville Treaty.

The university faculty was never fully in residence at any time after the war. In 1961 there were sixty-six professors abroad either teaching, doing independent research on Fulbright or special government grants, or serving one of the foreign liaisons of the university. The *Daily Student*, July 11, 1961, boasted this was the third largest number of absentee professors on foreign assignments of any American institution. If Indiana professors were frequently away from the campus, Bloomington became a haven for foreign scholars who joined the staffs of American universities. Among those at Indiana was Robert J. Champigny, a poet, who was awarded the Durchon-Louvet Prize in 1964 for his outstanding contributions to French letters and literature. This award was made annually to the French native living abroad who brought honor and glory to his mother country.

Many foreign-born scholars were to make major contributions in various fields at Indiana University. Vaclav Hlavaty, professor of mathematics, had once been a member of the Czechoslovakian parliament. He was blacklisted by the Czech Communists in 1948, because he refused to sign an oath of loyalty to the People's Democracy. In 1953 Professor Hlavaty solved the unbelievably complex and involved equation of Albert Einstein's "Unified Field Theory." This set of equations Einstein hoped would embrace a description of everything in the universe. Hlavaty told a New York *Herald-Tribune* reporter, July 30, 1953, that his solution provided the mathematical vehicle for understanding everything in the universe as Einstein had hoped. He said his solution described the process by which matter and energy could be described in terms of electromagnetic forces, and he thought it would prove a reconciliation of the apparent disparity between the relativity theory and quantum mechanics. The theory and the solution constituted the basis of the universe itself as it was held together by the electromagnetic fields.

Felix Haurowitz, who was also from Czechoslovakia, had been a professor of physiological chemistry at the University of Prague, 1925–30. Later he transferred to the Medical School of the University of Istanbul, and from there he came to the United States in 1948 as professor of biochemistry at Indiana University. In 1960 Haurowitz won the Paul Ehrlich Foundation Award of Frankfurt for his work in the field of antibiotics. He refuted the long-held theory that defensive reactions of antibodies were normal and healthy organisms. He discovered that they were "nothing but the formation of slightly modified proteins in response to the invading foreign agent," an agent called "antigen." Haurowitz's researches in this field attracted worldwide attention in the fields of chemistry and medicine.

Change was the normal condition and expectancy of the faculty from 1945 to 1970. New professors were hired every year, promising ones were lost to competing universities in search of topflight staffs, and old standbys either retired or died; always leaving personal voids on the campus. Despite the constant struggle to secure funds from public and private sources, Indiana University did comparatively well by its professors on its salary scale. In areas other than salaries it offered significant encouragement. There was beyond question a high degree of academic freedom, funds could always be found to finance research projects and special studies, and library facilities were expanded yearly. To encourage and reward maximum scholarly achievement the extraordinary rank of "Distinguished Service Professor" was created in June 1953. The first three professors elevated to this new classification were Hermann J. Muller, Tracy M. Sonneborn, and Stith Thompson. In future years other members of the staff were added to this prestigious list.

There was established in 1954 the Frederick Bachman Lieber Teaching Award in memory of the grandson of Katie D. Bachman, the donor. This cherished recognition of teaching given on Founders Day quickly became a mark of superior classroom performance on the part of the recipients. It has been won by such distinguished instructors as Byrum E. Carter, William R. Breneman, Robert G. Kelly, Marjorie Phillips, and Charles Hewitt. Other awards were established to recognize extraordinary services to the university by its professors and students.

The faculty voted by mail ballot in August 1955 to add Social Security to its retirement plan. By this action Indiana University became the first state agency to act on the recent authorization of the Indiana General Assembly to subscribe to the federal plan. Only forty professors opposed acceptance, reflecting by their action a last stand for rugged individualism. William C. Greenough ('35), a former assistant to the dean of the School of Business, and later assistant to the President, and President of Teachers Insurance and Annuity Association, said in January 1959 that his alma mater ranked at the top among colleges and universities in faculty benefits. Indiana administrative and School of Business staff members played active roles in the creation of the College Retirement Equities Fund subsidiary to TIAA. By 1965 the university assumed full payment of the 15 per cent of professorial salaries invested in the national retirement fund. Additional faculty benefits were provided in the fields of life and health insurance. The Board of Trustees, in June 1966, added a material sum to the latter programs to increase subscribed benefits in meeting medical and hospital costs.

By the time of his retirement from the presidency in 1962, Herman B Wells could take satisfaction in the fact that his intensive drive to organize a first-rate faculty had paid rich dividends in outstanding accomplishments in nearly every area of the institution's intellectual endeavors. President Elvis J. Stahr, Jr., reported in December 1963 that Indiana professors that year had produced 296 books and 1,430 articles; over two-thirds of the faculty had published something. Stahr, of course, could give no comparable quantitative report on teaching, but the increased outflow of undergraduates and successful graduate students was one mark of appraisal of faculty performance.

The crusade to hire and keep top-quality professors was ongoing. Ray E. Heffner, assistant to the dean of Faculties, told a *Daily Student* reporter, May 11, 1961, "We will have to get as much build-up in faculty as is available before competition gets too stiff." Indiana he said was hiring professors as fast as good ones could be persuaded to come to Bloomington; 55 per cent of the current faculty had been employed since 1955. Heffner made it sound as if the University was actually hoarding professors. There was, however, a limitation, and the administration still had to struggle to provide necessary funds to pay new professors' salaries.

These were the days of Camelot for the American university professor; for the first time in the nation's history the professorial "seller's market" was bullish. On the Indiana campus Stahr and his administrative colleagues expressed concern that prospective university staff members would find either governmental or business employment more seductive. The age had not arrived, however, when the teaching profession was on comfortable economic grounds. In a generation, economists said, the college professor had lost 50 per cent in economic status as compared with that of the average American. The AAUP study in 1958 indicated lawyer income had appreciated 34 per cent, dentists 54 per cent, and doctors 98 per cent, all of these far outranked professorial improvement of only 9 per cent.

President Stahr, in December 1963, said in his first *Annual Report*, "The need to attract and hold topflight faculty thus remains our number one priority. I hope all our faculty members, to the extent you can, will assist those directly engaged in the search for outstanding new people. You know at least as well as I that the key element in the strength of this institution, as of any other of decent reputation, is its faculty." That year Indiana added 127 faculty members, and suffered 62 losses. Stahr was favorably impressed with the new appointees, saying they were "Probably the largest and finest overall group every brought to the University in a single year." By 1966 there were on the faculty roll 2,103 full-ranked teaching staff, and 587 ancillary academic personnel.

When the Wells administration set out in 1937–38 to assemble a truly fine faculty, it perhaps had only a limited notion of the nature of the drama and intellectual excitement that would reward its labors. Indiana in the pre-World War II years hoped at best to improve its rather submerged position among the Big Ten universities. Wells and his energetic administrative colleagues could hardly have visualized that they were beginning to create on the banks of the River Jordan a faculty and the necessary academic equipment to produce works that would shake civilization itself. From poets, musicians, and artists to the most competent social and physical scientists, Indiana University in these years helped to usher in a new age for mankind in which social and political mores were now cast in new intellectual molds.

[V]

In the Toils of Mars

AT THE OPENING of the fall semester in 1937 a campus debate of mild proportions was in progress. Since 1918 the university had maintained a rather strong Reserve Officers Training Corps. At times in the intervening years students and professors had discussed whether or not there was further need for a military organization on the campus, and whether or not the university with its limited physical facilities should continue to expend energies and funds on officer training. There no doubt were fundamental philosophical reasons for opposing the reserve officers training program, at least the debate team discussed the two sides of the issue. The main point was the matter of compulsory military training.

The *Indiana Daily Student* opened a reconsideration of the subject of officer training by reserving a special column on its editorial page where students and professors were at liberty to present their views. This action was taken after Senator Gerald Nye had made his famous speech in Bloomington against the munition profiteers and the "nationless" warlords. The *Student* itself chose not to take a positive stand either way. Response was mild indeed, but even so the expression of opposition to compulsory officer training ran three to one.

The Indiana unit of the Reserve Officers Training Corps was commanded by Lieutenant Colonel W. R. Standiford, and then by Lieutenant Colonel John Frederick Landis. In the spring of 1938 there were 1,200 cadets, and the officers were busily polishing the corps to a fine finish for the annual inspection. Opposition at the moment was drowned in the competitive anticipation that Indiana for the third time would be awarded a gold star rating.

Cadets were dressed in "spit and polish" blue coats, white trousers, and dazzling black shoes. A soft feminine touch was given by five co-ed sponsors dressed in tight form-fitting skirts and shirtwaists, and carrying extravagant bouquets of flowers. This was militarism at its sweetest.

Whatever the nature of the low-key campus debate over the reserve officer program, it had little if any definable impact on the R.O.T.C. In the fall semester of 1938 enrollment in the corps increased from 1,392 in 1937 to 1,705, including the newly formed medical corps. Again in the spring review the shiny shoes smashed the sod of the athletic field in precision drill, and pretty girls put on a show to win another gold star. The next year more sex appeal was added to the campus army with the girls' drum, fife, and bugle corps. The parade ground that May came alive "in a swirl of white skirts and red coats," to say nothing of the shrill pipings of feminine Pans.

The Reserve Officers Association meeting in Vincennes in April 1940 adopted resolutions reminiscent of 1915 and 1916, asking Indiana University to construct an armory. No doubt on the urging of Colonel John Frederick Landis it was said the military facilities on the campus were "grossly inadequate."

President Wells was highly conscious of the fact that Indiana University was unprepared because of a shortage of space to conduct an efficient officer training program, and everything one could read in 1940 seemed to indicate that it was only a matter of time until the United States would be drawn into the second world war. In June that year he proposed to President A. C. Willard of the University of Illinois, and Chairman of the Committee on Military Affairs, National Association of State Universities, that an attempt be made to secure passage through Congress of national defense legislation for funds to construct R.O.T.C. armories on public campuses. President Willard reported the attitudes of his fellow committeemen in a letter to President John

J. Tigret of the University of Florida. The opinion of the group was evenly divided. Two members favored the Wells plan, and two opposed it. One member of the group strongly objected to the plan on the grounds that the army might come to use these facilities for officer training, taking them out of university hands. Too, he thought if the emergency were of short duration that the universities might be embarrassed by their defense ardor.

President Willard, despite the fact that Illinois had an excellent armory, was opposed to the proposal on the grounds that it might make the National Association of State Universities appear to be exploiting a national emergency. The proposal might actually result in a diversion of funds, and could introduce federal control into the universities, and finally the proposal seemed inconsistent with the stand of the association that in case of a great national emergency the state universities and colleges would function as civilian institutions so far as possible. "If the Federal Government builds new armories at such institutions," said Willard, "it would be common sense to use them to the utmost for training troops during the period of emergency." Willard nevertheless was willing to report Wells' proposal to the Executive Committee for further discussion, but nothing came of it. Indiana University in 1940 was still left where it was in 1916, without an armory.

Wells was almost as much aroused about the impending war as Bryan had been in World War I. He and six Middle Western university presidents in July 1940 endorsed the principles contained in a bill sponsored by the Military Training Camp Association which had been introduced in Congress on June 21, 1940, by Senator Edward R. Burke of Iowa. The presidents said they did not think an adequate force of well-trained men could be organized on a voluntary basis. They advocated immediate registration of all male citizens 18 to 65 years of age. They expressed themselves as strongly opposing a repetition of the Army Training Corps debacle of the first world war.

Within the year the temper of the nation itself underwent significant change. There remained little more than an echo of the booming Nye crusade. On October 16, 1940, 1,400 Indiana University students between the ages of 21 and 36 were registered for the draft, and few if any people remained uncertain about the United States' entry into the European war. Enrollment in the R.O.T.C. boomed, and again emphasis was placed upon physical conditioning of officer candidates. By the time the Japanese bombed Pearl Harbor the officer training program had been taken over completely by the War Department, and students were anxious to know what effect the Japanese attack would have on accelerating the draft.

The Army expanded its officer training program on the Indiana campus in June 1942 by adding a Quartermaster Reserve Officers Training Corps, one of three in the United States. President Wells said this was a recognition of the quality of the Indiana University School of Business. From this date on the university once again became about as much a military training camp as an educational institution. No special group became more war minded than the crack drill corps of Pershing Rifles. They injected imagined British commando ferocity into their training. They erected barriers along the Jordan just below Woodburn Hall and assaulted them. Crossing the placid little campus brook was a poor substitute for the great English Channel, and the gentle knoll beyond could hardly be called the chalk cliffs of Dover, but then there was the presidential castle which could be stormed if worst came to worst. Maybe Wells foresaw this possibility, because Colonel Raymond L. Shoemaker and Captain Tom Levi agreed to storming a site "somewhere east of Jordan Avenue" where there were more thorn bushes and bamboo briars.

There was now no debating the usefulness of the R.O.T.C., or the obligation of the unversity to make major efforts on many fronts to aid the national defense effort. Just as Indiana University had responded to the calls for service in 1916, it was again dedicated to an all out war effort in 1941.

Immediately after the bombing of Pearl Harbor on December 7, 1941, Indiana University was placed on a full wartime regimen. A student-faculty war council was formed which became responsible for drafting plans by which the university could best carry on its academic program. Any plan drafted had to encompass the fact that the various military and civilian branches of the Federal Government would make a heavy call on the institution. From January 7 to 14, 1942, a war planning committee composed of three administrators, twelve professors, and one student sat in continuous session discussing what changes should be made in university procedures to meet the increased national defense demands.

On January 17, 1942, Ward Biddle notified Uz McMurtrie

that the trustees were meeting and would remain in continued session to discuss war problems in "probably the most far reaching of any single Board meeting the university has had in many years. The President presented to them the plan to put Indiana University on an accelerated program which includes many things that the university seems to have need of." The program which had been drafted in nine days and nights was approved unanimously by the board.

President Wells announced on January 17 that Indiana University would adopt a three-semester plan by which the four-year program would be compressed into two and two-thirds years. The thought at the moment was to graduate as many students as possible before they were called into military service, and to avoid having them return to Bloomington at the war's end to complete a fragment of their education. The War Planning Council thought the new program would enable the university to live up to its historic role, "and would prevent unnecessarily large numbers of young men and women to face the present emergency and the post-war period without the benefits of a college education." Too, it was said a graduate would be more useful to the war effort. On January 17, 1942, the full text of the revised plan was published in the *Daily Student*. The new semesters would begin on January 24, May 10, and the first week in September. The period of annual faculty employment would be two and a half semesters, and salaries were to be adjusted according to the necessities of the moment.

From a long-range perspective the most significant result of the War Planning Council's recommendations was the institution of the Junior Division. Debate over this internal innovation had been intensive, but in the emotions and furor of war emergency, opponents of this plan were silenced by fear to debate the subject further, were on leave from the faculty, or were converted to the idea. After January 24, all students entering the university as freshmen were required to enroll in the Junior Division. Wells announced that the Faculty Council had unanimously approved the plan even though it made "an enormous increase in the work of the faculty and staff." To the president, "the unity demonstrated in the council sessions and later in the meetings of the entire faculty constitutes one of the brightest pages in the history of the University."

Adopting the War Planning Council's instructional plan

actually placed Indiana University on an immediate wartime basis. In communicating this fact to students, President Wells said that although Indiana University was not the first to announce such a plan, the Bloomington one was the most complete. "Our society," he said, "is faced with the necessity for a supreme military and productive effort. There is no shortage of manpower. There is a tremendous shortage of trained manpower."

Training manpower for wartime and military purposes involved radical changes within the university itself. The Army, during the first semester of 1940–41, inaugurated a new system of infantry training which would produce competent young officers. It then seemed certain that young college-trained men would be headed for extended military service. Students were urged to become proficient in all their work, and in order to represent the university in athletic events they were expected to present satisfactory records in the Reserve Officers Training Corps classes. The university went beyond this and removed the administration of military affairs from the College of Arts and Sciences. It also assumed heavy responsibilities in the organization of a medical corps, an enlisted reserve program, a quartermaster corps unit, and a civilian pilot training project.

The Medical Administrative Corps was of fundamental importance. This authority permitted the university to retain students between the ages of 18 and 45 who were bona fide matriculates in the medical and dental schools as well as premedical and predental enrollees, provided the latter had been accepted for admission to the professional programs by the beginning of the following term. All students so enrolled were members of the Medical Administrative Corps, and were exempted from being called to military duty by their local draft boards.

Indiana University had become actively engaged in war training in other specialized fields during the spring semester of 1939. In March of that year the War Department designated the institution as a cooperating school in the training of pilots for the Air Force. There was at that time on the campus a collegiate flying club under the direction of Joseph Crouch. There was not, however, a flying field available near Bloomington.

The first pilot allotment was for twenty pilots, but President Wells went to Washington to seek an increase in the number to fifty cadets. He also secured the assurance that the War Department planned an even more extensive program. Wells told military officials that already plans were underway to construct a public airfield just as soon as titles to farms on the site could be procured.

Both the romance of flying and the excitement of prospective military combat proved enticing to students. Those enrolling for pilot training were charged a fee of $40, and the university and the National Aeronautics Authority financed other costs. In addition, a research grant was made to the university so that Dr. W. N. Kellogg could determine how people without former aerial training could learn to fly. This experiment was expected to enable the university to produce pilots in the shortest space of time. The first class enrolled contained thirty fledgling airmen, and the War Department refused to increase the number because of the limitations of the local airfield; President Wells felt at that time the institution could not ask for an increased enrollment.

At the opening of the university in September 1940 it seemed certain the civilian pilot training program would be of limited duration. Both President Wells and Colonel John Frederick Landis expressed disappointment that work on the Bloomington airport had lagged. High tension power lines still blocked the landing path, and the runways remained unbanked. So poorly equipped was the field, in fact, that the Civil Aeronautics Authority considered it unsafe for training purposes. In January 1941 prospects for the pilot training program in the university brightened, however; an assembly room, repair shop, and hangar were under construction. Colonel Landis said the program was a great success. Twenty-eight of the first thirty students had passed their pilot tests, as compared with thirty-one of ninety candidates who had no formal training. Still, the airfield remained unapproved by the War Department, and Monroe County and Bloomington officials continued to procrastinate.

Colonel Roscoe Turner, the famous World War I ace, was appointed an inspector for the Civil Aeronautics Authority, and the Indiana Cadet Corps was assigned to the supervision of the Turner Flying Corporation for training. Turner came to Bloomington two or three times a week to oversee the program. An intensive course in air flight was begun on May 15, 1941, to include young non-college trained cadets. Chauncey E. Sanders of the Department of English was made director of the instructional courses in history, geography, and grammar. There were, however, too many physical problems beyond the classroom to promise success. When W. E. Barton of the Civil Aeronautics Authority inspected the Bloomington airport in June, he said work on the runways had not progressed sufficiently to meet the standards for safe instructional use. In response to this adverse report university officials called on Bloomington service and fraternal clubs to exert pressure on local officials to meet promptly the standards set by the military officials.

In the spring the air arm of Indiana University seemed much stronger. At that time, despite the earlier adverse reports, the university was designated by the War Department as a "focal center" for training flyers, and ten enlisted men were sent to the campus to begin a new training program. This was at least a ray of faint hope glimmering through a thick bank of gloom. President Wells, however, responded to a letter from W. T. Kinder on April 12, 1943, saying that the university would no longer train aviation cadets because of the conflict over unifying military commands within the institution.

The Bloomington *World Telephone* had another explanation why the university was dropping the air program. The paper said some officers of the War Training Service from Maxwell Field, Alabama, had flown into Bloomington expecting to increase the number of cadet flyers. When their plane landed, it plowed into a bank of soft mud, almost causing a fatal accident. They inspected the field's inadequate drainage system and took wing southward. A storm forced the officers to land at Bowling Green, Kentucky, where they decided to locate a pilot training center. Two months after this incident the Bloomington City Council offered to purchase the university's hangar and other aviation equipment.

By the time the pilot training program had come a cropper, Indiana University was engaged in far more promising military activities, one of which was the Naval Reserve Officers Training program. This corps perhaps had its inception on the campus when fourteen university students were accepted on a battleship cruise in the fall of 1940. When they finished their tour, they were apointed midshipmen in the N.R.O.T.C. at Northwestern University. From this stimulus Indiana University developed an interest in the Naval V-1 training program. This corps admitted freshmen and sophomores and gave them two years' deferment with a promise that they might seek a commission, provided they passed a comprehensive examination. They would then be transferred to the V-7 naval program.

The university extended its naval program considerably in July 1942, when 200 yeomen were assembled on the campus for four months of training. North Hall was vacated by students, and dining facilities and part of the instructional staff were made available to the Navy. Eventually it was said there would be 1,200 yeomen on hand to be trained by the Business School in the business and clerical methods of the Navy.

Prospects of so many sailors on the Indiana University campus stirred the Student War Council. This body planned dances, moving picture shows, and Bloomington home entertainment. No yeoman was to be left to pine away in loneliness. By mid-July 1942 life along the Jordan had taken on a nautical flavor. North Hall became a "vessel" and its small two-student rooms became cabins housing six yeomen. President Wells assured the sturdy "seamen" that everybody aboard the "good ship Indiana University" was glad the Navy had swung its hammock in Bloomington. The president said there was a fine staff of teachers on hand, and "the quarters are the best we can provide. All this has been provided because to the university the best is none too good for you."

Lieutenant Commander E. P. Jones agreed with the president. The "cabins" were ideal, and the classrooms, in the Business Building were far better than the Navy had anticipated. Naval instruction immediately preempted thirty-five classrooms, and under these conditions everybody was assured the Naval Training School would contribute its share toward achieving victory. The service schedule provided for five to six hours a day in classrooms. A sick bay was established to care for those who faltered. The university was designated the "Ship," and Bloomington was to be called the "Shore." Thus both the university and its crew put out to sea. The Y.M.C.A. and the Y.W.C.A. placed their organizations at the Navy's disposal and yeomen were made to feel they were aboard a hospitable ship. The *Daily Student* assured the "crew," "You men will 'keep 'em floating' during the next few months while the United Nations are winning the war. . . ." In a true fighting vein the editor hoped three months on the campus would make loyal fighting sons of Indiana of the yeomen. "If our university can help you sink another loyal Jap or Nazi ship, this school will feel well repaid for its contributions to your training."

The paper thought the land sailors would come to "love the place as we do." After six months the editor was certain the naval program was a success. "The Naval Training School established by the Navy Department on the campus last July, is one of the most prominent evidences that Indiana University is doing everything it can to help the country avenge the tragedy of Pearl Harbor."

Amidst an air of pageantry the first class of 273 yeomen was graduated on October 22, 1942. A select group of vocal sailors gave a musical revue entitled "Tattoo," and Marye Hulse was properly dubbed "Sweetheart of the Fleet." This first graduate contingent sailed away from the "Shore" too soon. A caravel load of SPARS was consigned to the "Ship" in June 1943. Indiana University was now converted into a training center for SPARS and WAVES in the latter year, and instead of 1,200 yeomen there were to be 1,200 women reserves. In preparation for the new contingent, the Navy proposed to train twenty-four bakers and cooks in the university kitchens. Wells said the university hoped that half the number would be men, and that no more than six apprentices would be in training at a time, because the kitchens were too busily engaged in feeding other military units to spare the time and space to the cook training program.

In response to what seems to have been a slightly critical query, President Wells wrote Lieutenant Governor Charles M. Dawson on May 26, 1944, that in nearly two years the Indiana University Naval Training School had trained 5,008 yeomen and storekeepers of both sexes for the Navy and the Marine Corps. He also assured Dawson that Indiana had consistently ranked at the top of the list of the 200 specialized schools operated by the Navy. A month later the naval training program was officially closed. The "good ship *Indiana University*," so far as the Navy was concerned was placed in mothballs, and somewhere "off shore" thousands of storekeepers and clerks helped to keep the naval supply system in a constant state of bureaucratic paper confusion.

While sailors learned the art of nautical storekeeping in the School of Business, a less dramatic military contingent occupied the Indiana campus. In June 1942 the Army announced that 23,000 inductees from the Fifth Corps Area would be accepted in the

Enlisted Reserve Program and would be allotted to colleges and universities on the basis of enrollment of male students. These reserves were chosen primarily to become officer candidates, and they were told they could expect to be assigned to officer schools at the end of the reserve training period. However, the Army changed its mind, and in May 1943 began calling up reservists. The first group of 60 men was notified to report for active duty, and there was indication that all 600 would soon be inducted. Medical and dental students were more fortunate. They were called into service, placed in uniforms, and returned to classrooms as members of the 1551st Service Unit.

Indiana University had sensed the coming of World War II at an early date, and by the opening of the first semester in 1940 possibilities had become almost certainties that the nation would now be actively engaged in a second world war. The international issues were more clearly defined, and there appeared to be close parallels with the era of 1916. Male students between the ages of 21 and 31 years faced a certainty that they would be called into military service either as draftees in the regular army or as national guardsmen. The impending Burke-Wadsworth selective service law established this fact. Immediately President Wells, who had strongly supported the bill, assured students that if they were drafted for the one-year service provided by the law they could return and resume classwork at the point they had reached when they departed the campus, and without having to comply with the university's established withdrawal and reentry procedures. Few acts of Congress agitated students so much as the Burke-Wadsworth Law. There was a rush on the campus to enroll in R.O.T.C. classes at all levels. The registrar reported that 52 per cent of the male student body fell within the draft ages.

On October 16, 1940, 5,313 men were registered for the draft in Monroe County, and of these 1,232 were Indiana students. More than 150 law students appeared at the registration booths in the gymnasium wearing derbies, swinging canes, and singing lustily "There is Power." Other students displayed signs saying, "Tanks," "Gas Masks Now," "We Been Subpoenaed," "From Commons to Tanks," "Those Meds Stink," and "From Commons to Camp." The "stinking" medics, not to be outdone, entered the gymnasium singing "We're in the Army Now." A faculty advisory committee consisting of K. P. Williams, Thomas A. Cookson, C.

E. Edmondson, and Julian Bryan was appointed to assist students in filling out selective service questionnaires.

Despite all this schoolboy excitement and the signs there was a blanket deferment of college students until July 1, 1941, but by that time they were required to have had their physical examinations. The new order of things placed considerable burden on the university. Most physical examinations took place on the campus. Also, the business office had the task of determining pro-rata refunds of fees based upon the actual number of days students had been enrolled, so that when they reentered the university they would know what reductions to make in payments. In every way the university attempted to oblige students who were subjected to the draft. A special convocation was held just prior to the Christmas holidays in 1941 at which President Wells explained the situation of students in regard to draft calls with the hope that they would go home for the holidays fully informed as to their immediate futures. The bombing of Pearl Harbor had made a material difference in students' status and morale.

On February 16, 1942, approximately 1,100 students were processed for the Monroe County Draft Board in Alumni Hall of the Memorial Union Building. At the same time Marine Corps officers opened recruiting headquarters in the Whittenberger Auditorium. During the next eighteen months a certain amount of student panic developed on the campus. Many of those above eighteen years of age began to feel it their patriotic duty to enlist. Professor Frank Horack, Jr., advised them to await their draft calls or to enlist in one of the reserve services then functioning on the campus. Throughout 1942 there was uncertainty as to the status of the eighteen- and nineteen-year-old students. Psychologically they were perhaps the most troubled of anyone on the campus, because they had no way of knowing when the War Department might decide to take them into service on a moment's notice. They were right.

President Roosevelt on November 13, 1944, signed the bill drafting the younger boys. There was a rumor afloat that major universities would be turned into military schools where underage boys would continue their schooling but in uniform and under light military discipline. However, university officials were informed that students registered in classes for the second semester would be allowed to remain in Bloomington until May at least, and the university would not be taken over by the armed services. The program for women would not be disrupted in any way, except maybe to dispense with physical education because of a lack of space. Paul McNutt, chairman of the Manpower Commission, urged university students, not immediately subject to the draft, to remain in the university. Juniors and seniors enrolled in R.O.T.C. classes were warned at the opening of the new semester that they would possibly be called into service in May.

The War Department, as usual, issued a multiplicity of directions on student status and at frequent intervals, so that it was difficult for even Professor Frank Horack to be certain what would happen next. Many of these directives pertained to universities and colleges with schools of engineering, dentistry, and medicine. Indiana had no college of engineering, but its students qualified for technical deferments in chemistry, mathematics, meteorology, physics, bacteriology, astronomy, medicine, and dentistry. Actually the specifications were such that only students majoring in or taking courses preliminary to majoring in these fields could hope to gain deferment. This, of course, left large numbers of Indiana University students still subject to the draft call of May 1943.

Never were the draft policies of the War Department relating to college students clearly settled. Every semester after 1942 opened amidst uncertainties about the immediate future. As a matter of fact, debate over the draft continued on beyond the cessation of hostilities. Injected into the discussion was the more fundamental issue of universal military training. In October 1945 Commander Edward N. Schaiberling of the American Legion asked the presidents of twelve major universities if their views had changed on the subject. He said a frank statement from the administrators would remove suspicion from the public mind that educational protests were merely stalling tactics to defeat post-war legislation on the issue of universal military training. An open letter was sent to the President of the United States on January 30, 1945, by university presidents which said in part: "It is urged that initiation of conscription debate be delayed at least until complete victory over Germany is achieved. A continuing program of public evaluation as to requirements of national defense is certainly in order, but we challenge the necessity of urging the Americans to act under tensions of war." This letter was signed by President Herman B Wells.

Indiana, like every other institution of higher education in America, experienced four years of wartime confusion and uncertainty about student enrollment. There were few if any moments when anybody could say with certainty what fundamental changes would be made in draft and deferment rules from one semester to the other. Male students had only the vaguest assurances that they would be allowed to stay in school for more than the semester in which they were registered. This condition of uncertainty worked hardships because no one knew what future commitments to make, and morale was seriously affected.

Generally speaking, the university itself operated a fairly low-level academic program after 1942. Enrollment of male students dropped phenomenally low. The special military programs, however, took up the slack in both enrollment and staff time. One of the most significant additions to the military programs was the organization of the Army Specialized Training Program. The first indication in Bloomington of the War Department's planning in this area came on March 16, 1943, when 226 infantry and quartermaster reserve corps students were advised they would be called to active duty when the AST Program contract was signed. University officials were told that the Army would begin campus training in language, social science, and institutional and military policy areas.

Between March and the latter part of May 1943, university personnel was left in the dark as to what would happen next. If the administration knew, it was prohibited from telling under the restrictions of the War Censorship Regulations Act. By the latter part of May, the early contract sailors, army storekeepers, and other specialized military units were withdrawn from the campus. Only a contingent of WAVES, said the *Daily Student*, were left behind. There was considerable excitement in anticipating the arrival of the ASTP soldiers, when at last their coming was advertised. Out of 150,000 men assigned to this duty nationally, Indiana University was led to believe it would receive from 5,000 to 5,500 men in all.

The period of anticipating the arrival of the new military contingent on the campus ended on May 29, when 104 men arrived aboard the Monon from the University of Nebraska and Michigan State College where they had been "processed." Other men were to be assigned immediately from the "Star" centers scattered about the Middle West. There were two classes of ASTP soldiers. The largest group was composed of college men who were to receive training in four or five basic fields. The others were carefully selected college graduates who were given intensive instruction in the field of European and Balkan languages. Nationally, the ASTP contingents were not without their humorous blunders in selection. There were soldiers with doctor's degrees who got assigned to elementary classes, and occasionally to areas of their specialties. There were doctorates who had to sit through the most elementary instruction in history and mathematics, and otherwise be bored by the whole program. Then there were men who had little or no college training, and sometimes were intellectually unequipped to carry prescribed class loads. No doubt the most costly blunders of the AST Program was the assignment of men who had spent long periods of basic military training in a specialized area only to have their training go for naught.

On the Indiana campus, Colonel Raymond L. Shoemaker commanded the military program, and Dean Bernard Gavit of the Law School directed the educational program. Girls were moved out of Memorial Hall, and the army was housed there, two to ten men in a room. All the university classes were in charge of the regular faculty, and the schedule was indeed spartan. Dean Gavit informed his colleagues that the ASTP unit would be administered on the West Point cadet system. Students were to be addressed as "Cadet," and cadets were to answer professorial addresses with "Sir!" and they would be required to stand to recite. In fact, they were to do everything but click their heels, and there was some of that. All cadets were instructed to be prompt, and professors were to hold classes for a full fifty minutes. On top of all this militaristic form there was tucked away in Princeton, New Jersey, a group of professional test-makers who caused instructors to look on the programs with wide-eyed wonder at how far the Princeton masterminds could miss the subject being taught. Dean Gavit imposed a kind of formalized austerity on the units in every phase of campus life. No university holidays were observed, and instructors were told not to assign more than an hour of study time per class hour for the week. Thus a weary phalanx of soldier-students stumbled in full order of march from one classroom to another to catch up on their napping.

The ASTP procedure was as erratic as the mind of the War

Department itself. Units of men came and went with the same degree of regularity of all military moves. In August 1943, 1,700 men arrived on the campus bringing the university's enrollment up to 7,000 students, and near the institution's highest peak. Housing was not readily available and this fresh contingent was bedded down in the Fieldhouse, the University School gymnasium, and some men were even quartered in tents. Women students were moved to other quarters to make room in the dormitories for soldiers. The university was now getting its first taste of providing emergency housing for students.

Indiana University was one of the first major institutions to grant credit for ASTP work. Each soldier was allowed seven hours toward graduation. The military training would also fulfill future R.O.T.C. requirements. Thus each cadet received approximately a semester's credit for each term. The first cadet class to graduate attended commencement exercises on December 2, 1943, when they heard the aging William Lowe Bryan make an eloquent plea for unity among the allied nations. With unity he told the young soldiers the allies would only barely be able to win the war, and with dissension the cause of civilization would be lost. "What Hitler has done in Europe," said Bryan, "Japan has done in Asia. Today we face the fact there is no nation in the world strong enough to defend its own life."

Army life on the campus fell somewhere between the pleasures of the university social swirl and the grim austerity of army barracks. Perhaps group exhaustion would have better characterized much of it. When Harriet Weaver of the Bloomington *World Telephone* visited Memorial Hall to observe the daily routine, she found two to ten men bedded down in tiny girl-sized cubicles. Thirty bags of mail came to the basement post office daily, and soldiers were out of bed by 6:00 A.M., and were kept on the move until 10:30 P.M. They did not even have time for that cherished army recreation, a barracks crap game. Somehow this student army preserved enough energy to attend campus dances on Saturday nights, and to produce *Soldiers in the Dark*, a wartime substitute for the Jordan Revue.

Just as suddenly as the ASTP horde swarmed down on the campus in 1943, it departed on April 1, 1944. The men left the campus to be assigned to active duty, some of them to fight against the last fierce German drives on the Western Front. Wells all but expressed relief that the climax of military activities on the campus was in sight, and soon thousands of veterans would return to Bloomington and more orderly academic life. He said, "It is agreed that the AST Program has been a success and has made a substantial contribution to the total training program for our armed forces." He thought it unfortunate that many of the boys would sit on campus for weeks, waiting to be reassigned. President Wells told the Board of Trustees privately that Secretary of War Henry L. Stimson "descended to sheer demagoguery in the statement of the disbandment by more or less accepting the point of view [that because such large numbers of boys were being trained in universities fathers were being drafted and sent to the fighting front]."

When the main body of the ASTP departed Bloomington 150 medical reserves were left behind to complete their professional training in Indianapolis. The grand finale of the ASTP experience was the citation awarded Colonel Raymond L. Shoemaker for the outstanding records of both R.O.T.C. and ASTP. Replacing the specialized training unit was the tag end of civilian military cooperation, the ASTRP. This latter group, composed of eighteen year olds, was poorly disciplined. Not even Colonel Shoemaker and Dean Gavit could win citations with this ragtag-and-bobtail contingent. These lads expected to go nowhere academically, and their chances of having to fight were almost nil. President Franklin D. Roosevelt on March 4, 1944, in a national radio address to American youth urged every American "who will be a high school graduate by July 1, to look seriously and immediately into the government's new plan for free college training of those too young for the draft." He thought it of the greatest importance for the youth of the nation to take the military examinations and to enter either the Army or Navy study programs. It would help them through the "awkward age" in wartime.

Between June 1943 and August 31, 1944, Indiana University helped to train approximately 3,000 soldiers in the general AST Program, in dentistry, medicine, and the specialized language areas. Besides this, the regular R.O.T.C. trained 90 candidates for assignment to officer training schools. More than 300 professors, staff members, and service personnel were employed in the military program over the five years, 1940–45. Dean Gavit informed President Wells in his final report, "on the whole the University's work in this field was very successfully done and the army's objectives were rather clearly met on a rather high plane. The instructional staff really worked at the job and deserves the highest commendation for the efforts put out and the results reached." What the law dean did not say in his report was that the formalized army instruction was often dull and onerous. Professors found that ASTP classrooms lacked the spontaneity of the civilian ones. The marching in full rank to recitations, the "cadet" heel clicking, standing recitations, and "sir" business destroyed a good part of the atmosphere of teaching and learning. The eternal testing by nonsensical formulas completed the job of intellectual manslaughter. Perhaps Dean Gavit never heard the lusty ASTP ballad which ended in the self-pitying refrain:

> When I grow old and take my grandson upon my knee
> Won't it be hell to tell him I fought the war in the ASTP.

While the university involved itself so deeply with the training of male soldiers and at all levels at the outset of the war, President Wells and Dean of Women Kate H. Mueller sought to locate on the campus a Women's Auxiliary Training Corps. This was a campus organization predating the arrival of various service-related women auxiliaries. In August 1942 university officials prepared to train these 600 women auxiliaries. Again the *Daily Student* was quick to boast that this was the first auxiliary program in the nation. The auxiliary program was only mildly military, requiring one hour drill a week. Students had to maintain a "B" average in their academic work. They were called WATC's on the campus, but the Navy referred to them as "yeomanettes." The girls were required to pass physical examinations and to wear uniforms on occasion. Freshmen and sophomores wore blue skirts, white blouses, and the unit's insignia. Juniors and seniors wore blue skirts, red jackets, and red overseas caps, red socks, and white saddle shoes. The line between the yeomanettes and the regular naval units is not always clearly drawn in the records, but apparently the two had little or nothing in common except loyalty to the Navy.

The main academic difference in the WATC academic program was the offering of more stenography and typing. The advanced courses required three class meetings a week and stressed such subjects as leadership, military courtesy, organized discipline, sanitation, first aid, organization of the army, military history, map reading, aerial photographs, mess management, military law, and defense against chemical warfare. Colonel Shoemaker told Captain George A. Sprecht that this program not only gave the co-eds an idea of military service, but it gave them a feeling of taking part in the war effort, and of participating in all the campus military activities.

The arrival of the 600 WAVES assigned from the official Navy auxiliary program was awaited on the campus with about the same anxious expectation as if they were bringing with them the battleship *Missouri.* On October 5, 1942, the first seven WAVE officers reached Bloomington, and four days later 601 recruits were on hand. The official auxiliary program was underway. The first feminine contingent completed its assignment detail February 1, 1943, and a second class of equal size replaced them. The full complement was supposed to be 1,200 women, but Indiana University lacked suitable housing space to care for so many girls. They could not be handily consigned to tents as were some of the ASTP soldiers. President Wells suggested the university drop physical education requirements for women, and use the women's gymnasium. "That requirement," he said, "was introduced for psychological reasons at the time the physical education program for men was inaugurated." He thought it not now necessary to continue the work.

Within twelve months, October 9, 1942, to October 8, 1943, Indiana University trained 1,800 WAVES, SPARS, and Marine women recruits. These were prepared to be storekeepers and radio operators. After that date only WAVES were to be trained. Aside from these the Indiana School of Nursing enrolled nursing cadets who agreed to go either into military or emergency civilian service for the duration of the war.

Just as with the training of the male naval contingent the Navy Department ordered discontinuance of the WAVE contract in March 1944. The last unit was to leave the campus in May, leaving behind a military void not to be filled until the G.I.'s came back to the university. Indiana University was one of 200 institutions which won the Navy's "A" rating for its storekeeper training center. By early spring 1944, the Navy determined that it had enough trained personnel to last out the war. Despite the fact Indiana was looking forward to a certain end of the war within twelve months, it was reluctant to close the naval program, and Senators Raymond E. Willis and Samuel D. Jackson undertook to persuade the Navy Department to reverse its decision to withdraw its personnel. Unless this was done, said university officials, the campus facilities would have to be converted to other uses.

Plans had been made by the Army prior to 1945 to locate the school for WAC officer training at Indiana, but these were changed and the school was placed at Purdue University. Indiana had been inspected and was actually making preparations to receive these officer cadets when the Monon and Illinois Central railroads cancelled their daytime services through Bloomington. The Army said satisfactory rail connections were necessary because WAC trainees came from various commands in the United States and from overseas and assembling them required adequate rail services.

Few if any state universities made a greater effort to serve the nation in time of war emergency. The war had a genuine impact on Indiana University. It came in the midst of an intensive program of rebuilding both staff and curriculum, and many of the experiences growing out of war services served to give new directions to postwar academic programs. It may even have been true that instructional approaches were revised in several fields because of the military requirements for immediate conditioning of personnel for service in sensitive areas. This was certainly true in the field of language instruction, in both methodology and breadth of coverage. Too, the whole field of physical education came under review, and after 1945 gained a new importance in the general university instructional program.

Aside from its extensive involvement in the various military training programs, Indiana University was called upon to serve a multiplicity of civilian demands. No doubt the most significant effort it made in this area was the major instructional program it offered across the state in industrial management and personnel supervision through the administration of the War Training Program. During the four years, 1941–45, 942 courses were given in 69 Indiana cities. This involved the services of 270 instructors who taught all sorts of war-related management courses. In these years 19,023 students were enrolled, 90 per cent of these took accounting and personnel supervision, and more than half of the registrants enrolled in supervisory courses. Women comprised a high percentage of the enrollment, "Because," it was said, "the women seemed to fit more readily into such courses as accounting, office management, personnel, and statistics than they did into many fields of engineering."

Professor Stanley Pressler of the School of Business said the War Training Program had far-reaching significance to both the university and Indiana private business. Business School professors had an opportunity to gain first-hand experience in the industrial parts of the state. The industrial community in turn acquired a considerable personnel resource through the efforts of the Management Defense Training Program administered nationally by the United States Department of Education.

In his report Professor Presser said, "Many men and women have been trained in the field of personnel and human relations, but during the last year and a half of the program, Washington officials felt that this training should be limited strictly to personnel work. This restriction substantially reduced training offered in this field." During the four war years, he said, almost every company in Indiana making any contribution to the war effort was represented among the registrants in the Indiana University training programs, and long after the war the impact of this emergency program would be felt in greater efficiency, especially in the fields of office management and accounting.

End of the fighting in both Europe and the Orient left major public policies to be decided. At the end of the war one of the most vital matters of concern to the universities and colleges was policies concerning the continuation of the draft. This question had been raised earlier by the American Legion and had drawn a response from a small group of university presidents. In November 1945 the *Indianapolis Star* carried the story that Congress was considering alternatives to compulsory military training. Thirty-five college and university presidents, including Herman B Wells of Indiana University and President-elect F. L. Hovde of Purdue, proposed to the House Military Affairs Committee that a national commission be created to discuss the draft. This body, said the presidents, should be charged to make a thorough study of military needs. Members would be "selected for their integrity, special knowledge and experience with large affairs and representing military, diplomatic, legislative, industrial, scientific, and educational establishments." The administrators said if the proposed commission should recommend universal military training they promised to support it.

Pending the appointment of the commission and the preparation of its report, the presidents also recommended that draftees be kept for only fifteen months' service. There should be a vigorous promotion of voluntary enlistments, better pay should be offered as inducement to men to join the defense forces, and the armed services should offer more vocational and specialized training, "Since it is only one element in a long-range, comprehensive program of national defense."

For Indiana University the year 1945 was a cardinal one. Its curriculum had been disrupted, the Wells' search for outstanding faculty members had been brought to a halt, the war revealed how inadequate the institution's physical plant was for the operation of a university with a highly diversified program, and it thrust the institution into both the broader national and international streams of educational activity. For Herman B Wells and many of his colleagues the war, however, had broken the tight band of provincialism that had bound the institution from its inception in 1820. By 1945 all of the elements that had come into existence since the outset of World War I reached a new stage of maturity. Returning to the classroom and the serious business of operating a major teaching and research institution required an almost complete departure from the customs and mores of the past. Pressures of the postwar era brought into focus new intellectual and functional demands which were world-wide in scope. No longer could the institution content itself with being merely a state university dealing with only local needs.

HERMAN B WELLS, *President, 1937–1962.*

THIS PICTURE SECTION selected from the archives gives some of the flavor of Indiana University in its maturity. Included are names, sights, scenes, and groups that helped shape the University.

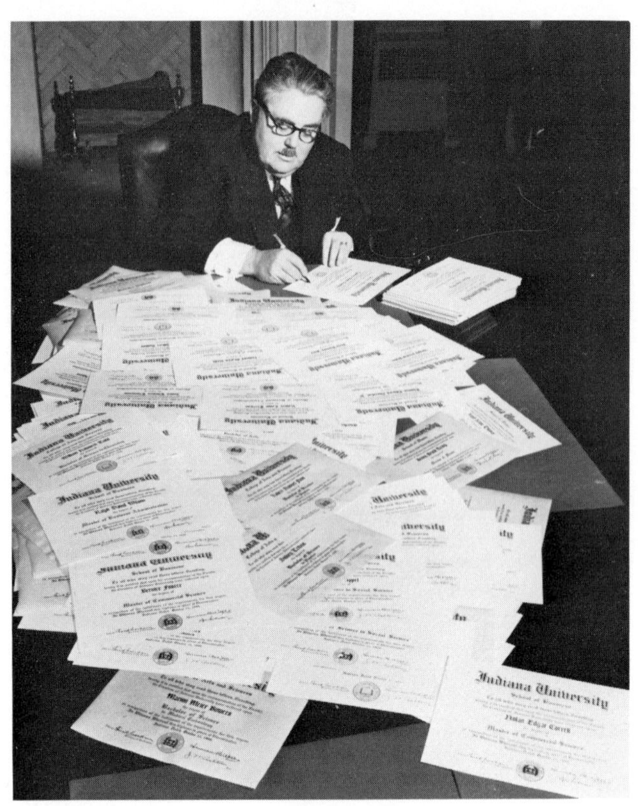

The President signing diplomas, 1950.

Herman B Wells and the Board of Trustees, 1949.

The inauguration of President Wells, 1938.

Paul Weatherwax and the Faculty Council remember President Wells' twentieth anniversary, 1957.

Santa Wells makes an annual appearance, December 1958.

WARD G. BIDDLE, *Comptroller, 1936–1942; Vice-President and Treasurer, 1942–1946.*

E. ROSS BARTLEY, *Director of University Relations and the News Bureau, 1938–1962.*

Three outstanding administrators, 1948: Charles E. Harrell, Thomas A. Cookson, and Joseph A. Franklin.

HERMAN T. BRISCOE, *Department of Chemistry, 1922–1941; Dean of the Faculties and Vice-President, 1940–1959.*

FERNANDUS PAYNE, *Department of Zoology, 1909–1951; Dean of the Graduate School, 1925–1947.*

The Auditorium, 1959.

Allan C. G. Mitchell, *Department of Physics, 1938–1963.*

Emil J. Konopinski, *Department of Physics, 1938–1977.*

Lawrence M. Langer, *Department of Physics, 1938– .*

Swain Hall, 1941.

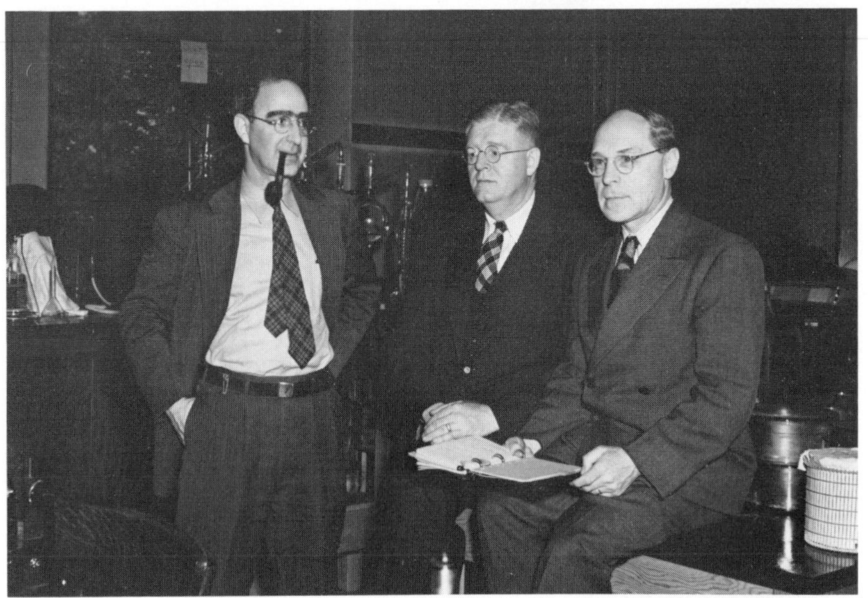

Three famous geneticists, 1946: Tracy M. Sonneborn, Ralph E. Cleland, and Hermann J. Muller.

Jordan Hall dedication, June 8, 1956: Leland S. McClung, Theodore Torrey, E. C. Stakman (a visiting speaker), Wells, and Cleland.

War Declared

EXTRA THE INDIANA DAILY STUDENT EXTRA

JAP BOMBS KILL 350 AT PEARL HARBOR

Honolulu Center Of Jap Attack

—EXTRA—

TOKYO, Dec., 8 (Monday) —(A. P.)— Japanese Imperial headquarters announced at 6 A.M. today that Japan had entered a state of war with the United States and Britain in the western Pacific as from dawn today.

Cabinet To Meet At 8:30 Tonight

U. S. Wins First Battle Is Report

Lieut.-Col. Shoemaker Says No Change In Program Here

WELLS PLEDGES FULL I.U. AID

The Indiana Daily Student, *December 7, 1941.*

John Stempel and Ernie Pyle, November 14, 1944.

The University War Council, 1942.

Indiana Air Cadet Corps, 1943.

WAVES, SPARS, and ASTS march to classes, 1943.

Postwar Planning Committee, 1944: Ford P. Hall, Robert T. Ittner, Ralph E. Cleland, Francis D. Wormuth, and Wendell W. Wright.

Dean Payne and President Wells admire the Nobel Prize medal with its winner, H. J. Muller, 1947.

The Law School, 1956.

RAYMOND L. SHOEMAKER, *Colonel, R.O.T.C., 1939–1944; Dean of Students, 1946–1955; Counselor, 1955–1958.*

BERNARD C. GAVIT, *School of Law, 1929–1954; Dean of the School of Law, 1933–1951.*

Law School alumni Sherman Minton and Paul V. McNutt with Governor Henry F. Schricker, 1950.

ALICE NELSON, *Director of the Halls of Residence, 1920–1965.*

KATE H. MUELLER, *Dean of Women, 1938–1949; School of Education, 1949–1969.*

EDITH B. SCHUMAN, *University Physician, 1938–1972.*

Student Veterans Living in the Board Room, October 1946.

A Trailer Courts Family, 1948.

Woodlawn Trailer Courts, 1946.

JOHN W. ASHTON, *English, 1946–1970; Dean, Arts and Sciences, 1946–1952; Vice-President, 1952–1958; Dean, Graduate School, 1958–1965.*

STITH THOMPSON, *English and Folklore, 1921–1955; Dean, Graduate School, 1947–1950.*

Alfred C. Kinsey, Clyde E. Martin, and Wardell B. Pomeroy, 1947.

Temporary Married Housing, 1947.

Forest Quadrangle, 1966.

Tulip Tree Apartments, 1965.

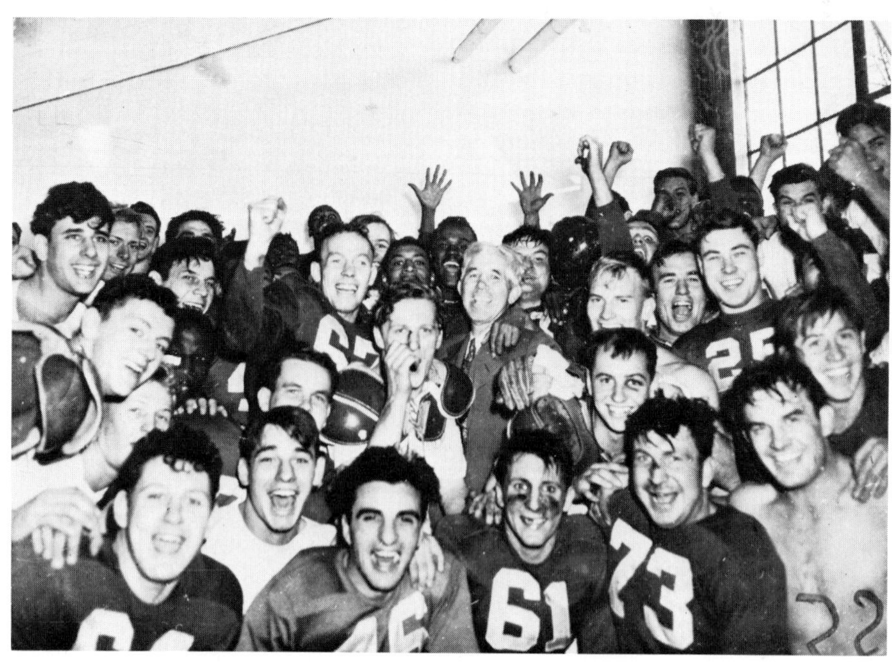

Big Ten Football Champions and Coach Bo McMillin, after defeating Purdue 26–0, November 24, 1945.

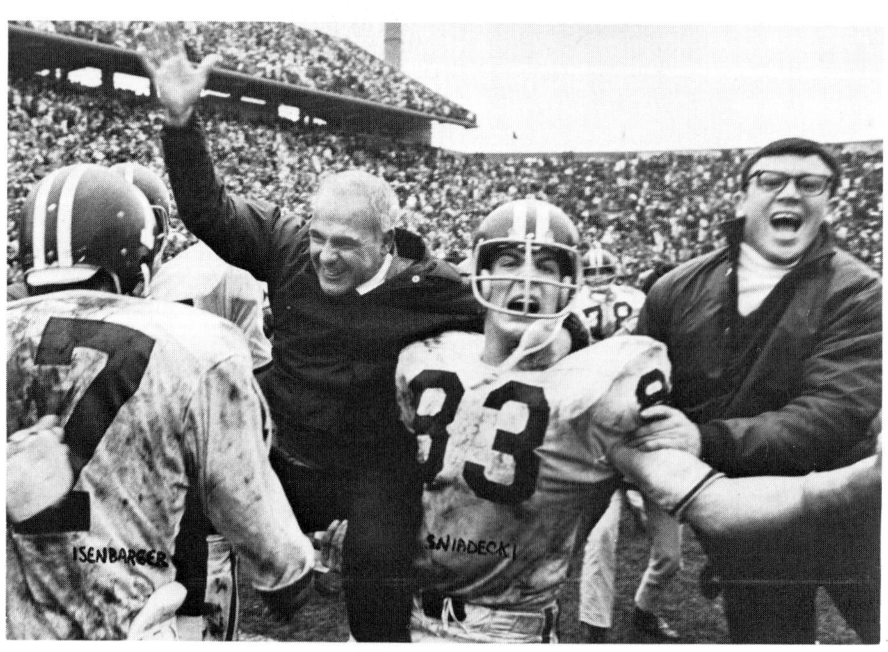

The football team and Coach John Pont celebrate the victory over Michigan State 14–13, November 11, 1967. The Big Ten Co-Champions played in the Rose Bowl, January 1, 1968.

[VI]

Meeting Demands Eternal

When Herman B Wells became acting president of Indiana University in mid-1937, he faced at least three challenges that seemed well-nigh insurmountable. First, he had to rebuild the faculty with good quality professors. That is, he and his administrative colleagues sought to hire the best staff members available and hoped they could find the money to pay them good salaries and to supply the necessary equipment for them to function as scholars. Second, despite the fact that Public Works Administration had assisted in the construction of new buildings, the university's physical plant was in grave need of modernization and expansion; for almost a century and a quarter it had been inadequate to meet the actual demands made upon it. A vast majority of male students were still without campus housing, and the instructional program suffered from lack of space. Had there been available to Indiana University in that year the best professors in America they could not have functioned adequately for lack of physical facilities. Finally, Indiana and Purdue universities were locked inseparably in a fiscal arrangement known as the "parity formula," adopted by general agreement in 1921. Six years later the General Assembly adopted a second formula for prorating funds to support capital improvements on the four state campuses, but it did not take into consideration their actual needs. At no time did this latter scheme fulfill its promise, and in 1939, with a tacit agreement of failure, it was abandoned with still three years to go.

Despite the great depression and the increasing world turmoil in the late 1930s, college enrollments increased in Indiana, and so did the costs of operating the university. As tangible as these facts were, it was extremely difficult to get governors and legislators to revise their traditional attitudes toward supporting higher education. Public education generally in Indiana suffered from precisely these same official failures. There was rigid resistance to a modernization of the general tax structure so necessary to produce sufficient revenue for advancing educational concepts. As a result, the colleges and universities came dangerously close to being placed in open competition with the public schools for funds. The financial history of Indiana University, 1937–62, was essentially an annual repetition of ancient struggles to break fiscal shackles.

Wells also had to tolerate comparisons with past university fiscal policies. There had been the criticism of William Lowe Bryan, that although he gave the university good intellectual leadership, he was too much a patrician to get money from Indiana governors and legislators. In truer perspective these critics seemed never to have stopped and reasoned that President Elliott of Purdue, and the presidents of the two state teachers colleges, fared no better. Parity had insured a degree of leveling of all four institutions.

President Wells wrote Judge Ora Wildermuth, October 24, 1939, "One fact which I think we must prepare to bring out in this state is that there has practically been no increase in appropriations since the depression year 1931." This was basically true despite the fact enrollment in the university had increased from 3,560 to 5,367. Some dramatic means had to be found to drive home the concept that the age demanded maximum returns from American universities provided with modernized facilities and the best professors.

Six months before Herman B Wells was made acting president, Ward G. Biddle wrote William A. Kunkel, January 11, 1937, a trustee and publisher of the Fort Wayne *Journal-Gazette*, that a group of selected persons should get busy and educate

Governor Cliff Townsend on the subject of adequately financing the university. He suggested that Kunkel arrange with the Governor to hold such a meeting, suggesting that they take with them "Skits" Simons, Dick Heller, and Herman B Wells. He thought it would be well to hold the meeting on Saturday afternoon when there would be no interruptions. Biddle said, "It is so vital to the University and will mean so much to Cliff's administration to see that these two state universities get on their feet that I think it would be time mighty well spent." This meeting seems never to have taken place, because the suggested date coincided with the second Roosevelt Inauguration, and all major Hoosier Democrats went to Washington to join the grand parade.

Kunkel must have spoken to Townsend, however, because on February 2 Biddle thanked him for his influence in securing a favorable biennial budget for the university. He told the trustee, "Bill, I am leaning heavily upon you in the next four years of our work here at Indiana. I know we can always depend upon you, and I know your power. With it we should go places." The four years of the Townsend administration were to be a period of phenomenal world, national, and even campus changes.

Although Biddle was spokesman for the university in this moment, of greater importance was the fact that Herman B Wells brought to the presidency a broad knowledge of Indiana politics and business from active participation in the field. As a banker he had gained considerable knowledge of accounting and monetary management and could fathom the complexities of state budgeting and appropriation procedures. He also had a sense of the campus reforms that were most urgent. Even so dominant a personality as Ward G. Biddle quickly perceived that the young president was competent to organize and conduct the university's financial crusades.

There were significant historical barriers in the way of Indiana's expansion program in 1937. In the past the state had supplied no more than 31 per cent of the cost of the physical plant, and had never appropriated as much as 50 per cent of the operational budget. The two-fifths of the five-cent tax levy provided for in the parity plan on February 14, 1921, always fell short of actual needs. In a more fundamental way there was the philosophical failure of both the universities and state officials to analyze the radically different functions of Indiana and Purdue. In this area about the only thing the two institutions shared in common was the eternal struggle to gain public support and a dedication to higher education. Functionally, their programs differed significantly, and it took more than a decade to bring this fact into clear focus.

In 1937 the Indiana University biennial appropriation was $3,940,000. During the last two years of the Public Works Administration activities on the campus the university incurred a considerable bonded indebtedness which necessitated provisions for its servicing. In addition land purchases were necessary to permit further campus expansion. That fall the Board of Trustees sought from the State Budget Committee $118,207 for these purposes, and received only $14,526.

The process of organizing Indiana college and university budgets followed a well-established procedure. The four colleges and universities prepared somewhat in common what they considered would be their needs for the next two years and presented their requests to the State Budget Committee. This body either approved the requests or pared them; almost without exception the committee reduced the suggested budgets. Whatever the Budget Committee recommended to the General Assembly was usually appropriated. There was a chance, however, that the final figure could be revised upward if the proper pressure was put upon individual legislators. The university lacked pressure power, however, and could only resort to persuasion.

Judge Ora L. Wildermuth wrote Herman B Wells, November 14, 1939, that "Nearly all the other states look with considerable jealousy upon the set-up as it exists in Indiana." He based his opinion on the fact that the central budgeting committee actually eliminated legislative lobbying by the universities. "You will never know how valuable to us is that Budget Committee," he told Wells, "until you understand what they have to do in some of the other states to get legislative action." It is to be questioned whether Judge Wildermuth's optimistic assessment of the work of the Budget Committee convinced those two realists, Wells and Biddle. Yearly they had seen the Budget Committee come to the campus and stay too brief a time to comprehend the actual needs of the university. They saw legislators lop off $800,000 from building requests and throw campus building hopelessly behind. As an example, the university's request for $257,000 to construct an urgently needed building for the Extension Center in Lake County was cut to $55,000. The general budget for operational funds for 1940 was $2,372,500, and for 1941 it was $2,430,000. The past fiscal year university expenditures were $3,241,072.02, and the legislative appropriation was $1,969,600. In later years Wells said he regarded the Budget Committee as helpful. He believed it kept the university from being strangled.

In an attempt to follow the sinuous course of budgetary proceedings, it must be noted that both budget committeemen and legislators seemed to believe that the institutions padded their requests, and the game was to guess how much to lop off. This is, of course, an unspoken and unrecorded matter, but there is more than an implication of this belief. The university administrators knew the price of eternal vigilance, and they also knew how costly stringency stampedes could be in the closing hours of legislative sessions. Wells and Biddle were indeed alert to the pressures, lobbying, and pulling and hauling which went on in capital corridors and chambers. Wells himself operated on the theory that persuasion and suggestion were much more efficacious than drawing the cord of commitment tightly around legislative necks; legislators must be left plenty of opportunity to maneuver. He gave some hint of this approach, July 28, 1938, in a letter to James Stuart, managing editor of the *Indianapolis Star*. He had previously sent Stuart some informational material which resulted in a highly useful editorial in the *Star*. This, said Wells, "made it easier for the men of the General Assembly to do what they wanted to do." The implication was that they were willing to follow a lead that helped them to make a show of decision and independence.

University administrators kept constant check on election results, and were quick to assess possible reactions of incoming legislators toward the university. It was indeed fortunate if alumni were elected. Because of the sizable number of School of Law graduates practicing in the state, the university no doubt enjoyed a possible advantage in the legislative body. A single incident seems to indicate this fact. In late July 1938 George W. Henley ('13), the university's attorney, and representative from Monroe County, was able to get $300,000 in capital funds restored to the general appropriation bill which enabled the university to go ahead with plans to build the Auditorium. The restoration was made by the Indiana Senate. Wells had been informed that the vote in the Senate could be changed, and he and Biddle visited that body. This appropriation was a landmark moment in both Indiana cultural history and the expansion of the campus in Bloomington.

Another alumnus, Senator Sherman Minton, was a major source of support, and the university called on him with considerable freedom. In a "tongue-in-cheek" response to a letter from Herman B Wells detailing costs to students attending the university, Minton said, "But when I look back to my days at Indiana, this average looks like criminal extravagance. I spent one whole summer term in Indiana for less than ten dollars a month. That was tops." He conceded youth had to be served, and "what the papas can't furnish, the New Deal does, and we keep up the big parade from the campus to the W. P. A." Minton said he felt between Herman Wells and Bo McMillin Indiana would somehow muddle through. Wells might well have replied to the frugal Senator that blackberries were in unusually short supply around Bloomington during the months of the regular university sessions. Minton claimed to have subsisted partly on this natural largess.

The General Assembly in 1937 had appropriated biennially $3,940,000, and in 1938 for 1939–41, $4,460,000. Even so there was internal dissatisfaction, especially in the School of Medicine. Dr. F. S. Crockett complained to President Wells about the difficulties in the school, and Wells replied, September 28, 1939, that there were no difficulties in Indianapolis that sufficient funds would not solve. He further outlined for the disgruntled Crockett the comparative financial position of the School of Medicine. Out of an "annual appropriation of $1,890,000 for 1937–1938," the School of Medicine had received $430,000 or 22.75 per cent of the total public appropriation. The school had an enrollment of 498 students as compared with a total university enrollment of 7,085, or 7.02 per cent of the total enrollment. Big Ten universities spent an average of 8 per cent in support of their medical schools. Wells told Dr. Crockett, "Surely, fairness to the remainder of the departments of the University would not allow us to go further than we have already gone in support of medical education." He said the only hope for further support would have to come from a total increase in university appropriations from the state. It appears, however, from the general financial records that legislators themselves may have favored the School of Medicine requests over other departments of the university.

One biennial university budget was hardly distributed to the departments before the administrative officials began the ordeal of making and pushing a new one through the Budget Committee and the General Assembly. Reflective of the 1939–41 budget was a request for supplementary funds with which to finance new buildings for which the university had received Public Works Administration grants. Ward G. Biddle told the Board of Trustees in March 1939 that the legislators had come to recognize the facts of the new era of bond retirements and interest payments incurred in the federal program of campus construction. He reviewed one of the curious bits of Indiana financial history. In 1927 the General Assembly had adopted the 2 per cent real estate Educational Improvement Fund Law to remain in force until 1942. The Assembly in 1939 repealed this law and instituted direct capital construction appropriations; Indiana University had collected approximately $270,000 annually under the 1927 law. Most of this fund had gone to modernize the School of Medicine plant, but general university demands far exceeded this annual dribble.

There were some disturbing signs in the wild confusion that marked the adjournment of the 1939 General Assembly. On March 7 it had exceeded the constitutional time limit of 61 days, and in a state of confusion bordering on general chaos had appropriated $2,150,000 annually to Indiana and Purdue. These were the years when Wells and Payne were crusading furiously for new and able staff members to strengthen the university's instructional and research programs, and this crusade demanded the sanest consideration by everybody with fiscal authority in the state.

In the situation created by the hectic closing hours of the General Assembly, Judge Ora L. Wildermuth revealed a somewhat strange anxiety in a letter to President Wells. Without saying so specifically, the Judge seemed to be disturbed by the 1939 drive and the promise of continuing ones. Wildermuth's concerns are reflected in Wells' reply, October 24, 1939. He quite agreed that all public institutions in Indiana had to put their administrative houses in proper order. He said, in the vein of an alert banker who expected the visitation of the bank examiner at any moment, that he and Ward G. Biddle had said repeatedly that day-to-day decisions in Indiana University were made as though a legislative investigating committee was at the moment marching up the steps of Bryan Administration Building. He denied Judge Wildermuth's statement that educational institutions spent money less carefully than did private business firms. Certainly this was not true at Indiana University. The institution, said Wells, had received no increase in its real appropriation since 1931, even though the Indiana tax burden had grown enormously. The universities had not shared in the increase in purchasing power. "It is my impression," he told the Board President, "there will be few states so situated. Of course, we all know that Wisconsin always gets dollars where we get dimes—at least for certain types of activities."

As activities of the university underwent expansion under Wells' leadership, there followed increasing demands for funds. Few critics stopped to raise the question of how badly had the university neglected these activities in the past? A question arose early in 1940 about how the institution's funds were being spent. A comparison between the early Wells' years, 1937–40, was made with the final Bryan year, 1936–37. Administrative costs had advanced to $134,105, but this included $57,500 to finance the retirement fund, and $30,000 to support student health and rehabilitation services. The College of Arts and Sciences' budget was increased $35,000 to strengthen the departments of physics and botany, the Library was given $40,000, and an additional sum of $66,280 went to Business, Music, the Graduate School, and Education. During the past three years these areas had received $309,625.30.

As the country began to recover from the economic pinch of depression, it experienced a second extreme inflation caused by increasing war pressures from abroad. Indiana University actually lost ground in its real purchasing power. Both Indiana and Purdue officials undertook in 1941 to protect the status of their incomes. They were able to have a cut of $410,000 restored in the final session of the Assembly. For this lift Wells wrote personal letters of appreciation to the governor and legislators. Indiana might enjoy an advantage in its alumni representation in the Assembly, but the parity formula locked it inside a general higher educational strait-jacket which mandated that the four colleges and universities confer and agree upon a composite request for operating budgets to be submitted to the State Budget Committee.

Any changes or increases had to be done largely in the form of extraordinary appropriations for capital outlays and to meet deficits. At times members of the General Assembly met in Bloomington for extensive inspections and discussions of the state's needs for higher education. At other times legislators singly and in groups were guests of the university at athletic events, and they were shown through the institution and had its work and needs explained to them.

Whatever the method of approach, Indiana University found it extremely difficult to make ends meet. The *Indianapolis Star*, December 29, 1942, quoted Herman B Wells as saying the university had accumulated a $429,000 deficit because of a greatly accelerated wartime program. Faculty salaries still remained the most disturbing fact of university operation. The average professor that year had no greater purchasing capability than he had a decade before. Governor Henry F. Schricker asked Wells to outline for him the actual salary situation. Wells reported 553 employees annually received less than $1,100; 422 received from $1,100 to 1,800; and the total number of employees on the campus who received less than $1,800 was 975. He then gave the governor a brief summary of students receiving war services training. It required two typed pages to list the various national activities supported in part by the Federal Government on the campus. Most of these were in the vital areas of scientific and medical research. "As our wartime leader," Wells told Schricker, "You have every reason to feel proud of the important role which the four state educational institutions are playing in these critical hours."

This analysis seems to have had no immediate effect on the governor or the legislature. The Director of the Budget Committee, C. Anderson Ketchum, and his colleagues slashed $642,761 from Indiana's request for biennial operational expenses of $6,793,436. Wells told the governor this left only $250,000 of new money, and the university was then operating at a deficit of $264,522.58. He reiterated that Indiana and Purdue had adopted what amounted to three semesters to serve wartime needs, and this meant a third increase in operational costs. The programs of the universities, he said, were entirely different from those of the teachers colleges, which had actually experienced little disruption because of the war.

Professorial salaries had to be increased in the 1940s, and

President Wells felt Indiana University would have to find an additional $100,000 just to meet inflated costs for supplies. Because of uncertainties some legislators suggested that appropriations be made on an annual basis to keep the support of the universities more nearly current with wartime inflation. The university received editorial support in this time of crisis from both the Indianapolis *News* and *Star*. The *News* said the university was using locker rooms and recreational halls for student living quarters. "The budget this year will have to make room for a new and intensive [building] program," said the *News*. "The school had enrolled the largest class in history, from 1934 to 1943 the number of graduates has nearly doubled."

Both Wells and the Board of Trustees undertook to convince C. Anderson Ketchum that an increase should be given the university. In a special emergency session, January 29, 1943, the trustees drafted a strong statement describing the university's plight. They told the budget director they were in disagreement with his decision, and unless he revised it they would appeal directly to Governor Schricker and the General Assembly. Ketchum and his committee colleagues seem to have had their attention focused directly upon budgetary tables rather than the changing needs of higher education, and they proved immovable. Ketchum wrote President Wells, February 3, 1943, that he had no further comment to make on the budget, "Except to say we have received expressions of virtually 100 per cent approval from all divisions and departments effected [*sic*] by our budget recommendations, except in the instance of Indiana University." He told Wells the new budget included a 15 per cent increase, but even so it represented $1,270,000 less than the university requested. The university could hope to recover $50,500 from the $150,000 contingency fund. Wells informed the deans and department heads, March 26, 1943, that the institution faced real stringencies in all phases of its operation. In a telegram to President W. C. Coffey of the University of Minnesota he said Michigan and Iowa had fared markedly better than had Indiana at the hands of their legislatures. The sum Indiana had received was at least $200,000 too low to meet the most carefully managed operational costs.

There was a constant fluctuation in the federal programs. Early in 1944 the Army abandoned its AST Program, a fact which injured the university, but Biddle told Wells it injured

Purdue more. He thought Indiana could avoid serious trouble for the moment, but he was not at all certain about a year hence. In the following April Lawrence Wheeler told an *Indianapolis Star* reporter that three-fifths of the university's annual operational budget, and an equal proportion of its physical assets, came from nontax sources.

The moment arrived when the end of the war seemed to be in sight, and indications in late fall 1944 were that within the foreseeable future, there would be a sufficient inrush of students to supplant the military enrollment. The General Assembly insisted that the university supply dormitory facilities on a self-liquidating basis. This it could do, but in the area of nonrevenue-producing buildings there was indeed a serious pinch. The state had a surplus of $34,000,000, and in November the university administration requested of the Budget Committee a capital outlay appropriation of $2,000,000. The following year the biennial budget request was for $7,256,531, and the Budget Committee followed its ritualistic custom and lopped off $1,006,531, and made no immediate provision for new buildings.

The General Assembly in 1945 was generous by former fiscal standards, but extremely shortsighted in terms of immediate and future educational demands. Governor Ralph Gates, said Wells in a letter to legislators, suggested a meeting of assemblymen in December 1946 on the Indiana campus so they could view first-hand the institution's physical needs. On December 16 Gates congratulated the president for his shrewd handling of the educating of the legislators, and he said he thought the effort would be productive in the forthcoming legislative session.

Both Wells and President Frederick L. Hovde of Purdue forecast a budget of $27,000,000 for the two schools, $15,000,000 of which would be used to finance new buildings. Wells said he believed Indiana University's enrollment would approach 14,000 (actually it was 11,003, up from 3,252 in 1944–45), and there would be urgent need for 250 to 300 new professors. He expressed the hope that $6,662,000 could be appropriated annually from the special liquor tax which was earmarked as a building fund. This tax had been highly productive since its passage in 1945, earning approximately $500,000 monthly. Both Wells and Hovde told legislators that unless generous appropriations were made to their universities, there was danger they would have to resort to selective admissions. In this instance they failed to gain full support from the *Indianapolis Star*, which seemed to be frightened by staggering postwar demands made on the state and its archaic tax system. "Nobody wants to make it hard for the state universities to do the job they must do, but other needs are equally pressing," said the *Star*. "In considering the requests of both universities the Governor and the state legislators must keep a proper balance among all state expenditures in Indiana."

This paper, December 27, 1946, analyzed further the record $52,000,000 (operational and capital funds) Indiana-Purdue requests. This meant $433 a year per capita cost as compared with the $100.30 statewide grade and high school per capita cost, and there were twenty-one times as many of the latter students. On top of this Robert H. Wyatt, executive secretary of the Indiana State Teachers Association, said more and more unqualified emergency teachers were being hired in order to keep the public schools open. This was a specious argument on the part of the *Star*, even though the public school cause was a truly basic one; the per capita costs had no meaningful relativity in fact.

The university's request for operational funds was traditionally reduced in 1947, from $11,400,000 to $9,000,000, and the capital outlay request was cut from $12,325,000 to $3,500,000. The capital outlay fund this year was especially significant because it was the first appropriation to be made for financing the ten-year building program, which finally was expected to total $26,000,000. President Wells informed the Board of Trustees in June 1947 that he estimated the full income for the university to be $9,075,000 and expenditures would total $8,965,901, or $4,-757,500 in excess of the state appropriation. At the same time he requested of the State Budget Committee an additional $700,000 from the Alcoholic Beverage Excise Tax to finance repairs on the Bloomington and School of Medicine campuses. He also asked for $35,524 to buy new medical and dental equipment. Included in the larger amount was the sum of $186,450 to finance the purchase of land adjacent to the campus, and to purchase the Andrew Wylie home at Second and Lincoln streets. The Budget Committee approved a grant of $595,999, and appropriated the $186,450 for land purchases. Governor Ralph Gates seemed to favor the purchase of the Wylie House after President Wells had driven him by the place.

Indiana and Purdue universities were by no means alone in their struggles to secure public funds. This was universal among the states. The national bill for higher education grew by leaps and bounds as enrollment went up and operational costs were inflated. Lloyd Morey, comptroller of the University of Illinois, told a National Work Conference on Higher Education in Indianapolis, October 14, 1947, that by 1960 need for higher education in the United States would require more than $2,000,000,000 in operational costs alone. He predicted there would be 3,700,000 students enrolled by the latter year, and each American family would be faced with an annual pro rata expenditure of $88. In order to maintain colleges and universities at the current level for the next twelve years would require appropriations of $1,370,000,000, a sum which would have to come from state and federal governments, student fees, and private endowments. The $2,000,000,000 sum he mentioned, he said, in answering a critical question from an auditor, was only 6 per cent of the $84,500,000,000 tax collection for 1945, and fell $7,000,000,000 under what Americans paid annually for alcohol, tobacco, amusements, and luxuries. To accommodate the predicted huge student enrollment, the nation in 1960 would have to spend $12,000,000,000 in enlarging physical plants of universities and colleges, which by the latter date would be worth $20,000,000,000. He startled his auditors when he suggested a 5 per cent increase in professorial salaries in order to raise academic incomes to a comparable level with current industrial wages and salaries. This would necessitate an annual increase of $218,000,000 of present appropriations.

Indiana University had long felt the pinch that Lloyd Morey described as a national educational phenomena. It operated, 1947–48, with a deficit of $1,500,000 just to maintain its past level of performance. That year it was confronted with a loss of $1,000,000 in Federal G.I. subsidies. In its next biennial budget the university requested $9,123,474 per annum, and Wells estimated the total institutional income from fees, hospital payments, and endowment would amount to $6,474,561, or more than 5 per cent of the maximum public appropriation. Entering freshmen in September 1949 added 4,547 students to increase the total enrollment to 11,414, a number which placed a maximum strain on every campus facility.

Viewing the rapid increase in student enrollment, the addition of new buildings, and the extension of general services, Claude J. Black, chief purchasing agent, said biennial operational costs had almost doubled. Coal was up 80 per cent; the annual electrical bill had tripled, to $94,000; and water had gone up from $12,000 in 1945 to $61,000 in 1948. Labor costs had advanced almost as rapidly, both in scale of wages and the number of employees needed to maintain the institution.

There was one bright spot, on paper at least. Joseph A. Franklin published the results of his study of the financial history of the physical plant and equipment January 25, 1949. The plant had an estimated value of $32,000,000. The State of Indiana had paid only 27 per cent of the cost; the Federal Government had supplied 12 per cent, borrowed capital accounted for 36 per cent, student fees and miscellaneous income 15 per cent, and endowment 9 per cent. That is, the State of Indiana had a capital stake of just over a quarter of the value of the plants in Bloomington and Indianapolis.

Despite all of the statistical arguments presented by university officials to sustain their budgetary requests, and all the national publicity about the crisis in higher education, the State Budget Committee, true to form, reduced the annual university budget from $9,123,474 to $6,800,000. The only item left untouched was a very modest request for $18,385 for the Medical School. Fortunately enough pressure was brought to bear on legislators. In a session-end jam the legislature raised the university's appropriation to $7,050,000, and appropriated an additional sum of $1,450,000 in deficiency funds, thus reducing the annual budgetary loss to $623,474. Even in the face of this generous restoration the editor of the Bloomington *World-Telephone*, March 3, 1949, wrote, "Indiana is more niggardly with its big educational institutions than most Middle-West states. Thus it is predicted that I. U. will lose some of its very best men in the immediate years ahead. Many professors can better themselves financially by leaving to drive busses or mine coal, or peddle milk." Wells responded to the 22 per cent cut by saying, "It means that the University's operations must be made to fit the amounts appropriated." The institution operated at a student per capita cost of $319 as compared with $856 at Illinois, $462 at Wisconsin, $460 at Michigan, and $338 at Iowa.

There appears to have been vigorous rivalry among the universities and colleges in the 1949 legislative session. In fact, there seems to be ample evidence of a disturbing amount of behind-the-scenes horse trading for legislative support. Senator Milford Annes claimed a million dollar appropriation for the School of Medicine was cut in half because of a deadlock battle between Indiana University and Purdue. He said this irresponsible action by legislators set back the "grand promise of great steps forward for improving public health in Indiana." It also helped set the stage for breaking the attempt to maintain equality between the two universities. The General Assembly in 1949 recognized the impossibility of maintaining the long outmoded practice of parity, a principle which was never truly applicable. The Assembly enacted legislation that became a truly significant milestone in Indiana higher educational history. It was decreed "That the four state universities and colleges shall co-operate in working out a formula to be presented periodically to the legislature and any other proper authorities for budgetary purposes. . . ."

President Wells expressed some satisfaction with the 1949–51 appropriation in a statement to the Faculty Council. He raised questions of how the money should be spent, and where the university should place its main emphases. He suggested a serious reevaluation of the entire instructional program with the idea of eliminating outmoded courses, and the halt of costly duplication. "Certainly we can all agree," he told his colleagues, "that we should provide for such additional programs as may seem desirable, as for example the contemplated University Press for scholarly publications. Of course, a new program like this and all such other new programs must be evaluated in the light of other needs." The task of modernizing the curriculum could be accomplished by careful management at all levels, even if some reduction in the general staff had to be made. Clearly there were opportunities to reduce many multiple courses, and to increase sizes of classes. "To my mind," said the president, "a time like this, while it is trying, may not be altogether a misfortune because it causes us to reevaluate that which we have done under relatively easy conditions; it makes us put first things first and put them in their proper perspective." He suggested that cuts in the programs be made in as dramatic a way as possible so as to demonstrate to the public and legislators what small appropriations meant in actual application. Too, an increase in fees would make that point eloquently to both students and parents.

By June 1949 cuts had been made in all departments. They

had been asked generally to reduce their budgets, and to tighten up their administration. The School of Medicine budget was reduced 2 per cent. President Wells wrote Governor Henry F. Schricker that 62 faculty members were being dropped, and 75 faculty positions were being left unfilled. At the same time 139 courses were being eliminated, and sections were being consolidated into much larger units. "This means," he told the governor, "that the University will not be able in the coming year to offer all of the subjects which its student constituency demands, and, worst of all, class sizes will be increased." Faculty salary increases had to be abandoned, and if the university lost professors because of this action, it could not replace them with comparable men even at an adjusted salary level.

The 1949–51 budget was the last one to be made under the provisions of the 1921 budgetary law. Results of the new legal provisions began to be revealed early in 1950 when preliminary surveys indicated differing costs of various services in Indiana and Purdue. Also, there were once again analyses of the sources of institutional incomes. The two schools were said to have had an enrollment of 40,000 students which cost $563 per capita. In-state students paid fees of $67.00, and those from out-of-state and G.I. students paid $272.00 and $328.90.

From the outset Herman B Wells had advocated independent budgets for Indiana public universities and colleges, but even he possibly did not anticipate the complexities that had arisen since 1921. There was far more involved than a mere independence in establishing the individual needs of the schools. Fundamentally, it was necessary to redefine the purposes of the four institutions, and to coordinate these with the general financial support of the state. It was not until March 1950 that a step was taken in this direction. A decision was made to begin a study to determine fair bases for formulating individual institutional needs and priorities. A central committee of the four presidents, Dean Wendell W. Wright, Dean Ray W. Kettler, comptroller of Purdue, headed the study group. Other Indiana University representatives were Herman T. Briscoe, Joseph A. Franklin, and Pressly S. Sikes. Frank M. Hart of the University of California, a specialist in academic physical plants, was employed to make an analysis of the physical facilities of the schools.

No one at the outset, including the presidents and deans,

seemed to realize what a vexing task the study requested by the legislature would become. (Indiana and Purdue had planted the idea in the minds of the legislators.) This was especially true when it became necessary to compare the Indiana and Purdue programs, and to define and reconcile their differences. The state teachers colleges were largely single-purpose schools, but this was not so with the two universities. There were so many fundamental differences between Indiana and Purdue that the study was seriously delayed, because President Hovde of Purdue expressed such positive opposition to some approaches to their resolution. Before compromises could be made, it was necessary for the schools to submit their 1950–52 budgets.

Late in November 1950 the four Indiana universities and colleges requested operational budgets totaling $47,820,000, an increase of $13,000,000 over the past biennium. Again substantial requests were made for cost of living salary raises, and the state was asked to assume losses from decreasing G.I. Bill of Rights enrollees. The presidents were summoned before the State Budget Committee and the Governor to give detailed explanation of their requests. Previously Governor Schricker had informed them that they must hold down costs on their campuses.

By the latter date budgeting studies had progressed to the point that the administrators had worked out a new formula for reckoning the needs of individual schools. They, however, had not completed the entire study, and could not do so for months to come; not only because complexities of programs and basic objectives of the four schools were involved, but because human emotions were aroused. Nevertheless the first budget request under the new law was made December 10, 1950. On that date the *Indiana Daily Student* said, "The twenty-five year old 'parity plan,' which gave the two universities equal appropriations and the teachers colleges a percentage thereof, went out the window by decree of the 1949 legislature. Repeated conflicts among the schools had come to the point where a final request was virtually unworkable." In later years Herman B Wells considered repeal of the stifling parity law the most significant accomplishment of a most fruitful administration of the university.

In carrying out the new legislative mandate of cooperative budget-making, the special committee of the universities and colleges sought information in four areas. These were direct teaching costs, financial operation of the institutions, administrative and service expenditures, and the utilization of present space availabilities and future building needs. Once the committee began making analyses of the various aspects of institutional operations it made some startling discoveries. Purdue had the highest outlay per student at the undergraduate level, and its comparative graduate costs could not be fully explained in terms of expenditures in the other three schools. Most costly was the upper level enrollment that had risen rapidly everywhere, and Indiana was high in this area. Differences in functions proved a thorny issue. Indiana had the professional school responsibility, while Purdue had agriculture, engineering, the technical areas, and agricultural extension services. Library needs and costs were much heavier at Indiana, but Purdue's need for scientific apparatus was much greater. Because of the demands of the School of Medicine Indiana had a high public service cost. There were areas where research costs of a comparable nature varied sharply, and professorial salaries at Indiana were consistently higher.

Frank Hart's survey of physical plants revealed that ninety buildings on the four campuses were ready for abandonment. During the past four years, 1945–48, the state had appropriated just slightly more than $1,000,000 for capital additions. He estimated costs for new buildings which would be needed badly at Indiana University by 1960 would total $39,235,075. Currently the university asked the General Assembly for $8,673,142 to finance buildings already in various stages of construction or to be started immediately. The university was faced with the problem of destroying dilapidated temporary structures and of rehabilitating several of its older permanent buildings. Administrative officials sought first priorities for the Life Sciences Building, and funds to begin construction of a new law building. In addition, there was urgent need for expansion of undergraduate library facilities to care for both students and books. With the rapidly rising enrollment it was estimated that a reading room seating 2,000 to 2,500 students was imminently necessary. Over and above the four Bloomington campus requests was one of $1,175,000 for additions to and modernization of the physical plant in the School of Medicine.

Under the new basis of actual need measurement, Indiana University sought operational funds in three biennial installments of $7,378,000, $10,500,000, and $9,671,000; two of these were greater than amounts sought by Purdue University. The General Assembly, true to its historical practices, cut to $9,671,900 the operational request, and to $4,103,571 the capital outlay fund, or 40 per cent of the amount requested. Though the general operational budget was the largest in the university's history, a significant portion of the increase was intended to make up the loss of G.I. fees. That year the university had thirty-seven alumni in the legislature, and their influence on the record of appropriations seems to have been significant, even though the basic requests were reduced.

While the comparative studies were still underway, Lytle J. Freehafer, director of the Budget Committee, decided in October 1952, that the four schools were not in compliance with the law of 1949, and, too, the four presidents had cavalierly ignored his warning of April 15, 1952. His letter to Herman B Wells was curt, if not peremptory. This drew from the president a direct eight-page reply in which he set the disturbed bureaucrat straight on the complexities of academic institutional organization and procedures. He said the report was incomplete because too much work had been involved to be accomplished in so short a time. The biggest delay was the fact the Quadripartite Standards Committee, which had the delicate task of assessing the individual needs of the four schools, had not been able to resolve some emotional problems. Wells said officials at Purdue had stated they were unwilling to accept anything less than $250,000 more than was appropriated to Indiana University, and threatened to withdraw from the committee if Indiana refused to agree to this formula; Purdue later reduced its differential demand to $137,000 between the Bloomington and Lafayette campuses.

In his letter to Freehafer, Wells said President Hovde sought to justify his stand on a comparative basis. "This computation," he said, "was based solely on present operations and did not use scientific or agreed standards of desirable operation." He then outlined in detail the intricate bases for differentiating the cost for the two universities. Fundamentally, Wells' analysis revealed that there was in fact an altogether different set of purposes for the two institutions. Computation of comparative costs, because of this fact, most often became an irrelevant game. An important point of irreconcilability was in the definition of extension work in the two institutions. Wells told Freehafer that Indiana University had followed good administrative policies throughout. "Our academic administration," he said, "is nationally recognized for its pioneering in cost controls of teaching operations. Representatives of other institutions have visited us for the purpose of studying our centralized method of class scheduling, academic staffing, and cost controls in order to receive equitable treatment between divisions." All of this system had helped to eliminate costly duplication of instructional and administrative management in both Bloomington and Indianapolis.

Between 1953 and 1962 the operational budget was increased phenomenally from $9,671,000 to $51,294,115. Within this decade the university conducted an intensive drive to secure more public funds. Biennially the fiscal story was monotonously the same; the institution consistently raised its budgetary requests for both operational and capital outlay funds, and just as consistently the Budget Committee and legislators reduced the requested sums. Both rising enrollment, inflationary costs, and demands for a more realistic salary base placed heavy pressures on everybody in a position to affect the budget. Reflective of these facts were the tensions that developed in the General Assembly. In March 1953 the university's appropriation was not approved until the closing moments of the badly troubled 88th session. An effort was made in the final vote to cut the university funds by 25 per cent.

Despite the tensions and bitter pullings and haulings the 1953 legislature made sufficient capital appropriations ($10,735,345) to complete the Life Sciences Building, the new power plant, the remodeling of the Journalism Building, and to make an addition to the Jeffersonville extension center. Wells told the Faculty Council March 17, 1953, that the General Assembly had finally appropriated sufficient funds to "achieve a long start toward the Medical School Building and also to complete the Service Building." He expressed the feeling this was "the most critical construction budget submitted by the University in the last twenty-five years." Once the Medical Science Building was provided for, it would become easier to secure capital funds for campus and extension center buildings. As generous as this appropriation was, the state had dropped behind schedule in meeting its "ten year" building fund commitments.

Before the 1954–55 budget was due, the interinstitutional cost studies were fairly well advanced; they were, however, still snagged on the problems of incomparability of the Indiana and Purdue programs. This nevertheless was not unique to the two Indiana institutions, it was a national problem which involved fundamental philosophy and objectives of public higher education. This in historical fact had been injected in American educational history by enactment of the Morrill Act in 1863.

A continuing discussion had been going on among the Big Ten schools as to how costs for the traditional arts and sciences programs could be reconciled with the practical or vocational programs of the land-grant universities. The Ford Foundation made a grant of $180,000 to study costs to the Midwestern universities, and to the Berkeley and Los Angeles divisions of the University of California. Stanford University and Wabash College were asked to participate in the study in order to supply private institutional costs for similar instructional services. This expanded study gave an entirely new dimension to the concepts of educational needs at higher levels in Indiana. Herman B Wells wrote Donald Clark, State Budget Director, September 7, 1954, "The study involving the Big Ten institutions and the University of California will provide comparisons and standards for comparable educational programs in a number of schools that were not possible when only Indiana institutions were being studied. Indiana state schools are almost unique in lack of duplication of programs, for instance, law, medicine, dentistry, music, business, etc., at Indiana University and agriculture, engineering, pharmacy, etc., at Purdue. Thus, in many programs which operate in one institution but not the other, there exists no basis for comparison and measurement until the information on comparable programs is available from other states."

The new budget year proved in many ways to have been the most successful in the university's long fiscal history. The administration requested $26,659,093 in operational funds, and the Budget Committee cut the amount to $24,655,140, a figure which Herman B Wells declared was the lowest possible one, and left no cushion for a contingency. The four state presidents told legislators that faculty take-home pay was less than that for 1939–40, and the new budget proposed to increase this level to the one of 1940–41.

Wells described to the Faculty Council, in January 1955, one of the unsettling problems which had at one time or another disturbed nearly every public university in the land. Purdue requested funds to enable it to organize a school of veterinary medicine. Nothing could throw an agricultural state legislature into a greater panic than this issue. An argument developed immediately that such a school would cater largely to out-of-state students. Impressive estimates were made of the amount of money which could be saved if all non-Indiana students were barred from the state schools—a move which would have rendered Indiana University a serious blow. There was some hue and cry in the press on this subject, but the four presidents were able to halt the discussion before it fully inflamed the General Assembly.

This was indeed the vintage year. In addition to the favorable operational budget, the legislature appropriated $6,100,800 for construction on the Bloomington campus and at the extension centers, and $3,350,000 for expansion of the physical plant of the School of Medicine. This latter appropriation was a direct result of breaking parity. These sums enabled the university to complete several major buildings, and to begin construction of others. In addition the General Assembly enacted the necessary legislation to permit university employees to participate in Social Security retirement benefits.

By November 1956 the Ford Foundation study was sufficiently advanced to reveal some significant comparative costs between Indiana University and Purdue. Indiana spent $404 per capita for freshmen, Purdue $539; sophomore differentials were $449 and $610; juniors $606 and $708; seniors $764 and $803; and graduates $1,040 and $1,020. It was said that Purdue required a greater number of hours for graduation, which accounted for the higher undergraduate costs. Legislators were told that the California-Big Ten study indicated that future new student enrollment in the four Indiana schools would increase costs for 1957–59 by $7,081,718. The study also revealed the fact that the Indiana public college enrollment had gone up in every decade for the past 130 years, and that by the most conservative estimate 42,000 students would enroll in the four schools in 1960. Actually on the latter date there were 26,791 in Indiana University alone.

During the decades of the 1950s and 1960s Indiana University conducted a vigorous publicity campaign to improve its financial position. This publicity stressed an almost feverish expansion in every one of the institution's activities. Legislators were told in a special article in the *Alumni Magazine*, February 1957, "It's your problem—The Crucial Age for Higher Education." The article stressed runaway enrollments, need for new buildings, the faculty salary crisis, and the inroads of inflation. Both the national Beardsley Ruml survey and the one made by the Indiana Chamber of Commerce revealed the exceedingly poor position of faculty incomes. In 1955 the Indiana professor's purchasing power, as compared with that of 1950, had changed only 4 per cent, while that of factory workers had improved 48 per cent, and doctors had gained 84 per cent. Inflation had reduced the purchasing power of the campus construction dollar to 72 cents, and it was said that if the state undertook to restore its 1951 building schedule in 1957–59, it would have to add more than $12,990,000 to its original estimate.

An attempt was made to catch up the university's building schedule in 1957, when the State Committee granted an authorization to spend $3,496,500 to complete work on Ballantine Hall, and $2,400,000 to construct the Extension Center at Gary. In September additional authority was given the university to go ahead with constructing and refurbishing the Health, Physical Education, and Recreation annex to the Fieldhouse, the Fine Arts-Radio and Television Building, the Lilly Library, and the conversion of the ancient Student Building into an undergraduate library. There was in this moment of diligent search for funds a bright note of cheer; the Alcoholic Beverage Tax yielded Indiana University $1,135,143 in 1960, and since 1945 this source had enriched the institution's income by $14,767,827.

There was no end in sight of need for new buildings. The campus expanded in vast rings of buildings, and well beyond limits anyone earlier would have conceived. With astute foresight, Wells had insisted, in the face of questioning, if not opposition, that the university purchase a large block of relatively cheap land on the northeastern and eastern rim of the campus. This turned out to be one of the most fortunate capital investments the institution ever made. The ease with which the expansion of the campus was made would otherwise have been impossible. There is no way of precisely estimating the differential between what the capital outlay for land actually was and what it might have been in the great building decade and in later years. In 1960 the administration sought approval for issuance of bonds to construct the vast 1,200-room self-liquidating student dormitory complex on Fee Lane (Foster Quadrangle) at a cost of $6,825,500. At the same time it sought an allotment of appropriated funds to refurbish Myers Hall, $641,091 to complete the Geology Building on Tenth Street, and $100,000 to build an addition to the Dental School. Most of these requests were approved in the approximate amounts suggested.

In 1960 the Budget Committee also approved the release of $2,200,000 additional state funds to finance construction of the addition to the Chemistry Building, and approved $60,029 to complete the remodeling of the Student Building. By this time Donald H. Clark, former director of the State Budget Committee, had joined the university staff as assistant to the Financial Vice President and Treasurer, Joseph A. Franklin. He was now on the other side of the budgetary table telling his former colleagues that Indiana University needed more than $24,000,000 to provide the necessary facilities for the rising yearly inrush of students. At that moment, January 1961, Wells was before two legislative committees requesting $9,572,019 in new building funds to finish the construction of seven buildings then underway. For this effort he received $6,698,571, and encouragement of more assistance in the future. The general operational budget of $51,294,115 enabled the university to raise faculty salaries 10 per cent in 1961–62, and 9 per cent in 1962–63. By 1962, the year of Wells' retirement, public support had slipped materially in the percentage of the total operational budget, but the president had been unusually successful in securing private support for the university.

Annually since 1945 student enrollment had climbed by approximately 2,000 additional registrations, and the total had risen from 28,975 in 1961–62 to 31,586 in 1962–63; in the next six years it increased to 52,101 in 1968–69, and approximately at the predicted level. Between 1950–55, enrollment followed an erratic and descending curve reflecting both the influx of veterans, and the haste with which they completed their courses. During the latter year, however, enrollment began climbing because of the larger number of Indiana high school graduates, the result of the higher birth rate during the late depression years, and a vastly improved economic condition in the nation. The affluence of the new age, plus emphasis on securing a college degree, had an impact well beyond even the most expansionistic concepts of many college administrators and legislators.

For Indiana University the problems of the new age were staggering. Enrollment for 1968, the 150th anniversary, was 2,551 greater than it had been for the whole first century. Many of the large lecture sections enrolled more students each semester than had attended the university in its first quarter of a century. The graduating class in 1968–69 came close to exceeding the number of graduates in all the first century. By a second standard of measurement, the physical plant had cost, by 1955, $66,650,840, and the state had supplied $16,471,839 of this amount; the remaining $51,179,001 had come from federal and private sources. By 1960 the State of Indiana had increased its investment to $31,927,923 on the Bloomington campus and at the extension centers, while the remaining $152,691,790 evaluation was represented in bonded obligations for academic buildings, federal growth, and private investments. In Indianapolis the School of Medicine plant was appraised at $32,924,410.

These decades were indeed the affluent age of American higher education, and Indiana University, through shrewd management, shared fully in its largess. In Bloomington a dramatic skyline of high-rise dormitories pushed up to encircle an equally impressive inner campus of modern academic structures. The outer buildings were the landmarks of an era of self-liquidating bond issues, rising fees, and general use of the principle of extended financing. In all of its struggles to enlist public support, the university administration demonstrated both pride and sensitivity about the sources of income. When a story in the *Daily Student*, October 13, 1960, indicated dormitories were financed by the state, the university administration sought immediate correction of the error.

The quarter century of Indiana University fiscal history, 1937–62, was one of the most exciting periods in American higher educational history, and maybe the most perplexing. There was greater public involvement in education at all levels than had ever been true. Generally Americans let their imaginations run unbridled in the boundless meadowland of educational megalomania. Except for abnormal conditions prevailing in wartime, there was scarcely a moment when educators were not predicting phenomenal increases in both student enrollment and demands for public services. Closer to Bloomington, the bases of both Indiana economy and society had undergone radical changes. Generally educational surveys, projections, and demands for financial support poured from national presses in continuous rolls. The spiral of growth appeared endless. So far as university administrators could tell from these studies, 1945–70, enrollment would continue to rise into an indefinite future.

Other surveys indicated properly trained professors would be in short supply, and some of the futuristic studies said it would be a herculean task for qualified graduate schools to serve both academia and American industry. This was the period when Indiana University came of age intellectually and physically. It not only cast its institutional nets into future waters, it balanced the books of history by overcoming the inert forces which so often had locked it in thralldom.

Academic administration in this quarter of a century departed sharply from that of the old patricians. It became as much a matter of accounting and entrepreneurial and political leadership as of intellectual guidance. Just as important was the operation of an officially public institution with a significant imbalance of bonded indebtedness and private support; which within itself became a general modern American social and cultural phenomena.

[VII]

Raising a New Horizon

TIMES, CONDITIONS, and fresh leadership converged in Indiana University's history during the decades 1940–60. For almost a century and a half the campus physically had come near a condition of stagnation. Lack of public support for the construction of new buildings held the institution in its tracks; it could not purchase additional land, construct new buildings, or open the way to accommodate numerical and program expansion. Huddled on its sylvan campus in an inverted "L" of relatively small academic buildings, the campus symbolized the patriarchialism of an institution which had striven so long to be a university but was held in a bondage of space. The William Lowe Bryan administration had begged repeatedly for legislative financial support to break this constriction without achieving much success. Ironically, the Roosevelt New Deal, the depression, and the general social fermentation of the late 1930s loosened the clutch of time and public penuriousness.

The new president, the Board of Trustees, and the faculty talked of staff expansion after 1937. In fact, the in-coming Wells administration had at the outset placed the most emphasis on selecting a staff that would fulfill most of the ideals implied in the growth of a progressive American university. Even the trustees caught the "excellence" fever and urged the president on in his avid search for major professors. Good professors, however, would have only limited meaning in the face of severe physical limitations that then threatened to grip Indiana University in the vise of mediocrity. The administrative search for professors was only one side of the coin; obversely, there was urgent need for buildings and scientific equipment in every phase of institutional operation. Tradition was powerful in Indiana history for niggardly support of the state universities. The New Deal, however, pointed the way to the federal till, and the principle of selling bonds to finance self-liquidating projects opened even wider avenues of fairly generous support. Hoosier legislators in the early 1930s were willing to give Indiana University fairly free headway in obligating portions of its income to finance the construction of new buildings by the sale of bonds to finance self-liquidating structures.

President William Lowe Bryan had paved the way for seeking federal New Deal support, but it was the succeeding Wells administration which sought and got major assistance from this source. Wells and his colleagues understood the implications of population projections, the approaching end of the depression, and the impact which a rising industrial urbanization in the state would have on Indiana University. They read the evil portents of allowing the institution to wallow in the stagnant mire of insufficient public support. When Wells came to office the University operated in 45 relatively small buildings on a 173-acre campus, and in 13 buildings of equal inadequacy for modern university operation in Indianapolis. Numbers, however, did not reflect the true situation on either campus. Most of the buildings were small, inflammable, some were shabby, and all were overcrowded. Except for two or three of the newer structures erected since 1930, they might well have been classed as archaic so far as effective instruction was concerned.

No doubt William Lowe Bryan, a good Hoosier Republican in the best Calvin Coolidge tradition, looked upon Franklin D. Roosevelt and his New Deal with genuine suspicion, but Indiana University's needs far outreached partisanship. There was a continuing clamor during the three decades, 1930–62, from students, alumni, and faculty for progress. Measured by the standards of Big Ten physical plants, the one at Indiana was low on the list.

Surprisingly, this fact was not clearly developed by the self-study committee. The timidity on the part of that special committee stemmed from the fact that Fowler Harper, professor of law, believed the only new building needed in 1939 was one for the School of Law. He expressed the belief that faculty additions and the library collection had higher priorities. It was difficult to assess the actual needs at that time because of the complex mixture of disciplines between Indiana University and Purdue University. No other Big Ten university was caught in this kind of academic bind.

Historically, the post-World War I Memorial Fund Drive and the subsequent federal grants gave Indiana University a chance to expand plant and program that might never have been possible with traditional legislative support. Indiana lacked both a tax system and a legislative willingness to devise one which would improve the Hoosier image.

When Herman B Wells came to the presidency in 1937 the Administration Building, later named the Bryan Administration Building, the School of Music, Myers Hall, the University School, the Journalism building, and the main body of the Union Building expansion were either completed or under way. The more the university built, however, the more severe became the pinch. The School of Education was desperately in need of new quarters. As a later critic said, it was little more than a squatter in various campus buildings. Business and the sciences were in need of modern quarters. In the latter case it was not alone a matter of space, but there was immediate need for a new building, designed and equipped to serve the advances in modern sciences. Exploration of the new field of nuclear physics would have been impossible in Lindley Hall. The Business School, also, was located in quarters that fell well below modern American business standards of equipment and physical surroundings.

If the instructional quarters of the university reflected an antiquity of academic operation, no institutional undertaking was more seriously handicapped by lack of respectable facilities than its general assembly and ceremonial functions. Assembly Hall was unfitted for proper ceremonial use the day its doors were opened at a cost of $12,000 as a men's gymnasium in 1896. Despite the fact that much warm university sentiment and tradition centered about the old building located east of Owen Hall, it was indeed a wretched symbol of Indiana culture and higher education.

Thus it was that the university administration and Board of Trustees sought heroically to pull the institution up by time-frayed bootstraps, and with hardly decent token help from the state government. There is no reliable standard by which to measure the impact of the Federal Government in the first phase of Indiana University expansion, 1932–43, but it was great. It is enough to say that this support exceeded at least four times the amount of money spent directly by the State of Indiana in the first century of the university's existence.

Herman B Wells reported to the Board of Trustees in 1942 that "The past five years have been the greatest single period of expansion in the physical plant of the University in its entire history. In this period fifteen new buildings have been constructed with an aggregate floor area of 667,390 square feet and 9,315,099 cubic feet." The building challenge that faced the young president was as great as that he assumed in organizing a capable faculty. The fact that Wells began his furious search for additions to his faculty before he actually had firm prospects for housing was in itself an act of faith bordering on recklessness. This was particularly true in the case of some of the scientists who needed highly specialized and sophisticated equipment along with generous allotments of space. Three building needs fell in this category: the Medical Building in Bloomington, expansion of the entire scientific plant in Indianapolis, and the projected Swain Hall to serve physics and mathematics.

A handicap in university history was that no major provision had been made for student housing, and the legislature had not been pressured to make provisions in this area. Male students had been left on their own, and private or memorial campaign funds had furnished a limited number of girls with campus housing. Included in the building program after 1937 were the dormitories, North, West, Morrison, Beech, and Sycamore halls. These buildings almost immediately upon their completion enabled the university to engage in a fairly extensive preliminary wartime program. The structures, however, proved woefully inadequate to meet the needs of an expanding student body after 1945.

Herman B Wells, Ward G. Biddle, Joseph A. Franklin, and some of the trustees proved adept at procuring federal building funds. In July 1938 the president sought to persuade the Public Works Administration that generous appropriations of funds to Indiana University would relieve classroom and housing shortages, would help alleviate unemployment in rural southern Indiana, and prevent a direct relief approach to solving social problems. He said Lawrence and Monroe counties had over 40 per cent of their population on relief. Besides, a liberal grant would help the Indiana limestone industry, which he said was probably the most seriously injured by depression of all national industries. His arguments were sustained by an extensive statistical review of the local unemployment situation and the university's building needs.

The university made its point with both state and federal governments. By 1942 it had spent $5,179,417 on new buildings, of which $2,199,809 had come from the Public Works Administration, and $713,445 from legislative appropriation. The remainder of this sum was dervied from sale of bonds. The General Assembly in February 1938 enacted a law that permitted institutions of higher learning to sell bonds, and the university specifically to construct the University School in connection with the School of Education. This too was a significant step in expanding the university's bonding authority as provided for in the initial law of 1935.

Though Wells was the central figure in pushing for rapid physical expansion of the university plant, it was Ward G. Biddle who actually saw the program through to completion. The president told the Board of Trustees in September 1938 that the building program and search for funds had consumed an inordinate amount of his time as well as that of his staff. He had conferred with Senators Sherman Minton and Frederick Van Nuys; he had enlisted the support of organized labor in Monroe County, and had interviewed officials "high in the organization of the Public Works Administration and I presented additional exhibits." He now felt, "The building program must go forward; I am confident that I, as well as the Board, can delegate practically all of that activity to the competent management of our comptroller, Mr. Biddle."

Biddle proved both persuasive and aggressive in his campaign for funds. He secured $386,100 from the Public Works Administration to initiate construction of the $858,000 laboratory school, and convinced the Indiana House Ways and Means Committee of the wisdom of selling bonds to make up the $500,000 differential.

The year 1937–38 was of major importance in campus expansion. Actually this was the year that Indiana University crossed over one of its historical divides. There was the move into the new Administration Building, the addition to the Union Building was almost completed, several men's residence halls were underway, and so were various classroom projects. The Bloomington *World Telephone* said on August 21, 1937, that classroom seating had been increased by 700, and laboratory and office spaces had also been expanded.

By mid-year 1937 the decision was made to raze the crumbling Assembly Hall even though its demolition might cloud many sentimental memories. It was said the old stage was hastily constructed over the murky men's swimming hole in preparation for the appearance of Maude Adams' troupe. In time it served Otis Skinner, Forbes Robinson, DeWolfe Hopper, and an endless procession of orating politicians, moral lecturers, and thirteen graduating classes. Time's passage with its inevitable freight of change made the revered spot more attractive, however, as a parking lot for the growing number of campus automobiles. In late fall the use-stained structure was dragged down scantling by scantling by W. P. A. workers. William Lowe Bryan said, "In wrecking Assembly Hall the W. P. A. is now working on one side and the termites on the other. According to the last report, the W. P. A., which considerably outnumbers the termites, is slightly ahead." Arthur B. Leible ('15), assistant professor of English, wrote "Dear Old Assembly's" obituary:

> Upon her stage Maude Adams knew
> More things than every woman knows.
> Here Otis Skinner sought for love,
> Behind her footlights singers came.
> Ex-Presidents her platform knew;
> The great she knew, and shared her fame.

Before the rafters were toppled on Assembly Hall the new Auditorium was advancing beyond the stages of a misty-eyed dreaming and hope. In a brief time the University was to climb from cultural rags to riches in the new structure, and a far more sophisticated image came to reflect the inner ambitions of the growing institution and of the people of Indiana.

The Wells' era rushed headlong into the future. Seven new buildings were ready for occupancy by the opening of the fall semester of 1938. The president had halted in his hunt for professors on occasions to seek building funds, and in September he told the trustees that the building program had become all demanding. "Both Mr. Biddle and I," he said, 'have spent much time working with architects and faculty groups in order that the plans which will be submitted to you at this meeting might be put in condition for presentation." His report to the board indicated that Indiana University had fared well at the hands of the Federal Government. He listed sixteen projects which had either been completed or were underway at a cost of $3,974,537.71, and the public in Indiana had supplied considerably less than half this amount. Four years later Wells reported an expenditure of $5,179,417 for new buildings. There were other large projects, such as the Business and Economics, School of Education, and Science buildings, not included in these reports. By February 1938 boarding spaces for men had been increased from 94 to 387, and from 326 to 670 for women. Perhaps nobody could be entirely precise about expenditures after 1937, because some buildings were nearing completion while others were still in planning stages, and published reports gave little more than overall notions of what was taking place on the campus. It would be difficult indeed to separate the overlapping amounts of money being spent at any one reporting period, or to isolate with certainty periodic increases in amounts.

Aside from the building program on the campus the university carried on a fairly extensive and expansive activity around its property borders. Over the years the university came into possession of several off-campus properties; among them the Woodburn, Mottier, and Knight houses. It acquired two private homes on Ninth Street, and purchased the Lutheran Institute in Fort Wayne for use as extension classrooms, laboratories, and offices. One of the most exciting off-campus collaborations was with the Goethe Link Observatory located between Martinsville and Indianapolis in the ridges above the White River. This institution was created by Dr. Goethe Link, an alumnus and distinguished Indianapolis surgeon. He was one of the first surgeons to perform successfully a goiter operation. The gift was to be named the Helen and Goethe Link Foundation to provide an astronomical observatory and a special research fellowship in the science. In 1939 a thirty-six-inch telescope was in place, a classroom seating a hundred persons was ready for use, and living quarters were ready to accommodate the first Link Fellow. The telescope was said to be powerful enough to photograph stars 200,000,000 light years away. Dr. James Cuffy of Harvard University was appointed the first fellow, and he soon began his residency in the Morgan County hills. A decade later Dr. Link gave title to the $300,000 observatory to the university.

One of the new campus buildings, Swain Hall, figured prominently in ushering in the new scientific age. In 1939 few if any mathematicians and physicists could have predicted with certainty the role of the new Indiana building and its nuclear equipment in world affairs. The hundred-ton cyclotron and photometer were installed as enticements to new scholars in physics. This building was designed to house both mathematics and physics, and before it was completed it was named for Joseph Swain, a mathematician and President of the University 1895–1903. Proudly the *Indiana Daily Student* boasted that the cyclotron and photometer would be the second of their kind in the United States, and second only to the equipment in the radiation laboratory in the University of California.

Not all of the $3,500,000 building program in 1938 was so promising. The lingering conflict between labor and contractors over job classifications and descriptions threatened the whole building activity. It seems the actual points involved in these delaying disputes were minor, but the consequences promised to be all but disastrous to university plans. The Public Works Administration personnel at one time was instructed to remove federal records from Bloomington, a move which actually threatened withdrawal of federal support and oversight. This dispute was settled, but labor continued to be unhappy, and eight months later again threatened to strike and bring construction of the Business and Economics Building, Beech, and West halls to a halt. The latter threat involved the wage scale and was quickly settled by an upward adjustment of the hourly rate of pay. By June 14, 1940, all work on the Business Building was completed when the Thomas Hart Benton murals depicting the state's economic history were placed on the auditorium walls. The Business School had moved into these new quarters in January, before the hall was actually finished. In June an announcement was made that an hour and a half open house would be held in the still unfinished Swain Hall so the public could get a glimmer of the wonders of both the new science and the new building.

Completion of these two major buildings marked the true beginnings of the new academic era in Indiana University. Although they greatly relieved intolerable pressures for space on the ancient plant, they served the more important function of symbolizing the opening of new approaches to the sciences and business. As the specialized departments moved out of old buildings, departments of the College of Arts and Sciences moved in with good effects on their future programs. There was, in the summer of 1940, almost a wholesale physical shifting of colleges and departments in the university plant. Some new departments, such as bacteriology and the speech and hearing clinic, were fitted into an already overcrowded plant.

Swain Hall was officially dedicated on October 25 and 26, 1940, when physicists from across the nation took part in a two-day colloqium devoted to nuclear physics. Professor H. A. Bethe of Cornell University lectured on the theory and forces of a single atomic nucleus. Professor Gregory Breit of the University of Wisconsin discussed the reaction of a single atomic nucleus with others. Other lecturers were Professor L. A. Durbridge of the University of Rochester and I. I. Rabi of Columbia. This was a landmark date in university history that capped a sustained interest in mathematics and physics since the founding of the institution. With the opening of Swain Hall and the settling of new faculty members in its laboratories and offices, the university demonstrated its will not only to interpret the main currents of modern science but to operate in the current of discovery itself. While physicists and mathematicians celebrated the opening of their new building, doctors in Indianapolis anticipated material expansions of the medical programs. The physical plant of the Medical School was enlarged not only to make available more laboratory and clinical space, but to include room for the Nursing School and associated sciences.

One dream, however, was thwarted. For decades supporters in and out of the university kept up a fairly persistent campaign to build a modern armory on the campus. Colonel John F. Landis, commandant, led a move to construct a military facility costing a million and a half dollars. He had the support of President Wells and Ward G. Biddle, and the Works Progress Administration officials sanctioned the project, as did the commander of the Army's Fifth Corps Area, but the War Department refused to violate its policy of appropriating more than $100,000 for the construction of armories. President Wells sought unsuccessfully to get the department to liberalize its policy.

Campus construction momentum halted in 1943. Fortunately a great deal of expansion had been completed before the demands of war on the physical plant placed the institution in an even tighter space squeeze. The past decade had witnessed a revolution in academic policy and expansion of the university's physical plant documented this fact. The Bryan administration, with the major assistance of the New Deal agencies, had begun this departure from the past, but it was the Wells administration that conceived of the larger and more significant academic and service functions of the institution. New objectives were set and university energy was devoted to expanding the campus to serve the new American concepts of public higher education.

When the seven new buildings on the Bloomington campus were nearly completed, the *Daily Student* in 1939 became actively interested in associating the new structures directly with the past. Wisely, the editor contended mere physical buildings played a small role in the making of a university. It was the spiritual human element that comprised vital tradition and meaning. The paper challenged students, faculty, and administration to combine wits in the selection of names for the new buildings. Only Swain Hall had been named. Thus far the other structures had functional, numerical, or sylvan names, all of which seemed unacceptably commonplace. Fortunately at this juncture the university had established a policy of good taste of not naming its buildings for living persons. This rule was further strengthened by that of the Works Progress Administration which forbade naming any project to which it was a contributor for a living person.

The *Daily Student* in September 1939 asked its readers to submit lists of names so a committee could choose the most appropriate ones. In October the editor complained that not a single suggestion had been received. Perhaps, he said, most students, but surely not faculty members, were too poorly informed about university history to make intelligent suggestions. A brief biographical sketch of David Starr Jordan was printed, and a list of other prominent university figures was offered as a stimulus. At the end of the year no responses were forthcoming and the paper challenged the honorary fraternities to assume leadership in naming the buildings, saying that thus far not one faculty member or student had offered a name. By February 1940 the *Student* announced there would soon be seventeen unnamed buildings on the campus, and it would be one of the largest campuses with the most "commonplace" names in American academia. Apparently no one but the editor was disturbed by this fact because in April he was still fussing, but the Blue Key honorary fraternity showed some interest by calling a meeting to compile a list of building names, so "not only will our buildings have names other than those of the points of the campus or species of trees, but the buildings will stand as tributes to some of I. U.'s great sons and daughters." This plea resulted in some action. William Lowe Bryan, James A. Woodburn, Dixie Heighway, and Ward G. Biddle were chosen consultants, and the *Alumni Magazine* was requested to seek names from graduates. Added pressure, however, produced no results, and the *Daily Student* announced only one letter suggesting a name had been received.

The naming crusade proved strangely fruitless except for the fact *Student* editors learned how indifferent professors and their charges could be about campus affairs, and how critical of action they could also be. World War II suspended the building program and left the naming of buildings unresolved. Nameless though they were, the campus buildings after 1940 bore a tremendous burden of war activities.

Before the last shout celebrating the Japanese surrender died away in late spring 1945, an almost frantic program to expand materially the physical facilities of the University was renewed on the Indiana campus. Swain Hall served the needs of only two of the major sciences, while the other scientific departments were left inadequately housed. It was now a far more expensive business to provide adequate quarters in a time when there was so much competition for skilled labor and building materials. University leadership saw more clearly than ever that if the University was to grow competitively with its Big Ten neighbors, then it had to offer its scholars housing and equipment in keeping with the revolution in learning wrought by the war.

Though the process of building came to a halt, 1941–43, there is evidence that some planning continued so the university would be ready to meet the demands of a greatly increased student body. The Board of Trustees predicted in November 1945 there would be an enrollment of 10,000 students almost immediately. It said, "The University cannot stand still. It must go forward, taking the lead and marking the path in the state's general advancement. To do this, there must be constant strengthening of its staff, its physical plant, and its course of study. This is particularly true for the immediate future." Wells said the university had less space per student in 1940 than it had at the outbreak of World War I. The trustees outlined a $25,000,000 urgent building plan, saying that $10,000,000 of this amount would be invested in self-liquidating types of buildings. This mammoth proposal made provisions for the Bloomington campus, the Medical School and Extension Center in Indianapolis, and the other centers in the state.

In projecting so large a program of expansion, the trustees felt that psychologically the people of Indiana were ready at last to support a good quality higher education. "The entire state," they said, "will have an unprecedented opportunity for increased well-being and wealth in the years immediately ahead. The building of war industry within its borders has provided the facilities for an exceptional economic advance. Its location at the center of national population affords as well the opportunity for national influence in social and cultural progress." Hoosiers, it was said, deserved educational advantages that would assure continuing economic, social, and cultural progress. In the past a smaller percentage of high school graduates had attended college than in other states. The trustees expressed the belief the people would no longer tolerate failure. Board members asked for one thing more, an enlarged and highly qualified faculty to justify the $25,000,000 expenditure.

Just talking about a $25,000,000 building program was heady business. Wells revealed some of the intoxication in his private papers when he speculated on whether or not to build on the agency contract plan or to adopt the war industry scheme of "cost plus." The suggestion of such a large sum of money overwhelmed the editor of the *Daily Student*. Forgetting the idea was at the moment only a projection, he wrote on November 3, 1945, "It means our campus will be one of the most outstanding in the country—its geographical location perfect, its standards tip-top." Current seniors, he said, would be "graduated from a university, the size and reputation of which will be unparalleled among Indiana colleges and universities."

Major new structures proposed would include almost twenty new buildings, among which would be one for the life sciences, a general classroom building in the School of Education, additions to the School of Medicine, new steam and power plants in both Bloomington and Indianapolis, a journalism building, law building, an enlarged library, health center, and infirmary. Dormitories were listed among the self-liquidating structures. In all, twenty-seven projects costing an estimated $17,125,000 were listed as early as 1943. The New York architects Eggers and Higgins were employed in February 1944 to create a master chart for a greatly expanded campus.

Dean Bernard C. Gavit, in between wartime assignments, drew tentative plans for a new law building. In his opinion about everything in the code book was wrong with Maxwell Hall, including a woeful lack of space, a damp and destructive library space, tiny classrooms, and an improper overall design. Many other persons relaxed from wartime demands by making plans and dreaming. One of these was Kurt F. Pantzer, an Indianapolis lawyer, who proposed in the closing phases of the war to Herman B Wells that the time was right for a public drive to raise $50,000,000 to aid two to five Indiana universities and colleges to raise their scholarly standards. He said he wanted to see Indiana professorial salaries made equal with those of Harvard and Columbia.

When Eggers and Higgins made their site report in mid-June 1944, they proposed a campus expansion that would extend north of the older buildings. The heart of the new addition would be bounded by Seventh, Tenth, Woodlawn and Indiana streets, an area covering approximately four large city blocks. They also proposed the present location of the heating and power plant in order to be near the railroad so coal would not have to be hauled across the campus. Eggers and Higgins conceived a northward rather than eastward spread of the ever-growing Memorial Union.

They took into consideration a system of campus roadways and even proposed a campus railway station on the nearby Illinois Central track to enable people to get in and out of the campus during athletic events.

On the heels of this report, Ward G. Biddle distributed to the Administrative Council a description of the proposed postwar buildings, and Wells asked his colleagues to suggest priorities to be presented to the Board of Trustees. He said, however, prospects were not bright. A year later Ward G. Biddle submitted to R. C. Ashton, division engineer of the Federal Works Agency, sixteen applications for funds. Five of these were given high priority, with the new science building included at the top of the list. There was a request for a School of Education building, two dormitories, and the Bloomington School of Medicine.

Obviously the major building included in the new list was the one for the life sciences to supplant old Science Hall, which had been overcrowded since the day its doors were opened to occupancy. The first big step forward in postwar expansion took place on September 26, 1945, when United States Senator Raymond Willis announced that the Federal Works Agency had approved a planning grant of $41,840 without interest to finance planning the life sciences building. At the same time Ward G. Biddle put pressure on Stephen C. Noland, chairman of the Indiana Economic Council, to secure planning funds for the School of Education, and the School of Medicine.

A question at the outset of the planning for the enlarged campus was whether the university should again seek private funds to finance the creation of a memorial to those who served in World War II. A joint committee of the Board of Trustees, the Alumni Association, and the Indiana Foundation agreed that a suitable memorial should be established on the campus, and that it should be paid for with private funds, and there should be some memorial scholarships. Indiana University, however, would not use as an excuse the memory of those who died in service to raise funds for operative purposes. Wisely, the joint committee told Wells that responsibility for supplying substantial building funds rested directly with the State of Indiana.

At the end of summer 1946 the university confronted the state with a whopping request for the long discussed $25,000,000 building fund to cover a projected ten-year program of enlarging campus facilities. This sum would be used for constructing buildings in Indianapolis, Bloomington, and the extension centers. The Medical School, for instance, needed research and testing laboratories, library quarters, a clinical building, and student housing. The three hospitals all needed additional space and equipment. Both law schools were in somewhat desperate need for new buildings. It seemed a certainty that the crush of students in the next decade would necessitate a new philosophy and approach to the support of higher education in Indiana.

The university, however, could not wait for the state to act, and continued to seek relief from its space crisis on the outside. It turned to the United States Army for help. The *Daily Student* observed, "I. U. is busting out all over—with quonset huts." These were used to provide instructional offices, classrooms, and storage. They were crammed into limited spaces between permanent buildings, in odd corners, and on prospective building sites. Thus the university stemmed expansion pressures at the same time it sought to provide permanent shelter for departments and growing hordes of students. The same thing was happening at the Medical School in Indianapolis. A two-story frame building was removed from the Bunker Hill Naval Air Station in December 1946. In Bloomington the huge "I" building was brought from the air station to be located between the new Business Building and the Auditorium. With its long central section and hundred foot wings it was the largest classroom building on the campus.

Prior to the university's large request, the legislature appropriated $25,000,000 in 1946 to finance construction of the four state school campuses. Funds to meet this appropriation were to be raised by a special liquor tax and Indiana University was given an extra $1,310,999 for temporary student housing and to improve the heating plant. The liquor tax proved a productive one, yielding over $2,000,000 a month. The Medical School alone was given $5,000,000 from this source. Besides non-university capital, special appropriations were made for the LaRue D. Carter Center and the Ball Memorial Nurses Home. These buildings were on the Medical School campus and directly benefited that institution.

Building operations on the campus were seriously disrupted during the winter months, 1945–46, because of another disagreement between contractors and laborers over the wage scale. This seems to have been an inescapable frustration of campus building, even though Indiana University itself obviously had no direct control over contractor wage policies.

Although the most dramatic part of campus expansion was the construction of new buildings, significant changes were taking place inside the older structures. One badly scattered department had scarcely abandoned the old Science Hall, Owen Hall, or Kirkwood, and Wylie before workmen gutted them and rearranged their interiors to serve new tenants. In Indianapolis endless remodeling took place in the Medical School plant. The Robert W. Long Memorial Hospital had new floors built on top of its east and west wings. The isolation ward was remodeled, and other major changes were made.

The more the university built and remodeled, however, the more crowded it seemed to become. Possibly half of the instruction in 1947 was conducted in temporary or outmoded quarters. Law had outgrown Maxwell Hall; music was already overcrowded, and from its ten-year-old building overflowed into the surplus military East Hall, a structure containing sixty practice rooms and an auditorium seating a thousand persons. The English Department functioned in scattered temporary quarters, as did geology, psychology, and many other departments.

Just as academic facilities were expanded the seating capacity of the Memorial Stadium was increased from 27,675 to 30,000 seats, and tiers of old wooden seats were replaced by collapsible steel ones that could be moved into the Fieldhouse to serve seasonal shortages there. In all, the university erected 105,776 square feet of temporary classrooms and storage space by 1947, and eight new buildings were opened for use on the Bloomington campus and in Indianapolis. Title to these temporary surplus military structures were delivered to the university on December 5, 1947.

The university was able to procure larger loans and appropriated funds in 1947 than at any time in its history. Ralph Gates was indeed a generous governor to the extent that he supported use of quickly constructed temporary buildings. He doubtless sensed a personal thrill in watching the university expansion in this respect. The story is told that he and Herman B Wells were riding down Second Street in Bloomington when he spotted Andrew Wylie's elegant old "Pennsylvania" house. As an outcome of his visit, Gates encouraged the university to purchase it from Mrs. Amos Hershey to be restored at considerable cost as a museum and institutional shrine.

Early in January 1948 the university purchased the Lumbermen's Mutual Insurance Building in Indianapolis to house the extension center. This was a rather conservative investment of $375,000 for the downtown property to be paid for in fifteen yearly self-liquidating installments. This structure was of sufficient size to provide extensive classrooms, services, and social needs of a growing evening class urban facility.

In Bloomington in April 1948 architects and engineers hurried along to complete plans for five new major buildings in Bloomington, the most important of which were the general classroom building of the School of Education and the Life Sciences Building, and remodeling the School of Dentistry building in Indianapolis. There was, however, no promise of surcease. President Wells in December asked the Faculty Council to reconsider its building priorities to determine if they should be changed and refined. Already in the planning stage was the original "$25,000,000" worth of buildings, and Wells was looking to the future. He requested funds to get professors and students out of basements, down from attics, and out of temporary buildings. He also set university sights on a new library.

An alumnus, Dr. Wemple Dodds, asked President Wells to inform him as to the sources of Indiana University's building funds. Wells replied that some buildings were to be financed from alumni contributions, some from student fees, but the academic buildings, constructed since 1930, were paid for in good part by federal grants and by the issuance of low interest-bearing bonds against future revenue. Since the enactment of the liquor levy, the Indiana legislature had been more generous toward the university. Swain Hall, the Business and Economics, Administration, and Music buildings were financed in part from the liquor revenue. These buildings alone, however, required $100,000 a year to service outstanding bond obligations. In keeping with the president's statement, Judge Ora L. Wildermuth, president of the Board of Trustees, informed Roscoe Freeman of the Indiana Budget Commission that the university expected to request as much fiscal aid as the federal and state governments would authorize for preliminary planning. He mentioned specifically the new Library, the Medical Building in Bloomington, and the Chemistry Annex along with four or five major service units.

Plans were completed and the State Budget Committee approved a request for $1,300,000 in 1949 for the School of Education general classroom building, and bids were solicited in September. A month later Johnson, Drake, and Piper of Terre Haute were given a contract to construct the four-story, twenty-eight-classroom building. The Bloomington *World Telephone* said this was the first permanent building to be constructed on the campus since the war.

In November 1949 the *Alumni Magazine* told graduates of the institution, "For the School of Education, quartered and moved from here to there over the campus in the past few years and currently housed in the condemned old dormitory for girls at Forest and Third, the last and long anticipated move is in sight. Construction has been started on the attractive location at Jordan and Third on a new $804,219 building to be erected as an addition to the University School completed in 1938." The story of the School of Education was paralleled in almost every other division of the university. No one ever stopped to figure out the loss of man-hours involved in the constant moving, or property losses due to wear and tear. Every move necessitated a considerable amount of renovation and rearranging of the interiors of older and even temporary buildings. Beyond this, academic moves always created a tremendous human emotional factor of being uprooted and of work being disrupted and delayed.

There was indeed a wide gap between the Bloomington campus of Indiana University and the statehouse in Indianapolis. Legislators no doubt were incapable of responding positively to the constant state of academic flux in the country, and certainly they were incapable of dealing with rising demands for buildings, the hiring of professors, and purchasing equipment at the rate these demands were generated. It seemed that the General Assembly lived in an altogether different world from that of the campus. President Wells informed the Board of Trustees, and anyone else who would read his *Annual Report* for 1948–49, that, "The space situation is the worst it has been in the past fifty years. We have only 110 square feet of academic space per student in contrast with a generally accepted required minimum of 250 square feet. Furthermore, about 25 per cent of the classes on the Bloomington campus are housed in temporary structures, which are deteriorating rapidly because of heavy usage." He thought the campus plant would have to be doubled in capacity before it would adequately serve the predicted student enrollment. In 1910 there were 200 square feet of space per student, and in 1949, 105 to 110 feet.

In some areas the Indiana University staff grew faster in reputation than the university was able to supply classroom space and laboratory accommodations. Wylie Hall, partially abandoned by some of the sciences when Swain Hall was completed, was renovated and equipped in 1950 to house Alfred C. Kinsey's Sex Institute, and Tracy M. Sonneborn's laboratories in zoological research. Kinsey had offices, a library, and nine soundproof interviewing rooms, while Sonneborn's laboratories and offices occupied the basement floor.

In order to deal with the housing shortages effectively the university adopted a crash program in 1950 of planning and building in terms of a ten-year interval. Such a program was submitted to the Indiana State Budget Committee on October 10, 1950, in which the university requested $6,875,000 to finance construction of three major permanent buildings in Bloomington. It also asked for $1,050,000 for major construction and renovation of the Indianapolis plant. The Bloomington projection again included the life sciences building, a new law building, and an undergraduate library. In Indianapolis plans were for cancer and heart research centers, a medical science building, and stores and shops. Earl Hoff of the University News Bureau was quick to say that the huge sum requested for the two campuses was an asking figure, no one knew what the future would bring.

Building on the Bloomington campus went on steadily, most of it financed by sale of bonds. The *Daily Student* and *Alumni Magazine* were proud of the new skyline which was rising above the Jordan. In May 1951 the general classroom section of the School of Education was completed, and the *Student* commented that the paint colors were the most attractive items about the new building. On May 19 and 20, the School of Education deserted Alpha Hall en masse. The teachers had gone modern in their new quarters; there were conduits for television, "blackboards" were passe having been replaced by green "chalkboards," and special chimes summoned Dean W. W. Wright and his administrative assistants from any place in the building. This structure, which was originally planned in 1937 as a wing of the University School, to be built at a cost of $231,000, cost $831,000 in 1951. The legislature turned down the first proposal because it believed the cost was too high. Not until 1949 did the General Assembly appropriate the necessary funds, and finally the building was dedicated in July 1951.

While educationists admired their new building, its special color scheme, and chortled over their "chalkboards" in the spring of 1951, the Board of Trustees approved the sale of $2,200,000 2½ per cent bonds to enlarge the Memorial Union and food services building. A special feature of the Union addition was to be a greatly enlarged hotel facility. The state appropriated $500,-000 to this project, and the Federal Government under the terms of the federal Hill-Burton Hospital Act granted $1,452,000 additional support.

After delays of all sorts the State Budget Committee authorized the university to advertise for bids for the construction of the huge life sciences building. This structure had been in the "talking" and planning stages for several years, the legislature had appropriated $3,700,000, and later the bids came within this amount no matter how much prices had increased. Fortunately the Hagerman Construction Company of Fort Wayne bid $2,892,-495 for the basic construction, and the equipment bids fell well under the appropriated sum.

At last the Life Sciences Building (Jordan Hall) was underway. Forest Avenue was closed to traffic. The *Daily Student* said on May 1, 1952, that automobile drivers were complaining because they had to take the long way around to reach the center of the campus. Colonel T. J. Louden's famous castle Alpha Hall now stood imperiled. It had been all things to both men and women, now it would be demolished some time in the future with no one to mourn its passing, least of all those soldiers who had been "bugged" or crammed into its rooms, three and four abed.

Vicarious tears, however, were wept by the *Daily Student* reporter for the obliteration of the Forest Avenue "Passion Pit" where many a young Hoosier had learned there was more to life than professors, deans of men and women, grade averages, and even more than Dr. Kinsey seemed to reflect. "Spooners," said the paper, "are weeping gentle tears for the passing of the pit and old-timers are remembering bygone days of Alpha classes. We will pause and mark the period and then watch with eagerness the construction of the Life Sciences Building. We will cheer as brick on brick builds it higher. And we will forget whatever was there before—That is progress." Progress, however, was not so fast that the ball and hammer were applied immediately to the gaunt walls of "Old Alpha."

During the decade, 1950–62, nothing seemed fixed on the Indiana campus. Five social studies departments moved into the abandoned Business and Commerce Hall in October 1952. The newly organized University Press was located in the Radio Building, optometry was crowded into Science Hall, and all across the campus departments moved bag-and-baggage in nomadic searches for more space. There was no end in sight for this academic hegira. Joseph A. Franklin informed Lytle J. Freehafer, director of the State Budget Committee, that Indiana University in 1952–53 would request $10,318,000 for eight projects; $555,-000 would be spent for enlargement and modernizing the relatively new Swain Hall, and $3,500,000 would be spent on a new power plant. In addition the University asked for $1,800,000 to modernize further its Medical School plant in Indianapolis.

The big push in the winter of 1952–53 was for the completion of the Life Sciences Building. Dean of Faculties Ralph L. Collins in December 1952 submitted an analysis of the space needs to President Wells. The amount of space to be released in older buildings when Jordan Hall was opened would amount to approximately half the floor area of the older permanent buildings in existence in 1920. Dean Collins' space survey was based partly on the expectation that a new law building would soon be constructed and Maxwell Hall would be released to the homeless Department of English. Maxwell, perhaps more than any other building on the campus, reflected the impact of constant departmental movement. Architecturally its admirers and detractors mutually agreed that it gave the appearance of being a Roman temple, a Hoosier schoolhouse, a trailing limestone arbutus, and an academic lean-to; so many changes had been wrought in its original plan. Out from its maze of halls, chambers, attic nooks, and subterranean dungeons had gone the library, the central administration, the registrar, deans of men and women, and of liberal arts. Law had pushed them out one by one, and now it was splitting the limestone cocoon and seeking new quarters. The *Alumni Magazine* observed "Although Maxwell Hall has undergone many changes in its 63-year life, many alumni who studied there think of the building as a symbol of the entire university. They'll tell you that a full appreciation of the I. U. tradition is impossible until a student has become acquainted with the winding maze of halls and rooms." Nevertheless, a city-wide fire inspection on February 17, 1953, found that "Dear Old Maxwell" was a blue-ribbon fire hazard.

Collins and Gavit were too hasty in planning to move the Law School. The legislature cut the university's budget request in half that year, leaving little more than enough money to finish the Life Sciences Building, and to make a start on construction of the new power plant.

Wells in 1953–54 still reported more than 20 per cent of the instructional program of the university housed in temporary and unsuitable quarters. Actually almost a third of the class hours were spent in the deteriorating ex-military housing. Only eleven square feet per student, he said, was available in most of the overcrowded rooms, and modern academic regulations specified 25 feet. He predicted conditions would become worse because an increase in enrollment was a certainty whereas adequate future construction was problematical. "We have made exhaustive studies of our Bloomington campus space situation," Wells told the Board of Trustees, "We shall require all the space to be made available by the completion of Jordan Hall of Biology and the erection of the new School of Law Building to carry us through the academic year beginning 1955 and 1956. Thus our ability to accept additional students in the academic years beginning in 1957 will depend upon the amount and the nature of the capital appropriation of the next session of the Assembly." The president said the internal plan was to keep classroom traffic within a range of 2,000 feet. For the first time he mentioned possible construction of a mammoth multi-story social science and humanities building on the Forest Place site. He thought at that time the new library would be placed in the general area of temporary East Hall.

The old stores and service building on Seventh Street was remodeled in 1953–54 as the Journalism Building. It contained 39,000 square feet, with a 47 x 68-foot city room for the *Daily*

Student, and there were the Don Mellett Auditorium and the Ernie Pyle Lounge. The latter contained Jo Davidson's bust of Pyle and a display of the famous reporter's news pictures and many of his personal mementos. The renovated building generally was arranged and equipped for dual instructional and newspaper publication purposes. In 1954 the building was named for Ernie Pyle, who in his student days could well have been called a peripatetic scholar.

Pressure from the lawyers for a new building ultimately produced results. The State Budget Committee in December 1954 agreed to an initial allotment of $1,117,908 to begin construction of a new home for the school. The university lost no time in getting construction underway. It terminated its lease with the Socony-Vacuum Oil Company which operated a service station on the site of the old Indiana School of Religion at the corner of Third Street and Indiana Avenue, and preparations were made to begin construction by January 1, 1955.

At the same time the site of the long-discussed power plant was located just south of the Illinois Central tracks and near the new service building, and within the year construction on this vital facility was begun. Eight more new projects were already in the drawing stage, among them Ballantine Hall, the Lilly Rare Books Library, the Women's Physical Education Building, the Health, Physical Education, and Recreation addition to the old Fieldhouse, and the new Stadium. At the moment construction was begun on the law building, bids were solicited for the construction of the five-story $8,000,000 Medical Service Building in Indianapolis. The legislature that spring appropriated to the university $5,500,000 in capital funds to complete the buildings then under construction. By commencement time, 1955, the ultramodern five-story Jordan Hall, which had cost $5,786,000, was ready for occupancy. Completion of this structure added 200,000 feet of floor space; a material addition indeed to the university's space availability. Ready to move into the offices and laboratories of Jordan Hall were eight of Indiana University's ablest scientists. These were Ralph E. Cleland, H. J. Muller, Tracy M. Sonneborn, Alfred C. Kinsey, D. Ebert, W. R. Breneman, Paul Weatherwax, and David Frey. When the impressive hall of biological sciences was dedicated on June 8, 1956, it was said to be one of the most modern scientific buildings on an American campus.

By no means were all the bottlenecks on the campus removed by the completion of Jordan Hall. One of the most serious was the 1907 library. Its stacks had long ago been filled, and there was neither space in which to put the overflow of materials nor seating for readers. Thousands of books were deteriorating in dead storage or were piled on floors. In midsummer the Indiana Budget Committee approved use of a half million dollars of the university appropriation to expand stack levels of the library. Wells assured the committee during its campus visitation that the addition would be adequate for 15 or 20 years. In notes outlining what he would say to the Budget Committee, the president at that time described his dreams for a "cultural quadrangle" surrounding the Auditorium. One of the buildings in that plan would draw some pressure away from the general library. He said Josiah Kirby Lilly, Jr., had indicated an interest in a rare books library and would perhaps make an annual gift to construct and maintain one.

At the time Wells discussed the possibility of a privately endowed rare books library with the Budget Committee, he also told it of the desirability of constructing a modern fine arts building which would be made self-liquidating by collection of special student fees as authorized by the legislature in 1929. He advanced more clearly the idea of Ballantine Hall by describing the programs that would be housed there. Then he introduced need for three more new buildings: geology, the School of Health, Physical Education, and Recreation, and the radio arts and television. There was a wise basic concept that the old physical plant would be left intact, and be surrounded by the new buildings.

Before the "cultural quadrangle" could be made more than an opening campaign for funds from the state, the ever-expanding School of Music made its third major demand since 1935 for additional building space. Plans were introduced in July 1956, for construction of a circular and windowless structure encompassing 106,000 square feet. This addition was to be built just north of the original Music Building, and was planned to give the greatest efficiency in practice and auditioning. Practice rooms were to be built in concentric circles, each heavily insulated against outside noise interference. It was not until April 1958, however, that bids were taken for the addition. Ground was broken on June 17, 1958, and the two and a half million dollar project was saluted with "A Fanfare for a New Building" composed by Professor Bernhard C. Heiden.

Using the self-liquidating plan to the fullest extent, the physical university was indeed a haven for contractors and workers. In late summer 1956, there was under construction buildings worth an estimated $23,000,000, most of which were of the self-liquidating type, such as the huge dormitory complexes and trailer courts. In 1952 the four houses remaining on Forest Place were finally cleared away from the site where the future Ballantine Hall would be constructed, and a new phase of the decade of building was begun. President Wells wrote Walter F. Woodburn, January 9, 1957, in an effort to clear up public confusion over conditions in the university. He said despite the fact Indiana University had since 1940 vastly increased its student enrollment, faculty research, and public services the state had financed only the construction of Jordan Hall, the power plant, the Law School, and additions to the Library and the School of Education. All other new academic buildings he said were of a temporary nature. Almost at the moment the president wrote this letter, the Indiana House Ways and Means Committee cut $2,000,000 out of the State Conservation Department budget which had been allotted to financing a new geology building in Bloomington to relieve the serious space plight of the State Geological Survey and the allied Department of Geology. It left, however, a million dollars in the university's budget for this purpose.

Cutting off two-thirds of the geology appropriation in 1957, however, scarcely made a dent in building activity on the two university campuses. In Bloomington the east section of the Memorial Union was in an advanced stage of construction. The foundation was being poured for Ballantine Hall, and work was about to begin on a new football stadium, basketball arena and a fieldhouse, the fine arts building, the radio and television building, the new library wing, and the Lilly Library. The *Daily Student* on September 17 told the visiting State Budget Committee, "Fortunately for the taxpayers of the state Indiana University has evolved a comprehensive plan whereby without use of state funds it will provide greatly needed facilities for research in fine arts, radio, television, and physical education, for its library, and valuable rare books collections, and for its athletic, intramural, and individual sports program."

There was a considerable lapse of time between the announcement of the decision to build a new stadium and the solicitation of bids; when finally six base bids were opened in mid-May 1957, and Huber, Hunt, and Nicholas of Indianapolis said they could construct the two high rise stands with a 47,000 seating capacity in 500 working days for $5,485,000, the project was underway. Site preparation required another $350,000, and there was to be an undetermined contractor's fee in addition to the bid price. The total amount involved was so large the university administration debated whether or not to build only the west stand at the time at an estimated cost of $3,500,000.

Wells' enthusiasm for the expansive building program was revealed in his reports. In the 1957–58 annual summary of university activities he predicted Ballantine Hall, containing 286,400 square feet, would be ready for tentative occupancy at least by September 1959. All the other projects, including the major addition to Swain Hall, the Medical Science Building, and the State Psychiatric Institute would be ready that fall. Lilly Library was being constructed, so were the Towers halls of residence, the Music School Annex, and the Stadium. The university had now raised an impressive horizon. In fact, it had become so thoroughly built up along the Jordan that Wells suggested that additional land had to be purchased before further expansion could be successfully undertaken.

"Indiana University," said the *Daily Student*, on May 21, 1959, "is big and it's getting bigger. As some construction is finished, plans for more building go into force, as the new replaces the old." The paper listed more than a dozen new structures which would soon be ready for occupancy, including 300 rooms in the Towers Center. At last Ballantine Hall was ready in late September 1959 to receive twelve departments in partially finished quarters. Removal to this building created the most significant amount of vacant space in the history of the university. This did not mean, however, that the towering hall would take up all the slack in space, and by the time it was dedicated in the following September enrollment was crowding the campus even more.

Ballantine Hall, an experiment in academic building, was so arranged that its floor area was about equally divided between offices and classrooms. The building was constructed under the partial oversight of a professorial committee. Professor Hulet H.

Cook of the Department of French and Italian was the ever-watchful chairman who assumed a patriarchal attitude toward the building. In May 1960 he informed his social studies and humanities colleagues that many hitches had developed during the past year. Contractors more interested in a future job than completing an old one had moved most of their workmen out of Ballantine before it was finished. The elaborate buzzer system failed to function to the annoyance of everyone. Heat came in spurts, and it took all year to discover that an improperly assembled master valve was the miscreant. The International Business Machine system of class bells went academic and upset not only the tenants of Ballantine but the whole campus by feeding an overcharge of electricity back into the clocks. Professors and administrators had planned three relatively small elevator cabs to haul people above the third floor; below this a privileged class would have keys to make stops. They believed Hoosier youth would walk the first three floors, the traditional flights of academia, without interfering with the flow of elevator traffic. It took a much lower I.Q. than was required for admission to the university to figure that it was a simple matter to ride up to the fourth floor and walk downward one or two flights of stairs. Professor Cook was indeed incensed that the thoughtless horde destroyed his carefully laid plan. "For me," he wrote his colleagues, "the bitterest pill of all has been to stand helplessly by as large numbers of robust youngsters surged and crowded into cabs in order to ride to the fourth floor and walk back down one or two floors at the most. Then I not infrequently saw irate and justifiably exasperated members of the faculty, some of them women nearing the age of retirement [being shoved aside]. . . . I was convinced that this disgraceful affront to the most elemental principles of common courtesy was being led by relatively small groups of brazen, arrogant, and extremely selfish students, many of whom, on the basis of their records, may well have no legitimate reason for being on the campus." Professor Cook learned the hard way that chivalry was dead on the American university campus, and the construction of Ballantine Hall with its elevator snarl had absolutely nothing to do with its demise.

Ballantine, to its professorial guardian, was a symbol of human unity. To him, "One of the most promising discoveries stemming from a study of modern civilizations is the high degree of uniformity in the abilities of the common people (whether in America, or the farthermost islands of the earth, in deepest Africa, or behind the thickest iron curtain) to comprehend and to appreciate, in whatever form they may appear, concepts which you and I know as peace, freedom, justice, equality, the moral worth and dignity of man no matter how hard the dictators, the oppressors, the detractors may work to confuse, to corrupt, to conceal their true meaning." Ballantine was to prevent this. Daniel Voorhies could not have said it more passionately, but the denizens of the campus "skyscraper," some of them at least, were cynical, and the professor knew it. In utter and self-inspired dejection he gazed down ten stories of dark elevator shafts and saw churning toward him profane herds of mentally deficient chumps, frantic maiden schoolteachers, and irate professors, and in an emotional peroration closed his seven-page sermon on human unity with "I don't give a damn if the last two or three pages do make you sick, I have tried only to express what I think and strongly feel. I would rather be a wild visionary vainly scanning the heavens for a star that has not yet risen—and may never rise—than the priest of doubt leaning over a dark well while repeating a litany of doom, and never daring to look up for fear of the fatal shock that would surely come into view."

In Bryan Administration Building the president was fairly isolated from the nagging irritations of the International Business Machine's irresponsible bells, he was not screamed at by furious professors "on the verge of retirement" jousting with students for standing room on the elevators, and he was well away from malfunctioning steam valves, which heated tempers one moment and froze intellectual enthusiasm the next. He thought Professor Cook's valedictory "a bit thick." He told the trustees "I guess that makes me a cynic," but nevertheless they should read the professor's soul-baring report. The root of the traffic problem in the new Ballantine Hall was the fact the building was originally planned to contain only five stories. As soon as the first plans were drawn, the faculty committee insisted on adding two more stories, and the added cost made it necessary to eliminate certain facilities, including larger elevators. There was a difference of philosophies between the faculty and Wells on this point. Wells said later, "I have always believed in an 'underbuilt institution.'" Some crowding, in his opinion, insured full usage of space, and lessened the drain on the housekeeping budget.

While Ballantine was rearing its stately shoulders well above its campus neighbors, the university entered into an interesting conditional agreement to purchase from the Storkline Corporation of Chicago the old Showers Furniture Company buildings. Here would be housed in its cavernous industrial bunkers the scattered Geological Survey and Department, the University Press, and the Stores Division. This would free more of Owen, Maxwell, and Wylie halls, and a quonset hut for central campus academic use. Involved in the July 22, 1959, purchase were three buildings totaling 54,000 square feet of floor space and two acres of land. Conditions of purchase were that the university would surrender the old plant if the Chamber of Commerce could find an industrial purchaser who would create a major source of local employment.

Before Professor Cook and his colleagues had comfortably settled themselves in Ballantine Hall, the trustees awarded the contract for the construction of a geology building on a choice lot on Tenth Street, and the contractor agreed to complete the building by 1962. This was to be a large and complex six-story structure of research laboratories, offices, classrooms, libraries, and service rooms. At the same time in 1960 request was made for a new psychology building next door to geology, and Business and Economics, hardly settled in its new building on Seventh Street, now sought larger and more luxurious quarters, which would fill in the frontier on Tenth Street. An eight-story addition was underway on the Chemistry Building, major remodeling was being made in the forty-year-old School of Medicine in Indianapolis, and the $3,600,000 addition was being made to the old Fieldhouse to serve Health, Physical Education, and Recreation, a structure which would be ready for occupancy in 1961. In January 1960 plans were further delayed to demolish decrepit Alpha Hall because the university needed its space.

The closing years of the decade were frantic ones. Joseph A. Franklin told a sparse Bloomington Chamber of Commerce audience in Whittenberger Auditorium in March 1961 that the university would not be able by 1962 to complete its "decade" of building plans. In a detailed summary H. H. Brooks, director of the physical plant, said that in 1961 the geology, fine arts, radio arts and television buildings plus at least a half-dozen major dormitories would be completed. This spurt of completions would include Foster Quadrangle, Rogers and Woodlawn centers, and the Showalter Fountain atop the traffic island in front of the Auditorium.

Beyond 1962 the campus planners foresaw a greater physical and academic challenge; they were still reading wartime birth statistics. Dean Samuel E. Braden said a basic goal of the university was to admit all qualified students who applied for admission. "If we do not do so, we will not be fulfilling our purpose as a state institution." Other university administrators expressed beliefs that enrollment would continue to rise and it would take one or two more structures of Ballantine proportions to serve them on the central campus. In 1962 President Wells said that Indiana University still had a low space provision per student (161 cubic feet as compared with 197 in 1939), and it utilized 50 per cent of its campus space as compared with 30 per cent national average. Donald Clark, assistant vice president and treasurer, advised the institution to begin immediately in 1962 a second decade of building because "it would be impossible to get enough money in one year for a crash construction program." He believed a steady program of construction a more sensible future approach because the institution, in May 1961, was just barely keeping even with an increasing enrollment.

There were some pronounced differences of opinion, however, between the Administration and the Faculty Council about future priorities. Joseph L. Sutton of political science and Robert F. Byrnes of history emphasized that a new library should have priority in the next ten-year plan. Byrnes said he could not conceive "of a project that should supersede the library as the no. 1 item in our building program. The only major dissatisfaction with the University among faculty and, even so, among students [is] the library. . . . We are now behind and we shall lose valuable faculty members if we don't get going right now."

President Wells, on the very eve of retirement in June 1962, while not specifically opposing the Faculty Council's arrangement of priorities that placed a new library first, thought such an arrangement might not be in the best interests of the faculty. Wells later made it clear that he did not oppose the building of a new library, but he felt the cost of $15,000,000 would place too serious a drain on faculty facilities and other buildings that had even greater priorities. Faculty and administration would have to confront the inevitabilities of rising enrollment with demands for more classroom and office space. He warned professors, "If we devote such a substantial proportion of the funds to a new library, we are inevitably going to be crowded. Faculty members will probably have to double up in offices; many departments that might have expected new buildings will have to be content with rehabilitated older buildings." Wells even suggested the necessity for scheduling unpopular hours for class meetings. Robert Miller, director of libraries, with Administrative Committee support, had already beckoned to the future by asking Eggers and Higgins to consider drafting plans for a modern library.

Indiana University fell short of the realization of its time and plan schedule for the first decade of major expansion, but even so it accomplished far more than anyone in 1945 could have imagined, and by 1964 the first phase of the building program was completed, and new plans were in various stages of being drafted for future expansion not only of buildings but for land purchases, the building of roadways, clearing away the worn-out temporary structures, and the recentering of the campus in general. In designing campus expansion certain provisions were made to preserve both natural beauty spots and the traditional center of the university. The old "L" of original buildings, facing Dunn Woods, was left intact. The woods were invaded to permit the location of the Bryan Administration Building and the new School of Law. The center of the campus, however, was shifted eastward to the Auditorium, Fine Arts Building, Education, Lilly Library, the new Library, and the Musical Arts Center. The campus was then embraced in a wider crescent formed by the Geology, Psychology, and the School of Business buildings. In an even wider crescent were the large housing quadrangles and groupings.

A traveler approaching the university from the east in 1962 could hardly fail to be impressed by the rising façade of large buildings outlining the campus that had moved largely away from the traditional site of university activities. It is doubtful that in the entire history of American higher education an institution had made proportionately greater efforts to serve a larger number of students in classroom, dormitories, and recreational facilities, scholars in libraries and laboratories, and to carry on a complexity of public functions. Every activity of the institution was influenced by this period of great expansion, but none so much as the image of Indiana University becoming a major American institution of higher education and assuming a significant degree of leadership in many fields. Completion of the Fine Arts Building, the great

Auditorium, the complex of music buildings, and construction of the Lilly Library placed the university in a category of service to the arts almost unequaled in most state universities. No historian could ever record on paper the enormous human energy, ingenuity, management, and human persuasion expended in the creation of the massive physical plant. Even though the Indiana General Assembly gave support, sometimes with reluctance, it was the use of federal and self-liquidating funds, according to the records, that actually opened the new era for Indiana University.

[VIII]

The Rise of an Academic Metropolis

For a hundred and twenty-five years Indiana University depended largely upon the housing accommodations offered by the landlords of Bloomington. Except for Alpha Hall, and later Memorial Hall for women, the institution did not make an effort to care for its students in campus housing. The depression of the 1930s and its accompanying unemployment ushered in a new era of university building. In the first years of the Wells administration Forest, South, Morrison, Sycamore, North, and West halls were placed under construction. These new buildings were financed partly by P.W.A. funds and partly by self-liquidating bonds. By 1940 the university could house 1,063 students out of a total enrollment of 5,000, an accomplishment it considered phenomenal.

Mrs. Alice Nelson reported to the president on June 30, 1942, that the halls of residence had accumulated a sinking fund surplus of a sufficient amount to pay off three years' obligations. Too, the dining halls were proving financially profitable; the university, however, was not yet able to feed more than a small percentage of its enrollment. Mrs. Nelson, director of residence halls, was caught in the tightest bind of anyone on the campus, and she was well equal to the challenge. She was said to be constantly on the move.

Forest Briscoe told the story of her rushing around from one housing unit to another with a urinal under each arm. Whatever she carried around with her in meeting the housing crush, she was a central figure in seeing that one more homeless waif was crammed into an already overcrowded room, and that his hygienic and dietary needs were properly served.

Coming with suddenness, World War II put a tremendous strain on Indiana University campus housing, and there was little or nothing the institution could do about it. Where building materials in 1939 had been in ample supply and at reasonable cost, the supply was now being severely restricted and prices were rising. Skilled and semiskilled labor suddenly dwindled as men who had been on relief or emergency work drifted away to other areas of wartime employment. If the university had had ample funds in 1940 it could not have constructed the housing it needed. To complicate matters further, the Navy took over the three men's dormitories, and somehow or other crammed 1,200 men into space which had accommodated 300 civilian men students. By this time, however, the male student population had dwindled to such a low figure that it could be housed in six former private homes owned by the university.

At the same time the Navy commandeered male housing facilities it brought onto the campus a heavy contingent of WAVES and SPARS that placed a severe strain on housing for women students. Again, the Navy placed two or three service women in Memorial Hall in spaces which had served one civilian co-ed. Before the end of the war in the university was virtually unable to provide any housing for men, and was severely limited in its ability to take care of the heavier feminine enrollment. By the middle of the war 2,400 Army Specialized Training Corps personnel were moved into girls' dormitories, and 801 women were forced to look elsewhere for rooms. Thus the university went from one housing crisis to another during the war years. The heavy crush, however, was to come in the latter part of 1945 and throughout 1946.

President Herman B Wells viewed the academic year of 1945–46 as one of anticipations and preparations comparable to that of a large family awaiting the blow of a heavily menacing cyclone. He and his staff devoted most of their energies to planning for the instant doubling of student enrollment during the next year. They studied projections of enrollment which had been made by various agencies, and it seemed certain that at least 9,500 students would crowd onto the campus by September 1946, and most of the new students would be married veterans who wanted not rooms but family apartments in which wives and young children could be housed.

Never in a century and a quarter of history had Indiana University been called on for so much expensive service by its student body. Never before had it been thrown so thoroughly upon its own resources to care for the great majority of its students. In 1946 the town of Bloomington offered less actual and proportional assistance than ever before. In many cases families had doubled up in homes during the depression and the war. Building had all but ceased, and many houses that were readily available before were now too dilapidated and outmoded to use. As a consequence, rooms available to students in 1945 were about half the number available in 1930. There was no promise that things would get better. A parting in town-university history had come, and the institution had to become suddenly aware of this fact. As nearly as university officials could tell conditions would grow worse, because no new buildings could be quickly constructed.

Wells and his administrative staff in 1945–48 viewed the housing situation as the major challenge facing Indiana University. They drafted a long-range plan for providing housing for the maximum number of students who might enroll in the future. This document, a cardinal one in the history of the university, reversed practices of the past. So important did the administration consider this program that the Board of Trustees was asked to meet at Camp Brosius in Wisconsin and well away from any disrupting influences in Bloomington or Indianapolis. The board was asked to approve two major propositions: First, borrowing large sums of money at low interest rates; the money to be paid back over an extended period of years, and from funds collected in the form of rent. Second, building on the university's surplus land tremendous facilities for the housing of an ever-increasing number of students. This proved to be a seminal plan, and bore heavily upon the institution's future.

No wartime emergency had created more anxiety than the certainty of a housing crisis in 1946. Every approach that could be imagined was used. In January 1946 an information center was established in the office of the Dean of Men, and Dorothy Lackey was given charge of an answering service to develop and send out information pertaining to housing. H. E. Pearson, superintendent of buildings and grounds, went in search of temporary shelter. He located seventy-five house trailers nearby at the Crane Naval Ammunition Depot. These, he said, could be moved onto the campus and made ready for veteran occupancy by the first of February. Pearson thought about a third of these units could be partitioned for use by two families.

The idea of using military trailers was Ward G. Biddle's. In the summer of 1945 he went to Washington in search of surplus housing. While talking with military officials, he discovered they were wondering what disposition they could make of hundreds of house trailers that had been located near war industries plants. Through the assistance of Senator Homer E. Capehart, Biddle was able to persuade the government to turn these portable units over to universities and colleges, and in a short time Indiana University found it had sharp competition for them. Immediately Indiana began a search for 150 more trailer units.

Early in February the Indiana State Economic Council announced an allotment of one thousand temporary housing units to the university, and at the same time Pearson was certain he would have 150 trailers on the ground, with 100 more arriving soon after that. A part of the Economic Council's allotment consisted of surplus military barracks. These cavernous structures would be partitioned into rooms accommodating eight men each. With the exception of a few refinements the veterans were right back in the army with their bunk beds, foot lockers, small mirrors, and folding chairs. Perhaps the chairs were the only real nonmilitary luxury the barracks-dwelling students enjoyed. By the middle of January 1946 Ward Biddle's scheme to acquire trailers bore further fruit. The National Housing Authority allotted 300 more of these tiny family hutches to the university, and they could be moved as soon as ground could be prepared and transportation provided.

The development of trailer towns on the American university campus was one of the most interesting social phenomena in postwar social and family readjustment. At Indiana the trailers were moved, reconditioned, and repainted a light tan by the Curry Construction Company. Ground, despite the wide open spaces of Monroe County, was at a premium and these tiny structures were placed in close harmony, mounted on their wooden underpinnings. To keep the brisk Hoosier winds from freezing the occupants, a stout liner of tarpaper roofing was nailed to the base and imbedded in the ground. Space oil heaters were used, and plumbing facilities met the barest minimum sanitary standards. Space inside and outside was cramped, and family life was the most compacted perhaps of any in the history of academia. Nevertheless, it became so attractive to many "trailerite" families that they refused to move when the university offered them more spacious and permanent types of apartments at low rates. In the spirit of the Indians of the Great Plains, the trailer was a haven within its tiny tepee ring, and that ring in a sense was home to the veteran-student and his brood.

There were many reasons why the veteran and his wife became attached to "trailer town." A feature article in the Bloomington *Star-Courier*, March 17, 1947, described the flow of life in Woodlawn Courts. Wives under pressure could have attended to their housekeeping chores in an hour, but in many instances they strung them out over the day, gossiping and visiting with "door" neighbors. Constantly something went wrong with the trailer and getting it repaired became a community concern that required much talking and commenting. One wife said if something went wrong in a multi-room house it was not immediately noticeable, but in a trailer a breakdown stood out like a sore thumb. Perhaps the most attractive feature of the court was the "community house," made by coupling three or four trailers together. A kitchen was available, and here couples whiled away evening hours talking and playing cards. The community laundry was ingeniously converted into a clubhouse almost on a moment's notice. Tubs were topped by doors taken off the utility "dog houses," and these were adorned with crepe paper to give the appearance of a dinner-cabaret. It was common practice for dancing couples to glide romantically about prosaic and camouflaged laundry tubs to the lilting tunes of Glenn Tucker, Guy Lombardo, and Sammy Kaye.

The campus trailer courts were great social and rank levelers. Colonels, majors, and captains lived door to door to sergeants, corporals, and dogfaced privates. Pilots of P-38's and B-24's who had shot it out with enemy planes over Anzio, Klagenfurt, Berlin, New Guinea, Tokyo, and Bataan were neighbors to pharmacist mates, tank drivers from Patton's corps, paratroopers, and even WACS, WAVES, and Red Cross nurses. The *Star-Courier* said, "When the fellows get together, there is a lot of 'batting the breeze,' and swapping tales about things they have seen, and places they have visited on pass, but the grim part of the war is seldom discussed."

The trailer court became a neighborly place indeed with its constant borrowings, and sharings. Troubles were passed around, and bad luck became a communal concern. During illnesses or family tragedies wives pitched in and kept the unfortunate's trailer going. Like Indiana pioneer families the "trailies" shared labor, baby-sitting, food, housekeeping chores, automobiles, and even gripes and displeasures at the university itself.

Veterans and their wives shared grave concern over the campus housing shortage. Perhaps the reason they adjusted as well as they did was the fact they felt lucky to have a humble roof and four walls for a home. The housing shortage was so grave in 1946–47 that families and single students, for that matter, were willing to accept any kind of quarters and overlook the lack of refinements and luxuries. This fact was borne out in Dorothy Lackey's office. This official was over-burdened with frantic appeals for student housing, and especially for family quarters. She asked the question in her bulletin if veteran husbands would accept rooms temporarily for themselves, and later move their families into more substantial apartments? If this idea was not acceptable, then would families accept housing where no cooking facilities were available?

In answer to Dorothy Lackey's questionnaire married veterans put university officials under enormous emotional strain. They contended they had either been separated from their families too long already, or that they should not be subjected to further deprivation and loneliness. This pressure also placed Alice Nelson in a most difficult position. A rumor went around the campus earlier that girls would have to move out of South Hall, and the *Daily Student* published this story as fact, and later had to retract it. Almost immediately Mrs. Nelson had to confirm the rumor by informing the girls that, after all, they would be moved. The *Daily Student* counseled the co-eds to accept their plight with good grace. The girls, and everybody else, were reminded that national predictions indicated that in September there would be at least 750,000 veterans in university classrooms. Everyone would be greatly inconvenienced by this inrush, and if the girls felt they had to blame someone or something then they could belabor the war. "Indiana University," said the paper, "is undergoing a crisis with the housing situation. A good policy would be stick by your school until it catches its breath and can overcome the problem with a workable solution." Actually there was little or no reason for emotion because North and South halls were actually being returned to their original purpose as men's dormitories.

Perhaps an even more trenchant fact for co-ed students was they would have to submit to many of the inconveniences the veterans and their families had experienced throughout the war. Privacy, in the earlier sense of college rooming, was virtually destroyed by girls having not only to double up, but in most cases to fill the rooms to ultimate capacity. Eight girls were to be placed in suites designed for six, they would have to sleep in double-decked beds, and use the "middle room" for dressing and study. They were assured there would be enough desks to go around, if they arrived on time. A few timid co-eds received Alice Nelson's dictum with the same dismay they would have accepted a hitch in the army. They ran to the phones and called their parents to rescue them, but for the most part the girls were understanding. Well they might have been, because Dean Kate H. Mueller said co-ed enrollment had increased almost as fast as that of men. By doubling up in the three-room suites 160 more women would be able to live in the dormitories than had lived there before the war and to enroll in the University. President Wells undertook to placate the girls by saying, "Even with the proposed re-arrangements of dormitory occupancy, students in the University-operated halls of residence will have more space facilities per student than those in the typical fraternity and sorority, even in pre-war times, in other words, the University is asking students in dormitories to sacrifice to the extent of roughing it fraternity and sorority style."

The problems of crowding co-eds in their rooming spaces were slight after all as compared with the possibility of having to turn veterans with long battlefield service away from the campus for lack of housing. This was a grim decision that faculty and administration refused to make. The veteran had already suffered unreasonable disruption of his life, and to ask him to wait until such a time as the institution could conveniently house him was out of the question. At the same time the university felt it must keep its commitments to the nonveteran student and not ask him further to suffer disruption of his life. Wells and his administrative staff took the attitude that housing of some sort had to be provided. The editor of the *Daily Student* agreed. "Before we begin thinking up any excuses," he said, "let us pause a moment in retrospect. These same veterans who now are seeking admission into our universities and colleges have sacrificed several years of their lives to make this country a better and safer place in which to live." These had been difficult years, some of the time for many veterans was spent under bombardment, and in hospitals recovering from ghastly battle wounds. The university was morally bound to serve all these applicants, deserving or not, with the fullest possible sincerity.

While university representatives searched through military installations for possible housing, arrangements were made to rent the Field Glove Factory Building in the center of Bloomington. Ward G. Biddle signed this lease to run until June 30, 1948. The Field Building had been used as a U. S. O. center, and it was said more than three quarters of a million people had passed through its doors during the war. This structure was temporarily named Town Hall and was of sufficient size to accommodate more than a hundred students, barracks style.

In early February 1946 plans were underway for the construction of two apartment buildings to house married students. The Board of Trustees approved the sale of self-liquidating bonds of over a million dollars to finance this construction. Alice Nelson, however, had warned students and trustees alike that such housing could not be made ready before 1948. These new structures were designed to contain 79 one-room and 36 two-room apartments, and would be located in the northeast quadrant above Third Street and near the Kappa Sigma house. There would be three stories of dormitory space with basement provisions for storage, recreational rooms, and laundry facilities.

The new apartments were no more than a gleam in the official university eye in February, and the need was pressing and immediate. More drastic efforts had to be made at the moment. Every estimate of veteran enrollment in Indiana was pushed upward. Early that year President Wells declared housing was the university's first priority. He assigned Ward G. Biddle to give intensive supervision to the emergency program. Biddle was a dogged searcher and he and his staff began a twenty-four-hour hunt for almost anything that had a roof and four walls. They sought barracks, trailers, furniture, bedding, tables, and chairs wherever they could be found, in or out of military installations. North and South Hoosier halls were erected on the high shoulder of land between the Fieldhouse and Seventh Street. Work was begun on the first unit of buildings on January 7, 1946, and on February 8, the first student occupants moved into their rooms. The eight dormitory units, mess hall, and washrooms were dismantled and moved by truck from Sharonville, Ohio. The open bays-barracks had accommodated thirty soldiers per unit, but on the Indiana campus they housed only eight students in comparable space. Unit two of the Hoosier halls complex was moved from Jeffersonville where it had originally comprised five old Civilian Conservation Corps buildings.

By the middle of February men students were moving onto the campus in droves, most of them wearing lapel buttons adorned with the "ruptured duck" indicating recent service severance. They left army camps only to return to eight-man sleeping cubicles on the campus, and most of them had to sleep in double-decked beds. The bifurcated Hoosier Hall structures before the Fieldhouse would accommodate 400 men. There were community study rooms, and communal bathing facilities. Heat was brought in through insulated overhead pipes from the Fieldhouse, and except for the partitions and the campus scene, the veteran had brought his coveted "duck" button back to the same army barracks for a three- to four-year stretch.

Woodlawn Courts were established as a trailer park where couples with children could rent two or three rooms. Childless couples were confined to a single room. Five acres were set aside on Henderson Street for another trailer camp to be called Hillcrest. In 1945 the university had received a $25,000,000 appropriation with which to construct new and permanent buildings, and it was decided that a substantial portion of this fund would go to the construction of dormitories. By now the university was set irreversibly on the course of housing most of its students in the future. Never before had its administrative personnel worked so assiduously to solve a problem. The search for temporary housing went on around the clock during seven-day weeks, and every projection of future enrollment made the task appear more impossible of accomplishment.

At the very height of the campus housing crisis, President

Harry Truman asked President Wells to go to Greece as his personal observer of that country's upcoming election. This was perhaps the most awkward moment such a request could have arrived in Bloomington. There was some light ahead, however. Ward G. Biddle's search was bearing fruit. He had located two warplant dormitories, one in Evansville and the other in northern Indiana at Walkerton. These buildings were spacious enough to house 600 students when they were finally in place in Bloomington. At the same time the City of Bloomington, through Mayor Loba "Jack" Bruner, requested that 25 new dwellings for veterans be approved by the Chicago Regional Office of the Federal Housing Authority.

When Wells finally thought it possible to leave the campus for Greece after the middle of February, he offered his home, the old Woodburn house on North College Avenue, as temporary student rooming quarters. Alice Nelson divided the house so each of three couples had a living and bedroom apartment, but they shared in common the kitchen and dining room, including the work of preparing meals, cleaning, and general housekeeping. These couples remained in the Woodburn house until past the middle of April and the president's return to Bloomington. On April 23, 1946, they prepared to move with the remark, "We were quite anxious about the date of President Wells' return. We felt sorry for the University being minus a President, but the longer he stayed, the longer we stayed." These couples had been chosen from the head of the list of applicants for apartments, and were desperate for housing because no more was available when their names were selected. Harley Preston said, "We spent a few days pinching ourselves to see if we were dreaming. We didn't expect such a thing to happen. It was only by chance that we were the applicants for trailers when the supply ran out."

Wisely, students themselves were drawn into sharing the anxieties of the housing crisis as advisors. At Town Hall meeting on March 5, the Council of Housing Representatives was made a formal member of the university's list of campus organizations, and this body planned semimonthly meetings to discuss housing issues as they arose from week to week. A representative was selected from each housing unit and attendance at meetings was made compulsory.

By April, twelve instead of two temporary men's dormitories, had arrived from Evansville and Walkerton and were being rebuilt on ground along Tenth Street between Service Drive and Union Street. These would house 600 men and would be ready by fall. Moving these large structures from the war plant areas was a herculean task within itself, but on the campus it was necessary to construct roadways, walks, bathroom and sewage facilities, and individual heating plants. These houses were divided into two groups, Rogers I and II. Rogers I contained eight two-story rectangular frame buildings covered with asbestos-shingle siding, and were lined with cellutex. Rogers II contained seven dormitories and a dining hall. These latter buildings were of concrete block, precast floor slabs. They were permanent structures designed by Burns and James of Indianapolis. The entire Rogers complex was designed to house 1,772 men students.

Lighting and heating on the campus proved to be a taxing problem, because never in its history had the university really solved this problem at any given moment. Under a headline, "No Wattage for Veterans So Candles Flicker Away," the *Daily Student* said, "Abe may have studied by fire light, but he had nothing on some of the modern vets on Indiana's campus who are studying by candle and kerosene, temporarily at least." Trailers were without lights, and veterans thronged the already crowded Library in search of seats and light, saying, "We're darned glad to have a place to stay." They said this even if they and their wives could not listen in privacy to "John's Other Wife," and they could not wear freshly ironed shirts.

Securing housing per se was only about half the problem of actually moving students into new living quarters. Providing heat, lights, water, sewage facilities, laundries, mess halls, and recreational facilities involved almost as much search for material and costs as the acquisition of buildings. Once the structures were in place the maintenance costs on the temporary buildings shot up to new highs for the university. Later when President Wells reported that the unbelievable number of 184 new buildings had been placed on the campus, he did not indicate the herculean task that a relatively small maintenance staff had to face, and even then were unable to satisfy all the calls and complaints about malfunctioning buildings and equipment.

Wilson Wyatt, former mayor of Louisville, and President Truman's housing expediter, on April 10, 1946, revised upward the estimate of housing needs in Indiana University. This came in response to a letter from President Wells detailing the institution's plight. Wells told the federal expediter, "It now appears that we will need 500 to 600 family units and 3,000 dormitory spaces for single men." Wells also endorsed the Mead Bill pending before the United States Senate, which proposed to provide more adequate housing for veterans and their families, and thus would enable most universities to solve their housing dilemmas.

Not only did Indiana University have to wrestle for the first time with the problems of married students, it had to be concerned with an entirely new kind of American academic community, the veteran village. The trailer and asbestos-siding housing where wives, children, dogs, and cars were crowded into miniscule space both within and without the house called for ingenuity in human management. Even barracks-broken veterans had to get used to this new way of life, along with making rather radical readjustment to civilian academic routine. In many cases both husbands and wives were enrolled in the university, and baby-sitting became a major problem with which the institution had to show some concern. Two trailers were set aside as nurseries. Nina Hassler, a graduate student in the School of Education, was employed as a fulltime supervisor of these nurseries. Dean Wendell W. Wright of the School of Education announced that students who were taking nursery training in credit-bearing courses would give part-time services on an apprentice basis. Dean of Women Kate H. Mueller sought the cooperation of the Y. W. C. A., the Dames Club, the Associated Women Students, and the Woodlawn Wives Association to acquire playground and nursery equipment, and to help keep children happy. More formally, a faculty committee was given oversight of this very delicate side of veteran life in the university. In some cases returning veterans developed a high degree of sensitivity and protectiveness about their family's welfare, and the crowded veterans' villages offered plenty of unavoidable offenses against privacy.

As the opening semester in the spring of 1946 advanced, Indiana University began to make some appreciable headway in solving the problems of its veterans. Congress appropriated $275,-727,000 to provide 102,000 housing units for the nation's colleges. The pinch, however, was locating already constructed units, or procuring building materials with which to construct new housing. In May, 266 new units were authorized for Indiana University by Orvil R. Olmstead, Regional Director of Federal Public Housing, but no one knew where these units could be found, or whether materials and labor to construct them could be brought to the campus. Ivan McDaniel, housing manager for men's residence halls, went on still another hunt through the military camps of the Middle West trying to locate overlooked buildings, or structures recently declared surplus. Strangely nothing appears in the record to indicate that Indiana University received any housing assistance from the giant Army base at Camp Atterbury, and only a few miles haul from the campus.

The summer of 1946 was indeed a frantic one for everybody; housing officials on the campus, and students at home awaiting word of room assignments. In June that year plans were matured to increase university housing to a capability of 500 per cent over its prewar facilities. A permanent dormitory group and a cafeteria serving 1,008 men would be constructed just east of the campus. In addition, 1,900 housing units for single men and women would be provided, and 288 married housing units would be brought to Bloomington if they could be found. On June 10, construction was actually begun on the new dormitories just south of Tenth Street. There were to be seven of these two-story buildings, each 230 feet long. A cafeteria measuring 140 x 160 feet was to be built in the complex. There would be little beauty about these box-like concrete block and slab structures designed by Edward D. James of Burns and James of Indianapolis, and built by J. L. Simons Company. The dormitories were scheduled to be ready for occupancy by the middle of September.

Housing for students was only one part of the university's woes. There was a serious shortage of classrooms and quarters for new faculty members, and the difficulty of building new private dwellings was almost too great to be overcome. It was all but impossible to find houses for rent in the town. This shortage came at a difficult time indeed. As returning veterans flooded into classrooms, there was an urgent need for new professors, and these had to come from a market in which every other university was seeking to enlarge instructional staffs. Also, President Wells was still engaged in his search for a faculty of high quality, and he was handicapped when the prospect of securing housing in Bloomington was mentioned in employment discussions. At a faculty meeting on

June 11, 1946, the president reported that a lack of faculty housing had prevented the university from securing staff replacements, and some instructors who had been hired had resigned out of frustration before they ever reached Bloomington because they could not find places to live. Partially to correct this situation three former faculty houses, now owned by the university, were remodeled to provide thirteen apartments. Orders were placed for thirty-five two- and three-bedroom prefabricated houses to be erected on the campus as faculty homes.

In addition to the above arrangements, Captain L. L. Hunter, commandant of the Crane Naval Depot, offered use of seventy apartments on that post at the modest monthly rates of $17.50 and $28.75 a month. Transportation to the campus would be provided by bus. In Bloomington some landlords were much less generous and understanding. Charges were made that they violated the Office of Price Administration's rent ceilings. A survey was made by the university to determine rates charged students to see how common chiseling might be. The *Daily Student* said of the violators, "It is, however, not feasible to prevent students from staying in unapproved houses. Unscrupulous landlords realize this as they increase rents two or three times the 1942 rates." Some of the price violators no doubt were among the most ardent patriots in 1943, but opportunities for personal gain in 1946 were too tempting for them to keep the flame of public concern alive. The Bloomington Chamber of Commerce concerned itself with this condition. The Ernie Pyle Post of the American Legion and its Auxiliary chapter undertook to deal with the Bloomington situation. To help meet this housing crisis faculty families were asked to board students. More than 150 veterans and their wives made a survey of the town in July to determine the availability of rooms and the conditions under which they could be rented. This group worked directly with Colonel R. L. Shoemaker, Dean of Students. The colonel said the university would be able to house 5,000 new students in September, provided there were no labor walkouts.

Next to Alice Nelson, Colonel Raymond L. Shoemaker was a major personality in handling both student housing and adjustment problems. The colonel was a man of strong personality, but he exercised finesse in dealing with young people. His broad experience in this area had equipped him for meeting just such a crisis as the leaping enrollment and the extraordinary housing demands it created. Never before had the American university system been called upon to give so much attention to the intimate details of human relationships in such a wide diversity of community housing. Indiana University was no exception, and Colonel Shoemaker contributed heavily to the fact that the institution at no time was confronted with a threat of student revolt or any other kind of upheaval. Complaints were accepted and adjustments were made within the limitations of physical facilities, and apparently to the general satisfaction of large numbers of students.

The veterans' survey turned up a hundred new rooms that could be rented at established ceiling prices. On the campus fourteen new buildings located around a central dining facility seemed assured for 290 married veterans at rental rates set by the Federal Housing Authority. At that point, however, nobody in the university knew from experience what hidden costs were involved in this new type of campus housing; the military standard of cost measurement was well-nigh worthless in determining civilian expenses.

In the middle of August 1946 the university administration was optimistic that all would be well by the middle of September. Students were assured there would be housing for them at the beginning of the new semester. The campus had the general appearance of a vast shipyard in full operation. Smithwood halls, the Hoosier halls, Rogers I and II, Woodlawn Courts, Cottage Grove Apartments, Forest Place, Sycamore and Memorial halls were either a-building or were being refurbished. Between Seventh and Tenth streets the permanent men's dormitories were underway. The expansion of the campus geographically was breathtaking. Fenwick T. Reed, assistant to the president, told the Bloomington Rotary and Kiwanis clubs that 70 buildings were under construction at once, and the eastern limits of the campus would be pushed back a half a mile.

Administrative pride in housing accomplishment received a boost when the St. Paul, Minnesota, *Pioneer Press* carried an extensive article by Howard Kahn, an Indiana graduate, describing the housing wonders being accomplished in Bloomington. Kahn admonished University of Minnesota officials to visit Bloomington to view the miracle wrought by the campus planners and builders. "Indiana University," he wrote, "has shocked a lot of public officials by building its trailer village and temporary dormitories on the loveliest sections of its fine campus. . . . Most schools and cities have sacrificed the rights of former GI's on the altar of aesthetics. . . . The policy at Indiana has been revolutionary. It can be stated in these words: 'provide a place for veterans to live. Even if the housing consists of unbeautiful trailers, dormitories and barracks, put them in attractive surroundings and beautify them as much as possible.' " Kahn said the housing shortage in Indiana University had not barred veterans from taking full advantage of the G.I. Bill of Rights.

What had been glowing optimism in August faded to dismal pessimism and doubt early in September. Campus housing would not after all be ready by the announced date of school opening in the middle of the month. The *Daily Student* said on September 5, 1946, "Four crises a day spells a lot of headache, but that is the schedule for Indiana University Administrators in regard to housing, says Col. Fenwick T. Reed, assistant to the President." At that time 300 trailers were on the campus plus 200 owned by students for which the university furnished space and facilities. Six one-story barracks were in place, twenty one-story buildings were almost ready for occupancy, and so were the seven permanent dormitories. In addition thirty-five one- and two-room apartment structures were approaching completion. Most of the temporary buildings had been hauled in from Crane Naval Depot, Walkerton, Bunker Hill, and Evansville in Indiana, Camp Grant and George Field in Illinois, and Lima and Sharonville in Ohio. The mere inventory of these buildings was a baffling task, and one wonders if anybody in fact had a precise notion of what had been accomplished.

This was not altogether true. President Wells made a regular morning tour of construction sites. He talked with contractors, foremen, workmen, and university personnel. He climbed through partially constructed buildings, inquired about schedules, and prayed for good weather, good labor relations, and speed. As in dealing with every other aspect of university operation, he viewed firsthand what was going on around him. No president of a major university was more conversant with what was actually going on in what appeared to be great confusion in crisis-construction.

By the first week in September there was enough information available to establish the fact that the university could not possibly open a new semester on September 23 as announced. Delay in the delivery of materials and labor shortages slowed progress on the buildings. The opening date was extended to October 16, except for the Evening School of Law, the Normal College of the Gymnastic Union, the Division of Social Services, and the extension centers. President Wells said the delay, which was common with other universities, would permit completion of housing. The decision, however, added further to the institution's burden, because all listed student applicants had to be notified by letter of the delay. When the university did begin its semester's work, students were told the area of the campus would be doubled, and there would be 108 new buildings, an increase that would almost necessitate a campus guide service.

Even with the delay, the university workmen needed much more time to complete construction work. There was desperate need for temporary housing. Again Governor Ralph Gates offered to lease the Canyon Inn in McCormick's Creek State Park, fourteen miles away from the campus. Rooms would be made available by Lyman C. Smith, manager, to disabled veterans in the Memorial Union Building, which could care for twenty-five handicapped persons. Other temporary student housing was provided in the University High School Gymnasium and the Men's Gymnasium. Sixty-four women were housed in the Student Building. Fifty families moved into Canyon Inn on November 1, and individuals located temporary lodging on their own. The most dramatic housing, however, was that given twelve men in the Board of Trustees' Room next door to President Wells' office. These lads were housed around George Ball's elegant boardroom table awaiting assignment to the Smithwood center as soon as workmen could make that place livable.

On October 24, 1943, Joseph A. Franklin announced that the Army had assigned 300 additional trailers to Indiana University. These were located at McCook and Kearney in Nebraska, a long haul indeed, but Franklin said they would be in Bloomington and ready for occupancy by the first of December. These were the last of the military houses. Only Michigan State University had exceeded Indiana in the acquisition of ex-military and warplant housing.

So sudden was the rise of the Cottage Grove Avenue and Woodlawn courts that a village was created almost overnight. It was inadequately provided for in the way of civic ordinances, and other community controls. Veteran residents organized a city form of management administered by themselves. This new type of American campus enclave was a sociological and political oddity functioning within the boundaries of both the university campus and the city of Bloomington. It was youthful in fact and tone. Young married couples, small children, and animals competed for space; especially limited were parking places for family cars.

Many a veteran lying on the beaches of New Guinea or storming the beachhead at Anzio, or rushing headlong with Patton's tank columns across France dreamed of the day when he would go home to something approaching a rose-covered bower. He was shocked into stern reality when he discovered that he was only taking his bride across the threshhold of drab military quarters which he had thought he was leaving behind forever. "Many of them," said the campus newspaper, "have visions of a barren two-by-four room with hardly room enough to pass without turning sidewise." This thwarted dream with its tiny kitchenette, dinette, and two cubbyhole bedrooms furnished and including gas, lights, heat, and water for $42.50 a month scattered a few rose petals anyway. It was comfortable and it was on the campus. Veterans depending largely on the G.I. Bill of Rights monthly check of $90.00 could hardly ask for more or expect less. Those who lived in trailers paid only $25.00 and $32.50, and while they enjoyed somewhat more privacy and independence, they shared many communal problems with neighborly concern. At least they had a wall on which to hang their fancy "Home Sweet Home" mottos, and maybe enough space before their doors to spread a modest WELCOME mat.

In all the frantic crush to provide housing for students there was even a bit of humor connected with the university's planning. Girls in the summer of 1946 were informed they would be given rooms in one of the Smithwood halls, and not knowing where these were located many co-eds rushed to Bloomington to inspect their future home. There were no buildings on the Smithwood site, and as far as the girls could see the wooded spot on Third Street back of the Kappa Sigma house was only a possible tenting ground. The so-called Smithwood halls were still standing as bachelor officer quarters at Bunker Hill Naval Air Station just north of Kokomo. By October 19, however, these structures had been moved to Bloomington and were almost ready for feminine occupancy, a radical change from their original purpose. There were eight dormitories in the Smithwood group. Because of the wooded location the various temporary buildings were given the arboreal names of oak, walnut, pine, hickory, and laurel, and were called the "trees" group. Following older patterns of earlier private housing in Bloomington the Smithwood halls came close to being mixed housing quarters. Laurel Hall housed 125 men, Pine Hall sheltered married veterans and their wives, plus 90 single girls. In all, about 200 men and 525 women lived in the wooded halls.

Fortunately there were no major accidents or calamities during the summer. In December, when the intense press for housing had subsided somewhat, 120 carpenters, members of the American Federation of Labor, went on strike against the Curry Construction Company. This crippling work stoppage continued past the middle of February and the opening of the new semester. This strike denied 300 men, mostly veterans, access to university housing. The only mitigating fact in this disruption was that severe winter weather conditions made the stoppage less crippling than it might have been otherwise, and work would have had to cease anyway. Vice President Joseph A. Franklin said, even with the strike, that with favorable weather the university could still house 75 per cent of the new students who would enroll for the second semester.

Not only was the university in a fairly stable situation for housing incoming students, it could now begin in January 1947 to move some of the 800 men out of the flimsy and overcrowded Hoosier halls into the more substantial Hickory Hall in Smithwood Center. This still left two men to the compartment in the old barracks. At the same time men were moved out of the Union Building and the two campus gymnasia. Some even came in from the country where they had found rooms.

All university dormitories were self-supporting, and this required astute management on the part of Alice Nelson. Up until January 1947, prices for all university services had been kept at a minimum, but in the latter month it became necessary to raise the charge for meals to $1.30 per diem; only the University of Iowa had a lower charge. Low fees and rentals were of vital importance to Hoosier veterans, and they could become emotional over any change in the structure. In May the Federal Public Housing Administration, which retained possession of the surplus military housing moved onto campus, created considerable anxiety by raising rents $10 a month. The veterans and their wives reacted vigorously against this announcement, and they had the active support of President Wells and his administration, including William Henry Snyder, the university's attorney. Wells told the press that students were no more opposed to the raise in rents than were university officials. In various campus meetings a very considerable amount of anger was generated. Some veterans declared they would refuse to pay the proposed increase. In this dispute veterans and their wives prepared a revealing inventory of what they got for their rent. Furnishings consisted of a dinette table, four folding chairs, a studio couch, two double-deck service-style bunks, a gas stove, an icebox, two mirrors, window shades, and screens. Much of this was furnished by the university. The Federal Public Housing Administration was accused of trying to institute a sliding scale of increases based upon a veteran's income, a plan which it was said would work a genuine hardship upon the disabled. In a sharply worded letter the Indiana students demanded to know who in Washington was responsible for the increased rent—a question which was never answered. They submitted a petition, and wrote their congressmen. Before it was over the whole Indiana delegation in Washington had not only been alerted, but had indeed been aroused.

As a result of the angry protests over rent rates, the federal housing officials took a characteristic bureaucratic way out of their blunder by assuring the Indiana University officials that a resurvey would be made of student and faculty housing. Announcement of this decision came in a telegram to Joseph A. Franklin, but it did not come before William H. Snyder, Senators Homer E. Capehart and William E. Jenner, and the entire Indiana congressional delegation had dealt directly with the housing officials.

The Federal Public Housing Administration still insisted on a sliding scale based on veteran income, a principle the Board of Trustees had already rejected. Both university and federal housing representatives agreed there was almost no basis for comparison of costs within the Big Nine area because few of the other schools had undertaken the construction and management of comparable apartment housing, or had government supplied dwelling quarters in operation.

At the moment the federal agency reversed itself in the matter of rents, which it did only after much pressure was exerted, the *Indianapolis Star* in a critical editorial said, "Alphabetical bureaucrats have no qualms about soaking former GI's and families trying to stretch a government allowance over high educational living costs at Indiana University. The landlord in this case is the Federal Public Housing Administration which owns apartments adjacent to the campus. The University merely collects the rent." The battle went on between Bloomington and Washington throughout May and the first half of June. During these weeks the face-saving resurvey was underway and involved primarily 280 family apartments. On June 13, 1947, the Federal Public Housing Administration capitulated and left rent rates at the original figure.

While the antirent campaign went on, the trailerites and apartment dwellers organized cooperatives to deal with other communal problems. The Woodlawn occupants elected a mayor and village council to see after public affairs. At the same time they organized a highly successful consumer cooperative that handled clothing and other staple family supplies. So successful was this cooperative venture that it even attracted the attention of Bloomington businessmen. Married students were now fairly well housed in university quarters, and hard-pressed campus officials could take a calmer look into the future.

The latter week of July 1947 Herman B Wells announced that after extensive negotiations the Board of Trustees had decided to begin a major building program that would house more than 1,000 single students and 232 married students and faculty families. This decision was reached after President Wells had been given a firm promise by the Bloomington building trades that their members would agree to maintain existing wage rates. Wells said, "The agreement between the University and the Bloomington building trades union to proceed with the buildings under present wage rates might well set a pattern of co-operation which if followed generally would do much to relieve the paralysis of the building industry workers."

As the university advanced toward a solution of the housing problem, it became clear that for all time in the future the married student would be a fact in American campus life, and that as a larger proportion of the high school population went to college the university would have to assume even greater responsibility for housing. This meant the institution would have to become efficient in building and funding permanent dormitories and apartments. Costs of the new buildings would be secured by the mortgaging of the structures themselves, and revenue from their rentals would be used to liquidate construction and maintenance costs. The projected new buildings in July 1947 were estimated to cost in the neighborhood of $4,500,000. J. L. Simons Company of Indianapolis was given the contract for their construction. Two three-story apartments were to be constructed at the corner of East Third and Jordan streets in the general form of a blocked "I" and of Indiana limestone. The new buildings would contain 234 one-bedroom apartments and there were to be recreational, lounge, and laundry facilities.

A new four-dormitory group to house men exclusively was to be constructed along Tenth Street east of Jordan Avenue and the Memorial Stadium. These were also to be three-story limestone structures of the simplest possible utilitarian design. Already there were 700 names of men on the waiting list for rooms, almost enough to fill the new dormitories. Even with the addition of the six new permanent buildings the university still could house under its own roofs only 21 per cent of its anticipated enrollment. In August Harold Jordan, chairman of the University Halls of Residence Committee, announced the hope that the apartment buildings at least would be open for occupancy by the opening of the fall semester in 1948. These apartments would house 234 students, a relatively small number in the face of the fact there were already 1,200 applicants for quarters before construction was actually begun.

At the opening of the fall semester in 1947, 350 rooms were available for single men, and 150 for single women. Married students, however, presented an altogether different problem since there were 1,276 applicants for 640 apartments. Again, it was necessary to seek housing for married students at the Crane Depot; again, Governor Ralph Gates offered use of the Canyon Inn at the end of the public park visitation season, and other housing off the campus was made available. President Wells said in August 1947 that, "Despite expansion of the University's housing facilities since last fall, the greater number of students who will be accommodated in fraternity and sorority houses, and the increase in rooms in private homes, it now appears that 600 men, mostly war veterans, will be unable to attend the University for the fall semester unless additional rooms can be found." Again a strong appeal was made to Bloomington householders to rent their spare bedrooms. It was said married students alone spent $120,000 during the school year in the town, and that university service personnel working in the community and town earned $35,000. In all, students were said to leave more than $300,000 annually in the town.

Although there was urgent need for additional housing, and the university was anxious to enroll every qualified applicant who appeared in the registrar's office, there was not the anxiety of opening the new semester in 1947 that had prevailed the year before. Nevertheless, the institution by this time was sorely struck with megalomania. The Bloomington *Star-Courier* reported September 19, "Roads and streets, trains and houses were crowded Thursday as thousands of students swarmed to the campus for the beginning of Indiana University's 124th academic year. All types of transportation was being utilized to bring boys and girls, men and women from every state in the Union. On the campus activities seemed to be more normal than at any time since Pearl Harbor." Freshmen were gathered into a compulsory convocation, and they filled the new auditorium. By this time classrooms, laboratories, and clinical facilities had been expanded by 81,000 square feet. The Federal Works agency had approved the construction of sixty new practice rooms for the School of Music. That summer Dr. John Van Nuys became the new dean of the School of Medicine, and Wilfred C. Bain of the School of Music; and both schools had expanded space. Fernandus Payne retired as graduate dean, and John W. Ashton was made acting dean in his place. There was a reduction in the number of freshmen entering the university, but a sharp upturn in the numbers of upperclassmen; in all, there were 11,003 students compared with 10,345 the year before. The registrar estimated that 2,000 applicants had been turned away for lack of housing or failure to meet admission standards. This was a crucial year in which the pattern of an enrollment increase of approximately a thousand students a year was set.

When all the hurly-burly of the opening of the new semester in 1947 had quieted down, the editor of the *Daily Student* indulged in a generous bit of self-adulation for the university.

"We look around our mushrooming campus again this fall," he wrote, "we can say 'Well Done, I. U.' This university, like no other such institution in the Mid-West, has met the housing problem head-on and has just defeated it. Everywhere, new dormitories, classrooms, and quonset huts are springing up." The progress had been difficult to achieve and had strained institutional finances mightily, labor resources were too limited to perform all the work, and a new type of campus management had to be created. The editor thought the new buildings had grace despite their hurried planning and construction. Rogers II "is as impressive a dormitory center as you'll find anywhere, with the colorful block buildings and newly planted, terraced grounds. The whole Nation might share our pride in the building feat that has been accomplished on this campus." A proud boast indeed from a temporary sojourner on the campus.

Even more impressive and permanent structures were erected on the campus. The Board of Trustees in late September of that year began the sale of $6,500,000 worth of bonds at unbelievably low interest rates. By a ruling of the Indiana Commissioner of Revenue on October 1, 1947, these 2½ per cent bonds were made tax-exempt. At the same time Carl and Violet Snoddy and Henry Pearson were granted a $308,000 Federal Housing Administration loan to build a forty-four unit apartment house on South Stull Avenue to house World War II veterans. Now housing needs were in a fair way to being served, and President Wells said in his *Annual Report* for 1947–48, that some available housing space actually remained vacant. In Bloomington almost a hundred private building permits had been issued. Several new apartments were under construction. In January 1948 the housing pinch had eased to the extent that the university turned "Town Hall" back to the Field Glove Company owners, and closed building "C" in the Rogers group to save fuel and electricity because of a falling off of enrollment for the second semester.

The transitional months from January to September 1948 were highly important in Indiana University's history. By summer of that year the institution was completely committed to the building and maintenance of what amounted to a small metropolitan community that necessitated a form of management for which neither the traditional university administration nor the trustees were conditioned by actual experience to handle. Joseph A. Franklin and Ward Biddle proved to be highly successful in the procurement of surplus housing from military and industrial installations and getting it transferred to the campus. Alice Nelson was masterful in managing campus residential properties. She was trained as a dietitian in the University of Chicago, and had managed the Indiana University dining facilities prior to the war, but during the years of the intensive housing pinch she made the transition from dining facility manager to an expert housing developer. One of her colleagues said she could communicate with contractors, building laborers, bankers, and government officials in brisk executive terms.

During these middle years of the 1940s the married student and his campus family became a fixed part of university-student relationships. This fact brought other changes in the mode of campus life. In the spring of 1948 a sharp break indeed was made with the past when it was decided to invest $30,000 in the installation of individual dormitory telephones. This involved the renting of 2,100 phones—a long step indeed from that spring day in 1894 when W. T. Hicks purchased the Bloomington Telephone franchise and strung a slender line to President Joseph Swain's office in Owen Hall.

More complex than the installation of the dormitory and apartment telephones system was the problem of offering educational facilities to children of married students. A move was begun to have the Bloomington City Council annex the apartment communities. This attempt was defeated by a single vote on the grounds that Bloomington was financially unable to cope with such a problem. The tax base of transient students, and even professors, was entirely too slender to raise more than a token percentage of the funds needed to care for campus children. The university was faced with reinstituting a program it had abandoned many years earlier by providing elementary school facilities within its campus organization. Failing to gain access to the Bloomington schools from dormitory and campus addresses, the married students formed the Hoosier Courts Cooperative Nursery Association to promote at least a nursery school. An old barn was converted into a schoolhouse by use of materials donated by the university. Plumbing, wiring, and gas fixtures were installed by volunteer parent labor. Mrs. Lifel Mueller was employed as director of the nursery, and the school was opened under the watchful supervision of a ten-member advisory board.

Periodically harassed university officials announced the housing problem had peaked, but each new semester brought its surprises and harassments. Too, the Federal Public Housing Administration could be unpredictable in its own bureaucratic ways. There came a break, however, in 1949. In transferring the surplus wartime housing to the campuses in Bloomington and Indianapolis, the housing authority had retained possession of the buildings because it lacked authority to give away the 77 larger buildings and 321 trailer units. Congress enacted a law in July 1948 that permitted the university to purchase these buildings. This perhaps placed the institution in somewhat of a dilemma. President Herman B Wells reported to the Board of Trustees that with present and expected enrollment the institution still needed housing for at least 1,000 single students, and 500 housekeeping apartments for married couples. He expressed the hope that the university could in the immediate future reduce occupany of some of the temporary housing, especially the Hoosier halls and trailers. At the same time he announced the closing of the shabby old former Civilian Conservation Corps section of Hoosier Hall.

In the first semester of 1948 the university enrolled 11,414 students, and of this number, said the president, the university housed 3,959 persons—1,715 single men, 2,800 single women, and 1,066 married couples—or 54 per cent of the student body. A Central Housing Office survey for that year indicated that 46 per cent of the university enrollment still had to find rooms in sorority and fraternity houses, and in private housing in Bloomington. When the second semester opened in February 1949, Alice Nelson said, for the first time the institution would furnish housing to all married student applicants. This optimism arose from the fact that the two new 118-unit apartment buildings off Third Street were ready for occupancy by students, faculty, and emeriti professors.

Genuine progress was made in the housing of single men. The new dormitory units (Wright Quadrangle) south of Tenth Street were opened to occupancy in September 1949 to 1,017 men, and on November 20 the general public was invited to an open house to inspect these modern living quarters with their fine lounges and dining facilities. This, said Joseph A. Franklin, would end both the housing shortage for men and relieve the crowding in older and perhaps substandard quarters. There was not, however, an appreciable drop in fresh demands for married student housing. Wells considered this too much of a burden for the university to bear alone. He called a meeting of Bloomington businessmen in his office and reviewed the significance of student monetary contributions to the town's economy. He undertook to stimulate construction by private means of sufficient residential quarters to care for a portion of the student body. Repeatedly, university statisticians had cited the amount of expenditures of students in the town, which in the aggregate were not inconsiderable, and married students, it was said, were even more promising customers.

Not only was there a lack of investment of private capital in student housing in town, but there were cases of chiseling on rent rates. One of these struck close home. The *Daily Student* reported that Professor William E. Ross of the School of Music and his wife had been named defendants in a suit filed by William J. Bowman accusing them of exceeding the rent ceilings. The Rosses rented a basement apartment at 402 North Park Avenue, and Bowman said they had overcharged several renters. There were other cases in town where overzealous landlords ignored rent ceilings and contracts and were hauled into court.

The presidential reports after 1945 all contained pleas for more housing. In 1950 President Wells informed the trustees that even more housing had to be constructed to meet married student demands. This despite the fact there were already available approximately 1,100 apartment units. At the same time Joseph A. Franklin announced in May 1950 that prospects were bright for the construction of a new experimental residence center for married students. It, said the vice president, would be located northeast of Hoosier Courts above Tenth Street. The new units would be low-cost one-story buildings designed by Edward D. James of Indianapolis. By August 10 construction was underway, and the cost was to be borne by the university without use of state funds. Wells and Franklin said it was hoped that the experimental project would point the way to a permanent solution of the married student housing problem. In the meantime the university offered for sale seventeen outmoded prefabricated houses which it had moved to the campus in 1946, and which had indicated a significant change in campus living.

While Franklin sold off dilapidated prefabricated housing,

abandoned one unit of Hoosier halls, and built more permanent housing structures, Alice Nelson did a "land-office" business in renting rooms and apartments. At the opening of the fall semester in September 1950 she said there was a "terrific demand" for married student housing. This was true because the university had greatly expanded its graduate programs. In many ways 1950 was a watershed year in university housing history. The university was now definitely committed to providing housing for more and more of its students, and housing had become not only big business, but a big community responsibility demanding a high degree of bureaucratic management. The Wells mandate that no qualified student be turned away from the campus was to be carried out in the decade 1950–60 in one of the most dramatic student housing programs in American academic history.

During the years since 1945 an entirely new type of school spirit had grown up on the campus. For couples moving into trailers and prefabricated ex-military buildings, living at the outset may have offered little more than grim practices, but in adversity there was a certain amount of strength and warm humanity. The organization of clubhouses, community entertainments, commissary cooperatives, nursery schools, and dames clubs drew students together in an entirely new pattern of association. There arose a community spirit and cooperativeness that concerned itself not at all with popularity contests, electing queens, sponsoring pep sessions, or with football and basketball for that matter. This was left to the life-everlasting campus sophomores. Instead there was concern with family matters, community living, and academic programs. Never in American history had so many wife-husband combinations interested themselves in things intellectual. To the veteran-student the immediate future held the challenge of making a living for a family already on hand, and a sound education shortened materially the apprentice years for doing this.

When the university began shifting its housing program and breaking up established student community centers, it ran into about as many emotional problems as it had experienced in 1946. Every official decision involved a human element of warm memory and loyalty which never before had to be considered. Not even the solid stone walls of Edward James' new one-story experimental houses compensated fully for the tender moments of grim necessity in the folksy plywood hutches where husbands, wives, children, dogs, and cats, all had to search out social solutions to their problems in the hard way of close-community living. It might even be true that an astute sociologist would find signs of the beginning of a significant new era in American family life itself.

Indiana University's experience with the inrush of veteran students after 1945 was by no means unique. This was the story all across the nation, and universities and colleges everywhere competed for housing and staff members. Decidedly a part of the heavy increase in enrollment in Bloomington and throughout the university system of off-campus divisions was the application of the Wells' desire to get as many people enrolled in the university as possible. While no active enlistment campaign was carried on, nothing was done to discourage admission to the university and its various branches. The new physical plant and faculty were built with this in mind. What was different was the fact that the university was isolated in a small town that fell miserably behind in house building during the years of war stringency for lack of labor and building materials, and when the crush came the institution had to face it with its own resources. Because of this peculiar local condition the university had to provide a greater proportion of its student housing than did almost any other major American university with comparable aspirations and objectives.

[IX]

The Last Rah Rah

As the 1940s tailed into the 1950s Indiana University was rapidly emerging into a major university with expansion affecting every phase of institutional operation. While buildings crowded the skyline along the Jordan and around the east and north meadows, new professorial faces appeared in the offices of the modern buildings. On the sidewalks great swarms of students drifted from one corner of the campus to the others during class changes. The predictions of the educational statisticians seemed to be coming true in full measure.

In 1950 Indiana University enrolled 14,810 students, with ten or more representing every county in the state. Marion County sent to Bloomington 2,150, or just slightly less than one-seventh of the student body. More than 80 per cent of the enrollment was native Hoosier, and more than 60 per cent came from the rural counties. The balance was heavily weighted in favor of the 10,450 men as compared with 4,370 women. An even more fascinating statistical fact was that women registered for work in every field offered by the university except graduate business. Between 1945 and 1950 were the flush years for American institutions generally, but immediately after that date enrollment dropped considerably as college-age years reached the slackened birthrate of the depression era, and the departure of large numbers of veterans. Indiana, however, suffered only a 2.4 per cent loss as compared with a national deficit of 8 per cent.

President Raymond Walters of the University of Cincinnati, a faithful compiler of college enrollment statistics, reported in *School and Society* the results of a survey of 713 institutions. Of thirty representative universities which he checked, Indiana had experienced the fastest proportionate growth the past year. At Commencement in June 1950, the university graduated 3,659 candidates, plus 472 who had received diplomas the previous February, making 4,136 degree recipients, the largest number in the history of the university.

President Herman B Wells in September said there would be more "family men" in school and fewer single men than in the previous year. Once again, however, the entering freshman class tipped the balance in favor of nonveterans. Besides their mere statistical weight, the freshmen were more sophisticated in the new ways of American life, and were more affluent than had been any entering students in the past. They brought to Bloomington after 1950 the usual number of "college Joes" and socially ambitious "Nellies," but theirs was an age when the "Big Men and Big Women on the Campus," like Digger Indians, were disappearing. These campus characters, however, did not pass off the scene without a stiff kick back at their protagonists, who were many, including student activities committees, the student governing bodies, tailors, watchmakers, and shifting organizational patterns.

Designers of men's clothing dropped the vest, and the watchmakers popularized wristwatches, thus making obsolete the belly-wide chains that had dangled fraternity and honorary keys in the same way South Sea islanders dangled shark's teeth necklaces. If this was not affront enough, a bill was before the Student Senate which proposed to limit the number of offices a student could hold. The measure when passed forced at least two students to surrender offices and threatened their organizations with probation if they did not drop the offenders. The *Daily Student* appeared quite concerned with this campus issue. In 1953 the Student Activities Office undertook to help along the timid but ambitious by finding niches for them. "They," said the campus paper, October 3, "serve the campus in many ways from working in an advisory capacity to campus organizations to helping the individual student who has activity participation problems."

The Indiana campus was highly organized and socially minded. During the academic year, 1952–53, 140 registered student organizations made 1,747 applications for mixed social events alone. The Student Activities Office, in the calendar year, 1952–53, held 925 meetings, and made 1,950 appointments of students to various organizational activities. This sounded like they were busier than the industrious university administration itself. By contrast a decade later the number of student organizations had decreased to 104.

Generally the American scene in 1950 was a mixture of well-being and freneticism caused by the Korean War. It was also an age made anxious by the witch-hunters and their reckless accusations. For the college student of draft age it was one made ominous and anxious by draft boards who stood ready to ensnare faltering scholars. On the other hand, the decade, 1950–60, was still one in which blithesome campus frivolity held sway. Bobby-soxers clouded the memories of flappers of another age, and "hot mamas" were now veterans' pregnant wives living in campus "married" housing. Campus dances became melees of loudness in what passed for ballroom music, and frantic jumping about in bunny hops and the jitterbug. Blaring notes of jazz orchestras reverberated across the campus in weekend jam sessions, and the popular tunes of the day represented the quality of popular campus existence in the new age. Hoosier students had by no means forgotten how to take life on the first hop. They rushed to the campus in automobiles, and fraternity and sorority house backlots often gave the appearance of being secondhand car dealers' displays. The new student had greater mobility, and both men and women were out to enjoy it. The Dean of Students undertook to restrict this sudden mechanization of the student body by forbidding freshmen to have cars on the campus, but not even the dean himself thought he would be able to enforce the rule with any degree of effectiveness. At times he found himself in the predicament of defining a "freshman," the "campus," and even an "automobile."

Undergraduate males were restive if not intelligently original in the 1950s. In fact, they were veritable sheep following unseen and unknown leaders. They swallowed live goldfish, crammed themselves into phone booths, Volkswagens, and piled "man on man" up into teetering pyramids. They engaged in "kiss-a-thons," "dance-a-thons," and as their professors and elders said every other kind of show-off except "work-a-thons." No matter where a silly student shenanigan originated, even in the most lowly institution in the land, "university men" followed suit if it brought them publicity.

In late spring 1952 the Indiana campus was the scene of panty or, euphemistically, "lingerie" raids. Like other forms of student madness, this one swept American academia with sheeplike imitation, but with savage behavior. The Indiana raids were unproductive, perhaps they were no more than puberty rites of adolescence anyway. The *Daily Student* said, "The girls fearfully hid behind closed curtains and giggled a lot." Alice Nelson was a realist; she understood adolescent psychology. She collected a barrel of panties and gave out notice that she would present any lad, who made application to her, a piece of keepsake lingerie.

Colonel R. L. Shoemaker, Dean of Students, was less whimsical about the caper. He warned on May 15, 1952, that students who could be identified as taking part in the recent panty raid would face dismissal. For the time being this seemed to have cooled boyish ardor. Three years later, October 1955, Dean of Students Robert H. Shaffer, in answer to inquiries about the fad said it had passed the limits of tolerance. Like his predecessor, Shaffer warned convincingly that every effort would be made to identify the raiders and they would be subjected to disciplinary action. Too, anyone damaging university property would be held liable for the damage. He also laid the law down to girls who encouraged or incited a panty raid. Any lass who opened a door or a window to admit raiders would be expelled. This fad died slowly at Indiana.

The American scene in the late Truman and Eisenhower years may have revealed a certain flatulent quality, caused partly by immense prosperity, and partly by the national leadership itself. Youth was influenced by the media of color movies, radio, and television. The year 1950 saw the introduction of the movies, *Father of the Bride*, *Asphalt Jungle*, *Twelve O'Clock High*, and *Annie Get Your Gun.* William Faulkner received the Nobel Prize for Literature for his writings in general. A. B. Guthrie, Jr., a native Hoosier, won the Pulitzer Prize for *The Way West.* Gerald

Johnson summed up a half-century journalistic career in an *Incredible Tale*, and Allan Nevins published the *Emergence of Lincoln.* Just then becoming the subject of countless sermons and coffee table conversations was George Orwell's sobering novel *1984.*

Strangely, students seemed to be little touched by their professors' concern in the opening Eisenhower era with the violations of academic freedom. They had most likely never heard of the earlier and voluminous report of the President's Commission on Higher Education which bore the pompous title *Higher Education for Democracy* (1927). One contemporary critic called it a "turgid" document. It advocated the free or open admission to college of a much larger proportion of young people then coming out of high schools even "at whatever cost to learning, in the name of democracy." This philosophy had spread abroad, and had resulted in at least two flagrant cases of violations of academic freedom, one at the University of Nevada and the other at Michigan State University. Outside critics sternly called the professional educationalists and their curricula into the court of public review. Professor Arthur E. Bestor, Jr., of the University of Illinois caused near revolt among their ranks with his *Educational Wastelands* (1953).

As the decade advanced a veritable stream of books poured from university and commercial presses. No other American generation had been so well served in a literary way. Perhaps the average student had little more than a glimmer of this fact, let alone having read the books. James Michener's popular *The Bridges at Toko-Ri*, James T. Farrell's *The Face of Time*, and J. D. Salinger's *Nine Stories* were among the popular titles of the early part of the period—all of them reflecting in some way the changing mores and tastes of American society.

By 1956 the musical taste of most students was set to both new and old cadences. Although he had enjoyed marked popularity at home since the early 1930s, Louis "Satchmo" Armstrong, the golden trumpeter, won international fame in a tour of the Middle East and Western Europe. Rivaling the famous jazz musician was the new "Memphis sound." Elvis Aaron Presley introduced to the new college generation the vogue of "rock 'n' roll." From 1955 on the Mississippi boy was to monopolize the affections of the screaming bobby-soxers, and their older campus brothers and sisters. An observer of the Presley frenzy wrote in 1956, "Watching him is like watching a strip teaser and a malted milk machine at the same time."

This generation of American university students closed out their era singing *My Heart Belongs to Only You*, *Catch a Falling Star*, *Davy Crockett*, *Autumn Leaves*, *Yellow Rose of Texas*, *Rock Around the Clock*, *Sixteen Tons*, and *Tammy*. They had mastered bebop, rock 'n' roll, and all the other musical and dance gyrations of the moment, especially those of Crazy Otto inspiration. The Indiana campus, like every other university in America, was visited by "name bands," and jive and jam sessions became noisier and rowdier with their insane gyrations that would have sent former Dean of Women Agnes Wells into a permanent state of shock. By the opening of the new decade the tempo of life in Bloomington had undergone fundamental changes, many of them reflecting the deep social ones of American society in general.

Just as the tone of American writing, the daily and periodical presses, radio and television reflected a deep note of concern in 1960, so did the tone of campus life. With the major federal court decisions lowering the ancient barriers of racial segregation, and the following incidents of the Little Rock Central High School, the University of Mississippi, the Selma March, and the youthful voter crusade in the Lower South, plus the Vietnam War, international uncertainties, and the impending presidential election of 1960, campus youth experienced sobering moments. The seeds of change in fact had been planted throughout the decade by the great "communist" witch hunts, the McCarthy debacle, and cases like that of Caryl Chessman, a condemned California kidnapper, who was executed, but not before he had stirred student reaction with his *Cell 2455, Death Row* (1959).

By no means did all Indiana University students drift through the "Eisenhower years" with no more on their minds than organizational frolics, the current popular tunes, the new dances, and movies. Paradoxically these were the years when the university was making its great reputation in the fields of music, the arts, and the sciences. In the social areas there were concerned students who sensed the implications of the great American hysteria.

Professors had perennially lamented the apathy of students, and well might they from observing many of the surface manifestations of their interests in the 1950s. Most of them, said faculty reports and comments, seemed to be indifferent to the serious implications of public events. When a student group did react positively their critics were stunned. From the perspective of a decade and a half one might well question whether or not the professors seriously wished students to be as concerned with public affairs as they pretended. At the height of the McCarthy hysteria in the mid-1950s when much of American leadership cowered behind its own murky screen of fear, there appeared on the Hoosier campus late in February 1954 an unsigned handbill which criticized the Wisconsin senator. The sheet claimed no official sponsor, and its creators were not registered with the Dean of Students. Colonel R. L. Shoemaker immediately banned the paper because it had been distributed without his permission.

Five students, two girls and three boys, calling themselves Robin Hood's Merry Men, stepped forward and admitted authorship. They asked permission to raise a modest sword against McCarthyism on the campus, saying they wished to breach campus apathy and bring the Senator's cowardly attacks out into the open. The five said they were members of the Baptist Youth Foundation, which proposed to generate public concern. They told the Dean they hoped to enlist other campus groups in their crusade, and that they had planned their strategy during coffee hours in the Memorial Union; not only had they distributed "literature" but they possessed an ample supply of "Robin Hood" buttons and more than a thousand green feathers.

Colonel Shoemaker was caught by surprise. After a preliminary examination, however, he told a *Daily Student* reporter that Robin Hood's Men did not pretend to reflect the public views of students or of the organized student body. "They have," he said, "used every means possible to prevent any indication of affiliation with the University." The neo-Sherwood Foresters objected to Senator McCarthy's infamous campaign of declaring guilt by association and thus injuring innocent persons. In an ambivalent editorial, March 2, 1954, the *Daily Student* accused the Green Feather apostles of using the Senator's tactic of prejudging, and of being dupes. Nevertheless, the editor believed, "They demonstrate the courage of their convictions by signing their names, posing for news photos and distributing the anti-McCarthy literature themselves. How about their adult sponsor? They pull puppet strings and jingle their pennies from the ranks of the anonymous." More than once the Green Feather students were to be charged with being the tools of an insidious outside influence, but the record is devoid of proof of this fact.

In the eyes of the campus newspaper the five students represented no organized body, but the editor conceded that minority groups could quickly win majority support in the American way. University officials were commended for holding that a student group once established and operating out in the open should be free. The paper thought Joseph McCarthy was in the same situation—he either won majority support in the American way or he should be silenced. "He is in the open. He is allowed to operate. His methods of success will succeed only as long as a majority of Americans want them to." The *Daily Student* indicated it had no fear of the five students, and it expressed none of the Wisconsin Senator and his highhanded practices. There was, however, on the campus fear of a shaking bush. "But we do hold horror for the puppet stringers who guide minority groups from the bushes of hidden identity—it is easy to determine the motives of those who work openly; it is next to impossible to ferret out the real purpose of those hidden elements who work mysteriously and deceptively to attain their aims. They can provide the real threat to America, and the hunt for them must continue, here and in every crack and cranny of our land." Dr. Frank O. Beck of the tiny campus chapel indicated in a letter to President Wells that he also thought there were outside agitators. This no doubt was the first time in American history that a Baptist congregation was suspected of having hidden purposes, if it was in fact the suspected outside sponsor. Dr. Beck had overreacted out of jealousy, so it was said, because a religious group, supported by the Rev. Douglas Rae of the First Baptist Church, had invaded his preserve.

Not only was the pixilating spell of the Ides of March upon the nation in the spring of 1954, the Indiana campus seemed equally as befuddled. Just as a suggestion of the burgeoning tips of hard maples along the Jordan were touched with a crimson hue, the Green Feathers seemed to assume a kindred shade. In Madison, Wisconsin, fifteen students formed a "merry band" and ordered literature, a thousand buttons, and a pillowcase full of green feathers from Bloomington. A similar order came from Purdue, and now arrows whistled toward the troublous Senator from these three academic forests, not devastating arrows, but visible.

There were other merry men in the campus woods. Six Indiana graduate students in psychology circulated petitions declaring, "We Believe [Senator William] Benton." At the same time the original Green Feathers complained that university officials had opposed the appearance of Senator William Fulbright on the campus for the avowed purpose of attacking his Republican colleague. They were told the trustees forbade use of university facilities for political or controversial purposes. In this connection the officials referred to the board ruling of July 16–17, 1945, which sought to restrict political activities on the campus to those of the Young Republicans and Young Democrats, and even they were to secure the permission of the Dean of Students and the Student Activities Office to meet.

Later in March the Green Feathers declined to draft a constitution and seek recognition by the official campus bodies, saying their fight was directed against Senator McCarthy and his red-baiting tactics. They had no desire to ask the university to take a stand. It was unnecessary, they believed, to create a constitution to promote a political point of view by every legitimate means, to stimulate campus discussion of the controversial issue of McCarthyism, or to uphold the principles of freedom and fairness. They were not trying, they said, to manipulate the public's mind.

By April the Green Feather group appears to have changed its mind. It did draft and submit a constitution to the Student Activities Office. A vigorous argument arose immediately in the Student Senate over the implication of the organization's name. Dick Cardwell, chairman of the health, safety, and traffic committee, was quoted by the *Daily Student*, April 2, 1954, as saying, "We are open to the blast. Should the Senate not place itself in the middle of a political matter? The words 'Green Feather' have an unfavorable connotation on the campus." Cardwell expressed the thought that if the organization had a broader purpose than just blasting Senator McCarthy the name should be changed. In the meantime the Green Feathers chilled the air even more by announcing the publication of an anti-McCarthy magazine with graduate student John Hollander as editor.

The "Robin Hood" controversy as well as the abuses of McCarthyism bubbled with more or less fury until mid-May, and had now assumed campuswide proportions. When the Green Feathers sought use of a meeting place in the Indiana Memorial Union, the manager, Lyman C. Smith, wrote President Herman

B Wells, May 18, 1954, that some years before the Union Board had created a town hall forum for discussing controversial issues. This he told the president is the best outlet for all segments of student opinion. "The Green Feather group," he wrote, "was organized for the purpose of controversial discussion. The Indiana Union, then, in continuance with its policies regarding Town Hall, invites and encourages this group to use Town Hall for public discussion." The *Daily Student*, May 20, quoted the university president as saying, "The University should not take a position pro or con on controversial issues." He did not favor the university associating itself with the anti-McCarthy group known as "Robin Hood's Merry Men." At that particular moment the national concern with the McCarthy tirade had reached in some quarters the condition of a schizophrenic panic. An overzealous woman asked that the Robin Hood books be removed from the nation's public libraries; once again this doughty English arboreal vigilante was being tried in the court of public opinion.

The troubles of the Green Feathers attracted the attention of faculty members, and Cletus J. Burke, associate professor of psychology and chairman of the academic freedom committee of the American Association of University Professors, introduced in that body a five-point resolution. Generally, these recognized the existence of the anti-McCarthy group, that recognition of the Green Feathers did not imply official university sanction of their purpose, and "that it would be difficult to explain to the public at large the distinction between approving the purposes of the organization and approving its right to pursue its aims." The local chapter of the association concluded that ". . . the Association feels that any university is failing in one of its most important functions if it bows to the views held by the uninformed partisan group instead of defending a considered position. In other words, the University should make sound decisions and then explain and defend them."

The Student Senate on April 1 had voted to recognize the Green Feathers, but on May 27 it rescinded its action by a vote of 16 to 7. This latter action was thinly veiled by the statement that the organization had been guilty of controversial discussions before seeking recognition. The Senate expressed the hopelessly ambivalent idea, "It may [upon recognition] choose any issue it desires to discuss, take any side it desires, and call in any outside speakers—but it hasn't obligated the University to defend its position. Academic freedom is granted—all the University asks is partisan developments after recognition." The constitution committee of the Student Senate expressed the hope the petitioners would not lose interest in forming a discussion group, but that it would shed its feathers and disavow Robin Hood.

Spring and summer 1954 may well be called the season of the arrows in the history of Indiana University. Denial of recognition of the Green Feathers bordered on campus paranoia. There followed a passionate in-flow of letters on the subject. Earlier the editor of the *Daily Student* had commented in an editorial, March 11, that the paper had received a "postmaster's nightmare" of correspondence supporting the Green Feather movement, and most of the letters were signed. After May 28 the flood was indeed at riptide.

Some writers expressed themselves as being appalled at the thought that no group seeking recognition should take a partisan stand before the fact, but it could be as controversial as it chose afterwards. Frank O. Beck, July 6, 1954, in a highly ambiguous letter viewed the Green Feather crusade largely as one stimulated by townspeople and graduate students, holding each group under suspicion. He expressed fear of what he called the "pro-McCarthy" students. In sharp contrast with the Dean of the Chapel, Professor Tracy M. Sonneborn of the Department of Biology gave a lucid statement of his views in his *Annual Report*, 1953–54. "I am aware," he wrote, "that strange pressures must have been brought to bear on the University in this case and that it is possible to take the view that some concessions must be made in order to survive and flourish. On the other hand, the Green Feather Movement spearheaded an awakening of student interest and concern with public questions of which any university should have been proud. The demoralizing effect of the action taken with this group is deplorable. If a university cannot tolerate, protect, and even foster such student activities it is in peril of losing one of the chief reasons for its existence. The arguments set forth in the justification of the University's action were too transparent not to be seen through by all, and they fall completely in the face of recognition given to the young Republicans whose stand on controversial questions was surely just as clear in advance or more so."

On March 1, 1968, the Student Senate in a tie vote, broken by Paul Helmke, speaker pro tem, proclaimed, somewhat nostalgically, "Today is Green Feather Day." Senator Daniel Cahill told the student legislature that, "It is my belief that the history of this body has been largely ignored. What happened to the Green Feather Organization is one of the nasty things that have happened at I. U. in the past which should be remembered and prevented in the future." No doubt many professors and university administrators agreed with Senator Cahill. The Green Feather incident was not a happy memory for the university, just as Senator McCarthy's wild forays on American freedoms were "nasty things." Looked at from the large end of the telescope of time, the McCarthy charges of communism under almost every national official bed shrink into small but ominous stains. For Indiana University in 1954, however, they appeared large, especially in a state where a fairly good number of home-grown witch hunters had troubled the waters on numerous occasions with charges of communism on the campus.

A student, Jack Spindle, wrote President Herman B Wells, May 21, 1954, "I was surprised and disappointed to read of your issued statement of disapproval of the group known as Green Feather. I am sure that you can agree that all the foundations of our society that we now accept were at one time controversial. It is the duty of our university by the very meaning of the word to allow and encourage the examination and discussion of all fields. Certainly the study of current issues facing society is important. . . . If you fear Indiana public opinion, if you fear Indianapolis newspapers, if you fear reprisal by state politicians your fears are baseless . . . suppression is not true neutrality." On July 1 President Wells responded to this letter. He told Spindle that "I find myself in hearty agreement with almost all the statements which you make in your letter; in fact, the official statement which the university administration made on this issue expresses in its first paragraph a position very similar to the one you take. I assure you that none of the 'fears' which you list near the end of your letter have entered into the making of our decision. This decision has been based on considerations which I believe are clearly explained in our statement, which I assume you have read." President Wells here referred to the statement of the Board of Trustees of July 1945, which was reissued in July 1954.

The Green Feather incident was ended when the United States Senate mustered enough courage behind the shrewd Boston attorney Joseph Welch to expose the fomentations of Senator McCarthy for what they were—the ravings of an irresponsible, if not mad, man. Nevertheless, for Indiana University it ushered in a new era of student-university relationships in which the foundation was laid for a much more independent reaction of students to the currents of the times.

Before the Green Feather incident disturbed the campus there had been student concern which went well beyond the pregame bonfire professions of loyalty. From time immemorial a major university problem had been associating the welfare of an institution with the highly transient nature of its student body. Classes were hardly acquainted with the operations of the university, before they graduated and scattered to the corners of the earth. In 1936 an alumni group organized the Indiana University Foundation which proposed to solicit funds from alumni and friends for the University. By 1950, it was said, there was hardly a department in the institution engaged in special work or research that did not receive some Foundation funds. Judge John Hastings, a Foundation director, recommended that students be drawn into the operation of the special group since they profited so much from its funds. On February 24, 1950, Howard S. Wilcox, executive director of the Foundation, appointed a six-member Student Foundation executive board. These six were asked to take over the direction of the Student Foundation Committee and coordinate its work with that of the parent body.

Later President Wells nominated thirty-six students to the Foundation Committee, and planned to hold a banquet immediately upon his return from Europe to generate enthusiasm for the new assignment. At the banquet Wells told students the committee had been formed to help develop an interest in the Indiana University Foundation, and to condition them for their roles as contributing alumni. Later in November the president increased the membership of the Student Foundation Committee by fifty-one new members.

Out of this greatly enlarged group grew the plans for the famous "Indiana Little 500," which would raise funds to aid working students. By April 1951 arrangements were virtually completed for an all-campus bicycle race and a general student spring carnival. This event was to follow somewhat the pattern of the nationally popular Indianapolis Speedway 500, which took place annually on Memorial Day. A combination of faculty and student committees planned the details, with Claude Rich, secretary of the Alumni Association, and John Mee of the Business School serving as major advisors.

From the outset the Little 500 captured student interest, was financially profitable, and drew into competition most of the organized campus groups. For weeks before the May race, roads and byways about Bloomington swarmed with bicycle riders building up stamina and speed. Curiously chalked designs appeared on broad stretches of concrete and asphalt, marking the practice racecourses for co-ed tricycle riders, who competed the day before the bicycle race. Coaches taught their charges how to mount tricycles on the run, how to make sharp turns without slackening momentum, and how to exchange riders without losing position.

Adding to the excitement of the spring carnival, popular entertainers and musicians were brought to the campus to pep up the races, and to join in the evening extravaganza following the contests. For instance, in 1963 the Smothers Brothers appeared in the Auditorium with Bobby Darin and Joey Dee with the Starlighters. Two years later Bob Hope made a return visit to the carnival. That year a record crowd of 23,790 persons crowded into Memorial Stadium to watch the race, this was an increase of 4,000 over 1964. In 1966 Connie Stevens and Roger Miller appeared with Ginny Tiu and her Orientals, the latter playing jazz, pop, and classical numbers.

Throughout the years of student unrest and protest the Little 500 Student Foundation Committee carried out its mission with the most tangible expression of concern for needy fellow students. Only one major matter marred slightly the festivities. A racial question arose over the election of a queen, and this feature was dropped from the program. In 1964 popular singer Molly Bee was chosen the Little 500 sweetheart, and she responded graciously by helping to award prizes to contestants, and then adding zest to the evening extravaganza.

In the general process of postwar expansion students were drawn into another area of university planning and operation. They were directly affected by housing conditions, whether they lived in dormitories or fraternity and sorority houses. Historically, Greek letter fraternities had been a part of Indiana University since 1845. In earlier years the organizations had made material contributions in solving a part of the student housing problems. Each decade after 1850 saw some expansion either in new chapters added, or by an increase in fraternity membership. By 1930 fraternities and sororities virtually dominated student social activities. The great depression, however, brought some changes in this area. Increasing enrollment tended to advance the importance of nonfraternity students, and during World War II some campus prophets predicted that the Greek letter organizations would shrink materially in importance, or that they might disappear altogether. It was thought returning veterans would have neither time nor interest in them; this proved rash prophecy. Women, said the prognosticators, would be slower to give up the organized way of life, largely because the alumnae would hold on to memories of the past. This also proved untrue in Bloomington. Students themselves sustained the system.

As attempts were made to restore the tenor of university life after 1945, there was a definite revival of interest in fraternity house living. The swirl of life about the chapter houses reached a rather high tempo. Once again inter-house rivalries became keen, weekly social affairs were lively, and so perhaps was some of the competition to achieve genteel academic standings. The numerous organized athletic contests helped to unify the brother- and sisterhoods in efforts to win honors for their lodges. The annual homecoming festival was a time of intense rivalry. In preparation for this occasion many an imaginative boy or girl applied more ingenuity to designing a decorative scheme for a house at that season than some of them applied to an entire semester of class work, or they gave more time to planning and holding dances than to maturing themselves intellectually in the Library.

In rushing seasons, members of the Greek orders somewhat resembled Hoosier livestock growers who periodically added new blood to their herds. Socially aspiring girls, dressed in their finest clothes and using their best party manners not infrequently subjected themselves to the most searching inspections by sorority sisterhoods, and many of them suffered disappointment and heartache upon being rejected. Fraternities were no less discriminating in the choice of brothers who would eat, drink, say grace by rote, submit to rigid "training," initiations, and the swearing of awesome oaths of eternal loyalty.

This was the segment of the Indiana student body that largely gave a tone of glamor to every student festive occasion on the campus. Photographic memoirs of these moments filled the latter quarter of the *Arbutus* with a lasting record of eternal youthfulness and tender adolescence escaping into man- and womanhood. In a somewhat more sedate manner the sororities displayed full pages of queens and their attendants, while the "big men on campus" were also put on display in less exciting forms. These were the last uninhibited flings at youth, sometimes expressed in the same vein of naughtiness that tempted some lads to festoon sorority house trees on Saturday nights with ribbons of toilet paper. Their grandfathers and fathers were up to the same sort of juvenile tricks, and grandma and mama had admired their lusty manliness.

The fraternity men on the Indiana campus collectively, at least, seldom demonstrated intellectual superiority to the sisterhoods. When the last intramural football game was history, and the chilling January rains had melted the last tendril of toilet paper into a soot-stained wad on a sorority house lawn, and Registrar Charles E. Harrell had recorded the academic results of the first semester for 1952, the women were well ahead of the men. Of 108 student organizations, dormitory women claimed the first twelve places. The thirteenth place went to a fifteen-man fraternity. In the first semester the next year 40 per cent of the fraternity pledges failed to make the necessary grade average to be initiated. Richard G. Speelman, activities counselor, made the astonishing statement that, "Nearly half of this year's pledges were drawn from the freshman group which were in the lower half of their high school graduating class." This indeed was the true mark of the "College Joe."

A decade later Harrell told the *Daily Student*, March 19, 1964, that sorority women had a grade point average of 2.77 out of a possible 4 points, fraternity men had an average of 2.352. The much larger number of women living in dormitories had an average of 2.510, and the all-men's average was 2.370 as compared with an all-university average of approximately 23,000 students of 2.472.

The university looked with favor upon the fraternities and sororities, despite the eternal threat of social snobbishness and other problems. In a small rural community such as Bloomington, the organizations gave a touch of glamor and sometimes grace to campus life. Too, sorority and fraternity houses were genuine aids in solving student housing problems. As the student body expanded in the postwar years of the late 1940s, many of the older houses were inadequate to accommodate their growing organizations. Also, new organizations were being formed and they found it difficult to obtain housing. The locating of suitable building sites, and the construction and financing of fraternity houses in Bloomington involved too much capital venture for the average fraternity chapter. Yet the university itself would be seriously burdened if it had to provide housing for the dozen fraternities and sororities that sought new quarters in 1948. This was the kind of problem that challenged the financial and planning ingenuity of Herman B Wells. In late spring 1949 he developed what came to be known as the "Indiana Plan" for fraternity house financing. This proposal was submitted to the Board of Trustees on June 10, 1949. A tract of seventeen to twenty acres of Fee and Rogers land north of the Illinois Central Railroad right-of-way would be reserved for fraternities and sororities. The president explained to the trustees that at least a dozen groups were then seeking residential sites of good size and away from the private residential areas of the town. The board adopted the proposal and appointed a special committee to devise a financial plan that would enable student organizations to purchase the land and build houses. Basically, the university would not issue its own funded obligation bonds to pay for building the houses. It would, however, agree to purchase funded obligations of any chapter that defaulted on its payments, and would use nontax funds to carry out fraternity financing. Finally the institution would not agree to guarantee any obligation but would purchase the balance of an unpaid loan. The trustees specified five sources of unrestricted funds that might be used to make such loans and purchases outlined in the plan. This action was approved by the Indiana Attorney General, November 13, 1952.

Administration of the Indiana Plan was placed in the hands of the newly created Fraternity House Plans Committee, which in turn devised an elaborate operational procedure and purchase and sales agreement. The first twenty-two lots surveyed contained approximately one and a third acre, and were priced at $7,500 each. By 1962 thirteen sororities and fraternities had purchased one or more lots, and all had either built houses or had buildings underway. So successful was the plan that in 1961 the so-called Third Subdivision with larger and more expensive lots was reserved.

By the end of its first decade of operation the Indiana Plan had helped finance houses for thirty-five organizations; some of which had secured loans to finance the enlargement of older houses. By 1968 the Indiana Greek letter organizations had developed an impressive community of semiprivate student housing. Loans and interests on the properties were as favorable as those granted other conventional university funding. Aside from the basic fact of providing a considerable amount of student housing on equitable financial terms, and without extending the university's borrowing capacity, the Indiana Plan solved the ancient problem of friction between fraternities and sororities and their private neighbors in the town. Equally as important, it brought this large assortment of student residences closer into the university system itself, and under the more direct safety and financial watch care of the institution. This perhaps stabilized most of the organizations and guaranteed them a way of life that they could not have purchased at the outset with their own private capital resources.

The ingenious Indiana Plan solved the problems of fraternity and sorority housing in a small county seat town with a high degree of satisfaction. For Hoosier students in general there were other and bigger problems demanding even more ingenious solutions. Nevertheless, students in Indiana University in 1960 were rather quiescent so far as most national and international issues were concerned. There existed the traditional political partisanships, with perhaps a majority of students supporting John F. Kennedy. There was concern with the race issue in the context of the recent Supreme Court decision (1954), and with the university's extraordinary effort to divest itself of the last vestiges of racial segregation. There was some tension over the Cuban revolution, and Korean War veterans filled much of the ranks of departed World War II veterans. There was, of course, deep student concern with what appeared to be an ambivalent draft policy of the Federal Government. Sociology, anthropology, some of the language areas, and international studies were popular. An increase of foreign students on the campus had helped to break down many of the older institutional folk mores.

There is no doubt that the influx of foreign students into

Indiana University after 1945 had an important leavening influence on the campus as a whole. Since the late 1930s Indiana had been attracting students from abroad, enough in fact that the *Daily Student* boasted, July 24, 1947, that, "Indiana University is rapidly becoming the melting pot of the Middle West." Students were said to be arriving from all over the world, which meant they came from fourteen countries largely to take the seven-weeks cram English course. In his *Annual Report* President Wells reviewed foreign student relationships with the university and said the visitors had maintained a grade average of 1.8 out of a possible 3 points. This was equal to or better than the all-university average.

China headed the list with 56 students, out of 181 from 56 countries. While he was in Germany as special advisor to General Lucius D. Clay, Herman B Wells inaugurated programs for the exchange of German students and professors with American institutions, many of whom came to Indiana. Generally both students and the university made amicable response to each other. In 1949 the visitors presented a limestone tablet to be placed in the south entrance of the Memorial Union Building. This memorial depicted a mother and daughter, symbol of intellectual nourishment and guidance.

During the summer, 1949, Indiana was one of ten American universities which provided a month of intensive "pre-advanced study orientation courses" to 300 Japanese students. A letter addressed to fourteen agencies which planned itineraries for foreign students, and over the signature of Herman T. Briscoe, November 27, 1950, expressed Indiana's interest in having non-American registrants. He said the university took "a keen interest in introducing our guests to the life of the University and the community," and offered openhanded access to the varied intellectual and human resources of the institution. Briscoe informed the agencies, "We would like to draw your attention to our readiness to continue to serve in this manner the cause of international friendship." Thus Indiana was erasing the image of Middle Western isolationism, and Bloomington provincialism.

There came to be special concern in the Wells administration by 1951 about the proper housing of foreign students, and especially those who came from the various official or governmental agencies. President Wells, Alice Nelson, and Leo Dowling, foreign student counselor, served as a committee to explore housing needs. They had in mind the creation of an international center which would be more of a club than a rules-bound dormitory. Leo Dowling suggested to his colleagues that Jordan Manor on Third Street appeared an ideal place if it could be made available.

Carrying his campaign to encourage international visitations even further, Herman B Wells, in a speech before the annual meeting of the American Association of Medical Schools at French Lick, urged the admission of more foreign students, because "American medical education would promote stability, prosperity, and western traditions which now may be of doubtful political and social orientation." Most of his auditors must have agreed with him, but wondered how they were going to stave off rampant criticism among Americans about limited admission of native students to medical schools across the country.

Dean Stith Thompson of the Graduate School observed in his *Annual Report*, 1952, that possibly Indiana University had the largest foreign student enrollment of any university which did not have a school of engineering. In Bloomington the visiting students studied in a wide variety of fields, an important area was education. The United States Department of Education had selected Indiana to provide training for special groups of educators, and during 1954–55, a rather heavy inflow of teachers came from abroad. In the two years, 1954–56, the School of Education had the largest foreign student enrollment on the campus, 67 per cent of whom were graduates pursuing advanced degrees.

As the years passed, the numbers of foreigners increased; in 1957–58 there were 677 registrants, and in March 1958 Dean Ralph E. Cleland wrote Indiana University would be one of seven American schools exchanging students with Russia. Twenty students from each country would spend a year abroad, the Americans would enroll in the universities of Moscow and Leningrad. The Russians would be enrolled in Princeton, Indiana, Chicago, Harvard, California, and Washington.

With 916 foreign students on the campus in 1962 the *Daily Student* boasted, "Indiana is host to the world." The university did have a generous representation from diverse national areas. President Elvis J. Stahr indicated two years later the number had risen to 1,234, a 30 per cent increase over the previous years. Leo R. Dowling was a highly successful counselor, and he had played a key role in the exchange programs. Apparently the campus went in for education of the whole man. Friedemann Moll, a German visitor, wrote, October 31, 1952: "But I shall not conclude this letter without thanking all the professors and students who helped us foreigners to make our stay at the University an agreeable and profitable one; especially in the beginning, when we did not yet know what a blue book, a comic strip, a jukebox, or a stag and drag party was. Indeed I had a high time on the campus of Bloomington: Three cheers for I. U.!"

In many respects the 1950s in Bloomington had been years of excitement as Friedemann Moll implied. This, however, in time gave way to deeper concern with conditions at home and abroad. By 1960 a restlessness had beset the American campus which could neither be clearly discerned nor explained. Indiana, in these years of ferment, largely reflected conditions that prevailed throughout American academia. Everywhere in the Big Ten, faculties, student organizations, and administrations undertook to isolate and adapt some of the elements of change. Student-university relationships were entering a new era as were parent-child-family relations. Every aspect of the lingering *in loco parentis* tradition was placed under severe strain. Not only had returning veterans from two recent international wars shattered the old controls, but even entering freshmen demanded more personal freedoms. They no longer obeyed many traditional parental rules at home, and they rebelled in the face of those in schools and colleges. The days of surrogate parental deans of men and women were near an end. After 1960 American universities and colleges were busily devising new codes establishing bounds of acceptable social behavior. This came about only partially because of currents of social and civil unrest in the nation; in the past decade universities had developed enormously complex social communities that revealed all the problems of urban society in general plus those peculiar to the campus. No American university in 1960 was sufficiently oriented to the new age to accept fully campus self-government, and, tragically, few or none recognized the inadequacy of the old rules. Indiana University was no exception as it learned from somewhat bitter experience.

[X]

Sexual Behavior and the Kinsey Perspective

NO UNIVERSITY in all of creation had ever been called upon to defend the freedom of investigation and publication in the highly personal area of human sexual behavior as Indiana University had to do in the 1940s and 1950s. Research in this sector of human life involved not only a deeply intimate matter but since the days of the ancient Hebrews had been spoken of in muted whispers. The Institute for Sex Research in Bloomington was in time to deal with most of the ancient moral and social mores in an open and statistically analytical fashion. Reports of the institute opened cracks in the heavily insulated wall of human reticence, and lifted the shades of hypocrisy. Institute researchers called into sober reconsideration moral and civil laws men had lived by, and revealed how in a startling percentage of the population archaic laws were violated in face of the realities of human behavior.

The organization, financing, and defense of the Institute for Sex Research in Indiana University was to become an ultimate test of academic freedom, freedom of investigation, and of publication. This was made even more trying by the location of the university in a conservative community and state. Progress of the institute from the outset was fraught with enormous emotional reactions if not actual resistance, a testing of university administrative courage, and the trauma of establishing at least two important landmarks in American intellectual freedom. Constantly Dr. Alfred Charles Kinsey and his able associates, Wardell B. Pomeroy, Clyde E. Martin, Paul H. Gebhard, and William Dellenback, were accused of setting back sex education in America, and in all civilization, for that matter. They were charged with frivolity, licentiousness, lack of proper scientific methodology, and social irresponsibility. To more frugal-minded Hoosiers they were charged with wasting the university's economic substance.

Few if any American universities ever faced such a delicate challenge of public relations, of public exposure, and of protecting the freedom of research and investigation. Almost constantly after 1945 President Herman B Wells and his senior administrative colleagues were called upon to justify the existence on the campus of the Institute for Sex Research. There is no reckoning of the time these officials spent in connection with the defense of the institute, and even in settling internal university staff wrangling. Alfred C. Kinsey was a strong-willed and dedicated man who had already established himself as an able entomologist before he became interested in human sexual behavior. His personality and private moral habits were tough shields against attacks upon him for frivolity or lasciviousness.

The defense of the institute would have been difficult enough in ordinary times, but the period of the 1940s and early 1950s was one of the most explosive in the history of American bigotry and public fears. It was an age charged with enormous anxieties, made tremendously more sensitive by the fulminations of Senator Joseph McCarthy against communism in and outside the context of the Federal Government itself. Both the press and the public were ready to capitalize on any departure from what was considered the social norm. The Kinsey research came within the scope of threat to the social status quo. Neither the critics of the McCarthy ilk nor the general public which had an inkling of the Kinsey Institute were able to differentiate between what was believed to be the threats of communism and threats of overturning folk mores and ancient beliefs and traditions.

Kinsey had a long association with Indiana University. Carl Eigenmann wrote William Lowe Bryan on May 12, 1920, that

Alfred C. Kinsey, a New Jerseyman, a graduate of Bowdoin College with a B.S. degree in 1916, and a doctorate from Harvard University, 1919, would be hired as an assistant professor in biology at a salary of $2,000. His duties would be to take charge of biology for home economics classes, and to teach entomology. The Graduate Dean explained that young Kinsey had been a laboratory assistant at both Radcliffe College and Harvard University. He had worked under the direction of M. W. Wheeler in the famous Bussey Institution, and there was a hint that he would be a safe instructor because he had been active in Boy Scout work, and had ten years' experience with boy's camps. Eigenmann was impressed by the fact that the new instructor was "studying a group of insects in Florida to California." This was reminiscent of his own hunt in this territory for blind cave fishes. To assist Kinsey in his pursuit of gall wasps the Department of Biology set aside $800 with which to purchase entomological equipment.

Bryan told the Indiana Board of Trustees on May 29, 1920, that he concurred "that Dr. Alfred C. Kinsey be elected to the position of assistant professor at $2,000 for the year 1920–1921." These were matter-of-fact recommendations for the employment of a lower-level professor. Not one of the three men in that centennial year of the university could possibly have envisioned the impact this slender young scientist would have on the university and on mankind in general.

Kinsey was reared in a conservative New Jersey family. The boy had a good high school record, but there was conflict between him and his father over the choice of a career. The father wanted Alfred to become a mechanical engineer; he, however went away to Bowdoin to become a scientist after two years of distasteful technological study. At the time of his appointment to the Indiana University faculty Alfred C. Kinsey was an intense and dedicated young scientist who pursued fervently the answers to several genetic-mutation-evolution and biological questions in an extensive investigation of oak gall wasps. During the summer and early fall of 1920 he held a Sheldon Traveling Fellowship to go on a collecting trip from Florida to California, a project which took him into thirty-six states. On October 20, 1920, the *Indiana Daily Student* reported that the new professor was in Bloomington with "an immense amount of material." There is no doubt that Kinsey impressed Eigenmann most favorably. His collecting trips had already yielded literally thousands of specimen of wasps and oak galls. At the end of the second semester in June 1922 Eigenmann wrote Bryan, "In regard to Dr. Kinsey, we all feel that he is a success as a teacher and investigator and if any promotions or increases in salaries are made for the coming year he should receive favorable consideration."

Kinsey's devotion to his research gained him a reputation early. In October 1923 he received as a gift a hundred specimens of gall wasps from Professor A. Trotter which had been collected along the Pacific Coast in California and Mexico by Dr. F. Silvestri, an Italian scientist. Of equal importance Kinsey's reputation continued to grow on the Indiana campus. In his final year as Dean of the Graduate School, Eigenmann wrote President Bryan at the end of the semester May 31, 1924, "I consider Dr. Kinsey one of the most brilliant of the younger men in the University," and he was happy the young professor had refused a seductive offer from the University of Illinois.

Not only did the tiny boxes and cases containing oak galls and wasps multiply by leaps and bounds as Kinsey went on annual searches for new materials; he was busy with the preparation of a 600-page textbook *Introduction to Biology*. When the manuscript was in an advanced stage of preparation, he submitted it to twenty-six biologists and to a number of experienced high school teachers for critical appraisal. He included illustrations and photographs from 300 artists. Kinsey told a reporter, "The most distinctive feature of the book is the style. I have attempted to employ the high school student's own language, and to use it in the same way that it is used around the camp fire or in the woods." He felt he had made a new approach to presenting physiology, heredity, ecology, distributive biology, and some of the other sciences.

At the moment when evolution and anti-evolution arguments swept the country, and fanatics, especially in Tennessee, Arkansas, Mississippi, and North Carolina, made capital issues of the subject, Alfred Kinsey was positive in his belief in the evolutionary processes of animal life, including man. He told the Indiana University Psychology Club in December 1926, that reflexes, tropisms, instinctive behavior, memory, and reasoning were traits which should be studied in lower animals in order to understand the complex behavior of humans.

Within a decade the young scientist had traveled 32,000 miles and had collected a phenomenal number of wasp specimens. In February 1930 he published his *The Gall Wasp Genus Cynips: A Study in the Origins of the Species*. Almost immediately he was off again on a semester-long expedition with Ancil Holloway and Donald McKeever, graduate students, to gather gall wasps in Mexico. Despite horrible roads and other handicaps these collectors were able to bring back to Bloomington a large and varied collection. By this time three distinctive traits characterized Professor Kinsey. He was a complex personality, a dedicated scientist, and a prodigious worker. Kinsey placed stress on quantitative statistics; for instance, on Nevember 6, 1934, the *Indiana Daily Student* said he had returned from a seventeen-day trip of 3,200 miles in which he collected six bushels of galls; in all, he had traveled 66,000 miles. A year later he was to add 10,000 miles more in travel with James H. Coon and Osmond P. Breland to southern Mexico, Guatemala, and El Salvador on a National Research Council grant and university funds in search of the origins of the species. This journey yielded 400 new insect species, and 50,000 specimens. In 1936 he published *The Origins of Higher Categories in Cynips*.

The passing years brought honors to Kinsey. In 1937 his name became a "starred" entry in *American Men of Science*. By that time his collection of wasps had grown to more than 4,000,000 specimens, representing a thousand species, and he boasted, "The annual additions to our collection exceed the insect collection of the National Museum at Washington or at the American Museum at New York." Despite the fact Kinsey's collection grew at the rate of 60,000 additions a year, and new evidence of mutations and species was constantly being revealed there was evidence the scientist was becoming somewhat disenchanted with Indiana University.

It is difficult from available documentary material to fit Alfred Kinsey into the Bloomington campus scene. He had a Methodist background, as did many southern Indiana Hoosiers, but this fact was scarcely discernible as compared with the zeal of his academic neighbors. He did, however, fix a part of his attachment to Indiana when he married Clara Bracken McMillen of Brookville in 1921, an Indiana graduate of that year. Kinsey enjoyed good recorded music, and later almost made a fetish of his "music nights." He was an avid gardener, taking special pride in his extensive iris beds. He perhaps had very few close friends in the university community, and most of his colleagues either did not know him well or regarded him with some degree of mixed feelings. He was often outspoken in faculty meetings, and frequently regarded committee meetings and many aimless faculty debates as a waste of time.

Before William Lowe Bryan retired, Kinsey was rather strong in his belief that Indiana University had reached a point of stagnation. Cornelia Vos Christenson has quoted a confidential letter on this subject in her *Kinsey: A Biography* (1972). "The President is seventy-five years old," he wrote, "and unwilling to settle any question, large or small. The whole University is in a mess; we get nothing done apart from the ancient routine—I would leave at the first opportunity offering comparable recompense and research opportunities." Bryan obviously did not suspect Kinsey's attitude when he wrote the entomologist after his retirement in June 1937, saying, "I have rejoiced always in what you have the ability to do and what you do. It is an extreme satisfaction for a man in my position to aid such a man as you to do his work." Even in 1938 when Wells became president, Kinsey was uncertain which way the university would go. No doubt part of his problem was that after the publication of his book the gall wasp project had lost some excitement and challenge.

Somewhat fortuitously a new challenge arose early in the Wells presidency which was to have significant impact on both men and the University. Kinsey never really forgot his scoutmaster concern for youth. As a biology professor and high school text author he naturally invited youthful confidences. The *Indiana Daily Student*, June 22, 1938, announced that a noncredit course of twelve lectures would deal with the legal, economic, sociological, psychological, and biological aspects of marriage during the forth-coming summer session. Men and women seniors and graduate students would be admitted to the lectures.

Almost from the outset of the marriage course, Kinsey and his colleagues faced parental, ministerial, and even medical opposition. When a Bloomington matron protested to young President Wells about the course, he admitted he knew little of its content and asked her to register for it and give him a report. She came away enthusiastic about Kinsey's lectures. Not so Dr. Thurman Rice of the Indiana University School of Medicine, and one of the lecturers. Throughout the rest of Kinsey's life Rice was to prove an irritant if not a nemesis.

Some faculty wives took the course and complained bitterly to Dean of Women Kate Mueller, but not about the content. They accused Kinsey of using the course to gather research materials for his private use. In a sense they were right because this was the beginning of long years of gathering sex histories to be used as basic information for several major studies on the subject.

By 1940 Kinsey had had enough of carping and complaining about the marriage course. He faced the alternatives, partly because of administrative prodding, of either toning down the boldness of the course, or of giving full time to sexual research apart from the general university program. Kinsey chose the latter, telling President Wells, "No scholar will voluntarily waive his right to disseminate information in the field in which he is especially qualified." Already he was embarked upon the sexual habits and behavior of the human animal. Even beyond this he concerned himself with the broad legal and social implications of human sexual behavior. Speaking in a Columbia University forum on crime, he was pessimistic that any appreciable modernization of sex laws would occur "in our life time" because of our persistent holding of ancient prejudices. He startled even his liberal audience by saying that only 5 per cent of sex crimes were really dangerous, the others were simply breaches of custom dating back three or four thousand years.

In the spring of 1941 Kinsey was informed that the committee for research in problems of sex of the National Research Council had given him a grant of $1,600 to enable him to get underway the program of the newly formed Institute for Sex Research in Indiana University. By that time Kinsey had recorded his 200th case of sex history and was aiming at 10,000 before he published his first study. To date the largest number of case histories taken in the field was 290. Half of the Kinsey cases filed by May 1941 were those of college students representing 140 institutions.

A year later the Research Council's special committee comprised of Robert M. Yerkes, George W. Corner, and Lowell J. Reed recommended a grant of $7,500 for 1942–43. In the meantime Kinsey had taken a thousand new sex histories. The three distinguished scientists of the committee visited Indiana University in December 1942 to determine the degree of future support needed to carry on the work of the institute. Already the public was beginning to get a severely perverted notion of the existence of Kinsey and his institute and there was some restiveness.

Alfred C. Kinsey sought sex histories from all levels of human society with a zeal seldom exhibited by even the most dedicated researcher. He was frequently oblivious to the necessity for establishing some degree of rapport with both people and the institution. President Wells' correspondence files reflect this fact. Dr. George N. Shuster, president of Hunter College, wrote Wells on February 4, 1943, that a problem had arisen on his campus. It had been discovered that a young woman was inducing students to meet with a Professor Alfred C. Kinsey to discuss their sex histories. The "procuress" received a dollar a head for each interviewee she brought the professor. Shuster said, "The problem which now presents itself to us is one of public relations. If girls who have been drawn into this project talk about it, we may very well have a story for some of the more sensational papers. They would undoubtedly try to suggest that Hunter is delving into the private lives of its students and that we are no doubt teaching love, etc." He asked President Wells to find out from Kinsey what actually went on. If he knew the facts he could better deal with any repercussions which might occur. Wells replied, explaining Kinsey's work, and saying he was certain the scientist would be glad to give Shuster the precise information he sought. In the meantime he felt the facts would offer no basis for scandal-mongering. This was only one of many times when the president was called upon to explain and defend the Kinsey project.

Kinsey had difficulty on this score at home. Mrs. Fred Hugill of Chicago wrote Dean Kate Mueller in February 1945, that her daughter Shirley had told her parents when she was at home for Christmas vacation that Kinsey had interviewed the members of a psychology class. Mrs. Hugill expressed no objection to the interviews, but she opposed Kinsey imparting voluntary sexual information, such as telling students "a very large percentage of college girls were not ignorant of sexual experience." Dean Mueller informed President Wells in a memorandum of February 19, 1945, that Kinsey always asked positive questions such as "When is the first time you have had such and such experience?" She said he refused to accept a negative reply. Wells noted on the memorandum "I am to see Kinsey when he returns."

Nothing, however, deterred the work of the institute. The medical division of the Rockefeller Foundation through the National Research Council upped its grants to $23,000 in June 1943, to $25,000 in 1944, to $28,000 in 1945, to $35,000 in 1946, and in 1947–48 it gave $40,000. By the latter date Kinsey had attained 3,000 personal sex histories. Now the problem was that of breaking the news of his research to the public. This he began to do locally when he addressed the Bloomington Rotary Club in September 1946. He told the service club that his study was then in its eighth year of research. He claimed 11,000 personal sex histories had been accumulated, but his objective was to take 100,000 histories. This latter number seemed to become an obsession with Kinsey. He announced that within a year the first volume, that on the sexual behavior of the male, would appear.

On December 30, 1946, the *Indianapolis Star* repeated Kinsey's report on his work, but added the sensational announcement that the human female matured much later than the male, shaking irrevocably an ancient folk belief. Females, he said, did not reach full sexual development until age 28, while males were mature at 16 years of age. This statement was to be repeated countless times by the American press. Kinsey told newsmen his was "a fact-finding survey, and there is no attempt to make any moral or social examination of the data." He felt people told him and his colleagues, Pomeroy and Martin, the truth because they believed the scientists would observe their obligation of confidentiality.

Kinsey's paper before the American Association for the Advancement of Science in Boston in late December 1946 was to bring his project much broader national publicity. While sex, he said, was important to marriage, personalities of husbands and wives were vital to lasting unions. If a marriage lasted until couples were forty or fifty years of age, it would last the rest of their lives, because the differing ages of sex maturity was a minor fact in middle-age adjustments. Some children began sexual activities at a very early age, patterns of sex behavior underwent few changes after adolescence, and mating ages showed a greater differential among better educated people. These statements were to receive wide news coverage, a fact which brought the university almost a frightening amount of publicity. Early in 1947 *Newsweek* said, "For 2,000 years, the belief has persisted that women mature at an earlier age than men. But last week Dr. Alfred C. Kinsey of

Indiana University upset this theory with a scientific report, the first of its kind on an eight year study of sex behavior." The magazine then repeated the age differentials of 16 and 28 between the sexes. In this way the Indiana University administration got a fore-taste of what both the institution and its professor of sex would face when the first volume of the institute's report was published.

Kinsey and his impending report on the sexual behavior of the human male had become highly newsworthy. This moment in fact was one in which the entire society of civilized man was emerging from an age of sexual muteness, if not secrecy, into one in which the subject would become a matter of extremely bold and open conversation. The New American Library published a $.25 paper-book entitled, *About the Kinsey Report: Observations by Eleven Experts on Sexual Behavior in the Human Male*. A 75,000-copy edition was sold in ten days, and the press gloated, "When new records are made, sex will make 'em." President Wells addressed a memorandum to the University's Executive Committee on October 30, 1947, in which he said the publication of the first Kinsey volume was near at hand; there would be eight reports in all. The national magazine and newspaper press would doubtless give the Kinsey material wide publicity. The first book would be published by one of the oldest and most reputable medical houses and it would prove of use to physicians, psychiatrists, social workers, and others of kindred professional interest. The president predicted the book would be controversial, but it was the product of scientific exploration, and "It seems to me it is essential that we stand firm in our support of the book and the research. We are not called upon to endorse the findings, but we are called upon to stand firm in support of the importance of the project and the right to publish it. Any less than that would be fatal. We would lose the respect and the services of our best faculty men and the respect of the scholarly world generally." Wells then expressed the belief that the work would be of fundamental importance and in time would be accepted as such by the public. He reminded the committee that Pasteur's researches had stirred controversy when they were publicized.

A month after President Wells had made his declaration to the Executive Committee, the *Indianapolis Star* revealed how much sensation could be generated by Kinsey's work. The paper said the Indiana University scientist had found that 50 per cent of all married men were unfaithful to their wives; men in the armed services were less active sexually than the civilian male at home, and slightly less than three-fourths of the male population were potent at seventy years of age, and the more education a man had the less apt he was to have premarital experience.

The selection of the publisher for Kinsey's books was undertaken with as much care and foresight as possible. Three top-flight commercial publishers were considered, but Herman B Wells urged Kinsey to seek an established medical publisher. In fact, throughout the early years Wells had tried to keep the scientific-medical aspect of the work in the forefront. Somewhat by fortuitous circumstances Kinsey met Laurence Saunders, president of the prestigious Philadelphia medical publishing house, and publication arrangements were made. When a contract was signed with this house, Helen Dietz, a senior editor, was given the task of working with the obstinate author. The editing of Kinsey's books became something of an epoch in publishing history. He was a determined cocksure man so far as his style and method of presenting his work were concerned, and he turned off editorial suggestions with great assurance.

The Saunders house, accustomed to issuing slow-selling professional books, had counted on selling an edition of 10,000 copies; this figure was arrived at after the report of what the company believed was a sophisticated market survey. Within two months after publication, the volume on male sexual behavior had sold 200,000 copies, and in time it had eleven printings. In Bloomington the campus bookstore sold out its first order on the afternoon of January 5, 1948, the day of publication.

True to Wells' prediction, the book was widely reviewed and commented upon by both the news and magazine presses. Kinsey told Henry Butler of the *Indianapolis Times*, "People have wanted a book of this kind. I think scientists have completely underestimated the public's desire to get a really unemotional, scientific book on sex." The *Army Times*, February 7, 1948, said, "Believe it or not department . . . that best selling . . . and well-nigh impossible to get *Sexual Behavior in the Human Male* by Dr. Alfred S. [*sic*] Kinsey . . . was originally planned as a scientific textbook. In fact, the dignified Philadelphia publishing firm . . . W. B. Saunders Co. . . . is knocked on its scientific heels by the overwhelming demand for the book."

The Associated Press quoted Dr. Fred Grundy, chairman of

the British Hygiene Council, as saying the Kinsey report had, "brought a breath of realism into the subject of sex behavior. . . ." The Boston *Globe*, February 18, 1949, said Dr. George Gallup "has only envy for Dr. Kinsey." The stories favorable and unfavorable broke fast after the publication of the first book. Wardell B. Pomeroy has said in his book *Dr. Kinsey and the Institute for Sex Research* (1972) that Kinsey was badly informed about the editorial ways and techniques of the American press, but at the outset he and his staff could assume a vast outpouring of publicity would greet the appearance of this rather bold study. Despite the fact the book was written in plain scientifically explanatory prose, and in many places was as literally unexciting as a biology text, it received no less attention. The elements of the book that stimulated the greatest amount of discussion were premarital sex, frequency of extramarital relations, homosexuality, and the commentary on out-of-date sex laws. These were subjects enough to provoke intense if not angry controversy.

Kinsey had to confront almost simultaneously several types of news media. There were the newsmen who either attended a news briefing in Bloomington or read advanced galley and page proof and wrote news stories that went through the various stages of newsroom rewritings and cuttings, and many times were further distorted by headline writers. The periodical press was somewhat more analytical, except in the case of the current news journals like *Life*, *Time*, and *Newsweek*. Then there were the monthlies which took a somewhat more extensive view of the book. Especially disturbing to Kinsey and the university officials was the excerpted article which appeared in the *Reader's Digest* for September 1948. This article was by Dr. Harold W. Dodds, president of Princeton University, and a member of the Rockefeller Foundation Committee. He wrote, "So far as my reading has gone, the recent sex survey reports seem to be acclaimed more by literary reviewers than by scientists who question the methodology of the reports and the significance of their findings. Perhaps the undergraduate newspaper that likened the reports to the work of small boys writing dirty words on fences touched off more profound scientific truth than is revealed in the surfeit of rather trivial graphs with which the reports are loaded."

Dr. Kinsey immediately sent the Dodds article to President Wells expressing fear that such caustic comment from so respected a source would result in the cutting off of Rockefeller Foundation support. On January 7, 1949, Kinsey also wrote Dr. George Corner of the Carnegie Institution of Washington and a committee member of the National Research Council, saying loss of Rockefeller support would jeopardize expansion of the sex research program, at a time when several good men were available to serve the project.

Kinsey took none of the royalties from his best selling book, which in its first year yielded $180,000. This money was turned back into the project. Indiana University paid only Kinsey's salary and supplied the institute housing. All other salaries and expenses were paid from Rockefeller funds and from royalties. The first was vital to the long-range work of the institute, which was incorporated April 8, 1947. Kinsey expressed a grim determination to continue the work of his institute, saying, "As I made plain in the early years of the research, before we had any outside support, we will continue this program, and we will expand it as we understand it must expand, irrespective of whether our support comes from one source or another. It will, however, definitely slow us up if we were to have to take too much time out to argue for a continuation of Rockefeller support, or if we have to go after funds from other sources, or if we have to support ourselves by lecture fees or popular writing." Wells suggested going to talk to President Dodds personally about his views toward the sex research project. However, Kinsey phoned the President on January 19, saying it would not be necessary to talk with President Dodds, but gave no explanation for his conclusion.

Kinsey, of course, faced a veritable army of reviewers. Out of all the commentaries, however, the one which perhaps stung deepest was the sixteen-page review-analysis by Lewis Madison Terman of Stanford University. This review appeared in the *Psychological Bulletin*, and was wounding in a highly professional sense. Terman was a native of Johnson County, Indiana, and had graduated from Indiana University in 1902. He and Kinsey had carried on a fairly extensive correspondence prior to 1948, and Terman had expressed himself as anxious to see the first report in print. When *Sexual Behavior in the Human Male* appeared, however, it contained a less than complimentary analysis of Terman's *Psychological Factors in Marital Happiness* (1938). Especially irritating to the famous psychologist were Kinsey's comments on pages 556–57 which strongly implied a high incidence of error in the Terman study. There were other famous critics to be reckoned with, including the Englishman Geoffrey Gorer, Lawrence S. Kubie, Margaret Mead, and Dr. Edmund Bergler.

Moralists spoke up on all sides. Some were ministers in Indiana and elsewhere. Kinsey was accused by some of publicizing sex when it should be left in the privacy of the bedroom. There was criticism of the report's frank discussion of homosexuality, premarital sex, and, perhaps, masturbation. Then there was criticism of the handling of statistics. Characteristic of the moralistic hue and cry was that of Dr. Claude E. Hadden, an Indiana University Medical School graduate. "Now I must sit in my office," he wrote President Wells on May 12, 1949, "and listen to patients sneeringly say, 'Oh, you're from Kinsey's school' when they see my diplomas. Their attitudes are far from complimentary. The impudent snoopery and the brazen exposition of his findings under the pretense of 'scientific research' is repugnant to the point of nauseation." Dr. Hadden said he had held his peace, but now he wanted to know if Wells and the trustees sanctioned such academic freedom. The enraged physician ended his letter with the moralistic peroration, "Next to the privilege of becoming the son of God and an heir to heaven I know of no greater privilege than the pious act of our sex life with which we become co-creators with God." As to Kinsey, the doctor said the Greeks had a word for him—"Mephistopheles." Wells responded with a calming letter explaining that Kinsey was entitled to freedom of investigation and publication while bearing scientific responsibility for his work.

Dr. Herman W. Kaebnick of Somerset, Pennsylvania, told the thirty-seventh general conference of the United Brethren's Commission on Social Action in November 1952, that Dr. Kinsey's report was "a direct challenge to the standards upheld by the Christian Church." The book served only as an additional reminder "of the sinfulness of man." All across the nation ministers, some of whom admitted they had not read the book, preached against it, or against what some newspaper story said it was.

Amidst all the furor of commentary on the Kinsey book, President Wells and his administrative colleagues had to deal with an intra-faculty squabble. Dr. Thurman B. Rice of the Indiana University School of Medicine, sometimes bitterly, if not viciously, attacked the Kinsey project. This feud may have started as early as the years of the marriage course when the two men were lecturers. A flurry of this lingering controversy resulted in the accumulation of a thick folder of letters in the President's office in December 1947. Rice quibbled with Kinsey, complained about all the publicity, and asked the identity of the Indiana township in which Kinsey said he had interviewed the entire populace. He said he wanted the latter information so he could personally check Kinsey's facts. He doubted also that the Quaker Church had endorsed Kinsey's work. Kinsey replied on December 9, 1947, that Rice would find most of the answers to his questions in the forthcoming volume which would appear on January 5, 1948. Then he denied responsibility for newspaper headlines and street corner gossip to which Rice listened. He sent a copy of this letter to Herman Briscoe and Fernandus Payne. Rice revealed a whining petulance to the deans which hardly made him appear an objective scientist. In a letter, December 15, 1947, he said President Wells, just then departing for Europe, had called Dean Van Nuys and himself aside and asked them "not to take after" Kinsey in the public press when his book appeared. "We told him that we would consider the University in everything and that we would not be starting a rumpus. (As a matter of fact that won't be necessary, others will start it.) I did not resign my right to think, to inquire, to object, to write and to speak, however, because that is part of the Bill of Rights guaranteed to me as well as to you." Briscoe and Payne wrote a placating reply to the medical professor saying they hoped the dispute would remain in private, otherwise there was much for the university to lose.

Rice's dispute did get outside the university. Professor Clifford R. Adams of Pennsylvania State University wrote Kinsey, February 20, 1948, that Rice and "certain prominent associates at Indiana University were making plans to demand your resignation on the grounds that you were reporting findings that were not actually justified by your data; that your work is setting back the cause of sex education and decent understanding of morality, and that you are a pernicious influence upon the student body of Indiana University and bring to the institution considerable disrepute." Rice had made a speech on the Pennsylvania campus, and Wardell B. Pomeroy says he told his audience that President Wells was "greatly concerned about Kinsey."

There was stinging criticism in Mrs. A. V. Spears' comment

in the "Public Letter Box" of the Parker, Indiana, paper, September 19, 1949. She felt it was bad enough that novelists wrote lewd literature, "but it was worse when our Indiana University sponsored the investigations such as Dr. Kinsey's and permit his findings to be published." This comment drew a response from Herman B Wells, who told her the research was financed by the Rockefeller Foundation and not by the university. Kinsey personally received no royalties from his books. "There is," he said, "a great difference of opinion concerning the publications by Dr. Kinsey. Research into such areas as were undertaken by this project, of course, must of necessity uncover controversial material. Dr. Kinsey, himself, however, is engaged in making a statistical study of what exists at the present time and carefully refrains from drawing recommendations from the data."

The following May a reader editorial appeared in the *Indianapolis Star*, which expressed the personal viewpoint, "I think the professor at Indiana University who does nothing but write on sex matters should be forced out of our schools. Must our children who attend our state schools be forced to listen to this depravity? Isn't it the Governor's place to see that we have suitable men to teach our university students? Some of us think it is time for a housecleaning among our university officials." Ross Bartley advised Wells to ignore this stricture unless it brought forth a rash of letters.

Reactions to the first study no doubt caught Kinsey and everybody else by surprise. Wisely the university administration prevailed on the scientist to seek a medical publisher, but even they were startled by the report of sales. Laurence Saunders told W. B. Rogers, the Associated Press editor of "Books and Art," that even the professional market survey service had told the company that "Its considered scientific opinion was 'that this best seller would not sell at all.' " Kinsey, however, had predicted a big sale. Wells made the modest statement in his *Annual Report*, 1947–48, "With the publication of the first volume of the Kinsey Report, the significance of at least one of the research programs associated with the University has become known to the public, here and abroad."

The president surely did not know just how widely known this published material would become. Neither the university nor Professor Kinsey counted on the razzle-dazzle of publicity or on the humorists and cartoonists. When Peter Arno published his famous cartoon, "Is There a Mrs. Kinsey?" in the *New Yorker Magazine*, May 1948, reporters scurried off to Bloomington to interview Clara McMillen Kinsey. Henry Butler from the *Indianapolis Times* published an extensive account of the Kinsey's courtship, marriage, and home-life. The June issue of *McCall's Magazine* contained an article about Mrs. Kinsey, Wardell B. Pomeroy, and Clyde M. Martin. President Wells visited Julian Huxley, then director-general of UNESCO, in his Paris office, and the conversation turned to the Kinsey research. Huxley knew Kinsey slightly, but under the influence of Peter Arno, he asked Wells, "Is there a Mrs. Kinsey?"

Not only was Professor Kinsey's volume on male sexuality subjected to intense scrutiny by scientists, but he was adjudged by more esoteric sex experts. The *Cosmopolitan Magazine* asked "a number of weighty Americans to comment on 'this Kinsey business.' " One of these, Mae West, said, "I supposed it would be dangerous to admit that at the best sex is fun." Miss West felt that Kinsey's defenders did not make enough allowance for romance. The daily press reported her as saying she was not surprised at anything in the Kinsey book. She too had made a more or less close study of the human male and agreed with the professor's findings. She had, however, used somewhat different approaches in her study because "I am afraid the only figure I employ is my own." She told Robert Ruark, the columnist, "I had the field licked before Kinsey ever saw it."

It was said erroneously that Kinsey asked Tallulah Bankhead if he might ask her a number of very personal questions. She readily agreed to be interviewed if in turn she could ask Kinsey equally as personal questions; and gossip had it, the Indiana professor departed at once. Martha Raye produced a phonograph record entitled, "Ooh Dr. Kinsey!" which was banned by the big broadcasting companies. Jack Lait, Jr., commented that people always did what they were told they should not do, and Martha Raye's record sold 500,000 copies. Kinsey no doubt stirred up some of this gossipy sex linkage when he went in search of sexual histories among the females of Hollywood in September 1949.

There was almost no end to the incidents and public chatter about the Kinsey report aside from the scientific comment. In Winston-Salem, North Carolina, lawyer Phil Horton was threatened with mayhem at the hands of enraged local women. They thought he had said that 75 per cent of the town's women lacked virtue; that is, the local newspaper said he had made the statement. What he actually said was that Kinsey was quoted as saying 75 per cent of college and high school girls were lacking in virtue. By November 1949 many people must have come to agree with the Bloomington *World-Telephone* reporter who wrote, "Dr. Kinsey will go down in history as the first writer to give a successful nitroglycerin transfusion to a statistic."

Whether the publicity was favorable or critical Kinsey almost overnight became a celebrity. Always he had been a popular lecturer, but now he was a sought-after attraction. In Buffalo, New York, he told an audience that anyone would reveal his sexual history if he were properly approached. He had interviewed all sorts of people in all kinds of places. Later he told the American Veterans' Committee that he wanted especially to take their sex histories, and those of veterans of the last world war. He repeated to the committee his conclusions about the age differentials in maturity between men and women. He felt the recently published volume of *Sexual Behavior in the Human Male* had as much value for women as for men because it could impart knowledge that would promote happier marriages.

Kinsey lectured frequently on the subject of social customs, sex offenses, the laws, and the courts. He told a New York City audience in May 1948 that 95 per cent of all persons brought to the courts for sex offenses had only "departed from customs." No question was raised as to the intrinsic harm they may or may not have rendered society. He commended that city's courts for the manner in which they handled sex offenders. He listed the categories of rape, coercion of older offenders against minors, compulsive exhibitionism, and incest, all four of these crimes would be punished under other laws, even if there were no statutory sex laws. He also listed as preventive laws those against nonmarital intercourse, dispensing information about contraceptives, associating with prostitutes, and campus petting. Kinsey thought these customs had originated three to four thousand years in the past. He told the American Psychopathological Association, June 4, 1948, that he thought social custom was a greater restraint on sexual perversion than were statute laws. Perversion did not harm the person but was regarded as an offense against nature, and

American perversion codes were derived indirectly from the Talmudic Code. The early Christian Church had adopted its sexual philosophy from the Jews, Greeks, and Romans. Because of the fear of statutory punishment the lives of many people "are made a perfect hell." Kinsey no doubt startled even his audiences of professionals when he said statistics established the fact that a great many people did at some time practice homosexuality where laws did not restrain people, "and in some segments of the population the practice runs to 50 to 60 per cent of the people."

In late August Kinsey addressed 500 delegates to the American Prison Association Congress in Boston. Again he discussed sex laws, sex offenders, and the courts, and garnered headlines. He told the congressional delegates that courts were gradually working out procedures. Convictions and prison sentences actually served no constructive purpose. "What happens?" he asked, "most often they are sent to penal institutions where homosexuality is practiced by 60 to 65 per cent of the inmates. Is that a cure?" Anyway 95 per cent of the male population at one time or another broke one or more of the twenty-one sex offense laws. The Boston *Daily Record*, September 1, 1948, said the remarks attributed to Dr. Kinsey were insults to the overwhelming majority of the people who try to lead decent lives. The paper asked in capital letters, "WHERE DOES THIS MAN GET HIS STATISTICS?" The editor thought the professor reached his conclusion of 95 per cent sex violations "by some process known only to himself."

Kinsey's speeches sometimes created almost as much heated criticism as did his books. The president of the university was often called upon to answer some of the complaints which followed published accounts of Kinsey's remarks, especially when alumni wrote him. Dr. Claude E. Hadden of Indianapolis responded to an unfavorable and out-of-context news report of a speech. Wells answered him in the most patient manner describing Kinsey's work. He admonished Dr. Hadden that it was always unsafe to draw conclusions from a press report. "I have myself seen the press with all good intentions completely miss the point of the speaker." Wells disclaimed, as he always did in his answers, that he had any competence in Kinsey's field, and the university had to rely upon the testimony of eminent medical scientists, physicians, clergymen, and social workers. Kinsey's project he told the doctor was not financed by the university.

Kinsey was constantly being called upon for professional advice and to serve as a consultant in areas involving sex laws and sexual behavior. At the same time he was working at his research for the volume on female sexual behavior. One such case was his work with the California legislature which was attempting to revise and modernize that state's sex laws. Kinsey gave a generous amount of time to this undertaking, but in the end the lawmakers lost their courage and enacted a traditional set of laws.

In June 1950 *Esquire Magazine* quoted Dr. Kinsey as saying he was not surprised by either the bitter attacks upon his book or by the flattering demand for it by the public. He had predicted all along that it would sell, maybe not the 300,000 copies it had sold at that date. With booming sales, the scientist's problems trebled. His attorneys Morris Ernst and David Loth wrote an article for *Redbook Magazine*, May 1950, previewing the forthcoming report on *Sexual Behavior in the American Female*. This with the threat of publication in the *Reader's Digest* was to create a great deal of anxiety in Bloomington. Ernst and Loth claimed to have worked closely with Kinsey and his staff, and they published conclusions which they said would appear in the second volume. Kinsey issued a rebuttal statement denying that many of the predictions contained in the article would be borne out in the published book. When *Life Magazine* proposed serialization of the female volume, President Wells telegraphed Kinsey in New York saying that he, Herman Briscoe, and Ross Bartley were skeptical of newspaper and magazine serialization. The three mildly favored a condensed book version for the public, although he and Briscoe actually favored the full text. Briscoe had written Wells earlier that he doubted production of such a book would, in fact, head off other publications.

While Kinsey and the university administration planned the serialization or condensation of the female volume, the scientist was drawn into the McCarthy charges of homosexuality among staff members of the United States Department of State. Representative Wayne N. Aspinall of Colorado had objected to Washington being called a Sodom and Gomorrah. Kinsey was of the opinion, sustained by his data, that the number of cases of homosexuality in the Federal Government offices was no higher than that in American society as a whole.

Kinsey and his colleagues were, after 1948, prime news sources wherever they went or whatever they said. As such they involved the university in constant publicity both favorable and unfavorable. Dr. Kinsey, Wardell B. Pomeroy, and Paul Gebhard went to Oregon State Agricultural College in June 1951, to gather data for a study of animal sexuality and fertility, especially in the area of homosexuality. This also had to do with the preparation of animals for artificial insemination. While the scientists were away from Bloomington on this trip, New England newspapers carried stories of a fake interviewer calling Radcliffe College girls on the telephone and asking them about their private lives. In San Diego, California, Ray Guttman, twenty-two years of age, was arrested for phoning women for interviews about their sexual behavior. A fake interviewer also called women in Washington in the name of the Kinsey Institute. This brought a warning to the public in general from the National Research Council about sex imposters. The Kinsey interviewers talked directly and in person with their interviewees, and never on the telephone.

From 1950 to 1954, the presence of the Institute for Sex Research on the Indiana University campus was a matter of constant challenge to the integrity of the institution. The record is clear that Herman B Wells and his administrative staff were constantly being brought under critical fire. The record is also clear that there was no reluctance to support to the fullest extent possible the researcher in pursuit of objective data. Frank Reid, an alumnus, wrote President Wells that he was disgusted with all the newspaper publicity. He said Kinsey "has dragged the name of Indiana University low enough and it is time to get rid of him." Wells replied that sociologists, anthropologists, and folklorists had long recognized the value of comparative cultures. Kinsey's statistical analysis was objective, and the theme of his work was not new. The largest library in existence on the subject of sex and pornography was in the Vatican in Rome. He said Kinsey's materials were no more obscene than were the illustrations in the old medical standby, *Gray's Anatomy*.

Wells suggested to Claude Rich that it might be wise to have a story about Kinsey's work in the *Alumni Magazine*. He thought the magazine should deal with more controversial matters and give the university's alumni data on which to form more objective attitudes toward social and public issues. Kinsey apparently took umbrage at the idea of a story, and Wells wrote him, April 18,

1951, "I did suggest to the Alumni Association that we have an article which fully covered your work and critical opinion about it. It occurred to me we owed it to our alumni to really give them the facts essential to their understanding of your project so they might defend you and the University when occasion arose. I may say that I was not prompted by any splurge of reaction but by the belief that in public relations the offensive and precautionary measures are the most effective."

Wells answered Governor Henry F. Schricker's enquiry about Kinsey's work by saying he had just attended a meeting of the Board of Stewards of the First Methodist Church, Bloomington. He went into the pastor's study for a visit and saw a copy of the *Sexual Behavior in the Human Male* on the desk. The minister told him the book had been of great assistance to him in counseling with parishoners who had marital and moral problems. He also told the governor great progress had been made in dealing with sex problems because of the frank recognition of their existence. Earlier Episcopal Bishop Karl Morgan Block wrote Kinsey he could wish for nothing better for clergymen of all communions than to confer with Kinsey. Wells attached a copy of Block's letter to his own to the governor. Alex Campbell, university trustee, also appended a note to copies of Wells' correspondence in which he said, "It seems to me that with all the bad publicity we have received, which of course I thoroughly understand, and all the attitudes the Governor, and other similar narrow-minded and uninformed outbursts by certain citizens over the country, including some alumnae—that we should capitalize in a careful and dignified manner the situation, as expressed by Reverend Karl Morgan Block."

So much criticism of Kinsey's work centered about the issue of the adequacy of his sampling, his statistical methods, and his use of graphs. The American Statistical Association sent a special committee to Bloomington to review the Kinsey project in the spring of 1952. This body released a story to the press on June 27, saying that the type of research carried on by the Kinsey team involved so many problems of sampling and measurements for which there were no satisfactory solutions. Nevertheless, the overall impression of the institute's work was favorable. By comparison with other sex study methods Kinsey's was outstanding. The committee listed five aspects in which the work was considered superior to all others, "The interviewing was the best." Adversely, more care should have been exercised in drawing bold conclusions from sample data. The statisticians recommended that the Kinsey group consider use of a probability sampling.

As the publication date of the *Sexual Behavior in the Human Female* approached, the university administration became more alarmed about the publicity and criticism which inevitably would follow. In April 1953 five articles by Robert S. Kloeckner had appeared in the Chicago *Sun-Times* which Ross Bartley thought were "all-in-all" good. On April 16, President Wells wrote Bartley, asking "that you work with Professor Kinsey on the form of his news release announcing his second volume, with particular reference to the medical advisory groups whom Professor Kinsey has drawn on as consultants."

Careful plans were made for a preliminary news briefing and press releases, and on May 15, 1953, Kinsey announced that a news release would be made on August 20, when writers would already have printer's proof. In the meantime some low-key publicity excitement was created by the visit of Christine Jorgensen, the highly publicized transvestite. She came to Bloomington on June 23 under the assumed name of "Miss King," and was met at the local airport by Dr. Kinsey who spent an intensive day, June 24, interviewing her. Then nearing the point of complete exhaustion he entered the Robert W. Long Memorial Hospital for a complete physical check. Christine Jorgensen told newsmen she gave Kinsey a full sexual report "the same as millions [*sic*] of other women have done." She called him a great man, and then created a sensation when she attended a show at the Indiana Theater.

While Kinsey was recovering from exhaustion, and was frantically preparing for the appearance of his second volume, the state budget committee arrived in Bloomington, July 2, with a mandate from Governor George N. Craig to scrutinize Purdue and Indiana universities with reference to professors who did consultative work on the side. Lawrence D. Baker of Kendall was chairman, and he inquired if "Dr. Kinsey teaches or merely heads the birds and bees department?" Repeatedly the university administration had to justify Kinsey's work to state committees, and repeated endlessly that only Kinsey's salary was paid from university funds. Kinsey took the lead in inviting committees to

Blomington to tour his offices and laboratories. He was a gracious host, and was free, up to a point, in answering his guests' questions.

Kinsey used every precaution to prevent either a newspaper scoop of the female volume or piracy of its contents. He allowed Inez Robb of the International News Service to see the proof on July 24, but cautioned her to keep the materials under lock and key. On July 27 Kinsey and his staff held a full day's briefing for newsmen. Eleanor Roehr, Kinsey's secretary, had prepared lunch for the seventeen reporters. Two weeks later Kinsey and his staff left Bloomington for three weeks, with Kinsey announcing "We've given as much time to the press as we intend to do for the time being." However, he said, "the press has been very nice." Kinsey believed the interval of three weeks was sufficient for leveler heads to prevail after the first burst of fury.

There was no doubt in anybody's mind in the responsible university community that there would indeed be generous publicity for the female study—clearly it would exceed that generated by the "male" volume. Already there was a flood of speculative and background articles in late July and early August. Jean Pearson of the Akron, Ohio, *Beacon-Journal*, for instance, ran an extensive background story on August 16. Kinsey and the university administration handled the newsbriefing and release as though a great national explosion was about to take place. The management of the press by Kinsey was indeed a landmark in control of news flow. Precautions were taken to have the contents of wastebaskets burned, institute keys were carefully guarded, janitors in Wylie Hall were placed under surveillance, and other security measures were taken. Those newsmen who were invited to the Sex Institute to read the proofs had to sign a pledge that they would not release their stories until 7:00 A.M., Eastern Standard Time, August 20, 1953. Bill Dyer said in his column, "Roundin' the Square," in the Bloomington *Herald-Telephone* August 19, 1953, "If you hear a roar like thunder at 6:30 A.M. tomorrow, it will probably be the various magazines hitting the local news stands with their articles on the new Kinsey book. We're told many of them long have had the thing printed, and have held up their usual magazine release date in order not to violate the story release date. Some of the magazines have been held by local distribution at least a week. Newspapers, too, are expected to enter the race tomorrow to beat their competition on the street with the story. Kinsey's ironclad release date has been set for August 20, at 6:30 A.M., CST." The town for several weeks had been a busy communications center with journalists coming and going.

The predicted flood of news and magazine stories took place. At home Kinsey and his staff were greeted on August 20 with an editorial in the *Herald-Telephone*, written with a slant reflecting Dr. Thurman Rice's strictures. The paper accused Kinsey of muddying the waters of sex, a subject the editor thought should be discussed only in the privacy of the home. "In fact, if it were not for local pride," he wrote, "we probably would be led to say that this Kinsey report deals too bluntly, and boldly, and too publicly with a subject that for hundreds upon hundreds of years has been confined to the doctor's office, the marriage counselor, the minister and the teacher—to a healthy degree." Despite this obtuse view, the paper boasted there was no doubt about it, August 20, was "K-Day in U.S.A." It said this was a publicity man's dream come true. No matter what controversy the book created, Kinsey had conducted "the most effective and complete [briefing of newsmen] in the history of modern journalism." On the streets of Bloomington the women, said the paper, greeted the news with a yawn, and planned to read about the book when they got around to it. The *Herald-Telephone* expressed the further opinion that frugal Hoosiers would refuse to pay $8.00 to learn about the sexual behavior of women.

Nationally there was an enormous splash with both newspapers and magazines giving major coverage to the Kinsey story. Perhaps few news stories in American social history brought a greater variety of expressions of snap judgments. Reporters and readers alike were quick to express uninhibited opinions. There was sharp contrast between what the *Chicago Tribune* and the *New York Herald-Tribune* had to say on August 21. The New York paper commented editorially, "The conclusions of a scientific work painstakingly and disinterestedly carried out deserves to be presented in a like spirit to the public. . . . Kinsey and his associates, whatever else they have done, have not shown moral standards are unnecessary or that the happy individual is one who responds to every lust and vagrant desire. . . . The scientist has done his part; from here on the moralist, the philosopher, and the religious leader must take over and do theirs." Conversely, the

Chicago Tribune said, "The report should not be taken too seriously as the methods used in collecting the data have been questioned and findings do not represent action of all women. Nor will the results alter our sexual behavior in the future."

The university administration and Dr. Kinsey had been correct concerning publicity of the female volume. Some newspapers on August 21 carried eight-column headlines, and used the story on front pages. The *Chicago American* devoted two full inside pages to the report. Equally as noticeable, however, was the fact the *Philadelphia Bulletin*, the *New York Times*, the *Christian Science Monitor*, the *San Francisco News*, the *Arkansas Daily Traveler*, and the *Oakland Tribune* carried no stories about the book. Editorials in some of these papers said they regarded Kinsey's books as being too much of a professional nature to be caried in family-type newspapers, and inadequate stories would only confuse readers. *Time Magazine* said the newspapers, which had failed to carry stories of the Kinsey book on the grounds that it was an offense to womanhood and the news was unfit for their readers, had committed a remarkable act of modern journalism. "This seems to us," said the Luce publication, "one of the most remarkable developments in modern American journalism. None of the censorious editors contended that Dr. Kinsey had faked his findings; some simply decreed that what he found about women was an affront to American womanhood, presumably because it might be true; others said they just didn't believe their readers could bear to face the facts." *Time* chided the editors, asking how many of them who had killed the Kinsey story had made speeches "proclaiming that the public has a right to know the truth and the full truth about everything. About everything, that is, except the facts of life."

Stories, rumors, some lewd humor, and gossip all sprang up overnight. The Kinsey myth grew like springtime Hoosier mushrooms. Reporters rushed to Hollywood to quiz movie and entertainment personalities about their reactions, and to seek their "scientific" opinions based upon what reporters implied was extensive practical research. Anne Baxter said, "I place my faith in the 80-odd million women who were not contacted." Sophie Tucker commented, "This is what I call a mark of progress." Gypsy Rose Lee was ready with a quote. "Sex and statistics don't mix," she told reporters, "I doubt whether I will read the book.

Statistics on sex bore me." Zsa Zsa Gabor commented that she was among Dr. Kinsey's 50 per cent of women who slept nude, but "the whole thing is too scientific."

In a much sterner vein Judge John L. Niblack of the Indianapolis Superior Court was quoted by the *Indianapolis News*, August 20, 1953, as saying Kinsey was guilty of "wasting the funds of my dear old Alma Mater. What Indiana University really needs so badly are some stalwart halfbacks to furnish good, clean mayhem on fall Saturdays." Thus the public chatter went on. Persons who had not seen the book, and who were never to read it were quick to render cocksure opinions on its contents. Women who called the *Indianapolis News*, with a single exception, were indignant about the Kinsey book, but those who were called by the *News* from random directory selection, with a single mild exception, expressed approval of the study. Only one man called to protest.

Alfred C. Kinsey was not noted for his jolly sense of humor, and certainly not so where his research was concerned. He no doubt was irritated almost as much by the frivolity that greeted his books as by the sniping criticism. The *New York Journal*, October 18, 1953, described a woman, looking at newsstands where Kinsey was emblazoned on every magazine cover save one, who remarked, "I wonder what angle *Popular Mechanics* will use." Danny's Hideaway in New York offered a Kinsey cocktail composed of two thirds Forbidden Fruit, one third Kinsey gin, and a dash of Strega brandy or Italian Witch. Jim O'Connor, the columnist said, "Stir well, sip slowly. But don't go around asking questions." Abner Silver, a popular song writer, composed *Puleeze, Mr. Kinsey!* which was also banned by the major radio networks. Nearer home, the *Indianapolis Star*, in a corny quip, suggested the two books be boxed together with one entitled "Dr. Kinsey's Misterpiece, and Mistress Piece."

The rest of Kinsey's life was spent in a swirl of publicity of every imaginable sort. As a serious-minded scientist in search of the truth, he appeared to think that every other compartment of professional life shared his zeal. He approached the press with the same self-assurance that characterized his research procedures and management of his laboratories. He was less experienced in this area in 1948 than in 1953 when he carried out intensive press briefings on the eve of the appearance of his second report. This time he understood something of the routine of reporting and newspaper publication, and certainly he had developed a sense of timing. Perhaps his summer briefings in 1953 were some of the most thoroughly managed news releases in the history of social and scientific reporting. Kinsey carried his will to manage news reporting over to coverage of his speeches. In October 1953 he spoke to a meeting of the Central Neuropsychiatric Association in the Claypool Hotel, and he demanded that reporters covering the meeting sign an agreement that they would show him their stories so he could correct factual errors. The psychiatrists had agreed to this condition before Kinsey agreed to speak to them. The *Indianapolis News*, October 13, 1953, said it had signed such an agreement prior to publication of the *Sexual Behavior in the Human Female*, but this time it was balking. "They figure the professor has gone far enough with this gimmick," said a news story, "next thing politicians will be asking to see stories on their doings before the readers see 'em."

This attempt to restrict reporters caused a bit of a furor, and the Indianapolis papers refused to abide by any restrictive agreement. Kinsey replied that he only wanted to protect the public from error. He said he had used his forty-word contract with reporters when he spoke to other scientific audiences, especially the parole officers in San Diego, California. This dispute obviously caught Kinsey by surprise. He and the university attempted partially to placate newsmen by taking Associated Press reporters through the Sex Institute's laboratories. The reporters were properly impressed "by the matter of fact way records were made and kept," and by filing arrangements and the library.

While reporters tramped through the laboratories in Bloomington, Kinsey apparently had a change of heart about the neuropsychiatric speech and agreed it could be opened freely to newsmen. The *Indianapolis News*, October 19, 1953, said he changed his announced subject of "Critical Points in Female Sexual Behavior" to "Concepts of Normality and Abnormality." If columnist Henry Butler spoke in any way for his paper, the *News* itself had a change of heart. Butler congratulated Professor Kinsey on his efficiency in handling the press prior to August 20, and publication of the second report.

Dr. Kinsey's existence after the publication of the female volume, September 14, 1953, was never dull. In October, and less than two months after the appearance of the second book, the United States Army in Europe banned the female volume from its libraries. The European headquarters in Heidelberg gave the unofficial reason that the Army "does not intend to spend money for that kind of book." A more pious reason was proffered, "The book is not thought to be of general interest to G.I.'s." Somehow these vapid censors overlooked the fact that post exchange newstands were crammed with magazines containing stories about Kinsey and his studies.

The Indiana scientist struck back at his critics, especially those who accused him of trying to change social policy. He told alumni of the Indiana School of Law on December 5, 1953, "You are mistaken if you think we went out to reach any solutions." Again, he repeated, "Despite what some people have said we said, the Kinsey group holds that sex is not necessarily the most important factor in the maintenance of a marriage."

By January 1954 the second volume had sold 210,000 copies, and by then the debate was in full swing as to the importance of the publications. A jury of fifteen editors appointed by the American Society of Editors said the announcement of the second volume's publication was the "most overplayed" story of the past year. The *New York Post*, January 10, 1954, disagreed, and so did Earl Ubell, science editor of the *New York Herald-Tribune*, who nominated it first in the "ten best scientific accomplishments of 1953."

Alfred C. Kinsey, an active taxonomist, was at heart a collector—of gall wasps, classical records, sex histories, a splendid scientific library, and all sorts of pornographic art objects and books. These latter materials he considered to be of historical and scientific significance in sex research. Despite the fact Kinsey had established a reputation as a collector, in this instance he had a second motive. Critics of his work had complained his material was too statistical. In the vast collection of erotica was to be found the subjective aspect of man's sex habits and mores, a substantiation of the statistical or objective image. If Kinsey ever had an erotic impulse, he kept it well concealed from the record. His collection of erotica came from all sorts of places around the world, but principally from correspondents in England, France, China, and Germany. In November 1950 U.S. Customs collector Alden H. Baker in Indianapolis bundled up two shipments of what he told the Bloomington *Herald-Telephone*, November 17, 1950, was "damned dirty stuff" consisting of pictures, statuary, and printed matter and refused to deliver them to the Institute for Sex Research. He ruled "there was nothing scientific about it." Some of this material was sent to Washington where customs officials declared the pictures too vulgar to go through the mails. Apparently other shipments were seized in New York in 1951 and 1952. These actions were justified under the tariff act of 1930. W. R. Johnson of the Washington office said the Kinsey materials had little intrinsic value, and the Revenue Code strictly "banned lewd, immoral or obscene material of any kind." To test this ruling further Indiana University made selections from the materials and returned them to England, so they could be reshipped to the United States.

Kinsey immediately prepared a press release in 1950 in which he declared his interest in the disputed materials to be purely scientific. He pointed out the vagueness of the revenue act and referred to exceptions to the law which had been made in connection with other artistic and scientific materials. He was able to cite precedential court and Customs Service decisions in this area, and the institute regarded its case as being broader than the condemnation of a single shipment of materials.

Kinsey told a Bloomington *Star-Courier* reporter, December 8, 1950, that the federal laws regulating admission of obscene materials were so narrow that some of the world's great masterpieces could not enter the country. He cited specifically the paintings of Michelangelo which hang in the Sistine Chapel of the Vatican. In light of the narrow interpretations of the Customs Service, the *Indianapolis Star* reported three years later, July 26, 1953, that the Indiana professor was supposed "to have tucked away in England a collection of sex research materials so juicy that it makes his last controversial collection of pictures look like 19th century parlor prints in comparison." These, it was said, were being held until a court ruling could be had on the shipments held in escrow by the customs officials.

Alfred Kinsey sent President Herman B Wells on December 13, 1950, a copy of the statement that the institute staff had prepared for the defense lawyers. It cited six scientific justifications for releasing the materials. He told the president that by that date the customs officials had actually released about 80 per cent of the impounded shipments, but he believed the university should secure a much broader ruling for future admissions. Kinsey was far too optimistic. His case dragged on for several years, even after his death, before it was finally settled. It was difficult to determine precisely what had stirred this moralistic wrath on the part of the customs officials, but perhaps it was the great amount of controversy over the *Sexual Behavior in the Human Male*, and the discussion of the forthcoming female volume. It may have been true that someone in Indianapolis had stimulated this action; at any rate it had a remarkable taint of prejudice. Actually it was discovered that Alden Baker of the Indianapolis customs office opened some of the Kinsey packages at the instigation of the Archbishop of Fort Wayne. It was said that he also supplied material to Governor Henry F. Schricker about the contents of the packages. This latter fact caused Dr. Merrill Davis, a university trustee, to purchase a standard volume of the world's great art masterpieces in order to give the governor a short course in art and the presentation of the human form in what from early times civilization has accepted as artistic forms of expression.

In October 1954 an announcement was made that a customs court would finally sit in Indianapolis for trial of the Kinsey shipments, and especially of the moving picture films. This meant a quasi-public showing of the materials to which Kinsey objected, saying the customs men were acting beyond their legal power. The university was represented by the distinguished Indianapolis firm of Barnes, Hubert, Hickam, and Pantzer. This firm had intimate connections with the university, Willis Hickam having served as president of the Board of Trustees, and it rendered its services at actual cost. The institute employed Harriet F. Pilpel of the New York firm of Greenbaum, Wolfe, and Ernst to represent it. In December 1955 she argued with Charles R. McNeill, assistant general counsel for the Treasury Department, that if the pornographic materials were to serve scientific purposes, then the department's actions in the Kinsey case "constituted a serious challenge to academic freedom and freedom of inquiry and one which cannot be allowed to pass unchallenged. . . ."

A year later the Treasury Department released some more selected materials, but Indiana University opposed this gesture, friendly though it may have appeared. In a letter to Governor George N. Craig on the subject, President Wells said, "I might add though the Department's attitude seems to be friendly and co-operative, that doesn't settle the case. The suit, of course, cost the Kinsey Institute a lot of money and could bring another wave of difficult publicity so we would like to avoid it if possible. . . ." Wells asked Governor Craig's assistance, which the Governor gave in a letter to George M. Humphrey, Dwight D. Eisenhower's Secretary of the Treasury. The Governor explained the purposes of the Kinsey research and asked that Humphrey attempt to get the issue terminated as quickly as possible. Daniel W. Kendall, Assistant Secretary of the Treasury, replied that materials coming under the heading of "classics" had at the discretion of the Secretary been released, and the other materials would have to await judicial decision. He said the Department of the Treasury then sought such guidance.

In the face of this ruling I.U. alumnus Douglas Whitlock, a Washington attorney, suggested that Indiana University seek institutional release of the materials. Wells believed the Board of Trustees would approve the idea, and he agreed that it would be hard for one branch of government to deny the request of another. A month later Wells wrote Harriet Pilpel an inquiry about the ultimate disposition of the Kinsey materials. He explained that under the articles of incorporation of the Institute for Sex Research these ultimately would go to the Rockefeller Foundation, or to an educational institution of repute and with a research facility which could make them available "to duly qualified students. . . ." Kinsey himself made clear the fact he did not favor the Library of Congress depository.

The Treasury Department proved unyielding, and on June 4, 1956, Harriet Pilpel informed President Wells that there seemed to be no other choice than to file libel proceedings as quickly as possible against the Government with the university acting as amicus curiae. She told the President that she wished to discuss the whole Kinsey issue with him when he came to Washington. A month later the Treasury Department spokesman, Assistant U.S. Attorney Alfred P. O'Hara, asked permission to destroy "photographs, paintings, statues, and books seized several years ago on their way to Dr. Alfred C. Kinsey at Indiana University." These materials were described by the government as obscene and immoral. The libel action that followed, said George Henley, the institute's Bloomington attorney, was filed at the university's request.

In affidavits filed on November 8, 1956, in the U.S. District Court, Southern District of New York, both Indiana University and Mrs. Alfred C. Kinsey contended the customs seizure was a deprivation of liberty and property without due process of law and in violation of the Fifth Amendment to the Constitution. The Institute for Sex Research made the additional contention that the actions of the customs service had deprived it of the right to free inquiry as guaranteed in the Ninth and Tenth Amendments. Assistant United States Attorney Benjamin T. Richards, Jr., undertook to confront this argument with the contention that the issue rested on whether or not scholars should have access to obscene materials denied to the general public, whatever the motive for studying the materials. Mrs. Pilpel maintained that the bigger issue of academic freedom was involved in the outcome of the case. Judge Edmund L. Palmieri replied to Richards that he gathered from the government's contention "that there is no such thing as obscenity in scientific research?" This action gave the university an opportunity to say for the court record that the materials in question were collected for scientific purposes. Repeatedly, Indiana University officials and the attorneys said that the Kinsey collection of pornography was second best only to that in the Vatican Library.

The federal case dragged on until July 15, 1957, when Judge Palmieri heard concluding arguments. In their presentation the government attorneys made such strong contentions of obscenity and immorality that Harriet Pilpel told reporters, "If the Government had taken the stand years ago that it is taking now, the Kinsey reports on sex behavior never could have been written."

The Associated Press reported November 4, 1957, that Judge Palmieri in a twenty-seven-page decision declared the statutes imposing a general ban on pornography did not apply in the collection of such materials for "a bona fide educational research institution for study by scholars." This decision was not only a victory for Indiana University and the Institute for Sex Research, but it was a landmark in the freedom of collecting basic research materials and the right to free access and use. Had the decision gone against the university and the institute, irreparable damage might have been done. No doubt they would have become defenseless targets for every bigoted critic in the land. It is significant, however, that not a single art gallery or library entered the Indiana suit as amicus curiae, yet many of them had suffered from the censorious acts of the United States Customs Service.

Already in this age of rampant McCarthyism the university

and the institute were being fired upon from another quarter. While customs officials were acting as protectors of public morals, the United States Congress itself offered a possible threat. Early in 1954 there was established under Resolution 217 a five-man committee charged with the responsibility of investigating the 38,000 organizations that enjoyed tax-exempt status. Particular interest centered upon those 6,000 that were designated "foundations." B. Carroll Reece, an East Tennessee Republican of rigid conservative if not reactionary views, was made chairman. Representative Reece's statesmanship perhaps rated no higher than the lintels of a back door to a rural courthouse. He told a New York *Journal-American* reporter that the committee might ask Dr. Kinsey to appear before it because the Institute for Sex Research had received funds from the Rockefeller Foundation. A story which appeared in the papers of the Scripps-Howard chain said the proposed investigation of the Kinsey Institute was prompted by letters to Congressmen asking that a check be made of the Indiana University project.

On the Indiana campus the *Daily Student*, January 7, 1954, stoutly defended the work of the Kinsey project. All the Reece committee needed to do, said the paper, was to examine the state auditor's report; all of the sources of funds for the institute were given there in detail. The Reece committee roiled the waters of academia and of the major foundations for all of 1954. Its final report was made in late December and was received with editorial shouts of condemnation and derision. A sample was the devastating attack made upon it by the *New York Post*, December 20, 1954. The paper said the Reece outpouring embodied "all the accumulated ignorance of American know-nothingism." The editor thought it read like the uncollected works of Westbrook Pegler. It was fundamentally a diatribe against the Carnegie and Rockefeller foundations, and The Ford Fund for the Republic. He said that B. Carroll Reece and his Republican colleagues engaged themselves in assaulting American public intelligence. "There is little pretense in the report," said the editor, "of dealing with anything that might legitimately be described as subversion. To Reece and his Republican associates, any idea unlisted in William McKinley's campaign program is heresy. They view sympathy for the United Nations as a clear symptom of un-Americanism; tolerance for Dr. Kinsey is equally beyond their comprehension."

The *Post* called the report a "manifesto of neanderthals." The two Democratic committee members, Gracie Pfost of Idaho and Wayne L. Hays of Ohio, termed Reece's outpourings "a stain on the House." Reece himself possibly should be awarded the snug niche in history of being the man who convinced most Congressmen that congressional investigation of this era had gotten out of hand.

From the outset there was sharp disagreement inside the Reece Committee as to its purpose. Rene A. Wormser, committee counsel, declared it was not to investigate sex, but almost at the outset Dr. Kinsey's name was injected into the hearing, which caused Wayne L. Hays to say sex had been dragged in by the back door. When Gracie Pfost questioned the relevance of mentioning Kinsey at all, Reece responded, "What disturbs me is why the foundations whose funds are made available by the people and by the government in foregoing taxes should be making grants for studies of this nature."

The committee heard the testimony of an assistant professor of sociology, Dr. A. H. Hobbs of the University of Pennsylvania, who said he had written several critiques of Kinsey's work. Professor Hobbs was of the learned opinion the books had wide influence and "were thought to be scientifically true." The Associated Press said Hobbs thought a reader might get the idea that homosexuality "is normal and right." He questioned the true science of Kinsey's work, and told the committee the foundations had backed projects harmful to the country. To show his objectivity he attacked Stuart Chase with the same wisdom.

Clearly some of the Reece inquisitors relished headlines and went far out from shore to seek them. They detected subversion not only in Dr. Kinsey's books but cited the Papal Encyclicals of 1891 and 1931 as possibly subversive. Wayne L. Hays constantly created commotion in the committee, but especially so when he suggested H. L. Hunt's Facts Forum should be investigated. The Ohio congressman was relentless in questioning witnesses, and he and Clark Clifford sawed off a host of slender political limbs, and in the end left the foundations still "poised at the Nation's jugular all summer."

It may be that the Reece report was one of the most bizarre official documents ever produced in the House of Representatives. This was indeed the final degeneracy of the era of McCarthy madness. No doubt some members of the Reece committee were stimulated, as was the chairman himself, by all the furor stirred up by Edmund Bergler and William S. Kroger's book *Kinsey's Myth of Female Sexuality* (1954). Bergler, a psychologist, and Kroger, a gynecologist, branded the Kinsey reports as "combinations of medical misinformation and psychological ignorance that ignores the element of tender human love."

All of this may have been madness, but it proved costly to the Institute for Sex Research. The grants committee of the National Research Council recommended in 1954 a grant of $50,000, but this was turned down by the Rockefeller Foundation Board in February after the great newspaper furor announcing the creation of the Reece Committee to investigate the tax-exempt foundations. It appeared that Dean Rusk was worried about the impending investigations, and especially about the incipient protest going on among conservative ministers and intellectuals, some of whom had no doubt inspired the creation of the congressional committee. Ironically, Robert Morrison of the Rockefeller staff told Chancellor Herman B Wells years later that the Kinsey research was one of the most important projects it had financed in its first fifty years.

By the time Kinsey met the Reece Committee head on he was at least knowledgable of the mores of congressmen. Earlier he was threatened with a slight difficulty by Congressman Louis B. Heller, a Brooklyn Democrat. This statesman asked Postmaster General Arthur Summerfield to ban the Kinsey books from the mails on the grounds they were "highly questionable, if not downright ridiculous." He charged Kinsey with representing "the bulk of American womanhood of having sinned before or after marriage." The *New York Post*, September 2, 1953, said, "Heller, who describes himself as a foe of censorship and a defender of 'freedom to read,' has concluded from not reading the book that, until a congressional committee investigates Dr. Kinsey's investigations, no one else should either." Heller was also quoted as saying "the 6,000 women interviewed by Kinsey and his associates were 'frustrated, neurotic outcasts of society.' "

This mad-hare stricture brought a cutting response from the New York Civil Liberties Union. "We are disturbed," wrote George E. Rundquist, executive director, "that not only did you urge a position condoning censorship, but went further and asked that a not yet published book [*sic*] be barred from the mails, precluding, theoretically, the possibility of any fair hearing into the alleged obscenity of the book."

For Indiana University and the Institute for Sex Research there was always the threat of devastating controversy with the church groups, especially with the Catholic Church. The *Indianapolis News*, October 20, 1953, quoted Archbishop Schulte of that city as saying "Every self-respecting Hoosier must profoundly regret the notoriety Dr. Kinsey has brought to our renowned University. There can be no valid objection to a scientific investigation of sexual behavior . . . but Dr. Kinsey has degraded science. Instead of circulating his findings among those competent to weigh their worth and apply them to the betterment of mankind, he publicizes them like a cheap charlatan and in most unscientific fashion makes them availabe to the young, the unlearned, the mentally deficient—to their great harm and the endangering of society." Obviously Archbishop Schulte had not read the Kinsey books or he would not have assumed the unlearned and mentally deficient could be misled by them.

The Archbishop's criticism was robust and seemed to be based in areas of morality and social reform, neither of which Kinsey espoused. At the same time the weekly *Indiana Catholic and Record* said Kinsey's work was "exploded on the public in totally unscientific form, it can become a moral hell-bomb!" The editor said Protestants marveled at the Catholic confessional, but after Kinsey Catholics marveled at the soul-baring that made his books possible.

President Wells was drawn into the controversy from several sides. On November 2, 1953, he wrote Mrs. William H. Louden of Indianapolis that he had already addressed a letter to the Knights of Columbus answering their objections, and in reply to her questions he had before him the book, *Twenty-Five Years of Sex Research: History of the National Research Council Committee for Research in the Problems of Sex, 1922–1947*. He offered to send her the book so she might gain some notion of the widespread attention the subject of sex was receiving. "The interest of men at Indiana University," he told Mrs. Louden, "is therefore not unique."

The *Indiana Catholic and Record* continued its attack upon Kinsey. The paper said neither Wells nor Kinsey was a communist, "but if you pressed us real hard we couldn't for sure tell you in what major aspect the Kinsey view of human nature and human morality differs from those of the communist." Kinsey, said the periodical, was trying to derive a new sex code from man's animal nature, and he rejected conscience and the law of God.

Wells immediately informed the Indiana University Board of Trustees of the Catholic attack, and at the same time referred to a sermon preached by Dr. Jean S. Milner, a Presbyterian minister of Indianapolis on the Kinsey books. The sermon was reported in an *Indianapolis Times* editorial. Neither Dr. Wells nor Professor Kinsey, said the minister, would like to follow naturalism to a brutal conclusion, "But we are suggesting that it is hardly fair to get so mad at communism, while being so complacent with those who pave the way for people to believe in communism and to act like communists." It seems rather clear from his attack that the Catholic editor had not read the books, and the Presbyterian said he had not and did not intend to do so.

The association of Kinsey's research with even a suggestion of communism brought an instant reply from President Wells. He answered both the Catholic editor and Dr. Milner on their charges. In a stout news release, February 17, 1954, he said there was a marked difference between America and Communist Russia in the field of freedom of investigation. The human race he said had been able to make some slow and painful progress because individuals had been left free to investigate all aspects of human life. Indiana University with its age-old policy neither approved nor disapproved the research findings of its faculty members. The verdict of validity was left to responsible professional workers in the same field. "To deny this right," he said, "is to deny one of the ways by which the human race attempts to reach the goals established for us by our divine Creator."

Less truculent was the tone of an editorial in the *Voice of St. Jude*, February 1954. The editor thought Catholic parents could react against the Kinsey Report by doing an adequate job of sex education on their own. He felt the Kinsey books had great potentials for good if they did no more than alert Americans to their moral decline.

A much stronger criticism was made of Kinsey, Wells, and Indiana University by the National Council of Catholic Women.

Their stricture indeed stung the university's administration. They asked, "Will our sons and daughters be exposed to the ideas of Dr. Kinsey? Dare we risk placing them in the charge of a university that seems willing to degrade science for the sake of sensational publicity? . . . We have not of course read his latest book."

President Wells on September 4, 1953, addressed letters to Mrs. Harold D. Brady, Anderson, Indiana, provincial director of the National Council of Catholic Women, and to Mrs. Alfred C. Brown, Brookville, president of the Indianapolis Archdiocese of the Council of Catholic Women. These were in response to the above charges, but also to a peremptory demand that the president clarify his own stand on the Kinsey sex research. His reply was a truly eloquent defense of freedom of investigation. With the backing of the Board of Trustees, he told the women Indiana University graduates compared favorably with those of all other institutions of higher learning in morals, ideals, highmindedness, and personal integrity. The university would defend itself in these areas against all attacks. He repeated the fact the institution neither approved nor disapproved of research findings, popular or unpopular as they might be. Teaching and the constant search for truth by research and investigation were the true functions of all universities.

Certainly no one, not even the angry Council of Catholic Women, was left in the dark as to the President's and Board of Trustees' stand when on August 21, they declared, "The University believes that the human race has been able to make progress because individuals have been free to investigate all aspects of life. It further believes that only through scientific knowledge so gained can we find the cures for the emotional and social maladies of our society." Further, Wells and the trustees said, they were proud to join the National Research Council and others in the support of the Kinsey project. As a final lick, Wells said, "I agree in saying we have large faith in the values of knowledge, little faith in ignorance."

In all the furor over the Kinsey books it became clear that the Catholic editors had either misread or more likely had not read Kinsey's books. Certainly they misinterpreted them, and completely missed the role of research in the free American university. Had their implied authoritarian control of the scholar prevailed no freedom of investigation would have been possible. The Indiana University chapter of the American Association of University Professors responded to the criticism in a heartening resolution on April 12, 1954. The resolution outlined the threats of the Catholic attacks, and commended President Wells for his "forthright defense of the scholar's right to do research regardless of the unpopularity of his conclusions." Further support appeared in Tracy M. Sonneborn's annual report for 1953–54. This distinguished geneticist commented, "As in the past, I continue to appreciate to the full the excellent qualities of the University Administration and leadership. An outstanding example of this was President Wells' statement in reply to certain attacks made on the work of Kinsey and his group." Wells had the foresight to understand that if Indiana University failed to confront the bigots, the university might as well disclaim all pretensions to being a free institution. It was clear from the outset that President Wells and his colleagues did not mean to lose this fight.

During the decade, 1945–55, Alfred C. Kinsey and his colleagues had set a furious pace for themselves. Gathering case histories, making special institutional investigations, acting as consultants, and, in Kinsey's case, speaking on numerous occasions, drained away an irreplaceable amount of physical and emotional energy. None of these, however, could have been more enervating than the emotional strains created by the publicity and criticism following the publication of each of the first two reports. For Indiana University officials there had also been considerable strain. It is not without significance that they referred to the criticism and publicity as "bitter," "disturbing," "threatening," and "fatal." Almost in any year after 1948 the institution could have been seriously crippled by the public and legislators.

Kinsey's fervor for gathering a case history file of a hundred thousand individuals drove him on. The two intervening years after 1953 were filled with this and other activities. In the autumn of 1955 Professor and Mrs. Kinsey visited Europe, somewhat on a "busman's holiday." Especially interesting were Kinsey's conversations with a professor in the medical school in Copenhagen who had collected an impressive amount of material on the homosexuality of Hans Christian Anderson. The Kinseys visited Sweden, Norway, England, France, Italy, and Spain. In all these countries the scientist had found readily available materials to serve his interests. The European journey was both a pleasure and an eyeopener as to the possibility of sex study in a much broader field. Kinsey was now able to establish comparative patterns of international society with greater certainty.

Upon his return to Bloomington, Kinsey resumed his exhausting pace. The critics were still unsettling if not obnoxious; there were more speeches and more consultations with state governing authorities and those of penal institutions. Before him were plans to prepare for publication at least eighteen more volumes in the sex and related fields. With this burdensome challenge Kinsey could have taken little real satisfaction in his accomplishments. In addition, the Institute for Sex Research faced financial problems. Royalties from the two published books had dropped from $209,079.64 in 1954 to $3,001.27 in 1955. The *Indianapolis News*, February 3, 1956, said the institute reported to the Indiana Secretary of State that it had to withdraw $74,000 from its reserves to finance its past year of operation. In all, the two books had earned $541,073.62 since 1948. In 1956 the institute had a cash backlog of $172,738.14.

On the campus the institute, in November 1955, moved its offices and laboratories from the basement of Wylie Hall to the third floor of the new biological center, Jordan Hall. On this occasion Dr. Kinsey conducted a tour for faculty, students, and townspeople through his private world of sex. He unlocked a safe and showed the visitors a case history in code. He said that when he, Pomeroy, Martin, and Gebhard traveled they did so separately so in case of a fatal accident someone would be left who knew the Kinsey code. The visitors were shown the office in which Dorothy Collins kept track of newspaper and periodical clippings, and performed duties as statistician. Especially impressive was the collection of primitive Peruvian pottery with its sexual symbols and information. The large library was also of a high degree of interest, especially after so much publicity about the refusal of customs officials to release certain materials. Kinsey announced publicly on March 17, 1956, that he planned to write a book on the sexual practices of the ancient Peruvians.

The *New York Times*, April 17, 1956, contained an article by Delmore Schwartz entitled "Survey of our National Phenomenon" in which Alfred Kinsey was labeled "an old-fashioned liberal." The author thought the qualities of compassion, sympathy, and tolerance showed through in his published books and in his speeches, but he revealed these human traits even more in discussing his aims while conducting his labortary tours. Schwartz compared Kinsey to the popular wartime news commentator Elmer Davis, also a Hoosier: "The tone, like Mr. Davis, is that of an old-fashioned liberal, and the motives of compassion and sympathy are as unquestionable as the chief social aim of his work—to provide a scientific basis for a greater degree of tolerance—an aim which is as characteristically American as our faith in facts and figures and the belief statistics don't lie."

Already by the time of the move to Jordan Hall Kinsey was a sick and exhausted man. He was worried about financing the institute, and had been unable to get money from one or two promising sources. This despite the words of one critic that his greatest accomplishment was that of securing money. He had automatically rejected federal funds, largely because he did not wish to surrender any degree of control over his research and publication plans. Kinsey ignored his physician's plea to slow down, and on August 25, 1956, he was dead at the age of sixty-two. In his death he left a personality void, and a mountain of raw data, enough it was said to document a small library of books in the behavioral sciences.

In November the Board of Trustees appointed Paul H. Gebhard, associate professor of anthropology, director of the Institute for Sex Research, and Wardell B. Pomeroy was made director of field research. Cornelia Vos Christenson, Theodore Torrey, head of the Department of Zoology, and Clara McMillen Kinsey were made trustees of the institute. Gebhard, an anthropologist, had joined the Kinsey staff in 1946, and almost immediately after he had completed work for the doctorate under the direction of Clyde Kluckhohn at Harvard. John F. Sembower said in his column in the Indianapolis *Eastern Sun*, November 8, 1956, that the appointment came as "a tribute to his executive ability and also as mute testimony that the backers of Dr. Kinsey's work are somewhat worried over the financial future." This was a transitional moment in the history of the Kinsey project. Eleanor L. Roehr, long-time secretary, resigned to become an executive officer in the university's public administration program in Thailand. Later Clyde Martin and Wardell Pomeroy left the institute.

Gebhard told an *Indianapolis News* reporter, December 12,

1956, that Kinsey had left behind enough research data to document two score books. He promised to carry on the institute's program without making radical departures from the Kinsey plan. "The next few years," he told the *News*, "will be devoted to analyzing and publishing data already collected. We've reached the stage where we can sit back, analyze, and digest." At that time there were eleven members of the staff to sit back and analyze.

Herman B Wells wrote Bernard Berelson, director of the Behaviorial Sciences of the Ford Foundation, March 6, 1957, that Indiana University expected to continue to support the work of the institute in the future. He stressed the need for financial assistance to carry on the work. The Federal Government gave vital assistance in April that year when the Public Health Service granted the institute $151,693 to make a study of sex offenders by analyzing approximately 2,000 sex histories of convicted persons, which were already in the institute's files. In September 1957 Gebhard announced that the third institute study, "Pregnancy, Birth, and Abortion," would be published early in 1958 by Harper and Brothers under the co-authorship of Gebhard, Pomeroy, Martin, and Christenson. *McCall's Magazine* bought two paraphrased installments of the forthcoming book to be published in its March and April issues.

In time new staff members were employed in the institute to replace Kinsey, Martin, Pomeroy, and Roehr. The institute broadened its fields of investigation and publication. By 1958 the institute's future seemed assured, even though a reporter asked newly appointed Indiana University President, Elvis J. Stahr, Jr., on May 5, 1962, what he expected to do with the Institute for Sex Research.

In historical perspective two side results of the Kinsey studies were significant. There can hardly be any doubt that the two earlier volumes lifted the veil on sex both as a scientific and social topic of primary interest, and engendered an openness of discussion of the fundamentally important procreative drive of the human animal. For the first time in the history of civilization this became a fact. This was eloquently documented by newspaper and periodical presses, by numerous lateral studies, and by an unestimated amount of public discussion. There is accumulated in the Institute for Sex Research on the Indiana University campus one of the most voluminous collections of press clippings, articles, personal correspondence, public addresses, and cartoon materials pertaining to any revolutionary movement in science history, with the possible exceptions of the nuclear bomb and the lunar explorations.

Amidst the noisy public fury stirred up by the first two volumes, American newspapers and periodicals themselves experienced moments of sharp revision of social attitudes and approaches in dealing with the Kinsey studies. In fact, press treatment of the subject was almost as significant a documentation of changes in American cultural and social history as were the basic conclusions of the Kinsey researches themselves. The decade, 1947–57, was a traumatic one in which none, including Alfred C. Kinsey, the Indiana University administration, or the American organs of publicity could comprehend with certainty the dimensions of the current social revolution. Certainly no one of these escaped the innate pains of this transitional era.

From the perspective of the 1970s, it is somewhat startling to realize how reluctant the public, including a good portion of the academic community itself, was to accept with dignified calmness the results of an objective scientific investigation. In even clearer fashion the publicizing of the Kinsey story brought about considerable changes in the reporting of scientific findings by the press. It is interesting that the Rockefeller Foundation financed a project of the National Asociation of Science Writers to study science reporting and its effect upon public reactions, and to bring about changes in this field of writing.

Nowhere in this chapter has it been a purpose to evaluate the work of Professor Kinsey, his staff, or the institute in any manner so far as their scientific contributions were concerned. The existence of the Institute for Sex Research on the campus of a public university was indeed a striking fact in the history of American higher education. The Indiana University administration experienced all sorts of soul-searching, public pressures, scientific sniping, and constant exposure by the American press. All of this tested administrative and Board of Trustee courage. Reflective of this fact is the sentence that appeared in the publisher's foreword to *Sexual Behavior in the Human Male* in which it is said, "It is based on surveys made by members of the staff of Indiana

University . . ." rather than by an integrated department of the university.

The frequent defenses made by President Herman B Wells, and Deans Herman T. Briscoe and Fernandus Payne were within themselves landmarks in the battle for academic freedom and the right to publish scientific findings. Earlier mention is made of the McCarthy era, but more than this, the 1950s were years in which most Americans at heart sought social stability if not social complacency. For a Middle Western university to support such a socially explosive and intimately personal program of research was indeed to adventure into an unexplored cavern of many unpredictable labyrinths—the most threatening of which was loss of institutional prestige and vital financial support.

On May 16, 1955, and after two jolting periods of public relations challenges, Herman B Wells wrote W. F. Pommeranke of the University of Rochester, "Indiana University stands today, as it has for fifteen years, firmly in support of the scientific project which has been undertaken and is being carried on by one of its eminent biological scientists, Dr. Alfred C. Kinsey." The president knew full well what the emotional cost of this resolution had been, and his colleagues on the Indiana faculty no doubt appreciated the dividends the university's stand returned to them in genuine academic freedom to do research and to publish objective findings.

[XI]

In Pursuit of the Unicorn

Between the fomentations of the Ku Klux Klan and the emotionalism of the Red scares, the people of Indiana were kept in an almost perpetual state of agitation during the 1920s and 1930s. The veterans' organizations, direct descendants of a still active Grand Army of the Republic in 1920, concerned themselves with protecting the Republic against all "isms." The American Legion and the Veterans of Foreign Wars were perhaps even more vociferous than the revered old G. A. R.s had been, and maintained a constant vigil over democracy.

In Bloomington in November 1938 the local American Legion Post forced a so-called Communist group to cancel an election eve meeting to be held in the Monroe County Courthouse, and requested Indiana University officials to deny them access to a meeting place. A local "anti-Red league" was planned to be comprised of the G. A. R., V. F. W. and the American Legion to crush Communist activities in and around Bloomington. Students and newspaper reporters were barred from the league's meeting on the grounds that they aided the "Reds." The *Indiana Daily Student* responded November 4, 1938, that the Communist Party was a legal organization in Indiana. The following day it carried a story that William Cavaness, secretary of the local Communist Party, said a meeting would be held in spite of opposition.

T. J. Louden, chairman of the ex-servicemen's organizations, told reporters that not even Governor M. Clifford Townsend, using the state militia, could prevent the disruption of the meeting, even if local officials requested such assistance. There followed a rash of letters in the *Daily Student*, most of them belittling the threat of danger from Communism in Bloomington or the University. The Westminster group aligned itself with those who opposed abridgment of free speech and commended the *Daily Student* for its courage. When all the smoke had cleared and election results were known, only two votes were cast for the Communist Party candidate, a fact which caused the student editor to observe, "This may make 'vigilantes' and misguided patriots realize the communist problem is not large in this city."

Karl D. Ketzer, author of a *Reader's Digest* article on Communism, evidently requested of President Wells a copy of the *Daily Student* containing the editorial. Wells wrote, November 12, 1938, "I am enclosing a copy of the *Daily Student* which contains an editorial entitled 'An Un-American Act,' dealing with a resolution of local organized groups to prevent the Communists from holding a meeting here the night before election. Perhaps we are a little too harsh on students, after all. I think this editorial excellent, particularly since it is a spontaneous expression of student viewpoint, when Indianapolis papers were all taking such a cowardly opposite position." A year later, June 28, 1940, the president replied to Hershel D. Newsom that if he had definite knowledge of Communist activities on the faculty he hoped he would give him specific names so he could "investigate the matter and get at the truth." Wells promised not to whitewash the matter, but there is no indication in presidential files that Newsom could deliver on his charge. For the moment there was an abeyance of Red-hunting on the campus because of the certain approach of World War II.

Four years of war created a hiatus in concern with Communism, not a cessation of fear. In 1945 Indiana University was caught up in phenomenal change in every aspect of its operation. Enrollment jumped from 6,821 in 1943 to 18,668 in 1946–47. There was a frantic hunt for instructors, classrooms, housing, boarding facilities, and everything else necessary to operate an expanding university-city. Returning veterans not only created a suffocating crush of numbers, but they were more mature and demanding of adequate instruction. The university's curriculum itself had been under fire since 1939 and had to be reordered well beyond the lines that had been recommended by the Self-Study Committee. Too, many of the committee's recommendations had been left dormant because of the war, and now they had to be carried out.

One of the most significant areas of change was in the field of broadening the university's educational program to encompass the area of international education. Indiana University, in the oppressive years of Hitler, had brought to its campus scores of German refugees, now it received a floodstream of foreigners who sought American university training at a time when their universities were so badly injured by the war. The various federal and international agencies concerned with world restoration made heavy demands on American universities. These ranged from the preliminary veterans' training programs at Shrivenham and Fontainebleau to supplying advisory and administrative assistance to educational agencies such as the United Nations Educational, Scientific, and Cultural Organization (UNESCO). All of this came at a time when universities were trying to draw faculty members back to campuses from the military and war services.

No one in Indiana University took time from all but overwhelming campus responsibilities to fully comprehend the reactions of such groups as the American Legion to changes brought on by events of the past decade. Few if any persons in Bloomington fathomed the rather sharp differences of points of view of the returning "G.I." and those of the Legionnaire veteran of World War I. The latter were still under the spell of the propaganda and preachments of that war and its immediate postwar years, which in Indiana in 1946 had more than a touch of isolationism in it. Too, there was in that year a generous dose of anti-Communism intermixed with the normal seasonal outbreak of Hoosier partisan politics. In the senatorial election in 1946 the Indiana Communist Party asked that its symbol and candidate's name be placed on the official ballot. The insigne was an outline of the state of Indiana with the slogan "Peace, Security, and Democracy" imprinted on it. The election commissioners not only refused the original request but ruled the use of the emblem was illegal, because it was common to the people of Indiana at large.

This action provoked a petition to Governor Ralph Gates signed by eleven citizens saying the ruling of the election commissioners was both undemocratic and illegal. The signers made clear at the outset that they were not in sympathy with the Communists and their objectives, but they felt they should have access to the free ballot. The *Indianapolis News* quoted Governor Gates as saying, "that he felt the board would give every consideration to the petition, and that it would include the Communist Party ticket along with those of other minority parties, providing petitions and filings were found to be in accordance with state law."

The majority of the eleven signers of the petition represented the Congress of Industrial Organizations. Dean Bernard C. Gavit of the Indiana University Law School, Fowler V. Harper, W. Howard Mann, associate professor of law, and John R. Shannon, professor of education in Indiana State Teachers College, were signers from the academic community. The petition said in part "The name of the Communist Party could not be left out as provided in section 106 of the official Election Code of Indiana."

The Indiana Department of the American Legion meeting in Indianapolis, August 19, 1946, received a petition from the Cass County Post 60 of Logansport urging Governor Gates to consider any Communistic tendencies among the state college and university faculty members as active grounds for dismissal. There followed an inordinate amount of newspaper publicity about the petition and signers, ironically, after the election commissioners had voted to include the names of the Communist Party's candidate on the ballot. The Legion's members seemed not to have pondered this fact, or to have thought of charging the election commissioners with having "Communistic tendencies." The three university signers were placed on the defensive; Dean Gavit said the professors were careful to point out that they were not sympathetic with the Communist Party, but "It was a matter of principle of basic civil rights." Harper was somewhat defiant in saying the doubts should be cleared up. He was a Democrat, a fact which perhaps brought him under some suspicion with some Hoosiers. Mann echoed his senior colleagues, saying the American Legion should encourage minor parties. If two major parties, he said, "gang up on minor parties, then we have no right to talk about the one-party governments of Europe." All four professors welcomed public investigation of their position.

The *Indianapolis Star*, August 21, 1946, quoted Governor Gates as saying he had not received the American Legion's petition, but when he did he would refer it to the trustees of the two institutions. He did this on September 5, and in a letter to Judge Ora L. Wildermuth, chairman of the Indiana University Board of Trustees, Gates said he did not question the right of any individual to assert his personal views, but he felt the acts of the professors of a tax-supported university were subject to scrutiny by the Board of Trustees. "I personally feel that subversive activities of any nature have no place in our state universities or colleges," he told Wildermuth. He requested that the Indiana Board investigate the professors and report their findings directly to him. There arose immediately the question of whether or not the professors signed titles of their positions on the petition. They denied this, saying the titles had been added by the American Legion and the press.

The publicity of the Gates' letter brought an offer of assistance from Roger N. Baldwin, director of the American Civil Liberties Union. Baldwin said the ACLU felt the letter "an extraordinary interference with the rights of citizens to promote political democracy." He hoped it had been made entirely clear that the signing of a petition to get a party's name and candidate on a ballot did not imply sympathy for the party itself. The Board of Trustees perhaps had never allowed itself to be maneuvered into such an anomalous situation as it found itself in on September 21, 1946. Judge Wildermuth was a man of unusually good sense and judgment, but he seems to have wavered at this moment. Governor Gates had been quoted as saying he favored placing the Communist Party on the ballot, and the election commissioners had voted to do so, yet four of the eleven petitioners were being investigated because they signed a petition to do what was required to be done legally.

Years later Herman B Wells said in an interview that Governor Gates followed a prearranged procedure. The American Legion officials had no desire to confront Judge Ora Wildermuth and Judge John Hastings or any other members of the Board of Trustees. By holding an open hearing the university could be cleared of all the charges, and at the same time faculty members and others accused of Communistic taint would have an opportunity to confront their accusers on the certain grounds of the Indiana University Board of Trustees room. In the end this strategy proved to be a wise one.

Investigation of Communism on the campus of the university began on September 24, when Judge Wildermuth and his colleagues asked individuals having knowledge of Communistic activities to come forward and present their evidence. He promised a thorough investigation of alleged subversive activities in the university. The law professors said they welcomed the investigation as a means of making clear their positions. In the meantime, however, Fowler V. Harper, a prominent member of the faculty since 1929, and one of the three members of the Self-Study Committee, resigned with a request for immediate leave of absence to accept the vice-chairmanship of the American League for a Free Palestine; Senator Guy M. Gillette of Iowa was president of the League. Harper was to manage the Washington office, and to have charge of the legal and international work of the organization.

The Board of Trustees held its first full meeting on the "Red Scare" on December 3, 1946, and almost a month after the senatorial election in November in which Elmer G. Johnson, the Communist candidate, polled 806 votes out of a total vote of 1,347,434. Democrats had cast 548,288 votes, and the Republicans cast 739,809 votes for William E. Jenner, an Indiana University graduate. In all, the minority parties collected 23,337 votes, hardly a threat even to the Marion County majority. There came into the Board Room in the Bryan Administration Building a veritable parade of witnesses to testify eloquently to their total lack of knowledge of Communistic activities on the campus. The freshmen who had been housed in the room during the acute housing shortage had hardly had time to grab their pajamas and run before the sessions opened. Prior to opening the hearings formally, the trustees met with Fred Beyer, industrial services director of the Indianapolis Chamber of Commerce and Patrick Cuddy, public relations director of the State Chamber of Commerce. Both men denied any knowledge of Communist activities in Bloomington, or anywhere else in Indiana for that matter.

First to appear as witnesses were W. I. Brunton, commander of the Indiana American Legion, and a resident of the southern Indiana town of Scottsburg. There were also State Adjutant William E. Seager, an assistant national Americanism director, and R. Worth Shumaker, all veterans of World War I. Too, there were Glenn R. Hillis of Kokomo, Joseph Lutz of Indianapolis, and Frank A. White, editor of the *Hoosier Legionnaire*. The *World-Telephone*, December 4, said "The Legion has been repeatedly ringing the gong during recent months on the subject of Communism, even to the extent of calling for the banning of names of Communist candidates from the Indiana ballots during last month's election. The Indiana election officials of both Democratic and Republican faiths, however, failed to find legal backing to keep the Communist off the ballot, and they did not heed the Legion's position in the matter." The paper said also the Communist symbol appearing on the ballot amounted to "very little," and implied the Board of Trustees hearing bordered on the ridiculous.

One sane voice cried out in supplication to the trustees. "Please let's not have any 'witch hunting' in Indiana University!" wrote B. E. Myers, director of the Department of Public Welfare for Indiana, "I am no Communist, I have no truck with them, and I despise their theories, but I believe they are people and have certain rights in this country. I am violently opposed, also, to printing the Communist label on everything not included in the majority political platforms, and then condemning everybody that has been labeled. In general terms, I am for academic freedom, if that is what is involved in the issue which is brought up by the American Legion, which I hope doesn't turn out to be the Un-American Legion."

Once on the campus the Legion representatives went fishing for "un-American" offenses, and asked the Board of Trustees "to investigate any act of any person engaged as instructor that may be classed as "pro-Communist" or "un-American" and urged immediate action. In a peroration Brunton asked that "those given the great trust of directing the destiny of this splendid school be alert to infiltration of Communists and Fascists alike."

President Herman B Wells asked the trustees to call before them the eleven campus deans as witnesses. Besides these, Dean Gavit appeared on his own behalf. Fowler V. Harper came back to visit his wife, and, incidentally he made it appear, to attend the hearings. Pressly S. Sikes, dean of the Junior Division, also appeared the first day. Harper was direct in his statement that "I am not a political sympathizer with the Communist Party nor have I ever been in sympathy with its philosophy, practices, or objectives. I have never attended a Communist meeting in my

NCAA Basketball Champions in Kansas City, after defeating the University of Kansas 60–42, March 30, 1940.

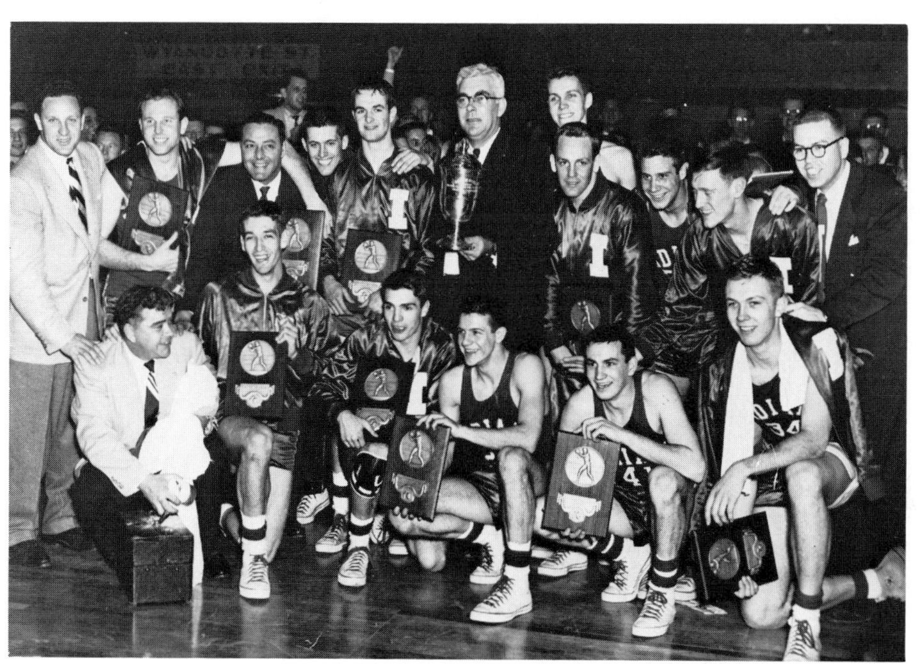

NCAA Basketball Champions and Coach Branch McCracken in Kansas City, after defeating the University of Kansas 69–68, March 18, 1953.

Tennis Team with Coach Dale Lewis, 1957.

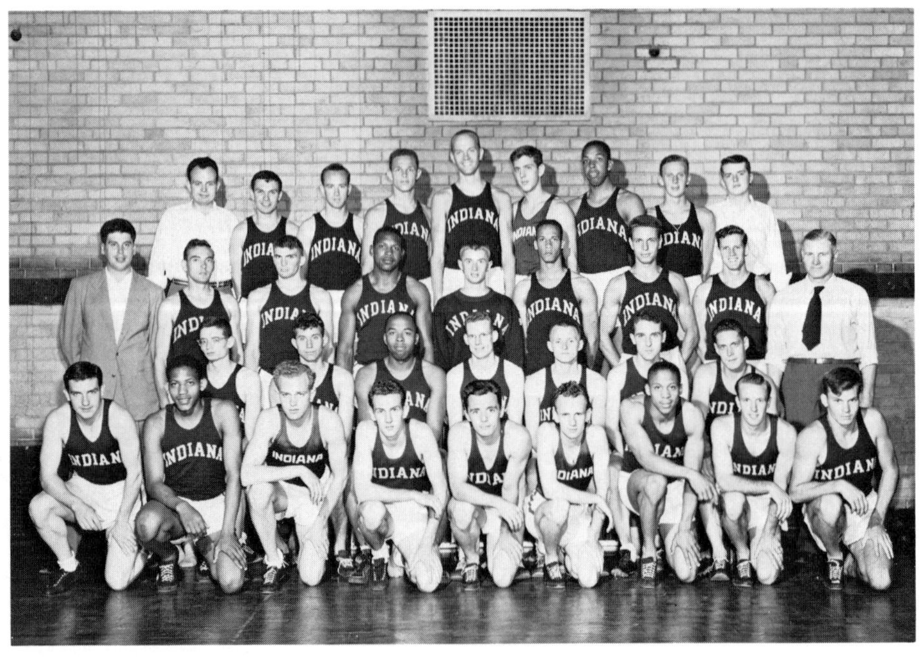

Big Ten Outdoor Track Champions with Coach Gordon Fisher, 1950.

Swimming Team with Coaches Hobie Billingsley and James (Doc) Counsilman, 1960.

Memorial Stadium, Assembly Hall, and the Fieldhouse.

William H. Crawford, *Dean of the School of Dentistry, 1940–1945.*

Maynard K. Hine, *Periodontics, 1944–1945; Dean, School of Dentistry, 1945–1968; Chancellor, IUPUI, 1968–1973.*

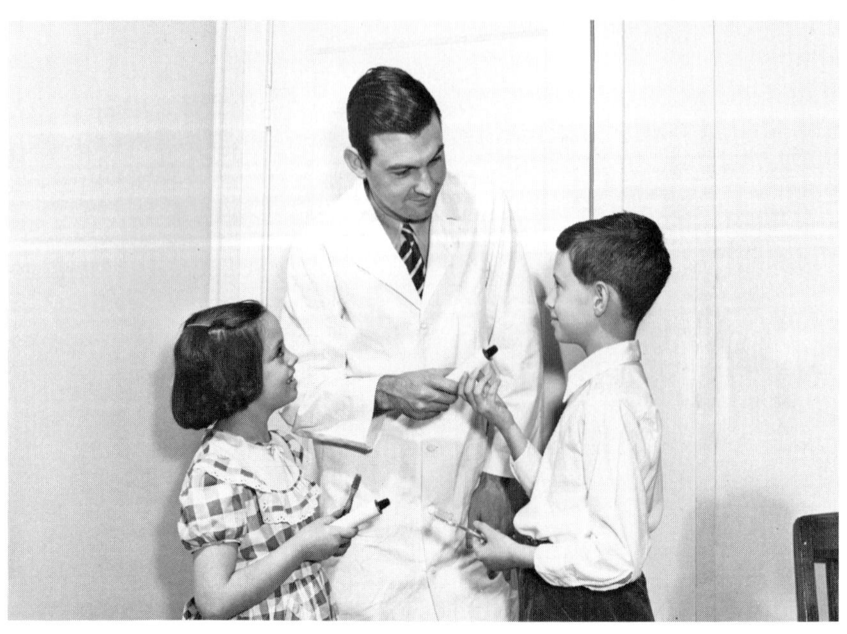

Joseph C. Muhler with two children in the dental study program, 1952.

WILLIS D. GATCH, *Dean of the School of Medicine, 1931–1946.*

JOHN D. VAN NUYS, *Director, Hospital Admissions, 1941–1946; Dean, School of Medicine, 1947–1964.*

The Indiana University School of Medicine—fifty years old in 1953.

Anne Meier, George Martin, William S. Armstrong, Elvis J. Stahr, and Bob Hope during the Little 500 Variety Show, 1967.

Football team skit, Jordan River Revue, 1952.

Law students inveigh against the Med students, 1951.

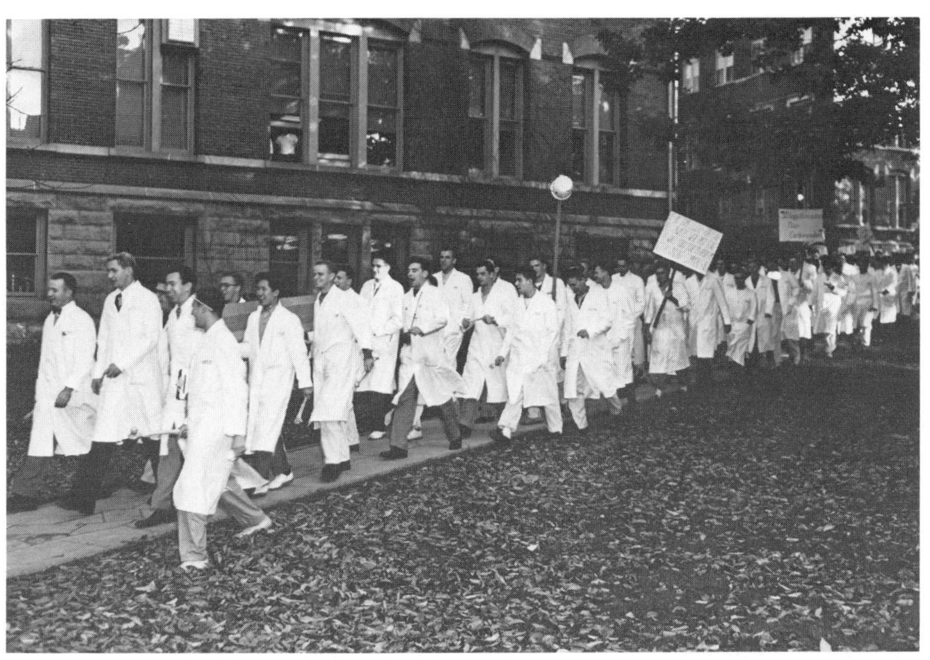

Medical students march against the Law students, 1951.

The Mini Race began in 1955 as part of the Little 500 Weekend.

The Little 500 Bicycle Race, an annual spring event since 1951, raises scholarship funds for students.

Hoosier Hall dance, 1946.

Dancing in Men's Residence Center to the music of Red Nichols and his Orchestra, 1941.

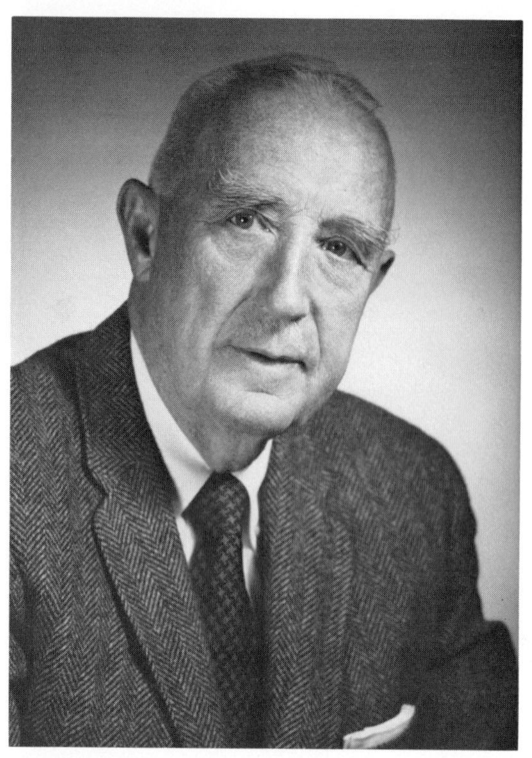

LEE NORVELLE, *Department of English, then Department of Speech and Theatre, 1925–1963.*

University Theatre, 1963.

Brown County Playhouse, 1951.

The showboat Majestic, *1962.*

The Madrigal Dinners, which began in 1947, are a popular annual series.

Scene from Madame Butterfly, *1958.*

Hans Busch and Parsifal *cast, 1951.*

Berkshire Quartet, 1950: David Dawson, Albert Lazan, Urico Rossi, and Fritz Magg.

Musical Arts Center.

Wilfred C. Bain, Ernst Hoffman, Marion Bell, and Kurt Weill discuss the première of Down in the Valley, *1948.*

The Belles of Indiana in the Benton Hall of Murals, 1952.

Lilly Library and Showalter Fountain, 1964.

The new Library, 1969.

Inauguration of a new President, 1962: Herman B Wells and Elvis J. Stahr, Jr.

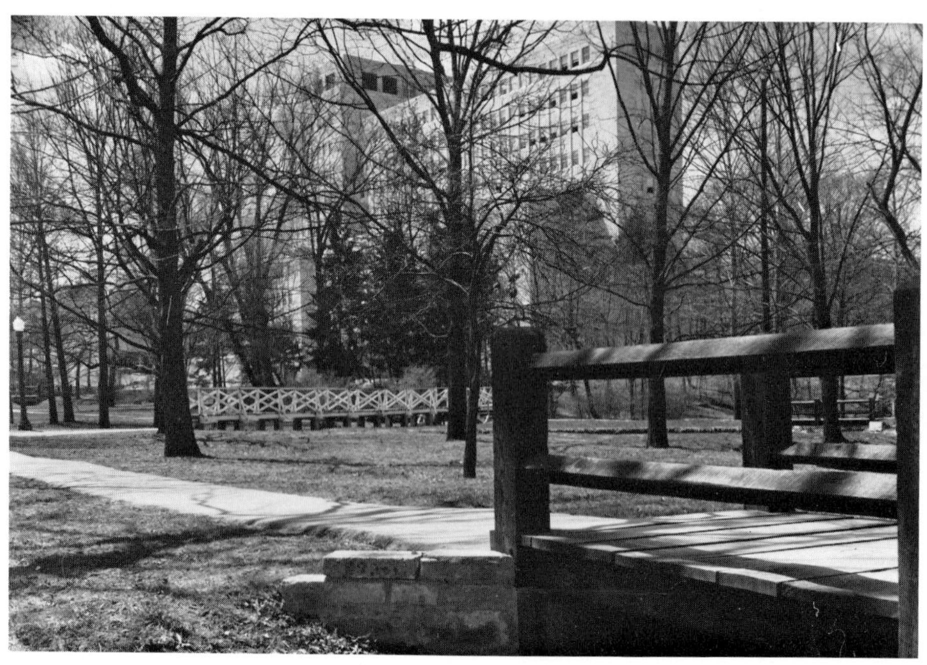

Ballantine Hall, 1962.

life. I am and have been for many years a member of the Democratic Party, and am in general accord with the political philosophy, practices and objectives of that party. . . . I support the right of all Americans to use the ballot to express their political convictions." He asked for a quick and formal resolution of the issue; in fact, he asked for a "100 per cent clean bill of health" or a formal hearing to examine evidence in which he could be represented by counsel. Gavit and Sikes denied as stoutly that there were any Communistic activities on the campus.

This set the pattern of testimony for the rest of the witnesses in Bryan Administration Building. Everybody denied knowledge of any un-American activities on the campus. One of this herd of witnesses, Mary Morrison, a junior, president of the Associated Women Students, and a Bryan scholar, answered the stock question, "Have you any knowledge of pro-Communist or un-American activities in Indiana University?" with a question of her own. She asked the trustees the embarrassing question, "What is a Communist?" This was said to have thrown the trustees into utter bewilderment. The *Indianapolis News* reported, December 6, 1946, "One report says the trustees cleared their throats, looked at one another, around the room, at the pictures of past presidents on the walls. And Miss Morrison waited. Various essays were made in the realm of definition, and then the trustees went into a huddle which produced, 'A Communist is a person who votes the Communist ticket, supports the policies of Moscow, advocates the overthrow of the American government by force.' " The paper said after a thoughtful pause Miss Morrison replied she had not seen anything of the kind the board described around Bloomington. Equally as disconcerting was the answer of Henry F. Schricker, Jr., who said he had no knowledge of Communist activities, "But I'm in the School of Business, and I wouldn't really know, because they're all Republicans there." These two were followed by leaders of campus organizations and students from the School of Law, all giving negative answers to the monotonous question of whether they knew of Communist activities, or un-American activities and teachings.

Deans and department heads reported there were no subversive teachings or activities on the campus. That sturdy old campus patriarch Dean Fernandus Payne spoke directly and positively for twenty departmental heads of the College of Arts and

Sciences; there were no un-American activities, no Communists, and no disloyalty to the Republic. Arthur Weimer found no irregularities among Henry F. Schricker, Jr.'s School of Business "Republicans." Colonel R. L. Shoemaker spoke for the students and assured the trustees he had received no complaints of radicalism among his charges. On this note Judge Wildermuth ended the two-day investigation—which in many respects was stranger than some of the scenes in the comic operas being performed on the Auditorium stage. Even the conservative Hoosier press had to view the hearings in this light. The chairman withdrew from Bloomington to digest the 400 pages of reports and to draft his findings for Governor Gates. The trustees, the Legionnaires, and the governor, however, turned the campus into a veritable hornet's nest of recrimination.

The angry comments that followed no doubt were unexpected. At once the differing points of view between the G.I. veterans and the older Legionnaires surfaced. A rash of letters appearing in the *Indiana Daily Student* discussed many of the issues involved. One furious correspondent on December 5, while the investigators were still on the campus, said the Indiana Constitution did not grant the American Legion authority to interfere with an individual's exercise of his rights. He felt "The Board of Trustees of Indiana University may send the American Legion about their business (which is not at Indiana University) but if the Board follows the suggestion of the American Legion, Indiana University might as well close its doors as an institution devoted to 'Lux et Veritas.' " He doubted if the Legion's representatives on the campus could define the term un-Americanism they "speak of without using meaningless terms. . . ." He concluded, "I resent the insult to the intelligence of every student, faculty member, and administrator at Indiana University which is implied by the American Legion. The implication is that we would not recognize communism if we saw it, whereas the American Legion is able to recognize it immediately." Max Cohen attacked the Legion on the issue of discrimination against minority groups. He said that in the state convention that summer the Legion had defeated a resolution to admit Negro veterans to equal membership. "In short," he wrote, "Negro veterans cannot attend the social functions of their fellow 'white' veterans." He criticized the organization for awarding William Randolph

Hearst a plaque for "Americanism." He thought "in the light of these facts, what is needed is not an investigation by the American Legion of Communism on the campus, but an investigation of the American Legion by the American People." Robert H. Harker declared that "In case the American Legion does not realize it, this is a University, not an over-sized soap box. We, as students, are here to learn to think, to be able to choose what we want and what is worthy of consideration." He asked Joseph Lutz to look carefully, he might find a Communist in the Indianapolis Orchestra.

Two former Legionnaires, enrolled as students, charged the organization with being all "top" and no "bottom." Decisions were made by a handful of top administrators. Why had not the local Ernie Pyle Post taken a stand to clear up the farcical investigations? They said, "When a staunch believer in civil rights is called a Communist, it's time to pack up. . . . What do you say, boys?" Donald G. Speyer of the Ernie Pyle Post, in a straddling reply, thought the Legion was "definitely wrong" in its charges against the three professors, even though their names on a petition might imply communist sympathy. Speyer expressed a strong belief in the democratic system, and opposed "mobocracy from the Ku Klux Klan to the German Bund." There was no end to the criticism that appeared in the press. "A [Paul] Robeson Fan" thought the Legion should investigate the cherished university colors of red and cream, the *Red Book*, the special Russian section in the Library, the forthcoming Ballet Russe, the appearance of Fabien Sevitzky, and a current affairs movie.

Never had so much energy and thought gone into letter writing. The echoes sounded and resounded long after Commander Brunton and his fellow Legionnaires had gone home to Scottsburg, Kokomo, Logansport, and Indianapolis. They took home with them knowledge of the humbling fact that Judge Wildermuth and the trustees had not uncovered even so much as a hint of Communism. The adjourned meeting of the trustees would be called back into final session on December 15 to put the finishing touches on their report. In the meantime George R. Nichols of North Hall sounded a bit of a benediction, "And so the American Legion has come to our campus to investigate our 'Reds!' Well! Well! Like a great herd of sheep, the American Legion, millions of them following the old ram. Jolly good boys! They drink beer at the post houses, slap each other on the back, cut up at conventions and tell themselves they've given their utmost for the country." Nichols was certain only a handful of members made the Legion's policies, the rest "listening between back slaps and songs for the tinkle of the old ram's bell." He invited Legion members to come out and talk openly about socialism, capitalism, democracy, communism, and all the other isms. These were proper subjects for young and inquiring minds in the University to tackle.

Marvin Kill, a student-veteran, wrote, December 10, 1946, a defense of the Legion against the other letter writers. He touched off almost as much of a row as did the hearings. One of his defenses was against the charge of racial discrimination, but in making his defense he may have incriminated the Legion more by his vague phraseology than the Legion did by its ambivalent policies on the subject. Kill declared himself bitterly opposed to Communism and un-American activity, however, he wrote, "I have never witnessed any evidence of subversive activity at Indiana University. I have always been confident that our faculty members were in no way connected with un-American activities, or any activity that would bring discredit to the University." He commended the professors for their willingness to face the fire of investigation. "Two former Legionnaires" all but demolished Kill in their reply. Maybe there was some truth in A. M. Folicks' reply, "The Legion wasn't looking for Communists. Its flag-waving and witch-hunting activities are far more realistic. It aims at the suppression of all liberal points of view and it is succeeding remarkably well. Many of our instructors have been intimidated."

The *Indianapolis News* absolved the university, and the *Times* said, "The Communists owe the American Legion a debt of gratitude for the front-page publicity the Reds of the state are receiving through the enquiry on communism in two of the state's largest schools."

True to Judge Wildermuth's promise, the Board of Trustees made its unanimous report to Governor Ralph Gates on December 15, 1946. In a four-part document the trustees said they found "no direct, circumstantial, or hearsay evidence of Communistic or any other subversive teaching anywhere in the University." The Communist Party polled only twenty-one votes in Monroe County. No faculty member was found to be engaged in any subversive activity, and the same thing applied to students. The three professors in question were cleared absolutely, and Fowler V. Harper clinched his innocence with Federal Bureau of Investigation clearance, and a certificate of merit signed jointly by the secretaries of War and Navy. The board reiterated its dedication to academic freedom, and officially at least, the Legion commotion was ended.

President Herman B Wells distributed the trustees' report to the faculty on December 23, and on January 6, 1947, the *Indianapolis News* quoted a letter he addressed to the American Legion officials. "Indiana University," he said, "is the child of our American democracy and stands in eternal opposition to any form of tyranny over the minds and hearts of men from whatever source, including Communism and Fascism." No Reds were found on the campus, and the institution would oppose subversive influences. In characteristic Wells' fashion he thanked the Legion officials graciously for their courtesy in coming to Bloomington and for "their helpful testimony." The Board of Trustees also eased its sharp denial of Legion implications of subversive activities by thanking its officials for the organization's concern for education.

While the president and the trustees were salving the Legion's wounds, Dean Bernard Gavit, Fowler V. Harper, and W. Howard Mann cooked a pot of brew for the Illinois Publishing Company and the publisher of the Chicago *Herald-American*, in the form of a $600,000 libel suit in federal court. The paper had strongly implied in an editorial entitled "Communism on the Campus" that the three were involved in Communist activities. They also filed suits for damages against the Hearst Corporation, Frank Taylor, and the Milwaukee *Sentinel*. The Hearst papers took this case seriously indeed. In an effort to get background information on the plaintiffs they sent their attorney to Bloomington to talk with President Wells, a source which gave them no comfort. These three professors were mainstays of the new Wells faculty, except now Harper was lost to another position. This furor over Communism may have been a main reason for his leaving Bloomington.

The *Indianapolis News* said on December 18, 1947, that a cash settlement of an undisclosed amount had been made by the Chicago *Herald-American*, New York *Journal-American*, Milwaukee *Sentinel*, Baltimore *News-Post* and *Sunday American*, and the Los Angeles *Examiner*. The papers agreed to publish the statement, "The editorial in question did not state either of these men [Gavit and Mann] were Communists, or had any Communist affiliations, and it was not the intent or purpose of this paper to so state or so to infer. This paper does not believe these men are Communists, Communist adherents or Communist sympathizers." Harper made a separate settlement with the papers, and on the same terms.

Indiana University was to see no peace in this fragile age of Red-baiting and Velde-McCarthyism. In 1929 the Indiana General Assembly had enacted a test oath law, which either had never been applied or had fallen by the wayside from disuse. As pressures built up over the latter part of the 1940s, the University Administrative Council on June 23, 1949, in "an extremely confidential" action decided to reactivate the test oath as a defensive mechanism. This was to be done by having the Dean of Faculties prepare blank forms to be distributed to the faculty, and to be included in the dossiers given new faculty members as conditions of their employment. This was a problem that troubled all the institutions, private and public, in Indiana. In November the university joined thirty other state universities and colleges in a declaration against the hiring of any person "who advocates the overthrowing of our form of government by violence or other unconstitutional means." Wells and Dean Wendell W. Wright were present at the formulation of this statement as the university's representatives.

This statement, however, failed to quiet the anxieties of the times. In January 1951 the General Assembly returned to the question of Communism and a test oath. These issues were taken up in separate actions simultaneously in the House and Senate. The House bill proposed to make membership in the Communist Party unlawful and a felony. Two sections dealt with teaching, publication, and writing, which might even have brought the university's library, and maybe some of its courses in European studies, under possible interdiction. The Senate bill placed more emphasis on a test oath or written statement, and provided that every person in the employ of the state or any private institution of learning should by April 1, 1951, file a statement of loyalty.

The *Indianapolis Star*, January 24, 1951, summarized the legislation in an editorial, and agreed the problem of protecting

America from Communists was a complex one. The paper said, however "well intended as this bill is, we do not believe its enactment is desirable. No such measure at the state level could really protect Indiana or America from the Communist menace. Yet its definition of subversion is so sweeping that it could possibly become the instrument for persecuting many non-Communists." The paper thought the Red threat lay elsewhere and no oath would have any effect on it. In April at a meeting of the American Civil Liberties Union, Harry Elmer Barnes said the doctrine of government by force was "the most fundamental of American political theory." There was lively discussion of the Indiana test oath bill by C. Leonard Lundin, Monroe C. Paulsen, and Harry E. Barnes. Barnes thought the best way to resist Communism was to "reverse our idiotic foreign policy" to permit peaceful coexistence of nations in the modern world.

Herman B Wells during much of this period had the dramatic firsthand experience of dealing directly with Russian Communists. In 1947 he served as cultural affairs advisor to General Lucius Clay in Germany. When he returned to Bloomington, he not only had developed a much broader concept of the main currents running loose in the postwar world, but he had some appreciation of what it took to resist Communism not only in Indiana but in Western Europe especially. In 1951 during the great debate in Indianapolis, he served as national chairman of the Crusade for Freedom, which operated the privately supported Radio Free Europe. On the campus in September 1951 the Student Senate voted to endorse "wholeheartedly" the Crusade for Freedom, and to make a drive for funds among students. This, however, proved disappointing when the campus, faculty and students, contributed only $326.62, and Monroe County fell short of raising its $2,000 quota.

Students nevertheless were free with their signatures when it came to signing petitions. The drive in December to bring home William F. Oates, Associated Press Chief in Red Czechoslovakia, received 3,747 signatures. Oates had been arrested in Prague and held incommunicado for seventy-two hours. He was taken before a mockery of a court and sentenced to ten years' imprisonment. The New York Bar labeled this a "travesty of justice," and set out to arouse students and congressmen on the subject.

The opening of the Velde-McCarthy era and the great Hollywood Red scare caused the editor of the *Daily Student* to turn introspective on the subject of resisting Communism. In his column "The Editor's Desk," he discussed the challenges of the moment. Congress, he thought, held a powerful legal weapon in the Smith Act against those who taught, plotted, or advocated the overthrow of the government by violent means. The Supreme Court, he said, had upheld the imprisonment of top Red leaders. Colleges, professors, and textbooks were under fire. Real Communists would scream loudly, but persons grown weary of witch hunts and fearful of infringement of their freedom would be more forceful. Surprisingly, the editor spoke critically of some defenders of academic freedom, saying they could become pawns of the Communists. He advocated "careful investigation" to weed out the real Communists. He concluded that "We now face a struggle with a strong opponent who will miss no opportunity to strike from within. We should welcome any honest investigation. Those with clean hands can lose nothing. It at least may shake us out of our day dreaming."

This column drew angry replies. Dick Ireland and Del H. Hymes, March 28, 1952, denied there was such a thing as a "properly conducted investigation." From Martin Dies to Harold Velde investigations had political and headline-snatching overtones. They were the resorts of opportunists and publicity seekers, and guilt by association had become a basic principle. The American Civil Liberties Union, they said, had always opposed this un-American approach, and guilt should never be assessed from a list of offenses drawn up by political appointees. They wrote, "Even to suggest an investigation insults the University. It implies that Indiana has failed so grossly in its job that only an outside force can cleanse it. It also implies democratic education is a mistake, that students cannot be trusted to think for themselves." Ireland and Hymes feared the conformity of the times and the disappearance of independent judgment. The *Daily Student* editor went on his way battling with the American Civil Liberties Union, advocating investigations, and placing his faith in the Smith Act. He still pretended to believe Communists used American freedom to threaten the Republic, and that they hid behind the bulwark of academic freedom.

This was a spring of debate, if not of frenetic anxiety. Dr.

Willard Uphaus ('15) spoke to the Student Progressive Party in the well-filled Union Lounge on May 20, 1952. He called himself a "Christian Socialist" who did not want Communism. He outlined a plan for peace that included changing our economy from one of war to one of peace. He wanted homes, medical care, and education guaranteed to everyone, "a world T.V.A.," he said. Dr. Uphaus said he was convinced competition in business was a wasteful luxury. Tender nerve ends were touched when the speaker suggested outright socialized medicine, the elimination of poverty, and winning the love and affection of underprivileged countries.

The following morning an *Indiana Daily Student* editorial said even though Dr. Uphaus claimed to have studied for the Methodist ministry, he "sang the communist line of thought, including social discrimination, war mongering, capitalists, Russia's love of peace, and negotiations (lasting for at least two decades) instead of armament." The editor endorsed freedom of speech, but denounced Dr. Uphaus for exercising it. Another critic said the "Doctor" left many questions unanswered. Before the second semester ended the roar of dissent was loud on the campus, with the idealistic spirit of Dr. Uphaus bubbling on, unsullied and unscathed. The campus editor, however, was staggered by the response from readers, saying that he was completely ignorant of the "basic tenets of freedom of speech." The American Civil Liberties Union ended the debate with, "If the editors of the *Student* feel that it is necessary to jail men, spiritually and physically, for their dissenting views, for heaven's sake, let them not do so in the name of democracy." Only Dwight Sherburne, treasurer of the Senite Metal Corporation, and William Kokariotis, director of Americanism of the American Legion, sponged the editorial bruises in this moment of self-inflicted defeat.

There must have been a silent prayer of thankfulness in the Ernie Pyle Journalism Building when a new sensation changed the subject of campus debate. One was not long in appearing. Hal Denman of Kokomo, editor of the *Counter Action Magazine* and a self-appointed defender of the Republic, charged in Indianapolis on June 20, 1952, in a meeting of the Veterans of Foreign Wars, that the Indiana University Library had become a "transmission belt for Communist propaganda." He waved to the audience materials in foreign languages bearing the library's stamp. In

Bloomington librarians said they had no notion to which publications Denman referred in his flamboyant accusation. Magazines were not permitted to be circulated, and there was no evidence of any being illegally removed. If Denman, in fact, had a periodical from the University Library, librarians could only wonder how he got it out of the building and to Indianapolis. They said, "But assuming the publications are from the Library and are Communistic in nature—we have no way of knowing if they are—but assuming they are, what does that prove? Indiana University would have a very inadequate library if it did not provide students with all types of literature. How else could scholars and students analyze and develop defenses against Communistic ideas and goals if documents and reports of Communistic materials were not available?" It was said there were scholars and students who studied propaganda just as they studied English, French, Russian, chemistry, and home economics.

As important as the attack on members of the faculty had been, the most dangerous assault was upon the library. It was easy enough to produce the tangible evidence that the collection contained materials of all sorts pertaining to Russia, Communism, and subversion. Any publicity campaign on this subject could disrupt support for the library, and most important of all cut off vital sources of research materials and disrupt the whole intellectual process in the university. Both administration and faculty took seriously the attempt to hold the institution up to public disdain. It would have been a simple matter to have influenced the General Assembly to cut appropriations for library purchases from abroad. While the U.S. Customs Service in the Kinsey case had attempted to censor materials being collected at Indiana University, the local critics would have completely denied the institution the right to house any "un-American" materials, or to teach in any area implied by such a collection. Fortunately this movement was checked, and in the end it appeared more as a shabby act in a comic opera, largely because Hal Denman made his appeal to a group that had already felt the sting of public investigation.

Beyond the campus, national anxieties and paranoia stirred the American people. Succeeding congressional elections seemed to bring to government new and more demagogic superpatriots. In 1953 Harold H. Velde of Illinois replaced Everett M. Dirksen in the House of Representatives, and became chairman of the House Un-American Activities Committee. He was a natural successor to Martin Dies in both philosophy and chicanery. An incident occurred early that year that indicated the shape of things to come. Mrs. Agnes Meyer, wife of the owner of the *Washington Post*, in speaking to the American Association of School Administrators, February 3, denounced McCarthy, Jenner, and Velde. She raised a question about Velde's I.Q. The Fort Wayne *Journal-Gazette*, February 19, quoted Mrs. Meyer as saying Velde was "a man who is conscienceless enough to use a deliberate lie." His committee was just then preparing to investigate American education. Velde was said to have confirmed Mrs. Meyer's low opinion of his intelligence quotient by accusing her of being a "pink" who wrote laudatory letters to a Russian magazine, and in turn was praised by *Pravda*. He confused her with a Mrs. Mayer of British Columbia, not the District of Columbia. No doubt every informed educator in the land was disturbed at what promised to be a first-class campus witch hunt.

In Bloomington on January 20 President Wells discussed the problems of congressional investigations. He advised his colleagues the "we should approach the problem with calmness, caution, and great deliberation." He thought there might be some storms ahead, but there were also some promising signs. If educators handled themselves well, they would find many responsible friends on their side. Two weeks later he announced he had appointed a committee to deal with the university's position in respect to a possible loyalty oath. This committee was composed of Leon Henry Wallace, chairman, Cleon H. Foust, William Hiram Fox, Ralph Leslie Lusk, Mary Crawford, Norman Pratt, William R. Breneman, Edward Buehrig, and Dean John Ashton. At the same time he said all thirty-three of Indiana's colleges and universities were trying to find a common position for all the institutions to take regarding loyalty oaths for faculty. Professor Harold Fabian Underhill responded to the president's remarks by saying it appeared to be a hopeless task to educate legislators on the futility of loyalty oaths, and the university should carefully evaluate the effect such oaths would have on the educational process. He felt Indiana University could formulate no adequate reaction until it had found an answer to the latter question.

While the campus committee pondered the loyalty oath issue, Professor Hermann J. Muller, a Nobel Laureate, in a closed-door session of the House Un-American Activities Committee said if the so-called "pinks" of the United States who were said to be sympathetic with the Communist line could live in Russia they would turn against the party. Muller had lived in Russia, 1933–37, and had his own bouts with the Red-scare masterminds. He said that education in Communism should not be confined to colleges and universities, but it should be taught at all levels of education. Both sides of the question should be discussed, and facts should be presented from both points of view. He implied strongly that Communistic premises were false.

Indiana University joined forces with the thirty-six institutions comprising the Association of American Universities. On March 30, 1953, the association announced the position that membership in the Communist Party "extinguishes the right to a university position." This announcement of policy was the outgrowth of a six-month study of the question of the academic man and the Party. The announcement of position was made by the Association's President, Harold W. Dodds of Princeton University. The report said specifically, "Appointment to a university and retention after appointment requires not only professional competence but involves the affirmative obligation of being diligent and loyal in citizenship. Above all, a scholar must have integrity and independence. This renders impossible adherence to such a regime as that of Russia and its satellites."

The association resolution held further that no person who accepted the principles of Communism or was a member of the Party had a place in a free and open university. This did not close the door to investigation, criticism, and full presentation of ideas, but all of these had to be nurtured in an atmosphere of "freedom and confidence." Academic freedom must be guaranteed to faculty members, and they must continue to inquire, criticize, and examine all ideas even the dangerous and abhorrent ones. Outside his special field of competence, the professor should remember he spoke as a layman. The report recommended that educators co-operate with congressional and legislative committees to redress abuses. Finally, universities should reevaluate the qualifications of professors who invoked the Fifth Amendment against self-incrimination in the refusal to answer questions.

On the day the association's report was published, President Wells made public through the Faculty Council a general statement applicable to Indiana University professors. He asked his colleagues to tell the truth and the whole truth if summoned before the congressional committee. He thought, however, there might be some individual cases where the protection of the Fifth Amendment should be invoked, but this should be done upon the advice of legal counsel. He suggested a procedure that should be followed in the university. If a faculty member were called before the Congressional Committee, he should have available to him all possible sources of advice. This meant one person on the university's staff should be designated to collect and convey such advice and information about the experiences of those who had testified. If a professor had been a former member of the Communist Party then he should admit it, and such testimony need not necessarily embarrass him or endanger his position. It did, however, create problems for other persons in a like situation, making the advice of counsel imperative.

The Indiana Faculty Council agreed generally that, "*It is desirable for any faculty member called to testify to talk with President Wells, Dean Briscoe, or to Professor Norman Pratt, President of the Indiana A. A. U. P. chapter, for information concerning such appearances. It was also taken by consent that it should be recognized that the mere fact of being called does not imply that a man is guilty of any offense, nor does it cast suspicion on him. His appearance may be for information only.*"

The *Indiana Daily Student* created some problems in these treacherous days when the disciples of Velde and McCarthy were running loose in the land. Sensitivity existed everywhere. Lieutenant Governor Harold W. Handley apparently had complained to President Wells about the paper. Wells wrote Handley, April 23, 1954, that the *Daily Student* was operated as a laboratory experience in journalism, but because of its publication as a daily it reached well beyond the bounds of the classroom. One resolution to Handley's problem, he thought, was that politically controversial articles would not be carried as editorials, and would bear the writer's name. "We think this procedure will work. At least we are giving it a trial," said the president. "We don't want to restrict free experience, but we want these students to know that freedom always is accompanied by responsibility."

The McCarthy year, 1954, brought to Indiana its peculiar problems in several forms. Miss Uta Hagen, a stage and screen star, was scheduled to address 900 high school students from thirty states in a campus gathering of the National Thespian Society. The American Legion charged her with having Communist leanings. The Legion listed fifteen Communist-front activities from 1940 onward with which Miss Hagen was alleged to have been associated. Her appearance in Bloomington was cancelled after much "disturbing political publicity."

Even following the disappearance of Harold H. Velde and Joseph R. McCarthy from Congress, the investigators went on at a somewhat reduced voltage. August E. Johansen of Michigan was made chairman of the Un-American Affairs Committee in January 1958. At the same time the Indiana General Assembly conducted its own hearings through its Senate Internal Security Committee. Subpoenas, said the *Indianapolis Star*, April 23, 1958, were issued to Ralph F. Fuchs of the Law School, Professor Russell J. Compton of DePauw University, and Professor Kenneth N. Cameron, a former Indiana University staff member who was then with the New York State Library. Also former Judge Norval K. Harris and eleven residents of Gary were issued subpoenas. Fuchs, a highly respected professor and campus leader in the American Association of University Professors, had been twice a special assistant to the United States Attorney General, national Secretary of the A. A. U. P., 1955–57, and had served in various capacities with the United States Civil Service Commission. On the campus he was an active advisor on the student-faculty relations committee, and to the local American Civil Liberties Union. Whatever the Hoosier senators had in mind, Professor Fuchs was never called to testify, nor was he ever informed what the committee thought he knew. Fuchs had a prior engagement in Denver and told the legislators he could not be present. Professor Compton of English birth, a former Rhodes Scholar, and former member of the Indiana University English Department, was editor of the *Shelley and His Circle Catalogue* at the Carl H. Pforzheimer Library in Purchase, New York. Maybe the senators thought Shelley was a subversive character.

While the tension of internal search for possible subversives built up mildly in Indiana in the spring and summer of 1958, Representative David R. Thayer, a teacher from the Shelbyville

School System, charged July 21, 1958, that prospective teachers then being trained at Indiana University were required to use texts favoring a socialistic form of government. Thayer said he had seen seven books in the School of Education reading room, six of which "were personally objectionable to me because they were too radical." He quoted from T. V. Smith and Edward C. Lindeman's *The Democratic Way of Life*. Likewise J. B. Berkson's *Education Faces the Future* impressed the legislator as being of a radical strain. Dean Wendell W. Wright of the School of Education made no comment, and Representative Thayer pretty well generated some unintentional answers to his problems. He especially objected to "emphasis on the equality of the entire human race instead of patriotism of a single nation," and especially to a suggestion of the equalization of personal and corporate incomes.

The 1959 version of legislative concern about subversion on the campus was supplied by Representative Chester W. Franke of Columbus. Franke was a dairy operator and chairman of the local American Legion's Americanism Commission. President Wells answered his charge of subversion on the campus, especially in the Department of History, which Franke said offered "sixteen courses in the history of China, Japan, Russia, the Far East, and the Baltic area," but none in Indiana history. He undoubtedly was sensitized on this subject at least from within the Department of History itself. Wells said a check of departmental offerings revealed twenty-eight different courses in American history, seven more in which American history was included, and twenty-two others in all areas of the world. Both semesters the history of the Middle West was offered. The Department of Government also offered twenty-two courses in American government, and many other departments offered American studies courses.

Wells told Franke he would "be glad to make a thorough and careful investigation of any kind desired by the legislature." He said that many years before as a banker he learned that the best way to operate a bank was to be ready at all times for the appearance of the bank examiner. Indiana University operated on the same principle, and was ready to stand investigation at any moment, no matter how bizarre the charges made against it.

In these decades of intense national emotions, red scares, and petulant political charges, Indiana University was constantly called upon to defend its basic principles of freedom against the inroads of the very groups and individuals who proclaimed the doctrine of democracy the loudest. These were years of significant social revolution, wrought by such actions as the Truman order desegregating the services, the Marshall Plan, *Brown* v. *Board of Education*, UNESCO, NATO, and many other revisions of earlier American institutional approaches to national and international problems. The coming of television, the great spurt of mechanization of life and business, and the tremendous commercialization of the American way of life had unsettling impacts on both human beings and institutions.

Even the applied constitutional principles themselves were brought under fresh scrutiny in numerous major court decisions that challenged the American university to define the goals of human freedom in terms of a modern open society. It was the university that ultimately became the primary bastion of defense of the newly defined freedoms. The loudest clamor of the overheated patriots died away at that moment when the House Un-American Affairs Committee lost its capabilities of producing sensational headlines. On the local scene the homegrown witch hunters in time made themselves ludicrous in attempts to dig up valid issues. Indiana University felt a far more active challenge in trying to keep its curriculum, staff, and libraries abreast of the challenges created by a world that was undergoing drastic changes.

[XII]

The Agony and the Glory

AFTER THREE YEARS of coaching at Indiana University, 1934–37, Alvin N. "Bo" McMillin had won twelve games, lost eight, and tied four. His teams had defeated Purdue twice and tied once. He, however, expressed the wish to do better. Early in 1937 he wrote President William Lowe Bryan that the university should create a large "scholarship" fund with which to subsidize football players. This proved to be a case of two men who were utterly unable to speak each other's language. More precisely, it was a case of two men who approached a common mountain but at different times and with sharply different perspectives. Bryan wrote his coach, February 19, 1937, that he had given thought to his proposal. "At the present time," he said, "there is strenuous competition for students along two lines: the one to secure star athletes; the other to secure men who give most promise of being star men after graduation. The two lines of men intersect. Some men meet both conditions. But two schools, one of which allots its scholarships primarily to secure athletes while the other allots its scholarships primarily to secure men of greatest promise for the future, will grow far apart." He then told Bo DePauw University was a good example of the latter policy. It had made a good showing in football with schools of its class, and with men of bright promise, and was forging ahead with students who would later distinguish the institution. Bryan referred to the Rector scholarships for men, which made DePauw "a poor man's school" and a "rich girl's college." He thought a large scholarship fund at Indiana devoted to securing athletes with no thought of academic excellence would be a calamity. Clearly he favored "first-rate athletes as well as first-rate men."

Bo McMillin and the Indiana fans were interested primarily in "first-rate" athletes, and the only "lines of convergence" that interested them was against the forward walls of animalistic strength of their Big Ten opponents. Maybe Bo did take the President's homily seriously. He had a 5-3-0 season in 1937, but lost to Purdue 13 to 7. His world fell apart in 1938, however, when Indiana won only one conference game, and that against Iowa 7 to 3.

McMillin won a good many moral victories, none greater than in the 1938 football season. He was given a ten-year extension of his contract in August before the great autumn disaster, and "millions of American fans" had chosen him over the Michigan and Notre Dame coaches to guide the college all-stars in their game against the professional Washington Redskins.

Herman B Wells in 1938 perhaps stood midway between the postures of William Lowe Bryan and Bo McMillin. He quickly came to appreciate the fact that Indiana University alumni and Hoosier fans in general placed high stakes on a winning football team in a state that produced a three-way competition for players and athletic glory. Excellence in football was simply another area in which the university was challenged to demonstrate an acceptable degree of competence. He was quoted by the *Chicago Tribune*, June 5, 1940, as saying, "Football unquestionably has an effect on the spirit of an institution, provided it is winning football. For that reason I wish for Indiana a winning football team. The spirit on the campus, the loyalty of alumni, and the attitude of the public toward a university are affected by the success of its football team." He said he thought it would be a cheering fact if the Indiana team could "knock the stuffing out of any other team." He preferred genuine Hoosier boys on the university's teams, and would like to see as many games as possible played in Bloomington.

While the president was voicing his views on football to a

Chicago Tribune reporter, a warm little controversy was brewing on the campus. Three women cheerleader pioneers appeared at the Indiana-Purdue basketball game dressed in slacks. The idea of girl cheerleaders was unsettling enough of tradition, but their dress was downright explosive. The argument centered around the fundamental issue of whether the girls should wear slacks or skirts. The *Daily Student* was quoted as saying, "Put 'em in skirts." Students interviewed about the matter were unanimous in saying, "If they're going to have girls out there they should dress them like girls." Rembrandt Hiller of Indianapolis, chairman of the Pep Session Committee which selected these daring first girl pep leaders, explained that the girls wore slacks "just to be on the safe side." The girls themselves said they preferred skirts.

Wells had to concern himself with the entire Indiana athletic program. Everett Dean had been a highly successful and popular basketball and baseball coach, even though his wins and losses balanced in 1937–38, his final year at Indiana. In June 1938 Branch McCracken, a former all-American at Indiana University and coach at Ball State Teachers College, was employed as Dean's successor. McCracken had been chosen all-American player in 1930, and had proved an efficient coach since then. In his first year at Indiana he won 17 and lost 3 games, splitting the two-game series with Purdue. He duplicated this record the next year, except his team defeated Purdue twice by almost identical scores. That year the Hoosiers were chosen for the NCAA tournament over the Big Ten champions Purdue because of a superior overall record. At Kansas City, March 30, 1940, Indiana defeated Phog Allen's University of Kansas champions 60 to 42 to win the National Collegiate Athletic Association championship. When this game ended, a middle-aged man broke through the cheering crowd to congratulate "Big Mac." He said his name was Naismith, "and I wish he [my father] could have been here to see this game tonight. This is the greatest basketball game I have ever seen."

The folks back in Bloomington agreed with Mr. Naismith. They thought it was the greatest game ever played. A yelling throng met the returning warriors on the outskirts of Bloomington. Coach McCracken was seated on a fire engine and was paraded to the gymnasium. There the coach read to the crowd the telegram that President Wells had sent him just before the Kansas contest. "Indiana University," said the president, "expects all its men to do their duty. I have confidence you will do yours."

Other athletes brought cheer to the banks of the Jordan. Roy Cochran on February 26, 1940, broke Ray Ellenwood's record to set a new world mark of 28.9 for the 440-yard indoor dash in a meet against Notre Dame, a meet which Chicago won 52 to 34. At the same time the Indiana wrestling team won the conference championship. The baseball team tied for seventh place in the now nine-member conference, because Chicago withdrew in 1939.

The spring victories of the various teams were sweet solace indeed, even if no Bloomington fire engines tore out to the Jordan with sirens going to deliver champion wrestlers and human speed demons to the campus. The supreme challenge, however, still remained the fielding of a championship football team. The best the McMillin tribe could do that season was win three of an eight-game schedule. They did defeat Purdue in a wobbly 3 to 0 game, an achievement which had added meaning to students in the form of an extra day of vacation.

In 1940–41 the basketball team duplicated its overall record, but bettered its conference standing by a single game, standing second to Wisconsin. Wayne Tolliver of the track team won the national championship in cross-country running. Other members of the team won both indoor and outdoor Big Ten championships. There was, however, still a trace of gloom over the year. Despite the fact Indiana had defeated Purdue 3 to 0, the football season had been largely cheerless because of five conference defeats. The *Daily Student*, partly at the suggestion of the football coach, opened its columns as a clearinghouse for all criticism of Coach McMillin.

At the annual football banquet Bo McMillin had also invited the critics of the football coaches and their team to come out in the open and speak their pieces. McMillin's contract had just been renewed for five more years, and the student newspaper hoped there would be both successful and spectacular games in the future. Since 1935 the flamboyant coach had won 25 games, lost 32, and tied 7. Critics of the 1941 team said the coaches used too many substitutes, ran too many plays, and that Bo McMillin was too indifferent to the student body.

The criticism of McMillin was acute enough that President Wells took notice of it. On December 2, 1941, he announced he had asked the University Faculty Committee on Athletics to review the letters relating to football which reached the *Indiana Daily Student*. Among the letters received by the paper was one from a freshman who wrote, "I think the *Daily Student* is fully justified in making a criticism of Indiana University's football season. Bo McMillin has been losing games for so long that his supply of excuses has [been] exhausted and all he can say is that 'the boys come out every Monday afternoon with determination to win the next one. . . !' " Clearly the fans indicated they wanted football victories. Some said the popular coach had failed. There were also stout defenders; one alumnus of 1934, condemned the *Daily Student* for raising doubts. "I think," he wrote, "it is obvious to sports followers over a wide area that one thing that Indiana has conscientiously tried is changing football coaches. This has given rise at one time or another to our University's gaining the reputation for being a graveyard of coaches." The paper, he thought, should engage in morale building instead of raising destructive doubts. A senior student questioned the wisdom of granting Bo McMillin such long-term contracts. Because of this he could not give the coach full support. A junior thought the coach had been on the job "long enough for him to produce results if he is ever going to." Another member of that class said he was weary of waiting for next year—why not hire Lou Little, who was then looking for a job.

One of the most interesting letters written in this season of criticism was that from Judge Ora L. Wildermuth to Herman B Wells, January 23, 1942. He thought Indiana's coaches and football team had an inferiority complex. "Indiana University has been for many generations," he said, "perfectly willing to be second-rate." Wells, he thought, had done much to change that, but "McMillin's background is not that of a first rank man." Judge Wildermuth discussed the coach's personal history, and concluded that percentages were against the university and its coach to rise up and smack the great football powers of the Big Ten. President Wells responded, February 4, "I am reminded of what George Cooke once said to me. He was a guest at my house. Looking at the dilapidated wreckage of the old Hill Mansion across the street, he remarked that 'Monroe County didn't produce big pumpkins, big ears of corn, or big men. . . .' "

The basketball team defeated Purdue by a single point in their

January meeting and this helped somewhat to change the subject of football criticism. That season McCracken's team won 15 games and lost 6 to stand second in the Western Conference. The team topped such great basketball powers as the University of California at Los Angeles, Minnesota, Wisconsin, Nebraska, Chicago, and Ohio State.

The turn of world history favored Bo McMillin in his moment of what seemed certain approaching crises. His fortunes during the war years improved so much that his renewed long-term contract seemed fully justified. These years, however, brought only limited glory because the power of the Big Ten competition was greatly reduced by the wartime depletion of football talent on the campuses. Indiana defeated Butler 42 to 0 in 1942; Kansas State 54 to 0, Fort Knox 20 to 0, and Purdue 20 to 0. These were the highest scores won by an Indiana team since the opening of Memorial Stadium in 1925.

In the flurry of high-scoring victories a committee of the Student War Council secured permission to have movies made of the football games to be sent to alumni in Army camps at home and abroad. This film was to be financed by a contribution of twenty-five cents from each student, and the Ohio State, Minnesota, and Purdue games were to be filmed. A "tag day" was designated in October 1942 to solicit additional funds to pay the cost of the films. The *Daily Student* reported, October 3, that 3,500 tags were sold, and $590 had been raised, perhaps enough with other student contributions to pay for three films; the record is unclear on this point. No doubt if sound had been added to the pictures the alumni would have been as furious as students and local fans at the naval yeomen who had cheered for Iowa on October 28, 1942, when Indiana lost 14 to 13. This, said a letter writer to the *Daily Student*, was caused by irritations between the students and the campus sailors. The yeomen, he thought, had been given no encouragement to develop the Indiana spirit.

The three years, 1941 to 1944, saw the Indiana athletic teams disastrously eroded by the drafting of upperclassmen into military service. For some reason, however, the football schedule was extended to ten games, with six of them requiring travel to other campuses, despite tire and gasoline rationing, and crowded railway trains. Bo McMillin said that even with green and inexperienced freshmen the football seasons would be continued. Zora

Clevenger also said the Faculty Athletic Committee favored continuing the sports programs in conformity with the war efforts. The basketball schedule was cut two games, and there were some trips away from the campus. In 1943 the team won second place in conference standing. The baseball schedule was also a light one with Indiana winning five of the six games played; three other games were cancelled because of rain.

Indiana University was seriously handicapped in its competition within the wartime situations that prevailed on other Big Ten campuses. Its military personnel was almost altogether Army, and this branch of the service did not permit its members to participate in intercollegiate sports. On some Big Ten campuses there were larger naval units than the one at Indiana and the Navy had no such restrictions. In many instances regular football players exchanged civilian status for naval duty and remained on Big Ten teams. To alleviate this pinch for athletes, the Big Ten board waived the conference's eligibility rules, leaving it up to individual member schools to set their own eligibility rules for players.

By July 1943 the entire membership of the Indiana baseball and basketball teams had been called into the military service. Billy Hayes was left with too few trackmen to enter a meet. Nevertheless, the three major sports schedules were maintained. Bo McMillin had only three lettermen left on the football team in September 1943. In his annual report to the president, Zora Clevenger said that the 1942 football team with Billy Hillenbrand as quarterback promised to be champions of the Big Ten Conference. Now the military draft had dimmed that rosy glow.

The Bloomington *World-Telephone*, November 4, 1943, said that Indiana was rated the best defensive team in the conference. Some of the scores that year resembled basketball tallies; the paper said although "underdog" Purdue won 7 to 0, it was a moral victory for Indiana because Purdue had played Navy men. Bo's freshmen had kept the Boilermakers on the defensive throughout the game.

Before the track season opened in 1944 the highly popular fifty-nine-year-old Billy Hayes died on December 16. He had been successful in producing some of Indiana's most competitive athletes, among them Charles Hornbostel, Ivan Fuqua, Donald Lash, Roger Poorman, Roy Cochran, Archie Harris, and

Campbell Kane. There were scores of others who had won glory on the track, and Billy Hayes had merited every commendable thing Zora Clevenger had said about him when he recommended his appointment to President Bryan in 1925.

Basketball not only suffered the loss of players, but early in 1943 Branch McCracken went away to the Navy and left Harry C. Good to coach the team for the three seasons, 1943–46. In these years Indiana ranged in the conference rankings from last to second position. Good started the 1943–44 season with an almost wholly inexperienced squad of eighteen-year-old freshmen who averaged 170 pounds in weight and 5′10″ in height. At the same time the co-ed organization, Oceanides, upheld Indiana aquatic fame in 1944 in a telegraphic swimming contest in which the university's team tallied 53.5 points. This was a cheering note indeed, made even brighter on November 26 when the football team defeated the Purdue "sailors" 14 to 6, bringing to a close a successful season of seven wins and three losses.

The ravages of war let up, and the football fortunes of Indiana University promised in 1945 to be bright. Bo McMillin was again given a ten-year contract extension, a vote of confidence that seemed warranted the following fall when his team won nine games and tied one to give Indiana the Big Ten championship. The Metro-Goldwyn-Mayer News filmed the game with Nebraska which Indiana won 54 to 14, and *Life Magazine* covered the same event with a generous story. The victorious season was indeed sweetened by the 26 to 0 defeat of Purdue before 27,000 fans on a fair day in November.

The championship team was made up of immediately returned military veterans. These men ranged from buck privates to captains. Lieutenant Pete Pihos and Sergeant Howard Brown were home on extended furloughs. Some of the men had flown B17 flying fortresses, some had driven tanks, and collectively they had seen service on almost all fronts of the war. They had earned enough campaign ribbons to deck Memorial Stadium itself. At the end of the 1945 season Bo McMillin said the defeat of Purdue by such a decisive score and the winning of the Big Ten championship was an even greater thrill than it had been to lead tiny Centre to victory over Harvard.

Before the last whistle had blown in the Purdue game, telegrams began arriving in the athletic offices. There were messages from Grantland Rice, Fritz Crisler, Christy Walsh, and the

Hoosier Hotshots of country dance fame. The United States Army invited Bo McMillin to visit Japan, and with Jeff Cravath, Henry Frnka, and E. E. Myten to organize divisional teams for G.I. competition. The *Daily Student* congratulated McMillin, saying, "And Bo, we thank you. . . . We like you, Bo, because you were just as happy as those boys who lifted you to their shoulders and carried you off the field after their victory." Pete Pihos made two touchdowns in the Purdue game and gained 410 yards rushing for the season. George Taliaferro, the giant black halfback, gained 602 yards, and Robert Ravensberg, left end, was chosen all-American.

There was a stir of excitement in Bloomington that year when a rumor gained some credence that Indiana might play West Point in a post-season game. Ted R. Gamble, head of the War Finance Division of the Treasury Department, asked the War Department if it would not remove its restrictions and allow Army to play in such a game against the Big Ten champion, Indiana. This was to be part of the drive to sell war debentures, and had originally been proposed by Congressman Gerald Landis of Linton, Indiana. Neither the congressman nor Ted Gamble had taken into consideration that the Big Ten (or Nine) Conference had a rule against postseason games. The year before, the conference had refused Ohio State University permission to play in the Rose Bowl. Indiana University officials objected to the proposed game saying that the football team had been disbanded and could not be reconditioned for such a game. In Washington the four Indiana and Illinois senators, Homer E. Capehart, Raymond E. Willis, C. Wayland Brooks, and Scott Lucas, undertook to persuade Dwight D. Eisenhower, Chief of Staff, to approve the game. National sports writers took up the hue and cry, and miscellaneous fans were vigorous in their supplications. Army rated first nationally and Indiana was fourth after Navy and Alabama. In the heat of public agitation the *Daily Student*, December 4, 1945, opposed the idea of postseason play on the grounds the extra game would be anticlimactic and a headache for coaches and players. Sensibly the editor said, "The conference championship, another 'I' link on the Old Oaken Bucket chain, and the first undefeated season in Indiana history are enough to keep the campus in good spirits until another football season rolls around next fall."

No doubt Bo McMillin and his players were of the same

opinion. If the coach suffered any disappointment over not playing the Army, it was quickly dissipated when he was chosen the eleventh national coach of the year by the Football Writers Association by twice as many votes as his nearest competitor, Earl Blaik of Army. At the same time it was announced that the same group had chosen Bob Ravensberg an all-American end, and he was to be thus honored five times in 1945. A day later the Associated Press announced that Indiana University's championship achievement was the second biggest surprise of the year, the first was the Great Lakes Naval Station's overwhelming defeat of Notre Dame.

The sweet fruits of victory were allowed to stand unspoiled. On December 10, a victory banquet was given in the Radio Corporation of America cafeteria in which Albert Benjamin Chandler, baseball commissioner, and Harold Van Orman were the speakers. *Life Magazine* at the same time honored Bo McMillin with a second story about his athletic career.

Not all of 1945, however, was a year of jubilation. On May 20 Jesse D. Ferguson died. Since 1914, except for two years, he had served as head trainer for Indiana athletes. Through good and bad years he had rubbed their sore muscles, bucked up their sagging spirits, and reminded them there would be another day with his famous salutation, "See you tomorrow." Except for the two years when he was trainer for Northwestern University teams, he was considered a permanent fixture along the Jordan. Long before his passing "Fergie" had become a campus tradition. Fate had denied him the pleasure of seeing Indiana win the conference championship.

In the white heat of celebrating the 1945 season a movement was begun at the victory dinner which in time caused Indiana University serious embarrassment. In a letter to the *World-Telephone*, Norman Neely, an alumnus and local attorney, suggested the organization of a boosters club, "which can play a considerable part in the football season of 1946, which may lead to another Big Ten championship and perhaps a national championship." Not a single man of the 1945 team was graduating, and future glory seemed assured. By December 11, 300 Bloomington fans had signed membership cards and the club aimed to maintain winning teams, to secure construction of a new stadium, and to increase the seating capacity of the Fieldhouse.

The *Indianapolis Star* said the boosters were "visioning Indiana football teams of the future as perpetual Western Conference champions."

Hardly had Norman Neely's oratory died away before the optimistic boosters were faced with the unsettling possibility that Lieutenant Branch McCracken might not return to coach the basketball team. On December 12 a pep rally was organized to demonstrate to McCracken, home from the war, that Indiana University truly wanted him to be its basketball coach. Signs were prepared, reading "Draft Back Branch McCracken." He had just been discharged from the Navy and announced to his admirers that he would not make a decision about the future until he had talked with Indiana athletic officials. Fear was rampant that he would accept an offer from Purdue, or possibly would be seduced to become commissioner of the professional National Basketball League. In their conversations Zora Clevenger and others were persuasive. McCracken announced in less than a week he would return to the Jordan to coach basketball. Already the season was underway with Harry C. Good as coach, and the team had won four and lost two games.

Campus football fortunes went up and down, in season and out. Early in 1946 "Big Ted" Kluszewski, a junior, was enticed away from amateur athletics with a contract to play baseball with the Cincinnati Reds. George Taliaferro, the sensational freshman member of the championship team, was drafted into the Army, and was later, in 1949, to join the Los Angeles Dons with one year of his college career to go. At the same time Bob Hoernschemeyer and George Sundheim, two ex-sailors, found themselves in scholastic trouble. Maybe a greater cloud was the announcement by Zora G. Clevenger that he would retire from the athletic directorship in August 1946. At the same time James DeWar, a halfback from Oak Park, Illinois, was discharged from the Army and would bring strength to the football team.

Every Hoosier supporter seems to have had his interest focused on the 1946 football season. The uppermost hope was that the team would repeat its former season's performance. In the meantime the university games had become potentially profitable to radio broadcasting. Harry F. Miedema, Jr., of the Petroleum Marketers Advertising Agency of Indianapolis protested to Governor Ralph Gates that the university charged his agency an excessive fee for the privilege of broadcasting the football games. Ross E. Bartley replied, August 6, 1946, that the reason for the fee was the fact that Miedema's program was a commercial one. All noncommercial programs, Bartley said, were given broadcasting privileges without cost.

The fates of football history were unkind to Indiana University. Bo McMillin and his teams were never to repeat their victories of 1945. In 1946 the season ended with six victories and three losses. Again the brightest spot was the 24 to 20 victory over Purdue. Michigan and Iowa were again powers to be reckoned with, and even lowly Cincinnati smote the Red warriors in the first game of the season. In his final season, 1947, McMillin's Hoosiers finished in their traditional slot of five season wins, three losses, and a tie, again falling victim to the Big Ten giants Iowa, Michigan, and Northwestern.

Branch McCracken came home to brighter promise. Good's team on January 6, 1947, beat Purdue 62 to 46 in what proved to be a tragic game for the Boilermakers. Bleachers in the Purdue fieldhouse collapsed, killing three persons and injuring "dozens" of others. The second game of the traditional series was played in the Butler fieldhouse because that at Indiana University was being enlarged to seat more fans. Despite the changing of coaches in midseason, the Purdue tragedy, and the revamping of the Fieldhouse, Indiana won 12 of 20 games, and tied Illinois for second place in Big Ten standing. This record was not again equaled for five years. Fans no doubt began to wonder about McCracken's optimism when it was said he looked at the new scoreboard in the Fieldhouse and expressed disappointment that it would not register a larger score than 99. The board, however, proved adequate until February 2, 1952, when Indiana defeated Butler 105 to 70, and three weeks later defeated Purdue 113 to 78. Earlier, Purdue had won both games of the 1947–48 season with Indiana, making identical scores for the two games, a coincidence that was to be repeated in Indiana's favor for the two following seasons.

Annually President Wells reported to the trustees on the fortunes of Indiana teams. In 1947–48 he took occasion to make a socioeconomic note that proved almost as revealing as a recitation of game statistics. The stadium and fieldhouse concessionaires reported selling 90,000 sandwiches, 145,500 bottles of soft drinks, 45,000 bags of peanuts, 16,000 bags of popcorn, 30,000 bars of ice cream, 4,000 cups of coffee, and campus dispensing machines disposed of an additional 938,264 bottles of drinks. It is doubtful that Ringling Brothers made a much better showing. Maybe nervous frustration accounted for so much eating and drinking.

Although the football season in 1947 was a fairly successful one, Bo McMillin was unable to achieve the ultimate by producing a championship team. At the end of that season he resigned with eight years to go on his new contract. When Zora Clevenger retired as athletic director, McMillin was most aggressive in seeking appointment to that post. He sought the administrative job even in the face of President Wells' advice that the office chores would prove onerous, if not completely frustrating. Quickly critics began to accuse the new athletic director of favoring football at the expense of other campus athletics. There developed friction among the various coaches and teams, and the coach-director's life was made difficult. He left Bloomington to accept the job of coaching the professional Detroit Lions and later the Philadelphia Eagles. No doubt the tremendously favorable financial arrangements he made with the Lions' owners also had much to do with Bo's forsaking college coaching.

Clyde B. Smith was appointed head football coach to replace Bo McMillin on March 16, 1948. The next five years were to be repetitive of Indiana's traditional football history. The Hoosiers suffered 20 losses to 8 victories and one tie. It did not add an "I" to the chain of the Old Oaken Bucket. Nevertheless, there were jubilant moments. On October 7, 1950, Indiana celebrated its fortieth homecoming. The surviving members of the 1900 team were seated on the Indiana players' bench where they saw their successors defeat Iowa on a soggy field. The *Daily Student*, October 10, observed critically that the local fans seemed subdued even in victory. The loudest noise they made was when the announcer said Purdue had defeated Notre Dame, breaking a 39-game winning streak for the Irish.

No doubt the complacent fans were conscious of the fact that in two weeks Indiana would have its turn with Notre Dame, and they wondered if the Iowa victory offered a ray of hope. If so, that hope was chilled by a 26 to 14 defeat by Ohio State University the following week. The Notre Dame game was played that year in Memorial Stadium on October 21, and ticket sales set a new campus record. Besides the pageantry of the event three major broadcasting companies had crews on hand to report the game. Where students had heretofore been indifferent to pep rallies, this time they turned out in full whooping ranks. The runaway spirit even satisfied the carping *Daily Student*. The Hoosiers won 20 to 7, the first time they had defeated Notre Dame in nearly a half century of intermittent competition. The Bloomington *Herald Telephone*, October 23, 1950, said "They [Hoosier fans] drank from the cup of victory over Notre Dame for the first time in forty-four years. Almost in reverence, they stood in a sort of thankful benediction. The Pilgrims standing on Plymouth Rock must have felt that way. And to Memorial Stadium Thanksgiving came a month early. . . . It [victory] made you think of Riley's immortal line, 'Ain't God good to Indiana.' "

Indiana students appeared to have thrown reason to the winds of frivolity after the Notre Dame game. A hundred cars loaded with demoniac Hoosiers rushed out of Bloomington at 1:00 A.M., October 23, headed for West Lafayette. They said they planned to join Purdue students in celebrating the downfall of mighty Notre Dame. Colonel R. L. Shoemaker had roadblocks set up at the White River bridge near Greencastle, and state police also waited for the caravan in Spencer and Crawfordsville, but even so a few cars slipped by and went on to Purdue. They dashed up and down fraternity row, arousing a few curious students who came down in pajamas to see what was happening. Unfortunately the Hoosiers dived into a one-way West Lafayette street and were hemmed up by the police. Their drivers' licenses were lifted, and they could be recovered only by going to the police station and promising to get out of town in twenty-five minutes; in fact, the police showed the unwelcome visitors the way to Bloomington. The victory celebration continued on the campus for a week, with students screaming, "No school all week." As in earlier days student mobs rushed the town square and virtually took over the village.

The Bloomington *Herald Telephone* said on October 23, "Clyde B. Smith, football coach, has come to Indiana University. He moved in two years ago. Saturday he arrived." The cost of victory was high. The paper said one football fan was killed, six offending drivers were arrested, a deer was slaughtered by an automobile, and hundreds of dollars worth of property was destroyed. William Lowe Bryan sat on the edge of this madness and composed his own thoughts to Coach Smith. "You and I know," he wrote, "those who blow horns at the head of the procession in time of victory then turn tail in time of defeat. We also know those whose pride is to stand by the fighting team and the fighting chief through every turn of fortune. With these I would be comrade." The time was near at hand when the "chief" would need such comradeship; in fact, the next week a more experienced Illinois team dimmed the Notre Dame victory 20 to 0. On October 31 the *Daily Student* commented, "And what has happened since then? Already we have heard students moaning about being 'let down' by the team."

Even in this most recent moment of adversity Clyde B. Smith had won the confidence of the Board of Trustees, and they extended his contract for three years. He thanked them by beating Marquette, but Purdue soured the season with a 13 to 0 victory. A fifteen-car Monon special train had hauled Indiana fans to Lafayette, but this time no one had to go by the police station to recover his driver's license or to be escorted out of town.

When Bo McMillin resigned the post of athletic director, Paul J. "Pooch" Harrell was selected for the office. Almost immediately he announced that Indiana University would construct on Fee Lane, north of the Illinois Central tracks, one of the most modern collegiate baseball fields in the country. President Herman B Wells was more explicit on this subject in his 1948–49 *Annual Report.* He said grading on the baseball diamond had already been started, and expressed the hope that the area just off the lane would be used as locations for a new fieldhouse, a stadium, a golf course, and other types of athletic fields. The first phases of this development, he thought, could be financed out of athletic department unappropriated receipts. Baseball at Indiana still enjoyed a great deal of popularity, and each season the team played twenty or more games with highly satisfactory success.

In other sports the university enjoyed most respectable results. Roy Cochran, a former track star, in July 1948, proved himself a major member of the United States Olympic team by setting a new world record of 51.1 seconds for the 400-meter hurdles. Fred Wilt ('43) was entered in the grueling 10,000-meter contest. He also contributed heavily to the breaking up of the Scandinavian combination by finishing second in the 5,000-meter contest. In 1949 five Indiana athletes were given Balfour awards for excellence. These were Don "Tex" Ritter in baseball; John McDonnell, football; Charles Peters, track; Andy Pachany, wrestling; and Lou Watson, basketball. That year Don Ritter was named all-American outfielder by the American Association of College Baseball Coaches; this honor came after Indiana had tied with Michigan and Iowa for the Big Ten baseball championship. In an indoor track meet with Purdue, Charles Peters set a new Indiana indoor record of 6.1 in the sixty-yard dash, an achievement that equaled the national record.

During the postwar years students were constantly being taken to task for lack of school spirit. Pep rallies were poorly attended, and in campus chatter students were critical of coaches and players following defeat. In February 1950 the Special Events Committee of the Student Senate decided Hoosier teams should have a mascot; maybe this would enliven school spirit. Dick Rhodes, a committeeman, said the athletic officials had approved the idea, provided students chose a suitable symbol. The past fall students had expressed a preference for a crimson bull. Rhodes thought this suggestion might be acceptable if someone would volunteer to be keeper of the animal. A month later the University Athletic Committee turned down the choice of a bull, crimson or otherwise. W. R. Breneman, chairman of the committee, said its members felt "the idea of a mascot excellent, but that they were not impressed with the idea of a crimson bull." They were convinced that student selection of such an animal had been stimulated by clever publicity for a humor magazine.

Athletic teams at Indiana University early became involved in wiping away barriers of racial discrimination, as did the university itself. In 1947 the National Association for the Advancement of Colored People held an institute on race relations in Indiana on the Bloomington campus. This meeting stimulated a disturbing amount of emotion among the people of Bloomington and in the state generally. President Wells, who said he was opposed to the NAACP stirring up animosities in the town, stated categorically that he wished to see the last barriers of racial discrimination in the university removed. This resulted in the organization of Lincoln House, the admission of three or four girls to dormitories, and ultimately in a generous expression of appreciation by parents and the NAACP for the university's actions. Earlier the university and one of its black students, Halson Eagelson, had been victimized in a racial incident on the way to a Purdue football game in Lafayette. Between 1948 and 1951 the coaches of the basketball team found it difficult to find housing and dining accommodations in St. Louis hotels and restaurants and elsewhere for Bill Garrett, who broke the basketball color barrier in the Big Ten; the team insisted on staying together on trips away from Bloomington.

The postwar years, 1948–55, saw considerable athletic activity in Indiana University, accompanied no doubt by an equal amount of frustration. Early in January 1949 the Los Angeles Dons signed George Taliaferro as a professional halfback after an unseemly tussle with the Chicago Bears. Loss of Taliaferro was indeed a blow to Hoosier football fortunes. Paul J. Harrell vigorously criticized professional managers for their shameless raiding of college teams for players who still had campus eligibility. To him, this kind of ethics threatened the future success of college football. The blow of losing a star halfback to a professional team was compounded in March of that year when it became known that Nick Sabel, Lou Kasonovich, and Milan Sellers had become ineligible to play because they had participated in a noncollegiate basketball game in Indianapolis. There was some brightness, however; Lou Watson and Don Ritter made capital showings on the basketball team. Before Watson finished his playing career the following year he had established himself as one of the all-time great Hoosier athletes.

A part of Indiana's troubles in this period seems to have originated in the athletic director's office. W. R. Breneman, chairman of the Athletic Committee, wrote President Wells, March 10, 1949, that the committee was confronted by three problems which were distressing. He said rumors had reached the committee and some alumni that there was dissension in the Athletic Department. The departmental organization undoubtedly was inadequate, and football weaknesses derived from coaching, lack of team spirit, and poor recruiting. Harrell, he said, failed to take positive action regarding departmental organization. He did not spend enough time in his office, even though his good will efforts were significant. Breneman told the president, "It should be pointed out that the executive committee felt that Mr. Harrell and his staff were doing many fine things for athletics and are developing an excellent long-range program. Since our meeting was called specifically to consider those things which were 'wrong' this letter must of necessity sound very critical." It is not clear how much an editorial in the *World-Telephone*, March 2, 1950, might have influenced the Indiana athletic administration. The paper quoted an unnamed man who had said he was chairman of the athletic committee of the Indiana University Alumni Association in Chicago. He charged the campus athletic leadership was incompetent and confused, and the coaches were not on a par with those in other Western Conference schools. Although quoting this man, the local paper refuted his statements by saying they were both uninformed and destructive. The editor thought the Indiana program a splendid one, and he was sure its managers were competent.

There was, nevertheless, campus criticism of the university's intramural program. The *Daily Student* said facilities were hopelessly inadequate. In twenty years enrollment had increased by 7,000 students, yet physical education and intramural facilities "are virtually the same." A case in point was that 970 freshmen men were signed up to take physical education when there was space for only 250, and so it was in the use of other athletic facilities available to students.

Frankly the tone of Indiana athletics was set by the rise and decline of football fortunes. In the years, 1948–55, the baseball team maintained a highly respectable record of wins and losses ratios, as did the basketball team.

The 1951 football season was barely underway when there was a muttering of dissatisfaction with both football coaches and players. Alumni in Bloomington, Indianapolis, and Chicago were displeased. Questionnaires of unknown origin appeared on the campus asking, "What is wrong with the football team?" The *Indianapolis News* said alumni in that city on the whole were willing to wait and see the season through. The Chicago alumni, however, were openly critical of Coach Clyde Smith. Frank Lindsley was quoted as saying, "We feel that Clyde Smith's record has shown that he can't give us the coaching we're entitled to. We have taken the leadership in what you might call the anti-Smith corps."

President Wells, said the Bloomington *Herald-Telephone*, had instructed the Athletic Department to produce a dynamic program. The faculty-student committee had been revamped, and the university showed signs of wishing to raise athletic standards to the level set for its academic departments. A month earlier Wells had received a letter from Robert W. McConnell, an attorney, saying the university was trying to play in a league to which it did not belong. He told the president, "If you want to make a contribution to Indiana University, far and above anything money can buy, then address the men, whoever they are, who arrange Indiana's football schedules. Let them know that the era of pipe dreaming is over; that Indiana is either going to have decent regard for the boys who come there to play, never again to grossly over-match them throughout any season, or the sport will be dropped. I believe a right thinking President can and would make such an edict stick." McConnell expressed the belief there was not one good argument for continuance of the present system. Football money was no more honorably earned than that grabbed by a "dive-taking fighter and his manager."

There may have been much to what the Indianapolis attorney said. Even Clyde B. Smith might have agreed with him on most points. On November 6, 1951, between defeats by Wisconsin and Minnesota, Smith resigned as head coach. He closed his coaching career in Bloomington with a 21 to 13 loss to Purdue. That season he won two games and lost seven; for his years at Indiana he won eight games and suffered twenty-eight losses and a tie. When his team lost to Michigan by three touchdowns in Ann Arbor on October 13, there was disturbing criticism but none of it seemed to be organized, not even the carping from the Chicago alumni. Students, and the *Daily Student* in particular, were generally kind in comments about Coach Smith. The paper said, "Nice guys like Clyde Smith have been hurt by the repercussions of 'you've gotta produce' theory before, and they will continue to have abuse heaped upon their shoulders in years to come until the sports-minded nation realizes that those men are doing their darndest for 'Dear Old Alma Mater.' " Plenty of people in Bloomington will miss the "little guy" when he is gone, said the editor. Even the *Herald-Telephone* came to his defense, commending him for his high standards and sportsmanship. It would be hard to find a man with his qualities for a future coach.

Clyde Smith said, November 28, 1951, the reasons he resigned were what he regarded as conflicting standards of principle in present athletic conduct, and he no longer proposed to compromise his players for the sake of winning. He felt the time had come for

Big Ten universities to reassess their sports programs. Modern coaches, said Smith, were selling their principles for messes of pottage, but he failed to define the pottage. Ralph E. Esarey wrote John F. Mee, Big Ten faculty representative, December 1, saying that he felt Smith was making a whipping boy of Indiana in trying to bring about a house cleaning of Western Conference athletics.

There was no doubt Smith's resignation opened Indiana to some criticism, and the veiled references in his speeches may even have brought it under some suspicion. Now that the break had been made the Allen County and Fort Wayne alumni thought the Athletic Department should undergo a complete shake-up, which should begin with the dismissal of Paul J. Harrell as director. In a more realistic sense the university was at a football crossroads. The *Daily Student* said it could go out and hire a high-powered coaching staff that would have enough prestige to draw players to Indiana, it could begin a highly competitive recruiting program, turn its back on the "Sanity Code," build a bigger stadium, and create a large athletic fund. Students themselves could fall victims to such a program by having to pay much higher athletic fees. Alternatively the university could balance its athletic program by supporting athletes with a degree of equality in all sports, or it could de-emphasize football by withdrawing from the Big Ten Conference.

There was much soul-searching about athletics, and football specifically, all across the campus. John F. Mee, Edward R. Edwards, and representatives of student organizations attempted in a highly publicized town-hall meeting to discuss the athletic program. Only 260 persons attended the meeting, and some of these hissed and booed Edwards' statement that the football team the past season came within a thin margin of being victorious. Mee said so long as he was chairman of the Athletic Committee Indiana would try to have a winning team, and he believed a football team not incompatible with a university of high academic standards. The *Daily Student* called the public meeting a failure. Frankly, said the paper, Indiana University had never had what could be called a football tradition. It said President Wells had declared on taking office "that Indiana University must continue its goal of above board athletics." Football, said the reporter, should continue "to be more of an entertainment than a sport."

Criticism flowed generously on the campus. Everybody seems to have wanted to voice an opinion. Malcolm S. Romine, president of the class of 1952, said Paul J. Harrell was head of the most criticized department on the campus. Yet he refused to attend the town-hall meeting to answer student questions. The town-hall meeting stirred up more friction than it gathered information or advice. Ralph Fuchs, faculty chairman of the Faculty-Student Committee, and John Sparks, student chairman, raised fundamental questions about athletic policies which apparently went unanswered.

While the wind of dissatisfaction ruffled the tenor of campus life, John Mee, Paul J. Harrell, and members of the Athletic Committee set out to find a new coach of "the high type integrity, moral character, and leadership that has been possessed by the university's football coaches in the past and is possessed by the coaching staff in other sports." They sought demonstrated coaching skill to train high-type athletes, a large order which many felt could not be filled within the context of Big Ten football rules and practices.

While the great campus debate went on about policies and principles, the Athletic Committee recommended on January 11, 1952, the appointment of Bernard Anthony Crimmins to be the sixteenth Indiana head coach of football. Crimmins was an assistant coach at Notre Dame, and as a player had been selected on an all-American team. He was given a five-year contract. At the same time Clyde B. Smith went to coach at Arizona State College. Ironically, his predecessor, Larry Siemering, at the southwestern school, had resigned in the wake of a scandal for having played an ineligible athlete the past season. Joe Matesic had played at Indiana under Smith, and then entered Arizona State under the assumed name of his brother Edward.

Kenneth L. "Tug" Wilson, Big Ten Commissioner of Athletics, wrote Paul J. Harrell on August 25, 1952, "I am firmly convinced Indiana University is slowly digging its own grave athletically in the state." He said the Hoosier coaches had believed they had to recruit players from outside the state. He thought the Indiana people had become convinced they stood little chance of attracting players to Bloomington, and fans also passed up the university. Harrell replied that there was not enough football talent in Indiana to enable three major universities to recruit teams to compete in the Big Ten. Besides, universities from outside the state tolled away some of the best high school players. He cited Michigan as a special offender. It was not too difficult to recruit fifteen basketball players from 800 high schools, but it was almost impossible to find likely football players in the 157 high schools that had football teams.

Questions were raised on every major college campus in 1952 about whether educational and athletic integrity might be undergoing a possible moral deterioration because of scandals which associated college players with professional gamblers, and with other unwholesome pressures. Kentucky, Bradley, New York University, and St. John's had all made the sports headlines with scandalous player conduct. There was considerable campus hysteria and soul-searching across the country, and Indiana in this tender moment was not to escape self-examination. Ross Bartley indicated concern on this point in a memorandum, April 1, 1952, in which he denied there was an overemphasis of athletics in the University. He quoted from a Louisville *Courier-Journal* story, saying President Wells had told a reporter, "Indiana University has every intention of continuing its moderate, faculty-controlled inter-collegiate program." Yet in Bartley's memorandum there was a strong overtone of fear that scandal could occur to upset such a collegiate program.

In December 1952 William Battle, an assistant coach, was placed on a seven-month "recruiting quarantine" by the Conference Faculty Committee of the Big Ten. He was charged with visiting high school athletes in attempts to influence them to enroll in Indiana University. This infraction was forerunner to what became a grim and tragic decade for Indiana athletics. Later, it began to seem football coaches were either incapable or too brazen to learn from history.

While the football team struggled through a dismal season of two wins and seven losses, Branch McCracken's basketball team had perhaps the best overall season in Indiana athletic history. It won 23 games to 3 losses, losing a single conference contest to Minnesota. For the first time the Hoosiers won the undisputed Big Ten championship by defeating Illinois 91 to 79, although they would win three more victories before the end of the season. The National Collegiate Athletic Association championship team of 1940 had finished second in the conference, but it was chosen because it had the best overall record. The *Herald-Telephone*, March 2, 1953, said, "The big roar found some 4,000 madly screaming students cheering the lionized Hoosier team in a 10:30 P.M. pep session at the Fieldhouse. It was one of the greatest single spontaneous celebrations ever given an Indiana University team. It was more spectacular because it came in the midst of a snow-swirling blizzard." Indiana, in regional tournament play, defeated DePaul and Notre Dame; they then defeated Louisiana State and Kansas for the NCAA Championship. The latter game, played in Kansas City on March 18, was nip and tuck for the Hoosiers, it was tied fourteen times, and Indiana led ten times; the final score was 69 to 68. Despite this thin margin, all the national rating polls that year placed Indiana first.

Aside from the national championship, the 1952–53 athletic season led to the establishment of several impressive individual player records. Bob Leonard, guard and captain of the team, and Don Schlundt, forward, were named to the all-conference team. Leonard and Burke Scott were selected all-tournament players in the regional contests, and Leonard and Schlundt were named on all-American teams. Leonard was the unanimous Big Ten coaches' choice in the Associated Press poll. Six members of the team shot above a .300 per cent average, with Schlundt achieving a .500 mark, and he set an individual scoring record of 47 points against Ohio State on February 27, 1953.

For the second time in a fortnight Bloomington was rocked by mad cheering. McCracken and his men were given a "mile long" parade tailed by 3,000 automobiles from Cascades Park to the Fieldhouse. President Wells said it exceeded that given Dwight D. Eisenhower two months earlier. Times were good for the basketball Hoosiers, and they repeated their next season with the championship team intact. Again Don Schlundt went on a record-smashing rampage, toppling ten of fourteen Big Ten records, including selection for three successive times to the all-Big Ten team. He was chosen a second time Helms all-American player, and he and Bob Leonard again were chosen in all-American selections. The Hoosiers fell short of the national championship, however, in a loss to Notre Dame.

Still the gridiron was Indiana's vale of thorns. Bernie Crimmins had indeed traveled from South Bend to Bloomington to serve Indiana under an evil star. In what the *Herald-Telephone* called the coach's darkest hour, November 21, 1953, the Hoosiers succumbed to Purdue in a runaway 30 to 0 game. Nevertheless, a neighborly throng of 5,000 fans looked to next year and gathered before the Crimmins' residence to shout their support. Such human warmth may have been good for the flagging spirits of a forlorn coach, but it accomplished nothing in reversing Indiana's football fortunes. From 1953 to 1957, the team won only twelve games while losing thirty-three, and between 1953 and 1961 the Hoosiers did not add an "I" to the Old Oaken Bucket chain. Crimmins and his colleagues perhaps found only one bit of solace in the fact the baseball team lost twenty-eight games in a row, and between 1950 and 1958 never finished higher than fourth place in the conference.

On February 22, 1954, the Bloomington paper announced the resignation of Paul J. Harrell as athletic director. He asked to be relieved of the job to assume other duties in the university. This news set off speculation as to his successor. The suggestion was made that Branch McCracken be appointed to that place. At this point, however, the administration considered the selection of a new athletic director crucial to the future of athletics. Criticism had been aimed at the director's office, and some disgruntled fans pretended to see in Harrell a source of athletic failures. There seems to have been little doubt that the Wells administration was vitally concerned. On December 6, 1954, the *Herald-Telephone* gave premature publicity to the fact that Paul W. Brechler of the University of Iowa had been chosen director. Brechler was highly regarded on his campus and President Virgil Hancher was able to persuade him to forgo a $3,000 salary differential to remain in his present job.

A month later the Board of Trustees announced that Frank E. Allen, superintendent of the South Bend schools, and a member of the Indiana Board of Trustees had been chosen to succeed Harrell, and to be professor of education. Allen was strongly prevailed upon by his colleagues to accept the appointment, even though his name had not appeared on the Athletic Committee's list of candidates.

Aside from the immediate problem of trying to improve the fortunes of football and baseball, the new director had to deal with the broader issue of intramural sports, the development of more student facilities, and the organization of an intercollegiate golf team. Plans were underway in the fall of 1954 to build an eighteen-hole course on a 250-acre tract of university watershed land. The lay of the land was conducive to establishing standard links without involving heavy construction costs for grading and filling.

Previously President Wells had reported that three new football practice fields were almost ready for use; these were located northwest of the new golf links, and immediately off Fee Lane. These, he said, would also be the site of the proposed new fieldhouse and indoor practice building. There were needs for expanding other athletic facilities brought about by a rising student enrollment. Coach Dale Lewis' tennis team won conference championships, 1953 and 1954, but they were not tailed home by howling mobs of admiring fans.

When the fall semester opened in 1955, the outward signs seemed right for the dawning of a new day in athletics, and for football in particular. Alumni were busy that spring among the Indiana high schools and abroad, and for the first time in history the Hoosiers would soon be able to field at least three full teams of about equal capabilities. President Wells, for what seemed to be the first time, made mention in his annual report of athletic scholarships. He said 54 varsity and freshmen players had qualified under Big Ten Conference rules for tuition grants. These grants placed an additional strain on the Athletic Department's budgetary capability; Frank E. Allen wrote Wells, May 18, 1956, that as things were going it would be impossible for the Athletic Department to remain as a self-sustaining enterprise. Costs inevitably would rise and have to be met in some way if Indiana chose to continue competing in the Western Conference. He suggested that the university attempt to secure an annual pledge of $50,000 from alumni.

Wells, in these years when the greatest expansion of the university generally was taking place, was drawn more and more into athletic problems. He indicated concern that endeavors in this sector be placed on a plane with all other institutional achievements. In September 1956 he outlined four steps for accomplishing this goal. These involved hiring the best available coaches, engendering new interest among faculty and alumni, mobilization of a student committee, and beginning "the long, difficult, and expensive process of building adequate athletic facilities." He said the university was more noted in most of its academic fields than in sports. Significantly, Wells said, "many impulsive solutions have been tried in the past but failed."

The president's statement was made a week before the football season opened on September 29, when Indiana lost to Iowa 27 to 0. That year Crimmins' team defeated only Northwestern in the Big Ten Conference, and in its final game, November 24, it lost to Purdue 39 to 0. This was the cataclysmic end for the 37-year-old "Smiling Irishman" Crimmins. Two days later with tears rolling down his cheeks he announced his resignation, saying, "I feel it is better for the athletic department if I step down. I know there are some good football players at Indiana and maybe my successor can do better. In my five years at Indiana we've never seemed to get the breaks."

The *Daily Student*, November 29, 1956, said Crimmins had lost fifteen pounds and had aged "considerably" in his five years as head coach. He returned to his former job as backfield coach at Notre Dame. Crimmins' record of 32 losses and 13 wins jeopardized somewhat the development of expanded physical facilities at the university. Now the hiring of an effective head football coach took on a strong element of fiscal meaning. In less than two months the Athletic Committee announced the appointment of Phil Dickens of Wyoming as head coach. Dickens, said the *Indiana Alumni Magazine*, was "called the tenth best coach in the Nation." A star player at the University of Tennessee, head coach at Wofford College, and successful in the Skyline Conference, he came with high expectations. He brought his full coaching staff from the West, and began his duties early in February 1957. Dickens possibly began preparations for the new season before he took time to read the Big Ten Conference rules and the most recent revision, or before anyone had the foresight to interpret them for him.

The conference on April 26, 1956, placed Ohio State University on probation for one year, forbidding it to participate in the Rose Bowl if invited, because of irregularities in finding jobs for football players. The followng August a special committee reported on proposed changes in "rule 7" granting financial assistance to athletes, and on December 8 the new rule was tentatively approved. Later, on February 22, 1957, and at the moment Dickens was getting settled at Indiana, the new rule 7 was confirmed.

No one at Indiana seems to have comprehended the fact that the coaching staff should be warned. Under the revision, conference schools could only extend aid to prospective athletes on basis of actual need as stated by the boy's parents. This was limited to cost of rooms, board, books, and fees. However, students in the upper fourth of their graduating classes could be given aid irrespective of demonstrated need.

Kenneth L. Wilson, conference commissioner, visited Indiana University on June 5 and 6 to inform President Wells that he was investigating the school's financial aid commitments to athletes. He had received complaints from both conference and nonconference schools that Coach Dickens had violated the new rule. It was said the coach had offered $15.00 in incidental money, and promised to pay transportation costs to Bloomington for prospective players. William F. Fox, a sportswriter on the *Indianapolis News* published a copyrighted story on July 1, saying Indiana was being investigated for rules infractions. He quoted President Wells as saying, "It would be wholly presumptuous on the part of anyone at Indiana University to make any statement on the subject at this time. It is the commissioner's job to enforce the rules, and we should in no way attempt to influence the procedure." The Conference Faculty Committee deemed Indiana in violation, and gave the institution alternate choices of placing Phil Dickens on a year's suspension or of withdrawing from the conference. Later John Mee told the Indiana Faculty Council that Indiana had drawn a lighter penalty because it had voluntarily taken steps to correct the offense.

Phil Dickens said in his defense, July 30, "I can say in good conscience that if I was in violation of the rules in statements attributed to me, I was not aware of it, nor did I intend to violate the rules." This statement came two days after the conference meeting in Chicago, at which both President Wells and John Mee were present. Wells told his colleagues in Bloomington, "Confronted with this alternative (suspension or withdrawal), Professor Mee and I, by authority of the Athletic Committee, advised that Indiana would comply by suspending Coach Dickens' employment as football coach for one year, effective August 5th. This action was in accordance with the University's 58 years of faith and confidence in the Conference as a regulatory body in collegiate athletics." The University was denied the right to petition for reinstatement of the coach until the following December meeting of the Conference Faculty Committee.

Frank E. Allen told his staff Dickens would continue to draw his $15,000 salary, but he could take no part in coaching football. He said the staff was instructed to abide carefully by this ruling. It was known Dickens could have no association with prospective players, but Kenneth L. Wilson and his assistant Bill Reed were vague in their statements of what the coach could do. He was permitted to observe games from the press box so long as he remained well away from the phone which connected directly with the players' bench. Bob Hicks, who had refused the head coaching job at Wyoming to follow Dickens to Bloomington, was made acting head coach.

Indiana sports writers, said the Associated Press, July 31, disagreed with the Conference Faculty Committee's ruling. Characteristic of the writers' comments were those of the *Herald-Telephone* reporter who said, "If all the sins in the entire conference are at our doorsteps, we should blush indeed. If we are but a scapegoat, we should be fighting mad. . . . We look to I. U. for the leadership that will preserve our pride, and ultimately, make a genuine competitor, if not the scourge of the Big Ten." The Lafayette *Journal* reporter said he had been told Dickens had escaped with a minor penalty for his 23 alleged violations of rules. He, however, regarded the penalty as too severe. The *Star* thought other Big Ten coaches were as guilty.

An even sharper reaction was that of Alexander Campbell, a former trustee, who wrote President Wells and Frank E. Allen, October 16, suggesting that Indiana University "hire a very fine, top-secret, former F. B. I. investigator," and select three Big Ten and two nonconference universities and spend several months investigating their athletic activities. He thought this the only way to overcome what he called "the Smith and Crimmins errors," and to free Phil Dickens to produce a winning team under existing conference rules. Although Campbell did not mention blackmail, there seemed to be more than an implication of it in the nature of his proposal.

As friendly as were the press commentaries, the blow of the conference ruling to Indiana was indeed discouraging. Wells addressed an informative letter to the university's alumni on August 12, in which he said, "We have suffered a great blow to our athletic program but we are not discouraged." A similar sentiment was expressed by Frank E. Allen. Neither man, however, at that point seemed to have realized there would be an inevitable blow from the infractions committee of the National Collegiate Athletic Association.

In October the national body's eighteen-member rules committee meeting in Kansas City placed Indiana on probation. President Wells made a gallant effort to prevent the action, pleading that any infractions of Big Ten rules that had occurred was unintentional. These restrictive rulings severely damaged Hoosier morale as Frank E. Allen told the Chicago Quarterback Club that month. By that time the Hoosiers had lost their first four games to opponents who had scored 183 points against them. There never had been an enthusiastic boosters club in Bloomington, he said, comparable to those in other Big Ten schools. Now there was one and, "perhaps," he said, "they were a little energetic and wanted to do things too fast." Recruiting, said the athletic director, was one of Indiana's hardest problems. It was forced to go outside the state to find enough good players. He told his audience the rumor was that the university had a special deal in Pennsylvania because fourteen members of the present team came from that state. Frankly, the director said, "We've run out of alibis at Indiana. We've been waiting 10 years for next year."

The wait indeed grew longer. Bob Hicks' team defeated only Villanova for a one and eight season. The suspension of Coach Dickens was revoked in December, and for the next six years, 1958–64, Indiana repeated rather faithfully its historic record. During those years it tied Purdue once, and won once. After the year of suspension trauma, and a disastrous football season, the Board of Trustees became deeply concerned. Early in December it broke silence and declared, "Football must be raised to the competitive [level] which the University has achieved with notable success." The board referred, of course, to the success of other campus sports. In 1956–57 Indiana had won Big Ten championships in indoor and outdoor track and basketball, and had won third and fourth places in tennis and swimming.

Baseball, however, was a cellar team. Its most notable accomplishment came in the field of race relations. For years the Hoosiers had played "conditioning" games in the Lower South, and against segregated teams. In 1956, two years after the Supreme Court rendered the *Brown* v. *Board of Education* decision, Coach Ernie Andres and Vice-President John W. Ashton canceled games in Florida and Georgia and decided that in the future Indiana would schedule no games in which Eddie Whitehead, a sophomore, was kept from playing. On a second front of social sensitivity, Gene S. Moll, an "interested parent," raised the question with Frank E. Allen of why there was not an intercollegiate athletic program for women.

There were three bright spots in the grim year 1957. James E. Counsilman was hired as swimming coach; Branch McCracken was elected to membership in the Helms Athletic Foundation's College Basketball Hall of Fame. In twenty-four years of coaching his teams had won 344 games against 138 losses; they had won three conference and two national championships. On June 24 the new eighteen-hole golf course was opened to competitive play, and it was hoped Indiana's standing in this sport would show an immediate rise.

The National Collegiate Athletic Association lifted its interdiction against Phil Dickens on October 22, 1958, and that year the football team won five games, lost three, and tied one. Phil Dickens was second choice after Paul Dietzel of Louisiana State University as national "coach of the year." This sunny break in the dark cloud of Hoosier football fortunes was of brief duration. On April 21, 1960, the National Collegiate Athletic Association again announced that Indiana University was being placed on probation for a period of four years for further infractions of recruiting rules. Wells said he and his administrative colleagues had defended the university against this second charge with the greatest vigor, but to no avail. The *Daily Student* pessimistically said the latter action hung an albatross about the neck of Indiana athletics for the next four years.

The university was charged with four specific violations. It was said an alumnus had offered a prospective player in New Jersey transportation to Bloomington to enroll in the university; another representative, a former Wofford College player under Dickens' coaching, had offered an Ohio prospect clothing and $50.00 to $75.00 a month; an alumnus and an assistant coach were charged with making a Virginia prospect an offer ranging from $100.00 to $300.00 a month and a monthly bonus of $50.00 to $75.00; and another Ohio prospect was offered $75.00 to $100.-00 and free vacation transportation.

Only football recruiting was involved, and the blame seemed to have rested largely with alumni, except for the one offense by an assistant coach. The *Daily Student* said, "Dr. Frank Allen, director of athletics, tells us, however, that there are more than 100,000 living alumni of the University, many of whom devote their principal efforts toward helping I.U. establish athletics. Many of these alumni are thousands of miles away, and university officials have no control over their actions. Yet the NCAA sees fit to hold colleges and universities responsible for the actions of their alumni under what are extreme circumstances, indeed."

The tragedy of this ruling was the fact that all Indiana athletes came under its interdiction, and were forbidden to compete for conference and national championships. The years 1960–64, promised to be unusually productive ones for basketball, track, swimming, wrestling, and gymnastics. Only one dim hope was left: Hoosiers could compete in Olympic trials. Perhaps the greatest sense of personal injury was suffered by President Wells. In a public statement he said, "I cannot and I do not wish to minimize the seriousness of the action that has been taken against Indiana University. It is a terrible blow and most certainly will affect our athletic program. The Athletic Department and I have spent not merely days and not only weeks but months on the matters involved. We made extensive painstaking investigations of our own. The result was we were unable honestly and objectively to concur in certain assumptions and conclusions on which action had been taken. On this firm basis, we presented our case with the greatest vigor and earnestness and with concurrence of the Board of Trustees and the Faculty Committee on Athletics. We still hold to our judgments." One of the judgments no doubt was that Indiana unhappily had been caught in a power squeeze between Kenneth L. Wilson of the Big Ten Conference and Walter Byers of the National Collegiate Athletic Association. Wilson had gone to Atlanta to ask for leniency toward Indiana.

On the campus in Bloomington petitions bearing 1,990 signatures were collected. These asked the Big Ten Conference not to suspend Phil Dickens a second time. Part of this concern about Dickens was caused by Jack Olsen's article in *Sports Illustrated* which said Big Ten football players generally were given "locker room payola." After each game, Olsen said, players were rewarded with "unsigned envelopes with 'honorariums' enclosed." He quoted a Big Ten recruiter as saying everybody "gave the boys a little on the side. But it's the way that Indiana did it that hurts recruiters everywhere. There was no finesse." This source said the actual passing of money should be left to "well-fixed alumni, thus avoiding any entangling alliances with players who might have a tendency to collect and tell." Dickens and his staff stoutly denied the allegations in the Olsen article, and so did university officials.

There was much campus speculation, said the *Daily Student*, May 19, 1960, as to what course Indiana University might take. This ranged from dropping out of the Big Ten Conference to Indiana and conference officials entering an injunction against the National Collegiate Athletic Association, and then investigating that body. The paper expressed the opinion that Wells and Allen "may reverse their stand and release Coach Dickens. This action, we think, can be expected." Wells and Allen, however, counseled everybody to remain calm in the face of adversity. A survey of Big Ten sentiment by the Associated Press indicated a preliminary feeling that Indiana had been dealt with too harshly and the Conference Committee would vote against further disciplinary action. The press was wrong, the conference placed Indiana on a year's probation.

Commissioner Kenneth L. Wilson wrote President Herman B Wells, July 29, 1960, "I find in these cases a widespread practice of offers of illegal financial assistance to prospective students and of the receipt of illegal financial assistance by students, once they have enrolled at Indiana University. . . . Significantly, it is a football player who is involved in each case. It is submitted by Indiana University that to the extent these practices existed, they were the workings of unknown, uninstructed, or irresponsible friends or alumni of the University. . . . I must say, however, that I have grave doubts any such practices on the scale suggested could possibly have been carried on without the knowledge, and, indeed, the approval of the football coaching staff." Wilson placed Indiana's membership in the conference on probation for one year and excluded it from sharing in football television receipts. Games played against conference opponents were not to be counted in reckoning standings.

The next day President Wells responded that the Board of Trustees and Faculy Athletic Committee had authorized him "to say to you that the University, though in disagreement with your conclusions, bows to your decisions. The University takes this step most reluctantly and only for overpowering reasons." These were the university's desire to remain in the Big Ten Conference, to end investigations of its athletic affairs by the regulatory bodies, and "We must now get on with our job, which is teaching, research, and public service." The university accepted the burden of penalties "confident that the Conference in its wisdom and sense of fair play, upon our further showing, will restore the University to good standing which is our aspiration in conference membership." Governor Harold W. Handley pleaded unsuccessfully with Commissioner Wilson to soften the probationary terms.

For the second time in five years Indiana's football fortunes crumbled, 1960–63; the team won only one game in 1960, two the next year, and three each of the next two seasons. Opponents scored 733 points to 313 for the Hoosiers, 599 of those points were scored by conference teams. Indiana won only four conference games, and one of these in 1962 against Purdue. In 1963 the home game against Ohio State University, October 5, set an attendance record of 42,296, and the season total was 136,761, a record. Nevertheless, ample internal evidence points to the fact that probation indeed had serious effects upon football.

The probationary penalties could hardly have been imposed at a more inopportune moment in Indiana University history. The new stadium was ready for occupancy early in the fall of 1960. On Sunday, October 2, a staff of more than 200 went through a practice drill in preparation for the formal opening the following Saturday. The new facility would seat 48,000 persons and had cost $6,072,860. Thirty-five years before Indiana had dedicated Memorial Stadium. Claude Rich, Alumni Secretary, recalled that its dedication on November 21, 1925, was blessed with a cold but fair day, and it had taken place just before the Hoosiers played Purdue in a 0 to 0 tie. This game had also initiated the tradition of the Old Oaken Bucket.

There must have been much introspection among the more concerned university officials as Governor Harold W. Handley formally presented the new stadium to the university administration on October 22, 1960, at the dedication game with Michigan State. Speakers were President Herman B Wells and Dr. Merrill Davis, captain of the 1910 Hoosiers (6 and 1) and then a member of the Board of Trustees. The dedication queen, Judy Curtis, had difficulty smashing a bottle of River Jordan water against a south goalpost.

The *Daily Student*, October 11, said "Oct. 8, 1960, will be remembered in Indiana University football history as the day the Fighting Hoosiers played their first game in a new, unequaled $4.5 [*sic*] million stadium. Other than that the day's events will probably go unnoticed. Nothing went right for Hoosier football fortunes Saturday. The weather was lousy, the crowd didn't even fill half the 48,344 seat stadium [*sic*] was disappointing, and the football team left something to be desired. For the third Saturday in a row the Hoosiers were plagued by inability to maintain a sustained offensive drive. Coach Phil Dickens said before the season opener against the University of Illinois that if anything, the defense was ahead of the offense." The Hoosiers lost that Saturday to Oregon State 20 to 6, and neither defense nor offense was ever ahead.

At the end of that October the *Daily Student* undertook to buck up the Hoosier's sense of humor if not courage by spelling Purdue henceforth with a lower case "p" and referring to it as "Cow College" and "Home Ec Tech." Phil Dickens was more realistic in his observation on November 22, after "Home Ec Tech" had defeated the Hoosiers 35 to 6. He said, "It's just like going bear hunting with a switch." The *Daily Student* said this summed up the whole season. "If Indiana is a team of professionals, as the NCAA and Big Ten have branded it, then there must be some higher form of animal in the Big Ten Conference's so-called amateurs."

Coach Phil Dickens' contract was renewed in December 1960, for five additional years. Frank E. Allen said, "We feel that Coach Dickens has done a remarkable job under most difficult conditions and that a good beginning has been made in developing a sound football program at I.U. I most certainly share the feeling of the university administration, the university faculty, and the many friends of I.U. that football is in good hands. . . ." Dickens remained head coach until December 22, 1964, when he wrote President Elvis J. Stahr: "By and large, though, our efforts have not yielded the results we had hoped for and which I am sure the University, the student body, and our loyal alumni and friends throughout the state have also hoped for. It seems wise for me, therefore, although I am reluctant to take this step, to provide you the opportunity to search for new leadership for the football program. Therefore under the terms of the new contract signed last September, I formally request to be relieved of my responsibilities as head football coach and ask that I be reassigned to another position within the University."

Dickens' teams had won nine games against twenty-six losses; they scored 539 points to their opponents 680, but they won only two conference games. One of the latter was a 12 to 7 victory over Purdue in 1964. Consistently Indiana would have stood at the foot of the conference if its games head been counted. In 1965 John Pont, who played at Miami in Ohio and was then head coach at Yale, was appointed successor to Phil Dickens, and he began all over again the climb into conference standing and good graces. This was accomplished in 1967 in a 9 and 2 season, the conference championship, and an invitation to the Rose Bowl, where the Hoosiers lost 14 to 3 to Southern California.

Branch McCracken resigned his position as head basketball coach, in March 1965, to accept a professorship in the School of Health, Physical Education, and Recreation. This ended a brilliant coaching career in which his teams compiled a combined record of 455 wins to 215 losses at Ball State and Indiana. These changes came at a time when there was a new athletic promise in Bloomington. An April 20, 1964, the National Collegiate Athletic Association removed Indiana from probation. An action which J. W. Orwig greeted with, "This is an extremely happy day for Indiana University and its athletic program. It is like breaking out of the clouds into the sunshine. The probation has been difficult and long. However, through the cooperation of many persons, we have been able to come through it in excellent shape. Our house is now in order and we intend to keep it that way. . . ."

In other ways the early 1960s were years of transition. Frank E. Allen reached the mandatory retirement age in 1961, and J. W. Orwig, a former all-American athlete from the University of Michigan, was chosen his successor. Robert C. Dro was continued in the post of assistant athletic director. The *Daily Student*, February 14, 1961, said of the new director, "Mr. Orwig—a trim, greying man—looks as if he were here on an athletic scholarship. He has experience in almost every major sport. He won letters in football, baseball, and swimming, at Scott High School in Toledo,

Ohio. He lettered in basketball and football at the University of Michigan in the late 1920s. . . . His appointment," said the paper, "was greeted by a mixture of surprise, anxiety, and unbridled curiosity as newsmen gathered to question Bill Orwig. . . ." The new director was able to relax questioners, and promised to work toward getting Indiana off probation.

Athletic fortunes, 1960–65, in sports other than football were indeed bright. The basketball team ranked fourth in the conference three years. Walt Bellamy and Gary Long rivaled Bob Leonard and Don Schlundt in player reputations, even if they broke no conference records. The point differentials between the Hoosiers and their opponents were remarkably slight, 2,089 to 2,112 in twenty-four games in 1961–62.

In this latter year a significant era came to a close when Gordon R. Fisher, the track coach, reached retirement age. Since 1944 he had established one of the most successful records in Big Ten track coaching history. His teams had won 81 dual meets to 29 losses, won ten state titles, set approximately a dozen conference individual records, won three Big Ten championships, and a conference championship in cross-country. He was succeeded by James A. Lavery.

While the gods frowned menacingly on Indiana football, James Counsilman's swimmers did much to temper the sting of their wrath. Such athletes as Chet Jastremski, Tom Stock, Frank McKinney, Bob Bennett, Gary Hall, and Charlie Hickox, and, later, Mark Spitz brought both national and international athletic glory to Indiana University. Several of these athletes proved themselves in grueling Olympic competition. For them, however, the period of suspension was a time of heartbreaking denial when they might have achieved a far more impressive record. There was more than a tinge of bitterness in James Counsilman's comment, January 11, 1962, that "naturally, we're disappointed. We're very disappointed. We've been called the No. 1 college swimming team in the country, and we'd like a chance to prove it. . . . The present I.U. swimming team has been called potentially the greatest in the Hoosiers' history." Thus the wound of indiscreet football recruiting was indeed deep and infectious, reaching out and denying a generation of top-quality athletes an opportunity to share in the glories of a conference which laid great store by physical excellence. One more transition was made in these days of Gethsemane.

John F. Mee, a truly scarred but able faculty chairman of athletics and the Hoosiers' conference representative, resigned that position, and President Wells announced the appointment of Edwin H. Cady, professor of American literature, in his place. This within itself was a promising wave to the future.

Whatever the facts in athletic history at Indiana University, it was an irony in academic history that football played such a disturbing role in an era when the institution was making such important intellectual strides. While some university officials searched for coaching talent, others helped to employ seminal scholars who would establish an illustrious intellectual reputation for the university. No one then or now, in all the soul-searching, has solved the riddle as to why Indiana football teams have not succeeded consistently in the Big Ten Conference. It is doubtful that reasons lay entirely with the constant succession of coaches and players. Maybe Hoosier supporters lacked finesse, as a Big Ten recruiter told Jack Olsen of *Sports Illustrated*, but this is a simplistic answer. Somewhere between the fact that historically Indiana high schools were heavily oriented toward basketball, as was the whole Ohio Valley, and the strong competition among three universities for local players lay at least one explanation. Traditionally the Indiana University administration placed major emphasis on the university's academic program, and this may have had an impact. At the heart of the issue involved in the suspension and probations was a matter of far more meaning than athletic fortunes. Indiana could not have made the choice of either being forced out of the Big Ten Conference or of voluntarily withdrawing. The whole history of the institution had been so intertwined with the growth of the Middle West that to have broken this association would have damaged both its regional image and seriously injured its pride. Traditionally its basic standards of comparing achievements in all fields had been made first with the schools of the Old Northwest, and no simple impulsive act could have undone this fact of history without ruinous results. No doubt such a move would have resulted in serious loss of legislative and alumni support.

Indiana alumni support was both strong and sentimental, but as Frank E. Allen said, it often tried to accomplish too much too fast. When all this is said, no one has defined with rationality what peculiar conditions existed at Indiana that did not prevail in other Big Ten schools. What, for instance, was the difference between Indiana and Iowa, or Wisconsin? Both schools operated in heavily agricultural states and were indeed academically oriented. Yet both enjoyed fairly consistent football success. Certainly lack of physical facilities at Bloomington was not a fact of consequence. Maybe Bernie Crimmins was right, Indiana never got the breaks. If this was so, however, the ill-luck was of long duration.

The history of football at Indiana University eclipsed the fact that in other sports the school enjoyed a remarkable success. The baseball team in the latter years finished its seasons with respectable standings. Basketball, track, tennis, and swimming stars pitted their skills against world records and toppled many of them. Counsilman's swimmers received universal acclaim, and Indiana became synonomous with aquatic attainments even though far removed from large bodies of water where swimming was a major recreational activity.

If Indiana demonstrated no other fact in its football history, it should be noted that, in both good times and bad times, the university suffered from no really perceptible punitive legislative attitudes and support. In the grim years of suspension and probation the Indiana General Assembly gave the university some of its most generous support. In a kindred vein, the alumni endured the trauma of conference quarantine with an abiding loyalty, born largely, no doubt, of adversity. The *Daily Student*, and some of the football coaches, may have complained about lack of demonstrable student excitement on the campus, but even these may have been the result of changing times and social conditions rather than to lack of fundamental institutional loyalty. Through almost a half century Indiana optimism never seemed to flag; there was always in the loyal fans' minds the eternal hope that in some way the next football season would be a Hoosier year.

[XIII]

The Capstone

IF THE GHOST of Carl Eigenmann hovered over the River Jordan in 1940, it would have sanctioned heartily the ambitions and priorities of the new university administration. The veteran dean in his pioneering days had vigorously promoted the proposition that Indiana University would never become a significant institution until it had capped off its educational structure with a competent graduate program, properly administered by a central graduate school.

In much of the university's earlier history, administrations had toyed with the idea of granting graduate degrees. David Starr Jordan had carried out, pro forma at least, the shadow of a graduate curriculum, but actually it was not until 1904 that a serious beginning was made in this area when advanced study was formalized under the watch care of a graduate dean. It was historically true that A. B. Philputt had been awarded a post-baccalaureate degree in 1882, but this was little more than a profession of aspirations. It was not until Carl Eigenmann was appointed dean of the Graduate School in 1908 that a serious beginning was made. Throughout his active career Eigenmann undertook to encourage the development of an effective graduate program. In his first year in office thirty Master's degrees were awarded, and in 1912 the first earned Doctor of Philosophy degree was conferred. This was a modest beginning, but the university did not take the second step of keeping pace with expanding American graduate schools during the next three decades.

Too little progress was made in Bloomington during the decades, 1908–38, in giving graduate work in Indiana University, other than according it a subsidiary status to the central undergraduate tradition. Neither the Board of Trustees nor the Indiana General Assembly gave the necessary attention to this phase of university expansion. The Bryan administration had given devoted attention to undergraduate instruction, and in a highly restricted fashion had encouraged some professorial research. No effort, in the modern sense, however, was made to develop a functioning graduate faculty capable of broadening the horizons of knowledge in various fields of intellectual interests. The Indiana graduate program in essence grew like an untended volunteer in the garden of instruction, each department designing its program, setting its standards, and certifying its students. From the outset these departmental domains became sacred areas walled off from invasion by central administrators. Graduate students who sought advanced degrees in the university did so largely on their own financial resources and as departmental wards. There were few or no fellowships, and only limited numbers of teaching and laboratory assistantships. In the same vein of austerity there were limited faculty leave concessions to do research.

Prior to 1938 a situation had developed in Indiana University that made centralized supervision of graduate studies extremely difficult, if not impossible. The professional schools of Business, Education, Medicine, and later Health, Physical Education, and Recreation, all developed graduate divisions which they guarded with fierce jealousy. This feudal possessiveness was perhaps not unique in the history of expanding American universities, but in Indiana University it had the disadvantage of fragmenting graduate offerings. Beyond this it bore directly upon the perennial efforts to secure financial support to establish a mature graduate program, the establishment and maintenance of standards, efficient use of research facilities, and final placement of postgraduates.

In a somewhat more intangible manner the image of Indiana University as a graduate institution in 1941 was far from being brilliant, or even an especially promising one in comparison with those of major private and public universities. The Self-Study Committee of 1939 said in brutal frankness, "Indiana does not deserve to be classed with other state institutions in the Middle West (except Purdue), much less the leading endowed schools in the country." For Herman B Wells, Herman T. Briscoe, and Dean Fernandus Payne the challenges, internal and external, were painfully visible. An assessment of the quality of graduate education in the United States, published in 1925, had listed only history at Indiana University in the first fifteen departments in the field nationally. No other Indiana department was even mentioned on the list.

This was at once a discouraging historical record for President Wells and his administrative colleagues to present prospective top-flight faculty recruits. They had, in fact, to sell the thought that the new and younger scholars would themselves build Indiana University into an institution of major significance. Also the Wells administration was able to argue in favor of graduate studies in seeking financial support for the university from varied sources. On the campus, administrators were faced with the prime necessity following World War II of supplying adequate building space, modern laboratory equipment, libraries, and professorial time for research. This had to be accomplished in an era when the entire university program was experiencing breathtaking expansion and reorganization. With a sure sense of destiny Herman B Wells took a direct hand in redirecting graduate work, and in insuring that it would quickly become a major endeavor of the university. An early action of his presidency was to persuade the Board of Trustees in the spring of 1941 to finance twenty-five graduate scholarships, which could be awarded the following year to attract to Bloomington the most promising students available. These stipends carried both cash awards and remission of tuition or registration fees. A committee composed of the deans of Music, Education, and Business was to select the scholarship students. This was an important pioneering step toward advancing graduate work in the institution. Aside from the availability of a limited number of teaching and laboratory assistants, Indiana had made little progress in supplementing its graduate students' financial resources.

Dean Payne reported in 1941 that 727 different students representing 159 colleges were enrolled for graduate work. Among these were 28 Southerners, eight of whom came from Western Kentucky Teachers College, and 28 blacks from ten Southern Black colleges. Painfully noticeable in this distribution was the fact that no student was registered from an Old Northwest state except Indiana. Ever one to search his academic soul with Calvinistic honesty, the graduate dean no doubt troubled the young president when he wrote, August 8, 1941, his views of future graduate work in the university. "During the year," he told Wells, "Professor Birge of the University of California, read a paper before the physics teachers of the country. He gave the number of Ph.D. degrees granted by universities over a period of years. Indiana stood high on the list. He then proceeded to state that Indiana did not even have a starred man in physics on its faculty. The inference was perfectly clear, and I agree with him, we should not have given so many degrees. We were not qualified. Our standards were low."

With this ego-shattering statement off his mind, Dean Payne then attempted to analyze the university's current situation. He said while neighboring state universities were nurturing significant graduate schools, Indiana was asleep. He wrote, "When they were at the peak, we were at the bottom." More desirable students he felt had gone to the prestigious rival schools, and now Indiana had to mount a vigorous campaign to redirect the established trend. Payne told Wells that since he had been President of the University considerable progress was already evident in the graduate program, "but we still have a long way to go." He indicated it would take at least four years for Indiana to begin competing with such well-established Big Ten graduate schools as Chicago, Wisconsin, and Michigan. Establishment of the Research Fund had already proved productive. Forty-five faculty members from thirteen departments had received grants ranging from $50 to $2,800. Besides these internal aids Alfred C. Kinsey had been awarded the sum of $1,600 from the National Research Council to carry on his research in human sex relations, and Oscar O. Winther and Harvey Locke had received Social Science Research Council grants. Francis D. Wormuth had been awarded a Guggenheim fellowship. English, history, and botany ranked high in campus esteem, and in national ratings. The addition of Harold Whitehall, R. L. Shriner, John Raper, Roger Shugg, and Carl

Voegelin to the Liberal Arts faculty, and Henry Hope and Otto Brendel in Fine Arts promised creative scholarship in the various areas of their experiences and training. Mathematics remained weak, because Wells and Payne had not been able to find an acceptable scholar to hire. In the midst of this moment of bubbling concern for the future of graduate work Herman T. Briscoe and Fernandus Payne held a series of conferences in the spring of 1941 hoping to devise plans for elevating Indiana's national standing. They evaluated with intensive care the departments of the College of Arts and Sciences, and then resolved to concentrate on twelve of them. The list included, in aphabetical order, botany, chemistry, economics, English, geology, government, history, mathematics, psychology, sociology, physics, and zoology. In order to develop the desired strength in these fields, the deans suggested that Payne be given increased controls over hirings, promotions, budgets, and scholarships.

This planning by Briscoe and Payne coincided with the thoughts of President Wells on the subject. In his ardent drive to strengthen the image of Indiana University he had expressed a determination to build a strong graduate school, perhaps without knowing how strongly encrusted professorial forces were in this area. One of his immediate concerns was procurement of the necessary funds from the Indiana General Assembly to accomplish his objectives. He needed solid assurances of financial support before he could make appreciable headway in the hiring of new graduate research professors, or in sustaining a meaningful research program. He also needed a considerable amount of immediately available funds with which to buy necessary scientific equipment, library collections, and to furnish adequate housing for them. Wells' task was an arduous one because he had to present a clear and convincing statement in the most simplified descriptive terms of the meaning of graduate education to Indiana students and citizens. In the fall of 1942, through his administrative assistant Robert Ittner, he sought to get from Dean Payne such a statement. This, however, was a case of two men approaching a common mountain, but from different perspectives. Dean Payne's devotion was to the academic thrust of graduate work of good quality, and the President's was for adequate financial support. Payne told Wells, "This need for advancement of knowledge is not easily explained to laymen, although it may be perfectly clear to you and me." All of this was factual and meaningful in terms of internal university aspirations in the graduate field, but pragmatically it was not the most perceptive political approach. The most tangible statement in Dean Payne's letter was, "Indiana is far below neighboring states in the research we do, in the students we train, and in the amount of money spent for these ends." Wells no doubt agreed with him, but he needed a statement that made a positive appeal to Hoosier pride. In an appended memorandum he told Ittner, "As I remember, this is not at all what we are after; but I think it probably impossible to get what we want from Payne. It will have to be dug out from other sources."

By 1943, President Wells had become deeply involved in the war effort. He was now spending as much or more time in Washington than in Bloomington. On those days when he was on campus too many problems associated with the university's wartime training programs demanded his attention. Nevertheless, even in these crowded months he kept close watch over graduate developments. He wrote Walter A. Jessup of the Carnegie Foundation, November 19, 1943, about the university's efforts to concentrate the expenditure of funds for the Library and for scientific equipment. He told Jessup that a substantial sum of money had been removed from departmental controls and had been put at the disposal of Robert Miller, the librarian, with the Graduate School exercising a guiding hand in the purchase of books and other research materials. Two years before, this same idea of centralizing budgetary resources had worked well in the purchase of scientific equipment. In this way departments were denied proprietary controls over both funds and equipment that could well serve the needs of several departments at once. The vice-president and treasurer had direct responsibility for making purchases, but, said the president, Dean Payne's "opinions determine the action of his [Graduate] Committee; so again he has an opportunity to chart the direction of the University's graduate program." There was an unusually cheerful note in Wells' letter. He said an "ever-increasing flood of money," was pouring into the university from outside sources. He believed the corporation tax of the state was indeed a boon to the university, and so was the income from institutional patent rights. The Graduate School had not taken an active part in the solicitation of gifts to the institution, which the president told Jessup he thought was a mistake.

The war, of course, reduced materially the number of graduate students enrolled; only 106 advanced degrees were awarded by the Graduate School in 1945, and many of these were in some way related to the military programs. By the latter date, however, the war was rapidly drawing to a close, and graduate work promised to take on a tremendously increased importance in the university's future operation. Dean Payne said in his annual report that he was certain the Graduate School would undergo significant expansion, but he hoped Indiana University administrative officials would not become too captivated by numbers alone. He reminded the president and trustees that his school was the one place on the campus where students were admitted on the basis of proven qualifications, and he advocated strict adherence to the standards that he and the Graduate Faculty had undertaken to establish. To the persistent dean "It seems strange that some teachers complain loudly about the admission of weak undergraduate students, yet when they have some responsibility for the admission of graduate students they are willing to accept almost anyone and coddle him along."

In the closing months of the war and before the inrush of students began Wells and Briscoe shared Dean Payne's concern about both the size of the student body and the standards of admission, but of necessity they had to be definitely concerned with the undergraduate program, especially since this was the area where most of the military veterans would be concentrated. Dean Payne and his colleagues had an internal problem to solve which was as great as the prospects of rising enrollment in the Graduate School. The autonomous control of graduate studies by the professional schools had grown more nearly by accretion than by any specific acts of planning. Earlier no one seems to have visualized the future meaning of this fact in the shaping of Indiana University's future reputation among American graduate schools. Since 1939 this diversified control and direction of graduate studies had been a bone of contention, sometimes a most frustrating one. By 1947 the concept was fully developed among the professional schools that they alone could determine the needs of their graduates, and set the standards for their advanced degrees. By this latter date university administrators began to realize more clearly the full meaning of this condition. They knew that any effort to centralize direction of all graduate work in a single school would cause injurious frictions in the various faculties. Business, Education, and Medicine especially would resist such a move with stubbornness. Dean Arthur Weimer of the School of Business perhaps expressed the views of his professional colleagues when he said he saw little advantage in centralization since the present plan seemed to be working satisfactorily. In the case of Education, Dean Payne and Dean Henry L. Smith had often taken opposing stands on the matter of standards and content of graduate work leading to the doctorate, and this conflict simmered on even after Dean Smith had retired. To the biologist-dean it seemed the work offered in the School of Education, and its degree standards were not of the highest quality.

A curious bit of academic folklore had grown up in the university which frightened some members of the professional schools. They seemed to believe that the graduate staffs of the College of Arts and Sciences would outvote them in graduate faculty meetings. Constantly this note of fear crept into the record. This timidity was based partly on the belief that liberal arts professors would be immovable on the subject of language requirements for doctoral candidates. If there were professional school faculty members who believed this fiction, they had a very limited knowledge of the rivalries that have traditionally prevailed among liberal arts departments.

Herman T. Briscoe set out to penetrate the barrier of resistance to centralized graduate work. He made two proposals to President Wells, September 8, 1947. First, he suggested that all graduate work in the university should be coordinated as much as possible in order to combine degrees and reduce duplications, and to remove the thorny issue of varying standards. Second, he proposed that the professional schools be allowed to set their own specialized standards and to control the content of their advanced instruction. He, however, was a scarred realist, and he told Wells, "To place all professional graduate degrees under one faculty, which would be dominated by one division [Arts and Sciences] of the University, would produce a situation of endless conflict." Dean Payne was retiring soon, said Briscoe, and he thought that would be the proper moment to take a firmer grasp of the university's graduate offerings. Again he had in hand multiple proposals which he gave the president, September 17, 1947. He suggested that, after a new dean of the Graduate School of Arts and Sciences was appointed, he should create a federated system of graduate work controlled by a representative council. Briscoe deemed the all-university plan an ideal one, but his courage wavered. He said in its operation it would be thwarted by endless conflict and bickering. With unusual timidity the Dean of Faculties suggested simply appointing a new dean and accepting for the time being the status quo.

Wells, however, seemed not to be willing to leave things as they were. Either Briscoe had planted in his mind the idea of federation of graduate studies, or he had conceived it independently as the most practical way out of a growing dilemma. Wherever the idea came from, this was more or less the approach he used until centralization was accomplished a decade later.

After canvassing the faculty in search of a successor to Dean Payne, President Wells wrote the eminent folklorist Stith Thompson, September 20, 1947, that the administration wished to appoint a new dean and to have him installed in office by the opening of the forthcoming year. Increasing enrollment of the crowded postwar year, plus the ambitions of the university to expand and strengthen its graduate program placed great pressure on the administration. In the meantime Dean John Ashton of the College of Arts and Sciences was acting as interim Dean of the Graduate School after July 1, and until a new appointment could be made. In a somewhat indirect and subtle manner Wells suggested to Professor Thompson the concept of eventually coordinating all graduate work offered in the university under a single faculty, and under the direction of a single dean of the Graduate School. The new dean, in the meantime, should consider the reappraisal of the current mode of examining doctoral candidates, the committee system, and the assortment of advanced degrees being offered. The president expressed the opinion that it might be wise to think about instituting a Doctor of Philosophy degree in the fields of teaching higher education subjects. He told Thompson, "In my opinion it is time for careful study of the objectives of our advanced programs of study, and consideration of the courses of study, research, etc., best suited to the accomplishment of these objectives." He then got to the heart of his administrative concern, "It is hoped that, someday not too far off, we may work out a graduate organization that will afford some measure, at least, of integration and university-wide supervision and direction. For the next few years, however, until such an organization can be agreed upon and its exact character determined, it seems best to proceed according to our present system, namely, the appointment of a Dean of the Graduate School to replace Dean Payne. . . ."

Thompson accepted appointment to the deanship. There were on the graduate rolls 1,031 students subject to his administration, and the number increased each semester thereafter. Dean Thompson moved the graduate office from the Department of Zoology with its stout smell of the presence of science and formaldehyde to the even more depressing confines of ancient Lindley Hall. His suite of three offices with their high ceilings and even higher window casements was far from being aesthetically impressive. If Indiana University expected to add luster to its graduate work, it had to do so through the personalities of its distinguished scholar-dean, and of the Associate Dean Oscar O. Winther—not with bright physical surroundings.

Thompson revealed optimism in his 1947–48 report. He was then looking back from a short but meaningful perspective in the vein of history. Not only had the graduate student enrollment increased, but most of the department programs seemed to be stronger. He told President Wells and the Board of Trustees, "part of this increase is to be ascribed to the very definite strengthening which has taken place in the departments so that students are now coming to Indiana University to study under particular professors. This I regard as a very healthy sign."

Wells emphasized to the trustees that the state central administration had given Indiana University special attention in bolstering the graduate program. He said a discernible shift in emphasis had been made in the recognition of the professional functions of the university. The graduate teaching staff had been enlarged, and at least a hundred hours of instructional time was devoted to the guidance of individual candidates.

Dean Stith Thompson proved a wise and thoughtful head of the Graduate School, and with the able administrative assistance of Oscar Winther he was able to visualize the bigger challenges of the postwar years. After he had been in office two full years, he wrote President Wells an extended letter in which he reviewed the position of graduate education in Indiana University. With entire candor he pointed out both the strengths and weaknesses of the program. He, like Dean Payne, had felt some anxiety about the divided nature of the administration of graduate studies in the institution. He did not, however, advocate immediate changes because he knew divisional and departmental emotions would be needlessly aroused. Nevertheless, he did suggest that it might become imperative in the future to consolidate supervision of the entire graduate program under the management of a single administrator. He mentioned specifically the plan used in the University of California as a good example of what he thought would yield the best results at Indiana. The California school had largely a federation of campus academic empires not unlike those in Bloomington. Harvard had at least four graduate schools operating under as many separate administrations.

President Conant wrote Thompson he was satisfied with this arrangement, but the dean did not regard the graduate program at Indiana as so well established as that at Harvard. He knew there was an almost unbridgeable chasm between the science departments producing exciting expansions on the horizons of knowledge in classrooms and laboratories, and the efforts of the School of Physical Education, Health, and Recreation. Frankly, Thompson told Wells, the present plan of operation, while relatively simple to administer so far as the Graduate School was concerned, was not in his opinion the best one with which to develop either a uniformly good graduate program or to improve the image of the university at large.

In somewhat more direct terms Dean Thompson indicated that he was not impressed with a report prepared by a special graduate committee that had been appointed to study the whole institutional procedures. In fact, he was so unimpressed that he had not bothered to present it to the Graduate School faculty. The committee had suggested so few changes that the Dean feared the debate it would provoke would actually do injury to the present mode of operation. He explained that many of the departments offered excellent advanced instruction, and others were showing definite signs of maturing. He listed zoology, botany, physics, geology, history, psychology, English, "and to a degree" chemistry. The linguistics program had already attracted national scholarly and student attention; so had anthropology and the limited folklore offerings. He also expressed pride in the comparative literature program, which was proving a fine entering wedge to instituting cross-disciplinary courses. With the Voegelins, Herzog, and Thompson giving advanced instruction in these areas Indiana University was acquiring a national reputation. Folklore especially was attracting widespread attention, even though the scope of offerings had to be severely limited because of a lack of staff. This newfound scholarly success seemed to indicate that the university should do more experimenting with cross-disciplinary offerings, but before much headway could be made in this direction the general graduate program had to be centralized or federated.

Without delaying to debate the question, Dean Thompson was a positive advocate of professorial research and publication, even to setting an excellent personal example in these areas. He had continued Payne's policy of summer grants to professors to do research and writings. The university maintained at least four series of scholarly publications, which opened outlets of presentation of research works by campus scholars. In addition to the monograph series nine academic journals were published on the campus. These represented a wide range of interest from the local specialized materials published in the *Indiana Magazine of History*, *Midwest Folklore*, *Slavic and East European Studies* to the nationally important *Mississippi Valley Historical Review*.

Remarkably, this rather extensive publication program had come into being on the campus without the dean of the Graduate School having much if anything to do with it. Thompson suggested to Wells that he felt he should at least have a place on the publications committee. Wells noted in the margin of the dean's letter that he approved of the idea. Characteristic of the university's history in moments of expansion there was a growing and unfulfilled demand for more funds with which to finance faculty research. As the Wells administration was able to employ professors of fine scholarly promise, this need for additional research funds became even more urgent. In 1951–53, the administration budgeted $51,000 to be awarded to selected professors of the teaching staff so they could have some time away from teaching duties. The highest grant from this appropriation, $2,500, went to Alfred C. Kinsey. At that moment he was just completing work on his second volume, *Sexual Behavior in the American*

Female (1953). Smaller stipends went to other professors, most of them seeking summer leaves.

During the years 1950–55, the university felt the financial pinch of dwindling G.I. enrollment and grants. The result of this was that the burden of subsidizing graduate students became heavier with each new semester. Not only was this true for American students, but the great inflow of foreigners seeking fellowship aid necessitated active efforts to develop new financial resources. In the past three years applications for graduate fellowships had increased from 50 to 180 in the Liberal Arts areas alone. Thompson said he was convinced it would be unfortunate if the graduate student body should soon be comprised of only those candidates who were able to pay all their expenses. If such a situation did arise then it would leave the university without access to some of the most highly desirable graduate students being trained in undergraduate colleges.

This matter of student aids had long been a serious consideration in the university. Reflective of this fact, Herman T. Briscoe reported to President Wells, February 21, 1951, that the Graduate Committee, representing all segments of advanced training on the campus, had reexamined the question of compensation for graduate assistants. As one way to increase stipends the committee voted to remit all fees for building and health services, and to raise the rate of compensation from $900 and $1,000 to $1,000 and $1,200 a year. A part of this recommendation at least was accepted, because on April 19, 1951, Dean Ralph E. Cleland announced the appointment of 33 fellows at stipends ranging from $600 to $1,200.

Times and social conditions changed rapidly in the decade of the 1950s, and these had bearings on graduate programs undreamed of a generation ago. Again in his letter-report to the president, Dean Thompson asked that the university administration give active attention to providing graduate housing for both married and single students in a common dormitory complex. A timid step had been made in this direction between 1945 and 1950 when a diligent hunt was made for surplus military housing to accommodate married students. During these years more and more student families were housed in these temporary structures located about the campus. While they enjoyed the delights and suffered many of the frustrations of crowded campus communal living, the graduate students themselves had only limited opportunities to share their thoughts and experiences with their fellows. The dean said he had discussed with Joseph A. Franklin the possibility of designating the Rogers II group of dormitories and living facilities for the exclusive occupation of graduate students and their families. This complex was largely self-contained with ample dining, meeting, and laundry facilities. Franklin responded this was not immediately possible because of commitments already made to undergraduates, but within a year possibly the suggestion could be carried out. This was done, and in 1954 graduate students were assigned to the Rogers complex. President Wells informed the Board of Trustees in June 1955, "Indiana University is one of a very small number of American universities which make provisions for the housing of graduate students. There is still a shortage especially for married housing. The Rogers II group housed 700 persons, most of them graduate students."

By the time Stith Thompson retired from the deanship in 1950 graduate school enrollment had climbed to 1,380 students, and there were enrolled in all the divisions giving graduate instruction 2,286 students, up from 1,599 the year before. These facts were ascertainable on the campus, but they had little or no bearing on the university's national rating. There was a longstanding administrative concern with Indiana's unfavorable comparative rating with such close academic neighbors as Wisconsin, Minnesota, Ohio State, and Michigan. In order to equal any of these Big Ten schools, with the exception of Michigan, said Dean Thompson, it would be necessary to consolidate the graduate offerings of Indiana and Purdue. The presence of engineering and agricultural colleges enabled many of the Middle Western schools to offer a much broader spectrum of graduate work than was possible in a "separate" university like Indiana.

The test of a good department, said Dean Thompson, was whether students came from afar to study under the direction of a particular professor. "We have that situation in perhaps six or eight departments or professors here," he told Wells, January 9, 1950. These departments and their able scholars, however, were not strength enough to make up for the lack of quality in less capable departments. The great momentary need was the breathing of intellectual life into the weaker departments so they too would attract the best graduate students available. In too many instances the university could accept only a fraction of the applications of promising students because of the inadequacy of departmental staffs. In translating the nature of this era of expansion and change to the Board of Trustees, Wells wrote in his *Annual Report*, 1950–51, "Several new programs of graduate study have been authorized, including a program of Slavic studies leading to an A. M. degree; a Ph.D. program in public address and forensics, and an A. M. program in radio. A training course in Finance Corps R. O. T. C. has been added to the military curriculum."

Of the 1,590 registrants in the Graduate School in 1950–51, a third were candidates for the Doctor of Philosophy degree, and more than half of these were married and in need of housing. When Stith Thompson retired from the deanship July 1, 1950, he could take some genuine satisfaction in the fact that he had planted several ideas, had clarified some campus views of graduate work, and had revealed conscientiously the strengths and weaknesses of the Indiana system.

Professor Ralph E. Cleland, the distinguished botanist, succeeded Thompson. He began his administration with the statement, "Since applied research must depend on basic research, and since one can never foretell in what fields those discoveries will occur upon which tomorrow's advances in practical applied areas are to come, it is essential to support all kinds of basic research in all the various fields of human interest." Because this was true the university must keep open all of its scholarly channels. At the end of the first year of his administration Dean Cleland informed his colleagues of the opportunities for employment of persons with graduate training, saying they had been greatly expanded, and that graduate enrollment nationally had advanced at an appreciable rate. With this inflow to the graduate schools had come a comparable need for fellowships, teaching assistantships, and other forms of student subsidies. At Indiana 446 registrants in the Graduate School were either teaching or research assistants, and most of their support was provided directly from departmental budgets. Only thirty-six students, he said, held nonservice fellowships, and four more received modest help from remission of fees. Dean Cleland was sensitive to the same pressures that had borne upon Payne and Thompson. As more graduate students appeared on the campus, and with husbands, wives, and children, the student welfare committee made more urgent pleas for graduate housing and social quarters. To meet this rising demand Dean Cleland also proposed organization of a graduate college in which all advanced students would be gathered into a single living complex, which would be largely accomplished by 1969 with the opening of Eigenmann Hall. This complex building had been in the planning stages for six or seven years, and it actually straddled the Wells and Stahr administrations in its planning and construction. Cleland also said the financial assistance was far too low to meet the advancing costs of attending graduate classes. This was especially so when Indiana compared its rate of pay with that of other major universities.

Every graduate school in America in the 1950s was brought under the artificial pressure of the deferment policy of the National Military Draft Authority. Not only did the rate of enrollment advance, but it was believed the standards of admission were threatened by the emotional appeals of less qualified applicants to be admitted so they could be deferred during the Korean War. Never before had universities been called upon to make such deeply human and moral decisions. By the same token, perhaps, universities had never experienced the pressures of such great nonacademic forces in the operation of an academic program as in these years. In 1950–51 Indiana University had 1,024 applications for admission to the Graduate School, and it accepted 616 new students.

The pressures and changes that occurred in these latter years made it more urgent than ever that the university give serious thought to a sharp revision of its procedures of admission to graduate instruction in all its divisions. A step in this direction was establishment of a graduate council of nine members in November 1951, which immediately began consideration of legislative problems governing advanced studies. This body, however, was unable to consider all the larger considerations of coordinating graduate work into a single administrative unit. So long as divisions had autonomy in making decisions in this area there were to be many differences and, maybe, weaknesses in admissions, instruction, and qualifications for degrees.

It was clear by 1953 that President Herman B Wells intended to bring about some centralized general direction of this function of the institution. Whatever the virtues of the old system it had five distinct disadvantages that tended to nullify them. These were, as had so often been cited, lack of common qualitative standards, an uncoordinated fellowship program, inability to concentrate on placement of Indiana graduates in the most desirable positions, the absence of a well-integrated appeal to the Indiana General Assembly for graduate support, and the control of graduate staff and instruction.

Without a doubt the most serious drawback to efficient graduate instruction was the internal rivalries and bickerings among the various schools and divisions. The President wrote Dean Cleland, May 18, 1953, "We need to give serious consideration to a plan for unifying all graduate work. There are many good reasons for doing so but one that comes to me regularly grows out of the fact our present system reflects only a part of our advanced degrees in national studies, etc., and this in turn places us in a disadvantageous position in national ratings. I despair of obtaining a union that would cause units to lose authority. Could we not, however, develop a federation under the banner of the Graduate School?"

Although President Wells had previously discussed the idea of federation, his letter to Dean Cleland no doubt was the actual planting of the germ of federation in future discussions of graduate administration. For the next four years the proposal was to be discussed by all segments of the faculty involved in graduate work. Wells' most active opponents of coordination were his former School of Business colleagues. Dean Arthur M. Weimer, March 11, 1954, wrote J. E. Hedges, professor of insurance, that just because other universities had concentrated administration of their graduate schools under a single dean and council was no valid reason why Indiana should do so. He felt the School of Business faculty should oppose such a plan in the university, except, possibly, "that there is co-ordination provided through the office of the Dean of Faculties." He told Hedges, "It seems to me there ought to be many philosophies represented in graduate study. I doubt that the University could secure so much support for graduate study through a centralized organization as through a decentralized one." Dean Weimer was clear in his statement of opposition to the creation of an overall deanship as suggested in Dean Cleland's latest memorandum on the subject.

President Wells appeared before the Graduate Council, May 6, 1954, to present his proposal of federation. He reviewed briefly the history of the graduate program at Indiana. He then described the present autonomous situation where schools and departments set their own standards for graduate work, and performed all of the other administrative functions. This was especially true in regard to work leading to the doctoral degrees. Characteristically, he made no demands, but discussed both the positive and negative sides of the issue. The record is unclear what the immediate response was to the president's gentle but persistent nudgings.

A year later a special report prepared by the Graduate Council was ready for consideration. This document said Indiana University was perhaps the only major state university in which administrative responsibility for all graduate work was not concentrated in a single coordinated graduate school. There was still little enthusiasm, however, on the Bloomington campus for the surrender of divisional autonomies. Faculty discussions of the report nevertheless implied at least that professors for certain specified reasons might approve a limited form of federation. These were for recruitment of new faculty and students, distribution of publicity data, and the procurement of financial support. Much of the faculty, however, did not wish to relinquish autonomy in making school and departmental budgets, designing curricula, faculty assignments and controls, admissions, and the setting of degree standards.

Paradoxically, the Graduate Council's report outlined five points for establishing an outstanding graduate school in Indiana University and everyone of them implied a unified administrative approach to accomplish their objectives. "The Graduate School of Indiana University has made great strides in the past, and it is the determination of everyone concerned with its administration and activity to ensure even more rapid progress in the near future, so that it may gain recognition as second to none in the Nation in the calibre of its student output and in the significance of its scholarly contributions." These were precisely the aims the president seems to have had in mind in his various statements to the Graduate School faculty.

Dean Cleland, a week after the Graduate Council's report was distributed, again put forth the president's suggested plan for federation. He emphasized two telling points: President Wells felt he could make a better presentation to the State Budget Commission and the General Assembly with the force of the unified Graduate

School behind him, and, on the record, Purdue University appeared to have an appreciably larger graduate school because its offerings were unified. Cautiously, it seemed, the dean proposed either a loose "paper federation," or the outright establishment of a good solid graduate school administered by a single dean, but making every effort to give all the individual entities as much autonomy as would be consistent with proper management. It now seemed on the surface that the faculty might be willing to concede at least the formation of a loose union.

This, however, was not to be. Two years later, May 14, 1956, the debate was still going on. A special committee had again made a study of the Graduate School, and had another report in hand. This time five suggested titles were offered for a federated division which ranged from "The School of Graduate Studies" to the "Federated Graduate Schools." Actually, the committee made no suggestions of major changes in the internal procedures of graduate instruction except in title, establishment of a central organization to appoint committees, to make a common approach to recruitment, publicity, and the solicitation of both public and private financial support. Interestingly, this report seems not to have considered the qualitative standards of work offered in the university to be sufficiently lacking to merit mention. Hopefully, the almost powerless proposed central organization would strive for uniformity among the departments and divisions giving graduate instruction, yet it would be without actual authority to impose its will on any division. All the faculties would still be adequately represented in awarding fellowships and degrees.

It may have been fortunate that this report was not adopted. Dean Cleland, however, was not satisfied to give up the effort to effect unification. He was back before the Graduate School faculty, February 12, 1957, saying that President Wells had asked him to prepare a proposal for coordinating the administration of the graduate studies in the university. He suggested that the Dean of the Graduate School be empowered to speak for all graduate work offered in the institution, and especially in national meetings. He again advanced the argument for uniformity of graduate studies administration centered in the hands of a dean with proper authority to oversee the graduate programs. Dean Cleland believed this would prove the most effective approach to both the foundations and the national government in making applications for grants and contracts. Negatively, he was of the opinion the various schools would lose a certain amount of power and control, and some present requirements would have to be revised. In expressing reactions to this latter suggestion, a few professors seemed to believe that unification would result in an actual lowering of some rigid departmental standards.

Despite the latter expression of fear, the minutes of the February meeting of the Graduate Council indicated Dean Cleland's proposal stimulated little debate. He asked the faculty to vote specifically on the test proposition, "Do you in general favor the proposal for the coordination of the Graduate Program?" This test indicator proved heartening and it appeared that at last the dean had made some solid gain toward achieving the administration's objective. The test vote, of course, had not committed the faculty to anything, but even so it did offer a glimmer of encouragement. Once more Dean Cleland, October 1, 1957, reviewed for the Faculty Council the central arguments favorable to unification. In fact, by this time the various points had been worn threadbare by frequent repetition over the years. By now it would seem that nobody, from janitor to trustee, was left in the dark as to reasons for coordinating graduate work. Dean Cleland told the Faculty Council that 62 of 75 major American institutions granting advanced degrees had centralized administrative programs, and that 50 of 52 state universities, including Purdue, were centralized. This may have placed Indiana in a class with Harvard, but in actual size of the graduate program and university objectives the comparison was meaningless. The reality was that Indiana University often found itself in a highly unfavorable situation in national meetings of graduate schools, in securing favorable publicity of the quality of its training, and in recruiting top-quality faculty and students. He asked the Faculty Council, for these reasons, to support coordination of graduate work.

President Wells tactfully revealed a determination to rectify the unhappy situation of the administration of graduate studies on the Indiana campus. Most of Dean Cleland's arguments contained points that formed the very heart of the Wells administration's crusade to create a major university. This was especially noticeable when Indiana University made less than a favorable showing on national comparative rating scales for any one of its areas of instruction and research. When the university's national image became involved, it stirred the emotions of the president, and to him this outweighed the imaginary losses of some campus departmental autonomy.

When Dean Ralph E. Cleland neared the time of his retirement as Dean of the Graduate School on July 1, 1958, President Herman B Wells took a long step toward effecting coordination of graduate studies by appointing Professor John W. Ashton to be Vice President and Dean of the Graduate School. He announced to the faculty that Dr. Ashton would also assume overall administration of the research centers and institutes in anthropology, folklore, linguistics, the School of Letters, the University Press, convocations, the promotion of outside research contracts, and solicitation of foundation grants. This move concentrated under Dr. Ashton's administrative control a considerable empire, and a tremendous amount of power in influencing all the university's graduate programs. Wells told the faculty, "As a part of his new responsibilities, Vice President Ashton has been asked to give high priority to exploring ways and means to bring greater coordination to the graduate programs of all divisions of the University." Never before in the history of Indiana had a dean been placed in such a powerful position and with such a big stick to hold over the heads of graduate directors in all schools and departments.

It did not take the new vice-president and dean long to capitalize on the efforts and experiences of his predecessors, and to realize his own sources of power. In a letter that literally shouted triumph Dean Ashton wrote Wells, April 15, 1959, "I am happy to report that all of the graduate divisions of the University except that of Health, Physical Education, and Recreation have now agreed to a proposal for the integration of graduate work which will involve the creation of the University Division of Graduate Studies to be administered by the Vice President and Dean of Graduate Development." There would be an advisory council composed of one representative from the Graduate School of Arts and Sciences, the School of Business, the School of Education, and the School of Music. Strangely, he did not mention Medicine. A generous amount of autonomy would be allowed as to degree requirements, standards, and fellowships to the various divisions. The new Graduate Council was expected to plan and integrate programs for the total university offerings.

Dean Cleland had reported in 1956–57 that there were 1,614 graduate students registered in forty-one Liberal Arts departments, and 608 of these sought the Doctor of Philosophy degree; in all, he estimated there were more than 3,000 advanced students in the entire university. Under the decentralized system perhaps no one could say precisely how many there were at the outset. The number of foreign students had increased appreciably by 1957, coming from perhaps 125 non-American institutions. The American registrants represented more than 300 colleges and universities. President Wells reported that year there were 377 members of the Graduate School faculty, and 81 of these had been awarded a total of $50,690.22 in research grants. Besides these, government and private industry had contributed $1,930,679.35 the past year in support of research and special scholarships. The Medical School in Indianapolis had received grants from various sources, greatly swelling this total.

By the time coordination of graduate work occurred in Indiana University the graduate student enrollment was increasing in considerable numbers. Dean Cleland earlier had observed that much stricter standards of admission should be applied to the flood of "Korean War" applications that poured into Bloomington with every mail. He was astounded by this development because it was largely the depression babies, measured on the scale of predictability, who should then be entering Graduate School. He did, however, recognize the extraordinary fact that without the draft threat many of the applicants would be following other pursuits.

In the latter moment of the highly contagious excitement over the new coordinate status of graduate work in Indiana University in 1958–59, President Wells informed the Board of Trustees what was taking place. "To the graduate schools throughout the country," he wrote, "is entrusted the responsibility of providing for the college teachers of the future. There are those who believe that the training of the research scholar and the college teacher should be in substantially different directions. This seems to me fallacious. It is quite true that many of the graduates will not become great, or even particularly significant research scholars with long lists of publications to their credit, but graduate research properly carried out is one of the most important and effective means of preparing a young man or woman for the profession of teaching. It is only in the graduate school that the student learns the kind of investigation and analyses which are the very essence of successful teaching and which distinguish successful teaching; that is, creative teaching from the more humdrum repetition of second-hand facts and materials. . . ." This was written at a time when all of the national educational and human resource surveys were predicting a major shortage of teachers at all levels by the late 1970s.

The president realized that not all the problems of advanced studies had been solved by the recent integration of graduate administration on the campus. American graduate schools generally were beset by all sorts of problems ranging from increasing numbers of students to constantly revising curricula, updating requirements for degrees, hiring adequate teaching staff, purchasing equipment for laboratories and books for libraries, and properly placing graduates. There flourished like grass in a Hoosier spring the perennial debate over the role of the research professor. Wells expressed the thought that research was the life blood of vigorous graduate instruction and direction. This, however, did not imply that teaching as such should ever be sacrificed on the altar of library and laboratory, and most of all the neglect of personal attention to individual students. Graduate schools had to assume heavy responsibilities for training teachers or members of the profession would wither away on the academic vine.

A new problem, which surfaced in the long struggle to unify graduate work on the campus, was that of maintaining the momentum Indiana University had built up during the war years in the area of linguistics and East European studies. Indiana had come to enjoy genuine international prestige in these fields, which President Wells recognized when he delegated such broad authority to Vice President Ashton to give oversight to these studies. Earlier Dean Cleland, July 22, 1954, had called attention to the fact that Indiana was perhaps unique among American universities in offering instruction in Finno-Ugric and East European languages. Professor Tom Sebeok, he said, had been an aggressive leader in developing the Air Force's language program on the campus, and in promoting linguistic studies in the postwar years. In 1954 he thought the university should review thoroughly this area where it had achieved so much success, and maybe redirect some of the program toward new objectives. The Department of Slavic Studies was developing its program more and more in the historical and political fields. In this way the department was departing from its original objectives and was then in danger of colliding with courses offered in history and political science. The dean proposed specifically that more emphasis be placed upon cross-disciplinary programs which would keep down departmental rivalries and duplications.

Dean Cleland later reported to the Faculty Council, May 1955, that in the past five years the fields of East European Studies, Library Science, Physiological Optics, the School of Letters, and Latin American Studies had appeared on the graduate firmament. The two latter fields had worked out efficient coordinations with other departments. He implied this was the trend that should be emulated throughout much of the departmental organization in the university.

While the relatively new fields of East European Studies, linguistics, Latin-American Studies, and anthropology extended instructional and research interests far abroad both organizationally and intellectually, Indiana University had not actually established branches of study in other countries. In 1958, however, it did enter into a joint agreement with Pakistan to establish a two-year graduate course in the basic medical sciences. The School of Medicine had been given a grant of $1,824,000 by the United States International Co-operative Administration to organize a three-year medical program in Pakistan. It was to train students in anatomy, physiology, microbiology, pathology, pharmacology, and biochemistry. Dean John D. Van Nuys had administrative charge of the project, and Dr. William Hugh Headlee, professor of parasitic diseases, was made coordinator. Dr. Paul Nicoll of the Indiana medical staff was sent to Pakistan to organize the school, and in April 1959 President Ayub and President Herman B Wells dedicated the new institution, which by June 1 had admitted seventeen students of advanced standing.

After 1958 the Indiana University Graduate School began to reflect the distinct advantages of coordination in nearly every area of its operation. In the commencement of 1959 it graduated 192 doctoral candidates as compared with 43 a decade before. The United States Department of Education approved the Graduate School for fellowships granted under Title IV of the National Defense Educational Act. Graduate enrollment had climbed to 2,797 in 1960–62, and 840 of these registrants sought the Doctor of Philosophy degree.

The *Indiana Daily Student*, October 6, 1961, chortled, "There is a new star blazing in the skies of graduate education—Indiana's Graduate School. It is now adding its light to that of those who have long dominated the skies." The paper realized the school had not yet exactly become a household name in either Hoosier homes or the halls of the General Assembly, but in the American academic community it was rapidly coming to be known for the excellent quality of its research and instruction. In his book *Graduate Education in the United States* (1960), Bernard Berelson, after having done research on 92 institutions, ranked Indiana in twelfth position. Individual departments in the university for two decades after 1940 had added greater luster to graduate work in Bloomington than had the collective departments and divisions comprising the Graduate School itself. Later this fact was to be reflected in Allan Cartter's searching survey, *An Assessment of Quality in Graduate Education* (1966).

The great struggle to establish the Indiana Graduate School on a unified basis as a principal division of the maturing university was conducted in less than inspiring physical surroundings. Even Herman B Wells admitted this fact in his communication to the trustees, June 1960. He told the board that the Graduate School had "moved from the dirty, cramped, and unattractive quarters in Lindley Hall to the spacious, well-lighted, and thoroughly prepossessing suite of offices in Kirkwood Hall." In this respect alone the *Daily Student* was not far wrong in its exuberant boasting that the Graduate School had burst onto a bright new physical and intellectual firmament.

The Special Study Committee composed of William Breneman, York Willbern, and George W. Wilson reported in February 1966, under the title "Growth and Change at Indiana University." They revealed an impressive expansion of the graduate program and enrollment. In 1965 more than 53 per cent of the degrees granted at Indiana University were postbaccalaureate, and in the decade since 1955, baccalaureate degrees had increased by 70 per cent, but the percentage of graduate degrees had increased 135 per cent. Somewhat more specifically, the university awarded 1,275 graduate degrees in 1955, and 2,991 in 1965. Fourteen broad areas offered work leading to Master's degrees, and seven conferred doctorates. The promise for the future was even brighter because there were 2,996 graduate students enrolled. The number of candidates seeking the Doctor of Philosophy degree in 1965 was 3.8 greater than in 1955.

By the end of the decade the Indiana graduate program had grown in complexity not only in departmental and cross-disciplinary organizations offering composite degrees, but specialized study centers and research areas had expanded beyond all expectations in 1955. Most of the 1966 survey on growth and change dealt with internal subject matter and disciplinary alignments in relationship to the traditional issue of departmental autonomy. "But there remains," said the three committeemen, "a need for deliberation and leadership from an all-university perspective." In order to insure an institution-wide perspective, the report contained rather elaborate recommendations for reorganizing the entire administration of graduate work, so as to be ready five years hence when a third or more of the university's enrollment on the Bloomington campus and in the Medical School in Indianapolis would be made up of postgraduate students. George W. Wilson, later to become dean of the Graduate School, expressed the opinion that departments and divisions should have greater latitude in altering, but not in eliminating, the language requirements for the Doctor of Philosophy degree. This had been a bone of contention in the long struggle to consolidate the direct-tion of graduate work. Some of the schools had looked upon this requirement as an intellectual scarecrow which frightened their prospective graduate students away.

There is little color or drama in the year-to-year operation of a graduate school inside a large university amidst all the tinsel and adolescent excitement of the undergraduate program with its social and athletic razzle-dazzle. The great organizational gains were often made after long and intensive faculty debate and study, but even the excitement of these discussions, though at times passionate, were scarcely newsworthy. The pathos associated with the human strains, stresses, and even disappointments in seeking a doctor's degree, like grief itself, were borne in silence. The true excitement of graduate education lay almost wholly in the creative quality of the finished human product it started on the road to scholarly achievement. Indiana University was to be richly rewarded in this area by its scholars of extraordinary capabilities.

No problem Herman B Wells and his aggressive administrative colleagues tackled after 1939 yielded more prestigious dividends than did the dogged crusade to unify and mature the Graduate School. The frustrating campaign to bring the administration of graduate work with all its internal campus ramifications under a single head represented in essence the direction in which the expanding university was headed after 1938. The struggle to achieve coordination had revealed a vast organizational mirror which reflected an uneven image of quality of instruction and direction of work from one department to another, the inability of the university to break through the rugged barrier of national comparison to assume its proper position on the rating scale of American graduate schools, and to make the proper presentation of its graduates to desirable employers.

In all the furor of the decade and a half of debating of graduate school issues, there prevailed an admirable expression of respect for individual initiative and autonomy, a precious jewel not to be plowed under in the bog of campus bureaucracy. There were heroes of the many battles. Dean Fernandus Payne with his unrelenting spartan courage had smote foes of his school right and left with the mighty sword of standards and quality. His gentler successors, Stith Thompson and Ralph E. Cleland, made no skull-cleaving thrusts at opponents nor did they make any unforgiving enemies of record, but rather they placed their faith in quiet logic, common sense, and persuasion to move the graduate program off dead center in the parochial concern for autonomy.

John W. Ashton was privileged to achieve final victory by bringing about the coordination of most of the programs of graduate schools, departments, and divisions. He was the first to help direct graduate education on the campus in a common thrust into highly complex areas of instruction and research. Beyond this he was able to bring about the broadening programs in the specialized fields, which used more efficiently the growing intellectual resources of the institution.

One rich reward of the long battle to unify and raise the standards of the Graduate School came quickly. Allan Cartter's *An Assessment of Quality in Graduate Education* (1966) gave a comparative appraisal of graduate schools in the United States. Four Indiana liberal arts departments were listed among the first ten in the nation, twenty were included among the first twenty, and twenty-three were in the first twenty-five departments with ratings from satisfactory to excellent. This was in sharp contrast to the 1957 rating when only nine departments were mentioned in the first twenty, and only four were listed in a similar survey in 1925. An even stronger measure of the progress made by the Graduate School in the past two decades was the fact that its graduates were employed as professors and scientific specialists in institutions all across America. Also, staff members hired after 1939, had already made professional reputations, which attracted a significant inflow of choice graduate students. These promised to give even more tangibility to the original university dream of an intellectual age of high competence.

[XIV]

"That They Might Have Life. . . ."

WHEN DR. CHARLES PHILLIPS EMERSON retired as Dean of the Indiana University Medical School in 1931, he could take satisfaction in the fact that in the face of great odds he had helped to establish a good medical program. Not only was medical education in Indiana yielding positive dividends in more doctors, the university offered greatly expanded services in the Robert W. Long Memorial Hospital and the James Whitcomb Riley Memorial Children's Hospital. In addition, special clinics and other sophisticated facilities served the state. All of these had become necessary teaching adjuncts to the training of doctors and nurses.

The biggest problem in the intervening years since World War I, was procurement of adequate financial support for the Medical Center, a nagging situation which continued on into the future. The Board of Trustees chose as his successor, Dr. Willis Dew Gatch, a surgeon, native of Aurora, Indiana, a graduate of Indiana University ('01), and graduate of the Johns Hopkins Medical School. Dr. Gatch was a rugged individualist often exercising the masterful hand of the surgeon on human relationships. He came to rule the Medical School with a tight rein, and like his predecessors, he wrestled mightily with the problems of bringing the school up to high standards of medical education, hiring promising staff members, and finding enough money to support his efforts.

It is doubtful that any other dean in the university enjoyed so much autonomy or lived so close to the public as did Dean Gatch. The very nature of his work brought him in touch with many realities of Hoosier life. Every legislative session produced some kind of threatening resolution, discussion, or attempted invasion of the School of Medicine. Constituents nagged legislators about medical training and many of them tried to make a show of action. Because the medical profession had such deep human implications, and because the two university hospitals offered so much direct public service there was an ever visible sensitivity about their operation. Too, perennial wails arose that the Medical School was not training enough doctors to keep abreast of the state's health needs. At the other extreme, the School of Medicine had to make enormous efforts to keep up with the rapidly advancing world of medical science, and to maintain a respectable rating among American medical schools. It is little wonder that the strong-willed Gatch looked upon his domain in Indianapolis as an imperial fiefdom.

When Herman B Wells became president of Indiana University, the School of Medicine's estimated budget, exclusive of the cost of the Clinical Building, was $912,590.00, a far too inadequate sum to satisfy demands made of the institution. In 1938 the General Assembly added a new unit to Dr. Gatch's administrative watch care when it appropriated $325,000 to construct the Indiana State Board of Health Building on the Medical Center campus. This was said to be the first such public service structure to be located in a medical school. This addition gave Indiana University direct access to the abundance of clinical materials of the State Board of Health. The addition of the new building was also an indication that at some time in the future a school of public health would be added to the university's medical program.

One of the first medical school debates which President Wells had to hear was that of concentrating all medical training in Indianapolis. Since 1903 this issue had been a tender one. Dr. Edmund D. Clark of the Indiana Medical Association suggested in October 1937 such a consolidation. His suggestion, however, came at a most inopportune moment for the proponents of the idea. University administrators and professors were dedicating with a jubilant expression of triumph, on November 20, 1937, the new Medical Building in Bloomington. This structure had been built by use of Works Progress Administration funds. Dean Burton Dorr Myers was a stout defender of the Bloomington program as Dr. Gatch was of that in Indianapolis. He declared the two-year school had an "A" rating, and the new building was perhaps the most modern one in the country. At the dedication favorite son, United States Senator Sherman D. Minton, said there had been built into the structure the "ideals, yes, the very lives of Gatch, Myers, Moenkhaus, and their colleagues." To him, it represented the spirit of Indiana in both history and aspiration.

Dean Myers refuted the critics who complained that out-of-state students were crowding into the classes in Bloomington to assure admission to the Medical School for the remainder of their work. He reported, September 28, 1938, that since 1927, there had been forty-nine out-of-state students, or an average of 4.9 per cent of each class, and in 1937 there was only 3.7 per cent. This compared with a national rate of 13 per cent. He told carping critics, "There has never been a time that a well-prepared state student has been excluded from enrollment by the [acceptance] of an out-of-state student." The error, if any had been committed, was on the side of admitting too few non-Hoosiers.

Whatever the merits of the organized medical profession's drive to concentrate all medical training in Indianapolis, prospective students seemed to sustain the university's position. In 1939 the school had received 1,000 student applications for admission. It was one of seven schools to receive such a large number, said the *Journal of the Association of American Medical Colleges*. Out of this deluge of applications Indiana accepted only 99 new students, and in May 1941 it accepted 140 from approximately the same number of applications.

In his first year in office President Wells reported completion of the Clinical Building in Indianapolis, and in 1939 he told the trustees this was "the most eventful [year] in the entire history of the Medical Center." The source of his jubilation was enactment of a state law which permitted the university to make service charges for care of the state's adult indigent patients. This added income had enabled the Medical School to open the fourth floor of the new building to accommodate eighty-five new patients, and to establish a seventeen-bed isolation ward in the West Wing of the Robert W. Long Hospital. In addition, operating rooms were opened on the fifth floor of the new Clinical Building. "Without this law," he told the trustees, "the School of Medicine could not have retained its standing as a first-rate school."

Time passed on for the mainstay of the Bloomington school. In 1940 Dean Burton D. Myers reached mandatory retirement age, and Dean W. D. Gatch would now be placed in administrative charge of both units. This would tend to unify medical training much more thoroughly than had ever been possible in the past. One further change was reported, Dr. Kime was appointed head of the Department of Anatomy replacing Dr. Myers.

In the immediate prewar years the Medical School made general progress both in operation and in important contributions to medical science. For instance, in 1938, Dr. Louis Mazzini, after six years of intensive investigation, announced a new test for detecting syphilis, which proved more accurate than the famous Wasserman test. The teaching in this course was said to be the best in the country. In another division, plans were made to utilize the fine subsidiary facility of the James Whitcomb Riley Memorial Hospital. A child guidance clinic was to be established in January 1940. This new division was to cooperate with the Indiana Child Welfare Agency and doctors throughout the state in efforts to correct personality maladjustments. This clinic was to be directed by Dr. David A. Boyd, head of the Department of Mental and Nervous Diseases. At the same time the Riley Hospital Board made provisions for emergency treatment of victims of infantile paralysis.

Not only were the organizational plans of the School of Medicine revised in 1939–42, but significant additions were made to the teaching staff. Besides Dr. David A. Boyd, Dr. John D. Van Nuys was appointed admitting physician, and Dr. Cyrus J. Clark was made head of the new Department of Medical Economics and Post-Graduate Instruction. Future promises for expansion were brightened when the Indianapolis campus was enlarged by a land exchange with the City of Indianapolis, and the purchase of additional acreage with standing buildings, which had an estimated value of $600,000.

Dean Gatch announced in January 1940 that the School of

Medicine would institute a two-year program intended specifically for training of general practitioners. The university established a $10,000 grant for this purpose, and the Indianapolis City Hospital Dispensary was converted into a practical training center for graduate physicians. This, said Gatch, meant a renewed emphasis on the training of more general practitioners, which Indiana so badly needed. Young physicians to be produced by this program would now have access to opportunities of working with the 600 patients who came daily into the clinics and hospitals. The closing years of the 1930s were especially promising ones. The *Quarterly Bulletin* of the Medical School in February 1940 reported "Progress of the University Medical Center during 1939 has made this year one of the most outstanding in the history of the institution. . . . Needed improvements in physical equipment, administrative organization and teaching techniques have been made to extend the training of the student body." Part of this improvement had come about because the addition of 3,800 square feet of the new State Board of Health Building had relieved cramped conditions that had actually blocked progress.

At the peak of the new optimism in 1940, conditions were changing rapidly for Indiana University's School of Medicine, and for the world. The bombing of Pearl Harbor, December 7, 1941, had set the nation on fire with anger and anxiety. President Wells reported in 1942 that since Pearl Harbor students and faculty of the Medical School had been stunned by events. It was obvious that most everyone with medical training would be called into some kind of military service. The international emergency had destroyed all hopes of young doctors for immediate entry into practice. After 1941 the Medical School's activities were dominated by wartime demands, and by spring 1942 thirty-eight younger members of the faculty had been called to serve the nation. For the second time in the century Indiana University was requested to organize a major medical unit to go to the battle front. Late in 1942 General Field Hospital 32 was organized, and was called into service in January 1943, taking with it fifteen more staff members. These professors left behind thirteen key staff vacancies which could not be filled immediately. Losses from the nonteaching staff ran as high as 60 per cent, and 104 nurses were called away from the hospitals for military services. General Hospital 32 took away forty-six more vitally needed nurses; this unit was staffed and equipped to care for a thousand-bed field operation.

Equally as hard hit was the Indiana system of special individual instruction by many graduate conference leaders and experienced quiz masters. After December 1942 only a small group of vitally needed student assistants was left on the campus, and these were kept on a standby military procurement basis. Wells wrote, "If we had not been able to hold these men it would have been almost impossible to keep the Medical Center running." After the first surge of losses of personnel the medical faculty was composed largely of men over fifty years of age, and many of these were private physicians who gave their services to the School of Medicine while serving their own patients. These doctors taught classes for little or no compensation, but wartime stringencies required that they give more time to an ever-increasing number of patients. Rather drastic steps were taken to revise the teaching program which required a much higher rate of student attendance at all exercises, a more tightly coordinated curriculum, and the institution of new courses in cancer, vascular diseases, first aid, neurology, and psychiatry. Future examinations were to be searching, and students were informed that they would have to be largely self-directed, and would get a good part of their medical education from attentive reading.

Tremendous energy was expended in speeding up the process of producing new physicians. In 1943 the new class was chosen in February instead of May, and Dean Gatch annonced the approval of 131 admissions. The new students would begin classes in May, and the training program would be continuous. A new class would be started every eight months, thus adding an extra semester every twelve months.

At the time readjustments were being made in the instructional program, the entire Medical School-hospital-clinic routine was being disrupted while getting the big General Field Hospital 32 ready for shipment overseas. Dr. Cyrus J. Clark, clinical professor of cardiology, and Dr. C. F. Thompson, professor of orthopedic surgery, were the chief organizers of the military hospital. They were commissioned colonels, and drew a large part of the new hospital's personnel from the doctor and nursing resources of the state. Fully staffed, the hospital required 75 medical officers, 120 nurses, 500 enlisted men, and 1,000 beds. This staff was inducted into the United States Army on May 13, 1942, which meant 692 persons were sworn into service in a joint ceremony.

The Medical School in Indianapolis in May 1942 was located on a sprawling seventy-six acre tract along West Michigan Avenue. It represented to date an investment of $6,000,000, 80 per cent of which had come from private donors. The complex consisted of the School of Medicine, the School of Dentistry, the Nurses Training Center, the Robert W. Long Memorial Hospital, the James Whitcomb Riley Memorial Hospital for Children with its Kiwanis and Rotary wings, the State Board of Health Building, the Clinic, the William H. Coleman Hospital for Women, and the Ball Residence for Nurses. In addition, there was the new Medical Building fifty-five miles away in Bloomington. This was the physical plant Indiana University had on hand to go through the war. Even with this impressive list of structures there seems to have been a pressing need for more space. The hospitals especially were called upon to render increased services.

It had become a ritual tradition that a thousand applicants would seek admission to the Medical School, and the supplicants in May 1942 were as numerous as ever. That year 128 new students were admitted to the first class operating on the new continuous schedule. Dr. Gatch and his colleagues had spent approximately two years devising a four-page questionnaire, an aptitude test, and a plan for gathering meaningful recommendations. When all of this material was in hand it was analyzed by a fourteen-man committee, a task that proved time consuming. The process was repeated every eight months to insure a steady flow of well-qualified students into the new classes. The Nurses Training School was equally as circumspect in its admission procedures. It was said to be the only nursing school in Indiana to require thirty hours of college credit for admission, and in May 1942 it accepted 150 new candidates. The university allowed nursing candidates with ninety-four hours credit and two years and four months of nurse's training to receive a Bachelor of Arts or Bachelor of Science degree.

The continuous year-round operation of the Medical School with a skeleton staff placed a heavy strain on professors. A second and unanticipated stress grew out of the war. As doctors from Indiana towns were drawn into military service, they left their indigent and most of their private patients without ample access to medical care. These had no place to go except to the public hospitals in the Medical Center. Inflationary costs of materials and equipment in wartime increased operational expenses of the school and hospitals by at least a third. At this desperate moment Dean Gatch told President Wells, "In this emergency the center has fortunately had the active assistance of the Governor, the Mayor, the draft officials, and the local procurement and assignment agency. . . . The medical School has also had the loyal support of every member of the faculty. Thanks to all of this, it is now prepared to carry on, not as usual, but we believe, with a high degree of efficiency." He thought the country needed nurses even more than doctors, and the Training School was giving refresher courses to nurses who had been out of training and was instituting a more generous admission of trainees and an extensive program of training nurse's aides.

Almost eclipsing the wartime emergency was the staggering problem of caring for hospital patients because of loss of doctors. By May 1942 the Clinic had admitted the record number of 60,161 out-patients, an increase of 4,000 over the last report. In addition, the number of inpatients in all the hospitals increased. The Riley Children's Hospital especially felt the impact of emergency conditions. A summary of wartime pressures was issued at the end of the academic year 1942. The Medical School staff had taught 353 students, cared for more than 5,500 charity in-patients, sorted through a list of 3,000 charity patient applications seeking admission to the hospitals, made 60,000 visits to the out-patient department, aided in the instruction of 187 student nurses, conducted schools for dietitians and laboratory technicians, and helped train WPA and NYA aids. In addition to these duties, the staff treated 11,053 in-patients, practically the same number as the year before when the full staff was on hand. The state police and Department of Health officials called on the staff, especially in cases of accidental poisonings and infectious outbreaks.

So serious was the shortage of nurses that President Wells wrote Dean Gatch, August 11, 1942, that some revisions should be made in the training program. He suggested an immediate campaign to increase the number of students in the fall classes, and that loans instead of scholarships be offered in-coming trainees. He thought the requirement of one year of college work should be waived, but that no one should be admitted from the lower one-third of high school classes. Students already accepted in another nursing school should be allowed to transfer to Indiana under the new rules. Wells had reason to be concerned. Since 1940 the number of nurses in training in Indianapolis had declined materially.

Despite wartime conditions and pressures the currents of Hoosier life flowed somewhat in traditional channels; a thousand babies were born, 1941-42, in the Coleman Hospital for Women. The James Whitcomb Riley Memorial Hospital for Children lived up to its scripturally inspired purpose, "That they might have life and have it more abundantly." The hospital's wards were kept filled with children being treated for a wide variety of afflictions. Early in 1940 Sister Elizabeth Kenny was invited to demonstrate her "fomenting" or hydro-turbulent treatment of victims of infantile paralysis.

The speed-up program promised three years of advancement for new students entering the Medical School after May 1942, and classes were filled to instructional capacity. In November 1942 a new class of 128 students chosen from 900 applications was admitted. This actually meant that compared with the traditional two-semester program, the new class was a major extra increase. Even so, there were perennial complaints that not enough students were being admitted to training. President Sparks of Wabash College complained to President Wells in September 1942 that the Medical School discriminated against Wabash students, and that Medical School professors had advised premedical students not to attend that school. Dean Gatch answered this criticism in a letter to Wells saying that the Admissions Board leaned over backwards not to show favoritism to Indiana students. The Dean said, however, he would not hesitate to choose Indiana students if it was deemed to be in the best interest of the medical profession to do so; although he could not recall anyone giving the advice that had irritated President Sparks.

Immediately after disposing of President Sparks' stricture, a fact-finding committee of the Indiana General Assembly submitted a report asking the 1943 session to provide funds to construct a new medical science building, supply additional hospital facilities for adult patients, and to make available funds with which to hire new faculty to teach an increased enrollment of students. This was hardly a realistic report because not a single one of its recommendations could be carried out in wartime.

None of the critics seemed to realize that however anxious the university was to strike at the sources of their complaints, it was bound by all of the limitations of every other institution that lacked personnel and materials. President Wells received a letter from a Mr. Jenkins, in September 1942, making a fairly extended list of observations. Jenkins professed friendship for the university and said it was being unduly criticized because of several administrative deficiencies. Among these was a too-complicated system of record-keeping, it was said President Wells and Ward Biddle did not give enough attention to the Medical Center, and because Negro patients were committed to the Medical Center but were actually treated in the Indianapolis City or Marion County General Hospital.

Even Dean Henry L. Smith of the School of Education joined the chorus for revising the program for training doctors and nurses. In a memorandum to President Wells, January 28, 1943, he suggested a four-point program for nurse's training, the burden of which was employment of a full-time instructor to teach classes by extension in the various nursing schools of the state. Dean Gatch's answer to all suggestions was, "It has been the feeling of the medical faculty that now is no time to lower standards, and the faculty believes that our men in the armed forces should have well-trained doctors." At that time, May 25, 1943, there was an enrollment in the Medical School of 504 students, and the Dean reported that despite loss of faculty the quality of student work had not been lowered.

From time-to-time President Wells sent memorandums to Dean Gatch regarding areas of Medical School concern. On one occasion he suggested that some special investigation be made of hay fever causes and treatment. He was constantly being approached about other problems in the Clinic and the hospitals. The public services of the Robert W. Long Memorial Hospital seemed to generate endless anxieties, ranging from the prompt admission of literally thousands of patients to supplying transportation for charity cases from various parts of the state. Inevitably, these problems irritated both President and Dean, and at times placed undue strains on their relations. Dean Gatch was ever a strong-willed man, and a sensitive one. Wells wrote President F. A. Middlebush of the University of Missouri, December 22, 1942, "Confidentially, I wish that we had no hospitals of our own, and that we were buying all of our clinical facilities from other hospitals. The Deans of Medical Schools all oppose this kind of arrangement, but I am confident that it is far less costly to the institutions and just as good from the clinical standpoint as to have hospitals under their own control. Most Deans of Schools of Medicine become so interested in hospital administration and they want to build bigger and bigger hospitals and have more and more beds, even though they use for teaching purposes a very small proportion of what they have."

By some mishap this letter got into the hands of Dean Gatch in the spring of 1943, and apparently it ruffled his feathers. In a meeting with the Board of Trustees in June that year, the President and Dean became involved in a somewhat heated expression of differences of opinion over the hiring of two new professors. Apparently Wells had favored their employment and Gatch opposed it. Judge John Hastings said in an interview in 1971 that the discussion became so heated that Wells threatened to resign. Certainly Judge Ora L. Wildermuth was disturbed by the turn of events. He wrote Dean Gatch, June 21, 1943, "I was gratified that you and Dr. Wells hashed out some of your disagreements Saturday night." As peacemaker, Judge Wildermuth said the two men actually had affection for each other and nothing should be permitted to embitter their feelings. He told Gatch, "It was most gracious of you Saturday night to accept the two men whose appointment was in question, and it was gracious of President Wells to agree if after a fair trial of one year they failed in your judgment then they would be removed, with that kind of co-operative spirit I can see for Indiana University and especially for the Medical School a brilliant future." Gatch replied that he and Wells had talked again about their problems and although they had differences of opinions there was no personal ill-feeling and they would work together in harmony. Wildermuth wrote Wells, enclosing a copy of Dean Gatch's letter, saying he thought it was all that could be hoped for. Clearly the source of irritation had not actually been removed in the mind of the president of the Board of Trustees.

The James Whitcomb Riley Hospital was without a doubt a

genuine clinical asset to the Medical School, and in turn the medical staff was indispensable to the Riley Hospital. Nevertheless, the financing and administration of the semi-private institution created moments of concern. President Wells wrote the banker-president of the Riley Memorial Foundation, Hugh McK. Landon, March 1, 1943, that Dean Gatch was concerned about the steady drop in the number of patients of late. The dean thought the children's hospital should begin accepting pay from some of its patients anyway. Without expressing a positive opinion about the Gatch proposal, Wells did say he was impressed by the statement at the last Riley Committee meeting that money continued to come to the foundation in increasing amounts from donors, and to accept paying patients might tend to dry up the source of this income.

James W. Carr, secretary of the James Whitcomb Riley Memorial Association, consulted Dr. Carl McCaskey, president of the Indiana Medical Association, as to his reactions to the acceptance of private patients in the public hospital. "His reaction," said Carr, "was immediate—almost bitter. He recalled that when the program started years ago many of the doctors outside of Indianapolis were opposed on the ground that eventually the hospital would become a pay institution." Dr. McCaskey expressed the belief that Indiana doctors would generally offer strong opposition to a changed policy. Beyond this he wanted to know who initiated the idea. He said the doctors believed acceptance of paying patients in a state hospital was a step toward socialized medicine. This was currently a sore subject with the doctors and they were organizing lay-committees "to fight the socialization trend." In April 1943 the Riley Memorial Association was informed that the Hospital might receive as much as $400,000 from the estate of the Terre Haute industrialist, William H. Yingling. In a short time other bequests were made to the hospital.

The Riley Association was, to say the least, irritated with Dean Gatch, and had James W. Carr revealed to the State Medical Association that he was the author of the pay proposal, the dean no doubt would have found himself involved in a heated controversy with his doctor colleagues. Generally it seems that Dean Gatch did not actively cultivate the good will of the Riley Board. When James W. Carr sought information of J. B. Martin, administrator of the Ball Nurses Home, he was informed by Dr.

Gatch that only his office could give out Medical Center information. This brought a stern letter from Hugh McK. Landon in which he said that every responsible person in the Medical Center knew James W. Carr was a thoroughly trustworthy official and could receive confidential information about the addition to the Nurses Home and treat it judiciously. "If the refusal to give him access to information is persisted in," Landon told Gatch, "I shall certainly report the matter to them [the Riley Board]. If you are trying to end their interest in the work of the Medical Center you are on the right track." A carbon copy of this letter was sent to President Wells with the typed notation, "This nonsense has gone so far that it is past endurance. Someone has to call this gentleman to order and perhaps it is well that it should be done by someone not connected with the University. The Riley directors are going to feel pretty sore if this matter has to be discussed with them."

Closely related to the general discussion of the Riley Hospital program was the matter of getting a physiotherapy treatment unit underway. President Wells had evinced an interest in this area, and had received from Dean Gatch an oral promise that he would investigate the matter. Wells followed this up with a written request that a report be given the administration so it could know "what is needed to get us started in this field." No doubt the president had been bombarded about the lack of some services in the Medical Center.

The Medical School had several hospital alternatives. Dean Gatch undoubtedly had reason to be concerned about a pending bill in the 1943 General Assembly that proposed to allow county judges to shift some, if not all, public medical responsibilities onto the university hospitals. He told Wells, March 2, 1943, that he had not changed his mind about the bill, but neither he nor his colleagues would oppose it publicly. This bill promised to place a heavy additional burden on an already troubled wartime hospital situation. It would open a funnel for indigent patients to pour into the Medical Center.

Whether the threat of the unfortunate bill pending before the legislature influenced the Medical School staff or not, a revision of procedures for admitting patients was instituted by the university, and especially as they related to the Riley Hospital. The institution later received a commendation for this change from the Crippled Children's Division of the United States

Department of Labor. President Wells wrote Thurmand Gottschalk of the State Department of Public Welfare, that he had "believed in the procedure from the day it was proposed, and I still do."

As the battles in Europe and the Pacific took their heavy tolls of human beings, there was an insatiable demand for nurses, and the Indiana Medical School in 1943 lacked the facilities to train as many as were demanded of it. In May the Federal Government granted $135,101 to finance the construction of a new wing to the Ball Nurses Home. The university supplied $83,000, $50,000 of which was raised by private subscriptions. The additional $200,000 wing would also contain classrooms and laboratories. Ninety per cent of the nurses then in training were already committed to military services upon graduation. The new wing would house 80 more students in addition to the 275 already enrolled. A second arrangement was made to step up the training of nurses by use of a semi-extension procedure. A telephonic lecture program was instituted by which medical school professors were enabled to lecture long-distance to nursing classes in other Indiana schools. The first of these programs was directed to the interns and staff of the St. Elizabeth Hospital in Lafayette in September 1944.

While the entire university was largely devoted to war services, no division was more heavily committed than the School of Medicine. Staff members were constantly being drawn away to perform highly specialized services. An example was enlistment of Dr. Sid Robinson, associate professor of physiology, who directed a group of scientists in the Harvard University laboratories in the study of fatigue in high altitude flying. Earlier on the Bloomington campus Dr. Robinson had constructed a fatigue measuring machine, and had conducted tests on groups of college athletes throughout the country. In 1939 he had conducted an interesting study of fatigue resulting from hard physical labor and its effects on the bodies of Mississippi Delta cotton sharecroppers. One of his military assignments was testing the adequacy of "C" rations issued to soldiers exposed to the tortures of the New Mexico desert. Many other members of the Medical School performed similar services in studying human exposures to the exigencies of war.

At the request of Dr. John R. Newcomb, vice chairman of the Procurement and Assignment Service for Indiana, President Wells addressed a general letter to the Indiana physicians in military service, April 8, 1943. He told the doctors that Indiana University was meeting all demands made upon the School of Medicine despite handicaps of making constant readjustments caused by shortages of all kinds. "Morale at the School of Medicine," he said, "is high. The students are aware of the seriousness of the preparation they are making and attendance at classes is at an unprecedented high average of 95 per cent."

When the end of the war seemed near in October 1944, the administration and staff of the School of Medicine began taking stock of their wartime experiences. In a news account in the *Indiana Daily Student*, October 31, 1944, the Medical School administration said, "The heaviest of wartime burdens placed on Indiana University have fallen on the Medical Center at Indianapolis. . . . The Center has thrived on adversity and faces the post-war period with confidence." The Medical Center comprised of five schools, three hospitals, and numerous clinics, said the spokesman, had encountered repeated challenges. At the time the Center carried on an extraordinarily heavy program of military-related services, it had shouldered an even heavier burden of civilian medical care. In the past year, 1943–44, the hospitals had administered to 10,739 in-patients, 35,309 out-patients, and had conducted 134,066 laboratory examinations. Staff members had also found time to make plans for extensive revisions of future medical educational procedures.

The Indiana General Field Hospital 32 was then in Aachen, Germany, where it remained until after July 1946. It was still one of the busiest medical units in Europe. Colonel Cyrus J. Clark, its commanding officer, wrote in July that its patient in-flow hovered around the 1,000 bed capacity. The hospital, he wrote, would remain in Germany for some time, but he was certain it would not be asked to become a part of the army of occupation. Major General Paul R. Hawley, Chief Surgeon of the European Theatre of Operations, wrote President Wells in July 1945, that "I find myself at a loss for words to describe the superb quality of medical personnel that came with this unit." He said of Colonel Clark, "His inspiring leadership has built up and kept the morale consistently high." Three years later the Navy Department awarded its Certificate of Achievement to the Medical School for its work both on the campus in Indianapolis and abroad.

End of the war brought as many exacting problems for Indiana

University as had arisen in the duration. The whole operation of the university reflected the impact of changes in conditions of American life. Heavy new academic demands made upon every department of the institution, in the face of shortages of every kind, produced new stringencies. There were demands for a wide variety of medical services by Hoosiers who were trying to make up for three years of partial neglect. This meant that needs for physicians and other trained medical personnel far exceeded the possibility of the university to train them. The abiding complaint that the School of Medicine was not training enough doctors troubled the university administration. A legislator stood ever ready to oblige critics by introducing legislation to force the training of more doctors. In this case State Senator C. Omer Free bombarded President Wells with letters during January 1945. He wanted information on how many doctors had been graduated, and how many had remained in Indiana. Before the month was out he had introduced a joint resolution in both houses amply adorned with "therefores" and "whereases," which boiled down to a request that a committee be appointed to investigate the School of Medicine's admission policies. The committee that resulted, despite Senator Free's impatience, did not report until February that "It has been the policy of the Indiana Medical Center not to limit the number of students entering said school and without regard to facilities available. . . . Your committee recommends that said Indiana Medical Center and its deans, personnel and staff connected therewith be commended for their splendid record of service, in maintaining said school upon a high standard, as it has in the past, which has merited high recognition in the Nation." This was hardly what the Senator had sought. Wells sent the trustees copies of the legislative committee's report with the notation, "Senator Free signed with reservations. He expressed his reservations in a speech which no one took seriously. All's well that ends well!" The motivation behind Senator Free's agitation was the fact that he sought to get his son admitted to the School of Medicine. This contention went on through two or three sessions of the legislature. The senator was finally persuaded that the best course for his son was to enter the School of Business, where he graduated, and then began a successful career with a pharmaceutical house. The admission policies remained intact, and the senator was placated.

Senator Free was by no means the only person raising the issue of Medical School admissions. Registrar Thomas A. Cookson pressured Judge Ora L. Wildermuth on the same subject. He wanted the president of the board to call a special meeting to discuss the senatorial resolution. Wildermuth told Cookson he understood clearly why the gates of admission could not be opened to all comers and he thought the Medical School in no danger from legislative action.

Despite the outside agitations there was a prevailing air of expansion inside the school. Professor Thurman B. Rice of the Medical School staff had campaigned for the development of a department of public health, and so had many Hoosier citizens. In February 1945 Governor Ralph F. Gates presented to the General Assembly a request for the enactment of legislation to permit a reorganization of the State Board of Health, codification of the Indiana health laws, the addition to the Board of Dental Health, and to deal with the diseases of middle and advanced ages. In the Medical School, the Department of Public Health would offer courses covering the whole spectrum of public health. Wells wrote Jesse C. Andrews, chairman of the Ways and Means Committee, February 17, 1945, that an addition of $50,000 should be made to the 1945–47 university budget to finance a modest beginning of an expanded public health program.

There was never any such thing as a status quo in either medical training or hospital operations. All things in social and scientific advancement worked to prevent a static condition. Human needs in modern society can never really be satisfied; this Indiana University was to learn in its day-by-day advance into the latter half of the twentieth century.

While Senator Free and his partisans were in hot pursuit of enrolling officers of the School of Medicine, Senator Charles A. Phelps of Fort Wayne nipped at the heels of the administration on another front. The impression got abroad, spread largely by Senator Phelps, that the university opposed the organization of a hospital for crippled children in northern Indiana. President Wells wrote Fred A. Miller, editor of the *South Bend Tribune*, January 29, 1945, that the university looked upon the establishment of another crippled children's hospital as purely the responsibility of the General Assembly. Instead of opposing such a move, the institution had offered to share its experience in operating the Riley Memorial Hospital with the northern committee. He told Miller that all university information was open to any public body that sought it.

The university had too many concerns of its own in the operation of the Riley Hospital to engage in a pettish sectional state controversy. There were demanding needs for modernization of the Riley plant, for improving all the hospital laboratories, and for development of an extensive research program. President Wells assured Hugh McK. Landon, February 7, 1945, that the university would move to make these improvements as rapidly as funds were forthcoming from state and private sources. The latter source was enlarged by a possible $300,000 bequest from the estate of the late Charles Olsen, former operator of the Lyric Theater in Indianapolis, and onetime national lightweight wrestling champion. This was welcome support for Riley Hospital. Despite Dean Gatch's earlier fears about the decreasing number of children admitted to its wards, it now showed marked annual increases. In 1944–45 the total number of children treated was up, and for the twenty years of its operation the number had climbed to more than 60,000.

For the School of Medicine as a whole Dean Gatch submitted a six-point outline as both a report and a projection for the modernization of medical education in Indiana. Two of his points dealt with the handicaps inflicted by lack of space and personnel. He advocated unifying the entire medical program of the university in Indianapolis, devoting a full floor in a new building to research, and creating a new mechanical shop for the building and repair of scientific equipment. The dean's proposal made a diametrically opposite approach to the development of a research program from that followed in the rest of the university. Somehow a copy of Dean Gatch's restricted proposal got into the hands of President Wells, and it provoked him into voicing a frank opinion. In a letter to James W. Carr he commented on the "outline of the so-called proposed programs," which he said was "of course meaningless." In Wells' thinking, research programs did not start with the provision of equipment and other necessary facilities before competent men were hired to use them. The President told Carr that he looked with disfavor on the proposal because at present every man on the Medical School staff had space and some type of laboratory for his research. He was even more direct in commenting upon Gatch's complaint of lack of personnel. "As to the lack of personnel . . ." he wrote, "had we had men capable of undertaking any of a hundred important government projects, the personnel would have been furnished as well as money for equipment. We did do such projects on this campus, one on malaria in the Chemistry Department, the other in physiology in the (Bloomington School of Medicine). . . . Dr. Gatch fought to the very end the program in physiology. He never gave any reason for fighting it." Wells said provisions were being made in the new buildings for research space. Then he uttered a concluding note of desperation that "a competent director could not be hired under the present circumstances at the School, and, if hired, would not stay more than ninety days. Time marches on!" Maybe at that moment in the university's history President Wells thought to himself if he wanted to give the devil a present he would offer him a medical school with a football team thrown in for good measure.

The two views presented in the dean's outline and the president's letter revealed sharp and fundamentally differing philosophies as to the administration of the Indiana School of Medicine. This was an era of planning, but the university's margin of public support was so narrow that it had to make certain that the future standing of its Medical School would not be marred by inadequate considerations.

Soon after the cessation of fighting in Europe, the General Assembly, in May 1945, enacted legislation permitting construction on the Medical Center campus of a mental hospital and clinic. An appropriation of $250,000 was made with a provision that, if needed, an additional $75,000 would be forthcoming. This legislation also provided that a mental health council composed of two Medical School faculty members and two alumni be appointed. Governor Gates appointed three doctors, LaRue D. Carter, Thurman B. Rice, and Norman M. Beatty, and Judge John M. Morris. By October 24 the committee's work was far enough advanced to discuss plans for the new building.

By the time the Mental Council was ready with its preliminary report, building plans for the entire Medical School complex were being discussed. Included in these were the blueprints for the Medical School, the State Board of Public Health, the James Whitcomb Riley Memorial Hospital, and other expansions. A major concern was how best to use the remaining thirty-five acres of vacant campus space. The new plans also demanded that close consideration be given to coordination of the entire public medical training and service facility. This was the first time the universty had so extensive an opportunity to do this.

Reconversion of the general teaching program from wartime emergency operation to a more relaxed peacetime routine required important readjustments in most areas of the Medical School's operation. First was the matter of reassembling a faculty and turning the teaching schedule back to the traditional nine-month, two-semester operation. The return to this plan reduced by at least 128 students the number of tri-annual admissions, which had occurred during the last two war years. There remained on the campus one last vestige of military obligation, the naval medical training unit contract which had to be liquidated. The Executive Committee of the Medical Center recommended that the out-of-state naval students then enrolled be allowed to complete their training by paying in-state fees when the federal contract expired. The committee felt that without this concession a number of promising students would transfer to other schools. At the same time it would be difficult for many of the naval students to transfer credits without losses.

By the latter quarter of 1945 several hundred doctors returned to general practice in Indiana. These doctors had been out of touch with the advances made in general medicine during their specialized services in military hospitals. A fivefold refresher or externe postgraduate course of six months' duration was offered them in the Medical School. The doctors were given opportunities to take resident training in the University hospitals, the Marion County General Hospital, and St. Elizabeth's Hospital in Lafayette. Course work was offered in anatomy, physiology, and pathology.

While the program to help returning medical veterans catch up on new medical knowledge and procedures was being formulated, the faculty in Indianapolis and the Indiana Medical Association once again opened the sensitive issue of consolidating all medical instruction in Indianapolis. This question was raised by the Department of Anatomy and Physiology, June 20, 1945, at the moment the end of the war was certain. Perhaps the faculty in Indianapolis had never really reconciled itself to the division of the instructional program, and maybe it never took time to understand the tremendous amount of historical emotion expended on this issue, or the expense in which the university had been involved over the years to maintain the Bloomington Medical School. Dr. Gastineau's planning committee strongly suggested to the Board of Trustees, July 26, 1945, "That the work of the first year of the Medical School be transferred at the earliest possible time from Bloomington to the Indianapolis campus, and that the first building constructed be an addition to the Medical School to provide room for the Department of Anatomy and Physiology." The departments involved, however, counseled further consideration of the matter. In fact they asked for postponement of this consideration until they could be relieved of pressures of the accelerated wartime schedule. The Board of Trustees accepted and filed away this report, hinting at the same time that Dr. W. D. Gatch might possibly retire from the deanship.

The board's action did not allay discussion of the consolidation. The Indiana Medical Association rather strongly advocated elimination of the School of Medicine program in Bloomington in its annual meeting. The doctors, said the *Indianapolis Star*, November 12, 1945, created about as much confusion as enlightenment on the subject. They became embroiled in an argument over the value of medical students having academic backgrounds, and possibly academic associations. The Medical Association nevertheless formulated an elaborate set of legalistic resolutions that called upon the Indiana School of Medicine to concentrate its entire training program in Indianapolis, improve the teaching of medicine, give advanced students opportunity to review basic medical science by serving as assistants, and, "That the Medical Center be placed under its own supervision and own budget that it may be able to secure the best medical talent for teaching." This latter request bore earmarks of having originated within either the medical staff or the dean's office, or both.

There was no lack of planning during the months at the war's end. Maybe some considerable internal political manipulation also took place during the period of transition. Issues raised by the various areas of interest in the Medical School and the hospital administrations seem to reflect a condition of unrest and impatience. The intervening year, July 1945 to June 1946, no doubt produced more internal fermentation than is revealed in the formal record. As meager as the documentary facts are for these months, two seem clear: there were rather sharp differences of points of view between the University President and the Medical School

Dean, and the Trustees supported the President. In its consideration of the Medical School report in July 1945, the Board gave somewhat more than a hint that it did not anticipate Dean Gatch to continue in his position much longer, despite the fact he had two years to go before he reached mandatory retirement age. Nevertheless, it appears that Dean Gatch's precipitate resignation, June 26, 1946, caught the Trustees by surprise. Gatch wrote Judge Ora L. Wildermuth, not President Wells, "I hereby resign all positions I have in Indiana University. Conditions several years ago made me consider resigning then, but the war prevented, I deemed it my duty to stay with the school until the war was over."

Publicly, Dean Gatch's actual resignation came without precise warning to the Board of Trustees, it was not, however, without considerable background of internal unpleasantness. The central facts behind this resignation was the dean's notion that the rules and regulations of the university did not apply to him personally. Clearly reflected in his actions as Dean of the School of Medicine was the fact that he considered that he operated an empire of his own, that he had only himself to answer to, and not the President of the University nor the Board of Trustees. This was especially true in regard to his retirement. On November 19, 1970, Judge John S. Hastings, in a taped interview, said, "Dr. Gatch said very bluntly, well, that plan [retirement] doesn't apply to me, and I won't follow it. I'm going to stay dean until I get ready to retire as dean." The President, said Judge Hastings, undertook to counsel with Dean Gatch, but this only angered the old surgeon. He became profane and abusive, especially of President Wells. The Board of Trustees was now faced with two ultimatums, resignation from the President, and refusal to retire from Dean Gatch. It was forced to tell Dean Gatch that he must resign, and gave President Wells direct instructions that he was still President of the University. This was indeed an unhappy moment in Indiana University's history. The board looked upon this incident as highly disturbing, and reminiscent of that moment in 1913 when President William Lowe Bryan had threatened to resign from the presidency. Gatch did resign, of course, but he left the university in a fit of anger, and as Judge Hastings said, "declared war on the Medical School and the University."

Dean Gatch did perform one gracious act in going. He praised the medical faculty for its loyalty and services. He then told the Board President that the faculty had made a comprehensive study of the conditions the Medical School would have to meet in the future. "The chief of these proposals," he wrote, "are that the first year's work be moved from Bloomington to Indianapolis, that much needed changes in the administration setup of the schools be made, that work of the School and the Center be controlled by physicians, and that the School be provided with facilities comparable to those possessed by medical schools in neighboring states doing research, for caring for the great number of patients it now turns away and, in general, to enable it to maintain its standing among the medical schools in the country." This sounded more like a blueprint than a letter of resignation. Had Dean Gatch left the matter of his resignation with the formal record, memory of his significant services to the university would be much softer and charitable. Unfortunately he uttered so many truculent oral statements before the trustees, and directed so many unseemly remarks to the President of the University, that he left no options open to the trustees. Judge Hastings said "We had an executive meeting of the Board in the Columbia Club in Indianapolis. Gatch in the meantime had been talking to others of the trustees. He really didn't try to pressure me. So the Board faced up to the thing, I think, as it actually existed. We did have an ultimatum. We had an ultimatum from both of them [President and Dean]. Gatch says either you fire the President if necessary, but I stay as Dean, or I resign as Dean. Herman very obviously said if you keep Gatch as Dean, I resign from the University. The session of the Board lasted quite some time, because the Board itself, was—I know I was—hurt that we were forced into that position."

This was one of the unhappiest moments in university history, only one other had equaled it in bitterness and that was the occasion when the long-time President of the Board of Trustees, James William Fesler, resigned in anger and turned against the institution he had so faithfully served over a long period of years. Judge Hastings observed of these two incidents: "It was entirely too bad to see two older men [Fesler and Gatch] with those long distinguished careers in the life of the University retire in anger and never forgive, which has always made me believe that most any position you can hold too long." With impeccable honesty and forthrightness, Judge Hastings said of the Gatch controversy,

"That one little unhappy episode, I think, should go in the record."

The Wells-Gatch confrontation involved a much broader issue than merely changing the deanship of the School of Medicine. Two cardinal facts were at stake. First, an appreciable number of faculty members had reached mandatory retirement age, and to have allowed Dean Gatch to make himself an exception to established retirement policy would have wrecked the entire system, and maybe have injured the payment of pensions. Second, Gatch had reached the age of sixty-five when administrators were required to accept a change of work status, and he refused to do so. President Wells offered him a distinguished professorship at a salary greater than the president's, and this he refused. Basically, Gatch's problem was that he never divested himself of the old Indiana proprietary view of operating a medical school.

Following the resignation of Dean Gatch, President Wells appointed an administrative committee consisting of doctors J. O. Ritchey, Matthew Winters, Frank Forry, and John D. Van Nuys to conduct the affairs of the Medical Center. Dr. Van Nuys was to act as executive secretary, which fundamentally meant he was acting dean. Earlier on April 25 Hugh McK. Landon retired as chairman of the James Whitcomb Riley Memorial Foundation, leaving a serious administrative gap in this area of the Medical Center. Landon had been a highly effective leader of the foundation, which was subjected to many sensitivities both on the part of donors and the staff of the Medical Center.

The first freshman class admitted after the war's end numbered 128 selectees, most of whom were veterans. As before, these had been chosen from among approximately 1,000 applicants. In August construction was begun on the 200-bed LaRue D. Carter Mental Health Memorial Hospital. The General Assembly had made available $325,000, and apparently Robert Frost Daggett, the architect, had completed plans for a five-floor double "Y" shaped structure that could be added to from time to time.

Documentary evidence indicates Dean W. D. Gatch's stewardship had been productive of rich professional returns, and the people of Indiana were indebted to him for many services. President Wells gave evidence of this when he reported in June 1946 that the School of Medicine had graduated in the period, December 20, 1942, to April 23, 1946, 637 physicians, 214 nurses, 47 medical technicians, and 69 dietitians. At the same time the hospitals had administered some type of medical service to 164,190 patients. "The faculty of the Medical School," said the president, "after due consideration, and with full realization of the undertaking, agreed to take over the medical care of patients in the Indianapolis Veterans Hospital according to plans of General Bradley and General Hanley." Wells said frankly the staff had no other choice. This placed a heavy added load on the School of Medicine, and because the Veterans Administration paid its doctors higher salaries, it no doubt placed a second strain on the institution's budget. Many doctors who had formerly taught in the Medical School without pay now would be drawn away to the high-paying veterans hospital service.

While expansion was occurring throughout the Medical Center, Dr. Thurman B. Rice actively promoted the idea that Indiana should develop one of the best departments of public health in the country. For the past two years his department had served largely as an exploratory venture in the field trying to discover the best lines of procedure. Indianapolis with its numerous schools, surrounding rich farming area, and rising industries promised to give department of public health access to all kinds of rich materials, such as sanitation, water purification, and general immunization. The department created by legislative action in 1945 lacked staff and equipment necessary for major growth. Dr. Rice told an *Indianapolis Star* reporter, January 27, 1947, that within five or six years Indiana University would have a school of public health. "This work," he said, "is going to cost a lot of money, one reason is that we will need a highly diversified faculty because everything a person comes in contact with can affect his health and also the health and welfare of the community. . . ." It was already clear that everything associated with the Medical Center would cost large sums of money. Dr. Rice outlined for the *Star* an elaborate program which he said would greatly influence future health conditions in Indiana.

The Indiana Medical Association had been able to make itself heard by the Board of Trustees. At its meeting, February 1, 1947, the board instructed President Wells to appoint a committee of medical faculty to study the whole question of consolidating the medical teaching program in Indianapolis. The trustees asked for a report on recommendations of action, a list of advantages and disadvantages, building requirements, and differences in prospective annual operating costs. The committee made a partial report to President Wells on July 15, 1947. It advanced three arguments favoring consolidation, saying members of the basic science departments of anatomy, biochemistry, and physiology should participate in clinics for the mutual benefits of all staff members, clinical applications should be taught particularly to residents, and the research facilities and staffs in the basic sciences should be used in the investigation of clinical problems. Finally, staff members should cooperate with clinicians and researchers. The committee speculated on whether the departments might become "service units" to the clinical departments. To find answers to these questions it was suggested that professors Kime and Harmon, with one or more members of the Indianapolis Center, be authorized to make an immediate study of these questions. The trustees must have had in mind another kind of report when they asked the committee to study consolidation of the Bloomington and Indianapolis programs. Answers to this problem still had to be found in the administrative areas of budgets and faculty assignments.

Throughout the more recent history of the School of Medicine committees played an important part in planning and directing the administrative course of medical training. In the case of the public or gubernatorial and legislative committees, the university administration had encouraged their formation as a means of exploring Medical School needs within the context of acceptable rules of operation. This procedure was characteristic of the Wells administration. It was in keeping with the president's philosophy that the noose should never be drawn tight around the necks of friends or foes, but allowance should be made for both constructive suggestions and face-saving solutions of problems.

Before the issue of consolidation could be thrashed out in committee, faculty, and administrative council, the Indiana General Assembly threatened to take a direct political approach, ignore all clinical-research discussion, and consolidate the schools by legislative enactment. When this seemed imminent, President Wells wrote Dr. Dillon Geiger, October 27, 1947, presenting arguments against having such academic matters handled by lawmakers. First, he said, it was essentially an internal academic and curricular matter, which must be decided in the best interests of faculty and students. Second, "If the doctors of the state ask to have the legislature dictate to the Board and the Faculty the curricular and academic policy in this respect, it will be setting a dangerous precedent. Many members of the legislature would be greatly pleased to have such a precedent set for it that would enable the legislature to dabble in such matters as numbers of students that might be taken, the grade averages that are to be required, the other types of requirements, the over-all enrollment of the Medical School, and so forth. We barely prevented the legislature from taking actions of this type from time to time. One of our strongest arguments has been that it is a matter of academic policy and not a fit subject for legislative action." Had the president been a prophet, he could have predicted that future legislators would attempt to dabble in academic affairs. Admission of more students to the Medical School was ever a viable issue.

This latter point was the sorest one with legislators who believed the Medical School staff had placed unreasonable limitations on admissions of freshmen students each spring. In this respect the university, if not vulnerable, was hard pressed to convince laymen why enrollment had to be limited. The *Indianapolis Star*, February 9, 1947, commented "Indiana University School of Medicine, the only one in the state, is in the path of a small avalanche and apparently lacks diverting fences for protection." In July 1947 Dean John D. Van Nuys estimated that 2,000 Indiana graduates of accredited premedical schools would seek to enter the Medical School that spring. Indiana had only 128 clinical spaces to serve them. Once or twice earlier Indiana had admitted 140 students, but Dr. Van Nuys said this would prevent effective training. Generally it was thought the state of Indiana needed 170 new physicians to meet its minimal medical needs, and the Medical School at most supplied only 100 of this number. The remaining seventy doctors had to come largely from the universities of Chicago, Wisconsin, and Michigan. Out of sixty-nine accredited medical schools in the United States in 1947, Indiana University stood sixth from the top in number of students graduated, and most of the top-rated schools had much larger budgets.

Dr. Van Nuys reported that the Indiana Medical School ran two shifts of classes in every subject taught. The teaching faculty's load was doubled because of this necessity. The school at that moment did not need more lecturing, instead, he said, "Intensive practical study under the most expert guidance must be provided." The General Assembly was being asked to provide $2,800,000 to construct a new classroom building, a central dining and service building, and an addition to the power plant. He also explained the methods of selecting students in a report for the *Star*. To the accusation of professional favoritism, Dr. Van Nuys explained that many doctors' sons were annually rejected by the school, and the backgrounds of students admitted were proofs of impartiality.

Somewhat helpful in relieving one part of the financial need was the bequest of Hugh McK. Landon's estate. Landon, the long-time and dedicated chairman of the James Whitcomb Riley Memorial Foundation, left the bulk of a $1,000,000 estate in various trusts to the Medical Center. He, however, would have been horrified to read J. W. Carr's confidential letter to President Wells, September 2, 1947, in which he said, "The other day two members of the Board of Governors were through the Riley Hospital. They were severely critical of the up-keep of the property. I, myself, have never seen it in worse condition. It certainly is not the show place it should be. . . ." Carr told the President that beds, walls, and other parts of the property were in "bad shape. Surely the University has money to care for this property." Joseph A. Franklin noted on the back of this letter, September 11, "Five painters started work on the wards of Riley Hospital today. It is intended that they will continue until they are finished with that building."

J. B. Martin, Medical Center administrator, gave the more cheering report that the hospitals had improved working conditions for nurses. These, he thought, now exceeded the recommendations of the Indiana Nurses and Hospital associations. Student nurses would be on duty forty-four hours a week, and night duty would be cut to seven hours. A full-time student counselor had been employed; nurses were to be given seven holidays a year, and were permitted to accumulate sixty days' sick leave at the rate of one day a month. Martin thought as a result applications for admission to nurses training had increased.

The Indiana Medical School in 1947 had reached a divisional point in its history. It had operated the past year without a dean, it was confronted by almost oppressive demands to expand all of its programs, to develop new ones, and to construct new buildings to house them. It stood challenged to apply a tremendous volume of new medical knowledge that came out of the four war years. Most important of all there were heavy demands for new research on the part of the staff. Dean Willis D. Gatch had brought the school through a trying era in which he had constantly struggled with maintaining a staff, the hospitals, and a greatly accelerated training period for students. Whatever may have been the personal clashes within the institution, the Indiana University School of Medicine had made a maximum response to public needs with the support given it. Notwithstanding, this was the history of a passing era in the history of the university. The promised land of full achievement lay on ahead and under the guidance of a more flexible and no less dedicated leadership.

[XV]

Horizons Afar

THERE COULD HAVE BEEN no more propitious time for a change in the administration of the Indiana University School of Medicine than 1947. Both the university and the school teetered on the brink of making major decisions to become significant institutions. Already visible in clear outline were the heavy human demands that would be made on public institutions in this new age, and especially upon the Medical School, which had to keep abreast of the revolution that was occurring in the teaching and practice of medicine. In the pinch for medical services during the war more and more Hoosiers came to look upon the Medical School and its associated hospitals as central public service centers.

During four years of war the staff of the Medical School was badly depleted by the loss of personnel to direct military services, and to the staffing of General Hospital 32. In 1947 returning doctor-veterans and freshman veterans sought admission to the school, thus placing an excessive strain upon its administration, staff, and facilities. Perhaps it was this inability to see in clear perspective what these demands would be, and to plan for the future that revealed Dean Gatch's greatest administrative weakness. Two immediate problems after 1945 had to be solved. A new dean had to be appointed to fill the vacancy left by Dean Gatch's somewhat hasty resignation, and immediate attention had to be given to restructuring the entire Medical School operation. Both its staff and physical plant had to be enlarged and modernized. To defer either of these would be to invite injurious reduction in the standing of the institution at a time when it sought to improve its rating.

Beyond the immediate problems of the deanship and reorganization of the plant was the challenge of instituting long-range research procedures, which not only would keep the Indiana School of Medicine abreast of modern medical science, but which would assure it a leadership position in the broadening search for scientific knowledge. This was an era in which the rest of Indiana University was beginning to make major contributions in many fields of research, and the School of Medicine could not afford to lag behind. Equally as important was that the practice of medicine generally in Indiana made increased demands for specialized services and leadership of the Medical Center in Indianapolis.

After a year of searching, the Board of Trustees, June 15, 1947, approved the appointment of Dr. John Ditmars Van Nuys to that position. This culminated a nationwide search for a new administrator in which the credentials of more than 200 prospective candidates were reviewed. Out of this large number of possible candidates eighty-five men were interviewed personally for the position of dean. National medical leaders, practicing in and out of Indiana, were asked to give their views and assistance in finding the right man. After all of this effort was made, Dean John D. Van Nuys, executive secretary of the Administrative Committee of the School of Medicine, was believed to be the best qualified man available.

At the time of his appointment to the deanship, Dr. Van Nuys was thirty-nine years of age, and was a third-generation physician in his family. His grandfather had practiced medicine in Waveland, Indiana, and then in Kansas. His father, Dr. W. C. Van Nuys, had been superintendent of Indiana Village for Epileptics in New Castle for the past forty-one years. His great-grandfather was a professor of chemistry in Indiana University. The new dean was a graduate of New Castle High School, Wabash College, and the Indiana School of Medicine ('39). He served his residency in internal medicine in the Medical Center, and during World War II he was director of admissions for the three Medical Center hospitals, and of the general hospitals. No previous dean was, before his appointment, more thoroughly familiar with the operation of the School of Medicine and all of its subsidiary services.

During Dr. Van Nuys' year as administrative secretary he in fact acted as surrogate dean, a seasoning experience that gave him the background necessary to tackle the larger problems of future expansion. Aside from the demands already mentioned there were those relating the School of Medicine to the Indiana State Board of Health, the Indiana Mental Health Council, the Veterans Bureau, and the impending consolidation of the Bloomington and Indianapolis divisions of the school. The Bloomington *World-Telephone*, September 27, 1947, carried the story that the Veterans Administration planned to locate its $10,000,000 hospital with a 500-bed capacity on grounds adjoining the Medical Center. This decision was said to be in line with national policy of locating veterans' medical facilities adjacent to medical schools. This gave them immediate access to both professional and research resources. The *Daily Student* quoted university officials as saying that locating the veterans hospital in Indianapolis was one of the major developments in the School of Medicine's history. Like most additions of this sort to the university program, there were diverse views that had to be reconciled. President Wells warned the trustees, "There has been considerable opposition in certain quarters to the location of this building adjacent to the Medical School, and the victory has been won, in my judgment, wholly because of the unwavering support of the *Indianapolis News*, which support of course emanated from Mr. McCarty, aided and abetted by Mr. Carr, and the determination of General Hawley. . . . We owe these three worthies a real debt of gratitude for their respective parts in this project."

Not all Hoosiers shared the university's enthusiasm for what seemed to be a tremendous asset in the federal medical facility. The 11th District of the American Legion protested the decision to build the new hospital near the School of Medicine. The legionnaires favored instead the enlargement of the existing Cold Springs Road hospital. John Samulowitz, state chairman of the legion's hospital committee, branded the proposed location of the hospital "a steal of the taxpayers' money." The American Legion also criticized what it called the inefficient handling of veteran patients by Dean Van Nuys' committee and a group of civilian doctors from the Medical Center.

This complaint fortunately did not represent the views of the majority of veterans, and nothing came of it. President Harry Truman informed the Indiana congressional delegation, September 8, 1947, that approval had positively been given to construct the government's hospital in Indianapolis as originally planned. General Omar Bradley had already instructed J. J. Rockefeller, head of the Veterans Administration Construction Section, to begin making plans for the Indiana installation. On the same date Senator Homer Capehart informed President Wells of the decision. President Wells told the Board of Trustees, "If the administration of our medical center is sufficiently imaginative the veterans' program can be made a powerful factor in promoting and developing scientific medicine and dentistry in Indiana."

Major General Paul R. Hawley, chief surgeon of the Veterans Administration, was direct in his statement. When he visited Indianapolis, October 6, 1947, he crossed swords with local legionnaire critics. He said he was unconvinced that the complainers represented the American Legion's majority views. He branded their proposal to enlarge the Cold Springs Road hospital a "piece meal" gesture. He said "The best medicine in the country—which is the best medicine in the world—is being practiced at the teaching hospitals," and that 60 of 124 veterans hospitals were associated directly with university medical centers. He stoutly defended the acceptance of the neighboring site to the Indiana Medical Center then being proffered by Indianapolis businessmen. General Hawley assured Hoosiers the 500-bed hospital would cost a minimum of $8,000,000, and he thought the proposed location would be worth at least $100,000 annually to the veterans facility.

The site offered by the business community for the new federal hospital was on 19.5 acres owned by the Indianapolis Park Board between the Fall Creek and White River parkways. In his public announcement President Truman emphasized the importance of readily available utilities and access to public transportation. Indianapolis merchants paid the Park Board $5,000 for the land in a controlled public auction, and in turn gave the tract to the Veterans Administration.

Expansion of the School of Medicine itself was almost equal

to that of the proposed veterans hospital. As a by-product of nuclear research and the explosion of the atomic bomb—a development greatly facilitated by Indiana University scientists—the School of Medicine in 1947 began experimental use of isotopes for the radioactivation of drugs to be used in the tracing and treating of cancer. Dr. John A. Campbell, chief radiologist of the Medical Center, had ordered a special type of Geiger counter to be used in tracing the passage of radioactive chemicals through the blood stream, and the detection of concentrations in diseased areas. This new field of research was one of several which required an expensive addition to the medical buildings.

Internally, the departmental organization of the Medical School underwent extensive revision and expansion. A new department of public health with Dr. Thurman B. Rice at its head was created. Dr. Randall L. Thompson, formerly a member of the Medical School of Virginia, was made head of the new Department of Microbiology. In this expansion Dean Van Nuys said Indiana University was one of the few American medical schools to offer an integrated course in microbiology.

Pressure for training of more doctors to practice in Indiana never let up. The admissions committee was constantly aware that more young Hoosiers aspired to becoming medical doctors than the School of Medicine could ever train under the most favorable of conditions. Annually more than a thousand applications were received, and all of them had to be considered. Screening these created an atmosphere of overstimulated emotions, and, no doubt, of eternal questioning about the making of correct decisions. In 1947 this onerous duty was made much more difficult by the flood of applications from well-qualified veterans and women. In August the school announced it had admitted 141 new candidates, 90 percent of whom were veterans taking advantage of the G.I. Bill of Rights, and all but six were native Hoosiers. This number represented the maximum that the School of Medicine faculty felt could be properly instructed with staff, buildings, and equipment available in the Medical Center.

No previous single year was more transitional than 1947 for the School of Medicine. Not only had a new dean been appointed, but needs for modernization and expansion came into clear focus. Both physical plant and staff had to be improved. Involved in this moment was the pressing matter of keeping the general instructional program abreast of modern scientific and medical teaching advances. Needs for improvements in the School of Medicine were highly reflective of the social and economic revolution then occurring in Indiana itself. In no decade of the state's history had so many fundamental changes occurred as in that since 1939. Every social demand made upon all public institutions had multiplied fourfold. The Medical Center was a primary area where increased pressures were first manifested. To begin to meet these challenges, construction was begun in August 1947 of a fifth floor over the east and west wings of the Robert W. Long Memorial Hospital. Although this improvement was being made at the modest cost of $150,000, financed jointly by public and Long bequest funds, it promised a vital addition of space to the hospital. The new floor provided for a twenty-four-bed isolation ward that would replace antiquated quarters in the west wing basement.

During the same semester the trustees approved a three-point enlargement of the School of Medicine staff by appointing on a geographical basis competent clinicians to engage in the offering of postgraduate programs in special work for local physicians. They also were asked to render special services to patients, at salaries of no more than $18,000, but were permitted to bill private patients to supplement their income. President Wells informed Dean Van Nuys that he was to devise detailed procedures for managing the new clinical programs.

There was little or no self-satisfaction in the university in 1947 with the comparative status of the Indiana School of Medicine. Within the institution continuing efforts were being exerted to effect changes, and forceful pressures were being exerted from without for improvements. The Indiana Medical Association in its 98th convention in October 1947 was extremely critical of public support of the School of Medicine. Dr. Floyd T. Rombarger of Lafayette, president of the Medical Association, was outspoken about "glaring weaknesses in Indiana's medical care picture." The *Indianapolis News*, October 29, 1947, gave Dr. Rombarger's speech full coverage. It said he accused legislators of "miserly niggardliness" in providing for the training of an adequate number of physicians, saying it would be necessary to spend millions of dollars to modernize the University Medical Center. Funds had to be forthcoming for construction of new buildings, to improve existing facilities, to employ many more full-time department heads, and to support a larger research program.

Touching Hoosier pride where it was tenderest, Dr. Rombarger said that Indiana was "justly proud of its roads and hogs and cattle while regarding with niggardliness the production and training of more physicians to care for its citizenry." He was positive the time had come to improve the School of Medicine, emphasizing that it must not be superseded by other class-A institutions. The State of Indiana, said the doctors, had a surplus fund of $61,000,000, $24,000,000 of which was deposited in locally and politically favored banks drawing no interest. If properly invested, said Dr. Rombarger, these funds would produce sufficient income to amortize a $15,000,000 loan for modernizing the Medical Center.

A basic concern of legislators, citizens, and doctors alike had long been the severely limited number of students admitted annually to the study of medicine. In 1947, 141 new students were selected for the incoming freshman class. In this year the number of first-rate student prospects might have run in excess of 250 out of a thousand or more applicants. Once again the state Medical Association urged the concentration of the four-year training program in Indianapolis, saying that Indiana was one of four schools in the country that did not offer their full medical programs in one center. Dean Van Nuys agreed with the doctors that it was now urgent that the entire training program be in Indianapolis. There was no indication that the university administration objected to this suggestion, perhaps it encouraged the move. However, if consolidation was to be accomplished it would take fully two years to construct the necessary new buildings to accommodate the additional students who would be transferred to the Indianapolis campus. Dean Van Nuys made public the fact that a special faculty study committee had almost finished compiling all necessary data concerning the problems of consolidation, and would soon make recommendations to the Board of Trustees.

This tender issue of combining the medical instructional program was akin to that of consolidating the administration of graduate work on the Bloomington campus. In order to end this half-century of discussion the university's postwar proposals for the Medical Center included a new instructional building, which was said to be "high on the list" of university construction. The doctors, afflicted somewhat with limited vision, recommended that the Medical Association "get tough" with members of the General Assembly who appeared reluctant to support an appropriation of the necessary funds for the university's School of Medicine; a move not in keeping with the institution's established legislative policies.

The Van Nuys administration of the Medical Center was active in expanding both instructional and medical programs. In November 1947 the public was told of the creation of two new divisions. A Department of Anesthesiology was to be organized in conjunction with the Division of Surgery. Dr. Kenneth Stolting, an Indiana graduate, was appointed head. This department, said the publicity statement, was one of only a few in the country that recognized the importance of the teaching of anesthesiology. Creation of this department was a part of the overall scheme for reorganizing the entire School of Medicine departmental structure. A year later a two-year residency was instituted to give further training to graduate physicians in the field of anesthetics.

A second step toward modernization was organization of a properly equipped nursery in the Carter Hospital for the care of premature babies. This nursery was located apart from the one caring for normal babies, and was equipped with glass-encased cribs, special temperature and humidity controls, and other environmental conditioning; each crib had oxygen inlets with safety pressure valves. For the first time Medical Center hospitals had a maternity ward that was provided with the sophisticated controls so necessary in dealing with premature births. This facility was an important advance in the teaching of obstetrics and pediatrics. Its creation, however, was to cause Indiana University some slight anxiety. Charles Darthard sued the Board of Trustees for damages of $125,000, claiming that both of his premature daughter's legs were broken as a result of careless handling while she was being kept in an incubator.

In these postwar years the James Whitcomb Riley Memorial Association received increased support. It in turn appropriated funds for added investigation of infectious diseases of childhood. This new research program was placed under the direction of Dr. Dwain N. Walcher of the Department of Pediatrics and Dr. John J. Mahoney of the Department of Experimental Medicine. This research sought to discover better therapeutic methods in the treatment of meningitis, scarlet fever, diphtheria, whooping cough, and tuberculosis. Plans were made also for investigation of the virus diseases and other ailments peculiar to childhood. Ultimately it was hoped these studies would reveal the effect which these diseases had upon the long-run physical development of children. There was, for instance, a special interest in the fevers and their effects on the endocrinal system. A colorful source of financial enrichment of the Riley Association was the sale of the historic Canal House and 600 acres of land of the estate of Finley Gray and his wife.

Before the seminal year of 1947 was ended there had been established in the School of Medicine a division or "foundation" for training of doctors, and for research in the field of dermato-syphilology in connection with the Marion County General Hospital. This new division was named in honor of Dr. Alembert Winthrop Brayton, the first professor of dermato-syphilology in the school. Funds for this foundation were raised by Dr. Brayton's former students. At the same time the Indiana Elks Association donated $21,000 to be used in cancer research.

The various grants to the Medical Center made mandatory the addition of a fairly large number of specialists to the staff. In January 1948 Dean Van Nuys told reporters he was in search of eighteen professors to fill new specialized positions in the faculty. Aside from grants by the Riley Association, the Elks Association, and the dermatologists, Junior League members of Indiana had diligently solicited research funds for the Medical Center hospitals. These special gifts were timely because they permitted staff expansions when the School of Medicine was trying to build up future momentum.

Because of the fermentation and excitement being generated in the School of Medicine, the Bloomington *World-Telephone*, February 27, 1948, praised Dean John D. Van Nuys for stressing the importance of modern medical education, and for expanding the sum total of the world's scientific knowledge in research laboratories. During the past year fifteen important research projects were underway in Indianapolis.

Not only were numerous research projects started, but efforts were made to broaden materially the traditional base of the School of Medicine's teaching program. Early in November 1947 the Board of Trustees approved the organization of an instructional center in Evansville in cooperation with the Vanderburgh County Medical Society. This center was designed to enable practicing physicians from southern Illinois, Indiana, and Kentucky to come for review of the latest developments and techniques in medicine.

By 1948 there had accumulated in Indianapolis an enormous volume of medical records dating back to the founding of the Long Memorial Hospital in 1914. Apparently these files had never been used to any extent for establishing a pattern of medical history in the state. In January 1948 these records, containing a quarter of a million individual medical histories, and weighing more than ten tons, were prepared for microfilming. It required more than 4,000,000 frames of film exposure to transfer them to a more flexible form of filing and usability. This body of material alone offered research materials that would require the attention of several specialists, and would in the end yield vital information about the continuity of the practice of medicine and its basic human involvements.

Dean Van Nuys announced June 24, 1948, the appointment of Dr. Harris B. Shumacher, associate professor of surgery at Yale University, to be professor of surgery at Indiana University. This was a significant appointment not only because of the importance of the subject in the medical curriculum, but because the new appointee became successor to Dean W. D. Gatch, who had made the position of professor of surgery a major one in the school. On the same date Dean Van Nuys announced that X-ray facilities were being doubled in the new construction. Approximately 5,600 square feet of floor space was being reserved for this sensitive work in the greatly expanded Department of Diagnostics.

One of the first moves of the medical program from Bloomington to Indianapolis was the transfer of Dean Edward Kime to the Medical Center faculty. In Bloomington the basic medical program underwent a rearrangement that meant substitution of clinical medicine for anatomy. At the Medical Center postgraduate study in anatomy and the other basic medical sciences were placed under the direction of Dr. Kime. This initial move brought an end to discussion of a controversial issue that had dogged the School of Medicine since its long-drawn-out controversy with Purdue University, 1903–10.

Important expansion was made in services of the James Whitcomb Riley Memorial Hospital. Late in November 1948 the Indiana courts approved settlement of several estate matters that yielded the association an additional $72,000. Already a $400,000 wing was planned for construction. The new three-story addition of approximately 5,600 square feet of space on each floor would house the extensive research facilities in children's diseases as well as office and laboratory facilities. Almost before the construction company had broken ground, the Riley Memorial Association received another $300,000 from the estate of Dr. Samuel Kennedy of Shelbyville. Under the Kennedy will these funds, so far as was possible, were to be expended for the benefit of the children of Shelby County.

There still remained, in February 1949, the unresolved question of the relationship of the Riley Hospital with the newly authorized Northern Indiana Childrens Hospital, or with the state for that matter. The 1947 General Assembly appropriated $466,000 a year for the next biennium to the newly created hospital, but in doing so it left unanswered many questions as to its organization and operation. But the most perplexing one was its relationships with the other public hospitals. James W. Carr, executive secretary of the Riley Memorial Association, claimed in a letter to President Herman B Wells that the legislature had discriminated against the Riley Hospital. He wrote Wells in the latter's capacity as vice president of the Riley Association. The Riley Hospital, he said, operated under a special Indiana statute that required it to charge minimum costs to county welfare departments for local children treated. Carr emphasized the fact that the state would pay practically all the cost of the new hospital, and leave the Riley Hospital dependent upon funds from the real property tax system. This he said meant the application of double taxation in nearly every county in the state, yet the new hospital served only one section of Indiana. Children in the Northern Indiana Hospital would have to pay only $5.00 a day for treatment, while those in the Riley Hospital could be charged up to $50.00 a day. Carr expressed the thought that this could be a serious threat to the latter institution.

The Indiana Attorney General said the discrimination could be resolved in one of two ways: a comparable million dollar appropriation could be made to the Riley Hospital, or the Northern Indiana Childrens Hospital could be placed on a comparable plan of fiscal operation with the Riley Hospital. To adopt the former plan would require Governor Henry F. Schricker to make an additional $1,000,000 available from his emergency fund. The Riley directors would agree to either plan, but they would protest making no adjustment at all.

In an extended meeting, June 4 to 11, 1949, the University

Board of Trustees approved sixteen revised rules for admission of children to the Riley Hospital. Among the new provisions were an outline of fees, a statement of responsibilities of both state and county welfare departments in certifying indigent children for admission, and the degree of financial responsibility to be assumed by parents and guardians. These rules applied to all children except those who were crippled; for the latter case the age limit was extended from sixteen to twenty years. Since its dedication in 1949, the Riley Memorial Hospital had administered to 375,000 children, 75,000 of whom were indigent.

Greatly aroused public concern over the ravages of crippling poliomyelitis in the 1940s gave special impetus to the Riley Hospital's expanded research program and enlarged physical facilities. The Riley directors announced a minimum grant of $1,200 research funds annually for an indefinite period by the trustees of the Herman H. and Mary H. Young Foundation. In the same month the Congress of Industrial Organizations (C.I.O.) pledged $400,000 for research support. This latter fund was to be used in combating rheumatic fever, poliomyelitis, and cancer. As a result of this new support, Donald J. Cassidy, medical director of the University Center, announced the organization of a special ward devoted to the treatment and care of children afflicted with infantile paralysis. This ward was especially wired and otherwise equipped to operate respirators enough to care for twenty-eight patients at a time.

University officials joined the directors of the James Whitcomb Riley Association on October 7, 1949, to lay the cornerstone for the new research wing of the hospital, a beginning that offered much brighter hopes for the welfare of Indiana children. Immediately the Riley Association began a campaign to raise $1,000,000 to supplement the state appropriation of $385,000. Herman B Wells was chairman of the Riley centennial celebration, and on March 10, 1950, he informed Governor Henry F. Schricker that more than a million Hoosiers had participated in programs celebrating the famous Indiana poet's hundredth anniversary. The drive for funds was encouraged greatly when the Union Trust Company of Indianapolis announced a gift of $50,000 from the estate of William G. Axt. At the same time the Damon Runyan Memorial Funds contributed $20,000 for cancer research on Riley Hospital patients.

In another area of the Medical Center the staff of the Robert

W. Long Memorial Hospital made a step into the future when it installed television cameras in the surgical unit. The installation of this modern viewing device enabled professor-surgeons to demonstrate operative procedures and techniques on the basis of electronic repetition and recall. Earlier the Medical Center had experimented with the use of open telephone lines for transmitting lectures well beyond the campus. This service was a supplement to the clinical plan then in operation. Professors in the Medical Center were enabled to lecture to off-campus nurses and doctors describing for them the newest techniques and treatments of injuries and diseases.

The new dean's first two years had indeed been innovative in the changes which were made. It was with justification that he wrote in his 1948–49 report that, "Some years hence the year just past may be recorded as the critical period in the development of the School of Medicine. It was the year in which the foundations were laid to bring the School to full university stature. It was also the period in which our activities were being re-evaluated by almost everyone having an interest in medical education and service, and, finally, it was the time during which the School's responsibilities in the social and economic structure of the state were being redefined."

Dean Van Nuys said the School of Medicine had received the fullest administrative support from the university. Significantly, he commented, "A meeting of minds of so large a faculty is ordinarily extremely difficult, but I am pleased to report that in introducing the plan for employment of geographical full-time clinicians, in making substantial additions to the faculty of the basic division, in enlarging post-graduate medical education, and in launching a more extensive research effort we had the full support of the faculty, endorsement by the alumni of the School, and approval of the Indiana Medical Association." The Dean commented this support, so necessary to the successful operation of the Indiana University School of Medicine, had come about because individuals were willing to subordinate personal interests to the welfare of the university. This was indeed a new note in Medical School history, one might say it seemed the day of jubilee had arrived. Clearly the School of Medicine was now operating on three broad fronts of teaching, research, and general therapy with both harmony and success.

Gradually as the staff multiplied and physical facilities were enlarged, the number of beginning students was increased slightly. In September 1950, 150 students from the traditional thousand applicants were admitted. There remained, however, public pressure to increase the number. Almost perennially legislators pretended at least to agonize over this subject. No doubt they were greatly agitated by parents, students themselves, and, perhaps, by local doctors. It was difficult for citizens and legislators alike to understand why it required so much money to train so few doctors in comparison with the expenditures on other university students.

On January 26, 1951, the Indiana General Assembly adopted a resolution that said, "The general public has manifested its interest and desire that an increased number of students be educated in modern scientific medicine to serve the people of the state in that field." Legislators asked that once again a special committee of five representatives be appointed to explore the possibilities of admitting more students to the School of Medicine. This resolution was offered jointly by Otis A. Kopp of Anderson and William M. Cockburn of Evansville.

In conformity with the resolution Governor Schricker appointed Dr. Merrill S. Davis, a University Trustee, as chairman with Virgil M. Simmons, Dr. O. P. Kretzmann, Carl F. Everleigh, and Leo J. Strunk as committee members. They were instructed to investigate the possibility of enlarging the freshman enrollment of the School of Medicine, and to report their findings within two years. As further provocation in this area, 322 Hoosiers sought admission to the Medical School and only 144 were accepted.

While legislators and committeemen fretted over limited admissions, the School of Medicine revived a technique used late in World War II; lectures were again offered in St. Elizabeth's Hospital in Lafayette by open telephone line. The first lecture was in the field of pediatrics, and Dean Van Nuys told reporters if the experiment succeeded then the faculty would be asked to extend their discussions into other fields, and to other assemblies of doctors. No doubt the renewal of this experiment was successful, because a year later county medical associations all over Indiana were listening to joint telephonic discussions sponsored by the State Medical Association and the Indiana Cancer Society.

In a final analysis the legislative resolution had no discernible impact on the school's admission policy. In 1952 only 150 freshmen were admitted. The report of the Indiana Medical School Expansion Study Committee revealed the fact that Indiana with a total of 542 undergraduate medical students stood fifth in the nation. Since 1948 and an enrollment of 438 students, it had advanced from twelfth place on the national scale. The fourth ranking school had only two more students than Indiana, and the four institutions were located in states with much larger populations than Indiana's. The committee also discovered that thirty-five medical schools in the nation had an enrollment of fewer than 300 students.

The Expansion Study Committee's report must have been a geniune disappointment to many legislators. It said the physical plant of the Medical Center was inadequate to accommodate efficiently the present enrollment, and that this was especially true in the teaching of the basic sciences at the sophomore level. Likewise space shortage for juniors and seniors would make a liberalization of enrollment policies decidedly unwise. Generally in the school there was a shortage of laboratory and office space. "All these deficiencies of space," reported the committee, "must be corrected before it will be possible to consider expansion." Corrective measures were suggested. A new medical science building would have to be constructed even to meet present needs, new appointments would have to be made to the faculty, and the first-year class would have to be moved from Bloomington as soon as space could be provided for classrooms and laboratories.

In order to insure an adequate inflow of new adult patients it would be necessary to project a 100-bed addition to the Robert W. Long Hospital. Then, too, the older sections of the hospital had to be put in suitable condition to meet current requirements. The report placed limitation of enrollment in the School of Medicine squarely upon the shoulders of the public itself. Even an increased enrollment did not necessarily insure Indiana an adequate supply of doctors. Under prevailing conditions the University graduated 134 physicians at commencement in June 1953, and these went to forty-seven hospitals in twenty-one states to serve their internships, a fact which may or may not have meant that most of them were lost to the state.

Modernization occurred in many departments in the School of Medicine after 1950. For instance, a new retina camera was installed in 1951 for photographing the interior of the eye, and this instrument facilitated research by both the School of Medicine and the Department of Ophthalmology in Bloomington. New laboratories and other clinical and research facilities were expanded in Indianapolis for research in cancer. The new building in which this project was housed was financed jointly by the United States Public Health Service and the Indiana General Assembly. The March of Dimes Crusade, in January 1953, contributed $12,975 to enable School of Medicine scientists to appraise the worth of certain drugs for the prevention and control of poliomyelitis.

Total funds available for medical research for the year, including those provided the Riley Hospital, exceeded $300,000 by May 1953. Virtually all of this money came from private sources. Dr. John J. Mahoney, assistant dean, indicated this sum represented a fifteenfold increase over the $200,000 outlay for research in 1947. In the area of public services, the load of the medical staff was considerably increased. The various off-campus clinics, the telephone lectures, counseling the Veterans Hospital administrators, and providing counseling and consultative services to the Indiana Public Health Hospital were time consuming. During the last nine months of the academic year, 1952–53, the university hospitals admitted 11,305 patients, an increase of 1,658 over the past year. These patients received 135,534 days of care, an increase of 20,000 days. The length of stay per patient was decreasing, a fact which somewhat offset inflating costs. The out-patient services of the four hospitals were furnished to 48,071 patient visitations, an increase within the year of 5,246. The largest number of the latter group were visitations of seasonal polio victims. These services were an inseparable part of the School of Medicine program, which could be clearly outlined to citizens and legislators in terms of elementary statistics, but it was difficult indeed to relate them to the school's admission and teaching policies.

In September 1953 the School of Medicine celebrated its fiftieth anniversary. It would be difficult indeed to imagine an institution whose history was colored by a greater variety of political, professional, and personal incidents. Its very foundation was troubled by the extended Indiana-Purdue-Medical College of Indiana contest. There was throughout the half-century the classical American struggle to secure adequate public financial support, then the serious disruptions of two world wars, and the unhappy administrative conflict that threatened to mar postwar readjustment prior to 1946.

In a positive vein, the half-century, 1903–53, was a golden age of medical science. These decades saw almost more solid scientific advances in the treatment of man's ills than ever before in the history of civilization. New techniques enabled physicians everywhere to exercise advanced life-saving skills. Introduction of new drugs not only added years of life to present generations, they helped to wipe out the deadly menace of several diseases. In this age research became a central fact in improving the healing art, not only in the field of actual accomplishments, but also in the area of immediate promise. Preventive medicine became equally as important as therapeutic medicine. One of the brightest chapters in the history of both American and Indiana medicine was the rising volume of aid from private contributions and endowments. In Indiana private assistance to the three Medical Center hospitals was within itself a noble achievement.

While Dean Van Nuys' report on the half-century of the School of Medicine was being distributed, the institution received $20,000 from the Indiana Heart Fund Association to experiment with the substitution of plastic tubing for natural blood vessels, and an attempt to study blood pressure and oxygen content of the heart chambers, cardiac catheterization, and the use of the artificial kidney in treatment of kidney and heart diseases. By December 1954 this latter machine was in operation in Long Hospital.

To celebrate the golden anniversary of the School of Medicine the Indiana General Assembly appropriated $5,035,345 for the construction of a new medical science building, a medical student union, and the acquisition of an adjacent fifteen-acre tract of land on which to place the new structures. In addition it was understood that equipment for the buildings would cost an additional quarter of a million dollars. This was a generous amount when compared with past appropriations, but it fell short of the $9,000,000 which the university administration requested, and far short of the $15,000,000 demanded by Dr. Floyd T. Rombarger and the Indiana Medical Association in October 1947. Construction of the student union and food service building progressed rapidly, and President Wells informed the Board of Trustees through his *Annual Report*, September 30, 1953, that it was ready to be dedicated.

During a quarter of a century of its existence, the Riley Association had contributed to the School of Medicine a half-million dollars in research aid. Much of the money that came to this hospital was in the nature of "seed grants." The James McKeen Catlett Fund of New York City contributed $3,250 to supplement research into individual psychological responses to lesions and brain damages caused by diseases and injuries. Medical education itself was aided by an annual grant of $15,000 plus $25.00 for each student enrolled in the School of Medicine, 1951–54, from the National Fund for Medical Education. In all, Indiana had received $165,495.34 from this source.

Dr. Max W. Briggs, holding both a Doctor of Medicine and a Doctor of Philosophy degree, was added to the medical staff upon the opening of the Cancer Research Building in 1954. By this latter year the school's research program, begun in 1947, was showing promising results in at least a half-dozen fields. A major one was the development of the $940,000 Indiana Mental Health Center just east of the Carter Memorial Hospital. This new unit promised to give the School of Medicine very real strength in the field of psychiatry. Dr. Margaret E. Morgan said, May 25, 1955, "It will be operating within a year and will be one of the finest in the world."

Closely related to the work of the developing Mental Health Center was that of the diagnostic clinic for treating epileptic and other neurological disorders. Estimates were that 20,000 Hoosiers needed serious medical attention in these areas. The new clinic was staffed by a team composed of a neurological specialist, a social worker, and a psychologist. It was designed not only to aid patients but to offer advice and services to Indiana physicians, especially those in general practice.

In the area of mental health, the delay in the appointment of a chairman of the Department of Psychiatry was a key factor in the resignations of six doctors in the summer of 1955. Dr. Margaret E. Morgan told reporters, December 2, 1955, that "Indiana mental institutions lost 51 doctors between July 1, 1953 and July 1, 1955, but the total number [employed] rose from 56 to 90 in the same period." She said the doctors who had resigned did so because they could obtain higher salaries in other states, notably Ohio. In the latter state assistant superintendents were paid $17,500 as compared with $10,500 to $13,500 in Indiana.

With the addition of several new buildings, the enlargement of the hospitals, provision of more laboratories, and employment of more staff members, the Medical School in 1955 was to increase its admissions to 156 freshmen. This increase, however, still kept it fixed in fifth rank of national admissions, and the next year the school dropped back to 150 admissions.

After fifty years of agitation over the division of the School of Medicine between Bloomington and Indianapolis, President Wells announced, in June 1957, that the coming year would be the last one for medical students on the Bloomington campus. Late in the spring of 1958 the basic medical science building in Indianapolis would be ready for occupancy. Ironically, the Bloomington building was named for Dean Burton Dorr Myers in September 1958, the year of the final move away from the campus.

In the same *Annual Report* the University President said that deans Cleland and Kime and Professor William R. Breneman had completed a study of the School of Medicine curriculum. They found that the level of instruction seemed to be set below the capabilities of the brightest students. As a result these students were not made to realize their full promise. This report resulted in the organization of a special program by which senior students in the upper third of their class were permitted to elect one to three months of special study instead of participating in the routine clerkship programs in the departments of Medicine and Surgery.

The medical challenges of the mid-twentieth century were greater than any single medical school could ever hope to meet. Research programs were constantly being expanded or started as the American public became more alert to the threats of cancer and other diseases, and the possibility of finding a cure for them. University specialists emphasized their greatly accelerated search for knowledge of these diseases. In 1958 the Indiana appropriation for cancer research was supplemented by two private contributions which totaled $34,000. At the same time a clinic was organized for the study of limited human vision. It was said that hundreds of Hoosiers suffered from loss of vision and threatening eye damage. The new vision clinic was placed under the direction of Dr. Fred M. Wilson, head of the Department of Ophthalmology. This study was supported partly by the Vocational Rehabilitation Office of the United States Department of Education.

In keeping with its drive for modernization, the School of

Medicine announced early in January 1958 that it was instituting another new departure in medical education. A carefully selected group of entering students would be introduced to a broad concept of the liberal arts through the study of human biology. The hope was that such an integrated course would attract more medical students to the fields of teaching and research. Under the new program selected students would be able to earn Bachelor and Master's degrees, and would have completed all but two years of clinical work toward the Doctor of Medicine degree. This curriculum was designed partly to fill the void left by the transfer of the first year of training from the Bloomington campus. Dr. Douglas A. McFayden told an *Indiana Daily Student* reporter, November 5, 1959, that the School of Medicine was the only institution offering such an alternative course. Under its requirements if a student chose he could pursue work leading to a Doctor of Philosophy degree in science and could teach or enter the practice of medicine with a more liberal background. The Johns Hopkins and Stanford universities also experimented with somewhat similar programs, but they did not go quite so far in professionalizing them.

President Herman B Wells reported in 1959 that the first students in the liberal arts-medicine-research curriculum had been enrolled the previous September, and the new department was housed in Myers Hall. Three years later the *Daily Student* commented that the day had passed when a doctor could treat diseases with a simplified knowledge of anatomy, traditional therapeutics, and a fistful of standard cures. Quoting professors of the new department, the campus paper said, "now in its third year of operation, Indiana University's special program in medical education is designed to develop the physician with a broadened background that will give the ability to cope with newer problems of medicine, particularly in the research field. Behind the practicing physician stands a dedicated group of researchers who seek answers that the doctors must have to cope with disease. . . ."

In addition to the liberal arts-medicine-research curriculum, the School of Medicine in late fall 1959 introduced an intensive two-year course intended to prepare young physicians especially for the general practice of medicine. They were to be trained to assume the traditional role of "family doctor" in keeping with suggestions of the American Medical Association and the American Academy of General Practice. This, said Dr. Donald Close, director of Postgraduate Medical Education, was to be a national pilot study in a new phase of medical training for public service.

Expansion was the key fact in the operation of the Indiana School of Medicine in 1959. More than a thousand people gathered in a tent on the grounds of the Medical Center on April 22 to dedicate the new $7,500,000 Medical Science Building. A three-day symposium was held on various phases of science, social responsibilities, and medical research. Participating in these seminars were the Indiana biologists John Mueller, William R. Breneman, and Donald E. Bowman. The new structure was opened to occupancy on June 1, and volunteer student helpers from the Student American Medical Association worked with a professional crew of movers to transfer in less than a day's time more than 50,000 volumes and the furniture of the library to the new building. Completion of the Medical Science Building was the culmination of plans that had been underway for more than a decade, and in fact was the realization of a dream of a quarter of a century. This addition to the Indianapolis campus not only released a large amount of space, but it opened the way to a much improved program of teaching and research. The Medical School could now expand its curriculum with a greater freedom.

Before the old Medical Science Building was vacated, plans were being made to convert it into quarters for the departments of Internal Medicine, Neurology, Surgery, and some phases of clinical research. The building, when reconditioned, was to be named for Dr. Charles Phillips Emerson, a fitting sentimental transition from one era of medical training to another.

In the transitional era some Medical School traditions were abandoned. Now there were to be interdepartmental research projects for the "free quarter" juniors and seniors. Indiana proposed to follow the national trend of replacing the rotating type of internship with a revised instructional program and internship in surgery and medicine. Dean Van Nuys predicted in 1959 in his annual report that within four or five years internships would be limited to medicine, surgery, and obstetrics. Finally, the School of Medicine in that year reverted to an earlier custom of requiring students to purchase their own microscopes.

Occupancy of the new Medical Science Building enabled the School to admit the record freshman class of 182 members in September 1959. This new class increased Indiana's freshman enrollment to 41 per cent as compared with 14 per cent for all other medical schools in the United States. Out of eighty-five institutions the School of Medicine now ranked fourth in the country; only Tennessee, Illinois, and Chicago had more beginners. Total medical enrollment in Indianapolis was 585 as compared with 744 in Michigan, 707 in Illinois, 677 in the Jefferson School of Medicine, and 658 in Tennessee. The hospitals also felt the impact of expansion, and admitted well over 1,000 in-patients each month from 1955 onward.

Constantly since its founding the Riley Children's Hospital stood challenged to discover new techniques and drugs for the treatment of the diseases of infancy and adolescence. The Board of Governors of the Riley Association awarded $105,000 in 1961 for research in leukemia, brain damage, heart and kidney diseases. The hospital staff performed approximately 300 operations a year to correct heart and heart-related defects in children. At the same time the cerebral palsy clinic had more than 600 children under treatment. The new funds were to be used to investigate almost the full spectrum of childrens' disease. This program was greatly benefited by the employment of Dr. Alfred Blalock, a pioneer in "blue baby" surgery, as George A. Ball visiting professor in surgery.

The School of Medicine research program was further encouraged in 1961 by three grants, totaling $5,891,698. The faculty joined with the United States Air Force to establish a cardio-pulmonary laboratory at the Wright-Patterson Base in Dayton, Ohio. This cooperative venture was organized to study the opening field of space medicine. The laboratories were designed specifically to determine the impact of acceleration, centrifuge, and temperature variations on the human system. A second research grant was from the National Heart Institute of the United States Public Health Service for the continuation of investigation in the area of heart ailments. This was a major project which President Herman B Wells thought required the employment of six senior faculty members plus supporting staff and laboratory facilities. The third grant, made by the National Institute for Mental Health, enabled the School of Medicine to organize a center for the study of schizophrenia in children. A further expansion and emphasis in the clinical sciences was the creation of the Department of Pharmacology under the supervision of Dr. James Ashmore.

The first Bachelor of Science degrees in the allied health sciences were awarded in June 1961. Amidst this proliferation of the various programs of the Medical Center there was a distinct note of progressivism in Dean Van Nuys' annual report. He told the Board of Trustees and the university administration, "The academic year 1960–61 represented a period of time crucial in the development of an increasingly felt philosophy on the Medical School campus. This is, that an atmosphere where knowledge is being created is a necessity for the optimum production of educated professional people whose major goal is the application of new health concepts to the service of the community. While the University School of Medicine faculty has always held training of students in the newest methods of clinical practice as its chief aim, optimum preparation was not available to the young man seeking to enter investigation or clinical teaching. The awards of large amounts of research and research training money from the United States Public Health Service to the medical school campus has permitted the addition of research-minded personnel to the staff as well as greater participation in research work by present staff members of the staff."

Now students were being exposed to research methods and philosophy throughout the whole four years of their enrollment in the school, and some were even introduced to research methods the summer prior to their enrollment as freshmen. Dean Van Nuys expressed special satisfaction with the postgraduate course in radiology during 1961, in which 124 physicians from twenty-four states were registered. The forty-sixth annual offering of the course in anatomical and clinical otolaryngology was oversubscribed by doctors coming from thirteen states. In all, nineteen special courses were offered as postgraduate training for practicing physicians. All of these new programs required additional staff, space, and specialized equipment. Dean Van Nuys said he and his staff had made careful plans to stretch the $2,000,000 state appropriation for a new clinical hospital as far as it would go, yet produce an efficient building. Two years before when work was begun on the renovation of the old medical science building the sum was adequate to modernize it, but by the time the work was completed in the fall of 1961, the structure would no longer adequately house the new clinical programs.

Great hopes were held for the experimental medicine program in Bloomington. Fourteen professional students had already registered, and as many more had elected the course for acedemic credit. Four new staff members had been appointed and as many more were to be employed. In the same burst of enthusiasm the School of Nursing had expanded its programs at a comparable rate with the ever-growing medical and hospital services.

On the eve of Herman B Wells' retirement from the presidency of Indiana University in 1962, the School of Medicine and the James Whitcomb Riley Memorial Association announced major plans for the addition of a $2,500,000 section to the Children's Hospital. These funds came from the state, the Riley Association, and the Hill-Burton Hospital Aid Administration. The new two-story wards were to be constructed between the existing wings, and when completed would house eight operating rooms, an intensive care unit, an X-ray unit, a diagnostic and treatment area, a urology diagnostic unit, and a rehabilitation section. This addition to a major segment of the Medical Center reflected the fact that research and concern in the field of children's medical needs had magnified the importance of this area of clinical medicine and research. Also, the heavy demands made upon the Riley Memorial Hospital revealed a greater awareness of the importance of modern medical care for Indiana children.

In the midst of this era of bright promise, Dean John Ditmars Van Nuys died, February 15, 1964. For the past seventeen years he had given the School of Medicine judicious and aggressive leadership. In 1964 it seemed obvious that he had met the challenges of an age when the art of medical training was undergoing constant and fundamental advances. Though the chief administrator overseeing a rather large instructional and applied medical empire, he was himself able only to make limited research contributions in articles relating to his professional specialty. Dean Van Nuys was denied the freedom of time and conditioning of mind to do intensive research.

The momentum which Dr. Van Nuys had helped to generate was not allowed to falter. In 1965 Dr. Glenn Ward Irwin, Jr., a forty-five-year-old native of Roachdale, Indiana, was appointed dean of the School of Medicine. He like Van Nuys was a graduate of the School ('44), and since 1950 he had been a member of the faculty. He was promoted to a professorship in 1961, and was an active teacher until 1964. He had served the Thyroid Association as president in 1959, and was active in the affairs of the organized diabetic specialists. He could hardly take time in 1965 to get adjusted to the new position, because there was pressing need for greater financial support from all sources.

In the public sector, the Indiana governors and legislators must have regarded the School of Medicine with its hospitals as a bottomless well into which they must pour an ever-increasing stream of money. Dr. Lawrence Wilsey, a special medical consultant, representing the firm of Booz, Allen, and Hamilton, told the Legislative Advisory Commission that the School of Medicine was "below average in virtually every standard. . . ." It would take, he said, a minimum of $26,000,000 worth of improvements to push existing facilities up to the average of other state-supported medical schools in the Middle West.

Dr. Wilsey further shattered legislative complacency by saying that if the Indiana University School of Medicine expected to accommodate "ballooning" enrollments, it would be necessary to expend between $62,000,000 and $73,000,000 in expanding existing facilities. Wilsey made the provocative suggestion that a second medical school should be established either in Gary or Evansville; he, however, favored Purdue University because of the "real academic advantages of its graduate schools."

President Elvis J. Stahr, Jr., who had become president in 1962, responded to the Wilsey proposal before the Indiana Publishers' Committee on Higher Education, October 19, 1964. This group had assembled on the Ball State University campus in Muncie to discuss with the presidents and other administrators problems facing the state-supported universities. Stahr told the publishers, "The first priority for medical education in Indiana is not the establishment of another school of medicine, but adequate support for the state's existing school." The problem of inadequate support for the Medical Center and the nagging question of a second school of medicine were to absorb a great deal of the president's and the dean's time after 1964.

Internally, the School of Medicine in 1964–65 was experiencing some significant readjustments. Without expressing an opinion as to whether or not the liaison with the Basic Medical Institute in Pakistan had succeeded, President Stahr announced, in June 1965, that the following October the university would terminate its obligation for the institute. It had granted eighty Master's degrees, a rather small return quantitatively, at least, for the time and money spent on the program. It may have been true that the "fruitful seeding" of medical training in the new country was worth the effort.

At home another program had failed to produce the anticipated results. Only seven professionally-oriented students had requested work in the science-medicine-research curriculum on the Bloomington campus. Dr. Douglas A. MacFayden resigned as director, a decision which President Stahr thought wise because the university was then able to reconsider the program in light of revised goals. Parenthetically, the president said in his *Annual Report* that admissions had increased to twenty-five students for 1965, an all-time high. Dr. Joseph McManus had been the key personal factor in holding the science-medicine-research experiment together, but he too submitted his resignation.

Conditions were far more propitious in Indianapolis. Ground was broken June 10, 1965, for the new Indiana University Teaching Hospital, an act which Dean Irwin said was "the largest faculty morale booster of the decade." This at the moment when the total available income for the Medical Center research activities was $6,100,000, a part of which was devoted to research training. The School of Medicine had just assumed responsibility for residency training at the Marion County General Hospital, and this absorbed some of the research-training allotment. During the past five years the Medical Center had admitted an average of 15,698 in-patients annually, and had rendered service to 81,078 out-patients. It was estimated in June 1965 that the hospital and student fee income would be $8,585,413, and personnel costs would be $505,499. Five registered pharmacists served the hospitals, and sales from the apothecary shops produced an income of $168,000.

The unusually heavy flow of patients through the Medical Center involved wear on equipment; much of which had to be replaced frequently. Some equipment had to be replaced because of the fairly rapid rate at which it became obsolete. President Stahr told the Board of Trustees this was especially true in the Sterile Supply Department which was still hand-washing utensils, syringes, thermometers, catheters, and other equipment. The hospitals needed both mechanical washers and modern sterilizers. In another housekeeping division it was recommended that the university follow the same policy in Indianapolis as in Bloomington of housing married students. In 1965 the Medical Center supplied 696 student beds in the Ball Residence Hall, Winona Village, Warthin Apartments, and the Student Union. In all, there were 1,327 students registered in the various medical training programs, 758 of whom were in the School of Medicine undergraduate classes. By 1965 this latter division had become so large that it was decided to drop the "out-of-state" registrants in pediatric nursing as soon as these nurses could find another affiliation. Part of this decision was based upon the fact that there was no weekend and evening supervision of women nursing students, and some disciplinary problems no doubt had arisen.

The School of Medicine in 1965 held a mirror up to itself to reflect its state of being. A special self-study committee under the chairmanship of Dr. William Deiss reported in preliminary findings a rather unsettling six-point observation concerning the clinical curriculum. The committee "was not surprised to find disharmony in the faculty-student relationships, but it was deeply concerned at the depth of these emotions of disinterest on both sides of the M.D. degree." Committee members expressed the opinion that the first two years of medical education in Indiana still adhered to a philosophy of "very traditional techniques." The interphase between preclinical and clinical teaching at the conclusion of the sophomore year was "fragmented" at the critical time "for proper integration and assimilation of material preparatory to the student's embarking on the clinical curriculum." Outpatient services showed marked variations in the degree and efficiency with which clinical materials were utilized for teaching, and, finally, no elective time was provided juniors and seniors in which they could measure their individual expressions of self-interest. These were harsh critical appraisals, somewhat reflective of lapses in the administration of the School of Medicine itself, but no doubt were more indicative of the pressures and lack of financial resources of the moment. The history of the School of Medicine for the past two decades had been one of trying to secure enough public financial aid to support an ambitious program of modern medicine in a constantly expanding physical plant. Dean Irwin believed that a positive morale builder was the beginning of construction of phase I of a six-story $30,000,000 adult patient hospital in 1965. This new teaching and research hospital, including the Krannert Pavilion, would eventually house 713 beds.

Fundamentally, the central mission of the Indiana University School of Medicine was to supply the largest number of trained physicians possible to serve the needs of the state. Toward this end there were 1,403 students enrolled in 1967, plus another thirty-eight taking the science-medicine-research courses. That June, 181 new doctors were awarded degrees, but 100 of these had accepted internships outside of Indiana, and possibly were lost to the state. At its last session the General Assembly had undertaken to prevent this costly out-flow of physicians by appropriating $2,500,000 for the biennium 1967–69 to finance statewide internships under the supervision of a five-man medical education board. This body was under the general direction of Dean Glenn W. Irwin, Jr., as chairman. Statewide interns were to be compensated from this fund, and it was hoped that they would both serve a useful apprenticeship in Hoosier medical facilities, and then remain in the state to practice medicine. The Regenstrief Foundation financed a study of various medical specialties, one of which was the training of primary or family doctors. This had ever been the basic need of Indiana.

In the six decades of its existence, 1903–67, the Indiana School of Medicine had maintained a fairly consistent level of growth. It admitted 203 students to the freshman class in the fall of 1967, but even this increase was a minus factor because the number of qualified applicants from the state's high schools had possibly tripled or quadrupled. In Indianapolis the physical plant had undergone major expansion, and with the projected adult patient hospital the clinical teaching capability would be tripled at least. But even so, the whole medical facility in Indianapolis represented an appreciably smaller rate of expansion than did the state's population growth, and the sensitive response of Hoosiers to modern medical treatment.

The budget for 1967–69, totaled $15,600,000, far short of the sum recommended by the professional consultants. The derivations of this budget reflected the distribution of responsibilities for providing American society with modern medical care. The Federal Government contributed 59.8 per cent, private philanthropies and foundations, plus hospital fees supplied 29.7 per cent, and the remaining 10.1 per cent came from the State of

Indiana. Aside from these sources of income, Dean Irwin said more than 600 private physicians had served as faculty members without pay, "and the value of their service is beyond calculation. We could not buy what they give the citizens of Indiana."

Possibly no other division of Indiana University came under so much constant public and professional gaze as the School of Medicine and its staffs. The school not only trained physicians as the only medical school in the state, it rendered an almost endless number of medical services to the public, it trained hundreds of nurses, conducted postgraduate courses, maintained the geographical clinics, and instituted further modern medical services in the new type of internships. The greatest driving force, however, was created by the whole world of modern medicine which made mandatory that teaching procedures and the curriculum be kept abreast of a fast-moving age of medical discovery, and a constantly broadening responsibility for public physical welfare. Nowhere in the nation was the challenge to maintain a respectable comparative standing of a medical school greater than among the Big Ten schools.

[X V I]

The Coming of Age of a Life Science

THE GROWTH OF professional schools within most American public universities reflects a curious evolution of national educational and social history. The growing needs and complexities of American society created demands that had to be served in the most practical way possible. It was also true that as universities matured and their faculties made scientific advances in various fields they created interrelationships which spread far beyond the old academic borders. It can be assumed that even the most visionary Indiana founder in 1820 had no concept that some day the rather primitive field of dentistry would become a recognized area of scientific academic research. Through approximately three quarters of the nineteenth century most of the practice of dentistry was scarcely more than that of a folk mechanical art with little or no scientific implications. Too, the borderline of practice was fine indeed, if in fact it existed, between the practice of medicine in broad rural areas and that of the elementary forms of dentistry. Doctors had neither formal training nor appreciable knowledge in this area of human suffering. Most of them administered treatment with painkilling drugs or removed the source of trouble by use of the most elementary equipment. Each decade after 1830 saw an increase in the Indiana population, and likewise rising needs for better health care in all the medical arts.

Not until the second half of the nineteenth century were efforts made to formulate the training and practice of dentistry in the United States into a professional guild with standards of training and ethics of practice. The first American dental school was organized in 1840 by four Maryland physicians. This proprietary school operated under a state charter, and with some degree of public restrictions. Alabama, Kentucky, Ohio, and New York enacted dental laws between 1841 and 1869. By 1879, the date of the founding of the Indiana Dental College, there were nineteen institutions, all of them of the proprietary class. There was opposition to these schools by some practitioners, and especially from suppliers of dental materials and instruments. These opponents conceived the training of dentists to be a matter of apprenticeships. None of the dental professors or other persons associated with the art seem to have had the remotest notion of the dietary and physiological implications of oral hygiene. There were, however, a few practitioners who saw need for more research and better training of practitioners. In Indiana there were the dental pioneers, John F. Johnston, P. G. C. and Andrew Hunt, W. R. Winston, and J. P. Ulrey. In 1858 the state's dentists formed the Indiana Dental Association, an organization that spent a considerable amount of time encouraging the enactment of regulatory legislation to alleviate quackery and malpractice.

No one in Indiana in 1860 had a notion of the capabilities of the state's dentists. Certainly few if any of them had much formal training for practicing their profession, and there was no dependable knowledge of how sound most apprenticeship training was. Hoosier practitioners no doubt ranged in qualifications from pure quacks to fairly well-trained apprentices. The status of dental medicine, no matter how successful the practitioners, went little beyond extractions, the making of crude fillings and false teeth, and efforts at administering painkilling drugs.

The Indiana General Assembly enacted a law, March 29, 1879, which provided for the establishment of an examining board selected from the State Dental Association. Graduates of a dental school were automatically permitted to practice without formal certification; all others were examined by representatives of the profession and approved or disapproved. At a called meeting, June 23, 1879, in the office of Dr. William Heiskall in Indianapolis, a proprietary dental school was organized under the title "The Indiana Dental College." The following October 1 six students were registered, and by March 1880 three of these were graduated.

In a highly enlightening history, Dr. Jack D. Carr, assistant professor of radiology of the Indiana School of Dentistry, has not only detailed the history of the Indiana Dental College (1957), but he has given an outline glimpse of the evolution of much of American dental education and the practice of oral medicine. Amazingly, the Indiana proprietary school seems never to have experienced difficulties because of a lack of funds. The school operated on stock issues and student fees, and remained solvent throughout its history. No other branch of Indiana University, historically, enjoyed such good fortune. Faculty members of the private school, however, were paid little more than token salaries until after the turn of the twentieth century, and plant and equipment costs were indeed modest. Early students paid little more than nominal fees, and their laboratory and equipment needs were kept at a minimum.

Three advances in the field of dentistry in the early decades of this century were of landmark importance. The Harvard Dental School began a crusade to organize a Dental Faculties Association of American Universities in 1903, and the next year the Dental Education Council of America was created. This latter body performed the function of devising standards and otherwise formalizing dental education. Admission requirements in the better schools were stiffened to include two years of high school training, and the prescribed curriculum was quickly extended into a four-year course.

Dr. Carr has written, "A school had to maintain the standards set by the Dental Education Council so that its diplomas would be accepted by most state boards of examiners. Therefore, as the standards had become so high, privately owned schools could not be operated at a reasonable profit. Such was the situation faced by Mr. Beeler and his wife, Maria Hunt Beeler, when they decided to sell the school [Indiana Dental College]." There were other background facts which by the 1920s began to have an important impact on the education of dentists. When Harvard University in 1903 insisted on the establishment of a four-year course, it immediately found itself involved in controversy with the National Association of Dental Faculties. Five years later it organized a collegiate body composed of Harvard, California, Iowa, Michigan, Minnesota, and Pennsylvania. This move was in time to steer dental training away from the proprietary schools and into the universities where higher standards of instruction could be established and maintained.

One phase of dental education in Indiana prior to 1925 has noteworthy significance. In 1896–97, a chapter of Xi Psi Phi fraternity was organized, and in 1901 a chapter of Delta Sigma Delta was established, to be followed by the creation of two more Greek letter organizations. These fraternities appear to have become active factors in both dental politics and interprofessional relationships. Years later letters contained in the files of President Herman B Wells referred to one of these fraternities as having an unwholesome influence upon the affairs of the School of Dentistry.

Immediately after World War I it seemed to be a fairly broadly recognized fact that the days of the proprietary Indiana Dental College were numbered. The school appeared to be in no position to control internal factors or to ward off the pressures which bore upon a nonacademic institution. In 1923 Dr. F. R. Henshaw admitted the days of the proprietary schools were numbered. However, he told the faculty there were no plans to discontinue the Indiana Dental College. Nevertheless, a move was begun soon thereafter to dispose of the school to Indiana University, following the earlier precedent of the sale of the proprietary medical schools. Back of this move was the usual amount of political pulling and hauling. Dr. Carr has said, "Strong political pressure groups in the legislature seemed determined to block the purchase unless they were paid handsomely for their votes." Opposition of the "grafters," however, was overcome and $35,000 was appropriated for the purchase of the college to be converted into a public institution. On June 1, 1925, Indiana University added the School of Dentistry to its college organization. In the transfer of the control of the school the university retained most of the private college dental faculty. It was said that with the addition of the new school and its faculty to the university, dentistry and medicine theoretically became intimately conjoined in many areas of training. As with medicine in 1909, the university had to create new courses, revise degree requirements, hire additional trained staff, and purchase new equipment to meet the standards of the Dental Educational Council of America.

One of the first administrative decisions made by Indiana University was the retention of the dean of the Indiana Dental School. Dr. Frederic Rich Henshaw, professor of operative dentistry, and who had served in this position since his appointment in 1920, continued as dean of the School of Dentistry until his death, May 27, 1938. Dr. Henshaw was succeeded by Dr. Gerald P. Timmons, acting dean until January 1, 1940, when Dr. William Hopkins Crawford of the University of Minnesota and Columbia University was appointed to the office. Later Dr. Timmons was made dean of the Temple University School of Dentistry. The facts of change were reflected in President Herman B Wells' reports in 1937–42. When the university took possession of the school in 1925, there were forty-two professors and lecturers, many of whom gave only a single course, and some of them offered little more than a lecture or two. Several of the "professors" were not even in the fields of the dental and medical sciences. Reflected in the extensive list was the fact that private dental practitioners, like medical doctors, cherished the added prestige which a professorship in the Dental School gave them. Wells said there were in 1938, seven full-time and twenty-eight part-time professors. Four years later Dean Crawford reported that he had a staff of twenty-five full-time professors, and twenty-two part-time lecturers. This faculty represented some changes of faces; in addition, there had been organized seven departments.

Among several innovations in the School of Dentistry after 1940 was the creation of three internships which gave students opportunities to gain direct hospital experience in the field of oral surgery. Too, the dental staff had become more research oriented than ever before. As new men were added to the staff, they helped to develop in both Bloomington and Indianapolis a higher standard of professional training. As some of the other university departments, such as chemistry and some of the fields of medicine, were strenghtened, dentistry itself made marked advances. The training in dentistry, as in medicine, was divided between Bloomington and the Medical Center in Indianapolis. First-year students were kept on the main university campus where they had readily available to them the foundation courses of the College of Arts and Sciences. In 1943, the mid-war year, the School of Dentistry had 169 registrants. The entering class was selected from 200 applicants, the lowest number to date, and fewer than half of these entered with the minimum of two years of college training. Forty-one seniors received degrees in August 1943, and forty-one of them went directly into the armed services. The remaining students were inducted into the Army and Navy Dental Reserve Corps and were placed on a simulated military regimen.

During his five years as dean, William H. Crawford had been able to accomplish some marked improvements in the School of Dentistry, even though he undertook the task during the stringencies of war when most of the students were members of one of the military services. In late March 1945 there appeared in President Wells' correspondence files several letters from Indianapolis dentists expressing regrets that Dr. Crawford was resigning his position. Dr. J. Thayer Waldo, wrote, March 19, 1945, that the past five years had been a new and progressive era for the School of Dentistry. "I am proud," he told President Wells, "to be identified with the movement which so strongly favored such a change. No one denies that this was not right and that over-all results are extremely gratifying." Dr. Waldo regretted, however, that "in one area," "we are in terrible shape. That is the relationship between the medical and dental departments. I am trying to express this honestly from both the medical and dental views,—it is deplorable. Dr. Gatch and Dr. Crawford never seemed to get along. In order to advance the dental school to the position which it should hold, as in other universities, this thing must be accomplished."

A week later Dr. Harry G. Jones, also of Indianapolis, commended President Wells for having selected Dr. Crawford. He said the selection of the Minnesotan had helped to get the School of Dentistry out of a difficult situation. A great majority of the Indiana dentists, he thought, were pleased, but in his opinion there still existed the old professional political clique, the Delta Sigma Delta fraternity, which had been so influential in the affairs of the proprietary school's affairs. "I might add," wrote Dr. Jones, "that this opposition is even greater now, inasmuch as many dentists, formerly neutral but now interested because of the school's fine programs, are very much concerned over the return of the former political faction." He expressed faith in Wells' and the trustees' sincere efforts to find a capable new dean, "so that harmony and progress attained by the school in the last five years will not be forfeited." He thought neither a Hoosier nor a member of Delta Sigma Delta fraternity "is capable of amalgamating these two factions." Dr. Jones was so strongly opposed to the fraternity's alleged domination that he believed even the choice of a Delta Sigma Delta affiliate from outside the state would prove a doubtful choice because he would soon become part of the old faction.

It is clear that sometime early in 1945 Dr. Crawford had informed President Wells orally that he planned to resign the deanship. It was not until June 19, however, that he confirmed his decision in writing. In light of the two letters quoted above, the dean's letter must have contained some veiled implications. He told the president, "I have been indeed fortunate in the opportunity I have had working with you. I know I have made many mistakes and I am leaving your dental school with many problems some of which are my own making and some I should have corrected. But my mistakes cannot be placed before any doorsteps but my own because the support I have received from you has been perfect."

Surely the internal politics of the professions must at times have put the professional politician to shame. Strangely, the Greek letter professional fraternities, on the record at least, seem to have played such an important role in the School of Dentistry. If the implications are to be trusted, they must at times have even superseded professional ethics and loyalties. In 1945 there were in the school five chapters plus the Student Dental Council and the Junior American Dental Association, a rather large number of organizations in ratio to student enrollment. Both of the latter professional groups were organized in 1939. President Wells reported at the end of Dean Crawford's administration that there were 126 students enrolled, and that since 1925 graduating classes had averaged forty-five members, however, in the latter year only twenty-one freshmen had been admitted, and there were thirty-nine seniors. For the first time since 1940 the entering class in 1946 was entirely of civilian orgin. The Army had concluded it had a sufficient number of dentists in its ranks and discontinued its training program at Indiana in August. Four months later the Navy ceased to support the training of more dentists.

Dr. Maynard Kiplinger Hine, a thirty-eight-year-old professor of histopathology and periodontics, was chosen as Dean William H. Crawford's successor. Dr. Hine, a native of Waterloo, Indiana, and a graduate of the University of Illinois School of Dentistry, was a member of Sigma Delta Sigma. He had received good training and had to his credit able teaching and administrative experience. His subsequent record revealed him as an active professional man holding to high academic standards. Certainly he came to the office of dean with knowledge of the needs of the Indiana School of Dentistry that he had gained by firsthand observation.

Dean Hine recommended in 1946 that in the future no more than sixty-four students be admitted to the School of Dentistry, and that preference be shown Indiana veterans and natives. This was the first year that the pressures of postwar applications were being felt. The Dean wrote in his first Annual Report, that "Recognizing the fact that there are a great number of Indiana veterans qualified to study dentistry who could not be accepted in dental school, President Wells has rightly taken the attitude that the dental faculty consider accepting a maximum number of students in dental school, we decided this number was sixty-four, but early in 1947, it was apparent that there would be many more than sixty-four qualified Indiana veterans who would desire to study dentistry at Indiana in 1947." Wells asked for an estimate of the cost of accepting additional students. The faculty decided that with added support the number could be increased to a maximum of ninety-one, and the President was able to get an additional appropriation of $25,682. In addition, he received promise of sufficient support to continue the training of the two expanded classes throughout their four years of enrollment. Ninety new students were admitted in September that year, which Dean Hine said represented a 40 per cent increase. Later, however, President Wells told the trustees that 71.5 per cent of all student applicants sufficiently well-trained to enter dental school had to be turned away.

While the student body was being expanded in numbers, there was a similar expansion taking place in both teaching and research programs. In 1948 Dean Hine wrote, "Our Department of Dental Materials is now recognized as one of the best in the country. In the past six months Professor Ralph Phillips has been offered appointments as head of departments of dental materials in Texas, Michigan, and Minnesota, all of which he refused to accept at least an additional year at Indiana."

Just as its sister school of medicine felt cramped because of a lack of modern and adequate space, the School of Dentistry was equally as pinched. During the academic year 1948, the Dental Building in the Medical Center was undergoing extensive remodeling. Part of this work was being done to permit the training of more students, to expand facilities for oral surgery, radiology, the children's clinic, and the library. It was necessary to excavate a deep basement under the fifteen-year-old building, to install forty new dental units for the clinic, and to permit the expansion of other facilities. There were registered in the three advanced classes 161 students, an increase of 58 over the previous year. Applications for admission had considerably exceeded the capacity of the school. Nationally in 1947, 10,313 individual students filed 17,671 applications for admission, and only 2,942 or 28 per cent were admitted; Indiana admitted 43 per cent of its applicants. The Council on Dental Education of the American Dental Association approved the expansion, and in the remodeled building the School of Dentistry was equally as well prepared as the School of Medicine to offer a broader curriculum of instruction.

Although the Army had withdrawn its support of a training unit in the School of Dentistry in 1945, it installed a Reserve Officer Training Corps unit in 1948 under the command of Major Julius C. Sexson. Students enrolled in this service were given special summer training and camp experience. Upon graduation they were commissioned officers in the Army dental reserve.

Pressures mounted in the School of Dentistry in the year 1948–49. The remodeling of the building had been disruptive, still this additional space had failed to provide adequately for the training of dental hygienists under the new auxiliary program. The faculty had been occupied with serving the needs of increasing numbers of students, and in trying to point new directions for the general programs. In the past three years enrollment had increased 123 per cent. Dean Hine expressed the opinion in this era that his school should concern itself principally with the training of students to become "general practitioners." Just as rapidly, he also hoped it would train a fair number of specialists, dental hygienists, assistants, and technicians. His problems seemed to be identical with those of the School of Medicine. Some of the reasons for the pressures on the School of Dentistry, as on Medicine, could be measured in precise social statistics. In 1949, 2,064 requests for applications were received in the office of admissions, 376 of which came from Indiana, but only 97 applicants were permitted to complete the process of application, and only 65 of these were approved, or at a ratio of approximately 6 to 1. This condition was to continue on into the future.

Dentistry in Indiana since 1874 had a distinctive male image. Occasionally, President Wells or Dean Hine spoke of "men and women" in their reports, but it was not until 1950 that specific plans were made for the training of women. For the first time in the school's history women were given special dental training in this academic year as hygienists. Two years later the program was accredited by the Council on Dental Education.

Despite the admission of women to the new courses, the School of Dentistry in 1952 admitted only 68 students because Dean Hine said there were no additional spaces for others. Increased admissions in the past years had pushed the total enrollment up to 315 students, fifteen of whom were postgraduates. This condition was to linger on, and was especially aggravated after 1951 when sixteen staff members were requisitioned for military service in the Korean War. No matter how many students were enrolled, the Indiana School of Dentistry was unable to train enough practitioners to serve the ever-expanding state population. In 1940 there was one dentist in Indiana to every 1,896 persons, one to 1,948 in 1950, and one to 2,048 in 1953. President Herman B Wells reported to the Board of Trustees in 1954 that the School of Dentistry had served capacity classes for the past four years, "So it is obvious that [with] our present plant, we cannot meet the needs of Indiana."

During the immediate postwar years the Indiana University School of Dentistry extended its activities over a fairly broad area of oral hygiene and care. In time this expansion was to involve a fairly wide spectrum of the University's scientific capability. In the great recruiting drive of the 1940s Dean Fernandus Payne was able to persuade Professor Harry Gilbert Day of the Johns Hopkins University to accept an appointment in the Department of Chemistry in 1940. In Baltimore the chemist had conducted experiments on the effects of a lack of zinc in the diets of animals, and had begun the study of dietary deficiencies in humans and their relationships to dental health. One of his experiments was an effort to determine the effects of fluorides on dental caries.

Later at Indiana Professor Day taught freshman dental students in special chemistry courses, and as research projects he had them carry out experiments in the general area of his interest. Some of them published papers on their findings in the use of fluorides. Two students, Joseph Charles Muhler of Fort Wayne and Thomas Boyd, elected to experiment further with the fluorides in 1944–45. Simultaneously, the Board of Trustees had accepted a gift of $2,000 from the Pepsodent Company to sustain three fellowships in the School of Dentistry on the condition that the name of the university would not be used commercially. The record is not clear whether either Muhler or Boyd received this scholarship aid; this, however, marked the beginning of a commercial interest in the research program. Nevertheless, the two carried on intensified investigations of the impact of mouth acids on tooth enamel. Already there had been some experiments in this area in the School of Dentistry. Tooth enamel had been reduced to uniform pulverized particles and the various fluorides had been applied to this material. No major results, however, had been published.

A comparable study of the fluorides had been made in the University of Rochester School of Dentistry in which the effects of acids were discussed in published materials. Apparently this latter experiment was carried no further. In the meantime Joseph C. Muhler had the idea of testing the effectiveness of a wide range of the fluorides in determining which if any had the most effect upon the preservation of enamel and in checking dental caries. Later Profesor Day made the observation that any chemist would have advised Muhler against such use of these chemicals. Fortunately none did. Muhler went to Bloomington to ransack the Chemistry Department's collection of fluorides. Professor Day took him to the laboratory of Dr. Frank Mather, a metallurgical chemist, and there they found a generous collection of the chemical, including one grime-encrusted bottle of stannous or "tin" fluoride. Subsequent applications of this particular chemical seemed to produce an encouraging difference from the others. In the excitement of Muhler's initial discovery Dean Maynard K. Hine asked Professor Day to assume oversight of Muhler's experiments. On Friday afternoons in the spring and summer of 1946

Day drove to the Medical Center laboratory in Indianapolis to review the past week's results of Muhler's research, and to go over the evolving hypothesis as to the effect of the fluorides on enamel preservation, and especially the promising results of stannous flouride.

In 1947 research grants totaling $7,740 were made to the School of Dentistry to continue the fluoride studies. These were awarded to the University by the National Institutes of Health of the United States Public Health Services, and were intended ostensibly to finance the studies of Dr. Grant Van Huysen and Dr. Ralph W. Phillips of the dental faculty. This agency had made a smaller grant the previous year, and the findings of the professors continued to be encouraging. The Van Huysen experiments involved the reduction of tooth enamel to solubility by use of both powdered and solid forms. Van Huysen and Phillips also demonstrated that stannous fluoride was more effective in enamel preservation than was the sodium form. As a result of this finding a public school experiment was begun under the supervision of Dr. Roy Smiley in 1949.

In the meantime Dr. Muhler and Dr. Van Huysen had jointly prepared a professional paper, which was received favorably by their professional colleagues. Muhler upon receiving his degree in dentistry, returned to Bloomington on a service fellowship to seek a doctorate in chemistry. He began an extensive series of tests on rats. He fed the animals caries-producing diets and treated separate groups with stannous and sodium fluorides. For the first time this produced a distinct contrast of the two chemicals on live enamels. As the end of four months the rats were killed and detailed examinations were made of the condition of their teeth. The experiment was conducted in such a way that Muhler had no knowledge at the outset of his examinations what treatment a specimen had received. He discovered, however, that those that had received the stannous flouride had withstood the diet with caries-forming properties with much better results.

The scientists found that it was not enough to prove that stannous fluoride was effective in controlling enamel decay, some means had also to be found for producing a more dependable supply of the chemical. Dr. W. H. Nebergall from the universities of Illinois and Minnesota joined the Indiana chemistry faculty in 1949. He and Dr. A. W. Radike, consultant in preventive dentistry, and their associates began a search to solve the problem of a fluoride supply. In the future they were to conduct more sophisticated experiments in the use of the chemical in a suspended form and in combination with a somewhat incompatible agency.

Again Muhler and his colleagues secured the cooperation of the Indiana State Board of Health in the testing of hundreds of schoolchildren. Also, Superintendent Hiram E. Binford of the Bloomington schools agreed to cooperate in the experiment. Once the testing started there was constant consultation with the Indiana State Board of Health to prevent any misunderstanding or outbreak of public indignation. The university scientists were able to secure use of a truck on which they mounted a secondhand X-ray machine in an improvised examination room. Now they were ready for the first time to begin applying their hypothesis on humans, and at an age when they were most vulnerable to the decaying effects of caries. The schoolchildren were divided into three groups, and their teeth were X-rayed and otherwise examined. Records were kept for each child. One group was given toothpaste containing sodium fluoride, the second received toothpaste containing stannous fluoride, and the third was placed on plain water. This routine was established on an interval of six months, at the end of which the initial examinations were repeated. In December 1952 the chemists reported a 36 per cent reduction in cavities among the children who had used the stannous fluoride toothpaste. In the use of the X ray, which perhaps was not too well installed in the truck examination room, the dentists and chemists stirred up a bit of controversy. Hermann Muller, then campaigning heavily against irresponsible use of X ray and other forms of X-ray exposure, raised objections to the Muhler experiment.

Though the first round of testing of the schoolchildren had confirmed the capability of stannous fluoride to lower the number of cavities, there still remained a fundamental problem. Stannous fluoride did not fare well in a suspended state, or at least the form used did not seem to do so. Dr. Nebergall and his colleagues went to work to develop a method of heating calcium-phosphate particles in an effort to reduce their reactions to the fluoride. A second problem was that in a standing state stannous fluoride underwent a reduction in effectiveness. Later Professor Day wrote, "The big breakthrough was in the discovery that a controlled heating process will make the conventional dicalcium phosphates compatible with stannous fluoride. Through the collaborative work by scientists in the Procter and Gamble Laboratories it was shown that when the treatment is properly controlled there is no substantial change in the abrasive characteristics of the phosphates. The heat treatment results in the formation of calcium pyrophosphates."

By 1950 the chemists and dentists had made sufficient headway with their experiments to give a progress report to the Chicago meeting of the International Dental Society. Following this meeting, Verling M. Votaw, an Indiana graduate and a representative of the Procter and Gamble Company, approached Professor Harry G. Day with the proposal that the company give the Muhler project financial support. Acceptance of this kind of financial aid in the development of such a potentially profitable commercial product involved numerous hazards for a public university. Dean Frank G. Gucker of the College of Arts and Sciences and former head of the Department of Chemistry approved procedures to determine the possibilities of accepting financial support in a reasonable amount, provided Indiana University could be assured freedom of publication, patent rights to research results, and otherwise assuring protection of the scientific findings of the institution.

Professor Harry Day prepared the memorandum of agreement in 1951 which outlined terms of a patent and its use, and provided for other scientific and research safeguards. All of this was done in consultation with Dean Gucker, Graduate Dean John Ashton, Dean of the Faculties Herman Briscoe, and Howard Wilcox, director of the Indiana University Foundation. The financial agreement was finally worked out between Procter and Gamble and Indiana University. By this time the scientists had solved most of the problems in the production of fluoride toothpaste. Now the dramatic moment was at hand for a final scientific testing of the reliability of stannous fluoride as an additive to toothpaste. Again, experiments had to be conducted on large numbers of schoolchildren. The new mass experiment was not begun, however, until both Joseph Muhler and the Procter and Gamble Company had conducted extensive toxicity tests: Muhler on rats, and the Procter and Gamble scientists on hamsters.

During the academic year, 1953–54, half of a quonset hut at

the corner of Jordan Avenue and Seventh Street in Bloomington was converted into an examination and distribution station. Following much the same procedures of the earlier clinical testing, examinations were made of the teeth of 1,600 Bloomington schoolchildren between the ages of six and fifteen years. Also, 450 college students were tested. This time, three types of toothpaste were distributed—plain, that containing sodium fluoride, and that with stannous fluoride. Enough of each sample was supplied to meet the needs of the entire families to assure no disruption of the experiment by use of unidentified dentrifices.

Results of the second testing seemed sufficiently clear by mid-May 1954. Dr. Muhler reported to the Indiana Dental Association that use of stannous fluoride definitely reduced the number of cavities by 60 to 70 per cent in children using it. Those who used sodium fluoride achieved only 30 to 40 per cent reductions. In the conclusion of this rather massive testing it was clear that ten years of intensive research had succeeded for Dr. Muhler and his colleagues in the School of Dentistry and in the Department of Chemistry. Bruce Blivens, Jr., science writer for *Collier's Magazine*, said the findings of the Indiana experiments had created a stir among the toothpaste manufacturers, who did $100,000,000 worth of business a year. The Indiana findings did more than this, they signaled a complete revolution in the manufacture and promotion of dentifrices.

University researches by members of two divisions of the institution and the cooperation of the Indiana public schools and of the State Board of Health yielded significant results in an area where there had ever been a certain amount of quackery and gross misinformation. Dentifrice manufacturers had plied their trades with far too little knowledge of what their products did or did not do for users. Although Dr. Joseph C. Muhler was the key scientist associated with the research that resulted in the new findings, the results were those of teamwork on the part of even more persons than those named above. In 1956 Muhler was thirty-three years of age, had earned two doctoral degrees, was secretary of the Dental Graduate School, was the author of eighty scientific papers, had contributed materials to the writing of textbooks, and was said to have written several mystery stories. He was indeed an energetic young man with a full commitment to his scientific interest. In the future he was to continue to be an industrious and productive scholar in the field of preventive dentistry and oral hygiene. In the School of Dentistry he was to become head of a major division with extensive space, staff, and a firm position in the curriculum for his specialty.

The use of stannous fluoride in toothpaste combined with the Nebergall process of suspension and preservation was patented in the name of the Indiana University Foundation. The Procter and Gamble Company agreed to pay royalties to the Foundation for permission to use the processes developed by the university scientists. The company began test marketing the new type of toothpaste in 1955 under the trade name of "Crest." This became the first dentifrice to be certified by the American Dental Association as containing an effective decay preventive agent. The prestigious Council of Dental Therapeutics of the American Dental Association reported in 1960, "After careful consideration of the results of clinical studies conducted on CREST toothpaste, manufactured by the Procter and Gamble Company, the Council of Dental Therapeutics has recognized the usefulness of the dentifrice as a caries preventive agent."

Although Joseph Muhler's experiments had resulted in the discovery of the effectiveness of stannous fluoride as a neutralizing and hardening dentifrice, researches continued in this area into 1956. The Office of the Surgeon General of the United States Army renewed its support of the use of fluorides in the prevention of enamel decay. This project was directed by Professor R. B. Fisher of the Department of Chemistry, and involved the use of highly specialized electronic instruments.

At the Atlantic City meeting of the International Association for Dental Research in 1957, Joseph C. Muhler and Charles Willis Gish of the School of Dentistry and C. L. Howell of the Indiana State Board of Health presented a professional paper on the Indiana experiments with stannous fluoride. By 1962 the Indiana experimenters had made more than 40,000 separate examinations of teeth, had made 5,000 X-ray exposures, had distributed approximately 200,000 tubes of toothpaste, and 37,000 toothbrushes. This extensive research had been conducted by at least a dozen chemists and dentists, and it resulted in revolutionizing an enormously profitable American health industry. For the first time in human history a scientific basis had been established for the determination of the quality of dentrifices. Far more important, of course, was the discovery of a substance that would reduce dental caries in an age when the American diet and food habits were highly conducive to tooth decay.

Other areas of research in the Indiana School of Dentistry made significant advances in the various fields of oral health and hygiene after Maynard K. Hine came to the deanship. The graduate program was instituted in 1946, and in time it gave the school distinction well beyond the borders of Indiana. By 1965 approximately 12 full- and part-time graduate students were enrolled, a fact which necessitated major revisions and expansion of the curriculum. This program of advanced training went far toward broadening the understanding of both the physiological and structural nature of oral medicine.

At the other end of the dental educational scale was the introduction of the innovative dental hygiene courses in Indianapolis and Fort Wayne under the direction of Dr. Ralph Schimmele. To the delight of local dentists thirty-six girls from the Fort Wayne area were enrolled in the dental hygiene classes with the promise that they would greatly lighten the burden of dental practice in Allen County in the future.

Since 1945 the School of Dentistry had promoted a program of research that received generous support from federal agencies, private industries, the Indiana State Board of Health, the Public Welfare Department, and from the specialized foundations. The private companies of Eli Lilly, Procter and Gamble, L. D. Caulk, and Mead Johnson were important supporters. Research scientists in 1965 justified this faith in the school of Dentistry when they placed two other new dental products on the market. At the same time faculty members produced an extraordinarily large number of scientific books and journal articles.

The record reflects the fact that Dean Hine was an aggressive administrator and his annual reports and communications fairly crackled with notes of pride and optimism. He and his colleagues appeared to take satisfaction in the large numbers of applications that annually flowed into the admissions office. That the school operated to its fullest capacity seemed further verification of dentistry as a medical science, as meaningful and respectable as that which was offered in the adjoining School of Medicine. In 1966, 1,800 prospective students made inquiries about admission, and of these 286 were permitted to complete their applications.

Ninety-nine new students were admitted, a level of admissions which remained fairly constant for the rest of the decade. The graduate program was equally attractive and reflected in the 350 applications the sense of the rapid advances being made in the practice of oral medicine. Ninety graduate students, some of them representing twelve foreign countries, including Canada, Ireland, France, and Japan, were accepted. In addition to the scientific courses, four new ones were instituted in 1966 by the School of Education for the purpose of training dental graduate students to become teachers in their fields of specialization. Dean Hine said he was convinced that the rise of the graduate program in his school reflected a significant parallelism with the growing importance of research at Indiana University during the past decade and a half.

Beneath the dean's heartening reports, however, could be discerned a lurking fear that his school would not be able to maintain its momentum in the future without substantially increased financial support. The University of Michigan had under construction a $17,500,000 dental educational facility. Ohio State University had just added a modern building, and Illinois had plans underway for a new school plant. These were costly improvements being made by Big Ten rivals and gave serious challenge to Indiana. Well beyond the fold of the Old Northwest there were serious threats of loss of faculty. Florida, Georgia, South Carolina, and, soon, neighboring Kentucky were organizing new dental schools and threatened to raid the Hoosier faculty for professors. These new schools entered the market for staff members offering $3,000 to $4,000 salary advances over those being paid at Indiana. Even young men who had only recently received Master's degrees were being offered salaries of 15 to 20 per cent more than those which were paid in dental schools two years earlier. That year Dean Hine reported the resignation of twenty-two faculty members without indicating reasons for the changes or where the professors went.

In almost the identical vein of arguments contained in the reports of the Dean of the School of Medicine, Dean Hine emphasized the public educational, health services, and research missions of his school. In some of his communications he listed as a major public service a staggering number of biopsies performed for the state's dentists. Interestingly, he told the university administration in 1967 that the School of Dentistry by force of academic and physical circumstance had become more exclusive in its admissions policies than was desirable. The hundred freshmen just admitted to the new class averaged 2.8 points on an academic scale of 3, and only 35 of Indiana's 92 counties were represented. At the other end of the scale, 124 applicants for graduate study had been accepted, 73 of whom were full-time students. The graduate program had become one of the largest in the country, partly because of the good quality of research performed by the faculty. Graduate students in oral surgery, pedodontics, and periodontics were assigned to hospital service to give them experience in working closely with physicians in a hospital environment.

As successful as dental training had been in Indiana University since 1925, the School of Dentistry had been unable to keep pace with the needs of the state. Indiana's ratio of patients to dentists in 1966 was slightly below the national average. In the five Old Northwest states, Indiana had the highest patient ratio; it had 2,164 as compared with 1,634 in Wisconsin and 1,714 in the nation. It was in this area that the School of Dentistry actually faced its greatest challenge, because it was in lowering the ratio that it had an opportunity to perform one of its major service functions.

Research activities continued at an all-time high with the university granting $1,222,914 in institutional funds to dentistry. In turn, faculty members were indeed productive in 1965–66. They reported publication of 117 professional papers, and 59 books. Joseph C. Muhler edited the Indiana Dental Association's *Journal*, David Mitchell was associate editor of the *Journal of Dental Research*, and Dean Maynard K. Hine edited the *Journal of Periodontology*. Besides these scholarly services, members of the dental faculty were elected to national offices in their various specialized organizations, with Dean Hine serving as president of the American Dental Association.

Despite advances made in the School of Dentistry in the past three decades, there still remained the handicaps of retaining the staff and a lack of adequate training space. Like the doctors, the dentists were hard pressed for quarters and clinical facilities in which to handle additional students or to expand the curriculum. Freshmen admissions topped off at 100, and graduates at 124. Thirteen of the latter came from abroad. There still was not room for full representation from all of the Indiana counties. The dental hygiene and trained assistants programs had been eminently successful. In fact, these latter services had succeeded far beyond original expectations. By 1968 it was impossible to fill demands for trained auxiliary personnel. The central or core faculty seems to have remained faithful by staying in Indianapolis, but otherwise there were phenomenal numbers of annual changes in instructional personnel. During the academic year, 1967–68, thirty-three staff members resigned, and sixteen new ones were employed. The records are unclear as to whether persons resigning were in fact temporary appointees or full-rank instructors in line for possible promotions and tenure.

An expansion and modernization of the dental curriculum took place in the years of the Stahr Administration. The Department of Preventive Dentistry was expanded and reorganized as the Preventive Dentistry Research Institute under the direction of Dr. Joseph C. Muhler. This modernization was made possible upon the completion of the 20,000-square-foot Preventive Dentistry Research Building. Occupation of the new quarters represented a long step indeed from the day when the director was gathering up a collection of grimy bottles of fluorides in the metallurgical chemistry laboratories in Bloomington. The past two decades of research and teaching had all but wrought a complete revolution in the field of preventive dentistry. Muhler and his colleagues continued their fight against dental caries. They sought to discover materials and techniques that would enable patients to self-administer treatments to control tooth decay. In 1968 they introduced a promising new form of stannous fluoride (zirconium silicate paste). To carry on their researches in this area the preventive dental scientists received approximately a half million dollars in new support. At the same time Dean Hine and his colleagues, in the area of periodontic research, spent a quarter of a million dollars on their projects.

Individual faculty members of the School of Dentistry received international recognition of both their teaching and research, Dr. William G. Shafer was appointed to the International Reference Center for the Histopathology of Odontogenic Tumors, a branch of the World Health Organization. At the same time he was asked to organize the International Reference Center for the Histopathology of Oral Precancerous Lesions. His colleague Dr.

Ralph W. Phillips served as president of the International Association for Dental Research. Dean Hine also served as president of this body.

No other division of Indiana University had reflected more clearly the rapid transition from a narrow past of proprietary control to the status of a professional academic school offering such widely recognized training in both undergraduate and graduate areas. Under the leadership of two highly competent deans after 1940, dentistry came to be a strong branch of Indiana University's offerings in the fields of the human life sciences. The School of Dentistry in its long private and public history reflected the rise in scientific consideration of an ancient art in the treatment of a basic human affliction.

Above all, however, was the development of teaching and research programs that demonstrated that oral medicine and hygiene had far broader physiological implications for general human welfare than scientists prior to 1925 had conceived. Broad findings by the Indiana scientists in the areas of diet and dental health alone helped to characterize the first three quarters of the twentieth century as one of major progress. Use of stannous fluoride to lessen the incidence of dental caries alleviated an incalculable amount of human suffering and loss of manpower energy. The fluoridization of public water supplies perhaps has had as much scientific significance as any general public health measure in history. Strangely, the established preventive measure touched off one of the most furious social debates of the age of modern science. Surely, the conclusion of this argument will someday come to be regarded as the surrender of the last great stronghold of superstition, folk ignorance, and fear. No scientist in a Bloomington laboratory in 1945 could possibly have apprehended the fears that so elementary an application of his findings would generate. Least of all he could not have anticipated the curious kind of socio-folk illogic that associated fluoridization of public water systems with alien political philosophies and international threats to a vast free body politic. Ironically, fluoridization was opposed in Bloomington by John Billman, a chemistry professor, William Dellenback, photographer for the Institute for Sex Research, and Dr. Hugh Ramsey, a local physician.

As impressive as it may have been to legislators, trustees, and the public for the university administrators to present the accomplishments of the School of Dentistry in terms of the ratio of Indiana population to practicing dentists, or in terms of enrollment and graduates, there was a more vital gauge of accomplishments. This was the degree to which the university in the space of three decades elevated to professional status a struggling proprietary school. Major research findings and the institution of continuing educational programs for established practitioners of oral medicine were achievements of broad human significance.

[XVII]

"And Bring All Heav'n Before Mine Eyes"

THE FACULTY and administration had long conceived one of the major functions of Indiana University to be the nurturing of the cultural arts. Almost from the opening of the first classroom door in the institution there was recognition that oratory, music, and acting had definite places in campus life. Even when the university was hard pressed in earlier years to meet its financial obligations the joint university-town Lecture and Art Association was successful in bringing to Bloomington remarkably varied programs of extraordinarily good quality. An index of these programs for more than a century reveals the appearance of far more sophisticated talent than might have been expected of a struggling public university in an intensively rural state. That William Lowe Bryan during much of his administration spent so much energy and time in a search for an able professor of music reflected a high degree of artistic dedication.

There was not so much administrative enthusiasm, however, for the theatrical arts as for other forms of expression. Bryan took a characteristic puritanical attitude toward the theater. To him, except in its most classic moods, acting was both superficial and unreal, if it did not in fact overstep the bounds of human probity. Lee Norvelle has said, "He had some interest in the classics. He liked Shakespeare; he liked Ibsen's plays. But the whole idea of the theater was rather hard on him because he was a deeply religious man, and there was still this business of the devil being in charge."

Most of rural Indiana no doubt shared many of President Bryan's views. The great majority of the people had no more concept of the place of the theater in society than that gathered from occasional appearances of roving stock companies which visited the county seat "opera houses." In Bloomington the Harris-Grand Theater was a popular stopping place for these "strolling companies" that visited the Middle West. Bloomington, however, was off limits to the rowdier burlesque companies. University administrators and townsmen both ruled against them.

As far as the university itself was concerned, there were little or no teaching facilities for the theatrical arts. Mitchell Hall was as inadequate for staging plays—any kind of plays—as it was for musical recitations. Lee Norvelle fitted up a 12 x 17-foot stage on the top floor of Kirkwood Hall, using temporary posts wired in place, and covered with monk's cloth; this was only the slightest gesture toward staging. The jerry-built stage in old Assembly Hall, despite the fact it had served a host of acting troupes, was seldom available, and was always inadequate.

After Lee Norvelle had nagged Ward G. Biddle about the university making better housing provisions for the theatrical arts, the administration proposed to purchase the 600-seat Ritz (later, the Von Lee) movie palace a half block off the campus facing on Kirkwood Avenue. Norvelle refused this proposal because he reasoned its purchase would prevent the location on the campus of a modern theater. With this, the campus actors and their instructors were left to cool their heels for almost a decade.

Even with the almost nonexistent physical facilities, there were also several student amateur theatrical organizations, chief of which was the famous Jordan River Revue. This popular informal student event had largely disintegrated after 1935. It was reorganized in 1938, stimulated largely by an invitation for students to participate in the Pontiac Hour on the National Broadcasting Company's national broadcast in November of that year. The Revue selected *Springtime for Henry*, a play which the *Daily Student* editor called "low-minded situation humor." Another theatrical production by students, *A Glimpse of Hollywood*, was given by the women's honorary organizations; this consisted largely of imitations of currently popular Hollywood actors and actresses.

Already the long struggle by the School of Music to escape the confines of Mitchell Hall to a modern music building was over. Completion of the Music Building in 1939 made available chaste Recital Hall which was designed for the presentation of both local musical recitals, and the more complex professional programs that were brought to the campus by the university and city music series.

Despite a lack of staging facilities, there appeared in Bloomington during the decade, 1932–42, an impressive number of individual artists and musical companies. These included Fritz Kreisler, Sergei Rachmaninoff, Gladys Swarthout, David Rubinoff, the Calumet Symphony Orchestra, the Indianapolis Symphony Orchestra, and the Ted Shawn Troupe. A veritable army of lecturers appeared in both Assembly Hall and the Alumni Hall auditorium in the Memorial Union. Every current subject that disturbed the American mind in this period was discussed by an outside speaker. There came in time William F. Ogburn, the sociologist, Father Edward J. Flanagan, president of Notre Dame University, James Bisset Pratt, Sir Hubert Ames, Paul H. Douglas, Max Lerner, and Erwin D. Canham. The university still held weekly convocations and many times faculty members joined the procession of outside speakers to keep students informed of the world about them. By 1937 there was no auditorium on the campus with the possible exception of the Men's Gymnasium, of sufficient size to gather more than a quarter of the students into an assembly, to say nothing of accommodating the public that traditionally attended university programs.

While not all of Indiana University's public assemblies took place in the outmoded Assembly Hall, enough of them did to give the university a feeling of inferiority so far as its aesthetic image was concerned. Wilbur B. Cogshall, editor in chief of the *Indiana Daily Student*, wrote as early as 1922 of "frenzied, desperate souls arriving hours before time of a performance to be on hand when the doors opened so they could get seats." He termed the spectacle of 3,000 people milling about the doors trying to force their way into a hall seating only 1,200 people a disgusting and disheartening sight. Once inside the audience was seated on slatbacked movable chairs, which rattled and growled as people shifted positions over the rough wooden floor trying to get out from behind numerous obstructing posts which supported the gallery. Not infrequently a chair collapsed, leaving a dazed if not injured patron sprawled on the floor. The floor was on a level with the stage, and spectators in backrows had great difficulty seeing what was going on. The editor said necks grew stiff in the extended periods of craning them. Ventilation was poor. In summer heat was punishment, and in winter aged radiators hissed and sputtered making indelicate thuds and screeches at inappropriate moments in speeches and plays.

In 1938 when the School of Music moved into its fine new building facing Third Street, the time had come when some positive decision had to be made concerning the theater and the convocations, and the restoration of injured pride from long years of tolerating inadequate public assembly space. In fact the administration and trustees had reached this point of decision as early as December 2, 1914, when they listed six new buildings which they thought necessary to serve adequately the growing institution's needs. Among these was an auditorium. Again in 1916, and at the outset of United States involvement in World War I, a large auditorium was listed as the primary need of the university.

When President William Lowe Bryan reported to the Board of Trustees in 1921 an alumni desire to start a memorial fund drive to raise a million dollars, he made the assumption that the Memorial Union Building would also contain a large auditorium. W. A. Alexander on October 24, 1921, described such a prospective facility to the trustees. He was supported in this by John W. Cravens, who said, "The need of an auditorium to seat three or four thousand people is very urgent. . . . Our present Assembly Hall looks like an immense barn with a rectangular silo attached. The choicest of Indiana's sons and daughters should no longer be compelled to occupy this building. They should have the inspiration that would come from a building in keeping with the great state of Indiana."

Cravens, the registrar, was no doubt earnest in his comments about a graceful auditorium promising to be an inspirational symbol of state culture, but he was also concerned about the fate of the ancient campus practice of herding the entire student body into chapel to receive some intellectual inspiration and a lot of religious instruction. Doggedly the university, like most of its fellow state universities, held onto this outmoded type of campus assembly down into the 1930s, even making regular provisions for chapel meetings in the daily class schedule. This was done despite the fact the student enrollment had expanded beyond any reasonable expectation of being seated.

After at least three decades of frustrated plans for improving the campus Assembly Hall, and plans were made for the three memorial structures in the late 1920s, it was decided to include in the Memorial Union only a small theater type of auditorium, and to seek additional funds from public sources to construct a building devoted solely to auditorium and theatrical use. It was not until May 1937, however, that the dream was actually turned into a concrete plan for its construction. A. M. Strauss, a Fort Wayne architect, prepared a preliminary floor plan for a building which would seat 4,300 people and presented it to the Board of Trustees on March 16, 1937. President Herman B Wells was instructed by the trustees to seek funds from the Indiana Bonding Authority, and on September 9, 1938, that agency granted the university $495,000. The Indiana General Assembly in special session appropriated $300,000 more, and authorized a bond issue of $305,000, making in all $1,000,000, a rather tidy sum at a moment when both labor and building materials were rather plentiful, and at the lowest cost since 1920.

Securing funds with which to build a luxurious auditorium on the Indiana campus was not quite so simple as the above paragraphs make it appear. Federal funds under some strange bureaucratic aberration could not be used to construct an auditorium or theater as such; they could, however, be applied to the building of a "hall of music." Somewhat ironically, Purdue University found itself in a common predicament with Indiana. Its Fowler Hall was an almost blood sister in both basic design and proposed general use. Purdue perhaps had a greater practical need for a larger seating capacity auditorium than Indiana. That university gave short courses and public lectures to thousands of people each year. Because of a lack of a large assembly hall these programs had to be repeated, some of them several times and at great expense and wear on the staff. This was particularly true of the summer programs for youthful farmers. By contrast, Indiana

University wanted a place to hold campus convocations, public lectures, and musical and theater productions. Indiana regarded its prospective auditorium as a center of liberal arts culture rather than as an informal instructional facility. Specific purposes, however, did not necessarily enter into the awarding of funds by the Public Works Administration.

Purdue received a grant of $495,000, and got from the Indiana Assembly the same appropriation and bonding authorization. That university chose to construct Elliott Hall, which would seat more than 6,500 persons. It was said President Elliott learned that by rearranging some of the radiator locations the Purdue hall could be made to seat more people than the Radio City Music Hall. This was done at the cost of other facilities. The stage in Elliott Hall was of band platform proportions, permitting the freest possible use for seating purposes on the floor.

Indiana University sought to make its "hall of music" the basic structure for what university planners and dreamers believed in time would become the hub of a huge cultural quadrangle. Because of this, it differed from the Purdue auditorium in three or four fundamental aspects. Floor plans included a large auditorium with a seating capacity for 3,738 persons. There was to be a vast operatic and theatrical stage with elaborate modern staging equipment and dressing rooms. In one corner of the building were located the offices and some classrooms for the speech and drama department. In the other quarter was the University Theatre, which seated 500 persons and shared a common stage with the main auditorium. Considerable space in the front of the building was devoted to a wide murals hall and a secondary entrance foyer.

In the overall plans of the new building Indiana University attempted to express fully three facts from its past. It was definitely turning its back on the somewhat agonizing days when 3,000 persons milled about before the doors of a cramped building in an unseemly scramble to claim 1,200 seats in a pillar-obscured hall. It was also accepting the fact that speech, music, and the performing arts constituted a fundamental part of a liberal arts education in a public university. Finally, there was expressed almost immediately a dream to bring to the campus the most sophisticated forms of musical and dramatic expression—grand opera. If this could be done, it would indeed be a fabulous erasure of the struggling cultural past. Ward G. Biddle had a genuine interest in music, and apparently was wholly uninhibited in what he believed could be accomplished at Indiana Unversity in this field. Fortunately he had the support of President Herman B Wells, who brought about some swift and decisive action in both financing and planning. The *Daily Student* quoted him as saying, "enough was enough. I. U. must have an adequate auditorium to improve its cultural offerings." In his inaugural address Wells had promised to take the university to the people of Indiana wherever they were to be found. The Auditorium promised to be one of the surest means by which the greatest number of people could be reached with sustained programs in theater, music, and discussion of public issues.

On December 4, 1938, ground was broken for the new building, and on January 25, 1941, the *Indianapolis Star* announced the Auditorium would be ready for dedication by March. The builders, Henke Construction Company of Chicago, almost accomplished a miracle in constructing such a complicated hall in so short a time. It is said that the first excavating firm made such a low depression-era bid, in which it did not take into consideration the fact that it might strike solid limestone near the surface of the ground, that it went bankrupt. Not only was the overall outside mass a challenging undertaking, but the construction of the modern theatrical interior was one of the most complicated tasks of any academic building in the country. Despite the fact William Lowe Bryan had attempted to organize a school of architecture, and Purdue had maintained an extensive engineering program from its founding, there was, in 1940, no school of architecture in Indiana. It was necessary for Indiana University to employ Professor F. R. Watson of the University of Illinois to supervise a part of the construction of the Auditorium. It was he who had responsibility for achieving satisfactory acoustical effects. The dedication ceremonies took place on schedule, March 22–26, when Governor Henry F. Schricker formally presented the Auditorium to the university community.

Hoosiers could say with justifiable pride that the building was a fine one. Albert Strauss and Eggers and Higgins, New York architects, not only designed a structure that would serve three functional purposes, they drew its three parts together into a tight unity that fitted well into its physical setting on one of the main campus divides. Professor Watson had achieved good acoustical results except for one or two spots. Lee Simonson, consulting stage designer, helped to place a huge mechanically operated staging and scenery facility in the vast hall while maintaining a sweeping harmony of rising orchestra and balcony seating. John Republic, the interior decorator, further tied the interior foyers, aisles, galleries, and body of the Auditorium into a high degree of easy intimacy for so large a hall.

In the great entry foyer, or hall of murals, the Thomas Hart Benton paintings were impressively displayed on the four overhead walls. These represent the people of Indiana in a multiplicity of historical poses and everyday activities and professions. They were prepared for the State to be displayed in the Indiana exhibit in the Century of Progress World's Fair in Chicago in 1933. When the Chicago fair closed and the Indiana Building was dismantled, the murals were shipped to Indianapolis and stored in the cowbarn on the state fairgrounds with no one having a clear notion how they might be displayed to a proper advantage in the future. When they were given to Indiana University, the architects and interior decorator planned space for all but four of the smaller ones, which had already been mounted in the Business and Economics Building auditorium.

Thomas Hart Benton came to Bloomington and worked for several weeks retouching the murals and fitting them into the broad panels that the architects had designed for them around the wide front entry foyer. In this way a precious exhibit of massive American genre art was preserved in a highly dignified setting. The subjects of the murals are purely Hoosier, and so are the portrayals of the state's activities. Some of the faces are those of Indiana University personalities, including William Lowe Bryan and Paul Vories McNutt. Also represented among the faces are James Whitcomb Riley and Thomas Hart Benton himself.

A humorous commotion developed between Benton and the interior decorator of the entry hall of murals. John Republic broke the blank spaces across each end by mounting a pair of Grecian urns atop fairly tall pilasters. When Benton first viewed his workaday and folksy paintings through this vista of ancient classicism he was taken aback, but not for long. He exclaimed in lusty Bentonian fashion, "Who placed those goddamned spittoons in the way?" This led to a stubborn testing of wills, and today the panorama of folksy industrial and professional Indiana is still viewed through the perspective of the symbols of the ancient world.

Building, stages, murals, Grecian urns, all were ready for public viewing in five grand days of joyous dedication in March 1941. Like a voice echoing from the far-distant past, William Lowe Bryan looked upon the great structure with Hebraic-focused eyes, and, no doubt with grating memories of rattling slat-bottomed chairs, rough floor boards, and cramped space, told a *Daily Student* reporter, "It is with our Hall of Music as with every first-rate thing that men do—it is old and new. Builders of genius in Egypt, Babylon, Athens, Canterbury were present within the man who conceived this new home of beauty." Another veteran out of the grim past, Guido H. Stempel, said, "The new Auditorium stands as a monument of importance in higher education of the expressive arts in general. The next step is the installation of an organ like the one in the Music Shed at Tanglewood in the Berkshire Hills."

On the evening of March 22, 1941, a proud procession marched on the new building as if it were a conquering horde approaching an impregnable citadel. The band boomed out the triumphant strains of Wagner's *Tannhäuser*. In that procession was the tall, white-haired Henry F. Schricker, Governor of the State, who had come to present the $1,170,000 Auditorium to the campus community and to the people of Indiana. Walter A. Jessup, long-time friend of Indiana University, advisor to Wells, and president of the Carnegie Foundation, spoke on the subject of "The University and the Larger Life." This was the premise on which the Auditorium was conceived and built.

After the formal dedicatory ceremonies the public was invited to tour the building on the following Sunday. Bishop James E. Freeman of the Washington Cathedral delivered the sermon dedicating the great structure to the glory of God, and the University Glee Club and Symphony Orchestra gave a concert. Then came the highlight of the five-day program when Alfred Lunt and Lynn Fontanne dedicated the theater and stage with Robert Sherwood's Pulitzer prize-winning play, *There Shall Be No Night*.

On Tuesday night the building was given a distinct musical dedication when Lotte Lehmann and Lauritz Melchior of the

Metropolitan Opera Company gave a concert. The programs were closed with a concert by the Indianapolis Symphony Orchestra directed by Fabien Sevitzky.

Herman B Wells, ever a man to enjoy a glorious moment, viewed the dedication of the Auditorium as a glorious affair in which Indiana University itself was celebrating a new advance in assuming cultural responsibilities. He told the people of Indiana the completion of the Auditorium was indeed a great dream come true. Its dedication came at the proper time when midterm examinations were ended, and he hoped students would sense the importance of the moment and enjoy a happy week of community celebration. He looked upon the completion of the Auditorium in much more durable terms than those expressed in ceremonial oratory. He felt it was truly the beginning of the fulfillment of a special university obligation to light a spark of creativity in Hoosier youth.

There was reason for rejoicing on March 27, when the crowds of visitors had gone home. Generally, the building had stood the rather intensive tests of performance and had proved satisfactory. Some dead acoustical spots were detected that had to be enlivened, and there were other adjustments that were necessary. A careful record was made of all of the discernible weaknesses of the structure that turned up during the week of dedication. In an oral interview in 1973 Harold Jordan said that generally the huge building functioned very well indeed. The Lunts, after a tour in the afternoon before their performance, said, "It is the finest theater we ever played in." Ward G. Biddle said on March 29 that the dedicatory program had been planned largely to test the Auditorium in every possible phase of its future use, and he expressed the opinion that "As a whole the building was in almost perfect condition, but no building of its size could possibly operate in the beginning without some adjustments." Biddle then expressed the hope that the dedicatory ceremonies would be but the beginning of the university's presentation of the best in the performing arts, including lecturers, for the benefit of all of the people of Indiana. He had reason to believe his wish would be fulfilled, because the first month the Auditorium was open its programs drew 37,476 patrons.

Biddle touched on the single most important element of uncertainty about the practicality of the Auditorium and that was its overwhelming size in both staging and main hall. An example of the fear of size was Katharine Cornell's refusal to play in a theater that seated more than 1,500 people. It took several years of negotiating on the part of Indiana University to persuade her to appear in the Auditorium. In December 1952 she appeared in Somerset Maugham's *The Constant Wife*. At the intermission she told Harold Jordan, "I am embarrassed with this simple little play I am doing tonight when I could have a few years back brought you my great performances of Joan d'Arc and others." She was back two years later and her contract still stipulated "no house over 1,500 except Indiana University."

The Auditorium quickly became a symbol not only of the university's cultural and intellectual dedication, but a significant business enterprise as well. It was necessary for the institution to recover a good part of the construction cost of the building, and also to cover the heavy operating and maintenance investments. Immediately the university administration devised a scale of rentals. A dividing curtain could be drawn to form a small seating area of 1,004 seats, and this could be rented for use of smaller audiences. It was not from the rental sources of campus use, however, that the university was to earn the necessary funds to justify its lavish expenditures on the building. With this objective in mind a rather heavy investment was made in staging space and mechanisms. In 1941 the combined auditorium and theater stages constituted one of the largest and most modern facilities of its kind.

Both the Auditorium and its internal mechanism had their first real tests on April 23 and 24, 1941, when the San Carlo Opera Company presented Bizet's *Carmen* sung by Madame Coe Glade, and *Madame Butterfly* in which Hizi Koyte sang the leading part of Cho-Cho-San. More than 3,000 persons attended each of these performances, and the Auditorium proved even more satisfactory than at the dedicatory performances a month before.

Guido H. Stempel expressed the desire to see a great organ installed in the building when a reporter interviewed him in 1941. This was a significant lack, which seems to have had no real explanation beyond heavy costs for such an installation. This condition was not to be remedied until 1948, when the famous Roosevelt Organ of the old Chicago Auditorium was rebuilt and installed in Bloomington. William H. Barnes, organ architect and recitalist, bought the historic organ at public auction and restored it. He gave it to Indiana University, and it was played for the first time May 13, 1948, by Virgil Fox, concert organist and minister of music in the New York Riverside Church. Fox's recital took place before 700 pipe organists who had come to Bloomington by special invitation as guests of the university.

There was no limit to Hoosier ambition. Now with a big auditorium with a "forty-acre" combination stage, university officials seemed determinded to erase the memory of past limitations by staging on the campus the grandest sort of theatrical and musical productions. A campaign was begun at the outset in 1941 to get professional plays and grand opera by the best companies to come to the Auditorium. The Metropolitan Opera Company made annual tours to Chicago, Boston, Cleveland, and Atlanta, but it had never considered the remote possibility that it might appear in a small university town. Ward G. Biddle, a serious music lover, had the support of President Wells, and, maybe, the reluctant support of the Board of Trustees. Biddle and Lee Norvelle, chairman of the Department of Speech and Drama, began both correspondence and visits with Edward Johnson, manager of the Metropolitan Opera Company. Johnson argued there was no college facility in America sufficiently well equipped to accommodate the Metropolitan. The Hoosiers brought out their blueprints, and Johnson replied, "Well, yes, physically you're set up so we could do it, but you can't afford it." He said the cost would be $13,500 in immediate post-depression cash "on the barrel head." Biddle and Norvelle figured they could sell $9,000 worth of seats, and could underwrite the remaining $4,500. The Board of Trustees agreed to supply $3,000, and the remainder had to be derived from either sales or private donations. This optimism assured the appearance of the Metropolitan Opera.

Since Indiana University was now involved in the all but staggering Metropolitan Opera venture, Biddle and Norvelle asked that the company produce the most demanding opera possible. The choice was *Aïda.* The opera company agreed to come, and not to book another engagement within a radius of 200 miles of Bloomington. This cut out Chicago, Cincinnati, St. Louis, Louisville, and Columbus. In order to accommodate the staging demands of *Aïda*, the university modified the joint theater and auditorium stages, and built a curved wall to make the triumphant march, which started on the theater stage, visible from the outset to four-fifths of the audience. Johnson continued to remain doubtful up to the point where the triumphant march began, but once it was underway he commented, "Well, I will say one thing, gentlemen. This is the most effective triumphant march we've ever been able to stage with *Aïda*, because the physical plant is excellent."

After the highly successful performance of *Aïda*, Edward Johnson told Ward G. Biddle, "The Metropolitan likes Indiana University, and Bloomington. So we are not saying 'goodbye' but only '*au revoir.*' " He said the impending war and other events would determine the Metropolitan's future planning of annual tours, "but when we again leave New York, Indiana University need only beckon."

This first operatic visitation drew patronage from Chicago, St. Louis, Louisville, and Cincinnati. The Auditorium was filled from the top-price front orchestra seats to the fifty-cent balcony student seats, and when the accounts were finally settled the university had netted a profit of $380. Indiana, however, had to relent in one case in its 200-mile contract restriction. Purdue University with its large Elliott Hall felt it, too, should have the right to seek a contract with the Metropolitan Opera Company. A compromise was reached in which Indiana University would have the privilege of selecting two operas from the Metropolitan's seasonal repertoire, and Purdue would select one. Purdue was successful in selling enough tickets to pay the cost of the performance and now the state of Indiana supported two appearances of the Metropolitan.

The reaction of individual performers, whether they came as single attractions or as leading men and women in group performances, was good. There followed on the heels of the first appearance of the Metropolitan Opera a veritable parade of American and foreign musical and theatrical talent. The index of auditorium programs virtually outlines the progress of the performing arts in America. In subsequent years the university never had an individual invitation refused. Also, the School of Music sought successfully the instructional services of individual performers and singers, some of whom were phasing out their operatic careers. One of the first of these performer-instructors was the highly esteemed Madame Dorothea Manski.

The Metropolitan Opera Company of 300 arrived early in the morning of April 12, 1942, by the Monon. The Graham Hotel on the square in Bloomington was accustomed to its drummer patrons arriving by taxi loads, and its management had never thought in terms of accommodating two trainloads of sophisticated New York musicians. In fact, it was out of the question. Orchestra and ballet personnel were housed in dormitory rooms in Rogers I, and alongside student neighbors. The management and a few of the stars occupied the twenty-eight lodging rooms of the Memorial Union.

Housing most of the opera personnel in dormitory rooms helped to break the barriers of stiff formality. This was demonstrated in 1947 when the residents of Rogers II serenaded the opera singers with the Indiana loyalty song. The opera singers sang back to them. The second night students packed the Rogers dining hall where the Metropolitan cast gave an impromptu program, most of which was sheer and relaxed buffoonery. The singers had hurriedly removed greasepaint and makeup and run through the rain to join in the celebration. This now became an annual affair. The "antics" party of 1949 was switched to the new Men's Quadrangle, where it was said more than 1,500 persons were in attendance, including President Herman B Wells, one of the first to arrive. At one of these frolics the opera cast remained up almost all night, before it was scheduled to catch an early morning train to Minneapolis.

Later appearances of the Metropolitan Opera Company in Bloomington not only caused serious housing problems, but in each succeeding year expenses were greater while patronage tended to level off. On May 28, 1956, E. Ross Bartley wrote Harold W. Jordan that if the company were to continue its annual Bloomington visitations some more ingenious way of selling tickets had to be devised. "In publicity and advertising," Bartley said, "it would seem we have reached a saturation point. I am not sure—in fact, I think it is unlikely—that more newspaper or billboard advertising would sell any more tickets. In publicity, we have for several years provided all the newspapers will print on the basis of news." He then outlined five steps for increasing sales. Wells suggested that in addition to Bartley's suggestions an intensive sales campaign be conducted among the students.

Bartley's worries were largely groundless, for the moment

at least. The Metropolitan Opera Association, under the management of Rudolf Bing, informed Indiana University in July 1956, that it would cancel its contract for future appearances. Bing said the cancellation was necessary because of points of disagreement between the management and the American Guild of Musical Artists, which represented the Metropolitan singers and ballet dancers. At that moment the opera company needed to borrow $500,000 to prepare for the next season, and it could not do so until it had settled its contract disputes. There is a serious hiatus in the history of Indiana University–Metropolitan Opera Company relations. Somehow the management-guild dispute was settled, and the company came back to Bloomington on May 20, 1957, when it gave Offenbach's *La Périchole* and Verdi's *La Traviata.* A year and a half later, December 18 and 19, 1959, it returned for the sixteenth time and presented Verdi's *Il Trovatore* and Mozart's *The Marriage of Figaro.* On its eighteenth and final visit, in May 1961, the Metropolitan Opera Company concluded its long and happy association with Indiana University by presenting Friedrich von Flotow's *Martha.*

When Edward Johnson was succeeded by Rudolf Bing as manager of the Metropolitan Opera Company, there was perhaps some fear that he might not prove so amicable toward the annual tour, and toward the Indiana Auditorium and its staging facilities. This fear, however, was dispelled when Bing, in an interview with a *New York Times* reporter, spoke most favorably of both the tour and the two Indiana universities. He told the reporter, "Stages throughout the country, with some notable exceptions like the new auditoriums at Indiana and Purdue universities, are not felicitous for opera."

Entertaining the Metropolitan Opera Company over such a long span of years was indeed a herculean undertaking for a public university. There were mixed reactions about this subject on the campus, but some of the university administration felt the appearance of the opera gave Indiana University a new cultural and intellectual image before the academic world. The Metropolitan gave generous publicity to the annual Metropolitan tours. The performances brought many important people to the campus who under other circumstances would have had no reason for visiting Bloomington. Some of these became generous donors in time, making possible the development of many programs for which there were no other sources of funds. For instance, Mr. and Mrs. Ralph Showalter, who had not visited the campus since Mrs. Showalter had graduated, came back for the opera performances, and later bequeathed the university a million dollars. Miss Elsie Sweeney of Columbus, a member of the Metropolitan Opera Board, became a generous patron of the School of Music. The performances and the accompanying interest in music which was stimulated did much not only to attract students, especially in the fields of the performing arts and music, but to bring into the university a highly sophisticated type of student.

The opening of the long Metropolitan series in the formative years of the Wells' administration had a significance of its own. The President was quick to sense the promise of prestige that the auditorium programs would bring to the institution. He wrote Ward G. Biddle, June 12, 1942, expressing the Board of Trustees' appreciation for his management not only of the opera appearance, but of the musical series in general. "May I add," he told Biddle, "my personal word of appreciation to that of the Board of Trustees. You have accomplished much for Indiana University in your years here, but no one thing more important than what you have done through the past semesters in the inauguration of an outstanding Auditorium year. I realize that the amazing success in the use of the Auditorium this year has reflected credit upon this administration, and I want you to know that I feel that success is due almost entirely to your own vision, and your promotional and managerial skill."

In an even more tangible way the era after 1941 was to see a sharp break in the traditional social and cultural isolation of Bloomington. The tours of the Metropolitan Opera Company revealed that rural Americans could be as culturally responsive as their metropolitan neighbors. They successfully combined an appreciation of the opera with a friendly informality, which was certainly a wholesome experience for the artistic community itself. No doubt the Indiana University audiences made favorable impressions on visiting artists. Ralph Helpmann, choreographer and player in the Old Vic production of *Midsummer Night's Dream*, said in October 1954, "It's wonderful to find a place where the people are so interested in drama. I'm surprised and pleased to find that your university has so many fine shows scheduled from outside the university. Your university must be quite a cultural center." His colleague Peter Johnson, playing the role of Philostrate, confirmed this observation and flattered the university by saying he found the Auditorium a more attractive place to play than the Metropolitan Opera House in New York. He liked especially the acoustics, the fan shape of the great hall, and the rising rows of seats.

In 1958–59 the School of Music announced a program of seven operas of its own production. These were presented in the Auditorium and in the cavernous and temporary East Hall. The first seven operas included Puccini's *Madame Butterfly*, Mozart's *Don Giovanni*, Wagner's *Parsifal*, and Prokofiev's *The Love for Three Oranges*. Wagner's *Parsifal* became an Indiana University tour de force. This entire opera was given in English first on Palm Sunday in 1948, and was repeated fourteen times by 1962, playing in these years before more than 40,000 persons.

There was on the campus even before 1941 a fairly extensive interest in opera. Individual opera singers had appeared from time to time in Assembly Hall, and Dean Winfred Merrill and his staff had produced several abbreviated versions of the more popular operas, sometimes doing little more than singing the musical numbers. When Dean Wilfred Bain came to Bloomington in 1947 he and the School of Music staff developed a sophisticated instructional and performance program on this traditional foundation.

Annually, the Auditorium management presented the "Auditorium Series." Scheduled for 1941–42 were fifteen attractions, some of which were Rossini's *Barber of Seville*, Marian Anderson, the Ballet Russe, the Don Cossack Chorus, José Iturbi, William Lyons Phelps, Clarence Day's *Life with Father*, and the second showing of William Saroyan's full length script, *Jim Dandy*.

There was little if any evidence that the musical and threatrical programs were seriously curtailed by war emergencies, 1941–45. In 1945 the Don Cossack Chorus overcame travel handicaps to appear in Bloomington. So did Sigmund Romberg's Orchestra and eight other performing groups. Annually, Lee Norvelle announced full theatrical programs, some of which involved extensive travel. The 1944 Auditorium Series was especially full with several large groups included. It was necessary to maintain a generous flow of popular programs in order to meet the self-liquidating obligations on the building bonds. Only one serious cancellation occurred and that was the Metropolitan Opera on March 1, 1945, because it was unable to reserve the necessary passenger train space to move the numerous company. Nevertheless, all the $12 and $14 tickets for that year were sold before October. Ticket sales in the immediate postwar months ran 32 per cent above the previous year's sales.

Ward G. Biddle wrote President Herman B Wells and members of the Board of Trustees on November 27, 1945, that he had been able to form a new contract with the Metropolitan Opera Company for the following spring. He said he had done this despite the fact "there was a nameless party [Purdue] who probably wants the Met."

During the decades, 1942–62, almost every major musical and theatrical personality in the United States and the touring troupes from abroad appeared either in the Theater or the Auditorium Series. This campus cultural center became a popular and "must" stop on the great American concert and theatrical circuit. Maybe more significantly Bloomington became an important point of contact with the larger world of culture between a large semirural Middle Western population and the sophisticated metropolitan world of arts. It is doubtful that many American university auditoriums and theater combinations fulfilled much more completely the charter mandates of their institutions to perform public services as well as instructional functions.

Even without the glamor and festive excitement that accompanied the Metropolitan Opera Company visitations, many of the other auditorium and theater programs gave distinct prestige to campus patronage of the arts. For instance, Maurice Evans played *Hamlet* on March 3, 1947, in an unusually fine presentation. That same month Lauritz Melchior, however, disappointed 3,000 patrons when his plane was grounded in Chicago because of a blinding hail-snow storm. He hired a Chicago chauffeur and instructed him to drive to Bloomington. At 7:00 P.M. he called Harold Jordan to say that he could not locate the Auditorium. He was near Bloomington, Illinois. The Dane's car was ditched on the icy road, and so was the wrecker trying to rescue it. The great tenor spent the night with a lodge brother of the local police commissioner. It was necessary to reschedule Melchior's appearance, and his manager, James A. Davidson, told reporters, "Mr. Melchior will be here if he has to walk."

For the student body and the university community in general the Auditorium seemed to be both a place to hold convocations and a public forum in which the problems of the postwar world could be discussed. Although it was never possible at any time of peak enrollment to get more than a seventh part of the entire student community into the building for a special program, its ready availability to campus groups placed it at the disposal of the entire student body. Occasionally the structure was put to a use that accommodated almost unlimited numbers of people without seating them. In April 1948 there was displayed in the foyers a selected collection of old masters from the Metropolitan Museum of Art. This collection, said the *Daily Student*, was valued at $1,350,000, $80,000 more than the building itself had cost.

Annually after 1941 President Wells reported to the Board of Trustees on the use of the Auditorium almost as if to justify its construction. During the first seven years of its existence it was used 596 times for major public events accommodating approximately a half million people. By 1961 there were 240 annual events with an attendance of 254,343 admission-paying patrons.

Not all of the impact of the Auditorium was felt immediately within the walls of the building. The enthusiasm generated by the annual programs plus those of Lee Norvelle and his staff led directly to the development of two interesting off-campus experiments. The Department of Speech and Theatre during the summer of 1949 opened the Brown County Theater in A. J. Rogers' Strawhat Theater in the resort-rural escape town of Nashville. Rogers had operated a theatrical program there, and at the same time had been a generous patron of university productions. The first season was so successful that the Brown County summer program seemed assured of a happy future.

A second off-campus theatrical venture had the genuine tug of nostalgic riverbank America. Herman B Wells discovered that Hiram College would possibly sell its showboat *Majestic* and its accompanying tug, then tied up at Point Pleasant, West Virginia. The boat, said Jeffrey Auer, the new chairman of the Department of Speech and Theatre, would be bought with private funds and operated by students and departmental staff members. After a visit to Point Pleasant by Lee Norvelle and Joseph A. Franklin, the purchase was made, and the boat ended its first season under the university flag in September 1960. Professor William E.

Kinzer directed the company in traditional riverboat melodramas which included *Ten Nights in a Bar Room*, *In Old Kentucky*, and *The Taming of the Shrew*. In 1961 a season was planned that took the floating troupe to thirty rivertowns between Cincinnati and Shawneetown, Illinois. The third tour was begun in June 1962 and offered *Rip Van Winkle* as its main play. The *Daily Student* boasted that the *Majestic* "is operating under the ownership of Indiana University and is the only remaining American river showboat making one-night stands. . . ." This venture added a good dash of color to Indiana University, which was bursting its seams in almost every phase of endeavor after 1945.

No one thing in the years of feverish institutional expansion did more to break the traditional restrictions of the university's self-consciousness of its geographical isolation and provinciality than did the building of the huge semi-Gothic Auditorium, and the support of vital musical and theatrical programs. Clearly 1941 was the year in which Indiana University actually assumed a new role of artistic refinement and sophistication dedicated to the cultivation of the finer sensibilites of its entire state constituency.

[XVIII]

"In Service High, and Anthems Clear"

ESTABLISHING A first-rate music school on the Indiana University campus was an unending challenge to William Lowe Bryan and Herman B Wells. Both men were aware that the cultural arts had genuine significance in the curriculum of a public liberal arts university. Beyond this, they no doubt were fully aware that middle America, and the Middle West in particular, was looked upon by sophisticated intellectuals in the East as a "Sahara of the Bozart." To lift this fog of vacuity required both determination and ingenuity. Two long steps in this direction were the completion of the Music Building in 1937 and the construction of the great Auditorium in 1938–41. Creators of these buildings not only hoped to broaden the cultural horizon of the university, but also that of the state of Indiana and the Midwest. By 1941 there existed on the campus ample basic facilities to accommodate an ever-expanding number of students and the musical and theatrical arts in sophisticated general surroundings.

In the nineteen years before his retirement, Dean Winfred Merrill had indeed performed yeoman service, first to the Department and then to the School of Music. No pioneering professor in Indiana University had striven harder to achieve a degree of excellence in his field than did Dean Merrill. In recording his academic background he indicated no formal advanced academic training, but he had studied with Joseph Joachim for three years at the Hochschule für Musik in Berlin, and with Bernhard Ziehn in Chicago. Throughout his life Merrill continued his studies and artistic travels, which was reflected in the music training at Indiana University. Despite the lack of funds to purchase even basic equipment to enable his charges to perform the more complicated forms of musical presentations, he at least pointed to the future when such a thing would be possible. As an example of the elementary handicaps of the Merrill period, the annual production of light opera during the fall semester of 1937 had to be delayed for lack of a suitable curtain in Recital Hall. Undaunted by this handicap, four talented campus musicians were selected to sing in the twentieth recital of the *Messiah* for the Christmas program. These were Douglas D. Nye, Helen Hodges, E. F. Dressler, and Freda Draper.

Curtain or no curtain, the fame of the new Music Building quickly spread abroad. Ernest Bacon, a San Francisco composer, interrupted a recital tour to come to Bloomington to inspect the building. He even enlisted the services of President Herman B Wells to arrange a tour of the building late at night. Bacon said he believed only the Music Building at the University of Wisconsin compared favorably with that in Bloomington for "up-to-dateness."

The Music Building was a sturdy monument to William Lowe Bryan and Winfred Merrill, but equally so it was a landmark to the imagination of the national New Deal agencies. After long years of planning and frustration, but ever hoping to gain a proper setting for the musical arts, Merrill retired in 1938, a cruel fate of the calendar which brought him to the very edge of the golden age of the arts at Indiana. He remained active, however, long enough to see a rising and rather enthusiastic interest in music established among Indiana students. George Blair in the year of the dean's retirement directed successfully a cabaret show. Seldon March, another graduate student, directed a cast of forty members in the *Mikado* as a presentation of the Pro Musica Club in Recital Hall.

Dean Merrill had encouraged such student productions even when much necessary equipment and staging properties were unavailable. He had developed a rather extensive music curriculum, organized administratively the School of Music itself in 1921, and greatly advanced the cause of formal music instruction on the campus. He left behind a good corps of music instructors who were well-oriented toward promoting their field in the public schools of Indiana, and with local music appreciation groups. Merrill's successor had the foundations of a good building and a competent staff on which to build further. Four of his capable colleagues were Ernest Hoffzimmer, Lennart von Zweyberg, Douglas D. Nye, and Winfred Merrill.

The new dean, Robert L. Sanders, a thirty-two-year-old composer from Chicago, came to Bloomington with high promise. He was a graduate of the Bush Conservatory and had a doctorate in musicology from the Chicago Conservatory, had served briefly as an instructor at the University of Chicago, and was for one year an assistant director of the Chicago Civic Opera. During his first year at Indiana he began extensive curricular revision. He abolished the separate harmony and ear training courses and replaced them with integrated sections in these areas. Robert S. Tangeman was employed in the history of music, Ora Hyde and William E. Ross were also employed to teach voice. A rather extensive list of part-time instructors, including the popular Ruby Lane Mosemiller, a faculty wife, were placed in charge of other instrumental work.

An expansion of the music library was begun, and in November 1939 Louise Lyman reported that the collection had been enlarged by the addition of the complete works of George Frederick Handel and the English composer Henry Purcell. In the meantime Dean Sanders' reputation as a composer was enhanced by his receiving the New York Philharmonic Symphony Society award for his *Little Symphony in G*. His *Scenes of Poverty and Toil* was performed by the Chicago, Washington, and Illinois symphonies, and in 1938 the Federal Theater in Chicago presented his ballet *L'Agya*.

Sanders and his colleagues in the School of Music enjoyed advantages that had not been the fortunes of their predecessors. The Works Progress Administration project for the initiation and promotion of musical activities throughout Indiana was given renewed encouragement in September 1940, when President Franklin D. Roosevelt approved an additional grant of $210,810. This appropriation was used largely in the areas of public school music instruction and in the presentation of public musical programs for Hoosier audiences across the state.

In another field the impact of the School of Music was greatly amplified. The year before Indiana University had begun radio broadcasting programs, which included rather generous musical programs. Quickly this media of performance gained wide popularity, and by 1940 the University Studio Ensemble had established a popular reputation. In October of that year the group broadcast its program nationally over a network of a hundred Mutual stations. This performance was recorded and was used in the future in spot broadcasts. Indiana by this time was savoring the exciting experience of broad national exposure, which brought the institution the honor of full-fledged membership in the National Association of Schools of Music.

The new Music Building in 1937 not only boosted morale of students and professors of music, but almost immediately new opportunities were opened to take musical instruction and performance well beyond the door of the traditional classroom and studio recitations. The dual programs of instruction and performance were given leeway that staff members could not have imagined five years earlier, when they were still cooped up in Mitchell Hall. On March 22, 1941, the cause of music on the Indiana campus was given still further encouragement by the addition of a second and central facility. Dedication of the luxurious Auditorium-theater in 1941, scarcely a block away from the Music Building and readily available for extensive use by the three arts—drama, speech, and music—introduced a new era of almost unlimited possibilities to Indiana University. None of the arts received more benefit from this new facility than music. It was now possible to produce physically the most complicated and demanding works composed by any musician in the past. Musical performances of any indoor dimension could be brought to Hoosiers on the university campus after this date, and many of them from the School of Music itself. Performances given by outside professional musicians yielded the invaluable dividend of comparative and demonstrative supplements to classroom teaching.

During the World War II years, 1941–45, the School of Music's activities had to be seriously curtailed because of a lack of performing talent, availability of transportation to move musical groups about the state, materials for creating stage settings, and from competition of other and more urgent campus wartime activities. The university's priorities of necessity had to be in areas that were more directly applicable to the defense of the nation. No sooner had the war with Japan ended, however, than the musical performance programs were revitalized. In the spring of 1945 the School of Music had two productions ready for presentation. In his Annual Report for the first postwar year Dean Sanders wrote, "Although the resources of talent on the campus did not strictly warrant such an ambitious undertaking, the School prepared and gave performances of the opera *Cavalleria Rusticana* and the operetta *Trial by Jury*. The performances were reasonably satisfactory, though they involved considerable compromise with perfection." These compromises, however, were steps far in advance of the gestures of performing only selected parts from the operas in the days when Dean Merrill tried gallantly to elevate the quality of musical taste on the campus.

Following the end of World War II, Indiana University experienced a material increase in all its fields of instruction, but none more so than in student demand for musical education. In less than a decade a building that had seemed so thoroughly adequate in 1937 proved to be too small to accommodate many of the new and ambitious programs. Joseph A. Franklin, university treasurer, announced September 22, 1947, that the Public Works Administration had approved the construction, just northeast of the Music Building, of a frame structure which measured 300 x 125 feet, and would contain a 1,000-seat auditorium, and 60 practice rooms. Like many other buildings springing up about the campus, this one was also a military surplus structure, a redesigned airplane hangar, brought to Bloomington from George Air Force Base at Lawrenceville, Illinois. Nevertheless, the new building, no matter how temporary it seemed to be in 1947, offered blessed release from pressure on the main music center. The new structure, not dignified enough to be given a commemorative name, was called East Hall. East Hall, however, made it possible for the School of Music to stage highly complicated performances within its own facility, and relieved it from having to subordinate its schedule of performances to those of the Auditorium Series, which operated quite apart from the administration of the School of Music.

Before East Hall had been installed, Robert L. Sanders resigned the deanship in the summer of 1947 to accept the chairmanship of the Department of Music in Brooklyn College. He was succeeded by Wilfred Connell Bain, a native of Shawville, Quebec. Dean Bain had been awarded degrees by Houghton College and New York University. He had received the doctorate in education from the latter institution in 1938, and had returned to Houghton College to teach music, later becoming Dean of Music in North Texas State University.

The thirty-nine-year-old Bain arrived in Bloomington in the fall of 1947, with well-developed ideas of how he wished to create a school of music of top quality. By the Christmas holidays he was prepared to make concrete recommendations to the administration. He outlined for Dean of Faculties Herman T. Briscoe an elaborate set of proposals, which included hiring Ernst Hoffman of the Houston Symphony as orchestra conductor. With Hoffman on the campus, he said, Indiana University students and faculty would be able to "put us in a position to perform opera." Bain told Briscoe that if Indiana wished to enable its School of Music to assume leadership in its field in the Middle West then there was "a great necessity for building a very strong instrumental, orchestral program." "It is impossible," he said, "to build a fine music school unless we use as the basis for the building, a very strong orchestral program and an A-No 1 theory department." For the moment, he thought, the theory and composition departments seemed good, but the orchestra was substandard, in fact, it was in Bain's judgment "very ordinary by comparison with high standards." Until the latter field was strengthened, he said, it would not be possible to attract promising student singers to Bloomington.

Dean Bain also told Briscoe that the School of Music needed to employ immediately professors in oboe and bassoon, so they could join with teachers of the flute and clarinet to form a woodwind ensemble. These four musicians should be given reduced teaching schedules to permit them to rehearse during the spring semester, so they could play concerts in the Indiana high schools and local music halls. Their expenses could be partially recovered at least by charging admission to their performances. These four professors could further reduce expenses by traveling together in a single automobile. There were also needs for another part-time teacher of theory, a teacher of percussion, and a distinguished teacher of violin. Shrewdly, Bain recommended that C. Lawrence Kingsbury of the School of Music and Department of Adult Education be used to promote the activities of the School of Music about the state of Indiana. It was hoped that this latter proposal would lead to a generous amount of public exposure for student musicians.

Already on the campus, the School of Music was embarked upon a joint enterprise with the Indiana Memorial Union Board. In 1947 choral students were given an opportunity to sing traditional English folk songs in a period program of pomp and ceremony centered about an evening of dining and convivial entertainment. This was the beginning of the tremendously popular Madrigal Dinners, which were to be repeated annually and with an ever-increasing demand for extended numbers of performances. Some of the future annual series were patronized by more than 5,000 guests. Dean Bain had a keen appreciation of the meaning of this kind of friendly public relations for the School of Music, and he was able to capitalize on it. By the opening of the first summer session the School of Music was ready to make some rewarding off-campus appearances. The Indiana University Chorus of 185 members presented Verdi's *Requiem* in Grant Park in Chicago in July. An appreciative audience gave the singers a rousing ovation. The *Indiana Daily Student*, July 29, said, "The music critics and the tens of thousands of music lovers cheered the singers with wild enthusiasm." No one said how many people were in Grant Park for the performance, but the student paper, in a burst of extravagant pride, may have overestimated the capacity of this Chicago music facility. In this moment of jubilation Dean Bain told the Bloomington *World-Telephone* that a company was ready to take to the road with the folk opera *Down in the Valley* and *Tales of Hoffman.* In exhibiting his professors and students before this kind of viewing and, sometimes, to critical appraisal, he was duplicating what he had done so successfully for eight years in Texas.

Earlier Bain had outlined for the university administration further needs of the School of Music for new staff members and instruments. He did not, however, mention the availability in the Auditorium of the fabulous Roosevelt-Barnes organ, which had once been used by the nationally popular Theodore Thomas

Orchestra of Chicago. The university had just spent $50,000 having the instrument installed, and it was to be used for the first time after its dedication in a major musical performance on January 11, 1949, when the Indianapolis Symphony appeared in a recital on the campus.

The constant flow of recommendations and correspondence which reached them from the School of Music surely convinced Herman B Wells and his administrative colleagues that Wilfred C. Bain had come to Bloomington in an "all-fired" hurry to build a top-quality school of music. In the dean's impatience he no doubt took some of the university officials by considerable surprise. They were used to a much more leisurely approach to selling culture and the arts to students and the public. Some of them even pretended to feel that all the publicity for music might actually be a liability. In the spring of 1948 there appears to have been pressure to establish a second school of music in connection with the extension center in Indianapolis, an undertaking which would have required a tremendously expensive and complicated rearranging of budgets, staffs, and equipment. Most important of all, this might have brought about a shuffling of university priorities. Bain wrote Herman T. Briscoe, April 16, 1948, that he did not see any way to organize an advanced program in Indianapolis, and to improve the Bloomington program at the same time. He wrote, "I think it would be very unwise for us to establish two complete schools of music within fifty miles of each other, and that is just what we would have to do if we should attempt to offer advanced work as well as elementary training at the Indianapolis center." He thought budgeting would be too difficult, and such an effort would rob other extension centers and the adult programs of vital services. Equally as important it would needlessly injure good public relations with the Jordan Conservatory and Butler University. Since President Wells was away in Germany, Bain told Briscoe nothing should be done at this time, "since he is familiar with this situation and the rest of us are not." Nevertheless, Dean Bain was anxious to experiment with a modest instructional program in music in at least one of the off-campus centers.

Wilfred Bain may have been Canadian by birth, but he arrived in Bloomington like a Texas twister. He was commended by the *Indiana Daily Student*, September 28, 1948, for getting opera going, expanding the graduate music program, hiring new professors, and bringing the famous Berkshire Quartet to the campus for a year-in-residence relationship to the School of Music. The campus reporter said, "He reminds you of the star of the opera, not the director." President Herman B Wells in his *Annual Report*, 1947–48, confirmed the campus paper's appraisal of the new Dean of the School of Music. He had made fundamental changes in an unbelievably short time, the greatest ones in the field of applied music. The teaching and training services of the school had been opened to university students in general, approximately 180 of whom had elected music courses as minor adjuncts to their major fields of study. Employment of Ernst Hoffman had focused much attention on the University's Symphony Orchestra, and also had led to the organization of the Opera Workshop.

No doubt the Opera Workshop encouraged the School of Music to institute a policy of initiating premiere performances of obviously new and unpredictable operas. In time, this custom was to bring the staff of the school great satisfaction. In 1948 and 1949 the staff and students gave premiere performances of Lukas Foss' *The Jumping Frog* and Kurt Weill's *Down in the Valley*. Beyond this, the staff and students rapidly matured their capability to present highly creditable performances of the traditional operas, and in the production of mature performances and ensemble programs, such as that on December 14, 1949, under the direction of George F. Krueger. This latter year was indeed one of triumph. President Wells reported that the Berkshire Quartet with Urico Rossi, first violin, Alfred Lazan, second violin, David Dawson, viola, and Fritz Magg, cello, had become members of the faculty with the rank of associate professors. By that time Hans Busch, son of Fritz Busch, had also joined the faculty, and he and Ernst Hoffman constituted a highly competent team for the production of opera. They began immediately to prepare operatic productions, chief of which was the Wagnerian *Parsifal*. This tremendous undertaking involved the services of 122 students as members of the choirs, the Symphony Orchestra, the band, and as soloists. Wells wrote, "This we hope, will have considerable effect on the extension of the influence not only of the School of Music, but of Indiana throughout the state."

All, however, was not unbridled enthusiasm and promise for the School of Music in the sparkling year 1949. The rapid growth of the school had created the problem of strengthening varied programs of training and performances. For instance, the teaching of theory, if not neglected, had not been properly modernized. Many instructors were involved in teaching the subject, but the results were confusing as to procedures, objectives, techniques, and course contents. Dean Bain said this fault could not be corrected until an independent department of theory was organized and properly staffed.

The music faculty felt, however, it had reached the stage where it could offer the doctor of education degee with a major in music, and except for the nature of the dissertation content, the degree would be more nearly comparable to the doctor of philosophy degree offered in the Graduate School. Another innovation was made in the field of church music in which competent choir directors and organists were to be trained for service in the churches of Indiana.

In a more pragmatic and historical sense musical training in Indiana University had as its grass roots objective the preparation of public school music teachers. Students majoring in the educational field of music emphasized training in vocal and instrumental areas. Work leading to the Bachelor of Music in Education was under the direction of a capable staff who perhaps attracted less public attention than those associated with the more dramatic direction and performance of opera roles, but fundamentally they reached far greater numbers of students. Almost as if the School of Music maintained a dual system of instruction, basic training was entrusted to Newell Long, Dorothy Kelly, Thurber Madison, and Gerald Doty. More creative students were tutored by Anis Fuleihan and Bernhard Heiden, composers. A distinct feature of the educational program was the evaluative sessions in which student accomplishments were appraised in collective staff judgments based upon improvement in performances as well as demonstrations of content knowledge indicated in traditional term examinations.

Wilfred C. Bain worked diligently on the two fronts. He knew the necessity for organizing a highly competent instructional faculty if his school was to achieve respectable professional standing. In this he was a determined, if not unyielding, administrator. At the same time he revealed a good sense of public relations, which caused him to parade professors and students before as many types of audiences as possible. An example of this occurred in February 1950, when the Indiana University Singers were taken on a tour of northern Indiana and Illinois. On this hurried trip they gave seventeen concerts and returned home to give a grand finale under the dean's direction. That summer the School of Music offered clinics, short courses, and held conferences for students and teachers from Indiana and the adjoining states. These programs attracted more than 200 outstanding school musicians who aspired to get on with their careers. The *Herald-Telephone*, July 19, 1950, said of the summer performances that the School of Music presented "the most varied and entertaining programs to be given this year" in the musical festival. The impact of the new programs was phenomenal in terms of the increase in staff numbers and student enrollment. In 1936–37, Dean Merrill's last year, 91 students were registered, in 1946–47, in Sanders' last year, 247, and in 1949–50, there were 425 students. Fees for applied music in the latter year amounted to only 29 per cent of the budget of the School, the remainder of the cost was derived from admissions to concerts and operas, and from the conventional sources of university income for instruction.

The university administration was to have no surcease from the School of Music. In his Annual Report for 1949–50, Dean Bain asked for more studios, rehearsal rooms, more instruments and equipment, and more support for opera productions. He explained that some smaller schools were better off in most of these areas than Indiana University. He and his staff, he told the president and trustees, had been so preoccupied with organizing the major fields of their discipline that they had given too little attention to nonmajors; 95 per cent of these had been taught by graduate students. As a result, there was too little concern with the maturity or talents of these student instructors. In 1950–51 he reported a registration of 425 music majors the first semester, and 403 the second semester.

Despite the excitement caused by a rising enrollment for work in the instructional fields, a tremendous amount of energy went into staging operas. In 1950 Hans Busch had matured plans to stage, with student talent, the Metropolitan Opera Company's adaptation of *Cavalleria Rusticana*. The *Daily Student* boasted that Indiana University had added another first in the United States to its already extensive list of distinctions. The School of Music was offering qualified students training in opera under the direction of a highly qualified professional staff. Ernst Hoffman and Hans Busch formed a solid instructional nucleus for such training. No less enthusiastic about the School of Music's accomplishments was the *Alumni Magazine* which chortled, "The School of Music, in its current vigor and activity might be compared to a gigantic *concerto grosso*, which is a composition that features, not one, but a number of performers in co-ordinated interplay with an orchestra." A variety of organized musicians comprised the school's music tour de force, all of them constituting highly pleasing public exhibits of the division's competence at home and abroad. A distinctly prestigous addition to the staff was the employment of the popular Anya Kaska of the Metropolitan Opera Company.

There is no doubt that the School of Music, professors and students, profited tremendously from the annual visitations of the Metropolitan Opera Company to the Auditorium. These not only gave a comparative stimulus to the university performers, but they went a long way toward gathering sustaining audiences for numerous local performances. Sophisticated and experienced artists revealed firsthand the fundamental importance of talent and training. At the same time the university was able to demonstrate its ambitions and capabilities in the field to artists who were potential future staff members, and many of these came to the campus to teach when their professional performing careers were ended.

The annual staging of *Parsifal* in the Lenten season became a barometer of campus musical maturity. The performance in March 1951 especially attracted widespread national attention. Ruth Merton of *Time Magazine*'s Chicago bureau spent several days in Bloomington reviewing the rehearsals and gathering information for an extended story. The presentation was indeed a test of local talent. Guy Owen Baker, a graduate student, sang the role of Parsifal in the first two acts of the opera. The *Christian Science Monitor* published a story of the opera, and Gene Cooke of *Life Magazine* also reviewed the performance. The Indianapolis and Louisville papers were generous in their coverage and praise. The cast consisted of 150 students, and Dean Bain directed the chorus while Ernst Hoffman directed the University Philharmonic Orchestra.

When the Metropolitan Opera Company came to Bloomington

in May 1951, School of Music students gave an afternoon performance of *Rigoletto* for the New York professionals. Jarmila Novotna said of the performance, "In Europe we have small opera groups but nothing to compare with this." Regina Resnick thought the Metropolitan singers could learn from the student performers. Hugh Thompson, Frank Guarrera, Mario Mazzoni, and Rudolph Bing all complimented the student performance. Bing said, jokingly, he would like to hire Claire Nunn as a teacher for some of his singers.

Fortunes of the School of Music grew more glowing with each passing academic year. Willi Apel, a musicologist with an international reputation, and author of the *Harvard Dictionary of Music*, was added to the staff. Student enrollment exceeded 500, and in June the first doctorate in music was awarded. There was now a full-time staff of fifty-one members and sixty-four graduate assistants. More and more the faculty roll began to read like that of former members of the Metropolitan Opera Company. This expansion did not, however, take place without considerable growing pains because it outran the capability of the university to supply space in keeping with the quality of its teaching and performance aspirations.

Each succeeding year saw the specialized music programs multiply, and public demands for performances increase. Promotion of the multiplicity of programs became a major cost factor in the operation of the School of Music, and maybe in competition with other divisions of the university. Ross Bartley of the Indiana University News Bureau wrote Vice President John Ashton, March 29, 1952, of his concern with the school's zeal in publicizing its programs. "An Indiana taxpayer." said Bartley, "in my opinion, might become irritated if he were a witness to the competition for admission-free audiences now in progress on the campus, particularly on the part of the Department of Bands and the School of Music. Further, the News Bureau would have difficulty in calming such irritation." He said the weekly campus calendar had carried for two weeks the notices of the Sunday band concert, and had sent individually typed letters to patrons costing eleven cents for preparation, plus three cents postage. Bartley thought "all of which indicates there is a competition on, at the expense of university funds, not merely to inform but to pressure elusive audiences."

The School of Music may indeed have wooed audiences with excessive enthusiasm for its multiplicity of programs, but Ross Bartley may also have been somewhat overcautious in calling them "elusive." There was no doubt that audiences had to be assembled in some way if all of the programs had patronage. Dean Bain's policy of demanding that every student participate in some kind of public performance did create competition for listeners, and as enrollment went up each year there was that much greater demand for auditors. The music programs were both numerous and varied, many of them attracting audiences assembled in Bloomington because of other public campus functions.

There was enough novelty in many of the School of Music programs, that this within itself captivated people. In December 1952 a cast under the stage direction of Hans Busch, and the musical direction of Ernst Hoffman and George Krueger, presented Benjamin Britten's *Billy Budd*. This was said to be the first time this opera had appeared on an American stage. President Wells reported to the trustees that a multiplicity of programs had been given on and off the campus. These included those of such groups as the Berkshire Quartet, the American Quintet, the Symphony Band, the summer operettas, and the operatic performances of *Parsifal* and *Billy Budd*.

Student enrollment climbed above 500 in 1952–53, and was divided almost equally between men and women. In commenting on this fact in his *Annual Report*, Wells said the School of Music needed to work more closely with the Indiana high schools in order to bring Hoosier students into more intimate association with Indiana University. He was perhaps provoked to make this observation because at this time students from all over the country were seeking admission to the growing school. Whether Dean Bain and his ever-lengthening list of highly specialized colleagues actually made efforts to reach out to the state's high schools in the sense that President Wells and Ross Bartley conceived to be most satisfactory may have been open to question. Student enrollment, nevertheless, continued to expand in the 1950s almost faster than the university could provide proper instruction and studio and classroom facilities to accommodate it. Every major performance now created its own wave of favorable publicity and in turn attracted an ever-widening pattern of student attention. *Life Magazine*, May 15, 1953, ran the picture of freshman Sallilee

Conlon on its front cover after she had posed unbelievably 232 times before the photographer was satisfied he had taken just the right picture. Inside the magazine ran thirteen pages of text describing various aspects of Midwest culture. The *Life* staff designated the Indiana School of Music as "the most outstanding in the Middle West." Special attention was given once again to the performance of *Parsifal*, which by this time had almost become the cultural benchmark of the Indiana School of Music. *Life* expressed the opinion that the campus performance of the demanding Wagnerian composition surpassed the Metropolitan Opera Company's staging and settings "hands down." The reporter was also impressed by the fact that the university presented 375 concerts and recitals a year. This was further borne out in Dean Bain's Annual Report, 1953–54, in which he wrote, "The University Administration is to be complimented and to be offered grateful thanks for a strong School of Music. The faculty and students are well aware of the key position which the Administration of the University has played in making Indiana University a great center of music and culture in the Midwest. The Administration has made possible the development of a desirable atmosphere in which the things of the spirit are given prominence, and where musical artists can find happiness and satisfaction in work and living." Bain no doubt sensed the fact that a growing university faculty, student body, and patronage from the peripheral geographical area were of enormous importance in giving the moral support so necessary to the success of the musical programs. Here were the sources of regionally generated audiences that formed strong loyalties to the campus musicians and the school.

As the fame of the School of Music spread well beyond the boundaries of Indiana, its ambitions reflected more than a touch of megalo-awareness. Staff and students, on May 26, 1954, gave a single performance of Moussorgsky's *Boris Godounov*. From the standpoint of complexity this was the most elaborate production in the history of the School of Music, and was said to be the first time that Moussorgsky's opera was presented by a nonprofessional cast. The following fall, November 28, the Philharmonic University Singers under the direction of Frank St. Leger presented a Sunday night concert in Carnegie Hall to a full audience. Among those present was the great prima donna Madame Dorothea Manski, then professor of voice in the School of Music. She called the New York program "an artistic rather than a student performance." The School of Music drew further critical praise. Jay Harrison, music editor of the *Herald-Tribune* wrote, "The facilities which allowed for a spotless performance of *The Ruby* are only some of the blessings bestowed by the State of Indiana on its University. The School of Music's resources, to cite no more than a single example, are vast beyond belief."

The Harrison praise also referred to a weekend of music festival, May 12 and 13, when local casts performed Della Joio's *The Ruby* and Leoncavallo's *I Pagliacci*. There were several national music critics in Bloomington to view the performances. Della Joio worked with the cast in the production of his opera; he had chosen Indiana because he thought no eastern university was capable of presenting such a work.

While students in Bloomington worked to produce two challenging operas, Eugene Bayless took his 75 "Belles of Indiana" on a barnstorming visit to the Far East. They spent eleven weeks on tour among American military installations in Japan and Korea. This was called a "morale building" tour. It was all of that plus the presentation of a series of able musical performances. At times, however, it was hard to tell whose morale was being boosted, the soldiers or the "Belles." Sue Unger, a sophomore, said it was "the most marvelous experience I'll probably ever have." The girls sang for President and Madame Syngman Rhee in the Seoul Palace, and all but turned Buddhists before the shrines in Tokyo. Other tours followed in these sparkling early days of musical fortunes at Indiana University, with each group coming home in the glow of success. Dark tragedy, however, stalked the School of Music in this period. Ernst Hoffman and his wife were killed in an automobile accident on January 3, 1956. This grievous misfortune removed from the teaching staff not only the tremendously successful leader of the Symphony Orchestra since 1948, but one of the modern founders of the School of Music.

Student enrollment leaped up to near the 600 mark in 1956, and the school was forced to become highly selective in admissions to many of the areas of its diversified program. It was said the Indiana high schools did not prepare outstanding students in the double reeds and strings, these had largely to come from elsewhere. For this reason the application of a gifted student from outside the state was given preferential consideration. No doubt the university administration at least accepted this fact with grace, wishing, however, conditions were different. President Wells wrote in 1956, "The School of Music continues to hold a place of leadership in American education in operatic training, it appears that there is no college or university providing a program of the scope of the operatic training program at Indiana University." He no doubt was right because the Indiana School had produced seven operas that year. This undertaking placed a severe strain on staff, students, and physical facilities. Students, said the president, were required to put in many extra hours because of the lack of facilities for proper rehearsal. The Berkshire Quartet lost the use of Lincoln House to make way for other expansion on the campus, the temporary Music Annex had to be torn down for the same reason, and it became necessary to convert two dwelling houses and the former Indiana School of Religion building on Third Street into rehearsal quarters. Demand for the smaller practice rooms had become so critical that it was said it was difficult to attract a distinguished faculty.

This latter condition may have posed a threat, but Charles Kullman, a Metropolitan Opera tenor, was employed in 1957 to teach voice and opera. There was a certain amount of pride in numbers in Indiana University so far as the School of Music was concerned, as if this was always a reassurance of success. It is little wonder that physical facilities were placed under such a severe strain before the new permanent addition was made to the Music Building. Although the school did not schedule an operatic premiere for 1957, it did print programs for 239 concerts and recitals, plus the traditional operatic performances. Dean Bain said, "This number continues to be the largest number of concerts presented by any university, college, conservatory, or school of music, studied or known to the author."

The death of Ernst Hoffman had created a serious vacancy in the opera program, a vacancy which had to be filled by the appointment of a professionally distinguished conductor if the School of Music hoped to keep up with its traditionally productive schedule. Tibor Kozma of the Metropolitan Opera Company was appointed Hoffman's successor in 1958. He was given the responsibility of conducting the Symphony Orchestra and helping to prepare half of the opera schedule. At the same time Roy

Harris, composer of 120 published compositions, including seven symphonies, was employed to give instruction in the symphonic area.

Production of seven operas in the academic year, 1957–58, was indeed a challenge that possibly no other academic institution in North America, or abroad for that matter, had attempted. This meant not only training casts, but the designing and construction of scenery, the coordination of schedules of performances with the Auditorium Series, and the holding of regularly scheduled credit-bearing classes. The opera list this year included *Don Pasquale*, *Candide*, *Cavalleria Rusticana*, *Amelia Goes to the Ball* (Cinderella), *Parsifal*, and *Albert Herring*. This was only a part of the general musical activities on and off the campus. While a small army of performers and singers charmed audiences in the great Auditorium, the Singing Hoosiers won the hearts of far less sophisticated, but no less appreciative, audiences in the European army installations of the American overseas forces.

The number of concerts and recitals rose to 253, including programs ranging from piano and voice to woodwinds and ballet. All of this kept up a constant pressure for instructional staff and facilities. The enrollment of the school had increased to 726 students, and women registrants in 1958 outnumbered men. During the preceding summer the unbelievable number of graduate students pursued work leading to the doctorate in music education. Again Dean Bain boasted that "For some years, the School of Music has had more students working toward a Ph.D. in music, musicology, theory, or music education than any other department or division in the University." The cry for space had now become a frantic wail. Classes, rehearsals, and practice sessions were held in eight different buildings on the campus, including the cavernous East Hall. Despite this wide dispersal of space across the campus, the School of Music maintained a solid reputation for the thoroughness of its instruction. Herbert Graf, stage director of the Metropolitan Opera Company, in Bloomington to direct a performance of *Belshazzar* in November 1959 said, "To my mind, I. U. has the best opera school in the country."

The advancing years of the Wells administration saw no let up in either enthusiasm or patronage of the School of Music. By September 1960 the faculty and student body had expanded sufficiently to permit a herculean number of opera performances.

Dean Wilfred C. Bain announced there would be an opera performance each Saturday night during the coming school year. This would include the performance of seven different operas in twenty-four repertory presentations. This, he said, would enable midwest opera patrons, "to hear the great operatic masterpieces on a regular basis, and will also give maximum experience to student singers, instrumentalists, dancers, and technicians."

The opening years of the new decade, 1960–70, saw a constant increase in students and the presentation of all sorts of public musical programs. These included 69 band concerts, and 350 more or less formal musical performances. At the end of this year Dean Bain was unusually cheerful in his declaration that, "A survey reveals that this astounding number of public recitals and concerts far exceeds that presented by any other college or university." He wrote that the problem of organizing choral groups was not easily solved because many audiences wanted to hear light entertainment while others wished to hear important works of music. He contrasted the difference between the musical programs of Indiana University and its sister rival Purdue. The latter school made no pretense of offering major musical instruction, and consequently it could use choral music as an extra-curricular activity for its students. At Indiana, however, musical programs constituted a vital part of the instructional procedures of a professional school of music. Student participation in ensemble and choral work was as fundamental a requirement as courses in physics and engineering. If their public presentations pleased and entertained audiences, that was to the good, but entertainment per se was not the primary objective of the School of Music.

Just as it had on that day, January 15, 1937, when Indiana University dedicated the opening of the Music Building, the institution experienced a moment of jubilation, April 13, 1962, when it dedicated the $3,000,000 addition to the older structure. This complex new wing consisting of ultramodern practice and classrooms brought once more the work of the School of Music into a unified physical plant, except for the use of East Hall. Five of the scattered temporary buildings were now returned to more prosaic usage. In his dedicatory speech, said the *Daily Student*, May 17, 1962, President Herman B Wells expressed great institutional pride in the Auditorium series, the annual appearances of the Metropolitan Opera Company, and the phenomenal growth of the School of Music. The latter, he said, had grown from departmental status "to one of the most renowned cultural institutions in the world." He continued, "Once upon a time music was looked upon as something easy and 'precious' in the higher education curriculum of America. Today, however, no division requires higher competence for admission and no other requires more hard grueling work for a degree."

Though celebrating the opening of a modern music facility, President Wells looked to the future. Already being planned was the structure which in 1971 would become a fabulous $10,123,000 Musical Arts Center. Even in the face of all this, the President declared his head would not rest easy on his shoulders nor could he find complete solace until the impact of the School of Music was felt everywhere in Indiana. "I'll not be satisfied," said Wells, "till we have a symphony orchestra in every county, singing societies and art classes for all who want them, and a little theater group in every town hall." This was indeed a dream of vast proportions that involved far more than the raising of massive limestone structures; its realization required a significant revision of the whole Hoosier approach to life and culture. Indiana townspeople, and even the denizens of the town halls, were proud in an abstract way of the university's cultural and artistic accomplishments. Both the School of Music and the Department of Speech and Theatre ran their tentacles into nearly every high school in the state, and into the larger and more sophisticated urban communities. The city halls and courthouses, however, were culture-resistant institutions with histories anchored solidly in the primordial past of rural American anti-art and anti-intellectualism. They were places of a far too mundane atmosphere to nurture cultivated man's finer sensibilities and accomplishments.

Speaking that day in May on the very eve of his retirement from the presidency, Herman B Wells gave no indication of lessening enthusiasm and energy. He and Dean Bain had formed an aggressive team who convinced a sufficient number of Hoosiers, legislators, and trustees of the great potential for artistic and cultural leadership in the Middle West. In Bain's report in 1962, he spoke over the retiring president's head to the trustees and public. "On behalf of the Faculty of the School of Music and its many students," he wrote, "I wish to thank the President of the University, the Board of Trustees, and the Administrative Committee for their continued efforts in creating and maintaining a climate in which the most advanced artist-teachers find satisfaction. The record of achievement of music at this University is a testament to the wise and vigorous leadership of one of America's great university presidents."

As though to prove its capabilities at least doublefold, the School of Music in 1964 instituted a year-round production of grand opera. The *Daily Student*, March 18, 1964, said, "Today Indiana University has the only opera company in the United States which operates the year-round. Each year it presents as many new productions as the Metropolitan Opera does." That summer Governor Matthew Welch invited the School of Music to present, in addition to a full campus program, its outdoor production of *Turandot* on "Indiana Day" at the New York World's Fair on August 17 and 18 in Singer Bowl. It was said these attracted the largest audiences ever to see an operatic performance in New York. The critics were also generous in their reviews and general appraisals of the musical maturity of the cast.

Growth was both pleasing and painful to the central university administration and that of the School of Music. Despite the mighty efforts to provide proper housing for the school, there was still a need for space in 1965. The librarian announced that with more than 70,000 volumes there was no place to store more books, and this, said President Elvis J. Stahr, handicapped the efficiency and effectiveness of the School of Music. He also reported that the entire curriculum of the undergraduate music education program was being revised in such a way as to meet changing demands for teachers and general musical training. This meant a realignment of the whole schedule of the undergraduate degree curricula, and even a changing philosophy in regard to methodology and purposes of training in this area. As a result of the revision, three baccalaureate degrees were provided for the future. Admissions and evaluation of the work of new students, especially transfers, became a perplexing chore. In 1964–65, 1,172 students were registered, 440 of whom were of graduate rank. Aside from this enormous instructional responsibility, the School of Music produced 676 programs of a public nature. It produced ten operas and operettas, which included *Madame Butterfly*, *Boris Godounov*, *Don Giovanni*, *Parsifal*, and the *Merry Widow*. Staging of these productions alone involved a major construction and equipment department to say nothing of providing the talent and audiences. Fortunately the music faculty contained major talent which made the heavy schedule of productions possible.

It may well have been true in the decades, 1950–70, that no other university anywhere had undertaken such a highly diversified and costly program of musical arts as did Indiana University. By 1971 the musical arts occupied three magnificent buildings, the School of Music turned away scores of students from all across the nation, and the faculty roll read like that of the professional field of music itself. The school had established a solid reputation for both teaching and performing. If ever in its history this part of the Midwest felt apologetic about its lowly state as a cultural wasteland, the Indiana School of Music with its associated arts and enthusiastic patronage destroyed the image. Beyond this, graduates of the school had an incalculable impact on music training and appreciation throughout the region. Even the churches of the Ohio Valley upgraded their music programs by the employment of Indiana-trained directors.

Ten grand operas a season was not exactly what the faculty and the Board of Trustees had in mind in 1921 when they voted, upon the recommendation of Dean Merrill, to change the Department of Music into an independent school. This, however, was not beyond the dreams of those pioneers who promoted with such vigor the procurement of a Public Works Administration grant to construct a temple in which the artistic spirit of man could be set free to soar as high as the ambition of man could take it.

No Mozart or Wagnerian opera could have been more dramatic than the change of eras which occurred in the history of the Indiana University School of Music on a cold evening in January 1968. Standing gaunt and virtually stripped of any former glory the old World War II hangar might have enjoyed as the seat of campus opera performances, East Hall vanished in a roar of flame and smoke. The ashes of the crumpling old building seeded the ground with symbolic continuity. Here the new Musical Arts Center would rise in all its glory to give the university a permanent leasehold on both musical and operatic art. Shimmering that night in the flame that melted the old hall away to a negligible handful of ashes might in fact have been the reenactment of Mozart's *Don Giovanni*, which itself had separated the ages of opera.

[XIX]

The World of Man Encompassed

INDIANA UNIVERSITY in 1950 was within sight of realizing several of the objectives that it had set for itself. The intensive Wells' crusade to recruit an able faculty had been rewarded by marked success, and there was now in Bloomington a community of scholars capable of the most sophisticated kind of creativity. The institution's libraries and laboratories had been expanded sufficiently to maintain major research programs in a variety of fields. For the first time in almost a century and a half Indiana began to feel the satisfying impulse of having achieved true university status. It also responded with sensitivity to the impact of immediate postwar and changing educational demands made upon institutions of higher learning throughout America. Also, developing a top-quality university had proved a heady experience for the Wells administration and the faculty, and what once had seemed limitations now appeared as challenges for the future. The university in its new and maturing status was called upon to take additional steps into an academic world that never before had seemed so vital to it.

An early call in the postwar era was for the organization of a scholarly book publishing program under the direction of an experienced director and editorial staff. Fortunately, Indiana University had not made the mistake, so common in the histories of many universities, of allowing the imprint, "Indiana University Press," to become established on the title pages of less than professionally produced publications prior to 1950. Likewise, it was not without significant coincidence that Indiana began to feel the urge to develop a professional publication outlet in order to maintain the scholarly momentum generated by a growing staff. There no doubt was in Bloomington the growing "publish or perish" view that infected all higher education.

The concept of the university as publisher has a background in a rich cultural history almost as extensive as that of the university itself. Oxford and Cambridge universities maintained presses of early vintages, which have survived and prospered since the fifteenth and sixteenth centuries. These British institutions accumulated financial support largely from the publication and sale of Bibles and other religious writings, a source of income denied modern American academic presses. These presses, however, made enduring publishing history by presenting such secular works as those of William Harvey on the circulatory system of the human body, Lord Clarendon's *History of the Rebellion* (1702), John Smith's *Map of Virginia* (1634), Francis Bacon's *Advancement of Learning* (1605), *A Prince's Looking Glass* (1603), and *A Remonstrance for the Rights of Kings* (1616). Over the centuries their backlists became a significant scholarly bibliography for the English-speaking world.

This university history had at least a partial bearing on the foundation of American university publishing. The idea of associating a press with the university in this country had its inception largely with Daniel Coit Gilman. When he became president of the Johns Hopkins University in 1876, he conceived a part of his mission to be promoting of research among the new faculty then being assembled, and if the works of these scholars were to have broad impact they had to be published. In 1878 the Johns Hopkins University Press was founded as a successful venture in publishing the *American Journal of Mathematics*, and then the *American Chemical Journal.* Cornell University established a press in 1860, but it was suspended in 1884, and not re-established until 1930. William Rainey Harper's University of Chicago organized a press in 1891; two years later presses were started at California and Columbia. In a second grouping, including Harvard, Yale, and Princeton, nine more presses were established before 1918. By 1950 there were forty-three university publishers, and when Indiana entered the field university presses were already producing an impressive number of scholarly nonfiction titles annually.

University publishing, as the older presses had learned, involved a number of factors peculiar to writing and research. Despite the fact professors did research, directed doctoral dissertations, and wrote books, a fairly large number of them had only the most elementary knowledge of publishing and book selling. Nearly all universities went through a common stage of press development. They supported print shops that produced administrative materials such as catalogs, schedules, and stationery; occasionally they produced a book, a periodical, or a specialized series. What this often amounted to was that a group of neighborly professors published each other's books and articles. In presidential and professorial minds these local publications could be used as foundations on which to establish a press. To a large extent this was true at Indiana prior to 1950.

Miss Ivy Chamness was editor of university publications, and the teaching and research staff produced several periodicals of subject-matter series, some books and monographs. The Woodburn and Myers histories of the University had been published in this way. In the early years of the Wells administration a faculty committee under the chairmanship of Professor Russell Noyes of the English Department made a report and a request on May 20, 1946, that an Indiana University Press be established as an organic part of the institution. Partly out of inexperience with publishing, but largely to bolster its plea, the committee argued that the creation of a literary magazine was highly desired, and there were other campus periodicals that could be drawn into an impressive consortium. Primarily the committee suggested the publication "of books of a scholarly or cultural interest," including the prestigious Patten and Powell lectures. Significantly, the faculty committee recommended "that the University Press be considered a division of the University but organized as a corporation somewhat after the pattern of the University Foundation." There was to be a board of directors appointed by the president, a majority of whom would be full-time faculty members. The committee thought it a good idea to appoint an alumnus who had publishing experience to the board. The director would be responsible for press policy, budgets, and all other publishing chores.

Wells either held the report for some time or his advisory sources were slow in making their recommendations. John W. Ashton, dean of the College of Arts and Sciences, wrote August 10, 1946, that he approved the central part of the faculty report. He thought the success of the Press would depend upon the quality of the man who was chosen to direct it. Ashton told Wells that such an undertaking would be an inevitable drain on the university's budget. Dean Fernandus Payne of the Graduate School took a more cautious line. He wrote the President on October 8 that he felt the suggestion of the committee was too ambitious. He would not start a press on the plan it suggesed. He would draw all the university publications into a common administrative press control. "To head them," he wrote, "we need at least one good man and a secretary," and then turn over to them the publication money in a single budget. A faculty committee could be established to help plan and edit the books. Dean Payne, indeed, was looking over his shoulder at past university publishing experiences.

The proposal to establish the University Press no doubt caused a generous amount of internal debating by both faculty and administration. Four years elapsed before the Board of Trustees approved on March 29, 1950, the establishment of the Indiana University Press. The board followed the recommendations made in the original Noyes report. In presenting the matter to the trustees, President Wells, much in the vein of Daniel Coit Gilman, said "The Press will be an ultimate expression of the influence of the University in scientific and intellectual publishing, while thoroughly aware of its primary function—that of publishing the results of scholarly research—the Press will make every effort to balance its program with books in all fields of learning which will appeal to the general reader." He viewed the university's entry into the field of publishing as an extension of the institution well beyond the teaching function of the formal classroom, and as an added intellectual stimulus on the campus.

In many respects the establishment of the Press was a major step in fulfilling the university's progress toward intellectual maturity. In his *Annual Report* for 1950, President Wells said, "The long hoped for Indiana University Press was launched in the early summer and a solid foundation already has been laid for growth and development."

Bernard Perry, a Harvard graduate and a trade publisher with sixteen years experience, was chosen director in March 1950. Perry had served as a college representative for W. W. Norton Company, as associate editor with E. P. Dutton, as associate editor and sales manager with Vanguard Press, and had established a book publishing division, which later became Hill and Wang, for A. A. Wyn, a magazine publisher. The new director was in Bloomington early in the spring and had set up an office in room 202 in Science Hall. A *Daily Studen*t story, December 2, 1950, said he felt teaching should go beyond the classroom, and "the Press' non-fiction books fill this bill." The paper also said the Press was in full swing, and already its offices had been moved to Heighway House at Seventh and Jordan. Edith Greenburg, also an experienced New York publisher, having served as a staff member of Vanguard Press, the Macmillan Company, and the Foreign Policy Association, was the first addition to the new staff as associate editor and production manager. Bernard Perry began making arrangements to have commission salesmen handle future University Press books. He ran advertisements in *Publishers Weekly*, the *New York Times*, and the *Saturday Review of Literature* promoting the first list. In spite of his best efforts to discourage them, faculty members began to ransack their desk drawers for "smoldering" manuscripts.

In December 1950 the first books were scheduled for publication. The first was *Poet of the People: An Evaluation of James Whitcomb Riley*, a collaborative critical appraisal by Jeannette Covert Nolan, Horace Gregory, and James T. Farrell. Also in press was Edward Seeber's translation of Edouard de Montulé's *Travels in America, 1816–1817*. The latter book had appeared under the title, *Voyage en Amérique, en Italie, en Sicile et en Egypte, pendant les années 1816, 1817, 1818 et 1819* (2 volumes; Paris, 1821), and an English edition was published the same year. It now appeared as "No. 9" in the Indiana Publications, Social Science series. Apparently this work had been accepted for publication before Perry arrived in Bloomington.

Looking to the future, Bernard Perry wrote President Wells, October 17, 1950, saying a university press gave dignity to a book and he would like to consider henceforth publishing those produced in the Institute for Sex Research. He told Wells that his publishing acquaintances were saying, "Isn't it too bad" the Press did not have the Kinsey books on its list. If the Press could have access to the forthcoming Institute studies, its salesmen would find ready welcomes from every bookseller in the country. Indiana he said could sell more copies than Saunders, because it could give more realistic discount rates to booksellers. Wells responded he would give the idea thought, but both the president and the Press director must have been conscious of the fact they had to deal with a strong-minded author in this case.

Within a year of its founding, the Indiana University Press announced it had in the process of production seven books, but it actually produced only four that year. In his first annual report, Bernard Perry wrote, "A new university publishing operation starts with many handicaps; lack of a name, lack of capital, lack of a back list of books to provide income for the business, lack of a sufficient staff, etc." He perhaps could have added lack of permanent and satisfactory office quarters; by this time the Press had moved for the third time from Science Hall to a quonset hut on Forest Place, and now to Heighway House.

Despite a rather extensive list of "lacks" the Press had bright prospects. Perry was busy making the Press' existence known by a modest advertising campaign and securing reviews in major journals, and Edith Greenburg was designing and preparing the first catalogs and books. He arranged for sales representation with three international agencies, and attended his first meeting of the Association of American University Presses. In lieu of a backlist of books of his own, he engaged in promoting the Indiana Monographs which were still in print, and the Indiana War History Commission's books, *Indiana at War: Civilian Directory*, and *Letters from Fighting Hoosiers*. In his *Annual Report* that year President Wells joined the Press director in saying that the Press could not emphasize scholarly works alone, but it must rely on appealing trade books to capture the general reader audience.

The future in 1951 was one of genuine expectation. The Indiana Historical Society had published R. Carlyle Buley's *The Old Northwest: Pioneer Period, 1815–1840* in two fat volumes, and it had won the Pulitzer Prize. This success had placed a heavier publication burden on the Society than it was equipped to handle, and the University Press acquired the title. Likewise in that year it secured the exciting Patten Lectures of Henri Frankfort, *The Birth of Civilization in the Near East.* A third successful title, and the first one commissioned by the Press, was *Hoosier Caravan* edited by the erudite bookseller, R. E. Banta of Crawfordsville. The latter book contained selections from the writings of native Hoosiers from General Lew Wallace to Elmer Davis and Pulitzer Prize winner, A. B. Guthrie, Jr., a native of Bedford.

There could now be no doubt the Indiana University Press was on its way to becoming a successful publisher. In a vein of optimism President Wells wrote August Frugé, chairman of the Committee on Admissions and Standards of the Association of American University Presses, April 5, 1952, seeking membership in that body. This optimism was justified. In 1952 the Press published Donald Sheehan's fascinating *This Was Publishing.* This author had gained access to the files of such famous old publishing houses as Harper Brothers, Charles Scribner and Sons, Henry Holt, and Dodd, Mead. The book gave real strength to the growing Indiana list.

A disappointment early in 1953 was the indifference of Hoosier readers and collectors to the republication of Logan Esarey's delightful and folksy essays, *The Indiana Home.* This slender volume first appeared in a limited boxed edition in 1947 under the imprint of R. E. Banta of Crawfordsville. R. C. Buley persuaded Bernard Perry to reproduce a much more elaborate edition in which he would prepare an introductory essay, Bruce Rogers would design the book, and Franklin Booth would supply the illustrations. Thus embodied in an elegant edition would be the work of four distinguished Hoosier authors and designers. Later, Perry wrote, "The handsome volume dropped into the publishing pond with a dull thud and, in spite of our efforts at sales promotion, especially at Christmastime, the book lay inert and neglected by the public." Despite the sales disappointment of the beautifully produced book, it did bring the Press a welcome reward when it was selected as one of the "Fifty Books of the Year" by the jury of the Institute of Graphic Arts. This experience no doubt convinced the editors that a university press had to seek a broader readership and market with books of greater general interest.

This the Press undertook to accomplish in the spring of 1953 when it announced it would begin publication of a poetry series under the editorship of Professor Samuel Yellen of the Department of English. The university had set aside a special fund to underwrite the publication of sixteen volumes in the next four years. It was expected, said the *New York Times*, May 24, 1953, that the poetry series would include the works of both beginners and established poets. The first two volumes, *The Gypsy Ballads of Garcia Lorca* translated by Rolfe Humphries, and David Wagoner's *Dry Sun, Dry Wind*, set high standards. In the same year the Press published in joint sponsorship with UNESCO and the Organization of American States a translation of a Latin American classic by Robert Graves, and the then unknown Samuel Beckett's translation of Octavio Paz' edition of *An Anthology of Mexican Poetry*. Unhappily, publication of the latter work was held up so long that the translator, who suddenly achieved fame because of his *Waiting for Godot*, was unable to give it the final attention that would have made it a work of even added quality.

The Press commissioned Muriel S. Wolle to write a book about the ghost towns of the Far West, which was published under the title *The Bonanza Trail* in 1953. This proved to be a highly successful venture from which the Press profited both in reputation and financial return. Bernard Perry said the sales of this book financed the Press' operation for a year. Two American regional titles in 1954 were successful as portrayals of life in the Midwest. These were Lewis Atherton's classic *Main Street on the Middle Border*, and Robert Price's *Johnny Appleseed, Man and Myth*.

There was certainty by mid-year 1953 that the Indiana University Press could carry out its mission as a scholarly and general publisher. In a somewhat optimistic memorandum Bernard Perry wrote President Wells on June 1, "A few further notes on the dilemma of a university press." A good university press, he said, would bring out "slow-moving, capital tying-up books." If it spent its energy on more popular trade books it would displease scholarly authors, while off-campus authors would be impressed by a "live" press that promoted its books. Perry told Wells the University Press was a very real business in that it sold a tangible product. The mission of the Press was one of performing the educational function "of interpreting and disseminating scholarly information"; otherwise it had little excuse for existing. He said he hoped that within fifteen or twenty years, and with a good back list, Indiana "might well be able to cover nearly all of its expenses without assistance." What the director did not say in this connection was that few if any people agreed as to the definition of a scholarly book, or attempted to draw a hard and fast borderline between a popular trade book and a scholarly one.

In that year the Press published *Theodor Storm's World in Pictures* by E. O. Wooley; the author had spent almost a lifetime studying the work of the great German author. At the same time it published Philip Wheelwright's *The Burning Fountain* as its first title in the field of philosophy. This book formed the foundation for a highly successful series in this subject field. Within four years the young Press had published an astonishing list of forty-eight books, and many of its titles had been favorably received by mature critics. The *Daily Student*, December 16, 1954, quoted a letter from Sterling North of the New York *World-Telegram-Sun*, saying "no regional or university press in America has made such sensational forward progress as the Indiana University Press." Harry Hansen of the *Chicago Tribune* wrote similar words; so did Lois Decker O'Neal of the Louisville *Courier-Journal*, and Van Allen Bradley of the Chicago *Daily News*. These paeans of praise had been evoked by publication of Robert Price's *Johnny Appleseed*.

There was hardly room for doubt that the Press deserved praise, for in a remarkably brief time it had become the established publishing arm of the University. By 1955 all the dogeared professorial dissertations and other forgotten literary productions had come out of seclusion for a brief moment of hope in such sunlight as beamed down on the editorial table, and were now back in their morgues awaiting the final dispersal of office files in moments of author retirements. In its first five years the Press published a few books of campus origin. Professor Edward Buehrig of political science offered *Woodrow Wilson and the Balance of Power*, Oscar O. Winther translated H. P. Hanssen's *Diary of a Dying Empire*, and there was a second printing of Richard Moody's *America Takes the Stage*. Alfred Kazin and Charles Shapiro offered *The Stature of Theodore Dreiser*, and Samuel Yellen had suggested a translation of Ovid's *Metamorphoses* by Rolfe Humphries. This last title was the foundation stone of a pioneering university press venture into paperback book publishing under the series title "Midland Books."

In 1957 the Press followed the suggestion of a member of its faculty committee, Oscar O. Winther, and anticipated the onrush of Civil War books when it republished with remarkable success William T. Sherman's voluminous *Memoirs*, along with J. F. C. Fuller's *Grant and Lee* and Thomas L. Livermore's *Numbers and Losses in the Civil War*. The books of the Civil War Centennial Series brought the Press a rich dividend in favorable national publicity in the pages of important review journals, including a front page review in the *New York Times*.

If there was disagreement over what precisely makes a scholarly book, there was none that Stith Thompson's monumental six-volume *Motif-Index of Folk Literature* fell safely within such honored classification. This new expanded edition, published in 1958, alone justified the organization of the Press. It received both national and international notice and approval. It went far toward systematizing and classifying the central folktale in human history. The first three books in the Civil War Centennial Series went into second printings almost immediately, and there was bright promise for most of the new list. The editorial and general staff had been increased to service a current list of thirty-two books and a growing backlist.

In these years of incipient affluence the Press had moved away from its temporary quarters in Heighway House to the stately old Andrew Wylie House at Second Street and Lincoln Avenue. There in the confines of the memorial of "Andrew the First," the editors could anticipate a future that the first president could never have envisioned. Publisher Perry had advanced upward not only in the steadily improving quality of his physical quarters, but in good fortunes in authorship and book sales. President Herman B Wells told the Board of Trustees that the Press may have reached its outer limits in 1958. "Having expanded its publication program to the optimum," he wrote, "commensurate with its budget and the University's overall activity, the Press is now faced with the problem of consolidation and stabilization, having published 32 titles in the calendar year 1958, it is necessary to retrench, at least, in terms of its expanded pace. It is doubtful whether the Press can do justice to its books and authors unless the total annual program is held to about thirty titles. This is easier said than done because the Press is always tempted to take on borderline manuscripts, that is, manuscripts which could not be done elsewhere or which present costly editorial problems; the reason for this is basically that publishers like our Press always prefer publication to rejection when they believe a service can be performed without lowering of scholarly and publication standards." This was indeed an interesting and percetpive comment coming from a university president.

A year later the Press made its fourth move to what promised to be a permanent home in the former office building of the Showers Furniture Company at Tenth and Morton streets. Sharing space with Erminie Voegelin, who did research for the United States Department of Interior in the suit brought by the Associated Great Lakes Indians to recover lands lost in the famous Treaty of Greenville, the Press offered a new booklist that seemed almost as expansive as its new offices. In 1960–61 Indiana participated in the Association of American University Press' program of translation and publication of Latin American titles. This project was financed by the Rockefeller Foundation, which sought to establish better understanding of the cultures of the Western Hemisphere. An American title on the new list was a facsimile edition of William Dean Howells' campaign biography of Abraham Lincoln. This unique copy owned originally by Samuel C. Parks, a Hoosier who had served in Congress with Lincoln and persuaded him to make interlinear and marginal corrections in the text, now belongs to the Illinois State Historical Society.

In the late 1950s, when federal funds enabled schools and libraries to buy books rather lavishly, the Indiana University Press title list expanded in length and significance. Its authors treated a wide diversity of subjects ranging from Raymond W. Thorp and Robert Bunker's *Crow Killer*, the bloodthirsty folk history of a mountain man who exacted deadly revenge from at least 300 Crow Indians because he accused the tribe of murdering his wife, to Bernard Berenson's *Sketch for a Self-Portrait*, *Paul Gauguin's Intimate Journals* edited by Van Wyck Brooks, and Albert Schweitzer's *African Notebook*. The Press' list was further distinguished by Morris Bishop's *Petrarch and His World* (1963) and his translation of *Letters from Petrarch* (1966), and William E. Wilson's incisive *The Angel and the Serpent* (1964). This latter title dealt for the first time in a compact way with the utopian experiments of George Rapp and Robert Owen at New Harmony on the Wabash. By 1962 the Press had approximately

300 books and monographs in its backlist, and its annual current lists increased the number by sixty or more titles.

When Elvis J. Stahr, Jr., was appointed the successor to Herman B Wells in 1962, Bernard Perry wrote him a five-page analysis of the Indiana University Press' history. He described its operational procedures, and gave more than a hint of its publishing problems. He recalled that he and Edith Greenburg had worked fifty to sixty hours a week "with professional publishing know-how, which we brought from New York." He told the new president he had no regrets, even though he and his staff had often been forced to substitute heroic effort for funds. The Press had begun operation with a budget of $20,000, and it might still operate on a comparable sum if it published only six or seven titles a year. Increased sales had only expanded financial demands. The report by Chester Kerr on the operation and maintenance of university presses in 1949 had recommended that no less than $100,000 be available for capital needs. Indiana had never enjoyed access to so much immediately available capital, and in its twelve-year history had received only two extensive appropriations for individual books. The Press paid salaries out of sales income, he said, and in 1961 it had overcommitted its book budget to authors and the anticipated Ford Foundation grant that required the university to assume fiscal responsibility for its personnel. Perry explained to Stahr that book manufacturing and sales promotion costs had to be paid immediately, but it took on the average five years to recover these costs from book sales.

After reviewing other fiscal policies, the Press Director said Indiana University had now to decide whether it wished to operate a professional publishing division on its current scale, which then was second only to Chicago in the Middle West, or to reduce its operations. University publishing, as most press directors knew by hard experience, was a constant struggle, and Indiana was no exception. Its program had grown into a fairly large one, and the demands made upon it for both publishing and administrative skills were no doubt awesome at times. A generous variety of manuscripts, treating a broad spectrum of subjects, had flowed into the editorial offices, and a good number of these had been turned into seminal books. For the university and scholar alike the book was at once a form of idea expression, a bastion of intellectual freedom, and tangible evidence of cultural advancement in the Middle West. In an equally important way, he said, the

Press extended both the university's intellectual and service arms. Perhaps in its first decade and a half it had reached out well beyond the narrowly conceived boundaries of scholarly books. Nevertheless, it had created a small library in its annual lists of books of distinctive literary worth.

The Press was to celebrate its two decades of publishing with the publication in 1971 of *The Carrey Drawings of the Parthenon Sculptures* edited by Theodore Bowie and Diether Thimme. This elegant publication was encouraged by Eli Lilly who had sustained an interest in the classics since early grade school days. His interest was further stimulated by the Carrey Drawings as they appeared in Henri Omont's *Athène au XVIIe Siècle* (1898). The new edition is an unusually fine piece of graphic art in which the Carrey Drawings are reproduced in color alongside black and white photographs of the surviving original sculptures. The production of this complicated book was a major challenge to the Indiana University Press to create a work of print reproduction and distinguished typography in keeping with the classical qualities of the subject itself. The monotype Centaur was designed by Bruce Rogers, who earlier had designed the Press' edition of the *Indiana Home*. The *Carrey Drawings*, with the scholarly text of Bowie and Thimme, constitutes a fitting and elegant testimonial to the sophisticated achievements of two decades of Indiana University publishing history.

Books, whether on the seasonal lists of the University Press, or in campus libraries, were basic to achieving the central scholarly objectives of the university, and to furthering the whole educational process in the Middle West. The struggle to accomplish this purpose was a long and frustrating one. Between 1908 and 1937 Indiana University had built a solid regional library with certain areas of better than ordinary strength, but its holdings were undistinguished because there was not a single strong special research collection. In 1903 the Board of Trustees made a gesture toward remedying this situation when it approved the purchase of a file of the *Indianapolis Journal*, and in 1913 Logan Esarey recommended the purchase of the McClelland Collection of Indiana and Western history materials. That same year W. E. Jenkins, the librarian, noted in his annual report that the university's library contained little material that would spread the fame of either library or university far abroad.

A condition of gradual accumulation of current books and

standard teaching materials and a modest research collection was reflected in the 1940 report of the librarian. Early in the decade, 1940–50, the university came into possession of the rather strong Robert S. Ellison Memorial Collection of 4,000 books and pamphlets of Western Americana. This material, though primarily of Far Western interest, constituted a significant foundation for the service of the United States Department of Justice in its research into the historical background of the associated tribes of Great Lakes Indians who had brought suit against the Government to reclaim lands they claimed were lost to them in illegal treaty negotiations. They sought to recover an estimated eight billion dollars worth of land, most of it surrendered in the Treaty of Greenville (1795). In time, and under the direction of Erminie and Carl Voegelin, historian-anthropologists, the Indiana University collection of materials dealing with the Indian in the Old Northwest, and especially that relating to the Anthony Wayne Campaign and the Treaty of Greenville in particular, grew into a significant regional library within itself. Besides this collection, there is an important cache of manuscripts, maps, original journals, and other documents relating to overland travels to the Rocky Mountain and Pacific Far West. Especially significant is the detailed sectional data map of the Platte-California-Oregon trails as compiled and drawn by J. K. Hosmer. Kathyrn Troxel said in 1956 that only the Coe Collection in the Yale Library and the Western materials in the Henry E. Huntington Library exceeded in importance that in Indiana University.

Closely related to the Ellison materials is the War of 1812 collection in the Lilly Library. There are also the Oakleaf Collection of Lincolniana and the Augustan Collection of British political and governmental manuscripts and documents, including the Daniel Defoe materials. In the literary field there is the Watkins Collection of Wordsworth manuscripts and rare published editions. All of these bodies of books and papers antedate the acquisition of the big central Lilly Library of rare books and manuscripts.

The Joseph B. Oakleaf Collection of Lincolniana was acquired in 1942 as a gift from the Ball Brothers Foundation of Muncie, Will Irwin, and Frank L. James. At that time this private library consisted of 10,615 volumes supplemented by photographs, etchings, busts, plaques, manuscripts, and medals. Originally it had been Oakleaf's intent to assemble what he believed would be approximately a hundred books printed about Lincoln. Over a period of forty-three years the Moline, Illinois, judge had found all but eighty-six known published items on Lincoln. His son J. L. Oakleaf continued the search for these and added the newly published titles which appeared after his father's death in 1930. He cared for the library in two rented apartments in Moline. Judge Oakleaf had asked that his collection be kept intact and that it be placed ultimately in a school or institutional library.

As significant as the earlier collections of books and manuscripts were, these did not elevate Indiana University Library holdings into a category of major status. This boost was to come with a single stroke in 1956, and without much prior knowledge on the part of university officials. President Herman B Wells informed the Board of Trustees in his *Annual Report*, 1955–56, that "The character of the University Library was changed almost overnight with the announcement of January 8, 1956, of the great gift of J. K. Lilly, Jr., of rare books, first editions, and manuscripts." This was one of the most significant gifts of its kind ever made to an American university. For Indiana University the Lilly gift promised revolutionary changes not only in substantive quality of the library, but likewise in its self-esteem and operation. As Wells told the trustees, "Our former concept of the Library as an agency of local service must be modified to include its new responsibility to national scholarship, to organize and make accessible the rich resources of Mr. Lilly's gift to faculty and students, and to lay the foundation for a wider scholarly use of its rare books and special collections. . . ."

A year later Robert Miller reported that the total university holdings amounted to 2,321,648 items. The four-story special depository in the Bryan Administration Building and other safety storage spaces were crammed with the new collections. The 1907 library building and its various built-on extensions were too overcrowded with the general library holdings and daily operations to permit housing of rare books within its walls. There was no place on the campus where the university staff could service properly such a large body of precious materials, or serve the "national scholarship" described by President Wells in his report to the trustees.

The Lilly gift was made with two conditions: the Foundation

would not support in perpetuity the administration and maintenance of the Library, and David A. Randall, a former manager of the famous Scribner's Fifth Avenue Book Store, would be employed as curator of the Lilly Collection. Randall had graduated from Lehigh University and had attended briefly the Harvard Law School. He, however, developed a greater interest in rare books and the book trade than in the law and withdrew to follow his interest. He began his apprenticeship in the rare book trade in 1929 under the tutelage of E. Byrne Hackett of the Brick Row Book Shops of New Haven, New York, and Princeton. In rapid succession he moved up in the fields of collecting and selling rare books. In June 1932, representing the dealer Max Harzof, he lugged a suitcase full of William D. Breaker's choice treasures out to Indianapolis to show them to Josiah Kirby Lilly, Jr. From that date until 1954 he was to have an active association with Mr. Lilly both as a book dealer and as a member of a special advisory committee for the preparation and publication of the multivolume *Bibliography of American Literature*.

In his tremendously interesting semi-autobiographical book *Dukedom Large Enough* (1969), Randall said that Josiah K. Lilly's zeal for rare book collecting had waned by 1954. He actually considered selling his superb collection, but lawyers convinced him that excessive capital gains taxes would make such a step too costly. It would be cheaper actually, said the lawyers, to give it to an institution. Randall said it was Mr. Lilly's independent decision to make a gift of his library to Indiana University, because he wished it to remain in the state. Though living only fifty-four miles from Bloomington, Mr. Lilly, a graduate of the University of Michigan, had never visited Indiana University.

In an interview on August 22, 1974, Herman B Wells said that he and Robert A. Miller, university librarian, had visited Josiah K. Lilly and had opened conversations with him about the possible disposition of his collection of books and manuscripts. Even though Mr. Lilly had not been to Bloomington, only fifty-four miles away, he was well-informed about the progress that the Indiana University Graduate School was making, and this fact was helpful in his decision to place his materials in the university. The Lilly gifts were made under four deeds of grants (November 26, 1954, May 20, 1955, January 19, 1956, and May

28, 1956). The first deed, made in the form of a personal letter to President Wells, stated, "You will note that in the Deed of Gift I have not undertaken to impose 'the dead hand,' and the University will accordingly be entirely free in the future to dispose of any of the items in such manner as the officials of the University shall deem advisable." The other deeds contained similar clauses. David A. Randall remained in Indianapolis for the next three years, and the deeds make no conditions concerning his employment by Indiana University as curator.

Announcement of the Lilly gift created national publicity, and the news was indeed exciting on the campus and in the town. There was much curiosity about the significance and size of the gift. Speaking before the Bloomington Rotary Club in April 1958, David A. Randall gave local businessmen some answers to their questions. The *Daily Student*, April 17, 1958, quoted him as saying, "The collection has been estimated by experts to be worth five million dollars. Mr. Randall added that it was difficult to appraise such a magnificant collection. This collection was assembled in thirty years by the Lilly family and consists of works dating back to the 15th century." He also told the Rotarians that some of the important items were four folios of Shakespearean plays, a fine edition of the *Compleat Angler* published during Izaak Walton's lifetime, and a remarkable collection of the writings of Robert Burns.

Cecil K. Byrd, associate director of libraries, had announced on July 19, 1957, that construction of a special $1,500,000 building to house the Lilly and other rare collections would probably be started in October. Egger and Higgins, New York architects, would draw the plans and A. M. Strauss would supervise construction of the building. The new structure would be located immediately east of the Business and Economics Building and diagonally across Seventh Street from the Auditorium. It was to be built on the site of the temporary war surplus speech and hearing clinic structure. Of greater significance this sloping site had been reserved for use as an outdoor theater, patterned after those on the Athenian Acropolis and at Epidaurus.

The 117 x 122-foot Indiana limestone building would be designed to harmonize with the massive Auditorium of modified Gothic lines. Byrd said there was to be stack space for 80,000 volumes and a comparable amount of manuscript storage facilities.

Most of this, he said, would be used to house the Lilly materials, which he estimated to be worth $6,000,000. There were to be special rooms in the building to accommodate the Ellison, Oakleaf, and other individual collections gathered in the university.

Byrd, in July 1957, was too optimistic; ground breaking for the Lilly Library did not take place until March 7, 1958. Members of the Lilly family were present, and the project was formally under way. In September 1959, the *Daily Student* announced that the new library was 90 per cent completed, and construction was on schedule. In the meantime more rare books and manuscripts were flowing into Bloomington. Among these was Frederic G. Melcher's collection of Vachel Lindsay papers and manuscripts; Melcher was editor of *Publishers' Weekly*. These new materials were placed with the 75,000 books and 1,250,000 manuscripts then in storage.

Several of the special rooms in the Lilly Library were designed in keeping with the nature of materials they would house. The Lincoln Room was furnished in the White House style of the 1860s, and contained facilities to accommodate the Oakleaf books, prints, the Springfield desk, and other memorabilia. A poetry room was furnished in late eighteenth century English library style, and an American frontier decor was adopted for the Ellison Collection. Local pride and joy were given free rein in Bloomington as the chaste Lilly Library raised its head on the campus horizon in the fall of 1959. *Time Magazine* said David A. Randall was one of the most knowledgeable authorities in the rare book field, "and one of the fastest moving speculators." The new curator also received the commendation of Herman W. Liebert, rare book curator of Yale University, as having helped to create one of the country's finest book and manuscript collections.

The *Indiana Daily Student*, December 15, 1959, was inspired to take a look at the Lilly Librarian. He was not, said the reporter, "a kind little old man, with rimless glasses setting on the end of his nose, lost in stacks and stacks of old, musty books." Instead he was described as a "dynamo of energy whose present ambition is to develop Indiana's rare book collection to a level with the best in the world." Randall gave the impression of being perpetually in motion. He traveled 10,000 miles a year to England and Europe in search of rare materials, and made innumerable trips to New York and the East in search of rarities. On one of these jaunts he brought home for the Oakleaf Collection an original copy of the Thirteenth Amendment signed by Abraham Lincoln and members of the Congress. He also acquired the notes of the physician who performed the autopsy on Lincoln's body.

The list of treasures grew almost monthly in anticipation of the happy date when the rare book temple would be opened to the public. Mary E. Smith, the Terre Haute maiden to whom Paul Dresser dedicated *On the Banks of the Wabash*, contributed letters from Dresser and his brother Theodore Dreiser. These were written between 1897 and 1906. Dresser was a faithful correspondent, writing Miss Smith from various points of his travels about the country. Among these are letters from New York, Chicago, West Baden, Attica Springs, and many other places. Of contemporary political interest were the papers of New York Congressman Joseph O'Connor, who enjoyed the distinction of being the only victim of Franklin D. Roosevelt's attempt to purge his enemies from office.

By late September 1960, Robert A. Miller upped Cecil Byrd's earlier estimate of space for rare books to 100,000 volumes, and 1,500,000 manuscripts; these were actually in place in the building. In fact, the space allotment would be for 300,000 books and 3,000,000 manuscripts. Frederick B. Adams, Jr., director of the Pierpont Morgan Library, said Miller, had been invited to give the dedicatory address. This ceremony took place on October 3, 1960. On that occasion a gold key to the building was presented to Mr. Lilly. Before Adams began his formal address, he presented to the Lilly Library twenty-seven missing manuscript pages from General Lew Wallace's *Ben-Hur*. Mr. Lilly had searched for these pages for a quarter of a century. General Wallace had separated them from the manuscript, and they had remained ever since in the Harper and Brothers' manuscript file until they were given to the Morgan Library. Mr. Lilly owned the rest of the manuscript. At the dedication ceremonies, which took place at the front of the building on Seventh Street, President Wells said the "Cultural Plaza" was a dream of twenty years, and it would be fulfilled with the addition of a fine arts building and a central fountain.

Behind the classical façade of the new Lilly Library reposed a truly magnificent interior housing an even finer collection of books and manuscripts of a highly varied character. There were manuscripts and first editions of most of the major English and American poets. Appealing mightily to Hoosier pride were the 1,400 James Whitcomb Riley manuscripts. There were manuscripts and books of and about most of the early explorers, including some precious Christopher Columbus items. Many of the American historical documents were the only ones of their kind west of the Appalachian Mountains. There was a vast collection of historical scientific manuscripts and books, including those of Euclid, Copernicus, Kepler, Boyle, Harvey, Einstein, Salk, Fleming, and Banting. There was a Gutenberg Bible, and generous representations from the historic presses of Europe and England.

The largest single corpus of coordinated materials were the eight tons of original manuscripts and writings of Upton and Mary Craig Sinclair acquired by the university in 1959. This was undoubtedly one of the largest volumes of paper ever accumulated by an American author, and constitutes an enormously keen insight into social and political change. These papers relate to the period, 1890 to 1959, but some of the manuscripts date back to 1818. In nominating Sinclair for the Nobel Prize, George Bernard Shaw wrote, "When people ask me what happened in my long lifetime, I do not refer them to newspaper files but to the novels of Upton Sinclair." This is the record that the Lilly Library acquired.

Other special collections added in the 1960s were H. B. Collamore's A. E. Housman materials and John C. Rugenstein's gift of the writings, scrapbooks, and memorabilia of Frank McKinney "Kin" Hubbard. Hubbard was creator of the folksy wit "Abe Martin." There are the Ricketts Collection of calligraphy, Andrew Lang's world-famous collection of children's books, and George A. Poole, Jr.'s collection of rare books and manuscripts. David A. Randall told President Wells that the Poole materials were the finest that remained in private hands on either side of the Atlantic. This library was purchased by friends of Indiana University from the Chicago antiquarian dealers, Hacker and Barker. Poole, a member of the Chicago printing family, had assembled the book and manuscripts in the remarkably short span of fifteen years. His library contained a generous number of pieces of incunabula dating from the seventh century. Five books are unique, seven of British origin are the only ones in America, and the 128 pages of the Gutenberg Bible is the copy found in 1828 in a peasant's cottage in Olewig, Germany. There is an extremely rare Gutenberg proof sheet, and a generous assortment of early European and American Bibles.

When the famous Midwestern publishing house, Bobbs-Merrill Company, was sold to Howard W. Sams & Company, Indiana University acquired the files that had accumulated in the older house for almost a century. These constitute an intimate history of a non-New York publisher and its distinguished Middle America authorship. Contained in the correspondence, book manuscripts, and financial records is as fascinating a publishing story as that presented in Donald Sheehan's *This Was Publishing*. Represented in these papers are the histories of a significant number of regional authors and their manuscripts, many of which were published because of the existence of the Bobbs-Merrill Company in the Middle West. Also in the records are the notes of the famous editor-manager David Laurance Chambers.

Of enormous importance in the Lilly Library is the collection assembled by Bernardo Mendel. This collection was acquired from Mendel in 1961, and it consists of rare manuscripts and books in two main categories. One of the categories relates to the world history of geographical discovery and exploration. Especially strong are the materials relating to the discovery and exploration of the Americas. With the addition of the Mendel Collection Indiana University came into possession in a single purchase of more than half the most important titles listed in Henry Harrisse, *Bibliotheca Americana Vetutissima*. The second category consists of major holdings of rare materials dealing with Latin America. Beginning with Cortes, and containing a vast number of Mexican imprints, the Spanish historical collection contains more than 30,000 titles.

After the acquisition of the Mendel Collection in 1961, the famous Austrian industrialist-collector continued to search for rare titles for the Lilly Library. He was able to add five major private collections from around the world to the library's holdings. Some of the latter were strong in the fields of music and German literature. When Bernardo Mendel died, June 1, 1967, his widow Hanse Mendel made a gift of his rare book firm and its collection to Indiana University. Later the Lathrop C. Harper business was sold, after books of special interest to the Lilly Library were removed.

Indiana University by 1960 had indeed established on its campus a solid backlog for research in many fields, especially in the humanities and cultural history. Since 1940 it had come into possession of extraordinary collections that gave it a decided edge over other public universities. By 1970 the cultural and creative potential of the university had assumed global distinction, and the long-standing objective of extending the intellectual impulse of the institution well beyond its immediate campus had become a reality.

The Indiana University Press and the Lilly Library were the accomplishments of an institution that had grown tremendously in its intellectual thrust and in academic maturity. The campus reach, however, was greatly lengthened in those years when the Press and the Library were becoming functional realities. Earlier Indiana University had extended its influence abroad in extension courses, special consultative services, and musical activities. The second quarter of the twentieth century presented an even brighter opportunity to communicate with masses of Hoosiers over a broader geographical pattern.

Radio communication had fascinated many groups on the campus, especially those interested in athletics. In 1937 this interest was broadened when Professor Lee Norvelle of the Department of Speech and Theatre made arrangements with the Indianapolis radio station WIRE to broadcast a series of fifteen-minute campus programs. These were to be transmitted to Indianapolis two or three times a week by long distance phone lines. In Bloomington the broadcasts would originate in an improvised "airless" studio in the Music Building. Actually the first program under this arrangement was a broadcast of the Indiana-Northwestern basektball game on January 12, 1938. Lake Walton recorded a running account on a recording machine, which was then rushed off to Indianapolis to be broadcast before midnight.

Although Indiana University had not participated in any significant way in organized broadcasting before this date, during World War I and afterwards it had maintained courses in the physics of wireless communication. Professor Rolla Ramsey was a pioneer in the field and was so recognized by the War Department. Now the institution was moving into an area of radio communication well removed from the physics laboratory and the theory of wireless transmission. Professor Norvelle had his quarter-hour access to station WIRE Wednesdays and Fridays, and he was ready to begin on Friday, February 13, 1938, a fact which may have explained some subsequent mishaps. President Herman B Wells advised the student radio committee that, "The programs should be representative of all interests of the Univeristy."

By the end of the first week in February Norvelle and his student committee had collected a modest amount of basic equipment which consisted of a public address system, a recording service, a phonograph, and three microphones. In the first broadcast the Glee Club sang Hoagy Carmichael's "Chimes of Indiana," then "Worship" and "Lo, How a Rose E'er Bloomin'." Frank Edmondson of astronomy interviewed Arthur M. Weimer and Willis C. Coval on the subject of federal housing, and Norvelle explained the new programs. Paul McNutt spoke on the second program, and the "Gentlemen from Indiana Quartet" sang. Following these beginnings the university programs ran a full gamut of campus interests, ranging from F. Lee Benns and Edward H. Buehrig's discussions of the problems of the Far East, Alfred C. Kinsey's descriptions of biological research, to the Debate Team discussing the Ludlow War Amendment. There was considerable debate among faculty and students regarding the new radio programs, mostly upon the issue of music versus discussions.

By May 1938 A. B. Hollingshed of sociology was placed in charge of the campus broadcasts. Their range was widened by sending transcribed records to stations in Fort Wayne, Terre Haute, and Evansville. After the university programs had been on the air for a year, a survey was made to try and determine what the public liked and disliked on radio in general. This investigation was financed by a grant of $60,000 from the United States Office of Education. Even more exciting, Indiana University had been invited to become a fourth member of the University Broadcasting Council, which was made up of DePaul, Northwestern, and the University of Chicago. Each member of this consortium agreed to produce for the National Broadcasting and Columbia Broadcasting companies two programs a week modeled after the famous University of Chicago Round Table.

In the meantime Lee Norvelle had made arrangements with

the Louisville *Courier-Journal* station, WHAS, to broadcast Sunday morning programs of music and timely comment. These broadcasts were entitled "Everyman's Campus," and began broadcasts in November 1939. The air waves in the Ohio Valley literally buzzed with Indiana University programs. Professors discussed world issues, singers charmed their listeners, and dramatists gave an even lighter touch to living in a world then hovering on the brink of disaster.

On the campus there was enthusiasm to develop radio broadcasts as educational communication. The Hoosier Radio Workshop produced a profile of listener interests and participation. Across the state there were 1.5 radios per home, these were 4.5 years old, to which 3.4 persons listened an average of four hours a day. News programs enjoyed first preference. This survey gave assuring evidence that the campus programs had a responsive potential audience across the cornfields of the state.

So successful had radio broadcasting become as a medium of instructional communication that Norvelle prepared an estimate of cost for the organization and operation of a university broadcasting station. On February 24, 1942, the Board of Trustees voted to seek precise cost estimates for building a frequency modulation station, and the operation of such a campus enterprise. President Herman B Wells in the meantime had some correspondence with S. A. Sisler of WGRC in Louisville. Sisler had made a tentative offer at least to establish a commercial broadcasting facility in Bloomington. Wells thought the trustees had come to the conclusion that any "responsible group wishing to establish a station in Bloomington and offering its facilities to us for laboratory purposes would be welcome." This proposal was held in abeyance because of wartime stringencies until February 1944, when a Louisville station prepared proposals to be considered by the Executive Committee of the Indiana University Foundation. At the same time the commercial station of the Indianapolis Broadcasting Company offered to cooperate with the Foundation, and without profit to itself. If necessary, the Indianapolis company would subscribe for all the stock, file for a broadcasting license, and hold stock in trust for the Foundation. When profits of sufficient amount had accumulated to liquidate 75 per cent of the cost, the broadcasting company would make the university a gift of the remaining 25 per cent. The university would be asked to provide studios and a transmitter tower site.

Perhaps few universities in the country faced the same peculiar problems of radio transmission as did Indiana. Just as the great limestone block beneath the southern Indiana countryside had created a problem of water supply, it also created curious interferences with radio waves. Also, in its isolated and thinly populated area, Indiana University would have to beam its broadcasts well beyond the twenty-five- or thirty-mile radius capability of a 1,000-watt station. E. Ross Bartley told President Wells, February 10, 1944, that the easiest way to overcome these handicaps was to seek from the Federal Communications Commission authority to establish a 10,000-watt station. Ten days earlier the Board of Trustees had approved application for such a station.

By the latter date H. J. Skornia had been made director of Radio Broadcasting. He wrote President Wells, September 6, 1944, that the university should establish a frequency modulation station at the earliest possible date if the university were to maintain the quality of its programs. He thought that the key moment had arrived to join with Ohio, Michigan, and Illinois in the establishment of a significant academic network. At that moment, he said, he had in preparation a rather detailed statement of Indiana's radio activities for President Howard L. Bevis of Ohio State University. He outlined more of a dream than a reality, but the statement was in line with his recommendations to President Wells. Skornia even said Indiana in its planning envisioned a television station.

This, however, proved to be more of a moment of great expectations than one of attainable certainties. The university administration and the trustees appeared convinced by the arguments presented to them, but obviously this was a venture into the world of communcation which, they implied, held for them many mysteries. Not so for Mrs. W. T. Morgan and her phalanx of the P. E. O. sisterhood of Bloomington. They resolved that the Board of Trustees should put the university into the broadcasting business immediately. Later Wells told Mrs. Morgan the board had received the P. E. O. resolutions kindly.

Despite the flurry of excitement in the fall of 1944, Indiana University was actually no nearer establishment of its own broadcasting station. Early in May President Wells wrote the management of WIRE in Indianapolis that the university was approaching the end of its ninth year of broadcasting, and he was indeed impressed with the services that organization had rendered education in Indiana. The University Round Table, and "Indiana Presents" programs "have made thousands familiar with the state's history and the works of its authors, composers, and scientists."

Wells noted in his *Annual Report* in December that the university had received an engineer's estimate of the problems and costs of establishing a campus station, and this would be incorporated in the application to the Federal Communications Commission for a license. In the meantime H. J. Skornia had set off on a different tack. He proposed to the president the establishment of an intercollegiate broadcasting circuit, using the campus phone and power lines to transmit a low-powered student service. This proposal was to generate a considerable amount of discussion and some controversy in the years to come.

Surely these were years of frustration for the director. There was no reason to doubt the popularity and usefulness of the university broadcast programs, but the institution was not only at the mercy of commercial broadcasters, it could not develop a more substantial program of educational broadcasts. Skornia told President Wells, September 17, 1945, that the Federal Communications Commission engineers had proposed that a 1,000-watt frequency modulation station could be established in Bloomington and beamed to a series of unattended transmitter or booster stations located about the state. This method had been tested successfully in the Washington area. He was anxious that the university get on with making decisions about the building of a station, selecting transmission equipment, and completing the application for an assigned frequency. The Board of Trustees, September 25, again decided to delay action without giving specific reasons for its decision.

The delay in establishing a campus broadcasting station appears not to have reduced radio activity on the campus. The "School of the Sky" was in its tenth year, the "Round Table" had become a fixture, and other series programs had gathered impressive followings. There was now no question as to whether the university could sustain a full broadcasting program for extended periods of "on the air" time. There was, however, a campus problem that had already caused disaster. Skornia wrote Vice President Joseph A. Franklin, October 13, 1947, that the control rooms and studios were insufferably hot. Two staff members and two participants had fainted during broadcasts. He said during months past he had helped carry several persons out of the studios, and had come near collapsing himself. In 1942 Captain William Glass McCaw had died from a heart attack while participating in a Round Table program. Repeated requests had been made of the campus maintenance division for proper ventilation, but so far nothing had been done.

While Professor Skornia and campus maintenance men struggled with problems of ventilation, two events occurred that had a bearing on campus broadcasting history. During the years of dormancy when nothing was accomplished in establishing an independent campus radio voice, students concerned themselves with the idea of campus broadcasting. E. Ross Bartley told the *World-Telephone* in Jannuary 1948 that two bright students had almost overnight decided to establish a radio station on the campus. They failed, however, to secure authority from the administration to carry out their plans. Announcement of this move had stirred up some excitement, if not opposition, in the town, because it was feared the commercial stations would lose listeners and revenue.

Extralegal though the student proposal was it did cause university groups to make inquiry about a trial membership in the larger Intercollegiate Broadcasting System. Such a membership was granted in March 1948, after the Faculty Radio Committee had approved the application. The Indiana station was organized with the call letters WVIS. Now student promoters had to secure from the Student Broadcasting System advice and instructions on the operation of a low-powered campus station.

Two years elapsed before further action was taken on establishing the student broadcasting facility. In January 1950 the Student Senate was told by Al Moellering, a junior, that the station, when established, would belong to the Intercollegiate Broadcasting System, which received a large amount of national advertising patronage. To raise the $7,000 necessary to establish the Indiana station, Moellering proposed assessing students a dollar each. Transmission could be carried over established phone and power lines, and the signal would be so weak that it would not be subject to Federal Communications Commission rules, nor would it interfere with commercial radio and television broadcasts.

Sarkes Tarzian, a Bloomington electronics manufacturer, secured a broadcasting license in 1948 and erected television station WTTV, for which he manufactured his own component parts. Establishment of this station opened a television outlet for the university. Significantly the near-at-hand television facility enabled university groups to appear on television without having to transport personnel and properties to the Indianapolis stations.

The university itself made slow progress toward establishing a campus broadcasting facility. Professor Skornia wrote Joseph A. Franklin in June 1950 that the need for sufficient technical broadcasting staff to handle campus programs had indeed become oppressive. He also proposed that the prospective university facility be called WFIU, and be referred to as a "laboratory" rather than a "station." The properties of abandoned WKMO of Kokomo had been purchased, and a transmitting tower was acquired from a similar station in Tuscola, Illinois. Skornia took pains to assure Franklin that thorough tests would be run on this equipment to assure there would be no electronic interference with commercial broadcasts.

At the end of a long period of indecision and struggle Indiana University was almost ready to begin independent broadcasting. The *Daily Student* announced, September 23, 1950, that WFIU was just about to broadcast its first program. It was a 10,000-watt station emitting its signals from a 244-foot tower. This structure straddled the temporary war surplus building used for nurses training, and as a library annex. It was located between the Sigma Alpha Epsilon fraternity house and Smithwood Hall. Four studios and three control rooms were built into the renovated building.

WFIU began broadcasting October 9, 1950. President Wells, just as he had done back in 1938 when the first university broadcasts were made, introduced the station to listeners. The university, he said, would offer thirty-five hours of broadcasts between Monday and Friday evening. Before the station had actually made its first broadcast it was known that it would create serious interference with the programs of the Indianapolis television station WFBM. Protest calls poured into the radio station. For instance, children watching cartoon programs would be treated to a highly sophisticated lecture on business trends by "Bugs Bunny." The *Daily Herald-Telephone* said, October 11, 1950, "Bloomington was enjoying the first thrills of the new entertainment era opened to us through television, still is disturbed by the meddlesome electronic tendencies of the new I. U. clinical station." The answer said the paper, was obvious; the university station should yield to WFBM until the trouble was eradicated.

A diligent search was begun to determine the cause of the radio interference; in the meantime WFIU temporarily suspended night broadcasting. The two electronics manufacturing companies, Sarkes Tarzian and Radio Corporation of America, both sought to correct the trouble. Sarkes Tarzian suggested relocation of the university tower at a site outside Bloomington. Radio Corporation of America engineers devised special wave traps, but before these could be used some discussion developed between the two companies as to their usefulness. While engineers argued their cases, the university remained without a solution to its broadcasting problem. So seriously did this puzzling electronics situation become that the university faced a real threat to its public good will. At the end of the summer session in 1951, WFIU suspended broadcasting altogether.

After a year of trauma Indiana applied for a new broadcasting frequency. President Wells informed the Board of Trustees that although the university was well within the rules of the Federal Communications Commission, "There was real danger . . . of doing permanent damage to the University's relations with the public if we persisted in being a source of annoyance to television viewers." That some of the public at least was wrought up by this situation was borne out in a letter from H. J. Skornia to President Wells, October 8, 1952. He said that "during this time [of the interference debacle] when I was being awakened at all hours of the night, when neighbor children were throwing rocks at our children because 'their dad was ruining their TV,' and when my wife was being snubbed, I tried to behave like a gentleman, even in the face of what I considered unfair abuse. . . ."

The Federal Communications Commission in its plodding way finally granted Indiana University's request for a new wave frequency and the campus station once again began broadcasting full weekly programs on March 31, 1952, and without further interference with the Indianapolis television beam. By July 1952 the university was broadcasting 3,306 programs of various sorts annually. The interference lapse did not disrupt the regular programs that were broadcast through commerical stations; if anything, the campus programs increased in both number and popularity.

On top of all the emotionalism stirred up in the first year

of independent campus broadcasting there arose some personal sensitivity on the part of H. J. Skornia. He had been most active in establishing Radio Free Europe programs and was out of the country much of the time. In 1952 Elmer G. Sulzer, head of the Department of Radio in the University of Kentucky, was employed to head up the Indiana program. Sulzer, a native of Madison and a former Indiana student, had attracted national attention with the Kentucky "Listening Centers," which sought to penetrate the great cultural void of Appalachia. Skornia expressed to President Wells the belief that he was being replaced because of the interference issue. Wells acknowledged that Skornia had worked diligently and had done his best in a most difficult situation. "I should point out, however, that the problem was settled by the relatively simple expedient of changing the wave length of the station." Whatever else might have been back of this exchange of letters, Skornia silenced it by resigning to accept the executive secretaryship of Educational Broadcasts.

The use of radio and television as a means of extending the instructional voice of the university was highly successful. The "School of the Sky" gave the institution an international reach with its rich variety of programs. It was broadcast over seventeen United States stations; in February 1953 it was commended by the International Broadcasting Union, because "This constitutes one of the most valuable contributions of the American radio in the cultural field." Earlier the professional journalists, through Sigma Delta Chi, selected the regular Tuesday broadcast, "It's Your World" as the outstanding public service radio program for 1949.

So satisfying were the educational radio programs that the College of Arts and Sciences in January 1950 approved the granting of a degree in radio. The contents of this new field were to be drawn from almost the entire university curriculum. The new course also took into consideration the fact that television was already a fact in American life. Sarkes Tarzian offered the university access to this media through use of his Bloomington station. In his *Annual Report* for 1951–52, President Wells expressed favor for this offer because the broadcasting station was nearby, and the university could possibly finance a two-camera subsidiary station for less than $80,000. Of greater importance the university could avail itself of practical experience, which would prevent the making of embarrassing and costly blunders in the future in the management of television broadcasting. A deterrent in this field had been the fact that the Federal Communications Commission only granted annual licenses for educational channels. The university, in fact, did not begin broadcasting from its own television station WTIU until March 3, 1969.

Because of the phenomenal success of the "School of the Sky" more requests for tapes reached Bloomington than the university could supply. These came from all across the country, not only for materials to be rebroadcast, but to be used in instructional laboratories. Nothing the university had done in almost a century and a half of existence had served so well its third objective of rendering public service. With radio and television demands booming, enlargement of course offerings in the relatively new vocational field was made mandatory. The Department of Radio and Television had indeed moved far beyond its pioneer beginnings when Lee Norvelle, H. J. Skornia, and a handful of professors and students had broadcast the first programs from a suffocating makeshift studio in the Music Building.

By 1960 Indiana University was through the birth pangs of broadcasting. President Herman B Wells in a statement that reflected both pride and relief said, "Our FM Station, WFIU, now is the most powerful broadcasting station of any type in Indiana, with an effective radiated power of 75,000 watts, we now lay down a good signal over at least half of the area in the State of Indiana." The Indiana station had been given a monopoly to broadcast the Saturday afternoon Metropolitan Opera programs, a fact which permitted the institution direct access to "upper level listeners."

It was to an "upper level" constituency that the Press, Lilly Library, and many of the broadcast programs appealed. In this audience, however, were those who appraised the quality of the institution by its accomplishments in significant areas of intellectual communication.

[X X]

A New Age—A New Helmsman

WHEN HERMAN B WELLS announced his intention to retire from the presidency of Indiana University in 1962, he caught the local academic community largely by surprise. For twenty-five years he had been a tremendous personal force in the institution, and it was difficult to imagine the university under any other leadership. He and his mother Mrs. Granville Wells had seemed permanent fixtures in the best of the Hoosier tradition. The era of the Wells administration was one of accomplishments measured in almost every standard of academic growth and maturity. The tangibles were visible on every hand in the form of modern buildings; the great Auditorium, the Lilly Library, the addition to the Music Building, Ballantine Hall, and a sprawling modern city of residence halls. Even more significant were the intangibles. A top-flight faculty enjoyed both financial support and the freedom of investigation and publication of the most controversial subjects. Classrooms and laboratories fed a constant procession of well-trained graduates into the national stream of specialized human beings. In Indianapolis the professional schools of Medicine, Dentistry, and Nursing had achieved national recognition by their contributions in several areas. Perhaps the retiring president had no greater accomplishment than breaking the parity formula, which was stifling higher education in Indiana, and creating a modern system of internal fiscal management.

In much greater detail this volume deals with the day-to-day operation of the university, with its victories and its frustrations. For both Wells and the university community there was the great human asset of affection and mutual respect. It was in this moment of high momentum that the trustees were asked to find a new president who could lead the institution to even greater expansion and achievements.

The search for a new president involved all the emotions of replacing a revered administrator, and at the same time finding a younger executive who could assume the all but awesome responsibilities of steering the university through the troubled decade, 1960–70. The board, acting with the aid of a committee of senior faculty members, sought suggestions from alumni, faculty, friends of the university, and from professional sources. Trustees visited the campuses of the Big Ten Schools and the major foundations. In all, said Mrs. Mary Maurer, a trustee, the board members considered the names of more than 150 possible candidates. Finally, on May 2, 1962, they were ready to announce their nominee, if President John F. Kennedy would accept his resignation as Secretary of the Army. The *Indiana Daily Student*, May 2, 1962, reported that a near-capacity audience had assembled in the Memorial Auditorium for Founders Day ceremonies. President Wells summarized the history of the university, and then told the assembly that "birthdays sometimes bring surprises." He introduced Willis Hickam, president of the Board of Trustees. This, said the reporter, caused a murmur in the audience, which now sensed the nature of the Trustees' announcement. President Hickam made the brief statement that Elvis Jacob Stahr, Jr., Secretary of the Army, had been chosen to be the new president of Indiana University. At the same time in Washington Secretary Stahr was submitting his resignation to President Kennedy. He requested that he be relieved of his cabinet post responsibilities by June 30, so he could assume the new appointment.

Stahr's letter of resignation brought warm commendation from the President of the United States. Kennedy wrote him, "You can take up your new and most important post at Indiana University with great satisfaction of a job well done, and a service truly performed for the government and the people of our country." Then he said, "Your conduct of Army affairs has been an outstanding example of good management. Your policies of recognition of young talent, of examination and adoption of new doctrines and techniques, and emphasis on vigorous leadership for our Army mark your tenure as Army Secretary." Stahr had often been the subject of news stories in the Washington and New York press. Some newsmen had hinted at a rift between Stahr and Secretary of Defense Robert McNamara, none of which seems to have had any real substance of truth. When Stahr's resignation was announced it received generous nationwide publicity, and so did his appointment as the new president at Indiana.

Even with the board's attempt at utmost secrecy, Secretary Stahr's selection was not actually a complete surprise. The *Indianapolis Star*, February 28, 1962, carried a story that he was the board's choice. It was said his name had been proposed by Donald C. Danielson of New Castle. The Indianapolis paper had added that Dr. Stahr was a registered Democrat. It would have been strange indeed if he had served in a cabinet position in the "days of Camelot" under any other registration.

Mary Maurer later told reporters the board had in fact considered Stahr fifteen months earlier and then dropped his name when he was appointed Secretary of the Army. Later his name was restored to the list of prospective candidates, and each member of the board had at different times visited Stahr in his Washington office. She told a *Daily Student* reporter, May 3, 1962, "We've been on our knees for 23 months."

Five days later the *Indianapolis News* carried a story that Indiana Congressman William Bray was unhappy about Secretary Stahr's announcement that the VI Army Corps headquarters was being moved from Fort Benjamin Harrison to Battle Creek, Michigan; this was not the happiest introduction of the trustees' candidate to many Hoosiers.

Elvis J. Stahr, Jr., was born in Hickman, Kentucky, in 1916. He had graduated with a Bachelor of Arts degree from the University of Kentucky, and with a perfect academic record. In fact, Stahr's achievement was the best four-year record in that institution's history. He had been most active in student affairs, including the office of cadet colonel in the Reserve Officers Training Corps. In his senior year he had been appointed a Rhodes Scholar in Oxford University for the years, 1936–39. He received from

Oxford the B. C. L. and M. A. degrees. In 1943 he was awarded the diploma in the Chinese languages from Yale University. Following service in World War II as a lieutenant colonel, Stahr became a senior associate in the Wall Street law firm of Mudge, Stone, Williams, and Tucker. In 1947 he returned to the University of Kentucky as associate professor of law, and a year later he was made dean of the Law School. Stahr remained dean of law for eight years before being appointed provost of the University in charge of making plans for the organization and construction of a new medical school. That same year he moved from Kentucky to the University of Pittsburgh as vice president for the Professional Schools, and in 1959 he was appointed president of the West Virginia University. Earlier he had served the Eisenhower administration as a consultant on education beyond the high schools. From 1961–62 he served in the Kennedy Administration as Secretary of the Army. Besides this breathtaking list of services the new Indiana president had served on numerous national committees and boards which acquainted him with many areas of national interests.

When news of the Indiana appointment was out, President Stahr told reporters, "As far as I am concerned, this is the top job in my profession. You can't imagine how happy I am." He said he felt like "a kid with a new toy." Two days after this news conference the Stahrs stopped at Weir Cook Airport in Indianapolis on their way to review the 101st Airborne Division at Fort Campbell, Kentucky. He assured reporters he might never fill Wells' shoes, and he refused to answer questions about compulsory ROTC and the Sex Institute. When asked if he would remain in the job a quarter of a century, he replied that at age 46, and under retirement rules of the university, this would be impossible for him to do so. Nevertheless, he expressed the desire to send down his roots in Bloomington. To the inevitable reporter's question about athletics, Stahr expressed an interest in both football and basketball and said he would be delighted if Indiana won the Big Ten championship in each of these sports. Dorothy Stahr answered the astute question as to what she expected her role to be in Bloomington with the statement, "raising children and pouring tea." The Stahrs did not come to Bloomington until June 2, and then for only a brief visit with President Wells and his mother, and to get a glimpse of the president's office.

Back in Washington Secretary Stahr was given a farewell review by the troops at Fort Myers, Virginia, June 28, and on Monday July 3, he was in the president's office in Bloomington to begin work. His first day on the campus consisted of conferences with the four vice presidents. In the afternoon at a farewell reception for retiring staff members the faculty greeted the new president and his wife, and said a final farewell to the new Chancellor Wells and Mrs. Granville Wells.

This was the formal beginning of a new administrative era at Indiana University. No other change of administration in the institution's history had received so much publicity or been accompanied by so much fanfare. The campus anticipated an exciting future of building on the solid foundation developed during the past quarter of a century.

Two days after he had taken up his duties as president, Dr. Stahr made his maiden speech before the American College Public Relations Association in White Sulphur Springs, West Virginia. He told the audience, "So long as we believe in government by and for the people—a concept the communists abhor—we must continue to find ways to exceed in educated brain power." After commenting on narrowly trained technicians, he said, "No mere fact-oriented education can fulfill our requirement." He thought "America must of course continue to train, and in increasing numbers, the highly educated person who can serve brilliantly on our scientific and technological frontiers if we are to feed, clothe, and sustain an 'exploding' population; if we are to help the rising nations learn how to satisfy the material aspirations of their people without sacrificing their yearning for freedom. . . ." This was the new president's educational philosophy. Universities and colleges had a large mission, and they were indispensable in "the ever-changing course of man's long adventure on earth."

For American universities in general the next six years of "man's long adventure on earth" were to be stormy ones. These were years in which the American campus became the scene of turmoil in which all sorts of forces and counterforces were at work. No other generation of university presidents had been confronted by so many complex issues, or the reexamination of so many old and comfortable human values. Academic freedom was to be threatened on all sides, both by radical and ultraconservative groups. President Stahr was to learn within a short time after his arrival on the Bloomington campus that the defense of freedom in the university had become far more than a platitudinous expression of ideals. There were the challenges of maintaining, and even increasing, the momentum which the university had generated in recent years, of hiring new and promising professors, of strengthening old departments, and developing new areas. It was still necessary to carry out a tremendous building program, to develop new degree-granting curricula at the regional campus centers, and to provide facilities and services for a phenomenally increasing student enrollment.

Added to the burden of the age was the startling exhibition in 1963 of Russian scientific advances in the launching of the orbital *Sputnik*. This event fired American imagination, stirred scientists into action, made inordinate drains on almost every research facility in the land, and challenged universities to redouble their efforts in all the scientific and technological areas. All of these pressures were exerted on Indiana University.

On top of getting himself oriented to his new job, President Stahr was called upon to make an almost ridiculous number of speeches. In Bloomington and across Indiana there seemed to have prevailed an almost pleading air that he would measure up to Wells. There seemed to have been an insatiable desire to know what he was like. What was his educational philosophy, and in a more ephemeral manner, how well would he serve the Hoosier tradition? To incoming students in September 1962, he emphasized need for more and better education. Speaking to the Indiana Bar Association two days earlier, he pleaded for support of education in America's fight against communism and the preservation of American opportunity. In other speeches he predicted a registration explosion when the wartime "babies" came knocking on the registrar's door. One wonders when and how the new president got all his speeches formulated for delivery, to say nothing of attending to the demanding duties of his office.

There was no end to the probing. Every move the new president made, a reporter was on hand to ask questions. For expert help in this area, he employed James R. Jordan of the State University of Iowa as head of the University News Bureau to replace the highly respected E. Ross Bartley, who had just retired, and also as assistant to the president in charge of university relations. Stahr appreciated the importance of good public relations, especially with the people in the Middle West who took deep satisfaction in their social and cultural attainments. At French Lick, October 12, 1962, he told the directors of the Indiana Chamber of Commerce, "Indiana University is, in simple fact, not only one of the Nation's best, but an extraordinarily well managed institution. Superior in this respect to any other institution with which I am familiar (and I have gained some familiarity with quite a number a few years ago, when I was with President Eisenhower's Committee on Education Beyond High School). In fact, as an old Wall Street lawyer, I would venture that the resources at Indiana University are used more efficiently than those of many business firms."

Thus the new president in speech after speech assured one group after another that he not only was dedicated to the ideals of higher education, but also to the philosophy of progress and improvement. Before he was formally inaugurated on November 19, he had received broad exposure on the campus and in the state. Already he had begun to take his place ex officio on public boards and committees, and to feel comfortable in speaking in behalf of the university.

The inauguration took place in the Auditorium with 750 academic delegates present. For the first time in Indiana University history a new president was presented with the mace, jewel, and collar as physical symbols of his office. Stahr's inaugural address was a thoughtful outline of aspirations, balanced between expressions of sentimentalities and serious statements of purposes. He discussed the new place of the university in society, the educational process and opportunity, research, the role of the professional schools, and the rising importance of the community or off-campus colleges in the university system.

The inaugural was a warm and friendly occasion of rededication of Indiana University to its central purposes in an affluent era of staggering political and social changes. American political, economic, and educational leadership of the period spoke generally in terms of ceaseless expansion in every phase of institutional operation. Only slightly visible in November 1962 was the rising cloud bank of student restlessness and revolt which would prove so disruptive of traditional educational procedures. The United States Supreme Court in April 1954 had brought into focus the matter of co-racial educational equalities, and perhaps unleashed an enormous sense of guilt North and South in this field. Although

Indiana University had already desegregated its classes, dormitories, and all other public facilities, there were now demands for a much deeper racial integration. Some of these were to be made in the forms of new curricular approaches to black history and culture, semiprivate social organizational revision, and additions to the teaching and administrative staffs. All areas of American public life were being subjected to the acceptances of new social codes, new human relations, and shifting if not fading sentimentalities. President Stahr spoke of these things in his address, but he could not have anticipated their full implications for the future of Indiana University.

In Bloomington there were two portents of the future on inauguration day. The *Indianapolis Star*, November 20, 1962, said that although classes had been dismissed only approximately 500 students lined the parade route. The second was newspaper criticism of the general Indiana institutional budget requests for support of higher education. Only the day before his inauguration the new president had to answer this criticism. He explained to budget officials that within five years Indiana University student enrollment would increase from 17,829 to 31,000. Needs for additional faculty were urgent, and the State of Indiana had not assumed its fair share of higher educational expenses in the past. He cited the fact that in the case of the university, the state had paid only 26 percent of the cost of land and buildings, 40 percent of the operating budget, and 30 percent of the current building maintenance. The four public universities had asked for $228,000,000 for the next biennium, an increase of $92,000,000. Of this amount Indiana University sought $94,800,000 from the state, while the entire university budget was projected at $253,700,000. Many times in the next six years of his administration, Elvis J. Stahr was to justify requests for funds from the state.

In his first *State of the University Report*, December 1963, President Stahr revealed how fast the honeymoon of a new public university administration could be brought to a close. "My first year here," he wrote, "despite 'sweating out' the General Assembly session(s); the acrobatics of those terribly exercised in various ways about a now defunct group called YSA; and some of the inevitable, and I fear eternal headaches associated with 'football for the alumni, sex for the students, and parking for the faculty (and the sophomores),' was a happy one for my family and me."

Stahr mentioned the postponement of a football game, the dismissal of classes, and the memorial services for President John F. Kennedy that year. Jacqueline Kennedy had accepted Stahr's invitation to speak before the Golden Anniversary Convention of the Association of College Unions. This, of course, was cancelled. In the same report the new president set forth the Jeffersonian philosophy of little direct administrative government and more presidential-professorial partnership. This was in fact a subtle but distinct statement of administrative-faculty policy that was never fully grasped on the campus. All administrative branches of the university government, he said, existed to create the environment and tools in which the learning process could best thrive. In a subsequent speech in Washington, D.C., he said that it was the unique role of the university "to be ahead of the society to provide a seed bed of development, growth, and above all innovation to meet new requirements. It is the job of the University not merely to commence and transmit the knowledge and values which it receives but to question, criticize, and improve upon existing knowledge."

Stahr's speeches and his rather lengthy "State of the University" statements revealed a high degree of thoughtfulness. At the same time this was an age of questioning, criticizing, and maybe improving upon existing knowledge. He indicated a realization that the American university system was under fire because of its dedication to freedom of research, publication, and professorial securities. Every day Indiana University was brought under some kind of fire for the acts of its faculty, or for lack of action. On December 17, 1963, Stahr outlined plans before the Faculty Council for the undertaking of an "all-over survey of Indiana University." He told his colleagues American public higher education was entering a new era in which it faced both traditional and new problems. Numbers of students and costs were two knotty challenges of the immediate future.

Professor York Willbern of the Department of Government and an experienced institutional analyst, William R. Breneman of Zoology, and George Wilton Wilson of Economics formed the Self-Study Committee, which was given access to all phases of the institution's operation. During the next three years these scholars were diligent in making an investigation of the entire university program. On May 29, 1966, they issued their extensive two-volume report, a document which was in fact a blueprint for the university's projection into the future.

Before the Self-Study Committee could complete its investigation, the private *Bowker Report* was published by the American Statistical Association in March 1965. This report dealt with graduate competence, and Indiana University ranked ninth in the humanities and social studies. A year later a second analysis by Education and World Affairs, *The University Looks Abroad*, said "Indiana University by any measure of strength among American universities must be rated near the top." This publication also made the observation that there was no ready explanation "Why this small frontier college should grow into a university with a world-wide reputation and strong international commitments." It undertook to answer its question by saying, "Strong personalities have left their mark on Indiana University," and it mentioned specifically Herman B Wells and Elvis J. Stahr.

Simultaneously with the latter report was the much more thorough one, *An Assessment of Quality in Graduate Education* compiled by Allan M. Cartter for the American Council on Higher Education. This survey was made in 1964 when 4,000 of the nation's established scholars were asked to evaluate qualitatively the work in twenty-four disciplines. Every department in which Indiana University offered graduate courses leading to the doctorate was ranked in the top half of all American universities, and seven—Astronomy, Botany, English, German, Linguistics, Russian, and Zoology—were ranked in the first ten. Eleven more were in the first twenty. The Cartter report did not include Business, Dentistry, and Music, areas in which Indiana was especially strong. Three departments—Chemistry, Mathematics, and Physics—were rated 20th, 25th, and "Good." These were areas in which the Stahr Administration sought to establish national strength. Generally Indiana was rated as one of the top twenty-five schools in the United States.

Since the 1950s a significant issue was whether or not the administration should give the construction of a new library a higher priority than other new buildings and university needs. This issue had been the subject of earnest discussion in the Faculty Council on several occasions during the Wells administration. The old library structure was inadequate by every standard of measurement. It could no longer house the growing collection.

Already it was so crowded that research space for faculty use was severely limited. Student traffic became more burdensome with each succeeding year, even with the addition of the undergraduate student library located next door in the old Student Building.

In submitting the budget request for 1964, Indiana University asked for $11,900,000 with which to build a modern library plant. Robert A. Miller, director of Libraries, told a *Daily Student* reporter, October 27, 1964, that if the General Assembly appropriated this sum it would take three years to plan and construct the new building. A year later the two United States Senators from Indiana informed the university that the Department of Health, Education, and Welfare had allotted to Indiana University $2,132,456 to help finance the undergraduate portion of the new building. In time, this large new and modern library facility was to become President Stahr's most significant physical landmark on the campus.

More important than the new building was the fact that under Robert Miller's administration the book, pamphlet, and periodical collections had grown phenomenally. During the years of faculty, plant, and program expansion after 1945, Indiana University became a major purchaser in both the rare and current book markets. Even when there was lack of shelf space or staff to process them, materials were purchased and stored. As the university expanded its language, international fields, science programs, and artistic and cultural offerings, the library made heroic efforts to keep abreast of the ever-broadening demands. With the opening of the Lilly Library the rare books were isolated in this major research depository. The mid-twentieth century not only saw the publication of a phenomenally large number of books throughout the world, but the tide of periodicals, pamphlets, public documents, and official reports was almost overwhelming. Indiana University was forced to acquire a highly representative body of this material to serve its research scholars, and to maintain its rank in the field of advanced studies.

Other major buildings were to be planned and constructed during the Stahr years, but for the moment there were other and more pressing issues which shortened the orientation period of the president. As both Wells and Stahr pointed out to legislators almost every two years, Indiana University had never operated in any year of its existence solely with funds appropriated to it by the General Assembly. It was not until after the Civil War that the state made direct financial grants to the institution, and then only in modest sums. Funds were derived from various sources including land sales, student fees, gifts, and limited returns from capital funds. In the intensive fund drive in the 1920s to collect money with which to finance four memorial buildings and facilities, the university made its first modern plant expansion. This, however, was insufficient to care for the urgent needs for additional physical facilities, staff increases, and support of the various university services. This was especially true in the 1930s when matching funds were needed to take advantage of federal grants.

In the earlier drives for funds it seemed clear to the Board of Trustees that Indiana University alumni were not giving significant amounts of money to help modernize their institution. The board began in 1935 to discuss the possibility of creating a nonprofit agency for the sole purpose of aiding the university, and which would prevent the commingling of private money with public funds. Complete control of funds was to be lodged with the university, and donors were to be assured faithful execution of their wishes in perpetuity.

The Indiana University Foundation was organized in 1936 to serve at least three fiscal purposes. First, to create a semiprivate agency for the solicitation and management of restricted gifts from bureaucratic red tape, and to open a channel by which private donors could make contributions to the university without giving the state an excuse for reducing its appropriations. Second, to create an agency to manage the new federal funds which were derived from central government sources, and, third, to open the way for receiving corporate gifts and grants which could be earmarked for special research projects and services.

Beginning modestly, the Indiana University Foundation prospered in a limited way, and by 1960 it had become rather affluent. The idea had proved sound, and the device was imminently workable. It was not to exist, however, without misunderstandings and criticism. To the uninformed, the Foundation appeared to be a private conclave that controlled the institution itself. Some critics looked upon it as being beyond the direct control and review of the various public accounting agencies. There were some who objected to it because of its tax-exempt status that gave it an investment advantage, and some regarded it as a competitive device for discriminating against local businesses and government. These were the standard criticisms that Americans since the second decade of the nineteenth century had raised against public colleges and universities.

Fortunately, after 1936 the Indiana University was able to cultivate a substantial number of supporting friends and to receive appreciable gifts and grants. Its accounts were audited annually by certified public accountants, and its general fiscal operations were open to public viewing. By 1962 the Foundation had proved an indispensable operative device that helped the University solicit and administer its funds to the best advantage. The critics were ill-informed as to the financial history of the institution, and little appreciated the impact of tradition upon this aspect of its development.

For the Wells administration, with rather substantial income from research grants, royalties from Crest toothpaste, and numerous other sources, the Foundation was a necessary management and fiscal agency. Beyond this the capital resources accumulated in the Foundation gave the University the necessary margin between hiring able and productive men and supporting their research, and accepting a condition of mediocrity. Too, the scholarships and fellowships supported from Foundation funds made a tremendous impact on the quality of advanced students attracted to the graduate departments.

In 1962 the wolf cry was loud in the land; some unspecified persons again protested the public auditor should audit the Foundation books. The implication was that something irregular was taking place. E. Ross Bartley, public relations director, said that Governor Matthew Welsh in October that year had declared the State of Indiana "would not, or had no desire to, audit the books of the Foundation." Governor Welsh said, "The Foundation has been the organ through which much of the research work of the University has been financed, and the Foundation has performed an extremely valuable service to the state."

Two years later the Monroe County prosecutor, Thomas A. Hoadley, filed a formal complaint in June 1964, against the Indiana University Foundation, the Hoosier Realty Corporation, and the Board of Trustees. He hoped to force the three bodies to open their books for auditing by the Indiana Board of Public

Accounts. Hoadley contended in Circuit Court before Judge Nat U. Hill that under the terms of a Bloomington ordinance of 1909 it was a misdemeanor to refuse to submit to a public audit.

Herman B Wells, president of the Foundation, told a *Daily Student* reporter, June 23, 1964, that "The Foundation, as a private state-chartered non-profit corporation welcomes a test of its powers under Indiana Statutes and of its procedures." He explained the books were audited annually by certified public accountants, and all Foundation policies were made by a board of respectable Indiana citizens. The Hoosier Realty Corporation was created to purchase and hold land for future university expansion. This land remained on the tax rolls, and was assessed in the same way as private property. Wells explained that if the university bought land directly it would become tax exempt. Fenwick T. Reed, Secretary of the Board of Trustees, was uninformed at that date of Hoadley's complaint against that body. E. Ross Bartley told the reporter an adverse decision by Judge Hill could be costly. For one thing it would destroy the anonymity of donors, and no doubt would prevent many individuals and corporations from making further gifts to the university.

Throughout the summer the arguments over ownership of property by the Hoosier Realty Company, and the question of tax payments were reported in the press. In mid-July Chancellor Wells issued a detailed statement of property ownership by both the foundation and the realty company. He listed taxes paid, and indicated the parcels of land that had come to the university as gifts. Hoadley continued his campaign, claiming the Foundation hid behind its tax-exempt status. President Stahr replied to the Hoadley charges three years later, March 8, 1967, that "Indiana University Foundation is a private nonprofit corporation, but it is not a secret corporation. Its books are audited annually by certified public accountants." A new charge was made that the university had been either offered or given funds by the United States Central Intelligence Agency. Stahr again answered that funds had been received from the Institute of International Education, the Asia Foundation, and the African-American Institute. These grants were made and used for specific educational purposes connected with the United States foreign policy procedures. When the university had sought such funds, it wished to support specific programs that were planned by its staff. Stahr said the university had entered into no classified contracts with the United States or any other governments. He informed the public, "neither the University nor the Foundation knows or could know all of the sources of funds of all the foundations, corporations, or individuals which have made grants to them over the years. However, in accepting any gift or grant from any source, we do know in each and every instance the purpose for which the funds are intended, and of course, how they are to be used."

The Hoadley charges went unsustained by court decision. How much they may have influenced either donors or public opinion is an unanswerable question, and perhaps not at all. What they did portend, however, was the great educational irrelevancy of much of the agitation of the 1960s. Charges against the Indiana University Foundation and the Hoosier Realty Corporation were puffed up to demagogic proportions without the accuser having to answer directly to the question of why they were suspect or detrimental to the educational purposes of the university.

For the first time in its thirty-one year history, the Indiana University Foundation, in September 1967, published a report of its holdings as determined by the accounting firm of Dieterle, Cinkaske, and Ennis. At that time it had total assets of $8,600,000. It had handled $74,000,000 in public contracts, and in the past fiscal year had paid the university $22,000,000 of this amount. It had earned in the past year $2,600,000, $1,009,411 of which was classed as "contract income." The Foundation had expended $2,400,000 and had an excess of income of $143,716. Possibly the most important revelation was the fact that the Foundation had received $1,149,611 in contributions for the employment of new faculty members, and for salary increases, student aid, and departmental support. The accountants uncovered no suspicious secret accounts, and no Central Intelligence Agency spies were listed in the report.

The Foundation gained a considerable amount of unsolicited publicity because of the Hoadley charges. It seemed certain the public was made conscious of both its existence and usefulness. In a prefatory note to the published report Herman B Wells took the opportunity to explain the mission of such a foundation in the operation of a public university.

The ridiculous furor over the more private fiscal affairs of Indiana University in more settled times would have been little more than comical local political antics, but in the 1960s it reflected the tenor of the age. President Stahr's honeymoon in Bloomington was at best a short one. He, like almost every other president of a public university in the land, discovered that there was a broad chasm between the ideals one expressed in maiden speeches and an inaugural address and the nature of the forces that beset an expanding university struggling under both a great educational and public service responsibility. Each succeeding year of the decade was to bring its emotional upheavals, almost none of which came within the traditional context of Indiana University's history. Not only was the institution itself searching for clearer directions to the future, the public also sought answers to the problems of a world in upheaval which focused more than ever before in the halls of academe. Because of its great struggle to establish freedom of research, publication, and teaching the university was the one place where voices of protest could be raised with the greatest assurance against political and public recrimination. Amazingly, the great momentum which Indiana University had built up since 1945 helped to thrust it forward despite the agonizingly disruptive forces that surfaced after 1965. The internal programs of the institution were little deterred by the noise and clamor of the moment.

[XXI]

An Age of Moral Ambiguities

Modern universities, in a postwar American society that had either ignored or revised a significant portion of the old puritanical code, could no longer function as bastions of the social system. The impact of the automobile, the movies, the book and magazine press, television, the changing relations between the sexes, and the feeling of greater individual freedom on the part of youth in determining the course of their lives came into full blossom by 1960.

No doubt the presence on the campus of a large number of married students, and especially of married undergraduates, helped to revise university attitudes. Nothing, however, had greater impact than the affluent condition of the average family. Children in earlier periods of American history had been forced to assume economic responsibilities during their college years, but now they did less to help maintain themselves. This created the paradoxical condition of unrest because individuals developed guilt complexes and began searching for that elusive thing, personal identity. This social yearning showed itself in classrooms, in counseling sessions, and in campus organizations. Students appeared not to have realized that human beings since the beginning of civiliation itself have searched for self-identity as part of the adventure of living. By 1960 it appeared evident that Indiana University was caught up in some form of incipient student revolt.

Forces which brought changes originated partly beyond the boundaries of Bloomington. The age confronting the American campus in the coming decade was one of a great hailstorm of "alphabetical" national and campus student organizations. In 1959 the old Student League for Industrial Democracy of Jack London and Upton Sinclair fame went through at least a couple of metamorphic stages to emerge as Students for a Democratic Society. Already there were in existence the various racially or civil rights oriented organizations, such as the National Association for the Advancement of Colored People, Congress of Racial Equality, and the Student Nonviolent Coordinating Committee. Students at the University of California had protested both the execution of Caryl Chessman, and the actions of the Associated Students of the University of California. In Greensboro, North Carolina, black students had introduced the "sit-in" movement in an attempt to desegregate a 5-and-10-cent-store lunch counter. Highly irritating was the disappearance of three CORE workers in Philadelphia, Mississippi, later proved to have been murdered by the despicable Ku Klux Klan. All of these occurrences fed the flames of the new student left. In Michigan and Wisconsin Robert Alan Haber and Tom Hayden developed the Students for a Democratic Society into a force that destroyed the complacency of many campuses. They collected headlines as the movement grew. In mid-1962 at a meeting of various student leftist groups in the United Auto Workers' summer camp in Port Huron, Michigan, SDS adopted the *Student Manifesto*. This sixty-page document was a recitation of every reform that Tom Hayden could think of at the time. Adoption of this document signaled the emergence of the new student left as a clearly identifiable force on the American campus. The *Manifesto* criticized the apathetic state of the American university, and challenged students to upgrade it by joining the "now generation."

Indiana University had developed over the years a rather voluminous set of rules and codes relating to student decorum and relationships within various areas of the university. Some of these enjoyed no other distinction than being the cumulative statutory barnacles that no group had bothered to scrape away, others flowed out of successive faculty council and student legislative meetings. The administration's attempts to establish rules of management of the new living complexes also created myriad codes and regulations applying to student conduct. By 1964 most of this cumbersome body of materials came under fire from someone.

In October 1968, and in the midst of a considerable amount of student unrest, Interim President Herman B Wells observed in a "State of the University Address" that David Starr Jordan in 1885 had revoked all student rules but two: They should not set buildings on fire or shoot a professor. This was one of Jordan's more whimsical utterances which not even he observed. Jordan demonstrated on several occasions his support of the old surrogate parental rule. Besides, neither Jordan nor Indiana University in 1885 assumed any direct responsibility for housing the student body, which at that time was overwhelmingly male. In 1968 the number of male and female registrants was almost in balance, and the university was a major landlord.

The national youth revolt, as exemplified in the tawdry Haight-Ashbury community in a blighted portion of San Francisco, came into full flower by 1968. Attempts were made in this California center, and at other places in the nation, to fuse political radicalism, social revolt, drug usage, and, maybe, a literary revolt. All the elements of the subculture were drawn together in this drug-hazed community. Here Abbie Hoffman, Jerry Rubin, and Ed Sanders founded the Yippies, or Youth International Party. Vaguely associated with the social upheavals following the famous Supreme Court decision, *Brown* v. *Board of Education* (1954), there had arisen across America a new literary bohemia in which such figures as Dave Dellinger, A. J. Muste, Erich Fromm, Allen Ginsberg, and Allan Watts became central figures. The new poetry with its strong tones of protest against established institutions and ideas, plus the rising popularity of Zen Buddhism, exerted new influences. Even the diplomatic historian William Appleman Williams had charged the United States with being overcentralized in its economics, and overaggressive in its international approaches.

Across the country the student revolt was to manifest itself in the form of sit-ins, endless agitation, destruction of campus properties, presentation of innumerable demands for voices in decision-making, including professorial salaries, promotions, and grants of tenure. Indiana University was to share in this era of turmoil, and its campus felt the impact of student unrest, and even of their strident demands.

In the opening of the troubled decade there was a multiplicity of problems in dealing with students. Shoplifting and theft of university property became matters of concern. The Board of Trustees adopted a formal rule in July 1962, permitting the Dean of Students to expel those persons convicted of thievery either from downtown stores or the university. Dean Robert Shaffer was promptly confronted with a case the following September of three students charged with stealing examination questions the previous April. The three students accused directly were suspended, and eighty others, plus five fraternities, were placed on probation. The *Indianapolis Star*, September 22, 1962, commented that student behavior in this case reflected the increasing college pressures that made "honest students attempt to cheat."

Almost every public cause and issue that troubled the public mind absorbed student time and attention in Bloomington. For instance, student body president Mike Donovan called an emergency session of the Student Senate to condemn the "deplorable action" of Mississippi public officials in the James Meredith case. He asked for a resolution supporting President Kennedy, and $15.00 with which to purchase postal cards for students to write Governor Ross A. Barnett.

While the Meredith case was being discussed in the press, President John F. Kennedy visited Indianapolis in October 1962. A group of Butler, Purdue, and Indiana University Medical School students demonstrated at the Weir Cook Airport, both to protest and to support the President's Cuba blockade policy. The largest number of supporters were from the Young Americans for Freedom and the Student Medical Association. Protesters were representatives of the Student Ad Hoc Committee to Oppose United States Aggression, and they handed out handbills critical of the national action. A fourth group was students active in the Fair Play for Cuba Committee. This assemblage of such divergent groups resulted in some physical beating and shoving of students by the crowd while police did little or nothing to prevent violence.

On the campus in Bloomington a corporal's guard of fifteen students met at 2:45 P.M. to protest the Kennedy blockade. The

Indianapolis News reporter estimated that a crowd of 3,000 disrupted the pitiful little parade which marched down Seventh Street, through the campus, out the gate across Indiana Avenue, and down Kirkwood Avenue. Fights occurred, most of them started by nonstudents. It was said by the *Indianapolis Star* reporter that a man from Spencer was one of the provocaters. Dennis R. Bryant, manager of the Swing Inn Pizzeria, was said to be on his way to the campus to make a delivery when the demonstration occurred. In the melee he grabbed a sign away from Mrs. Polly Smith, who said she had joined the Cuba defenders in protest against their ill treatment. The Cuba Committee was led by James E. Bingham, a graduate student and son of an Indianapolis attorney. The anti-Cubans presented signs reading, "Pinks Stink!" "Yanqui si," "Cuba no!" and "Block that Ship!" The *Indianapolis Star*, October 25, 1962, estimated the crowd at 3,000 to 5,000. President Stahr, however, thought only 200 or 300 were present. "I think," he told reporters, "it is significant that out of a student body of 17,804, only a few hundred were unable to refrain from heckling the members of the so-called 'committee.' "

Three days later the Young Americans for Freedom held a rally attended by approximately 1,000 persons at the State Fairgrounds in Indianapolis. Joseph C. Scholl, Richard M. Nixon's Republican opponent for the governorship in the California primary, was the speaker. The YAF made awards to Jameson G. Campaigne, editor of the *Star*, Mrs. Dorothy Gardner, Clarence Manion and Gerhart Niemeyer of Notre Dame University, and the singer Pat Boone for their devotion to victory over Communism. Later President Stahr discussed the various demonstrations and counter-demonstrations with the Faculty Council. He said he was in New York City at the time of the campus commotion attending a meeting of the American Association of Universities. There he learned that comparable demonstrations were taking place on other campuses. In Bloomington the Division of Safety had made hurried plans to prevent the outbreak of violence. In the face of possible clashes, both Stahr and Wells had made calming statements to the *Daily Student* urging moderation. The efforts to prevent violence, said President Stahr, had been generally successful. One professor had been mauled a bit when he was accidentally caught in the milling crowd, but no one seemed to know by whom. Stahr asked for the freedom and protection of those with whom the majority disagreed, and made it clear that he had no intention, "to play the fool for totalitarians" either of the left or right. He informed the council he hoped there would be no recurrence of the shoving incidents, and, "there is evidence that such demonstrations are not indigenous to this campus. However, it is possible that our students may have learned that mob responses to demonstrations are not the way to combat them."

Earlier incidents of lesser fury had stirred the Indianapolis press if not the campus. On October 30, 1960, Keith Cuffel, a Butler Christian Theological Institute student in Indianapolis, was indicted for selling copies of Henry Miller's *Tropic of Cancer* and *Tropic of Capricorn*. Cuffel was a clerk in Curry's Bookstore. In Bloomington eighty students and an instructor signed a petition seeking a quashing of the indictment.

Members of a campus fraternity secured some anti-United Nations literature and gave it to children who came to the door collecting funds for UNICEF. Bill Jenner, son of Senator William E. Jenner, was a member of the fraternity, but he was not in the house when the incident occurred. His membership in the fraternity, said the *Indianapolis Times*, December 7, 1962, made the issue newsworthy, a curious bit of association.

If President Stahr and the Faculty Council believed the disturbances over the Cuba Committee were at an end, they were sadly disappointed when Thomas Hoadley, the new Monroe County prosecutor, asked the grand jury in January 1963, to investigate both the Fair Play for Cuba Committee and the Young Socialist Alliance. The Louisville *Courier-Journal*, January 16, 1963, quoted Hoadley as saying, "I am not convinced that the total blame of this near riot should be placed on the shoulders of these two [the two men charged with assault and battery] anti-demonstrators, as certain professors, committees, and other people suggest." He ordered charges dismissed. "A high source in the University Administration," was quoted by the Bloomington *Star-Courier* as being astonished at the prosecutor's announced plans. It was feared this would jeopardize the university's budget request then before the legislature. The Young Socialist group had been recognized by the Student Senate, December 19, 1962, after it had been denied recognition on two previous occasions. This was the youth wing of the Trotskyite Socialist Party. While

Prosecutor Hoadley threatened a grand jury investigation, Tom Charles Huston, a senior, and a regional director of Young Americans for Freedom, said the *Indianapolis Times*, February 4, 1963, was in Washington accusing Dean Robert Shaffer of capitulating to the leftists.

David Rogers, Bloomington representative in the General Assembly, rushed to the defense of the university and called Hoadley's efforts to ban the Young Socialist Alliance from the campus ridiculous. He told reporters, "These kids are just a bunch of beatniks who like to play chess and raise a ruckus." The YSA was not listed by the United States Attorney General as a subversive organization, and President Stahr asked the Indiana Attorney General, Edwin K. Stone, Jr., for an opinion as to whether the organization violated state law.

These were historic days when Indiana University faced nagging problems with athletic irregularities, expanding every phase of its operation, taking care of annual increases in student numbers, securing adequate support from the legislature, and guarding freedom on the campus while Thomas Hoadley made menacing sounds at the Monroe County Court House. Fifteen YSA members shouting for Cuba, and the Young Americans for Freedom opposing Communists at every turn, even those who lurked inside the Peace Corps, made times seem a bit out of focus. When YAF, through the National Committee for Effective Social Welfare, expressed fear that VISTA would undercut the Red Cross, Boy Scouts of America, and the Salvation Army, the university administration must have wondered if the campus was still on the same planet where it had originated.

The tomtoms of anxiety boomed through blustery March with Prosecutor Hoadley provoking angry student letters, while the Bloomington *Star-Courier* gave him less than a favorable press. The YAF added zest by bringing Senator Barry Goldwater to Bloomington to cheer on the Young Republican Club in a Wright Quad assembly of 3,000 students who chanted the original call, "We want Barry!" Former United States Senator William E. Jenner introduced his colleague who in turn criticized President Kennedy's proposal for Medicare and VISTA. Goldwater was reported to have expressed the belief Kennedy could be defeated in 1964. Outside the building delegates to the Little United Nations picketed the Senator with signs, "True Americans support the U.N." and "LUNA Protests the Arizona Lunatic."

The troubled atmosphere was cleared somewhat when the local press and university officials were able to persuade Thomas Hoadley to hold up a grand jury investigation of YSA, at least he was said to have promised not to call the grand jury into session until after the legislators had gone home. He, however, in a public letter called attention of the officials to the fact that YSA was a "Trotskyite Communist revolutionary group," and the officials replied that it was not on the Attorney General's subversive list.

Before the Cuba riot could be disposed of by the court, a greater sensation distracted the prosecutor's attention. A co-ed's farmhouse apartment was raided and a half pound of marijuana was confiscated. The *Indianapolis News*, April 13, 1963, said a graduate student from Cedar Rapids, Iowa, was accused of placing a note in a coffee can, reading, "Nancy, this is your week's supply. Fritz." He was also accused of promising to mail her more "grass" from Chicago. The co-ed was suspended by Dean Shaffer, and he awaited further investigation of the graduate student. In the meantime police found a list of twenty names in the co-ed's car. The Bloomington *Star-Courier*, April 18, 1963, indicated the prosecutor had appeared on national radio, television, and before news reporters discussing the case. The *Indianapolis News* said, April 19, that the night before Frederick C. Fisher had surrendered on a charge of possessing drugs, and that he and Nancy Dillingham were held under a $2,000 bond to appear in the Monroe County Circuit Court. A week later it was reported locally that Hoadley would agree to drop the charges if the pair would leave Indiana University and Monroe County, and furnish the names of other marijuana users.

A resolution was introduced in the Faculty Council in April 1963, seeking to prevent further debacles over freedom of speech, protests, and orderly demonstrations by setting aside a place on the campus where anyone could speak freely to any audience, or to no audience. It was suggested that a corner of Dunn Meadow be used for this purpose. The committee making the proposal said the experiment had been tried at Wisconsin and Minnesota. On May 7, 1963, the council discussed a recommendation to the Board of Trustees, and then fearing the Trustees would not favor use of the Meadow offered the amendment, "or some other open, accessible space to be designated by the Board of Trustees." This move, the council believed, would "perhaps relieve some of the tension over dissatisfaction with the Indiana University Administration and policies." The board adopted this proposal, and in the fall the "neutral ground" in Dunn Meadow was made available to the "University Community in which any group can speak about and debate the issues of the day which concern its members."

Just before the Christmas holidays Dean Shaffer assured the Student Board of Academic Review that the Dunn Meadow arrangement in no way limited individual freedom. Professor Ralph E. Fuchs, former chairman of the Faculty Council, told the board the rule was made to prevent injury, traffic problems, and disturbances of classes. The Dunn Meadow forum, declared Dean Shaffer, was a place "where any group can discuss literally anything." It was also away from the classrooms where the noise could not be heard. An individual, said the dean, might picket or express his ideas elsewhere on the campus so long as he did not disrupt classes or impede traffic.

By March 1965 the Dunn Meadow neutral ground rang with a mixture of jeers, firecracker explosions, and applause. The Ad Hoc Committee to End the War in Vietnam outlined its stand to bring about a cease fire and to stop the bombings, to begin immediate negotiations, and to withdraw American forces before an audience of 3,000 persons. Three professors and a student spoke for an hour and a half amidst the noise and the efforts of pro-United States policy supporters to capture the podium.

A second gathering of 650 marchers expressed sympathy for the Selma Negroes who protested against the ancient Black Belt Alabama stronghold of peonage and racial discrimination. The *Daily Student*, March 13, 1965, was highly critical of the various Dunn Meadow gatherings. It said, "The same sophomoric minds which came up with the endearing chant, 'Block that Ship!' during the Cuban missile crisis in 1962 produced a similar bit of whimsy yesterday in '2-4-6-8, we want to escalate!'" The editor reminded his fellow students that free speech was important, "If those who ridiculed them from the midst of an anonymous crowd cannot realize this, the battles in Viet Nam, Selma, and on every other frontier of freedom have been waged in vain."

Nevertheless, the Dunn Meadow forum remained lively. In May 1965 Students for a Democratic Society organized a series of "vox forums" which indeed engendered vigorous expressions pro and con on a half dozen current topics; by 1968 the meadow forum idea had more than proved its usefulness.

In 1963 three incidents indicated that for students in general not all campus life was gathered up in the feverish excitement over Cuba, VISTA, marijuana, or the Boy Scouts. Not even the approaching presidential election of 1964 distracted some students' attention. Vice President Samuel E. Braden bore the horrendous tidings, July 9, 1964, from the Board of Trustees that in the fall sophomores would not be allowed to operate automobiles in Monroe County. In a comment reported in the *Daily Student* Dr. Braden thought "The student automobile on the campus is falling victim to its own increase in numbers, somewhat like the rabbits in Australia." The rule may have been as difficult to enforce in Bloomington as birth control among the rabbits of the "out back bush."

Assistant Dean Virginia H. Rogers sought to deal one of America's classic frauds a quick knock-out blow. Under the guise of being the "320 Club" the ancient chain-letter fraud found some takers. Dean Rogers promised disciplinary probation to practitioners, and suspension to the ring leaders who brought the chain letter onto the campus. The sucker bought a letter for $10, and hoped to keep the chain unbroken until he had collected $320.

Student dignity was further bruised when an eighteen-year-old pledge to Sigma Alpha Nu Fraternity was surrounded by a band of Bloomington teen-agers in the woods back of Swain Hall and robbed of his green pledge "pod." University students ran after the beanie-snatchers and caught one who claimed he was a seventeen-year-old visitor from Texas and was totally unacquainted with his companions. The *Daily Student* commented the Safety Division refused to discuss the affair. Had they been historically oriented, they might have observed that this surely was the last freshman cap ever to be snatched on the Indiana University campus. Local freshmen no longer merited the wearing of the "green." That fall 26 per cent of them had graduated in the top 10 per cent of their high school classes, and 83 per cent had graduated in the upper half. More of them were eligible to enter sophomore classes at the outset than ever before.

Not all students wore calluses on their hands brandishing placards, or bruised their larnyxes shouting slogans and epithets. In fact, large numbers appeared unconcerned with the emotional outbursts over the various headline issues. In February 1964 the Student Senate called for the condemnation of Steve Smith, president of the student body, for some reflection on the Communists, and suggested the study of student conduct. It considered the establishment of an international week, and in the same legislative breath requested free bus service to basketball games. Also, a genuine spark of righteous anger was struck by Senator Vukovich over an investigation of kissing in Sycamore Hall. He claimed this was an attempt by the university to dictate private moral behavior. The Senate resolved to allow the Board of Standards to produce a code of student conduct, "especially in kiss-ins." This was indeed a vital issue which had resulted from a well-publicized "kiss-in." Apparently the *Daily Student* had staged the incident to emphasize Valentine's Day. There were thirty onlookers and thirty newsmen present, and more than sixty girls huddled behind darkened windows. They heard the girl say, "Oh damnit!" and she kissed him. In the next issue the paper admitted the "Valentine Day Kiss-in at Sycamore Hall was a flop. . . ."

In another area students reluctantly did a good turn by their lapses. Fines for infractions of rules for automobiles showed a $5,000 increase over the previous year. These levies went into a scholarship fund, which on April 28, 1964, amounted to $19,555. Students, like their parents, had become legless except on dance nights. More than 5,000 male students again responding to the sappiness of spring roared across the campus on the night of May 27, 1966, babbling "We want panties." Campus and city policemen stood by as the adolescent pack went from door to door uttering its primordial mating call. It was perhaps the last appearance on the campus of cave men. This time Alice Nelson was not on hand with her barrel of "lingerie" to shame the savages. They disappeared behind their own self-constructed mound of adolescent frustration and ignominy.

While resurrected "lingerie" raiders were on the loose, the Board of Aeons issued its revision of "Students' Rights and Responsibilities at Indiana University." The board said it had considered the impact of state and federal laws, and the possibility of outraging the source of financial support, and concluded that rules governing student lives were unjustified in a more modern era. In the six proposed rule changes graduate students were to be given full exemption from *in loco parentis* restrictions, including entertainment of members of the opposite sex in their rooms. No student should be disciplined for offenses committed off-campus, university officials should stay out of students' rooms, and rules for upper-class women were declared archaic. Later that year Dean Shaffer also recommended liberalizing rules relating to upper-class women over twenty-one years of age.

President Elvis J. Stahr, Jr., like other members of his administration, demonstrated concern for students and their welfare, but at the same time viewed the student movements of the 1960s with a high degree of caution. In his second "State of the University Report," December 14, 1964, he said of entering freshmen, "They are important, not just because our appropriations are directly related to how many students come and stay, but because freshmen are at the most difficult interface in our educational system and because they are upper-classmen of the near future." Then he struck at the weakness of the whole system of the 1960s in his plea, "We must offer them excellent teachers."

As time went on, President Stahr expressed deeper concern about students. He told the *Indiana Alumni Magazine*, September 1966, a major concern was "a growing student unrest around the country. . . . I am worried about the deeper implications. This is not, as some suggest, something associated solely with bigness. I don't want to stifle students. I want them to be curious and free to explore and question and dissent—but to do it responsibly. They must not become sheep running off after every agitator. This is the opposite of exploring and questioning." A year later the president expressed fear to his deans that the new left "may be beating the game and doing damage to the University both within and in terms of its public relations." At that time the number of incompleted courses, he said, had reached disgraceful proportions. Graduate assistants who participated actively and competitively in politics with their students created unusual tensions. Yet to attempt to regulate them would be to raise a storm.

On Friday, May 10, 1968, a traditional university event that seemed safely out of the line of fire of campus protests was challenged. For months the Little 500 Committee of 650 juniors and seniors had made plans for the 1968 carnival and bicycle race for the purpose of raising scholarship funds for working students. Following the girls' tricycle race on the Friday evening before the main event, a group of fifty black students announced they planned to "sit-in" on the bicycle track on Saturday, May 11, in protest against the racial policies of the campus fraternities, and especially in opposition to those which had "acceptance clauses" in their charters. The blacks asked that all the Indiana University fraternities sign waivers from their national rules, and begin definite plans for desegregating the local chapters. The *Indiana Daily Student*, May 11, 1968, published a generally critical editorial of the Little 500 on the grounds it was a scheme to get money away from students, the committee would not allow reporters to examine income-expense accounts, the Indiana University Foundation seemed to regard students as immature, the carnival board was unrepresentative, and the event was not for all students. Concluding his generous number of strictures, the carping editor wrote, "The great college weekends of this year have been at Harvard and Columbia universities. There the students have become mature and have carved their way into the university structure. They didn't do it in a bicycle race."

The fifty blacks said the bigoted representatives of the four fraternities which had "acceptance clauses" in their charters would not ride—or nobody would ride. Clarence Turner, a graduate student and presumed spokesman for the protesting group, was quoted by the *Daily Student*, May 11, 1968, that if the blacks were attacked they were prepared to defend themselves. This threat seemed to imply that the blacks were ready to make a violent response if they were molested.

By 1:00 P.M., May 11, twenty of the twenty-four fraternities had complied with the blacks' demands starting the removal of "acceptance clauses" and other racially restrictive matter from their charters. Also, in other ways these fraternities were conforming with the university's nondiscriminatory policies. The Panhellenic and Inter-Fraternity councils and the Student Government affirmed, "The fact that were such a clause to be included in a house's national constitution, a waiver from such a clause has been obtained. . . ." These student leaders assured the blacks that all organized groups "are in complete sympathy with the motives of the black students." They said, however, the time span set by the protesters was entirely too short to permit the formulation of plans for ending all discriminations.

The weekend of the Little 500 on the campus that year promised to be a gloomy one. If an attempt was made to hold the bicycle race, it would most certainly lead to some kind of an incident; no one knew how serious it might be. There were only fifty blacks involved in the sit-in, and there was considerable sentiment to remove them by force. No one could predict what mixed reactions the potential crowd of 25,000 spectators might have. Fortunately such a confrontation was avoided because a heavy rain fell on the Saturday afternoon of the scheduled race, and if there had been no protesters the race would have been called off anyway, and for the first time in its quarter of a century history.

For thirty-eight hours, Friday to Sunday, student leaders, members of the university administration, professors, and fraternity officers remained in constant meetings trying to resolve the problems of racial discrimination on the part of the four fraternities directly in question. Only one of them, in fact, was seriously involved, and that was Phi Delta Theta. The fraternity was in the process of removing its acceptance clause later that year at its annual convention, and the Indiana chapter was powerless to act on its own initiative. This fact was revealed in the chapter's notarized statement given the blacks, and they objected to it. At 6:00 A.M., Sunday, May 12, President Stahr was called by a member of his administrative staff to compare the fraternity statements of policy, and it was determined that of Phi Delta Theta was in fact sufficiently different in both substance and form to justify asking its members to withdraw from the bicycle race. President Stahr later wrote, "I myself concluded that the statement did not comply with the agreement of the previous afternoon between the Black Students and the President of the Student Body and that a subsequent statement signed by another member of the fraternity had not cured the effect." The president of the Phi Delta Theta chapter withdrew his fraternity's team "for the good of the University." President Stahr then accompanied the fraternity's representative to the Phi Delta Theta house and explained the reasons for the action, assuming personal responsibility for the decision.

After sitting through a day and a half of rain, reading the fraternity statements, and discussing among themselves the issues raised, the blacks removed themselves from the bicycle track. Before they gave up their vigil, however, President Stahr said they had begun to dig holes in the track, and had started bonfires with bleacher materials. There was a touch of classicism in this last stand. The blacks had equipped themselves with garbage can lid shields, and had pipe hand spikes. The race was run on Sunday afternoon, and the Phi Delta Theta group received a special tribute from the contestants for their action. The winning team rode by the Phi Delta Theta section and tossed up the winning bicycle as a trophy for their act of withdrawal.

There, however, were some repercussions among the blacks. Professor Orlando Taylor, a speech and theatre staff member, told the *Daily Student* reporter, May 14, that "the actions of black students over the week-end was just a beginning of what could be 'the world's greatest week-end.'" He said the big story of the past four days of emotional strain and excitement was not the winning of the bicycle race but rather the gains made "by determined black people and enlightened white people." The professor uttered the disturbing opinion that the conflict had not ended. Black student protesters were said to be concerned that in all the meetings and discussions the public statements of the fraternity leaders might be interpreted by the public that they had taken the lead in desegregating their chapters; the fact that all but four of them had done so was proved by the black's immediate acceptance of their notarized assurances that this was so.

The actions of black students in the "Little 500" incident were almost futile. No one could have really believed that the issue of the fraternity acceptance clauses had any substance at all. In every case the fraternities had either removed the discriminatory sections of their by-laws or were in the process of doing so. Behind this incident was a somewhat tragic fact. One of the leaders, a football player, had a brother killed in the bitter Detroit race riot of 1967, and he was out to get "whitey" in every way possible. It was said that it was this embittered boy who kept the boycotters on the bicycle track until almost the last moment. At the other extreme some campus officials sought to have President Stahr act precipitately and have the blacks removed forcibly. In this case the university administration had to proceed in an extremely narrow channel and with utmost calmness and sincerity to prevent an unhappy racial incident of tragic proportions.

The Bloomington *Herald-Telephone*, May 12, 1968, regarded the sit-in on the bicycle track as part of the whole radical dissent of the 1960s. "But the danger, as the case is in today's planned demonstration, is that protestors become more absorbed in the tactics than in the causes, certainly the tactics at today's race is adapted to a cause in which the morality is obscure." The paper thought the black students might stir resentment that would impair the Negro student's voice on the campus in the future. There did not appear in the record even a hint of the policies of the university's black fraternities. Presumably their sentiments were represented in the expressions of the twenty organizations that had already removed all discriminatory barriers. In retrospect, the Little 500 protest was a dramatic after the fact demonstration that certainly lacked the full force of pertinence. The fraternities were either already desegregated by their own initiative or were in the process of removing the discriminatory barriers. The hints that "the world's greatest college week-end" might take the form of the destructive Harvard and Columbia demonstrations proved to be meaningless. In a deeper philosophical vein the black students had picked a rather weak objective to dramatize their feelings of being discriminated against on the campus.

In 1968 Indiana University had a fairly long history of dealing with racial issues. Since the 1920s there were a fair number of black students registered in its classes, and there were three Negro fraternities on the campus. Blacks had been prominent on some of the athletic teams, and in the music programs. Over the past decades the institution had become a first port of call for black academic emigrants moving up from the Lower South. The mere crossing of the Ohio River, however, did not mean an escape from either racial prejudice or discrimination. There was not an appreciable difference of racial attitudes between the people of southern Indiana and those of western Tennessee or the other Southern states.

Since 1938 especially the Wells administration had worked at lowering racial barriers. The services of the Student Union were made available on an equal basis to all students, and so was campus housing. The academic program was desegregated, and some progress had been made in removing all recognizable forms of segregation in day-to-day human associations within the university. One of the great problems at Indiana, and elsewhere throughout the country, was the matter of interracial communication as to the forms and manifestations of discrimination. The clearest formal statement of the university's attitudes and approaches to the problems of whites and blacks in higher education in Indiana was made by President Stahr on March 23, 1968, in a campus conference of statewide consideration of the problems. He told the conference audience that an understanding should be established as to the sources of differing attitudes. It was difficult to learn "what the Negro really thinks and what *he feels* discriminated against. By far the most illuminating comments and thus most helpful guidance to us at I. U. have come from concerned Negroes who *wanted* the University to know where it was failing because they accepted the University's good faith. Some of them have sought out an administrator and informed him with specific details what practices—or omissions—of the University gave offense to the Negro, often unknown to the University." An alumnus had discussed with two deans some areas of sensitivities. University publications had not carried pictures of Negroes, and the public relations brochures were guilty of the same oversights.

The blacks, on the other hand, had created islands of segregation of their own. They tended to congregate among themselves, and a residence quadrangle had attracted large numbers of black student tenants, reducing the possibilities of other halls being desegregated. Black athletic prospects who had been invited to the campus were often housed in one of the three Negro fraternities with the thought that this was a most hospitable gesture, but the black athletes had adversely interpreted this as "pairing."

In many other ways blacks were sensitized by university policies and operations that basically were not intentionally discriminatory against anyone. The fact that Indiana was an equal opportunity employer was not properly publicized. The School of Education had no black professor, yet it trained teachers who taught large numbers of Indiana's blacks. It was said the various placement agencies did not send out Negroes' papers to prospective employers, a belief proved to be wrong. A professor asked a black girl out of idle curiosity why she chose Indiana over a Negro school, and she resented the implications she imagined to be in the question. Finally, there were no black cheerleaders, this despite the fact that a black girl had been chosen "Miss Indiana University," and a Negro had served as president of the student body.

During the summer of 1967 the Board of Trustees had adopted a resolution directing the university's administration to take necessary steps to remove every vestige of discrimination based upon race, creed, or national origin. In 1966 the university had introduced at the Fort Wayne and Indianapolis regional centers divisions of general technical studies aimed at training students of all races to fit into employment patterns of the state. At Indianapolis and in Bloomington, Indiana University—as had Washington University and the University of Wisconsin—introduced on an experimental basis preparatory courses leading to advanced studies in several practical fields. Well beyond the periphery of university operation, the institution in 1966 organized cooperative programs with Stillman College in Tuscaloosa, Alabama, and Texas Southern in Houston, Texas, in an attempt to improve areas of instruction and management in those institutions. At Stillman an Indiana professor performed the chore of reorganizing the Department of English and its basic course offerings. In turn, Stillman and Texas Southern professors came to Bloomington to pursue advanced graduate education. There was at Indiana University a program of helping more Negro students finish the work of the twelfth grade and to prepare to enter college. "The plain, hard fact," said President Stahr, "is that until more of these youths complete high school and enter college, college campuses will remain disproportionately 'white.'" This same condition was true of advanced students seeking university faculty status; they had to complete doctoral work in order to compete for positions on former all-white faculties.

The frank Stahr statement in March 1968 failed to satisfy militant campus blacks, perhaps none of them had read it. They conceived of campus discriminations that did not in fact exist. No one could be sure, but there seemed to be fairly good evidence that there was a broad spectrum of black protests based upon generalized rather than specific local conditions. In May 1968 President Stahr was in Chicago attending a meeting of the Midwest Accrediting Commission when he received a telephone call from a black militant leader demanding that he return immediately to the campus because of an impending black confrontation with the administration. He refused to leave the meeting, but the following day he was back in Bloomington. John Snyder met him in Indianapolis and told him that a hundred blacks had paraded in Dunn Meadow, then had marched downtown, and were then assembled in the president's flower garden at the Bryan House, where they awaited Stahr's arrival. They were accompanied by about twenty-five white members of the Students for a Democratic Society. Rollo Turner, a graduate student and black leader, however, refused to allow the whites to join them in their protest, and even forced them to remain silently in the background. The march was frightening to Mrs. Stahr and the Stahr children. On another occasion, so it was said by the press, the president's house had been stoned, there was fear of an assault this time. The president talked with the blacks and assured them he would meet them the following Monday in the Whittenberger Auditorium and answer their questions and complaints. When he did meet with them, he discovered that a considerable number of their formal questions had no relevance whatsoever to Indiana University, and some of those which did apply had already been solved. It seemed that the Chicago Black Panthers had prepared and sent the questions to Bloomington. When President Stahr asked why the blacks asked such irrelevant questions, he was told they just wanted to hear his answers.

One of the students' demands was the reservation of a separate wing of a dormitory for black occupancy only, and for other segregated facilities. For instance, when blacks were asked about their objectives in pushing for elimination of racial discrimination from fraternity charters they replied they did not want to join the chapters; they merely wished to establish the privilege of doing so. Thus it was that the process of totally desegregating Indiana University involved a long and complicated history, plus deeply rooted folk mores that were integral parts of the generally disturbed state of affairs on American university campuses. The Indiana experience in these years clearly revealed that it took patience and extensive planning to make the necessary transitions demanded by the stepped-up tempo of destroying ancient social and folk barriers. Most of all it required astute soul-searching to identify the problems of black students inside a university so thoroughly committed to maturing the best educational and service programs possible, and to the employment of highly qualified professorial personnel. By 1968 many of the acts of discrimination had grown out of a change of objectives and desires of black students themselves. Many of them sought to institute a kind of resegregation in violation of the new court mandates, faculty and trustee rules, and general student body responses. Although the black studies program had been expanded and black administrators and staff employed, there were still protests, some of which seemed to want an inverted type of racial segregation. Sometimes it seemed that these students had almost lost sight of the tremendous gains they had made, and of the need of consolidating these gains.

By 1968, and the date of Stahr's resignation as president on the grounds of physical and emotional exhaustion, student activism had grown more intense. In a statement to the Board of Trustees on "Dissent vs. Disruption," Dr. Stahr wrote, "Some of the events of this year on campuses across the Nation have suggested some searching reflection upon the principles which undergird the academic community. The very soul of the environment for scholars is complete freedom for each to enquire, to debate and to criticise, a freedom that must be preserved against attack from within the University as well as from outside." He hoped administrators, board, faculty, and students would reassert the intent to keep the Indiana campus free from disruption and the menace of coercive actions. At the same time Vice President John Snyder recommended that the university seize the opportunity to devote all of the institution's resources to teaching, and to taking steps to return the faculty to a sense of responsibility for undergraduate students who pay the bill. Because it had failed to do these things, the university had been "holding the bag and responding to the leftists. The University is not a democracy. Students should have a voice but they are not responsible." Dean Charles Hagen commented that the faculty had failed graduate students. If they were kept properly busy, they would not have time for undergraduate activities.

Interim President Herman B Wells, in his "State of the University Address," October 10, 1968, said, "In the perspective of time, I believe that the management of change affecting students at I. U. will be heralded as a signal characteristic of the Stahr era." Both Stahr and Wells spoke of student affairs in the troubled year, 1967–68, with intimate knowledge of the campus undercurrents and sources of unrest. The *Daily Student*, April 12, 1967, ran an editorial saying the Student Government was in trouble. Dean Aulick would leave its presidency in May, and three candidates sought to succeed him. Marty Zohn ran on the Tryus ticket, Jim Durkott on Action, and Guy Loftman, a senior and a dark horse, on the Progressive Reform ticket. Loftman, said the paper, admitted he was of the radical New Left. He had actively participated in rallies, sit-ins, and demonstrations. His running mate was Barry Wheeler, chairman of the Academic Board of Review, and was also said to be of the New Left.

With these prospects for management of student government, the *Daily Student* commented, "If Student Government is to become a moving force on campus, as we believe it should be, Mr. Loftman is the only one who can save it." The editorial was signed by the whole editorial staff. Loftman received the highest individual number of votes, 3,418 out of 8,129 cast.

Upon his election Loftman, former local president of Students for a Democratic Society, said that " 'radical' meant only 'getting at the root of the problem.' " According to the campus paper, April 15, 1967, "The University could expect at least a year of concerted student efforts aimed at standing up for things students called 'student rights.' " In his inaugural address Loftman outlined at least three major areas of action. He proposed to evaluate the Remak Report on Academic Affairs, to establish student committees for each department to help solve its problems, and to establish a Board of Administrative Review, comparable to the Board of Academic Review, to do research into the way the university allocated its funds and reached decisions affecting students, and to concern itself with other administrative matters. In concluding, the new Student Government president said he hoped during his administration to make great advances in freedom, the gaining of power, and responsibility.

In attempting to carry out his administrative review Loftman, August 9, 1967, asked Indiana Attorney General John J. Dillon to give him an opinion on the Indiana Anti-Secrecy Act as it related to Indiana University. He told this official that he and his staff had been doing extensive research "about the past and present state of Indiana University finances." He said on August 4 President Stahr and the vice presidents ruled that students would no longer be given direct access to university financial information.

Addressing a meeting of the local chapter of the American Association of University Professors, the *Daily Student* said, "Guy Loftman, Student-Body President, fiercely attacked what he called the authoritarian administration of Indiana University last night and was met with resounding applause from a group of over 100 faculty members and administrators." He told the audience

Indiana was "tragically anti-education and devoted to bureaucratic waste." He asked "that faculty and students join together to reshape Indiana University into a truly educational institution."

After President Stahr had retired from the presidency, Students for a Democratic Society and the Young Socialist Alliance demanded in mid-October 1968 that Interim President Herman B Wells state his views on six major questions. Previously Wells had agreed to address a general student gathering on various issues of concern to them. When he was confronted with the six demands, however, he cancelled his personal appearance and replied in an extensive statement through the *Daily Student*, November 1. Two of the questions raised were about military recruiting activities in student recreational areas, and "learning how to kill in our classrooms." It is doubtful whether Wells' answers satisfied members of the two organizations that quizzed him, but certainly they seemed to have satisfied a large number of other students, and the campus experienced a considerable cooling off as a result.

The Indiana University faculty and administration learned after 1965 that they functioned in an American society that had either come to ignore or had revised nearly all of its revered puritanical code. The impact of the automobile, the modern media, sprawling suburbia, changing sex attitudes, and an expressed desire to assume greater personal responsibility for their lives, all of these things came into full bloom for American youth. No doubt the presence on campuses of an ever-increasing number of married undergraduates helped to change some attitudes.

Against this background youth in the 1960s became assertive of its rights and privileges, and a fairly large number all but rejected all forms of disciplinary controls whether at home or in college. In the youth revolt, as exemplified in the Haight-Ashbury community in San Francisco, the orgies of "rock 'n' roll festivals," and the rise of "hippyism," there was a loud clamor for freedom, even from some of the laws of nature in the abuse of their bodies. In many institutions the "underground or off-campus press" flaunted traditional social conventions in both language and stated points of view. In dress and personal appearance both men and women students responded to the youthful tendency to sloppiness. Following European and English trends, girls' skirts were shortened, to what an older generation considered above the line of decency. When the *Daily Student*, November 6, 1966, carried a story about dress regulations in a New York high school, a jocular Indiana student wrote a trenchant comment under the title "Raise the Hemline." He thought educational administrators should consider what he called his "morally enlightened argument." First he thought this was a man's world, and miniskirts tended to bring the males to classes, they kept the boys awake, and males learned more if they were awake. "Therefore, miniskirts, etc., contribute to the social, economic, and technological advancement of our nation." As he said, in the face of such compelling logic the antiquarian educators could find no arguments. Logic or not, college girls shortened their skirts, deepened their necklines, threw brassieres to the wind, wore panty hose, and defied other conventions. In less appealing fashion some girls went to the other extreme: they wore sloppy blue jeans, discarded army jackets, patched the knees and crotches of their britches with loud scraps of cloth, and otherwise looked like they had just been dragged from the bottom of the Jordan River.

Men students in large numbers allowed their hair and whiskers to flourish without threat from razor or comb. Their dress was as casual as sawmill workers, and many of them gave more than a hint that shower baths were the infernal machinations of Dow Chemical and International Telephone and Telegraph. Historically there was little originality in the growing of campus beards. Earlier Indiana University students had equated beards with manifestations of intellect, and the modern lads fell into the same snare and delusion.

The American corporation both encouraged and capitalized on student social revolt. American motor corporations set out to snatch the Volkswagen and sports car trade away from foreigners. They produced Cougars, Gremlins, Mustangs, Colts, and Chargers with specialized body designs, racing stripes, psychedelic colors, special engines, "four-on-the floor" transmissions, emblazoned tires, and wheel covers. They even popularized the van for the free campus swingers to win the eternal hatred of dealers in second-hand hearses who had enjoyed a flourishing market for these otherwise worthless vehicles.

Along with all other changes some college youth began smoking "pot" or taking amphetamines and hallucinogenic drugs, thus involving themselves in clashes with law enforcement officials. There were campus seers and prophets, many of them from faculty ranks, who defended smoking marijuana, and were only mildly opposed to use of the new drugs. In the case of marijuana some persons of supposedly trustworthy scientific background maintained it was no more harmful than smoking cigarettes.

The ever-growing student body at Indiana in these years responded to the general tenor of the decade. It was no worse and no better than the classes of other years, except they had been exposed to more modern educational preparation. Most students had actually lived more sheltered lives, and were more pampered than those of their parents' generation. In the tremendous expansion of housing, dining, and recreational facilities, the "new" university offered students a comfortable if not luxurious way of life. It could not, however, afford them much privacy.

Early in 1968 some students began to crusade for "open" residence halls. They wanted women's residences, especially, opened to men visitors. Proponents argued students were mature and socially responsible, and such visitations would take place in a socially controlled environment; this latter term was undefined.

For most Hoosiers, including the university administration, faculty, and Board of Trustees, the student proposal was disturbing. The Faculty Council, May 30, 1968, expressed its good faith "in the capability of students to act responsibly in matters of intervisitation; it also recognizes some of the problems attendant to the workability of intervisitation plans submitted by individual student units. . . ." The council agreed to an experiment to "run from about the first of May until the end of the semester. . . ." Subsequently it refused to extend the experiment through summer school because of "differing circumstances."

Dr. Elizabeth Greenleaf, director of Residence Halls and Activities, reported to Vice President John Snyder, June 6, 1968, that a major difficulty had been "an inability to adequately control the environment," and lack of staff authority to act independently to correct weaknesses. In her survey report Dr. Greenleaf outlined six positive points that ranged from accepting visitation as a principle to good working relationships between student officers and the resident assistant. She made the observation, "The 'public display of affection' was less visible as fewer people were using the lounges." In a ten-point negative reflection, the director listed problems ranging from "unescorted males in women's units" to liquor, shower bath problems, roommate difficulties, and breakdown of procedures in the final week.

Before Dr. Greenleaf finished her report, David Cahill of the

Student Affairs Committee wrote Professor Ralph E. Fuchs, saying the month's experiment produced significant evidence that the halls were quieter. He told Fuchs, "I cannot emphasize too strongly the large amount of identification students have with the plan which they have made and are enforcing. It gives them a vital sense of power over their own lives, instead of fostering a sense of impotent fury against a distant and unresponsive 'administration.' " He declared "Visitation is certainly the most popular program in the residence halls."

President Elvis Stahr addressed a letter to the *Indiana Daily Student*, June 18, 1968, outlining the Faculty Council's actions, the conditions of the visitation experiment, and reasons for not continuing the plan into the summer. David Cahill took exception to the letter the next day in the "Jordan River Forum" of the student paper. Professor Robert L. Turner responded to the Cahill letter repeating essentially President Stahr's statement of the council's actions—which he said the graduate student had clearly understood on June 4.

The issue of "open guest hours" reached the Board of Trustees on September 20, and after a two-hour debate that body by a five to three vote agreed to a three-day-a-week visitation period from 1 P.M. to 2 A.M. Previously the Faculty Council had voted open visitation, but did not specify the women's residences. Students had asked for full week visitation. Prior to the trustees' discussion, Interim President Herman B Wells told them that the first dormitory was built in the 1920s, and this was done upon the request of students. Indiana, he said, was a pioneer in the construction of coeducational residence centers which provided dining, social, and library facilities. Wells assured the trustees that he had confidence in the moral integrity of students. Robert Menke, an alumni trustee and Huntingburg business man, expressed a similar veiw. He said he had lived in Bloomington two years and had associated with students and had come to look upon them in a more trustful light.

When the trustees approved the open visitation plan, Frank B. Jones, Alumni secretary, prepared a special publication for alumni circulation entitled *Indiana University in Perspective*, September 30, 1968. He explained the issue of "open house guests," reviewing the background of the three weeks' test the past spring. He told the alumni, "First, before going on, I would like to say that in this case, your Alma Mater is not the first to have open visiting or open housing, or whatever terminology one wants to give it. In fact, Indiana University is one of the last. The other Big Ten Schools with similar plans include Wisconsin, Ohio State, Iowa, Northwestern, Michigan State, and Michigan."

The *Indiana Daily Student*, November 9, 1968, quoted Charles Kendall, president of the Inter-Residence Hall Association, as saying some problems had developed, but these were being solved as students came to realize their responsibilities. All the womens' residences except Read Hall voted from 70 to 100 per cent to open their residences; the voting thus far involved 9,818 students. The first plan went into effect on October 12, 1968, without the university coming apart at its moral seams, or with students gamboling with complete bachannalian abandon upon the elysian green of romantic freedom. There still remained the "crowd," the roommate, the modest co-ed on the way to the shower bath, and the "unescorted males" mentioned by Dr. Elizabeth Greenleaf, but even so the campus world managed to hold together.

The administration was never without its concern for students. Since 1960 both professors and administrators had from time to time raised questions about the effects of "bigness." Some administrators contended that actually this had little bearing on student attitudes and reactions. It is doubtful indeed, in the face of events, that this point of view could be entirely sustained in a careful consideration of all the facts of university operation and way of life. In 1964 plans were underway to expand the Student Health Center. Dr. John Miller explained that $200,000 worth of new equipment would be added to existing facilities. Two additional physicians would be employed, and two full-time psychiatrists would be appointed. Dr. Miller denied that the creation of the latter division reflected an increased need for psychiatric care among students, but rather the meeting of a long-time need for broadening student services. A new student group insurance plan was offered in 1965 that gave individuals much better access to health care.

President Stahr that year reported that out of a student population of 20,125, a third or 7,031 had received direct and repeated medical attention in the Health Center, and in all there were 64,249 student visitations to the facility. There had been fourteen attempted student suicides, and forty-three withdrawals for mental or other health reasons. The sex balance by now was almost precisely even between men and women, with 51 per cent males. Unmarried students accounted for 82.5 per cent of the campus population, and class distribution ranged from 19 per cent freshmen to 12.5 per cent seniors, and 32 per cent graduate students. Significantly the Registrar noted the presence of 1.5 per cent non-students, a factor which was later reflected in campus disturbances, and even in the strident demands made of institutional management.

Within the two decades, 1950–70, succeeding student generations in Indiana University reflected significant changes. Dean Pressly S. Sikes of the Junior Division reported in February 1950 that the current freshman class made better grades than had those of previous years, and there were 62 per cent fewer withdrawals for academic reasons. Of the new class 15 per cent maintained a "B" average. He attributed this favorable condition to better counseling to help bridge the gap between high school and college, and to the maintenance of small classes of thirty to thirty-five students. Twenty-three veterans' wives living in university apartments achieved the best grade average in the university, and sixty-seven members of Kappa Kappa Gamma sorority led the organizations with a "B" average in 1951, the highest organizational average in university history. They, however, lost their lead to the Kappa Alpha Thetas in 1952.

Two years later 357 freshmen, or 17 per cent of the entering class, had a "B" average or better, and of these 197 were women. As the decade advanced, the various categories of students showed marked improvements, and in 1956 dismissal of freshmen for academic reasons was 11 per cent below the past six-year average. Indicative of this heartening condition an old student institution passed into history in 1956–57. The Junior Division promoted faculty legislation to discontinue the traditional mid-term "smoke-up." This practice had an early origin, and was the source of much student anxiety, and some parental anger. If a student had failing grades at mid-term his dean sent his parents a report, and this often resulted in panic all around. The installation of International Business Machines, said President Wells, made it possible to issue mid-term grade estimates rather than the grim reports that traditionally had conveyed such a note of finality.

Both students and faculty, with neither being satisfied with any scheme, attacked grading practices. The last change in the

Indiana system had been made in 1917 when the three-point A-B-C plan was adopted. On October 21, 1965, Charles E. Harrell, Registrar, announced that both the Bloomington and Indianapolis campuses would adopt a four-letter, four-point system, with "C" bearing two quality points. He explained there had always been difficulty under the three-letter grading system because an "F" meant a minus one quality point. Machine computation was possible under the new grade range, and, besides, about four out of five American universities used the four-letter, four-point method of grading.

Undergraduate grade achievements continued to climb in 1965, and the whole student-body averaged above a "C." In June, 264 seniors graduated with honors. These were encouraging facts, but they raised questions and refuted contentions. Freshmen reached the university more adequately prepared than those of other years. Whether or not their instructors recognized this fact and challenged them was a bothersome question. Was the grading too lax? Apparently the "bigness" of the university had no actual bearing on individual performance, and, finally, how much did lack of genuine intellectual challenge contribute to student unrest? New students arriving in Bloomington had the broadest frame of general knowledge reference, and suffered almost not at all because of the traditional gap between high school and college.

In the face of gripping changes, Indiana University weathered the storms of the 1960s without serious disruption of any part of the institution's operation. No buildings were destroyed in student riots, no one was seriously injured or killed, some dignity was bruised, there was serious embarrassment caused by unseemly heckling of Secretary of State Dean Rusk when he visited the campus, and everyone experienced some anxiety. The vast majority of students, however, took little or no part in the demonstrations, placard snatchings, shouting of profanity and obscenities, shovings, and kickings. For students and university this was a transitional period in relationships. The administration and faculty engaged in considerable introspection as to whether many practices and rules had not become too outmoded to serve a free intellectual society trying to exist in sharply revised national and social contexts. In a more direct sense the time had come when educational, family, and political mores faced fundamental change. A new age of moral ambiguities was upon the country.

[XXII]

Years of the Bitter Harvest

DURING THE Vietnam War patriotic and public emotions were easily stirred by rumor, slanted news reporting, and, perhaps, some downright deception. In 1962 Robert Francis Byrnes, professor of Russian history with a broad diplomatic service background, became chairman of the Department of History. This was the first time in Indiana University history that a non-American specialist had held this position, and in a department which had long emphasized American and regional studies. Byrnes was imaginative and energetic and he stirred much consideration of the history of the new world age. In departmental discussions suggestions were made that, in the light of international commitments by Americans, an attempt must be made to give students a clearer understanding of the shrinking world about them. This same dilemma and confused probing was going on in every progressive department of history in the country.

On November 12, 1962, a featured column under the by-line of Sexson Humphreys appeared in the *Indianapolis News* bearing the exaggerated headline, "U. S. History Slighted?" The columnist discussed a proposed new course which would combine study of Western Europe and the United States since 1950. It was said this new course would replace the traditional freshman introductory one in United States history. Entering students would be required to gain an understanding of the history of Europe before they tackled that of their own country. Humphreys quoted Byrnes' critics as saying some analytical surveys revealed Indiana high school students had only the sketchiest notion of the Constitution and American traditions, a fact which was eloquently documented in the substantial Baxter, Ferrell, Wiltz survey of the teaching of American history in the Indiana schools. The old introductory courses, said Humphreys, would be elevated to the sophomore level. He wrote, "The I. U. history department has approved the new course, but not unanimously. There has been editorial criticism of the proposal by Bloomington, Indianapolis, and Fort Wayne newspapers. The leading faculty critic of Byrnes' plan for the course refuses, however, to speak for publication, and administrative officials of the University prefer to withhold comment until full consideration has been given." This was indeed a tempest in the academic teapot, stirred up perhaps more by personal pettishness than by objective investigation of facts. The established courses were left unimpaired. Byrnes denied that any de-emphasis of American history had either occurred or been contemplated. This was the old provincial issue all over again, but this time in a moment of national sensitivity about the United States' world responsibilities.

In a broader vein the Humphreys column said, "The charge is also made that 'exotic' history courses like Turkish history and civilization before the Mongol Conquest are multiplying and American history courses are standing still." Byrnes denied the charge because there were fifty-nine American courses and sixty-seven non-American ones, a rather heavy imbalance in favor of the former. He was quoted as saying there had been a steady rise in American course enrollments, and staff members in the field had been increased from five to twelve in five years.

There was more publicity on the subject of the history curriculum, this time from an extremely conservative and impassioned quarter. Dr. George W. Crane, in his syndicated column in the *Indianapolis Star* and the Bloomington *Herald-Telephone*, September 13, 1963, fanned anew the flames over the slighting of American history. He said Indiana University students "are offered a single two-hour course in American history covering 1865 to the present," while the "history department lists dozens of courses on

Russian and communism subjects, as well as Latin American courses ad infinitum." In some way a wild wind had blown this angry thistle of falsehood into Dr. Crane's garden, and he demonstrated a naïve willingness to accept it. All the critics were reading the news as they wanted to believe it, and failed to read that less spectacular source of academic information, the semester course schedules.

When Indiana University announced, July 10, 1962, that it had received a Ford Foundation grant for $2,300,000 to be expended over a period of ten years to develop courses in East Asian languages with emphasis on Korean, Chinese, and Japanese it stirred the resistance even more. "A Taxpayer" in a letter to the *Indianapolis Star*, December 8, asked why should Indiana University be "called upon to support the biggest East Asian-Russian program in the United States?" He suggested legislators should examine the university's budget to "consider whether this program is really one of the major functions of Indiana University."

These ill-conceived and ill-aimed blasts had little or no effect on attempts to enrich the Indiana curriculum. Three years later, February 1965, the Board of Trustees, after five years of planning, approved the creation of a Department of Near Eastern Languages and Literature with Wadie Jwaideh as head. This department was an expansion into an area little explored by American public universities, and it began to offer courses in Arabic, Hebrew, and the Persian languages and literature. This time the shrill critics were in pursuit of Cuban revolutionary supporters, unshorn and unbathed hippies, peace corpsmen, and freedom marchers, and had little or no time to pursue the offering of cultural insights into the ancient holy lands and their histories.

Internally, the Stahr administration undertook to tighten up class schedules, no matter the content of courses. President Stahr announced in April 1963 that 200 more Saturday classes involving 6,000 students would be added in order to take up the slack in a reduced instructional budget. At the same time fees would be increased. The administration was indeed striking at the granite-like barriers of student resistance. Saturday had come to be considered, largely by student-generated tradition, as a "free day." In this they had considerable faculty sympathy.

Rigid registration rules were made to ensure that freshmen

and sophomores would remain in the classrooms on Saturday, and to ensnare as many juniors and seniors as possible. Dean Robert E. Shaffer explained that bounding enrollments made such rules mandatory if somewhat limited facilities were to be used effectively. At the same time efforts were made to avoid duplicative educational procedures and to relieve pressures on lower-level classes. Entering freshmen were encouraged in September 1963 to take advance placement examinations in basic courses to determine if they should not be advanced to more challenging work.

The Faculty Council in June 1965 threatened the complacency of another campus custom by proposing to advance class periods from 45 to 60 minutes with 15-minute class breaks. Proponents of this move argued that such a change would make Indiana University one of the pioneers in the nation with full-hour recitation periods. There, however, seemed to have been a limited amount of adventurous pioneering spirit among the faculty. The full hour proposal stirred up considerable published discussion, but no action resulted. Another and somewhat more timid assault was made upon the nervous curricular outposts when the "pass-fail" grading system was promoted by students. President Stahr appeared before the Student Senate, April 20, 1967, to announce that with the opening of the fall semester juniors and seniors in good departmental standing could take classes on a pass-fail basis. When the president had departed the chamber, the Senate was turned into what the *Indiana Daily Student* called "a wild shouting match." Hardly had the youthful senators settled back in their seats after the uproarious discussion of the pass-fail issue before students were preparing for their day in academic court by grading their professors. On May 1, 1967, it was said that more than 35,000 questionaires were stuffed into student mailboxes as the culminating act of more than a thousand man hours of labor in preparing to evaluate both professors and their courses. It is doubtful, however, that this idea ultimately had the impact that its proponents hoped for; the students found it as difficult to grade a professor as it was for a professor to grade a student.

In more substantive ways the university curriculum experienced some changes and several important expansions. A joint arrangement was made in July 1962 between Indiana University and the United Steelworkers of America to offer a pioneering course in labor education, with an ultimate goal of conferring a degree in the subject. Two years later physiology, bacteriology, botany, and zoology were united into the new division of Biological Sciences with Tracy M. Sonneborn, Distinguished Service Professor of Zoology and Genetics, as temporary chairman. At the same time President Stahr appeared before a special legislative subcommittee, June 25, 1964, to advocate the organization in Indiana University of a school of architecture. Much earlier in the university's history William Lowe Bryan had sought such a school in his attempt to broaden the institution's professional curriculum. The state legislative subcommittee in 1964 visited several possible sites for the location of a publicly supported school. Stahr made a strong argument as to why it should be located in Bloomington. He told the legislators the university already offered many courses in the disciplines basic to the study of architecture. The visitors toured the university plant and listened to descriptions of courses, visited the libraries and the Department of Fine Arts, and inspected laboratories and other facilities. All of this, however, was in vain because the subcommittee recommended in August 1964 that the new state college of architecture and planning should be located in Ball State University at Muncie.

Though the Indiana School of Architecture was lost to the university, there were solid gains in two other areas. The highly successful Division of Library Science introduced its doctoral program that fall with the avowed purpose of filling the need for highly qualified library directors and research personnel. Three years later the university supplemented its campus program in the fine arts by the addition in Indianapolis of the John Herron School of Art. This was the absorption of still another proprietary school which had come out of the nineteenth century, and which now needed the support of a public university to survive. These were major landmark changes that occurred during the Stahr years. Actually the process of change was manifested more fundamentally in the year-to-year departmental and college curricular revisions. The minutes of the Faculty Council and the Board of Trustees became chronicles of growth and change.

While professors and administrators struggled with the problems of broadening the curriculum and making the instructional program more effective, the Indiana University community was engaged in carrying on an ancient tradition. Almost since the founding of the institution lecturers had come to Bloomington to discuss contemporary issues and to expound learned theories. The decades, 1950–70, were no different, in fact this might well be characterized as the era in which campus audiences seemed to hope that the next lecturer would bring finite answers for a good number of civilized man's problems, or offer reasons why he was failing. The current American scene of the 1960s with John F. Kennedy and then Lyndon Baines Johnson in the White House, the freedom crusades, the Vietnam War, the sex revolution, the youth revolts, the emerging space science, and a dozen other issues produced prophets of all sorts.

Barry Goldwater came to the campus in February 1963 to assure already convinced Republicans, gathered in the great Wright Quadrangle Assembly Area, that their party represented the wave of the future. "Today's so-called liberals will be known in history as radicals," he assured the audience of 3,000 persons. He thought the liberals turned radicals would seek to destroy individual liberties in the United States.

Facing toward an altogether different frontier, Wernher von Braun told a convocation assembly that man was going to the moon and he had the capacity to carry out this objective. James E. Webb, administrator of the National Aeronautics and Space Administration, was equally as certain Americans would conquer outer space because of their accumulated scientific knowledge. Three months after Webb had lectured on the campus Judge Willie Lay told an Auditorium gathering, "I predict that in the foreseeable future the United States will have a permanent man in space and through Project Apollo two men will have been on the moon at least once." In a short time Colonel John H. Glenn came as a living exhibit of the new space age man. The *Indiana Daily Student*, April 9, 1965, reported that "Colonel John H. Glenn is the kind of man who makes a person feel like standing up and saying the pledge of allegience. His blue eyes twinkle and he grins disarmingly. His sun tan looks as if he has just got home from a camping trip with Annie and the kids." Glenn spoke on the value of technology utilization, and described his triple orbits of the earth in 1962 in *Friendship 7*.

In these years the American people were in orbit with a different kind of challenge. Since 1945 Indiana University had been deeply concerned with the whole spectrum of racial relations. The classic constitutional decision of *Brown* v. *Board of Education* was a social rip cord which had opened the subject to renewed discussion and reaction. The stormy Southern resistance movement, and the persistent legislative and court battles had gathered daily headlines. It seemed that everybody wanted to say something in public. Adam Clayton Powell, the well-publicized Harlem minister and congressman, came to Bloomington on April 14, 1964, to speak on the "Black Revolution," and following him came Governor George Corley Wallace of Alabama to "stand in the schoolhouse door" for white supremacy. Management of the Great Issues Forum found itself overwhelmed by the crowds which attended the lectures. Preliminary to the Wallace speech, Dean Robert Shaffer ruled that only students could attend, and in this way he hoped to forestall a Ku Klux Klan demonstration and incident on the campus. The audience was checked and rather careful security precautious were taken to insure peaceable assembly. A full-page advertisement appeared in the campus newspaper, April 23, 1964, paid for by the Young Democrats, the National Association for the Advancement of Colored People, and the Protestant Campus Council stating a policy and making a protest. The protest was a statement of disagreement with Governor Wallace's theories of human worth. The group deplored racially inspired inequalities in American society, and called on members of the university community to wear the black and white badge of equality. Wallace, they said, should be listened to with dignity, and he was. The *Daily Student* said the lecture itself went off without incident, but it divided the campus on the civil rights issue.

The following year two former Southern governors came to the university. Each of them had been actively associated with civil rights protests and actions, and each had been staunch in his defense of the southern way of life. Secretary of Commerce Luther H. Hodges came on November 17–18, 1965, to speak on the aerospace program. By that time he had begun to voice an almost about-face philosophy of race relations from that which he had espoused as Governor of North Carolina. Both as Governor and then as Secretary of Commerce, Hodges was a far more moderate man than Strom Thurmond, former Governor of South Carolina. Thurmond had been one of the chief promoters of the famous "Southern Manifesto," and had raised a loud voice in the United States Senate against the Supreme Court decision of 1954.

In 1948 he was the presidential nominee of the State's Rights Party.

Answering in part for the Federal Court's position in the field of racial discrimination, Justice Tom C. Clark described for a "Great Issues" audience in 1965 the behind the scenes working of the Supreme Court, and voiced a radically different philosophy from that of the governors. Speaking with a high degree of personal authority, James H. Meredith described the "American Negro in Mississippi." Meredith had endured the trauma of desegregating the University of Mississippi, and had become spokesman for the Negro generally in his home state. In July 1965, when he appeared in Bloomington, he had just returned from a lecture tour in Africa and the Middle East. Later Indiana University Press was to publish his book describing his experiences on being a pioneer in a highly transitional period in national social history.

Interspersed with the civil rights-related speakers came a small army of lecturers discussing world affairs in 1964 and 1965. Turner Catledge of the *New York Times* analyzed the presidential campaign of 1964 from an editorial point of view. George A. Morgan of the United States Embassy in Moscow described conditions in Russia; William F. Buckley, Jr., propounded the new brand of intellectual conservatism. In his speech on the campus, Wayne Morse, a senatorial liberal from Oregon, accused President Lyndon B. Johnson of passing up the last opportunity to save the world from another major war. Richard M. Nixon, preparing the ground for another try at the presidency, spoke on his observations in the Far East, and on American foreign policy in that area. Partially answering the Nixon pronouncements, Melvin R. Laird took Republicans to task for their views of American policies and actions in Southeast Asia.

No student in the years of the 1950s and early 1960s could have pleaded lack of exposure to full-scale and variegated views of the world about him. The oratorical parade was endless, and the ideas they enunciated appeared to be seamless. Negatively, some of the lecturers stirred political emotions, some aroused racial antagonisms, and others offended the community's sense of social propriety. There were three of the latter category in the spring semester of 1966. The poet Allen Ginsberg, accompanied by his companion Peter Orlovsky, stopped in Bloomington on his way to New York to talk with an Indiana sociologist about the history of narcotics legislation. In turn, the professor asked him to meet with a graduate seminar on deviant behavior. The English Department also asked Ginsberg to participate, without fee, in its program dealing with modern poetry; no one knew before hand that Orlovsky would also lecture. Their lecture held in Ballantine Hall before a standing room audience, March 1, 1966, proved a sensation on a campus that had been conditioned to rather frank discussions of deviant sexual behavior during the Kinsey era. The *Daily Student*, March 2, 1966, said, "Allen Ginsberg, a bearded poet in white denims, was accompanied by Peter Orlovsky, who sported faded blue jeans and hair cut well below shoulder length. Ballantine 013 was packed beyond capacity as nearly 600 students listened anxiously to Mr. Ginsberg and his companion, Mr. Orlovsky." The poets opened their lectures with religious invocational chants sung in both Japanese and English. Then there was a sermon on the "Highest Perfect Wisdom," and Peter Orlovsky read a pop art poem on Dick Tracy, followed by some poetry describing a sexual situation in which he said he and Ginsberg had participated. Ginsberg's poems covered a range of subjects from religious sects, Vietnam, and sexual relations, and in the process of reading he uttered aside observations on politics, governments, and public officials. Earl Hoff, editor of the University News Bureau, said the program "was more lurid than anticipated and that the [university] officials were embarrassed by the program."

The Ginsberg-Orlovsky performance received wide and somewhat sensational newspaper publicity. On March 4, Richard C. Bodine, Speaker of the Indiana House of Representatives, denied the Legislative Research Commission was engaged in a "witch hunt," but if he found the facts of the poets' appearance and remarks on the campus raised a question of obscenity, then he would ask the commission to investigate the matter. There followed a discussion of the Ginsberg affair between President Elvis J. Stahr and Speaker Bodine in South Bend. Stahr told the press that he expected to confer with his colleagues on the campus before making a public statement. Later he wrote the Speaker of the House two eloquent letters, March 8 and 12, which were reminiscent of his talent as a college debater. He reviewed all of the ascertainable facts, and in a ringing peroration he told Bodine, "In summary, as long as the world about us is not without flaw, and as long as we study the world, there will be an occasional performance which will not match the standards of the great majority of us. Nevertheless, I have confidence in the competence of the Indiana University Faculty and academic administrators, and the University's total record supports that confidence abundantly." Stahr told the Speaker further that it was impossible to know in advance what any lecturers would say except in the cases where they submitted manuscripts for publicity purposes. He expressed pride in the atmosphere of freedom on the university's campus, and in the students who could "not be swept off their feet by fads, fancies, or phoneys." He said two ministers who had heard the lecturers had expressed to him approval of them. Perhaps the St. Louis *Post Dispatch* wrung the last drop of interest out of the Ginsberg incident in a story on March 13, which by that time was well out of context in fact and point.

Before the Ginsberg dust had settled there was another speaker, and another furor. On May 3, 1966, Frank E. McKinney, president of the Board of Trustees, issued a statement through the Indiana News Bureau regarding the appearance of Herbert Aptheker in Bloomington. Possibly no two men ever lived in worlds further apart than McKinney and Aptheker. The board president and Indianapolis banker said Aptheker was an American citizen who was an avowed member of the Communist Party. He thought, however, many people would unwittingly have the university deny the constitutional guarantee of freedom of speech in the anger and frustration aroused by the "world situation at this point in history." The university administration, he said, loathed Communism because it would undermine and destroy freedom. "We will not assist the communist conspiracy," he informed the public, "by denying freedom of speech and thereby martyring its mouthpiece. To martyr this man or to flatter him as a dangerous man to let open his mouth is to grant him victory, because he will then have forced us to abandon our own principles." McKinney also expressed strong faith in the intelligence of students to expose the hypocrisy of the communist system.

The *Indianapolis News* editorially condemned the appearance of Herbert Aptheker in Bloomington. The paper felt the university administration had badly served the people of the state by allowing a highly publicized Communist to speak on the campus.

On May 9, 1966, the *News*, however, had a change of heart. It carried the apology, "*I. U. we're sorry.* In this column last Friday we indulged in comment about the officials of Indiana University in connection with the visit to the I. U. campus of Herbert Aptheker, a recognized spokesman for the Communist Party. The *News* was ill-advised regarding the circumstance surrounding Aptheker's visit to Bloomington. Our comment and criticism was harsh and unjustified. We are sorry. . . ." The Aptheker commotion was indeed a tempest in a very small teapot. No one was known to have been converted to communism, and a week later the vast majority of students could not have recalled his visit, yet the university's stand for freedom of discussion was another measure of its intellectual integrity.

Lecturers came and went with regularity. Some of them promised that there would be a new era in television broadcasting, the war in Vietnam would be won or lost in the Mekong Delta, or, as Jesse Unruh of the California legislature said, there would soon appear a new "American politician." Maybe Unruh was thinking of himself in that role. Senator Abraham Ribicoff, February 10, 1967, told an Indiana audience, trying eagerly to peer into the future, that there was no magic formula for curing America's current social ills beyond the commitment of time, money, and talent. Dr. Clark Kerr, former president of the University of California, came to Bloomington to deliver the prestigious Patten Lectures in October of that year. A smart-aleck nonstudent dressed in a Halloween suit and mask dashed onto the platform at the beginning of the first lecture and slapped a pie in Dr. Kerr's face, to the shock and embarrassment of the audience. When the boy was finally caught, he was found to be the son of an administrative official of an Iowa university.

In an era of world unrest and unprecedented student anxiety Indiana University invited to its campus a wide variety of speakers who discussed almost every current topic under the sun. Some even came and discussed non-subjects. Some were prophets of doom while others brought glad tidings of a "new era." For the university itself, the central issue in the troubled years of the late 1960s was maintaining consistently the principle and privilege of free speech and open discussion in the face of stubborn public opposition, including that of the public press which should have been an unflinching ally. The Stahr administration was challenged from its inception in 1962 to maintain freedom as no other administration in a century and a half of university history had been challenged.

Indiana University in the post World War II decades was acutely aware of changing conditions in the world. Its students were drawn from around the globe, and its professors went everywhere. They served in sensitive governmental positions, in foreign classrooms, as advisors to businesses, and to all sorts of national policy-making agencies. Both the Korean and Vietnam conflicts drew heavily on the faculty and student body, and on the campus there was a keen awareness of these struggles. A constant debate went on in classroom and public forum over policies, moral commitments, and the relationship of the individual to the government. Southeast Asia was far removed from Bloomington, but the evolving issues over South Vietnam built up intensive emotional concern, especially for male students who were on the campus almost by reprieve from local draft boards, and who were convinced their "2-S" classification could be changed almost instantaneously.

The war in Vietnam came into full focus for much of the academic world on May 14, 1965, when the Inter-University Committee for a Public Hearing on Vietnam sponsored a nationwide "teach-in" on the subject. In Bloomington the discussions were organized by Students for a Democratic Society. McGeorge Bundy of the United States State Department was questioned by five professors over a nationwide telephone hook-up. On the Indiana campus, following the Bundy program, twelve professors debated the Vietnam issue.

Perhaps only a minimum number of students heard either McGeorge Bundy and his professorial protagonists, or the warm debate by local talent in Ballantine Hall. A large number of them, however, saw the editorial in the *Indiana Daily Student*, July 29, 1965, admonishing them to check their draft status. The editor warned that marriage was no guarantee of exemption, but having a child would bring about a reclassification to "III-A," a slightly lower category. Later that summer Students for a Democratic Society angered the editor when the organization proposed a draft card burning in Washington in protest of the war. He wrote, "This draft card burning will not only be a criminal offense, it will be a disgusting display of the Students for a Democratic Society's lack of maturity." The editor granted that the organization had a perfect right to criticize the Government's policies, but it had no right to advocate destroying draft cards, and cited the provisions for stiff fines and prison terms for committing such an act. "So," he said, "those who burn their cards can expect to pay for the pyre."

Early in 1965 professors and students on American university campuses searched for answers to one of the most baffling moral and policy issues in American history. Those at Indiana University were no exception. Both students and professors took sides in the great debate, some of them exhibiting an old conservatism toward governmental authority while others proposed to challenge it. When Richard M. Nixon visited the campus on Sunday evening October 18, 1965, he spoke to a crowded auditorium of students and townsfolk. In his speech he adhered closely to the mainstream of current American foreign policy, supporting to some degree President Lyndon B. Johnson and Secretary of State Dean Rusk in their actions. Outside the Auditorium 150 Students for a Democratic Society, Young Socialist Alliance, and Americans for Democratic Action marched around the Showalter Fountain bearing antiwar signs. Counter marching were about 50 Young Americans for Freedom, Young Republicans, and Young Democrats. Their signs said "I. U. Students say Win in Viet," and the Young Republicans proclaimed "Young Republicans Support L. B. J. in Viet." Perhaps the sign bearers impressed no one much but themselves; in the Auditorium Richard M. Nixon sought to bring solace to Republicans and wavering Democrats.

Somewhat reflective of a sizable segment of student opinion, the editor of the *Indiana Daily Student* neither supported the war nor approved of the protesters. He saw more in the antiwar marchers than mere blurred men and women, "We also noticed what the people looked like—specifically, their physical appearance. It did not take too long to recognize a majority of the demonstrators were non-comformists (according to American Society) in dress and grooming. . . ." The editor thought the clean-cut type would appear more effectively before the citizens, otherwise the beatnik types would nullify their good ideas by people labeling them "crackpots." Richard M. Nixon, inside the palatial Auditorium, seems not to have generated nearly so much commotion with his conventional Republican line as did the ragtag stragglers outside belaboring Venus with their shouts and their waving signs.

On the heels of Nixon's visit there arose a second minor commotion. Guy Loftman, president of the Indiana chapter of Students for a Democratic Society, raised an objection to campus participation in the Red Cross' "bleed-in" for the armed forces in South Vietnam. Loftman's protest, raised in the Student Senate, was futile as he was defeated by a vote of 20 to 3. The Red Cross collected 1,276 pints of blood, and a thousand of the donors requested that their contributions be sent to Vietnam. The *Daily Student*, November 6, 1965, said that a large majority of the blood donors most conscientiously wished to support the American armed forces. In the Senate Lynn Everoad objected to the use of the "bleed-in" success story to say that politically the entire student body supported the United States in its involvement in Southeast Asia. She undertook unsuccessfully to bring about a campus-wide referendum on the subject.

By late October of that year it was difficult at times to discern how much of the discussions, protests, demonstrations, and other displays of opposition were to the point of opposing the Vietnam War, and how much had become parliamentary maneuvering and an attempt to snatch at campus political power. Opposition to the war in Vietnam was indeed an active issue among all campus groups where expressions of points of view were pertinent, but no one seems to have been able to differentiate clearly the nature of the current struggle and that of the two previous world wars in which Indiana University had been so deeply involved. Reminiscent of those wars, co-eds from thirty-six sororities and residence halls set to work early in December to bake 12,000 cookies for troops in Vietnam. They called their undertaking "Operation Cheer Up," and for good measure many of the girls wrote letters to troops to be sent along with the cookies. Local merchants contributed ingredients for the cookies, brownies, and fudge, and Sears, Roebuck and Company permitted the girls to do their cooking in public view in their store. The activity was a success, and more than 500 pounds of their baking were sent to Vietnam by special handling. There are no records of the "cookie romances" that may have developed.

There was less festivity for male students that December, for them the Vietnam War took on ominous meaning. The student editor wrote, December 9, "Seven thousand miles away amid steaming jungle rubber plantations and swampy rice paddies, there's a little war growing larger." The time was at hand when male students had reason to be deeply concerned. The only thing which separated them from the Marines in the jungles was a tiny billfold card bearing the legend "2-S," a status which could be changed by local draft boards. Students interviewed by *Daily Student* reporters that month expressed varying opinions from full support of the country's policies, the bombing of the Hanoi-Haiphong industrial complex, to open opposition of involvement. Steve Schlosser, a junior, was quoted as saying, "Since we called off the Viet Nam elections in 1956 and have set up a series of military dictatorships, we can hardly say we are fighting for democracy. The morality of genocide by B-52 bombers is also hard to defend. The war's only redeeming aspect is that it keeps our economy going." Overall there was a note of hopelessness that the war could not be ended after ten years of bitter jungle fighting.

Obviously the Johnson Administration was actuely aware of campus unrest over the subject of its foreign policies. In time a procession of official apologists visited the Indiana campus to explain the Johnson-Rusk decisions. One of the first of these to appear was General Maxwell D. Taylor, consultant to the President of the United States. For several days before the General's appearance in the Auditorium there prevailed an air of some anxiety over what might happen in militant confrontations. There was an indication that there would be a major antiwar demonstration when General Taylor arrived at the Auditorium to speak. On February 25, 1966, about 250 persons marched around the Showalter Fountain, some protesting involvement in the war, and some shouting for victory in Vietnam. A lone G.I. in army fatigues stood silently before the Lilly Library bearing a sign saying "Support the GIs." This lad was D. D. Arney, a senior who had served six months in Southeast Asia, and had promised his colleagues he would lift a banner in their support. Mixed in with the protesters were supporters of Senator Vance Hartke bearing signs emblazoned with various slogans and pronouncements. The weather was rather bleak, and the demonstrators made little if any headway for their causes, whatever points of view they espoused. Even that zealous and mysterious crusader who circled the fountain in a foreign car bearing a sign which read, "Red propaganda Produces Yellow Youth, Appeasement is for Fools, Liberty is for Patriots," failed to create much excitement, except to call attention to the fact that he was a less hardy soul than those who bared their breasts to the wintry evening in their march. Inside the Auditorium General Taylor delivered his speech without incident and perhaps without knowledge that a few hearty souls outside took opposite views.

General Taylor was followed in May by General Lewis B. Hershey, a native of Steuben County, Indiana, and director of the Selective Services. Between February and May a considerable amount of anxiety had built up over the draft. The *Daily Student*, April 30, 1966, reflected this fact when it ran a four-page analysis of student relations to the war. The story indicated the war was escalating, and the draft was edging nearer to the campus. The paper said that uncertainty over draft status for most students was the top worry of graduating seniors. When General Hershey spoke in the Auditorium on May 2, 1966, more than 2,000 demonstrators shouting pro and con sentiments marched around the Showalter Fountain for an hour. A student group calling itself "University Students for America" appeared to outnumber the hecklers, or the Independent Committee to End the War. Students for America not only heckled the Vietnam critics, they engaged in throwing three or four showers of eggs, an act which Dean of Students Robert Shaffer branded as "a display of pseudo patriotism and disgraceful in view of Indiana University's long history of academic freedom." The dean assured students they could not dismiss grave international problems by engaging in "sophomoric antics."

In contrast, the 300 supporters of the Independent Committee paraded in orderly fashion along the well-worn path of protest about the fountain. They seemed to have received the egg showers with the aplomb of martyrdom, thus making their point even more strongly. Somewhat relieving the solemnity and anger of the occasion was the humor created by an independent marcher. He bore a sign in behalf of "Students Wildly Indignant About Nearly Everything" or SWINE. His banner read, "I don't like almost anybody."

Inside the Auditorium General Hershey emphasized the fact that most selective service policy was made by local draft boards.

No doubt he expected student protests before he came to Bloomington, and by long experience he was able to accept them with granite-like fortitude.

Either by design or because of the inconvenience of travel, Lyndon B. Johnson did not brave the protesters in Bloomington. On July 23 he spoke in Indianapolis in defense of his national policies. On hand to greet him were members of the Independent Committee to End the War. Some of these people were arrested and roughed up unnecessarily by the Indianapolis police and were placed under bonds ranging from $100 to $250. There were a few injuries resulting from scuffles with the officers, and in sober retrospect the incident reflected upon the judgment and responsibility of the Indianapolis police. Back in Bloomington the committee scheduled a downtown march and demonstration to raise funds to pay fines and other personal losses. David Starr, a member of the body's executive committee, told newspaper reporters, "The focus of the demonstration will be against war, which, as our experience shows, is forcing Americans to deny basic freedoms in our country." Only about 175 faculty members, students, and some children marched and demonstrated. Later at Whittenberger Auditorium the announced "teach-in" turned into a rather warm debate, much of it among members of the Independent Committee themselves. This chapter in the protest movement was an unhappy one. There was clear evidence the Indianapolis police had overreacted, even to the point of unnecessary physical abuse, and trampling of the constitutional rights of individuals. There seemed to have prevailed an attitude of "We'll show the college folks the light 'Texas Style.' " Back in Bloomington, police and committee "ushers" prevented incidents during the march down Kirkwood Avenue and around the Court House Square. Members of the Delta Upsilon fraternity caricatured the march by lagging along in the rear of the marchers carrying placards bearing the legends, "Ban the Beard," and "Send Soap."

Hardly had the wrath over the Indianapolis experience cooled before Vice President Hubert Humphrey appeared on the campus scene. He spoke in the Auditorium on September 23, 1966, and both Students for a Democratic Society and members of the Independent Committee engaged in what by now had become almost a ceremonial march around the Showalter Fountain. Approximately a hundred persons bore placards denouncing the war and

American policy in Southeast Asia. Taking a somewhat different tact from his predecessors, the Vice President urged, by implication at least, that members of the large audience deny recognition to the controversial W. E. B. DuBois Club. He said that organization was a Communist front, and that it was then under investigation by the Federal Government. His warning was somewhat late because at that time the DuBois Club had been dropped by Indiana University from the list of registered campus organizations. Nevertheless, there were still active members of the body on the campus, and the university administration was still highly sensitive about the activities of this extremist group.

Scarcely a week passed on the Indiana campus after 1966 when there was not some form of protest against national policies and the war or some university policy. On May 6, 1967, the *New Republic* published an article under the headline, "Just a Drop Can Kill. A Secret Work on Gas and Germ Warfare." It mentioned Indiana University twice as one of the places where research on the chemical had been done. Vice President Lynne Merritt, Jr., denied the institution had any contracts involving classified research. The university had, said the Indiana University Foundation, accepted within the past two years thirty-two contracts from the Army, Navy, and Air Force for research on military-related projects. Guy Loftman, the student body president, entered into correspondence with the *New Republic* to determine the extent of the university's involvement.

As the year wore on, there were "love-ins," marches, "teach-ins," demonstrations, debates, and charges against the university for its various relations with the Federal Government. Almost every activity, administrative and research, came under some kind of scrutiny. In October 1967 it was said that approximately 205 Indiana students had joined the Hoosier College Cavalcade to Washington to participate in a draft card burning demonstration. On October 27 President Johnson, in a speech to a group of commercial employees in the Shoreham Hotel, said the United States would not be swayed from pursuing its goal in Southeast Asia. This seemed to be an answer to the draft card burners. Out of the 300 Indiana University students who reached the Capitol, only one, Irina Johnson, was arrested when she ignored a military policeman's order to move on.

The draft card burners were hardly back in Bloomington before a protesting group of students crowded into the School of Business Building and disrupted a job interview session conducted by a Dow Chemical Company representative. The crowd of approximately a hundred demanded that the Dow representative leave the building in five minutes, otherwise the mob would break into the room. When the demonstrators did push into the room and refused to leave, the Bloomington police were called to quell the riot. They placed the crowd under arrest. Two students were injured in the melee, and in protest several students fell limp on the floor, forcing the officers to remove them bodily.

The School of Business commotion occurred on the eve of Secretary of State Dean Rusk's visit to the campus on October 31, 1967. Rusk appeared to have come to Bloomington as a self-invited guest. Later, the *Daily Student*, November 2, 1967, said this was not quite true. The Secretary was invited to speak by Ernest K. Lindley ('20), and then special assistant to the Secretary. Rusk seems not to have brought with him a prepared speech—as one observer said later, he came to enter into an open discussion, and directed his remarks along this line; above all, he made no major policy statement. He no doubt was trying out some policy ideas in an attempt to discern the reactions of the campus mind to them. If this was true, he did not fully reveal his thoughts. He spoke in the morning at 10:00 o'clock, but by 9:45 the Auditorium was filled to its 3,800 seating capacity. That morning the *Daily Student* most cordially welcomed Rusk to the campus, and asked its readers to give him a dignified hearing. The paper later said the Secretary spoke "to an emotionally up-tight audience. He was speaking to college students—many of whom are better informed on the Vietnam issue than the general public, and most of whom are emotionally tied to it because it does—or will—affect them directly soon." A week later President Elvis J. Stahr told the Faculty Council, "Everyone in the University knows that the interference with the speech of Dean Rusk was neither spontaneous nor the result of something he said; it was premeditated and carefully planned and organized; there were even handbills printed in advance to instruct in how to carry it out."

When Secretary Rusk appeared on the stage, he was greeted with screams of "Murderer," "Eichmann," and "Napalm Baby." His friends, however, all but drowned out the hecklers with their standing ovation. As his speech progressed the audience became more involved in a general hassle with itself. One enraged woman hit an obnoxious male protester over the head with her parasol, an act which was not wholly without grim humor. The angry lady's comments were heard plainly in the fine acoustical hall, and they provoked loud laughter from the audience, a fact which went far to break the mounting tension. Rusk commented upon the general confusion by saying, "I came prepared to be your guest—I am not going to engage in a shouting contest with anyone." When he had finished speaking, President Stahr before opening a question and answer session, told the audience, "This University has a tradition of free speech. Premeditated disruption is unworthy of Indiana University. Your rights do not include the right to prevent others from listening." At the end of the session Rusk was escorted from the Auditorium by police to a waiting car, a precaution which may have been unnecessary. Only a small but raucous part of the audience had been rude and unmannerly, but it gave no direct evidence of being violent.

There was an interesting sequence of incidents in the history of protests on the Indiana campus at this point. The Dow Chemical recruiters incident had occurred in the School of Business on October 3, 1967, and Secretary Rusk appeared the next day. The protest leaders who might have created a violent incident were in jail, and as a result the disruptions were largely disorganized and leaderless. President Stahr was warned that there would be possible bloodshed, and he said the Rusk visit for him was a harrowing experience.

The day following, Keith Owen, a graduate student, submitted an open letter to the *Daily Student* apologizing for the rudeness to Secretary Rusk. He agreed with President Stahr that premeditated disruption was a denial of free speech. He said, "Such antics should be reserved for the east stands of the football stadium, where I am sure they will be much more appreciated or at least in order." The notion seems to have prevailed that the Secretary had not actually been allowed to finish his speech. The editor of the *Daily Student* wrote him, December 1, inviting him to come back to Bloomington and take up where he left off. The editors were mistaken, Rusk had finished what he had to say, and no doubt had learned what he had come to find out.

The Rusk incident received worldwide publicity to the humiliation of Indiana University. Immediately students became aware of this fact and began circulating an apology seeking signatures of endorsement. Quickly this statement was signed by 14,000 students, and on November 12, 1967, it was taken to Washington by seniors Jim Durkott and Jayne Grote; their expenses to the capital were paid by two friends of the univeristy. The seniors carried along with the signed petition several letters from officers of the university, and from those of various campus organizations. When they presented their apology and letters to Rusk, they stated that they were apologizing only for the rude reception he had received on the campus, but were not endorsing the war, a point the Secretary reiterated for them, and on November 18, 1967, the *Daily Student* published a letter from Secretary Rusk. He said he and Mrs. Rusk realized the disturbers comprised only a tiny fraction of the audience. "The others present were most generous with their ovations—and the initiative taken by leaders of so many of your student organizations should remove any remaining doubt anywhere about the fidelity of a large majority of your university community to a fine tradition of courtesy and to a basic function of the University; the search for understanding and sound conclusions through orderly discussion."

There was a considerable amount of postmortem comment on the Rusk incident. Professor Leonard Lundin, of the Department of History, in an open letter November 4, 1967, expressed forthright convictions. Professor Lundin, a man of impeccable integrity and courage, thought from newspaper and television reports that some members of the audience "were extremely unmannerly." Some months previously he said he had experienced similar rudeness when he presided at a meeting in which pro-war advocates had undertaken to disrupt an anti-war discussion by using much the same tactics as those which had disrupted Rusk. The Secretary of State came to the campus, said Lundin, as a "very high official, and active director of events, a foremost representative and presumably one of the architects of our war policy, a symbolic figure, a sort of 'Mr. Viet Nam War.'" He reviewed the possibility of getting young men of the audience killed on the battlefield, of destroying Vietnam villages, of using napalm, and guns. "It is not easy," he wrote, "to be polite to someone who seems determined to make you a corpse, an arsonist, a murderer, or a bully." Professor Lundin was unconvinced that the United States was on a quest for peace. He said, "possibly there are worse things than bad manners toward a public speaker. Possibly one worse thing is a government's lying to its people."

In a calmer moment the *Daily Student* editor, November 28, 1967, thought "It is apparent Mr. Rusk visited I. U. for a reason —however ulterior it might have been. He was here to feel the pulse of this part of the Nation, to test responses, to sound the administration's popularity." The editor believed Rusk knew what he could expect before he left Washington because he had received many letters, pro and con, on the subject of the escalating war. In simpler terms, students were reacting to the Tet offensive.

President Stahr reviewed the official university position on the Rusk incident in an eighteen-page statement to the Faculty Council, November 7, 1967. He emphasized the point that Indiana University had three indispensable requisites: a commitment to freedom of inquiry, freedom of expression, and the freedom to differ. He viewed recent events on the campus as a wave of anti-intellectualism that was lashing the American campus in general. At Indiana, he thought, a defiance of the university's values posed serious dangers. "In short," he told his colleagues, "it is not open dissent or disagreement I fear, but disruption, whether calculated or provoked, I fear the possibility that in the minds of a good many the lines are being drawn to challenge principles and pressures which we must preserve and protect if we are to sustain our common enterprise." By that date a considerable amount of tension had developed and the future promised even more disruptions.

The week before President Stahr addressed the Faculty Council, 125 students had assembled outside his office to protest the university's relations with the Dow Chemical Company. They demanded the privilege of presenting to Stahr a list of mandates. The president refused to see them, but Dean Robert Shaffer made arrangements for a calmer and later meeting. When they did meet with Dr. Stahr, the protesting students had reduced their mandates to four demands. They wanted the university to stop Dow representatives from recruiting on the campus, it must not call in outside police to quell student incidents, that all charges arising out of the School of Business incident be dropped, and that the university "strive for intellectual integrity by not having an 'obligation to the people who might need napalm.' "

President Stahr responded to these demands by saying that almost everything Indiana University did in some way supported the war effort if someone chose to make such an interpretation. The president's office did not make School of Business policy or that of the Placement Bureau. Police were called when the protesters used force and there was a clear indication of danger and violence beyond the conventional capability of the campus police to stop. He thought Indiana University had an excellent record of intellectual integrity, and it expected to maintain that record. He would favor dropping charges against the students who had been arrested if upon full investigation they were proved to be groundless. At the moment the issue was in the hands of the Dean of Student Affairs and the Student Conduct Committee.

When Dean Robert Shaffer and the Student Conduct Committee did investigate the Dow Chemical incident, they recommended to the faculty, November 8, 1967, that forty students be placed on critical disciplinary probation, and that three of the gravest offenders be placed on notice of immediate suspension if they violated university rules in the future. Those who were found guilty of resisting police and authorized university personnel were to be placed on critical disciplinary probation for the rest of their college careers. All students were to be placed on notice that immediate suspension would follow future violations of university rules on picketing and demonstrations, this ruling to cover both demonstrators and counter-demonstrators. The Dean cited as a reason for such positive action the "vital importance of laying a clear and thoroughly understood basis for the prevention of such occurrences in the future. . . ."

The same day that Dean Shaffer reported the findings of his office and the Student Conduct Committee, President Stahr addressed a letter to the Board of Trustees in which he stressed the fact that Indiana University looked to the future in creating a solid base for insuring the strongest possible unity in the institution in dealing with incidents like the Dow commotion. "If they are not prevented," he wrote, "from getting rid of the ones we believe most responsible for them," then there was no remedy. He told the trustees that the university administration was not unmindful of the importance of public opinion disapproving the behavior of student activists, "much of which we share, and we are going as far with it as we can without precipitating what could be a fatal cleavage between the faculty and administration."

There was faculty reaction to the handling of the Dow incident. The Continuing Committee of Indiana University Faculty Members was formed. It investigated the incident, and implied, if it did not ask directly, that a more complete report than the one given the Faculty Council in the past November meeting should be formulated. The committee felt possibly a complete reappraisal of university rules should be undertaken with a view to humanizing them. Members thought it crucial "that communication among administration, faculty, and students could be improved." Three faculty members independently suggested, December 7, 1967, that members of the peace groups and the campus and Bloomington police be brought together in a discussion of issues. They felt the university should institute a course for police which would deal with antiwar demonstrators, student life, "hippies," right-wing movements, race relations, narcotics, liquor, etc." Thus the great debate within a debate went on with no end in sight. University values, traditions, official actions, and institutional commitments were challenged in many ways.

In these stirring months there was a rumbling of ominous thunder on both the right and left. A challenge of debate originated between the Students for a Democratic Society and the local Ku Klux Klan on the subject of the Vietnam War. It was at once evident that the students would manhandle the Ku Klux debaters in the area of subject matter and information, but the university was quite willing for the debate to take place as an expression of freedom of discussion. President Stahr was informed by the Mayor of Bloomington, however, that the police had found that automobiles and trucks of Klansmen contained guns, and in one case dynamite, and that there was a genuine possibility that physical violence might result. In a second call the mayor asked the president to call off the debate because he and the police were convinced the debate would get completely out of hand, and this was done. It was clear that the possibility of a flash explosion of brutal violence on the part of direct actionists haunted both campus and town along with the lingering protests and confrontations.

The rutted road to Indiana University's one hundred and fiftieth anniversary on January 20, 1968, had been an arduous one. For most of that long span of years no one could have imagined the turmoil that would beset the campus in the closing decade of this era. The academic community was sorely troubled, and there was some sharp division among its various campus constituencies. The moral and intellectual courage of faculty and administration was challenged on numerous occasions after 1965. The ancient values, traditions, and moral and intellectual commitments, which historically had been considered the rock-hard foundation of the university, had come under fire in areas of academic freedom, racial relations, civil order, and the broad and complex programs of the institution. Faculty-student relationships were troubled, and the administration had become a ready target of criticism and questioning.

In a calmer present moment when the whirling storm of protests and confrontations have simmered down to even less than a whisper, there has remained the question of what the age of near paranoia produced. For one thing there was a reassessment of many older values, careful scrutiny of emerging ones, and a more precise drawing of a line between honest discussion and debate and willful disruption. There crept into faculty relations within the university an element of what President Elvis Stahr referred to as the "referee attitude" of some professors, a phenomenon which he acknowledged to be nationwide.

From the apex of the administrative pyramid Stahr made a careful reappraisal of his own. On February 14, 1967, he wrote, "If anywhere an administration and a faculty can work effectively, it ought to be right here where they have worked together so well for so long. . . . But if those bent on disruption can drive a wedge between us, it will be driven, I assure you. If they can alienate the students from either or both of us they will gleefully do so, I assure you. If those bent on either disruption or control can alienate public support from us, they will joyously do so, I can assure you."

President Stahr was disturbed by the staging of student tests of authority, and by some of them parroting "lines" given them by disruptive sources. He thought, "the sit-ins and other forms of protests" were "borrowed from that long frustrated segment of society whose seriously disadvantaged plight has often led to genuine desperation." He believed this departure would do the same for students. Stahr said he refused to believe that much of the current protests could be translated as freedom, or that freedom was automatically abandoned when the university and faculty refused to cooperate with the radical campus dissidents of the "new left." "To me," he wrote, "academic freedom is the freedom to be as objective as human integrity can be. Is its cloak really meant, I question, to cover dogma and conspiracy and deceit? Surely we can deplore the denial of academic freedom to a Galileo without having to insist that his persecutors should have the same defense. Isn't one of the triumphs of academic freedom that it made possible the unmasking of witch doctors?" There were plenty of witch doctors peddling a varied assortment of wares, both on the campus and in the country in these years. They flailed out left and right, paying little or no attention to the classic freedoms of the past. Many of them presented new nostrums of freedom of instant brewing and without clinical testing.

By the time the creeping arbutus on the historic lovers' stamping ground near Bloomington had beckoned to the rising sap of campus romantics in May 1968, the roar of dissent in Bloomington had all but drowned out the ancient love calls. Within the past year the events of disruption came with nerve shattering frequency. The forum in Dunn Meadow grew more raucous in support of various causes, or for noncauses for that matter. The border about Venus' bowl at the Showalter Fountain had been tramped bare, and there were still to be more marches. At Founder's Day that year the face of protest on the campus had become lined in anger. Behind it seemed to boil the urge of disruption and belittlement of all the day with its citations for good scholarship, good teaching, and all other intellectual achievements represented. Even some of those who had been elected to Phi Beta Kappa membership spurned the honor, and marches out of the Auditorium services left gaping holes in the audience. President Stahr fervently pleaded for compassionate concern in solving acknowledged problems. Above all, he asked the university community to keep its sights fixed on "the individual human being and his genuine assessment and acceptance as an individual. The goal," he said, "is not lip service, nor is it surface compliance with more deadlines or decrees, or punishment of offenders. It is a positive goal. . . ."

Somewhat away from the maddening throng the Board of Trustees, on May 24, 1968, was impatient with the disruption of university programs, and injury to its reputation. Its members reaffirmed the university's long-standing commitment to provide the maximum educational opportunity for all of its students, and to preserve the rights of all the university body to question, debate, criticize, and to dissent peaceably. They were positive, however, that they did not intend to tolerate disruption, coercion, physical restraint, or the threatening of persons with intimidation or harm. The university would enforce with firmness its policies and rules relating to picketing, demonstrations, and related activities. Students would be expelled who resorted to disruptive violence or threats of violence, or who usurped university property and facilities. Specifically this meant summary dismissal from the student body. Except for its statement of its regard for freedoms, there was missing a note of amelioration in the trustees' statement. This was within itself a reappraisal of that body's authority in the face of both academic and physical challenge and disruption. Pointedly it referred to the occupation of an office in the School of Business in the Dow Chemical incident.

The years after 1965 had borne heavily upon the President of the University. On one occasion a graduate student had read, out of context, a statement that Stahr had made about Communism and had published a letter in the *Indianapolis Star* accusing him of being disloyal to the country, an incident which aroused Stahr's anger. This spring semester 1967–68 had subjected the president to serious separation from his basic responsibilities, and had drawn him into frequent confrontations with dissident groups presenting demands, mandates, and petitions. Even the faculty "referees" took their emotional tolls. On July 6, 1968, President Stahr addressed an eloquent letter of resignation to the Board of Trustees. An administration that had begun so full of expectations and promising long-range associations in 1962 had since 1965 grown burdensome and frustrating indeed. Like President Herman B Wells before him, Stahr had carried on a constant fight to procure funds from the Indiana General Assembly, to locate and hire top-flight faculty members, and to complete a mammoth building program. On top of this Stahr, like all of his predecessors in the presidential office, assumed an onerous burden of public relations both in Indiana and across the nation. As a former Secretary of War, he was in demand as a speaker for all sorts of organizations, educational and business. His speech file over the six years fattened, and his subjects ranged from discussion of the evils of communism, education as the bedrock of the nation, to banking and newspapering. All of this, plus the day-to-day administrative demands, sapped away his energy and spirit. The furor of the Vietnam years was in fact the sustenance of the flames about the sacrificial pyre of university presidents, and Stahr was to a large degree a victim of the fires.

President Stahr wrote the trustees he was giving up the presidency of Indiana University on September 1, 1968. His reason was, "For the last two years I have been increasingly aware that the heavy and growing pressures of the University Presidency were levying a great toll. By the end of the past academic year, I had to face the plain fact that I have succumbed to what one resigning president aptly called 'presidential fatigue.'" Stahr said he was resigning before the "super pressures" of the moment rendered him ineffective.

At Indiana Elvis Stahr had been subjected to the same kinds of pressures and frustrations that had confronted presidents George W. Beadle of Chicago, Fred Harrington of Wisconsin, Nathan M. Pusey of Harvard, Grayson Kirk at Columbia, and Clark Kerr at California. There was not, however, dissension between the President and the Board of Trustees, or between him and the great majority of faculty and students. Happily no insane rage had resulted in the bombing and burning of buildings or the ransacking of office files, the pilfering of presidential relics, or any other extreme physical manifestation of dissent. No one was killed and there was little personal injury. In resigning from the presidency, Stahr declared deep affection for both the university and the state, and expressed the desire to remain a member of the faculty. It was even suggested that he accept a part-time appointment at least as an officer of the Indiana University Foundation. He even went so far as to purchase a home in a faculty community, and upon recovery from his occupational virus he planned to settle down in a law professorship. Almost immediately he was offered the presidency of the National Audubon Society, and the course of his life took a sudden and much calmer turn into quieter waters.

Despite all of the writings inspired by the years of protests and confrontations on the American university campus in the decade after 1965, there still has not elapsed enough time to plumb its depth of meaning in terms of changes that may have occurred in university management at all levels, or in internal university relationships; the succeeding calm has proved almost as unfathomable. Herman B Wells was called back as interim President by the Board of Trustees and had to deal with the lessening confrontations that delivered to him mandates and demands. Soon the eye of the storm moved on, and the university turned to consideration of its academic and service roles in the succeeding age of wavering economics, and the sudden reversal of many of the educational predictions and projections made in those building years of expanding social and economic growth of the country.

[XXIII]

"Knowledge Is Our Sword and Shield. . . ."

When Elvis J. Stahr became President of Indiana University in 1962, the institution was nearing a century and a half of operation. In the latter half of the twentieth century, as in the years of the university's beginnings in the 1820s, the nation was in a state of social and economic ferment. Both eras presented their particular challenges, with the latter being a period when the country paradoxically was attempting to settle itself into a longed-for era of peace and economic stability, and at the same time was yearly becoming more deeply involved in the political-military frustrations of southeastern Asia.

Nearer home the state of Indiana was prosperous, perhaps more so than it had ever been in its history. In the charter year of 1820 there was a population of 147,178 persons, and these were largely confined to the Ohio River shore and the southern counties. In 1960 there were 4,662,000, an 18.5 per cent increase within the past decade, and the urban population was growing phenomenally inside this traditionally agrarian state. The balance was now decidedly tilted in favor of the urban community, 2,910,000 to 1,752,000 rural dwellers. Just as this shift had marked effects upon the state, so it was to influence the course of affairs in the university.

The new challenges to Indiana University were once again to chart the mission of a modern institution in its efforts to meet the needs of a more sophisticated modern student and service clientele. High schools in Indiana in 1958 graduated 40,164 students out of a total school enrollment of 935,000, a substantial increase over the year before. Every educational indicator pointed to the fact that even larger classes would be graduated in future years. This horde of high school graduates flocked to the universities demanding better teaching, greater depth and relevance of course materials, and clearer directions in career planning. At the same time the Indiana faculty was being urged to perform more sophisticated research and to assume an increasingly heavy load of public service. In the post-Korean War years the lines of governmental and industrial endeavors drew into closer parallels with those of educational institutions than ever before in American history.

In Bloomington President Stahr and his colleagues faced most of the problems of faculty recruitment that had characterized the first decade of Herman B Wells' presidency. Retirements, resignations, and deaths created major vacancies in positions that had to be filled from a highly competitive market. Among the names of those leaving the faculty were those "wheel horses" who for years had personified to off-campus colleagues Indiana University's expanding programs. No greater problem faced Stahr than that of maintaining and even increasing the momentum of the university that had developed so dramatically over the past two decades. Internally, traditional programs were being revised and expanded, and new ones were being added. Almost every meeting of the Faculty Council and the Board of Trustees resulted in approval of some kind of innovative expansion.

Beyond the Bloomington campus Indiana University entered into numerous agreements with the Federal Government, and foreign governments and universities to supply highly competent consultants, specialized public servants, professors, and lecturers. The Committee on Sabbatical Leaves reported fifty-seven faculty absences in 1964–65, and sixty-eight the following year. Even a greater number of professors were on special leaves to serve in governmental and foreign service posts or to do independent research. The Leaves Committee said in 1965 that the requests for leaves of absence had become so numerous that it felt the time had come to devise a new approach to recording and giving oversight to them. Almost every leave granted a staff member necessitated the employment of a temporary professor to maintain normal instructional programs.

At the outset of the Stahr administration the university was organized into eleven divisions, and already in an advanced formative stage was a move to grant to four of the off-campus extension centers much wider scope of operation and greater autonomy. This prospect also necessitated serious faculty considerations for the expanded curricula.

No general or statistical report by faculty or the Dean of Faculties could possibly convey a dependable notion of the quality of the staff in terms of its reported published materials. Annually the university administration requested of faculty members that they report their activities in the three categories of teaching, public service, and publication. In 1964–65 a thousand professors, out of an instructional staff of 1,625 full-time members, reported 698 publications. More than half of these must be considered by their titles alone as peripheral in character. Nevertheless, there were important works included in this list. What, if any, mature publications were produced by nonreporting professors must as a matter of record remain unknown.

The drive was vigorous and eternal to hire productive professor-scholars who aspired to achieve the levels of such veterans as Kinsey, Cleland, Mueller, Sonneborn, Breneman, and the other stars coming from the Wells administration. Likewise the more recent generation of students, on paper at least, appeared to make greater demands for quality instruction. This was especially true of those who came to the university after the qualitative levels of admission had been raised in 1964. The revised standards required four years of high school English, nine units in the social and physical sciences, and qualification in some foreign language. In addition, students had to achieve standings in the upper half of their graduating classes, and score above the median point on the College Board and ACT examinations. Admissions officers undertook to bring to the Bloomington campus the better graduates of the Indiana high schools. By 1965 the results of the tighter rules of admission were evident in the student body. The Division of Undergraduate Studies observed in its annual report that not only were grade point averages significantly better, but a greater number of freshmen had moved up to sophomore standing by taking special examinations than at any time in the past.

In the mid-1960s Indiana University was caught in the unhappy dilemma of admitting a better qualified student and of being unable to offer a significant amount of individual instruction in many areas. Under the most favorable conditions the institution would have been unable to solve fully the problems of mass instruction or student management in many divisions of its operations.

Indiana was by no means alone in confronting the instructional problems of this uproarious decade. All across the land universities faced the dilemma of serving ever-increasing numbers of students while at the same time trying to develop more effective programs of teaching and research. The crush of numbers overwhelmed both faculty and institution; keeping records alone was a massive undertaking. No longer could a faithful professor or recorder carry in their memories many of the key decisions that were being made. The historic position of registrar all but became outmoded in the new inrush of professors and students; the position became rather one of records management. Charles E. Harrell, registrar and director of Records and Admissions, reported in June 1965 that his office had taken "giant strides toward automation of the enrollment and records system of the University." By use of what he called a "remote console" the time of registering an individual student was reduced from forty-five to three minutes. Indiana, it was said, had become a national leader in the mechanical processes of registration and records management. This, however, was not accomplished without bureaucratic trauma and confusion. Harrell said, "The new registration system has caught the imagination of the academic world and we are pleased that it worked so well and that the University and the staff is [*sic*] receiving so much nationwide publicity." In the first full year of operation of the new procedure the registrar's office recorded almost a half million grades, supplied 48,000 transcripts, and conferred with more than 18,000 persons. No area of the university reflected so clearly the precise statistics of growth and change than did the recording division of the registrar's office. There were, however, no mechanical systems that could be substituted for the human associations of the professor-student-classroom routine. Many mechanical and electronic innovations were introduced, but the human needs were in no way lessened.

The system of lecturer-quiz master was fully instituted, but basically there remained the almost insatiable demand for the personification and humanizing of the instructional process. In fact the 1960s unrest seemed to reflect much of the dehumanization which had gone on in American universities.

Despite increased efficiency in removing various petty sources of irritation which beset students in their efforts to enter the university and to settle themselves into a comfortable routine of campus life, there was by 1964 a rising current of restlessness and dissent. Extracurricular life became more and more a dominant fact in student-university relationships. Each year students made additional demands that they be set as free in their personal and social actions as the man on the streets of Bloomington. They challenged much of the university authority in these areas as they had already challenged their parents' controls. The military draft, the lowering of the legal voting age, and greater emphases in placement procedures in the admission of superior high school students all worked against the maintenance of traditional academic relationships and procedures. For the past two decades the university had pleaded with its students to assert an intellectual independence; it had encouraged the greatest possible freedom of discussion and debate, yet it was somewhat stampeded when its administration and faculty confronted many of the realities of the new freedoms. In many of his speeches and public statements President Stahr dwelt upon the subject of freedom, perhaps thinking in terms of the classical academic freedoms of teaching, research, and publication rather than those in social behaviors. It was inevitable that much of this spirit would filter down to the student body. The Director of Student Personnel wrote in June 1965 that "Despite the traditional stand of the University upholding freedom and relevant activity, there appears to be a need for continued interpretation of the nature of a university to students, alumni, parents, and the public in general."

For the Stahr administration and the faculty this was the crucial human challenge of the modern university. No matter how modernized the registrar's office, the plant, or living conditions had become, or how productive the faculty, it was the rising mass of bright students making postadolescent assumptions of adulthood that all but erased the lines between authoritarianism and personal freedom. Annually a greater number of articulate students came to Bloomington to raise questions, to demand establishment of social and subject matter relevancy, and to drag along with them the mores of an Amercian society caught in crisis and confusion.

The Indiana student body had by the mid-sixties become as mobile as the parental society from which it sprang. In 1964–65 students paid $24,103 in fines for automobile violations, and $3,312.25 in Bloomington court fines. The prediction was made that by 1973, 10,000 student automobiles would seek as much parking space for automobiles as that occupied by the central academic buildings themselves. It was even suggested that computers should be installed in the traffic office to keep track of the roaring, fuming horde of mobile registrants.

When and if students found parking spaces for their cars, they crowded onto sidewalks and into corridors and classrooms which only a decade before architects and builders had conceived to be ample for the forseeable future. There persisted a chronic shortage of classrooms, and especially large lecture halls. Faculty bodies debated how best to handle large numbers of students with the most constructive use of instructional talents, energies, and space. Oftentimes these reflected greater concern for management than for actual enrichment and effectiveness of instruction. A special committee recommended that the Dean of Faculties consider the designing and construction of a large classroom building embodying minimal standards of design and equipment. It was said that the sheer size of the modern campus made it necessary to reconsider traditional practices; one proposal was that the institution be robbed of two class periods by extending recitation time to a full hour. Because of limited classrooms and the forty-five minute recitation periods it was said that too much time was lost by the frequency of class changes. An Arts and Sciences committee said, "pedagogical principles cannot be given full weight under the prevailing practices." There can be little doubt that this statement had a high degree of relevance in the solution of pressing needs for internal reforms and reconsideration of undergraduate instruction. Despite the fact that rising enrollment statistics made an impressive exhibit for governors and legislators, Indiana University was caught up in a baffling numbers game which further restricted educational objectives and philosophy with every semester's registration session. A large inflow of students into overcrowded classrooms further befogged the idealistic intellectual and educational objectives of an institutional striving for a high degree of excellence in its instructional programs.

This was a challenge that neither new classrooms nor topflight faculty could promise readily to meet and solve. It was essentially in this heads-on crush of the past with a vague and uncertain future that generated almost a decade of student unrest. Closely associated with this fact was the vacuity of national purposes in a time of a Far Eastern war in which official justifications and rationalizations became as indefinite and undependable as the underlying forces of the times. There could, however, be little mystery as to many of the provocations of this era of student unrest and campus revolt. The nation itself was, despite a running dialogue of assertions from the White House and official Washington, unclear about some of its basic aims.

In the field of graduate studies, Indiana University faced even more urgent demands. By 1965 there were already clouds of uncertainty rising above the horizon of many of the disciplines. Never in American history had so many people in social and cultural fields made so many wrong guesses as to future demands for highly trained specialized personnel in so many fields. Rapidly changing educational and public policies in certain areas of the world also bore upon the advanced American educational programs. It was not so much that the United States and the world no longer needed highly trained personnel as it was the fact that needs had become pragmatic and specialized in new contexts.

Consolidation of all graduate work under the administrative oversight of the highly competent John Ashton did not solve many lingering and some new problems. This part of the university's programs may be assumed to have reached a decided watershed by 1965. John Ashton went away to Washington to become administrator of graduate facilities under Title II, a division created under the terms of the Educational Facilities Act. In Bloomington a change was made in the area of administering both graduate studies and research. Lynne Merritt, Jr., was made vice president for Research and dean of the Graduate School. Vice President Merritt assumed an expanded responsibility because the supervision of research activities was transferred to his office from that of the Dean of Faculties.

This change in administration, said President Stahr, signaled a broader search for funds for university-wide research and reorganization of the Graduate School. This was an era when universities across the country were competing for federal funds made available by various agencies and under the several public title projects. Indiana University especially sought funds for advanced fellowships to meet the needs of increasing numbers of graduate students and postdoctoral training. For several years previous to 1965 Vice President John Ashton had warned that funds for student support had lagged behind the increased number of students. By the latter year annual graduate enrollment had risen to 5,435 students, slightly more than a sixth of the entire Bloomington student body.

One of the most far-reaching reorganizations that occurred during the Stahr administration was the conversion of the Indiana University Extension System into a series of four-year degree-granting colleges. In the spring of 1965 the Indiana General Assembly enacted legislation that permitted the development of such programs at the Northwest, South Bend, and Fort Wayne centers. This enlargement of the off-campus program resulted in an immediate increase in student enrollment and in demands for more staff and enlarged physical facilities. Fortunately an improved highway system, better means of communication, and reorganized library procedures enabled the central library to deliver books to any of the centers within twenty-four hours. That year five students were awarded Master's of Business Administration degrees, with all the work being completed on the downtown campus in Indianapolis.

A building program of major proportions was carried on in the regional campus centers. Indiana and Purdue conjointly constructed a new and greatly enlarged plant at Fort Wayne to accommodate both an enlarged student body and instructional program. The number of full-time students increased and so did early daytime classes. When the centers were allowed to expand to four-year degree-granting institutions, they created a demand for enlarged full-time faculties. At Fort Wayne, for instance, there were fifteen full-time and sixty-five part-time instructors.

The Indianapolis division operated up to 1968 in a converted downtown business building that was ill-suited either for expansion or the offering of a fully modernized university program. Classes were offered in the afternoon and evening. There was, however, a growing demand for full-day instruction. Because of a rising enrollment and the changed status of the major regional centers, a decision was made in 1964–65 to relocate the Indianapolis branch in new buildings on a campus near the Medical Center.

There was little if any difference in the experience and needs of the regional centers. All of them underwent significant expansion in demands, and there was an important shifting over from being afternoon and evening schools to being full-time colleges in need of new faculty members, enlarged curricula, new buildings, and greater dependence on advice and support from Bloomington. Likewise there was need after 1965 for programs of greater social and cultural maturity to meet the demands of the new breed of students now entering what had formerly been primarily extension centers catering largely to prospective teachers. This meant that Bloomington was forced to supply a good amount of leadership in making the conversion conform with the broader objectives of the university.

In other ways Indiana University extended its programs far beyond campus boundaries. Its audio-visual facility distributed and showed an unusually large volume of teaching materials that ranged from films of a descriptive nature to those of a more sophisticated content for use in specialized seminars in medical, biological, and geographical subjects. A phenomenal amount of visual instructional materials were distributed in both the United States and abroad. By 1968 the collection of audio-visual films and other types of instructional materials had become one of the most significant in the nation.

Every decade after 1945 saw Indiana University challenged not only to develop a good research program that would produce substantial pioneering works in several fields, but to bring imagination and ingenuity to the teaching and learning processes. President Stahr had sensed this fact on assuming the presidency, and on numerous occasions he stressed the importance of teaching, and the improvement of the means by which the classroom could be made a more exciting place for its transient tenants. Vocally at least, the work of the classroom was the front line of criticism by dissatisfied auditors who either failed to find all the rewards they anticipated, or they made impossible demands on their instructors. On the other hand, the professorial staff in good numbers had their complaints against both the institutional changes and the loss of many human associations with the ever-expanding university.

One of the great paradoxes in Indiana University history was the fact that while the bitterest of student unrest was being manifested on the campus in the mid- and later 1960s plans were underway for the broadening of administrative management of the institution. Operating in an ever-expanding field of education and public services, administration of the highly varied university activities got out beyond the traditional form of central campus management. On April 19, 1968, President Stahr presented to the Board of Trustees a blueprint for a complete restructuring of the central administration. He informed the board that the present system had become so heavily overburdened with the details of management that serious inefficiencies had developed because campus officials frankly lacked the knowledge and time to give the necessary oversight to the needs of the widely diffused and diversified programs which were then in operation. Unnecessary irritations were developing internally which had to be halted. The proposal given the trustees was, in fact, both an administrative and philosophical redirection of the university as it attempted to carry on its many basic functions.

For almost precisely a century and a half Indiana University had operated under a highly centralized administration that had concentrated almost all basic authority in the hands of the president, his administrative staff, the deans, and the faculty. Historically, decisions had been made within the limitations of direct needs in Bloomington, and all other divisions of the university were subordinated to the mother source of direction. In introducing the proposed new administrative plan Stahr told members of the board that the university had grown too large and too complex to be directed in the traditional manner, and prospects were clear that even more growth and complexities would occur in the immediate future. Not only had Indiana University grown in terms of numbers, it, like American business, churches, government, and the press, had associated itself with fields of endeavor that in another age would have appeared to have no direct educational implications. In many respects, it, in a more restricted fashion, was becoming as much a conglomerate as were many modern industries.

During the six years of the Stahr administration there was a 52 per cent increase in enrollment in Bloomington alone, and on all the campuses there was a 50.9 per cent increase. Pressures of all sorts, internal and external, exerted themselves on the university. The internal or self-study committee in 1965 suggested some rather drastic changes in both instructional policies and a realignment and reassertion of university purposes. Heavy student and service pressures since 1945 had as a matter of course forced changes; sometimes they were brought about largely in the forms of momentary expediencies rather than as well-planned and coordinated revisions. The professions of law, medicine, education, and business were continuously caught up in the vortex of trying to make progress, and to ignore this fact further, even slightly, threatened the university and its separate entities with costly outdating. Collectively these responsibilities placed enormous weight of immediate decision and action upon the central administration, and, as President Stahr said, there was too little time left for planning or to develop fresh perspectives.

Inherent in the new administrative plan was a tacit admission that decisions made in Bloomington frequently failed to satisfy needs of off-campus centers. Too often administrators had failed to understand problems fully in the contexts of their backgrounds. Too, there was the ever-delicate matter of dealing with faculty and staff personnel at a distance, and communication became unsatisfactory and too impersonal to encourage the best possible esprit de corps.

Because of the nature of the organization of Indiana University the areas which made direct and immediate demands for realignment were the off-campus centers, plus the professional schools in Indianapolis. Approximately a third of the 47,642 students registered in university classes in 1968 were on the regional and Indianapolis campuses. There were six general educational centers which had passed through fairly rapid metamorphic stages from being extension centers to becoming full-blown regional collegiate institutions, with each stage demanding more precise consideration of policies. In addition, there was concentrated in Indianapolis the somewhat loosely gathered professional schools of law, the associated medical sciences, dentistry, the Normal College of the American Gymnastic Union, the School of Social Service, and the John Herron Art Center; each of which required specialized administrative oversight. None of these branches, Stahr informed the trustees, could function freely so long as the basic academic and administrative policy was made in Bloomington. The time had come in 1968 for the university to view its commitments in a fresh light, and in conformity with the findings published in the Indiana High School Commission *Report* of 1962.

The reorganization plan put forward by the President in April involved four main points, which included the creation of a consolidated Indiana University in Indianapolis under the administration of a chancellor, and partly in cooperation with Purdue University. Further, the university administration would be divided into three parts or units; one would be centered in Bloomington and would comprise the central university, one would oversee the Indianapolis consolidations, and the other the regional campuses. The latter would be under the direction of a vice president, with the separate units being administered by chancellors. All six regional branches were to be renamed, with the title "Indiana University" preceding the locational names. The Board of Trustees approved this proposal at its April meeting in 1968, to become effective on July first.

Almost immediately President Stahr announced the appointment of John Ryan to be vice president in charge of the off-campus centers or regional campuses. Actually Ryan was appointed to succeed Samuel E. Braden who had resigned as vice president of the University and dean for Undergraduate Development to become president of Illinois State University. Ryan had received two graduate degrees from Indiana, had served as a vice president of Arizona State University, a research analyst in the Kentucky Department of Revenue, was chancellor of the University of Massachusetts, 1965–68, and he had served briefly as an associate professor of government in the University of Wisconsin. In time, he was to become president of Indiana University.

Reserved to the central administration were overall responsibilities for making financial policies, budgeting, planning, research, graduate studies, general student policies, public relations, and the setting of all major academic standards and policies. Thus a century and a half after being conceived in a somewhat vague and uncertain charter act, Indiana University, with a student enrollment of approximately 48,000 students, wrestled with the dilemma of both numbers and cumbersome operation and management. It was one thing to devise a different plan of operation, but a much more difficult one to coordinate university services and resources such as libraries, laboratories and materials, computer centers, telecommunication, and seasoned faculty experiences. On the latter point it was a severe challenge indeed for the university to assure anything like an evenness of instructional and intellectual stimulation and prestige to its various units with the same effectiveness as in Bloomington.

On the main campus the thrust of the times was upon the university. Rapidly the scales of sexual balance were being drawn into equality between the enrollment of male and female registrants, a fact which necessitated even more drastic internal revision, if not changes in many future purposes and perspectives. In 1967, 43.5 female registrants were undergraduates in Bloomington and 49.5 per cent in the collective undergraduate student body. Freshman enrollment had slowed down to an annual increase of 2.5 per cent in Bloomington, reflecting no doubt the impact of the regional campuses and their prospective four-year degree-granting programs.

Maintenance of the faculty during these years of sharp revision in the program for what amounted to seven universities presented constant challenges to administration and departments. There were in 1968, 1,967 members of the staff with the rank of assistant professor or above, an increase of 56.2 per cent over the number in 1962. State appropriations were still insufficient to enable the institution to push its two top professional ranks up to competitive ratings on the American Association of University Professors' scale of salaries, even though the two lower ranks were rated high. It seemed clear after 1965 that, although Indiana University had made phenomenal progress in the organization and maintenance of an able faculty since 1938, there could be no let-up in the drive to hire and retain a distinguished faculty. So far as the future could be foretold competition in this area would grow even more intense. Every higher educational indicator seemed to point to continued expansion.

With almost chamber-of-commerce-like pride the administrators of Indiana University after 1960, predicted ever-increasing enrollments of students and accompanying needs for faculty and plant additions. In the most tangible manner possible they backed their prognostications by building towering student residence centers financed with revenue-bearing bonds. Thus the university avoided the inevitable delays and confusions that would have arisen from the procurement of necessary state funds in large amounts. In fact, this mode of financing, skillfully manipulated, had placed Indiana University well in the lead of other Indiana schools, and even ahead of comparable universities and colleges nationally. Classrooms were in woefully short supply, despite the tremendous amount of plant expansion which had occurred since 1945. For instance, if the policy of holding introductory freshman English sections to a maximum of twenty-five students had been strictly observed, there would have been a yearly demand for no fewer than three or four additional new classrooms. Members of the Department of English, said, "The problem is where to put them?" Already Saturday and night classes took up much of the slack, "but the Registrar's office refused to schedule classes on Saturday afternoon or anymore evening sections." Professor Scherer was quoted by the *Indiana Daily Student*, December 17, 1963, as saying, "Indiana University has earned the reputation of being a 'cultural oasis.' By scheduling more evening classes, we would be depriving students of access to this side of university life." Students living on the Bloomington campus, as Professor Scherer suggested, lived by an altogether different tempo from most of those enrolled on the regional campuses. Generally they favored daytime classes offered on the traditional 8:00 to 5:00 schedule. This permitted them also to participate in the non-academic programs of the university.

In 1962 plans for a new School of Business building had been advanced to the stage where bids could be sought for its construction by late spring 1963. This rapidly growing division of the university, like the schools of Music, Medicine, and Dentistry, was dispersed about the campus in several buildings. The Business and Economics Building, later to become Woodburn Hall, was both too small and antiquated to serve the School of Business with its rising inflow of students, and the annual visitations of representatives of more than 500 state and national industries. J. Edgar Hedges, professor of insurance and chairman of the building committee, said School of Business classes and professorial offices were located in shabby Hoosier Hall, Ernie Pyle Building, the Business and Economics Building, the Law Building, and in two antiquated residences on Tenth Street.

The new School of Business Building was to be located at the corner of Tenth Street and Fee Lane on a promontory which overlooked the general campus. Ground was broken for it in March 1964. The new seven-story limestone structure with its large stadia-type lecture rooms, modern seminar facilities, generous library space, professional offices, and conference rooms actually provided little more space than had been formerly occupied in the various buildings about the campus, but the entire functioning of the School of Business was concentrated in a single place.

It took more than three years to construct the elaborate and even luxurious building with its sophisticated modern facilities. In some parts of the structure there were even plush quarters which served in many ways as special public relations quarters. On November 12, 1966, the *Daily Student* annonuced "The computers, the swivel chairs, the typewriters, and even the students are in place at last, as student, faculty, and staff members of the School of Business look forward to next week's formal dedication of their new $5-million building." Boastfully it was said the hall "has been called 'the finest physical plant for a school of business to be found in the country.' "

In opening the dedicatory services, J. Irwin Miller, chairman of the board of the Cummins Engine Company of Columbus, told a selected audience of 250 professors, students, and businessmen that the completion of the new building was a confirmation of the fact that "business is not only important but that it can be taught. This is contrary to what businessmen themselves have felt for many years." Following the dedicatory services there was a week-long program in which Dr. Ottino Caralciolo de Forino of Rome and head of the Organization for Economic Co-operation and Development, Oscar L. Dunn, vice president of the General Electric Company, Stanley Marcus of the Nieman-Marcus Company of Dallas, and President Elvis J. Stahr spoke. Nearly all of the week of oratory and seminar discussions was in fact a moment of recognizing the fact that modern American corporate business had come to be operated and managed more and more within the context of a science—as much so as engineering, the manufacturing process, or of medicine.

From the more prosaic perspective of campus housekeeping occupation of the new School of Business Building actually did little to relax the campus space crisis. The new structure was erected at a cost of $5,500,000 and symbolized one of the main objectives of the university. Business training was in large measure one of Indiana's efforts to broaden its academic base, acting in part as an answer to the lack of a school of engineering. Planners of the building anticipated increasing enrollments. There was seating space for 2,200 students, provisions for closed circuit television between the two auditoriums, and other specialized equipment was in keeping with the modernity of the plant.

Reflecting the university's projection into the wide domain of industry and business, the various speakers during the dedicatory week denoted their attitudes toward the training of the future operators of modern business in American society. J. Irwin Miller said education for business had become a necessity because modern businessmen had developed a code of ethics, public images, and were subjected to a never-ending stream of federal regulation that were both complicated and demanding. Oscar L. Dunn no doubt startled some members of his audience with the statement that, despite the fact many of society's values and operations were greatly influenced by the business segment of the American system, "the image of the businessman is often a dull and unimaginative one. Bright students, perhaps resentful of the shameless devotion to the profit motive, may major in areas they feel will make fuller use of their varied talents."

There were those in the audience who could recall the long struggle of Dean William A. Rawles and William Lowe Bryan to broaden the university curriculum in this direction in earlier years. These pioneers had molded a commerce-business program out of parts extracted from the liberal arts curriculum. The first professors were almost altogether academics who taught classical economic and commercial principles rather than pragmatic details of industries operating from day to day producing goods for a highly competitive and profit-oriented society. The pioneer professors of business were little more than neophytes feeling their way into a sprawling jungle of trust-ladened and laissez-faire materialism. Unlike their successors on Tenth Street they knew little if anything about the magic of business prophecy and counseling.

While embryo businessmen and their professors sat by and saw their great stone castle dedicated to the everyday practical affairs of a prospering American commerce, anxious hearts on other parts of the campus pulsated to an altogether different measure. Astronomers occupied a new addition to Swain Hall in 1965, and at the corner of Jordan and Tenth streets the Student Health Center was housed in new and somewhat elegant quarters. Psychology and geology were next-door neighbors to business along Tenth Street. The large structures which housed them, said President Stahr, were completed and occupied by 1967 (although the Psychology Building was completed early in April 1963). That same year the Chemistry Annex was completed by March even though a disastrous fire had delayed construction of the building.

In all the flurry to complete the academic buildings an interesting private experiment in student housing was projected. West of Indiana Avenue at the corners of Dunn, Grant, and Seventh streets the Southern Area Developers, Incorporated, began construction of a modern successor to the old-style Bloomington rooming houses in an eight-story building, the Poplars, to accommodate 483 women, to be occupied primarily by Indiana University co-eds. Over the years, however, this project failed to achieve its objectives and wound up in the hands of the university.

Throughout the Stahr administration lack of space was a major problem, both in Bloomington and on the regional campuses. President Stahr informed the Board of Trustees, December 18, 1963, that "Our most serious deficiency, and clearly our number one worry in Bloomington and at the Medical Center and certain other locations, continues to be a shortage of adequate academic facilities." There was a stifling four-months delay by the State in beginning to collect the recently enacted retail sales tax, a fact which greatly reduced revenues necessary for the university to be able to match already meager capital appropriations. At the same time the university's share of the alcoholic beverage levy had already been obligated to expand the power plant. At that moment he hoped the General Assembly would make available necessary funds to begin construction of new buildings. As an example of the use made of the existing plant, he said, "Statistics indicate that Ballantine may well be the most heavily utilized classroom building in America."

There was a never-ending scramble for academic space. One instructional department moved out of an overcrowded building and a smaller one moved in only to outgrow rooms and offices before modernization could be accomplished. That ancient structure, Lindley Hall, which stood in such worn grace with its high ceilings, sprawling hallways, and dingy walls was subjected to a face lifting. Structurally, however, it could not tolerate a full occupancy on the upper floors because of an ingenious and theoretical plan of framing and timbering devised by a professor of physics at the time of its construction.

At times in the crowded six years, 1962–68, President Stahr and his administration must have had space nightmares. In his "State of the University Address," December 18, 1963, the president said the Indianapolis Medical Center had even worse housing problems than existed in Bloomington. The Teaching Hospital was archaic, the Long Hospital was largely obsolete, and the university had "thus far not received a dime of nearly $4-million needed for other construction and rehabilitation for Dentistry, Nursing, and Medicine." The Indianapolis Law School operated in an ancient building, and the other regional centers rented unsuitable quarters for classes and offices. "No matter what we do," he wrote, "and we shall do all we can—our minimum needs for academic space remain inordinately unsatisfied, and we have exhausted our flexibility. Overcrowding in faculty offices will continue for sometime. . . . Our genuine concern about it was reflected in the decision to take over a residence hall this year, primarily for faculty offices."

When the School of Business moved from what later was named Woodburn Hall, it left behind the usual dinginess and outmoded furnishings which has since the beginning of academic time characterized the interiors of classrooms and halls. Nevertheless, "Woodburn 100" was an extraordinary example of a "hand-me-down" chamber of instruction. It was dark, dingy, ill-equipped, and acoustically defective. Even the sunniest professor had to work hard to keep his spirits up in that forlorn setting. The room seated approximately 400 students and on rainy days it became stuffy and noisome. All of this Professor Tracy M. Sonneborn discovered when he lectured in that room the first semester of 1967–68. On February 29, 1968, he wrote Dean Richard Young of Arts and Sciences, "You also know my utter disgust with the University's failure to provide the physical facilities needed for classroom instruction. Woodburn 100 was an ordeal I shall absolutely refuse to endure another time; extreme overheating (abetted by 400 bodies), useless blackboards, horrible acoustics, dim lighting, no possibility of controlling light to permit note-taking while slides are being projected, no screen for projection,—my adrenalin rises at the thought of the room. I *want* to teach as many students as wish to take Genetics—I firmly believe everyone should!—but I will limit enrollment to what can be handled in a good lecture room rather than go through again what I went through last semester. And I will refuse to believe that this University is honestly and seriously interested in good teaching for large numbers of students unless it promptly provides good and well-equipped classrooms for them." About the only part Tracy left intact of Woodburn 100 were the industrial murals painted by Thomas Hart Benton, and he perhaps found the room so dark he did not see them. Nevertheless, the famous genetics professor made his point, and David Derge, dean of Faculties, began collecting incriminating evidence against the two large lecture rooms in Woodburn with the intention of having them refurbished. The administration should have sent the Distinguished Professor of Genetics to delineate the space problems of the university to legislators. He no doubt could have been both graphic and forceful in informing them that successful teaching also depended upon the proper surroundings and classroom decor.

Stahr had been in office only four months when the Library Review and Planning Committee made its *Interim Report II* in November 1962. In a pleasant preamble the committee wrote "A new library building enjoys the position of first priority on the list of new construction for the Bloomington campus." Funds were being sought to begin its construction. Eggers and Higgins of New York City were again employed to make preliminary studies. It had already been decided that there should be two distinct divisions of the new structure, but they should rise above a massive common foundation. Provisions were to be made for an undergraduate library, and more extensive ones for the main graduate library and service divisions. The site at the corner of Tenth and Jordan streets had been confirmed, and this was diagonally across from that of the future School of Business.

It was not until January 18, 1966, however, that specific plans to construct the library were gotten underway. President Stahr wrote Governor Roger D. Branigan requesting authority to award contracts for the construction of the large building. In 1962 planners had estimated that the new plant would cost approximately $12,500,000, and in 1964 the General Assembly had appropriated $687,000 to finance preliminary planning and site exploration. In four years the cost had risen to $14,371,000. Stahr told the governor that the new building was planned to seat 3,000 undergraduate and 2,000 graduate students; the undergraduate section would house 100,000 volumes, and the general and graduate section would accommodate 1,500,000 volumes. "An investment of this magnitude," he wrote, "should be kept safely in a building that provides ultimate protection from fire, water, insects and humidity extremes. The new library center will offer this protection." Stahr was no longer president, however, when the Library was finally constructed and ready for occupancy, though ground was broken for it before his resignation.

Two other capital buildings were to create some discussion and controversy. When the university first suggested to Governor Branigan the construction of an elaborate Musical Arts Center early in 1967, he disapproved the idea, but immediately the semi-abandoned old Air Force hangar East Hall burned before wreckers could destroy it, and the governor and the State Budget Commission approved, June 29, 1967, the building of the projected $10,300,000 structure, to be financed partly by bonds and private gifts. It cost ultimately more than the original estimate, and when completed was perhaps one of the most elaborate specialized buildings on an American university campus.

At the same time there was a renewal of plans projected in 1950 to construct a massive assembly hall between the Fieldhouse and the new Memorial Stadium. The new building was designed to contain a seating capacity of 18,000 and was to be used for a multiplicity of purposes when extraordinarily large audiences were assembled. President Stahr no doubt came nearer declaring its central purpose when he said, "The University today has the smallest basketball facility in the Big Ten and has already been forced to ration basketball tickets among students, faculty, alumni, and others." Appealing further for public support, he said the new building could be used by the Hoosier Girls' and Boys' State, the Order of the Arrow, and the Indiana High School State Basketball Tournament. It would be available for use when such "distinguished visitors as Vice President Richard Nixon and General Maxwell D. Taylor" came to Bloomington to speak.

Guy R. Loftman, president of the student body, addressed a letter to the university community in general on September 14, 1967, in which he said that he, David Cahill, and others had been engaged the past summer in an investigation of the "University Events Stadium." He raised four questions which dealt with cost, sources of funds, need for the building, and arguments which could be offered against construction of the center. He raised questions about the priorities in the future plans for campus construction. Loftman said the university was in desperate need of more and better teachers and teaching facilities. It needed to humanize its treatment of employees and students, and should not waste time and money on facilities which made no direct contribution to educational excellence. A week later he addressed a letter to the Board of Trustees, saying he had a petition signed by 2,700 students who requested that plans be dropped for the proposed general assembly hall, and asked that $850,000 be earmarked annually from student fees (approximately the amount that would be taken from that source to pay for the new building) to be used to pay faculty salaries, for library acquisitions, for nonsalaried employees, for student aid, and for improvement of the educational plant. The board in answer said that the 2,700 signers of the petition seemed to reflect considerable lack of unanimity among students. It perhaps reacted more pointedly to the supplementary request that citizens be allowed to inspect university records, and that nonregistered student groups be allowed to use the Student Organization Accounts Office for the purchase of supplies and exercise of other privileges.

Robert Menke, alumni trustee from Huntingburg, responded to a request from Joseph R. Ewers, assistant to the President of the University, October 9, 1967, to counter the Loftman proposals. Menke said he favored construction of the special events building because "As a citizen taxpayer, I'm pleased that our legislature and our Governor have approved this building. After several hundred thousands of dollars had been spent on architectual planning, it seems a bit ludicrous and mysterious that at this point johnny-come-lately critics of I. U. have so exhausted their repertory of 'issues' that they can only find a lame duck to shoot at. Is it not unsportsmanlike to malign the I. U. administration for implementing the will of the people, as unmistakably expressed by their elected representatives, including the Governor?" Menke knew the Hoosier mind better than Loftman, and he was certain the public approved the construction of the big building even if it openly and admittedly was proclaimed a "palace of basketball." He said, "The Assembly Hall will give us a place where we can work off the pressures of daily life and learn consensus and unity. A confrontation on the issue of Assembly Hall is a good point around which most Hoosiers would be very glad to rally." The contract for construction of the large public building, for whatever purpose it might be used, was awarded on September 22, 1967, and construction was begun early in December. Original estimates were that the 330 x 370-foot building, containing 9,520,000 cubic feet, would cost no less than $12,600,000. Eighty per cent of the construction cost would be raised by a bonded loan secured by the athletic sinking fund and a reserve of $35 from each student's annual fees.

When the argument over Assembly Hall had faded away to a faint echo, and construction got underway, the bold outline of the campus was completed. Like ancient Rome or Athens one vast stone building after another had pushed up almost shoulder to shoulder to comprise a tremendously impressive physical academic plant. There was a fairly successful harmonization of the past with the contemporary as older buildings were refurbished and modernized. Even ballooning over its unorthodox framing and counter-leverage, Lindley Hall raised its head anew with something approaching the dignity of seniority. Set within appealing natural settings the monotony of so much gray limestone was toned down, and even the massiveness of many of the buildings was subdued by tall trees growing up close to their foundations. Almost as meaningful as the construction of the new classroom and library buildings was the fact that the functional center of Indiana University had shifted a considerable distance away from its location in 1940.

New construction on the regional campuses greatly facilitated the growing autonomy of these units. A specific example was the separation of the Bloomington Law School from that in Indianapolis in March 1968. The latter school had an enrollment of 529 students, and was accredited by the Association of American Law Schools. Dean William B. Harvey presided over the Bloomington school, and Dean Cleon H. Foust directed the one in Indianapolis. With the granting of autonomy to the Indianapolis School of

Law, immediate plans were made to begin construction of a $3,300,000 building to house it on the new urban campus.

The construction and modernization of buildings on a university campus is as continuous a matter as extending the educational curriculum itself. No single president or generation of professors can lay claim to initiating and seeing through to completion so vast an undertaking as that of expanding the physical plant as Indiana undertook to do after 1950. Many of the ideas that finally took form in the huge stone structures in the 1960s had been advanced in earlier years; some of them, like the Library, were held in escrow until money, planning, and building talents were available in sufficient quantities to see the projects through to completion. Elvis J. Stahr saw nearly all of the greater master plan completed, but he, like his presidential predecessors, could not solve the eternal plea for more space in which to teach annually increasing numbers of students, and in which to carry on expanded programs of research.

During the Stahr years Indiana University student enrollment increased from 21,908 in 1962–63 to 35,569 full-time students registered during the second semester, 1967–68, in all divisions of the university. Perhaps as many as 7,000 students had actually registered for some classes and were present on one of the campuses. By the latter year there were 20,801 men registrants and 14,768 women, of these 25,539 were undergraduates and 7,605 were graduates, and 2,425 were registered in one of the professional curricula. The professional and graduate registrations accounted for the imbalance between men and women in the graduate enrollment; the undergraduate enrollment was almost balanced. Claude Rich, long-time secretary of the Alumni Association, retired from that position in June 1968. He reported there were 30,000 alumni in 1927, and in 1968 there were 182,464 graduates, 107,464 of whom had graduated since 1948. Between 1962 and 1968 the Indiana student body had grown by 50.9 per cent.

Elvis J. Stahr left the presidency two years before the celebration of the university's first century and a half of existence ended. Appended to his letter of resignation in the official record is a list of his accomplishments during his six years in Bloomington. This included caring for an increased enrollment, making genuine headway with racially desegregating the institution, not only in fact but in spirit, the self-study of 1965, establishment of the Graduate Library School, the advanced School of Social Service, and the absorption of the John Herron School of Art into the university system. During one year early in the 1960s the university had focused major attention on the city and its problems with substantial results. In Stahr's expressed opinion the most far-reaching accomplishment of his years was the inauguration of the new administrative program which gave autonomy to the regional campuses, and the reorganization which resulted in major changes in the complex Indianapolis divisions.

These tangibles could be appraised in fairly precise terms. Despite this list, possibly Stahr's finest accomplishment was the maintenance of academic freedom in all that term implies. The American system of higher education during the years 1962–68 was heavily challenged in many of its traditional areas of standards and freedoms. Even old verities came under heavy fire. Robert H. Shaffer, dean of students, in October 1968, clearly stated the Indiana University position in this era of change and disruption. "The University," he told a student assembly, "still has to be very much concerned about providing the best quality environment for effective education. Educators, alumni, parents and citizens in general should welcome the new trend for young people to be concerned about the nature, direction and depth of the education which the university provides them. Only by involving the student in his own education will that education be relevant to the issues and problems he faces today." This was an attempt on the part of an intelligent administrator to distinguish the fine line that Americans and their universities sought to establish as guidance for the future.

In a forceful manner the Faculty Council in 1968 made clear the foundation policy of the university, "Indiana University considers the freedom of inquiry and discussion essential to a student's development," said the professors, "Thus, each student shall have freedom of speech and assembly, and freedom to publish and distribute any material at any time and place, subject only to legal limitations, provided that he does not unreasonably disturb the peace of the good order of any University activity or unreasonably interfere with the movement of vehicular and pedestrian traffic." In the broader field of academic freedom the university staff gained even wider access to full exercise of all the prerogatives of intellectuals functioning in a free and open society. At the same time the grave responsibility of the academic individual enjoying the most clearly defined privileges of any segment of the national society were more clearly defined.

Herman B Wells moved back into Bryan Administration Building in September 1968 as interim president. In returning to the office he had held for a quarter of a century he recognized that times and conditions had undergone remarkable changes since he had retired from the presidency. There was still student unrest. Students made strident demands of him and sought a direct confrontation and a revision of university authority over their activities. They even demanded a revision of university obligations in several areas that contributed to the conduct of the Vietnam War. Wells refused both a direct personal confrontation or the immediate recognition on students demands and their rights to invade the administrative operation of the institution. He gave, instead, his answer in a masterful published statement in the *Daily Student*. The statement combined a distinct tone of reasonableness with one of firmness, and it had a marked calming influence on campus emotions. When Wells did meet with students, it was to discuss the conditions under which both they, the administration, and the faculty could function in a free university in the pursuit of a freely sought and freely offered education. His answers to the major extremists' questions were too challenging for even the most blatant radicals to confront this much revered man in their customary raucous debates.

Wells was more nearly at home in taking the first steps toward readjusting the whole university system to the mandated realignments of the Self-Study Committee of 1965, and in advancing the administrative reorganization authorized by the trustees in April 1968. So much of the reorganization contained in the two outlines dealt with phases of university operation which the interim President himself had suggested earlier. The fundamental problems of decision-making in the broader areas differed little from what had been true prior to 1962; the scope and implications of needed change, however, had grown much more complex. The awesome burden of managing the details of creating a broadly based university operating within a statewide campus system, plus an equally demanding professionalization of much of the university's expanded educational offerings, had become great.

Academically in 1968, Indiana University operated on both a

national and international scale. With programs in Latin America, the Far East, and Europe its faculty was scattered almost around the globe. At home in Bloomington professors came and went on temporary appointments or leaves to serve agencies of the Federal Government and the State. School of Business professors, for instance, served not only governmental agencies, but acted as consultants to private businesses and organizations. This external activity placed a strain upon some instructional functions which annually had grown more demanding. As better qualified students came to Bloomington, and as the retention rate of entering freshmen and sophomores in unprecedented numbers swelled the ranks of upper classes, the demands for better and more mature teaching grew in like proportions. It was partly because of this improved quality of students that much restlessness and criticism was generated in the latter years. Indiana, like every major American institution of research and learning, felt the impact of the "post-Sputnik" age. Not only were demands made upon scientists, but upon the whole academic community. Almost with national frenzy Americans became critical of the quality of past educational training and demanded that a supreme effort be made in this area by the university in the immediate future.

Not only were professors and administrators called upon to devise new and imaginative pedagogical approaches to teaching, the newer generation of bright college students sought richer and more challenging learning experiences. One of the most difficult challenges was that of humanizing the entire university association with students. At Indiana this had to be accomplished inside a burgeoning academic metropolis constantly being beset by adolescent irritations and dissatisfactions derived in large measure from a vigorous questing of the individual student for personal fulfillment in a society which itself struggled mightily to define and reevaluate many old and trusted values.

Edward W. Najam, Jr., defined in a perceptive manner student thinking in October 1968. "Closely related to student objections to teaching itself," he wrote, "is the question of relevance. This point, which is the basic cause for student protest, is so well hidden that the public finds it hard to recognize. Thus far, most institutions of higher learning, including Indiana University, have demonstrated a remarkable ability to divorce what is taught in the classroom from what is going on in the outside world, principally in the world of the student himself. . . . This is largely attributable to the University's failure to integrate classroom work with your total personality development. . . . Our generation is inordinately preoccupied with the meaning of life and with trying to make the individual significant in a technological world. It is not difficult to see why we students, who come to the University to seek better understanding of ourselves and of others and greater intellectual and aesthetic awareness, become frustrated."

In 1968 Indiana University stood squarely on a firm bench, if not at the crest, of a mountain of a century and a half of advancement from being a tiny frontier seminary of learning with a prophetic title to a broadly based university with a high degree of aspiration toward excellence in American higher education. The final annual report made by Elvis J. Stahr, Jr., when compared with one made by Andrew Wylie, established a historical benchmark of progress. There were, of course, sharp contrasts of the ages in American culture, economic and social maturation, ages through which the university had survived and prospered. In far more formal manner Indiana University had made good those ancient backwoods oratorical pleas that it serve the people, whether it be in supplying teachers to rural schools, a doctor to a desperately ill child in Peru, lawyers to staff the city offices in Indianapolis, businessmen to serve the Cummins Engine Company in Columbus, or members of the United States Senate—it had done all those things and more.

Governor James Ray in addressing the Indiana General Assembly, December 8, 1826, on the subject of Indiana Seminary, expressed the underlying philosophy of developing a university of high quality in the state. "With such ample resources in land as we possess for building up and patronizing a great state institution of learning, in Indiana, she should no longer indulge herself in a state of passivity on this subject, but at once admit the truism, that letters and intelligence are the precursors of power. Education made the Greeks good members of the commonwealth enabling them to acquire arts and habits, as rendered their services available, in peace and war. In the most flourishing period of the Roman republic, literature had a patron in every great man; and instruction prepared all orders of their youth for the senate, the bar, or the field. But here in this land of freedom more than anywhere else, knowledge is our sword and shield—hence let us gird upon posterity this formidable panoply, and the republic is safe." It was this formidably girded panoply that spurred Indiana on for a century and a half in the preparation of all orders of the state's youth for "the senate, the bar, and the field."

[XXIV]

Epilogue

INDIANA UNIVERSITY's first century and a half, 1820 to 1970, covered the broad scope of the history of American higher education. During this long span of years the nation achieved cultural and scientific maturity, and assumed a position of leadership in many areas of civilized endeavors. The state of Indiana itself evolved from a raw backwoods frontier into a prosperous Midwestern agricultural and industrial region. Its university was an active central force in nurturing the spirit of refinement and of intellectual growth. It reflected in its history many of the broader social experiences of Americans everywhere who worked to fan the spark of learning into a flame of intellectual maturity. For Indiana the struggle to progress was often made needlessly difficult by lack of public concern and support.

In isolated Bloomington, the tiny university undertook to meet the challenges and overcome the frustrations of establishing a valid liberal educational tradition. It did this in a public setting which was more concerned with clearing away the woods, building towns, railroads, and factories than with schools. A university was a desirable social luxury if it could take a meager public land grant and sustain itself. In a century and a half it experienced changes of leadership on many occasions, and endured almost every crisis to which Americans have been heirs.

Little could that handful of constitutional delegates in Corydon in 1816 have visualized the tremendous changes and social demands which in time would be made of Indiana University. Their eloquent avowals of intellectual ideals in the long run of time proved to be durable articles of faith. Subsequently legislators and trustees helped to make the miracle of higher education become a reality in Indiana. In passing decades presidents and professors enlarged upon the formally stated objectives of the university in the application of emerging educational formulas and experiences. The central objective of preparing youthful Hoosiers to become more productive citizens endured throughout unshaken and unchanged. Only the methods and means of attaining this objetcive were revised.

David Maxwell, a founding godfather, conceived a goal of the infant backwoods university to be the training of technicians who would make it easier for the frontier state to deal with its vast physical problems. Only in this way could the people of Indiana hope to achieve the social and cultural refinements of the good life. The first president, Andrew Wylie, was deeply committed to the classical tradition in the truest *Yale Report* manner. He subscribed to a fundamental educational philosophy of teaching the ancient wisdom and lore of civilization. He asserted Indiana frontiersmen needed first to ground themselves intellectually in the basic knowledge of languages, philosophy, mathematics, and moral ethics. Then the so-called practical or applied sciences could be based on such knowledge. Thus from the outset in Bloomington there was outlined a fundamental conflict of philosophies and intellectual concepts, a condition which has prevailed throughout the history of Indiana University.

Through the years Indiana University has struggled to broaden its objectives, and to serve the cultural, professional, and practical needs of the state. In the founding decades it sought to meets its obligations within the context of the mandate that it was to be the capstone of the public educational pyramid. Because of this fact the university during its first century gave the appearance of being largely a teacher-training institution. It enjoyed remarkable success in this area, so much so that in later years its supporters boasted about the unusually large number of graduates who became college and university presidents. While voicing a much broadened concept of the role of the university, both constitutional delegates and early legislators unwittingly forced this condition upon the school. It took the passage of many decades and monstrous social and cultural changes to obliterate this limiting condition.

Creation of a School of Law in 1841 was an initial step into professionalism. From this date onward Indiana slipped many of the restrictive liberal arts shackles by expanding outward from its departments into more highly specialized professional areas. Few American universities have moved up from such a limiting base of tradition, penury, special interests, and wavering public support as did Indiana University. This was especially true during the vital formative years down to 1867 when the Indiana General Assembly made its first direct appropriation for the support of the university. Of the first five presidents of the institution none perceived necessity for expanding its scope of training more clearly than did the Methodist preacher-president, Cyrus Nutt. Failure to reach this goal in these years was a crucial fact. When Indiana University was denied the privilege of becoming the land-grant college of Indiana its limited position was fixed more firmly than ever in remaining a "separate" liberal arts university in a predominantly agrarian state. This occurred at the time when a national philosophy of applied scientific public higher education, as expressed earlier by David Maxwell, became a dynamic force in American life.

Creation of Purdue University in 1869 not only brought into existence an active and influential competitor for public support, it created a further curricular circumscription for Indiana University. This condition in future years bred some traumatic rivalries and conflicts which required the most astute tactfulness to make constant and fundamental readjustments.

For Indiana University in 1884 good fortune grew out of a mild social scandal, and David Starr Jordan was elected to the presidency. He was a man for all seasons, and he brought to office an unquenchable spark of imagination and foresight, a fact which quickly elevated him to a leadership position of national stature. In the critical years of America's mauve decade the new Indiana president wrought curricular changes, vitalized institutional outlook, and established new approaches to offering university instruction. Jordan was acutely sensitive of the intellectual revolution that was occurring in national higher education. He more than any of his predecessors had a clearer perspective of progress being made in better American universities. As a Cornell University trustee he was able to view firsthand some of the vital innovations at that important public institution.

In Bloomington, Jordan's more tangible accomplishments were establishing modernized departments in the sciences, instituting the elective system, getting Hoosiers to tolerate, if not accept, the elementary facts of biological evolution, eugenics, and the possibilities of social progress. Through tireless campaigning he made them aware of their university. During his administration there was established in the university a sense of intellectual freedom in its broadest implications. With this Jordan helped to implant the principle that freedom of research and publication were also vital parts of the liberal arts tradition.

The tradition of good teaching antedates David Starr Jordan's presidency, but he gave it fresh impetus. He organized a good faculty, even though he was unable to obliterate all traces of the narrower concepts of classical university education. Personally Jordan was a man of several startling contradictions. Intellectually he was liberal-minded and courageous. In dealing with professors and students from day-to-day, however, he was puritanical and authoritarian about matters of lesser import. Nevertheless he enjoyed the loyalty of most of his colleagues and of the Board of Trustees. This enabled him to project a program well beyond the actual level of financial support which Indiana was willing to give its university.

From its opening in 1825 onward Indiana University was forced to operate well beyond the limits of the direct support prescribed by the Indiana General Assembly. Certainly the concept of sustaining a university in an expanding state with two township grants of cheap public land was false. For a century and a half there were few intervals in university history when the institution was not trying to overcome handicaps imposed by lack of public financial support. In every case where presidential administrations demonstrated progressive leadership, the president was astute in procuring special and private funds to make up for the public lack in general support.

Just as David Starr Jordan brought personal and institutional vitality to a decade of Indiana University history, William Lowe Bryan in three and a half decades gave the institution devoted and intelligent leadership. The two men made different approaches. Bryan, puritanical and patrician, was a highly complex personality. Professionally he had early showed promise of becoming an important pioneer in the field of psychology. This he forsook for a long career in university administration. Never a liberal in the Jordanian sense, he nevertheless was dedicated to the philosophy of the importance of liberal education. He demonstrated a belief that all professional training rested on the foundation of the arts and sciences. Within limits Bryan was an intellectual progressive. He organized and maintained a reasonably good faculty, and at all times he exercised an authoritarian hand in university management. Surprisingly the Indiana University faculty made constructive and oftentime progressive responses to the institution's enlarged challenges. Many of its members produced important research and critical works, and made important contributions in their specialized fields.

In his long term in office William Lowe Bryan faced some major crises which would have exhausted a less hardy and courageous man. First, there was the eternal biennial struggle of trying to persuade reluctant legislators to provide vitally needed operational funds. Then there was the most devastating threat of all when Purdue University and the Medical College of Indiana joined forces to establish a school of medicine in Lafayette. No previous threat contained such grave implications for Indiana University's future progress. Bryan, the trustees, and many professors saw this move as promising certain disaster. It promised to block the one academic avenue by which the liberal arts university in the first decade of this century could hope to enter upon a broader stage of curricular activity. To lose the privilege of organizing a school of medicine would have been a far heavier setback than earlier failure to become the land-grant college of the state.

The fight to nullify the Purdue-Medical College merger to create a public school of medicine was long, drawn-out, and bitter. The ultimate victory for Indiana University, however, was of such significance as to justify taking the risk of exposing the two schools to considerable adverse public reactions. Gaining the exclusive privilege to operate a school of medicine vastly increased the university's financial needs. For the first time in its history the university was concerned with the maintenance and operation of an enormously costly professional school which had to be maintained at sufficiently high standards to be accredited in an extraordinarily competitive field.

Hardly had Indiana University begun to meet the demands of its School of Medicine before World War I occurred. This conflict proved for the institution, as for all other American universities, an unsettling crisis. It generated onerous challenges in areas of broad public war efforts while drawing away professors and students. Costs were inflated, and it was necessary to make substantial curricular changes and plans of operation. The four years of war taxed Indiana University's staff and plant to meet national demands. The great impact, however, came with the end of the war and the ushering in of a new era in which returning veterans and the American people in general looked to the universities to supply greater intellectual and cultural leadership. The world of the university was greatly expanded after 1914. In Bloomington President Bryan and his faculty colleagues were subjected to social and intellectual pressures beyond anything they had experienced before. The university found it more difficult to respond to postwar demands without bringing about major changes in institutional programs and approaches. The great war involved only the armed might of the western world, but in doing so it revealed many of the shortcomings of democratic society itself. Indiana University found it difficult to respond as dynamically to the new age in the same manner as some of its Big Ten neighbors. Both administration and faculty had to become reconciled to the fact there could be no return to prewar procedures and mores. Tragically the largely stagnant Harding-Coolidge-Hoover era in American history failed to reflect the sapient dynamism of the American people. This also was a failing of many universities. In the state of Indiana a fundamental conservatism reflected the lack of understanding of the revolutionary forces which were at work. There appeared the isolationists, the super-patriots, the Ku Klux Klan, the revival of fundamentalist religious attitudes, and the inertia of public indifference and lack of understanding.

William Lowe Bryan and Indiana University felt the effects of the age, plus others of purely local origin. The Great Depression, while not posing in Bloomington some of the grim prospects of severe curtailment in the general university program, nevertheless had a stagnating impact. In this latter period the aged president and many of his administrative and faculty colleagues had reached advanced ages and were time-worn and wearied in the service. Drastic change, whether willed or otherwise, was inevitable. To meet this crisis Bryan and the trustees were successful in instituting a retirement program supported by the state which enabled aged professors and administrators to retire and live in some degree of economic security and dignity. Adoption of a new pension system virtually removed the older faculty leadership within the brief space of two or three years. Bryan himself was among the first to be retired.

The retirement of William Lowe Bryan was an event of tremendous importance to the future history of the school. In 1938 the institution was in a position to take advantage of the upswing of the national economy and the opening of a new era in American higher education. To close the hiatus of the Bryan departure the Board of Trustees elected Herman B Wells to be acting president. Wells, Dean of the School of Business, was a young man with substantial banking experience. It was believed his temporary appointment would give the trustees time to make broad searches for a permanent president. No one left recorded evidence, at least, that he would serve for more than a year. There, however, is sharp contradiction in evidentiary fact. In office the acting president made positive and aggressive decisions. Like David Starr Jordan of another generation he began to set a new institutional course. He went in search of funds, private and public, to enable the university to undertake a more mature academic program. He worked diligently at organizing a productive faculty, and effected the creation of a small self-study committee to undertake a searching analysis of the university and its current state. This committee of three produced a startling profile that detailed weaknesses and recommended modes of changing the entire institutional structure. In time the self-study brought about a broadening of university objectives and approaches to serving a new constituency. Nowhere does the university's documentary record indicate that Wells served with the customary timidity and stultifying caution of a "stand-in" president. A year later he was elevated to the presidency, an event which gave rise to considerable national publicity.

The quarter of a century of Herman B Wells' presidency was

generally an expansive one in the history of American higher education. It was also one of constantly shifting means of obtaining somewhat diffuse objectives in university operation. In Bloomington the shackling provincial and curricular bonds that had historically hobbled Indiana University were cut away. The vigorous campaign to locate and employ able professors was productive. Organization of a comprehensive library was begun, expensive scientific laboratories with modern equipment were organized at costs well in excess of the amount of money provided by the state. New divisions of the university were created, and older ones were rejuvenated. Rising along the Jordan River and symbolizing the changes of the new era new units spread out well beyond the confines of original boundaries.

Although grounded in a narrow liberal arts tradition, the university was no longer its spiritual captive. Concepts and objectives were broadened almost in every faculty survey report. Never a classical educational philosopher, President Wells personally blended a native sense of everyday practicality with a dreamer's vision. Assisting him in this were the realistic educational statesmen Fernandus Payne, Herman Briscoe, and members of the Self-Study Committee. In concept they set a future course of action and realization.

The new regime had scarcely gathered momentum before World War II disrupted its plans. In many respects this gripping international crisis proved both a deterrent and an expansive influence. During the war years the university rendered services on a wide diversity of fronts. It contributed basic assistance in specialized areas of medicine, business management, languages, service training, and international policy making. The exigencies of war produced a fermentative yeast of change on the campus. In a positive way it produced a clearer perspective of the role of the public university in both national and international relationships. Beyond this it destroyed almost the last vestiges of ancient Midwestern provincialism and isolationism which in the past had influenced university operation.

At war's end the Wells' administration was more mature, intellectually and realistically, and more responsive to fundamental social and cultural changes than was that of William Lowe Bryan in 1918. Expansion of university functions on a multiplicity of educational fronts after 1945 became an impressive fact in national higher education generally. In these years Indiana University not only struggled with its internal realities, it made progress in improving its position as a major university in a region where academic competition was dramatically intense.

In the past half century the Midwest, or Big Ten, universities had become academically strong. They made tremendous advances as measured against that of the entire national university system. In face of this awesome fact Indiana University had to work its way upward from well down in the list in competition with such mature neighbors as Michigan, Chicago, Wisconsin, Illinois, and Ohio State. It was able to expand almost miraculously in the face of such competition, an expansion accomplished through the determination and imagination of administration and faculty.

The tangible accomplishments of the Wells' period became readily visible on the campus in the rise of such landmarks as the great Auditorium, the Lilly Library, Ballantine and Jordan halls, the enlarged schools of Music and Education, the Indiana Memorial Union, and clusters of residential quadrangles and fraternity houses. Less clearly defined were the early purchases of lands that have insured the university growing room with enough margin against commercial intrusion. Organization of the Indiana University Foundation, a semi-private arm of the university, has yielded incalculable dividends. This facility has enabled Indiana University to expand and operate beyond the limits of direct state and other governmental financial support. Without it the institution could never have achieved its important mid-twentieth century expansion. Beyond this was courageous use of the university's borrowing capability which permitted enormous plant expansion by sale of low-yield bonds to finance self-liquidating projects.

Those were the material achievements. In less tangible but vital spiritual areas of academic freedom the university won major victories after 1945. Blighting and obstructive forces attempted to interfere with academic freedom on several levels. These forced administration and faculty to take rigid, even militant, stands against self-anointed guardians of the American way of life such as American Legionnaires, apostles of every stripe of Americanism, religious and scientific bigots who denounced the Kinsey researches and publications in human sexual behavior, and the lowly anti-intellectual prowlers who infested the library corridors searching for incriminating evidence of communism. Of fundamental national importance was the court victory over the excessively vigilant United States Custom Service and the Department of Commerce involving the privilege of educational and cultural institutions to import research and artistic materials no matter the moral reservations of a censorious branch of the Federal Government.

The decades, 1938 to 1962, were filled with many of the complexities of American university history. In these years Indiana University increased its cultural and intellectual assets tenfold. The sweep of its intellectual and social perspective was universal and international. Rising out of the heartland of rural middle America there appeared a university that overwhelmed, if it did not defy, every tradition and provincial more of the region. Herman B Wells personally was a sensitive and skillful man who was able to protect the university's past image without allowing its former narrow provinciality to obstruct the current thrust of a sophisticated modern academic institution.

Obviously the strands of an evolving modern Indiana University are numerous and varied in nature. They are woven in and out of the mazes of many social and cultural contradictions of Hoosier folksiness, and of bold academic pioneering that often undermined the old ways. The organization of a vastly expanded library, the gathering of the rare and specialized Lilly Library, creation of the Indiana University Press, and the expansion of programs of the School of Music and the creative arts involved the kind of leadership that concerned itself with far more than the subleties and conflicts of a state political system, and a conservative folk culture. The genius of this era of molding Indiana University into a major institution of learning was astute management and direction of the processes of change, and of keeping the modernizing forces within the bounds of orderly expansion.

After 1962 Indiana University operated on at least three levels of professionalism. Its associated schools of medicine, dentistry, law, and business were realizations of the age-old objective of broadening its institutional base so as to keep the university in the mainstream of public needs and services. The wide dispersion of many of its programs over a broad geographical pattern substantially increased the impact of its domestic influence. The organization of special international programs took the institution farther afield than its earlier leadership could have ever conceived.

When Elvis J. Stahr became president in 1962, he assumed the ancient burden of maintaining a high degree of institutional momentum with inadequate funding. Student enrollment increased even beyond optimistic long-range projections. There was scarcely a let-up in demands for housing, classrooms, and professors. In some of his earlier annual reports President Stahr emphasized need for faculty recruitment in a competitive job market.

Unlike his predecessors, President Stahr faced locally generated social problems which threatened marked changes in student-university relationships. Too, following the historic decision of the United States Supreme Court in *Brown* v. *Board of Education*, the university had to give serious reconsideration to its racial policies and practices. Student protests growing out of the Vietnam War at times all but obscured the central objectives of the university in another of its recurring transitional eras. In the latter years the overall building plan was completed, except for the big central library. There were urgent needs to consolidate the gains of three decades of expansion, to reassess qualitative standards, and to redefine the purposes and nature of public higher education. Perhaps there had never been a time in Indiana University history when leadership was so concerned with the maintenance and direction of institutional thrust and in such a confused age.

The protection of academic and personal freedoms became demanding challenges. These two had to be clarified and redefined within the context of an age of conflict and social uncertainties. It became more and more difficult to separate individual and academic freedom from the raucous and distracting protestations of injustices and discrimination. Although no great and abiding solutions to fundamental problems came out of the 1960s, no trusted and established freedoms were seriously abused or lost. Of far more important long-range meaning was the fact that the teaching and administrative processes were considered ready for sober reevaluation. Even the broader modern objectives of the university were redefined and updated in a fresh self-study. Occurrences on the Bloomington campus reflected the unrest and uncertainties that gripped American academia in general.

Thus Indiana University ended its first century and a half of operation in 1970. The historian is denied the privilege of scaling the full measure of its history. Much of it is deeply imbedded in the dedication of individual professors, of trustees, alumni, and nameless friends across the country. It is little short of tragedy that the history of Indiana, or any other university, cannot be written in the richer and fuller terms of professorial contributions. It has been the professor who has most clearly translated the goals and objectives of the institution by competent classroom teaching, interminable student conferences, the grading of an endless stream of papers, and by serving as members of wearying work-a-day committees. In addition, the professors have ever answered calls for public service.

An individual professor lecturing to a class has always been in microcosm the university in action. In kindred manner an inquisitive and tireless research professor laboring in library, laboratory, or over the keyboard of a typewriter has been maker and guardian of the univesity's scholarly image. By force of organizational design presidents and deans have personified much of Indiana University history, but in this they have been largely surrogate personalities. They have served as spokesmen and before the public have been the visual representatives of the institution. Behind them a small army of unsung and highly worthy yeomen have served in professorial ranks. It was they who fired student imaginations, stirred ambitions, and lifted visions to faraway horizons or learning. By their very numbers and personal and professional diversities they devised their own historical anonymity; they have survived, however, in the mellowing memories of students and alumni, and in the solid monuments of their scholarly accomplishments.

The ultimate measure of Indiana University's mission is found in the collective accomplishments of its graduates and these have been heartening. In dramatic terms Indiana graduates have filled public, state, and national offices; they have sat on high courts as judges; they have been college and university presidents, newspaper editors and topflight reporters, corporation executives, counselors to governments and institutions, and teachers. They have been authors, musicians, creative artists, scientists, physicians, lawyers, and diplomats. Through the years alumni have returned rich dividends to justify that far-off dream of 1816. Names and notations of accomplishments that appear periodically in alumni publications are little more than minority reports. Again it has been graduates applying their talents to their callings without fanfare who have kept the faith and glorified the mission. They have more than justified public support of the university, and the constant vigil to keep it free.

With it all the essential challenge has been one of keeping abreast of the needs of the next entering class, the current age, and of trying to discern what lies immediately beyond the next intellectual and cultural horizon. The history of Indiana University has ever been prologue in the eternal effort to impart the timeliness of ancient ideals and dreams to succeeding generations of Hoosiers so that they might maintain social and cultural momentum in dealing with the unsettling issues of each passing age.

It seems self-evident that creation of autonomous units of Indiana University about the state has in it the possibility of lessening the centralizing influence of the institution in Bloomington. In a positive manner, however, the institution has finally loosened the old restrictions which so long held it captive as a "separate" liberal arts university. The decision to grant autonomy to off-campus centers in 1968 was historically a revolutionary act. Comparable to David Starr Jordan's revolt against the past by instituting the elective system, creation of the new independent branches was a direct response to current demands of local Indiana society. Loss of the land-grant college designation in 1869 was a stifling institutional blow, but development of the widely dispersed centers perhaps more than compensated for it. Certainly the collateral institutions represent a realistic response to immediate current educational needs. Essentially their creation is a rational compromise between the traditional liberal arts curriculum and an ascending demand for the offering of a professional-vocational curriculum.

By fortuitous circumstance the conclusion to end this history in 1968 coincided with the shading off of the early tradition of American higher education into a much broader and more diffuse modern one. In the case of Indiana University it was possible down to 1968 to focus largely upon the Bloomington scene and its emanating influences. Up to the latter date presidents of the university had stood firmly at the apex of university authority, and in the main the Bloomington faculty made basic educational policies, and had assumed direct watchcare over the university as a functional intellectual enterprise. By like token the Board of

Trustees focused their attention largely upon the Bloomington operation, treating the off-campus branches as adjuncts of the central body. Up to the latter date Bloomington had been sole residuary of that precious spiritual part of university life and tradition; alumni affairs, athletic contests, major cultural programs, the grand student festivals, the big commencement, homecomings, conferences, and that most intangible of all collegiate assets, the "university spirit" were centered there. Intellectually in 1968 Bloomington remained the seat of the great libraries, the research laboratories, the Indiana University Foundation, the vast physical plant, the famous professors, and the university focal center.

Of utmost historical importance Indiana University, in a century and a half of operation, has nurtured a cultural spark which it fanned into full flame in the past half century, as epitomized in its libraries, its free academic spirit, in the fine arts, and the magnificent School of Music. The university's intellectual empire has matured in both breadth and depth in its extensive history. There still remains for it the enduring challenge of constantly redefining the processes of education and intellectual leadership in terms of ever-changing times and the nature of the society which supports and patronizes it.

Bibliography

Indiana University
Correspondence, Manuscripts, and Papers

Correspondence File, William Lowe Bryan Administration, 1902–1937.
Correspondence File, Herman B Wells Administration, 1937–1962.
Correspondence File and Papers, Office of the Chancellor of the University, 1962–1970.
Correspondence File, Elvis J. Stahr Administration, 1962–1968.
Departmental Reports File, University Archives, 1937–1970.
Faculty Personnel Records, 1830–1968. This is a loose leaf file comprising the curriculum vitae of former faculty members. Included are details of their services to Indiana University, and records of subsequent employment.
Hastings, John S., Correspondence File, September 23, 1937–June 25, 1940.
McNutt, Paul Vories, Papers, 1932–1950, Lilly Library, Indiana University.
Self-Study Committee, Correspondence and Papers, 1938–1940, Indiana University Archives.
Speech File, Herman B Wells, September 1935–June 1962, 23 bound volumes, Owen Hall file, Indiana University.
Speech File, Elvis J. Stahr, July 1962–November 1968, Indiana University Archives.
Dedication Papers, 1941–1942, Indiana University Auditorium, Indiana University Archives.
Presidential Reports, 1937–1970, including "State of the University" analyses, University Archives.
Herman B Wells to Stith Thompson, July 20, 1937–May 17, 1955, Lilly Library, Indiana University.

Indiana University
Official Minutes and Reports

Minutes, Indiana University Board of Trustees, July 1937–November 1970.

Minutes, Indiana University Board of Trustees Executive Committee, July 1937–November 1970.

Minutes, Faculty Council, 1947–1968.

Report of the Self-Study Committee to the Board of Trustees of Indiana University, Parts I and II, March 21, 1939.

The President's Agenda for the Board of Trustees, 1957–1968.

The Presidents' *Annual Reports*, 1937–1970.

Annual Departmental, Division, and School Reports, 1937–1970. In the period covered by these reports Indiana University required each operative unit of the institution to file an annual review of the past year's activities. From these reports the presidents formulated their own *Annual Reports*, as cited above. In turn, the professorial and major administrative staff members were required to report to their respective schools and divisions. This material is voluminous and constitutes almost a detailed view of year-to-year operations.

Report of the Indiana University Language Program, 1962–1968.

Five-Year Report of the East Asian Language and Literature Program, 1962–1967.

Report of the Schaap Committee on the Indiana University Physical Plant with special emphases on the Bloomington Campus Master Plan, December 16, 1966.

President Herman B Wells' Report on Acquisition of Lake Lemon Property, January 1959.

Indiana University Official and Campus Publications

The Arbutus, Indiana University student yearbook, 1936–1970, 34 vols.

Indiana University *Bulletin* (Catalogue), 1936–1970, 34 issues.

Indiana University *Register*, 1951–1970, 29 issues.

Indiana University *Alumni Quarterly*, 1914–1937, 25 vols.

Indiana *Alumni Magazine*, 1938–1970, 31 vols.

Indiana University *Alumni Newsletter*, 1913–1940, 28 vols.

Indiana University *Newsletter*, 1935–1945, 10 vols.

Indiana University *Museum Annual Reports*, 1964–1970, 6 vols.

Indiana University Auditorium *Publications*, 1941–1946.

Indiana University Auditorium *Programs* (collected file), 1942–1970.

Indiana University Auditorium, *Twenty-Fifth Anniversary Festival*, 1966.

Bernardo Mendel, Bookman Extraordinary, 1895–1967, Bloomington, 1973.

Bernardo Mendel Collection, Dedication of the Mendel Room, Lilly Library, 1964.

Daily Family Memorial Collection of Art, Bloomington, n. d.

Thomas Hart Benton Murals, Bloomington, n. d.

Official Handbook: Paul V. McNutt Quadrangle of Indiana University, 1968–69, Bloomington 1969.

Bibliography

Interviews

Allen, Howard W. New York City, January 18, 1973.
Allen, Ross. Bloomington, Indiana, March 21, 1970.
Bain, Wilfred C. Bloomington, May 12, 1973.
Barnhart, Dean L., and George E. Gill. Indianapolis, Indiana, April 1970. By Kemp Harshman, Joseph Kasarko, and Thomas D. Clark.
Blough, Earl. Providence, Rhode Island, May 11, 1971.
Bradfield, Joseph L. Indianapolis, March 27, 1969.
Buehrig, Edward H. Bloomington, April 19, 1973.
Byrnes, Robert F. Bloomington, December 20, 1968.
Cady, Edwin H. Bloomington, April 24, 1973.
Chamness, Ivy Leone. Bloomington, January 24, 1969.
Clevenger, Zora. Bloomington, November 24, 1969.
Collins, Dorothy. Bloomington, December 15, 1973.
Davidson, Frank J. Bloomington, January 1, 1969.
Edwards, Edward, and Herman B Wells. Bloomington, August 5, 1974. By Thomas D. Clark and Dorothy Collins.
Franklin, Joseph A. Bloomington, September 29, 1969.
Hastings, John S. with Dorothy Collins, Chicago, November 17, 1970.
Jordan, Harold. Bloomington, May 2, 1973.
Kinsey, Clara McMillen. Bloomington, February 17, 1969.
Kohlmeier, Lucy, Bloomington, November 11, 1968.
Konopinski, Emil J. Bloomington, February 19, 1973.
Langer, Lawrence. Bloomington, December 14, 1973.
Lundin, Leonard. Bloomington, October 10, 1972.
Mathers, Frank. Bloomington, October 25, 1972. By Harry G. Day and Thomas D. Clark.
McClintock, Lander. Bloomigton, December 10, 1968. By Thomas D. Clark and Oscar Winther.
McNutt, Ruth. Indianapolis, May 27, 1969.
Nelson, Alice. Bloomington, April 28, 1969. By Thomas D. Clark and Victoria Cuffel.
Norvelle, Lee. Bloomington, February 19, March 6, 1970.
Payne, Fernandus. Bloomington, October 8, 12, 15, November 2, 1968. By Thomas D. Clark and Oscar Winther.
Prickett, Alva Leroy. Bloomington, October 24, 1968.
Shrock, Robert. Bloomington, April 13, 1972.
Snow, Charles Wilbert. Bloomington, May 2, 1970.
Sollitt, R. V. Greenwich, Connecticut, June 23, 1971.
Stahr, Elvis J. Bloomington, November 5, December 12, 1968; New York City, August 1970; Greenwich, Connecticut, April 16, 1975.
Stempel, John. Bloomington, April 14, 1970. By Thomas D. Clark and Barbara Benson.
Sulzer, Elmer G. Bloomington, December 18, 1968.
Thompson, Stith. Bloomington, November 10, 1968. By Oscar Winther and Thomas D. Clark.

Thornbury, William D. Indianapolis, May 21, 1969.
Von Tress, Edward. Bloomington, November 24, 1969.
Wallace, Leon. Bloomington, May 2, 1969.
Warren, Winifred Merrill. Bloomington, May 27, 1969.
Weatherwax, Paul. Bloomington, March 5, 1969.
Wells, Herman B. Bloomington, January 25, 1968, and March 6, 10, 1971.

UNPUBLISHED THESES AND PAPERS

Day, Harry G., "On Making Stannous Fluoride Useful," Phi Beta Kappa Address, Indiana University, April 16, 1975, in author's files.
Deputy, Manfred Wolfe, "The Philosophical Ideas and Related Achievements of William Lowe Bryan," 1947, Indiana University Library.
Lowell, Mildred Hawksworth, "Indiana University Libraries, 1829–1942," Doctoral dissertation, University of Chicago, 1957.

ARTICLES

Bailey, Gilbert, "Picture of a Postwar Campus," *New York Times Magazine*, December 21, 1947.
"Indiana University: *Life* Takes a Farewell Look at Doomed Campus Folkways, *Life*, November 23, 1943, vol. 12, pp. 90–96.
"Letters to the Editor," *Life*, December 14, 1942, vol. 12, pp. 4–6.
"Speaking of Pictures. . . . With These *Life* Makes Its Apologies for an Injustice Done to Indiana University," *Life*, February 1, 1944, vol. 13, pp. 12–15.
Kinsey, Alfred Charles. "Homosexuality: Criteria for a Hormone Explanation of the Homosexual," *Journal of Clinical Endocrinology*, I, no. 5, May 1945.
Myers, Burton D. "A Study of Faculty Appointments at Indiana University," *Indiana Magazine of History*, June 1944, XL: 129–153.

INDIANA LAWS AND COMPILED STATUTES

Laws of the State of Indiana, Indianapolis, 1935–1970, 18 vols.
The Indiana Code of 1971, Titles 19–21, Article 5, Indianapolis, 1971.
Journal of the House of Representatives, 1937–1970, 18 vols.
Journal of the Senate, 1937–1970, 18 vols.
Reynolds, Clifford, comp., *Biographical Directory of the American Congress, 1774–1961*, Washington, D.C., 1961.

INTERCOLLEGIATE ATHLETICS

Indiana University Department of Athletics Records File, 1937–1970. This particular file was gathered and organized as a special record for this study. It does not constitute the separate sports files which are kept by the Athletics Office.

Indiana University Department of Athletics Statistical Files and Record Books, 1930–1970. This record is compiled by individual sports, and it varies in form from one sport to another. The composite file, however, comprises a fairly complete record of all competitive athletics.

The National Collegiate Athletic Association *Yearbook*, 1950–1970.

The National Collegiate Athletic Association, Chicago, 1963.

Correspondence File between Herman B Wells and the National Athletic Association on Hearings and Rulings on Indiana University Athletic Infractions, April to December, 1960.

Confidential Files of Correspondence from the National Collegiate Athletic Association on Infractions to the Chief Officer of Indiana University, 1958–1959.

Confidential Files, National Collegiate Athletic Association, Correspondence to Herman B Wells, and Wells' Replies and Report, February 1960.

Confidential Official Statement from Indiana University to the National Collegiate Athletic Association Council, April 1960.

J. Frank Lindsey to Elvis J. Stahr, August 11, 1962, concerning Indiana University's probationary standing.

Evis J. Stahr to J. Frank Lindsey, August 23, 1962. University Archives.

The Kinsey Studies

The newspaper and clipping file covering the Kinsey Studies is an extensive one. Publication years for the first two sexual behavior books received broad newspaper and periodical coverage, too broad to be listed in a bibliography of this type. This material is contained in the files of the Institute for Sex Research and in the clippings scrapbooks compiled by the University Archives. This is also true for the large volume of books, pamphlets, and objects collected by the Institute. The correspondence files of the Institute are also extensive; the contents of the interviews are recorded in a special symbolized shorthand and are closed.

Newspapers

Bloomington (Ind.) *Courier-Tribune*, May 1968–July 1970.
Bloomington (Ind.) *Daily Telephone*, 1937–October 4, 1943.
Bloomington (Ind.) *Daily Herald-Telephone*, July 1, 1950–July 1, 1970.
Bloomington (Ind.) *Daily Herald*, December 29–June 30, 1950.
Bloomington (Ind.) *Evening World*, January 1, 1938–October 4, 1943.
Bloomington (Ind.) *World*, January 1, 1936–June 1, 1941.
Bloomington (Ind.) *World-Telephone*, October 5, 1943–July 1, 1950.
Bloomington (Ind.) *Star-Weekly*, 1943.
Bloomington (Ind.) *Star-Courier*, October 8, 1943–May 1, 1968.
Indiana (University) *Daily Student*, 1936–1970.

Indianapolis (Ind.) *News*, 1937–1970.
Indianapolis (Ind.) *Star*, 1937–1970.
Indianapolis (Ind.) *Times*, September 1943–October 1965.
Louisville (Ky.) *Courier-Journal*, 1937–1970.
Louisville (Ky.) *Times*, 1937–1970.
Indiana University Clippings Scrapbooks, 1937–1965, and the clippings collection, unfiled, 1965–1970.
News releases and clippings files kept by Earl Michael Hoff, Director of the Indiana University News Bureau, in private posession of Earl Hoff.

BOOKS

Barzun, Jacques. *The American University: How It Runs, Where It is Going*, New York, 1968.
Beck, Frank O. *Some Aspects of Race Relations at Indiana University*, Bloomington, 1959.
Big Ten Record Book, *The Encyclopedia of Big Ten Athletics, 1948–1970*, n. p., 1970.
Bishop, Morris. *A History of Cornell University*, Ithaca, 1962.
Blake, George I. *Paul V. McNutt: Portrait of a Hoosier Statesman*, Indianapolis, 1966.
Boucher, Chauncey S., and A. J. Brumfield. *The Chicago College Plan*, Chicago, 1940.
Bryan, William Lowe. *Farewells*, Bloomington, 1938.
——— and Charlotte Lowe Bryan. *Last Words*, Bloomington, 1951.
Carmichael, Hoagy, with Stephen Longstreet, *Sometimes I Wonder: The Story of Hoagy Carmichael*, New York, 1965.
Cartter, Allan M. *An Assessment of Quality in Graduate Education: A Comparative Study of Graduate Departments in 29 Academic Disciplines*, Washington, D.C., 1966.
Chalmers, David M. *Hooded Americanism*, *The History of the Ku Klux Klan with a New Epilogue by the Author*, Chicago, 1965.
Christenson, Cornelia Vos. *Kinsey, a Biography*, Bloomington, 1971.
Curti, Merle, and Vernon Carstensen. *The University of Wisconsin, 1848–1925*, 2 vols., Madison, 1949.
East, C. Earl. *Relieve It with C. Earl East: Stirring Stories which Really Happened*, Mission, Kansas, 1963.
Eells, Walter Crosby. *Survey of American Higher Education*, New York, 1937.
Evans, Norman C. *Spring Mill, Hidden Valley Village*, Mitchell, Indiana, n. d.
Fisher, Karl. *The First Hundred Years of Beta Theta Pi at Indiana University, 1845–1945*, Menasha, Wis., 1947.
Goodman, Walter. *The Committee: The Extraordinary Career of the House Committee on Un-American Activities*, New York, 1968.
Gray, James. *The University of Minnesota, 1851–1951*, Minneapolis, 1951.

Havighurst, Walter. *The Miami Years, 1809–1959*, New York, 1959.

The Ideas and Practice of General Education: An Account of the College of the University of Chicago, by Present and Former Members of the Faculty, Chicago, 1950.

Jackson, Kenneth T. *The Ku Klux Klan in the City, 1915–1930*, New York, 1967.

Jencks, Christopher, and David Riesman, *The Academic Revolution*, Garden City, N.Y., 1968.

Kinsey, Alfred Charles, with W. B. Pomeroy and C. E. Martin. *Sexual Behavior in the Human Male*, Philadelphia, 1948.

———, with W. B. Pomeroy, C. E. Martin, and P. H. Gebhard. *Sexual Behavior in the Human Female*, Philadelphia, 1953.

Leuchtenburg, William E. *Franklin D. Roosevelt and the New Deal, 1922–1940*, New York, 1963.

Lipset, Seymour Martin, and Gerald M. Schflander. *Passion and Politics: Student Activism in America*, Boston, 1971.

Manchester, William. *The Glory and the Dream*, Boston, 1973.

Marquette, Ray. *Indiana University Basketball*, Bloomington, 1975.

Michael, W. Miles. *The Radical Probe*, New York, 1971.

Myers, Burton Dorr. *Trustees and Officers of Indiana University, 1820–1950*. Bloomington, 1951.

Nichols, David C. *Perspective on Campus Tensions*, Washington, 1970.

Payne, Fernandus. *Memoirs and Reflections*, Bloomington, 1975.

Peckham, Howard. *The Making of the University of Michigan 1817–1967*, Ann Arbor, 1967.

Perley, Maie Clements. *Without My Gloves*, Philadelphia, 1940.

Pomeroy, Wardell B. *Dr. Kinsey and the Institute for Sex Research*, New York, 1972.

Randall, David Anton. *Dukedom Large Enough*, New York, 1969.

Rinsch, Emil. *History of the Normal College of the American Gymnastic Union of Indiana University, 1866–1966*, Indianapolis, 1966.

Rock, Dorcas Irene. *A History of the Indiana University Training School for Nurses*, Bloomington, 1956.

Rudolph, Frederick, *The American College and University: A History*, New York, 1962.

Sampson, Edward E., and Harold A. Corn, and associates. *Student Activism and Protest*, San Francisco, 1970.

Schmidt, George P. *The Liberal Arts College: A Chapter in American Cultural History*, New Brunswick, N.J., 1957.

Unger, Irwin. *The Movement: A History of the American New Left, 1959–1972*, New York, 1974.

Veysey, Laurence R. *The Emergence of the American University*, Chicago, 1965.

Wilson, Kenneth (Tug), and Jerry Brodfield. *The Big Ten*, New York, 1967.

Index

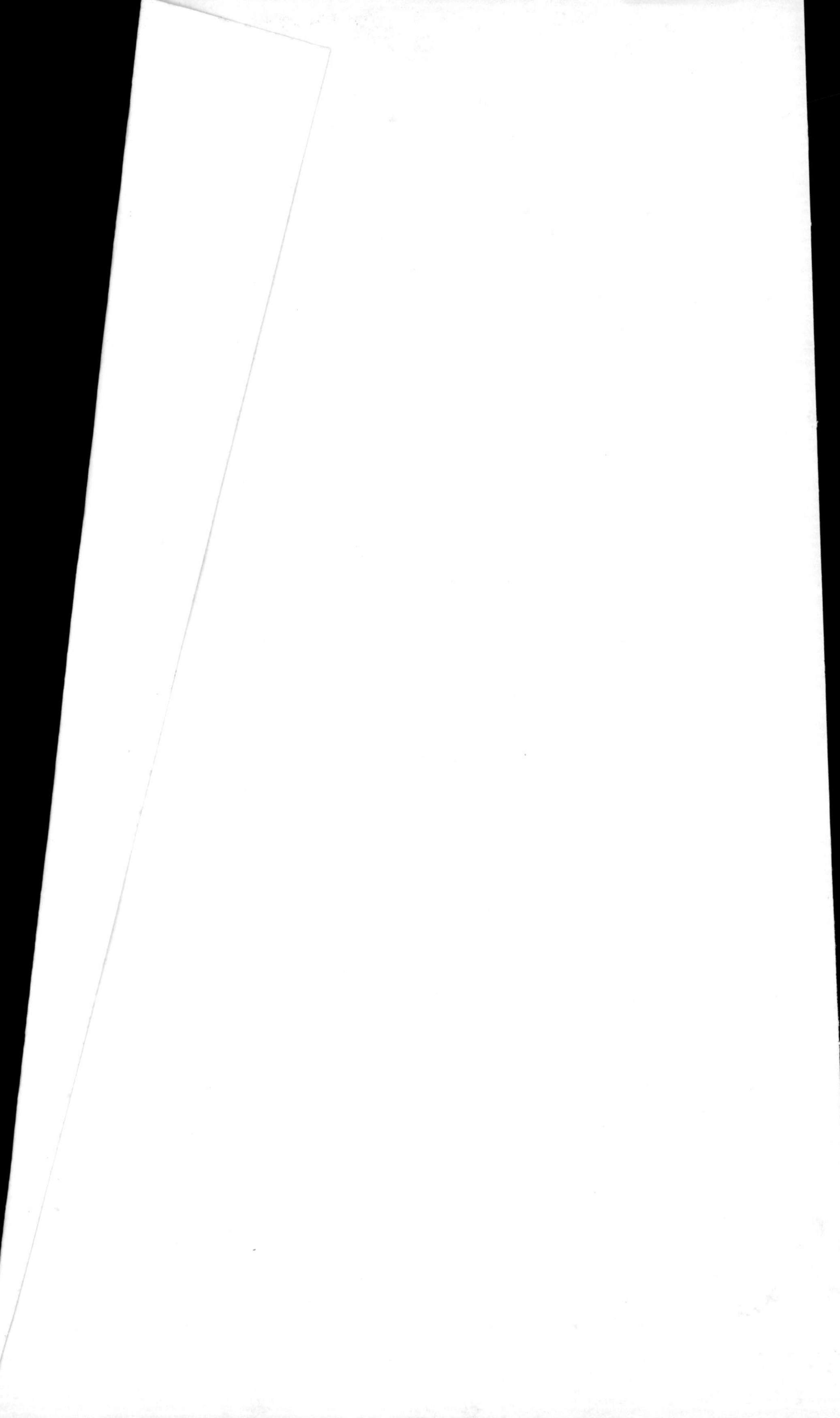